The Sixth Annual International Symposium in Economic Theory and Econometrics was dedicated to Jacques Drèze on the occasion of his retirement. During his career, he worked on the development, extension, and applications of general equilibrium theory, and he also was essential to the founding of the Center for Operations Research and Econometrics (CORE) in Louvain-la-Neuve, Belgium. The papers in this volume are those given at the conference, and present some of the recent developments in general equilibrium theory in perspective of actual and potential applications.

Equilibrium theory and applications

International Symposia in Economic Theory and Econometrics

Editor
William A. Barnett, *Washington University in St. Louis*

Other books in the series

William A. Barnett and A. Ronald Gallant
New approaches to modeling, specification selection, and econometric inference

William A. Barnett and Kenneth J. Singleton
New approaches to monetary economics

William A. Barnett, Ernst R. Berndt, and Halbert White
Dynamic econometric modeling

William A. Barnett, John Geweke, and Karl Shell
Economic complexity

William A. Barnett, James Powell, and George E. Tauchen
Nonparametric and semiparametric methods in econometrics and statistics

Equilibrium theory and applications

Proceedings of the Sixth International Symposium in Economic Theory and Econometrics

Edited by

WILLIAM A. BARNETT
Washington University in St. Louis

BERNARD CORNET
Université de Paris and
Laboratoire d'Econométrie de l'Ecole Polytechnique

CLAUDE D'ASPREMONT
CORE Université Catholique de Louvain

JEAN GABSZEWICZ
CORE Université Catholique de Louvain

ANDREU MAS-COLELL
Harvard University

The right of the University of Cambridge to print and sell all manner of books was granted by Henry VIII in 1534. The University has printed and published continuously since 1584.

CAMBRIDGE UNIVERSITY PRESS

Cambridge
New York Port Chester Melbourne Sydney

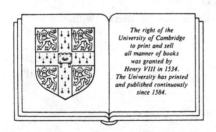

CAMBRIDGE UNIVERSITY PRESS
Cambridge, New York, Melbourne, Madrid, Cape Town, Singapore, São Paulo, Delhi

Cambridge University Press
The Edinburgh Building, Cambridge CB2 8RU, UK

Published in the United States of America by Cambridge University Press, New York

www.cambridge.org
Information on this title: www.cambridge.org/9780521392198

First published 1991
This digitally printed version 2008

A catalogue record for this publication is available from the British Library

Library of Congress Cataloguing in Publication data

International Symposium in Economic Theory and Econometrics (6th :
1989 : Louvain-la-Neuve, Belgium)

Equilibrium theory and applications : proceedings of the Sixth
International Symposium in Economic Theory and Econometrics / edited
by William A. Barnett ... [et al.].

p. cm. – (International symposia in economic theory and
econometrics)

ISBN 0-521-39219-5 (hardback)

1. Equilibrium (Economics) – Congresses. I. Barnett, William A.
II. Title. III. Series.
HB145.I59 1989
330′.01′5195 – dc20 91–10539
CIP

ISBN 978-0-521-39219-8 hardback
ISBN 978-0-521-08825-1 paperback

Jacques Drèze

Contents

Editors' preface

The contents of this volume comprise the proceedings of the conference, "Equilibrium Theory and Applications," held at the Center for Operations Research and Econometrics (CORE), at Louvain-la-Neuve, Belgium, on June 9–10, 1989. The objective was to present some of the recent developments in general equilibrium theory in the perspective of actual and potential applications.

The conference was organized in honor of Jacques Drèze on the occasion of his sixtieth birthday and the end of his academic career. Before his leaving for a world sailing tour, all of the participants wanted to testify their debt to his scientific work, essentially devoted to the development, the extension, and the applications of general equilibrium theory. Held at CORE, it was also the unanimous recognition, stressed by Gérard Debreu in his address, of his role as "the architect and the builder" of this Center.

The introductory address by Gérard Debreu comprises Part I of the volume. The rest of the volume is divided into four parts, spanning the scope of the conference. Part II is on incomplete markets, increasing returns, and information. Part III is on equilibrium and dynamics. Part IV is on employment, imperfect competition, and macroeconomics. Part V is on applied general equilibrium models.

The conference that produced this proceedings volume is the sixth in a conference series, called *International Symposia in Economic Theory and Econometrics*. The proceedings series is under the general editorship of William A. Barnett. Individual volumes in the series generally have coeditors, and the series has a permanent Board of Advisory Editors. The symposia in the series are sponsored by the Innovation, Creativity, and Capital Institute at the University of Texas at Austin and are cosponsored by the RGK Foundation. This sixth conference also was cosponsored by CORE and the Department of Economics, the Graduate School of Business, and the Center for Statistical Sciences at the University of Texas at Austin.

The first conference in the series was coorganized by William A. Barnett and A. Ronald Gallant, who also coedited the proceedings volume. That volume appeared as the volume 30, October–November 1985 edition of the *Journal of Econometrics* and was reprinted as a volume in this Cambridge University Press monograph series, entitled *New Approaches to Modeling, Specification Selection, and Econometric Inference.*

Beginning with the second symposium in the series, the proceedings of the symposia appeared directly as volumes in this Cambridge University Press monograph series. The coorganizers of the second symposium and co-editors of its proceedings volume were William A. Barnett and Kenneth J. Singleton. The topic was *New Approaches to Monetary Economics.* The coorganizers of the third symposium, which was on *Dynamic Econometric Modeling,* were William A. Barnett and Ernst Berndt; and the co-editors of that proceedings volume were William A. Barnett, Ernst Berndt, and Halbert White. The coorganizers of the fourth symposium and co-editors of its proceedings volume, *Economic Complexity: Chaos, Sunspots, Bubbles, and Nonlinearity,* were William A. Barnett, John Geweke, and Karl Shell. The coorganizers and proceedings co-editors of the fifth symposium, *Nonparametric and Semiparametric Methods in Econometrics and Statistics,* were William A. Barnett, James Powell, and George E. Tauchen.

The coorganizers and proceedings coeditors of the sixth symposium, which produced the current volume, are William A. Barnett, Bernard Cornet, Claude d'Aspremont, Jean Gabszewicz, and Andreu Mas-Colell. The seventh symposium in the series will be held in 1991 at Washington University in St. Louis on the interface between economics, political science, and monetary policy.

The intention of the volumes in the proceedings series is to provide refereed journal-quality collections of research papers of unusual importance in areas of currently highly visible activity within the economics profession. Because of the refereeing requirements associated with the editing of the proceedings, the volumes in the series will not necessarily contain all of the papers presented at the corresponding symposia.

William A. Barnett
Washington University in St. Louis

Bernard Cornet
Université de Paris and Laboratoire d'Econometrie de l'Ecole Polytechnique

Claude d'Aspremont
CORE Université Catholique de Louvain

Jean Gabszewicz
CORE Université Catholique de Louvain

Andreu Mas-Colell
Harvard University

Contributors

William A. Barnett
Department of Economics
Washington University in St. Louis

Jean-Pascal Benassy
CEPREMAP

Jean-Marc Bonnisseau
Laboratoire d'Econométrie
Ecole Polytechnique

Bernard Cornet
Université de Paris I
(Panthéon-Sorbonne)

Jean-Pierre Danthine
Batiment du Rectorat et de
l'Administration Centrale
Université de Lausanne

Claude d'Aspremont
CORE
Université Catholique de Louvain

Gérard Debreu
Department of Economics
University of California

Egbert Dierker
Institute für Wirtschaftswissenschaften
der Universität Wien

John B. Donaldson
Graduate School of Business
Columbia University

Rodolphe Dos Santos Ferreira
Faculté des Sciences Economiques
Université Louis Pasteur

Jacques Drèze
CORE
Université Catholique de Louvain

Jayasri Dutta
CORE
Université Catholique de Louvain

Françoise Forges
CORE
Université Catholique de Louvain

Jean Gabszewicz
CORE
Université Catholique de Louvain

Louis-André Gérard-Varet
GREQE
Hospice de la Vieille Charite

John Geweke
Institute of Statistics and Decision Science
Duke University

Jean-Michel Grandmont
CEPREMAP

Roger Guesnerie
Ecole des Hautes Etudes en Sciences
Sociales

Jean-Jacques Laffont
CRES
Université des Sciences Sociales

Guy Laroque
CEPREMAP

Michael Magill
Department of Economics
University of Southern California

Edmond Malinvaud
Chaire d'Analyse Economique
Collège de France

Andreu Mas-Colell
Department of Economics
Harvard University

Philippe Michel
Université de Paris I
(Panthéon-Sorbonne)

Heraklis Polemarchakis
CORE
Université Catholique de Louvain

Martine Quinzii
Department of Economics
University of Southern California

Paul Romer
Department of Economics
University of Chicago

Alasadair Smith
School of European Studies
University of Sussex

Jean Tirole
Department of Economics
Massachusetts Institute of Technology

Anthony J. Venables
University of Southampton

Michael Wolfe
School of Business
University of West Virginia

Michael Woodford
Graduate School of Business
University of Chicago

PART I

Introduction

CHAPTER 1

Address in honor of Jacques Drèze

Gérard Debreu

The next two days will be given to a scrutiny of the everwidening horizon that Léon Walras contemplated first. General equilibrium was fated then to become a central concept in economic theory, and its destiny is manifest in the program of our Conference, which will discuss several of the most active research areas it has stimulated in the recent past. Incomplete markets and money, increasing returns, information, and dynamics are on the agenda. So are applied general equilibrium models, and non-Walrasian equilibria. The work done at CORE in those areas, and the results obtained in Heverlee and in Louvain-la-Neuve make it entirely proper for us to gather here for that discussion. To the many participants for whom this visit is only the latest in a long sequence, to those for whom it is almost a homecoming, and to the members of CORE, the choice of venue for our Colloquium also makes an exceptional reunion possible.

But a far more compelling reason brought us together today. Jacques Drèze, who has yet to celebrate his sixtieth birthday, decided to gain several degrees of freedom by dropping the constraints that formal teaching has imposed on him since 1958 when he obtained his Ph.D. from Columbia University, and became Chargé de Cours de l'Université Catholique de Louvain, an unconventional decision in which the hand of an expert on decision making is visible. What Jacques accomplished in the 31 years he spent on the faculty of his university could fill several brilliant academic careers and it is above all to honor him that we are meeting.

The volume of Jacques' articles is already so large as to daunt an editor who would prematurely consider collecting his papers. One hundred articles including more than 2000 pages would claim his attention. Permission to reprint them would have to be sought from 48 co-authors, whose list goes from Aumann to Zellner, so numerous that only his three most frequent collaborators, Pierre Dehez, Jean Gabszewicz, and Franco Modigliani, will be mentioned. In that number alone, one can read Jacques' uncommon availability to his colleagues. Organizing Jacques' papers in any way other than the trivial chronological order would also be fraught with difficulties, for the main themes that run through them often interact. The first of these themes is the approach to economic uncertainty that Jacques began to develop in the early 1950s. The utility function that von Neumann and Morgenstern placed at the basis of their theory of games in 1944 had become widely accepted, and Savage's *Foundations of Statistics* was published in 1954 as Jacques completed a 2-year visit to the United States as a graduate fellow. His first two articles on economic theory, which appeared in *Economie Appliquée* in 1959 and 1960, offered a subtle critical analysis of several aspects of the position taken by the new Bayesian school. They did not foretell that Jacques was to become one of its masters. In a long series of important articles spanning three decades, Jacques turned his attention to many of the main problems of the economic theory of uncertainty: the foundations of cardinal utility and of personal probability, moral hazard, consumption, saving and investment decisions, market allocation and equilibrium. One of the most recent of these studies (still unpublished) is devoted to a question in the theory of incomplete markets, an area of intensive research activity in the past few years. In another major, parallel research program, Jacques has been one of the outstanding proponents of the Bayesian approach to econometrics. Attaining great distinction in econometrics as well as in economic theory, Jacques performed a feat that is rare in our profession.

As CORE was beginning its own career in 1966, Jacques was turning to the study of the core and contributing to an article on economies composed of giants and dwarfs. It was the starting point of a new line of research and of a series of papers on the core of an economy with atomic agents, which, like many of his articles, were in the framework of the theory of general equilibrium. Later Jacques was drawn more deeply into game theory and contributed to several papers in that field, the last one (in *Econometrica* 1986) so complex that the two authors thought it advisable to guide the reader through the proof of the main theorem by means of a marvelous flow chart.

Also in the first years of CORE, Jacques contributed to the formulation of a process for the allocation of public goods. Parelleling some of the work done by Malinvaud on that topic at that time, the process became known, and widely discussed, as the MDP procedure.

Price rigidities and unemployment have been long-standing concerns of Jacques. They made him, in an article published belatedly in 1975, one of the originators of the theory of fixed-price economics and one of its main contributors. Jacques, who has written at length on abstract, mathematical economic theory as well as on applied problems of economic policy, has often shown acute awareness of the tension between the intellectual demands made by different approaches to economics. His work on fixed-price equilibrium was one of his main contributions to the resolution of that tension.

In spite of their richness and of the wide range that they cover, the contributions to economic theory and to econometrics to which I alluded are but a minor fraction of Jacques' scientific output. Many other theoretical problems challenged his inquisitive mind, which kept perceiving unanswered questions in the economic world around him. His sensitivity to social problems and his interest in concrete economic issues led him throughout his career to write a large number of articles where his command of economic theory and of econometrics is allied with an analysis of economic data in discussions of economic policy. The example of versatility that he set puts him in a sparse set of economists.

The large debt of our profession to Jacques is immensely increased by the leading role that he played in the creation of CORE in 1966 and in its development. By the end of the 1960s, CORE had become the major research center in mathematical economics outside the United States. Since then, it has remained at the edge of the exponentially expanding universe of mathematical economics and game theory, operations research, and econometrics. On the occasion of the twentieth anniversary of CORE, which was celebrated in January 1987, Werner Hildenbrand reminisced about the heady days when CORE moved into its new building in Heverlee in the fall of 1968. Since my first long visit began at that time, I had the chance of being carried for an entire academic year by the wave of enthusiasm that he described. The distance traveled by CORE since then has been great, and long ago, it became a regular stopover on the international circuit of wandering economists and operations researchers. For this, we must thank Jacques, who, more than anyone else, has been the architect and the builder of CORE, and who, for more than two decades, has made an essential contribution to its unique atmosphere.

Neither Jacques' teaching and his supervision of 20 doctoral dissertations, nor his research and his writing, nor his contribution to CORE preempted his willingness to accept many other time-consuming responsibilities. Thus, he became Co-Editor of *Econometrica* for five years in 1965, and he played a major role in the creation of the European Doctoral Program in Quantitative Economics. Recognition of Jacques' multifaceted achievements came in many forms. He was President of the Econometric Society and of the European Economic Association. He is a member, or foreign member, of several academies. Over the past nine years, he has received nine Honoris Causa Doctorates.

This sketch of Jacques could have remained purely academic if he and Monique had not made another unconventional decision. Next month, they will embark on their sailboat for a year-long voyage in a definitive demonstration of Jacques' new freedom. Many eminent scientists can be suspected of trying to prove in their persons that perpetual motion is possible. Following the trajectory of a particular high-energy physicist, one may discover that he travels more than 600,000 km in a year, achieving an average speed in excess of 68 km/h. But those two numbers are highly misleading since his center of gravity remains essentially at rest most of the time. Jacques' simulation of perpetual motion during the coming year will be much more convincing, for his center of gravity will maintain a significant speed for several weeks on end.

As he sails over the Atlantic Ocean, cut off from the support system of seminars, working papers, computers, fax machines, during many long, lonely watches, Jacques will steadily look at economics from an unfamiliar perspective. Few economists' courses would be unaltered by that experience, and the landfall that will mark the end of Jacques' voyage may also mark the beginning of a second career. For that career and for your voyage, dear Jacques, I will speak for all inside this room and for many outside in expressing our warmest wishes.

PART II

Incomplete markets, increasing returns, and information

CHAPTER 2

Asset pricing and observability

Jayasri Dutta and Heraklis Polemarchakis

1 Introduction

We explore observable restrictions on asset prices. We consider an exchange economy with diverse preferences and endowments. The asset structure may be incomplete, with fewer assets than states of nature.

Asset prices do not allow for arbitrage: a portfolio of assets with positive payoff does not have a zero price. This nonarbitrage condition is equivalent to the existence of a positive price associated with each state of nature (Ross, 1978; Harrison and Kreps, 1979; also Geanakoplos and Polemarchakis, 1986). State prices are the implicit prices for elementary securities, often referred to as Arrow prices (Arrow, 1953).

In fact, the nonarbitrage condition is exhaustive. Neither equilibrium nor optimality have any observable implications for asset prices other than those derived from the nonarbitrage condition. If the asset market is in equilibrium, Arrow prices exist, irrespective of the asset structure, and are positive; and, conversely, if the Arrow prices implied by the asset payoffs and prices are positive, it is possible to construct an economy that yields these prices at a competitive equilibrium (Harrison and Kreps, 1979). Perhaps more strongly, it is possible to construct an economy for which these prices characterize an optimum, even if the number of assets is smaller than the number of states of nature; this construction is valid locally to an equilibrium (Geanakoplos and Polemarchakis, 1990).

When the asset market is complete, the Arrow prices that support any nonarbitrage asset prices are unique, and they are fully recoverable from the asset payoffs and prices. All possible assets are attainable, since their payoffs are in the span of the payoffs of the marketed assets, so that it is possible to speak of fully determinate nonarbitrage prices for all

This work was supported by the Deutscheforschungsgemeinschaft, Sondersforschungsbereich 303 and the Gottfried-Willhelm-Leibniz-Förderpreis during BoWo '89. It was completed while we were visiting the Department of Economics of the University of Bonn.

assets. When the asset market is incomplete, there are many Arrow prices compatible with every vector of asset prices; generically, assets that are not attainable cannot be unambiguously valued by nonarbitrage.

Asset pricing in the theory of finance is concerned with empirical statements about the prices of assets. We use the term empirical in a broad sense. This includes predictions that relate the prices and returns of assets to the means and variances of their payoffs, expectations, and variances taken with respect to an empirical probability measure. In addition, it includes restrictions on asset prices, such as subspace restrictions, stated in terms of observables.

What does the nonarbitrage condition imply for the empirical properties of asset prices? To derive this, we first use the normalized Arrow prices as a probability measure. The nonarbitrage restriction is then equivalent to the condition that asset prices equal expected payoffs - the martingale property - when expectations are taken with respect to the Arrow measure. Generically, this measure is different from the empirical measure, even if the empirical measure is the commonly held prior distribution of all individuals (Drèze, 1971; also Lucas, 1978; Bewley, 1980). Then, we show that, empirically, the price of all attainable assets must equal their expected payoffs, with a correction factor. This factor represents the covariance of asset payoffs with a random variable that is the likelihood ratio that transforms the Arrow measure to the empirical one.

Evidently, there are as many distinct likelihood ratios as there are distinct Arrow prices that support the asset prices, so that this pricing rule is not unambiguous if the asset market is incomplete. However, only one such likelihood ratio is observable: it is the return to a portfolio of marketed assets. We call this the "benchmark" portfolio. Any attainable asset is unambiguously priced by its expected return and its covariance with the return of the benchmark portfolio. In addition, the benchmark portfolio weights can be derived, in closed form. The weights depend only on the empirical expectation and variance-covariance matrices of returns on the marketed assets, that is, the portfolio is of the familiar mean-variance form. Clearly, if the asset market is complete, the benchmark portfolio recovers the unique Arrow prices. Otherwise, it selects one of the many state prices compatible with equilibrium, the selected one being linear in the payoffs of marketed assets. Since all assets are priced relative to it, this portfolio provides a summary measure of the attitudes toward risk in a competitive market.

Once the benchmark portfolio is available, we can use it to derive asset pricing rules. For example, the Capital Asset Pricing Model (Lintner, 1965; Mossin, 1966; Sharpe, 1964; Treynor, 1961) posits a relation between the return of any asset and its covariance with the return of the market, the aggregate consumption portfolio; and the relation is valid only if all individuals choose portfolios that trade off expectation for variance in returns, which is only possible with restrictive assumptions on preferences or on the structure of payoffs. We show that the same relation is valid with general preferences and asset payoffs as long as we define the "market" portfolio appropriately and restrict attention to attainable assets. Once again, this representation is equivalent to the nonarbitrage condition; the market portfolio is stated entirely in terms of observables.

Even with fewer assets than states of nature, the asset market may be effectively complete: it may be possible to price assets, not necessarily attainable, so that, if marketed, they would leave the solutions to the optimization problems of all individuals essentially unaffected. Under restrictive assumptions on the utility functions and initial endowments of individuals and on the asset structure, 2-fund separation obtains and every asset, not necessarily attainable, can be priced by its expected payoff and its covariance with the return of the benchmark portfolio. Also the Capital Asset Pricing Model holds with respect to the return of the aggregate consumption portfolio.

Since the benchmark portfolio does select one out of the many possible Arrow prices, it can be used to approximately price nonattainable assets even when the asset market fails to be effectively complete. Formally, the pricing rule operates as follows. Consider an asset whose payoff is not spanned by those of marketed assets. Find the portfolio of marketed assets that yields the return closest to the return of this asset – closest in empirically weighted Euclidean distance. The market price of this portfolio is the "projection" price of the asset. We give an example of the projection pricing rule to determine the price of a nonattainable asset. Of course, this is only one of many possible approximate prices. More importantly, it abstracts from the fact that, generically, the introduction of a previously nonattainable asset in an incomplete asset market affects nontrivially the solution to the optimization problems of individuals. Interestingly, it is precisely this caveat that turns projection pricing into an empirical implication.

2 The asset market

Economic activity extends over two periods, 1 and 2, under uncertainty. States of nature are $s=1,\dots,S$; all uncertainty is resolved in the second period. Date-event pairs are 1 and $(2,1),\dots,(2,S)$.

Commodities $l=1,\dots,L$ are marketed and consumed in both periods. A commodity bundle is

$$x = (x(1), x(2)) = (x(1), \ldots, x(2,s), \ldots),$$

a vector of dimension $L(S+1)$.

Individuals are $h = 1, \ldots, H$. An individual is described by his utility function u^h defined on the consumption set X^h, a set of commodity bundles; and by his initial endowment w^h, a consumption bundle.

For $h = 1, \ldots, H$, the consumption set is

$$X^h = \{x : x \gg 0\},$$

the set of strictly positive commodity bundles.

For $h = 1, \ldots, H$, the utility function u^h is twice continuously differentiable; $Du^h \gg 0$ and D^2u^h is negative definite on $[Du^h]^\perp$; for $(x_n : n = 1, \ldots)$, a sequence of consumption bundles, and for $x \neq 0$, a commodity bundle on the boundary of the consumption set,

$$\lim_{n \to \infty} x_n = x \Rightarrow \lim_{n \to \infty} \frac{x_n' Du^h(x_n)}{\|Du^h(x_n)\|} = 0.$$

For $h = 1, \ldots, H$, the initial endowment is

$$w^h \gg 0,$$

a consumption bundle.

These are strong but standard.

Individuals' utility functions may, but need not, satisfy the expected utility hypothesis. The probability of occurrence of the states of nature may not be agreed upon, even defined.

Assets $a = 1, \ldots, A$ are marketed in the first period and pay off in the second. A portfolio is

$$y = (\ldots, y_a, \ldots).$$

A marketed asset is described by its payoff, b_a.

For $a = 1, \ldots, A$, the payoff is

$$b_a = (\ldots, b_a(2,s), \ldots),$$

a second-period commodity bundle of dimension $LS \times 1$. The asset structure is a matrix of payoffs of marketed assets,

$$B = (\ldots, b_a, \ldots) = (\ldots, B(2,s), \ldots),$$

of dimension $LS \times A$.

The matrix of payoffs of marketed assets has full column rank:

$$\dim[B] = A.$$

This eliminates redundant assets.

There exists a portfolio $\bar{y}$ such that

$$B(2,s)\bar{y} > 0, \quad s = 1, \ldots, S.$$

This allows commodity prices to be normalized so that the portfolio $\bar{y}$ has a state-independent payoff in terms of revenue.

An economy is parametrized by the array of initial endowments, and possibly by the array of utility functions and the asset structure. The family of economies can be identified with a finite dimensional open set.

A property holds generically if and only if it holds for a generic set of economies: an open set of full Lebesgue measure. A property is robust if and only if it holds for an open set of economies.

Commodity prices are

$$p = (p(1), p(2)) = (p(1), \ldots, p(2,s), \ldots),$$

where

$$p(1) = (\ldots, p_l(1), \ldots)$$

and

$$p(2,s) = (\ldots, p_l(2,s), \ldots), \quad s = 1, \ldots, S.$$

At commodity prices p, for $a = 1, \ldots, A$, the payoff in terms of revenue is

$$d_a(p) = P(2)'b_a,$$

where

$$P(2) = \text{diag}(\ldots, p(2,s), \ldots).$$

The matrix of payoffs of marketed assets in terms of revenue is

$$D(p) = P(2)'B,$$

a matrix of dimension $S \times A$.

We restrict attention to strictly positive commodity prices such that

$$\dim[D(p)] = A,$$

which we normalize so that

$$p(1)'1^L = 1 \quad \text{and} \quad D(p)\bar{y} = 1^S.$$

The payoff in terms of revenue of the portfolio $\bar{y}$ is state-independent. This is simply a normalization; the portfolio $\bar{y}$ is not risk-free, which would require a payoff at each state of nature inversely proportional to the marginal utility of income of each individual.

Prices of marketed assets are

$$q = q(1) = (\ldots, q_a, \ldots).$$

At commodity prices p, prices q for marketed assets do not allow for arbitrage if and only if

$$D(p)y>0 \Rightarrow q'y>0.$$

At commodity prices p, the attainable reallocations of revenue across states of nature coincide with

$$[D(p)],$$

the column span of the matrix of asset payoffs in terms of revenue. The asset market is complete if and only if

$$\dim[D(p)]=S;$$

all reallocations of revenue across states of nature are then attainable. Evidently, the asset market is complete whenever

$$A=S.$$

Otherwise it is incomplete.

At prices (p,q), an individual solves the following optimization problem: for $h=1,\ldots,H$,

$$\operatorname{Max} u^h(x)$$

subject to the budget constraints

$$P(2)'(x(2)-w^h(2))\leq D(p)y,$$

in the second-period commodity markets, and

$$p(1)'(x(1)-w^h(1))+q'y\leq 0,$$

in the first-period commodity and asset market.

A solution to the individual optimization problem exists, is unique, and is characterized by the following first-order necessary and sufficient conditions: for $h=1,\ldots,H$,

$$Du^h(2)=P(2)\gamma^h(2),$$

in the second-period commodity markets,

$$Du^h(1)=p(1)\gamma^h(1),$$

in the first-period commodity market, and

$$D(p)'\gamma^h(2)=q\gamma^h(1),$$

in the first-period asset market, for some

$$\gamma^h(1)>0 \quad\text{and}\quad \gamma^h(2)=(\ldots,\gamma^h(2,s),\ldots)\gg 0.$$

Evidently, $\gamma^h(1)$ is the individual's marginal utility of revenue in the first-period commodity and asset market, and $\gamma^h(2)$ the state-dependent marginal utility of revenue in the second-period commodity markets.

At prices (p, q), the asset market is effectively complete if and only if, for $h=1,\dots,H$,

$$\frac{1}{\gamma^h(1)}\gamma^h(2)=\gamma$$

for some

$$\gamma=(\dots,\gamma(2,s),\dots)\gg 0.$$

Evidently, when $A=S$ and the asset market is complete, it is effectively complete.

When $A<S$ and the asset market is incomplete, generically, the asset market is not effectively complete.

An asset, i, marketed or not, is described by its payoff in terms of revenue

$$d_i=(\dots,d_i(s),\dots).$$

At commodity prices, p, an asset is attainable if and only if

$$d_i\in[D(p)];$$

equivalently, an attainable asset is identified by the unique portfolio of marketed assets such that

$$d_i=D(p)y_i.$$

At prices q for marketed assets, the price of an attainable asset is

$$q_i=q'y_i.$$

An asset is nonattainable if and only if

$$d_i\notin[D].$$

Attainable assets are priced at the unique prices at which if marketed they would leave the solutions to the optimization problems of all individuals essentially unaffected. For nonattainable assets, generically, such prices do not exist.

The return of an asset is

$$r_i=\frac{1}{q_i}d_i-1^S;$$

evidently, this is an abuse of language for a nonattainable asset.

The matrix of returns of the marketed assets is

$$R(p,q)=(\dots,r_a(p,q),\dots).$$

The return on the portfolio $\bar{y}$ is state-independent and equal to

$$\rho(q)=\frac{1}{q'\bar{y}}-1;$$

this is its expected return for any probability measure on the states of nature.

We chose units of measurement for the marketed assets such that

$$q=1^A,$$

and restrict attention to portfolios with

$$y'1^A=1;$$

it follows that the return to any portfolio is

$$r(y)=Ry.$$

A return is attainable if and only if it is the return to a portfolio.

3 Nonarbitrage asset prices

All properties of asset prices or returns follow from the nonarbitrage condition alone. The following result characterizes the set of prices for marketed assets which do not allow for arbitrage.

Proposition 1 (Geanakoplos and Polemarchakis, 1986). *At commodity prices p, prices q for marketed assets do not allow for arbitrage if and only if they satisfy the nonarbitrage condition:*

$$q=D(p)'\lambda$$

for some

$$\lambda=(\dots,\lambda(2,s),\dots)\gg 0.$$

Proof: Let

$$\bar{Q}(p)=\{q: q=D(p)'\lambda \text{ for some } \lambda\geq 0\}.$$

By construction, $\bar{Q}(p)$ is a finite cone. All finite cones are convex and closed. Since $D(p)$ has linearly independent columns, the interior of this cone is a non-empty open set and coincides with

$$Q(p)=\{q: q=D(p)'\lambda \text{ for some } \lambda\gg 0\}.$$

Let $\tilde{q} \in Q(p)$; then $\tilde{q} = D(p)'\lambda$ for some $\lambda \gg 0$. Now suppose $D(p)y > 0$ for some y, while $\tilde{q}'y \leq 0$. Since $\lambda \gg 0$, this is a contradiction. Thus, if $\tilde{q} \in Q(p)$, $D(p)y > 0 \Rightarrow \tilde{q}'y > 0$. The open cone $Q(p)$ consists only of prices that do not allow for arbitrage.

Note that $D(p)\bar{y} = 1^S > 0$. It follows that $0 \notin Q(p)$ and hence that $\bar{Q}(p) \neq \mathcal{E}^A$.

Let $\tilde{q} \notin Q(p)$. Since $Q(p)$ is convex, there exists a nontrivial hyperplane, $\mathcal{H}_{\hat{y}} = \{q : q'\hat{y} = \tilde{q}'\hat{y}\}$, with $\hat{y} \neq 0$, through $\tilde{q}$, such that $q'\hat{y} \geq \tilde{q}'\hat{y}$ for all $q \in Q(p)$. Since $0 \in \bar{Q}(p)$, $\tilde{q}'\hat{y} \leq 0$, and $q'\hat{y} \geq 0$ for all $q \in \bar{Q}(p)$; equivalently, $\lambda' D(p)\hat{y} \geq 0$ for all $\lambda \geq 0$. Since $\hat{y} \neq 0$ and $D(p)$ has full column rank, $D(p)\hat{y} > 0$. Thus, if $\tilde{q} \notin Q(p)$, there exists a portfolio $\hat{y}$ such that $D(p)\hat{y} > 0$ while $\tilde{q}'\hat{y} \leq 0$. Asset prices not in $Q(p)$ allow for arbitrage.

Note that in the previous argument, if $\tilde{q}$ is on the boundary of $Q(p)$, there is an arbitrage portfolio, $\hat{y}$, with $\tilde{q}'\hat{y} = 0$. □

We refer to λ as the Arrow prices.

We argue at given prices (p, q). We omit the reference to prices when no confusion arises; also the distinction between asset payoffs and asset payoffs in terms of revenue.

Let the set of Arrow prices compatible with asset payoffs D and prices q for marketed assets be

$$\Lambda = \{\lambda \gg 0 : D'\lambda = q\}.$$

When the asset market is incomplete, Arrow prices are not unique:

$$\dim(\Lambda) = S - A,$$

with

$$\lambda_1, \lambda_2 \in \Lambda \Rightarrow (\lambda_1 - \lambda_2) \in [D]^{\perp}.$$

Note that, for $h = 1, \ldots, H$,

$$\frac{1}{\gamma^h(1)} \gamma^h(2) \in \Lambda.$$

Evidently, the prices of attainable assets are independent of the choice of Arrow prices compatible with the payoffs and prices of the marketed assets.

3.1 *The martingale property*

Asset prices satisfy the martingale property with respect to a probability measure ν on the states of nature if and only if, for some $\rho > 0$, and for every attainable asset,

$$E_\nu r_i = \rho;$$

equivalently, if and only if

$$\nu' R = 1^A \rho.$$

Asset prices satisfy the martingale property if and only if they satisfy the martingale property with respect to some measure.

Asset prices do not allow for arbitrage if and only if they satisfy the martingale property for some strictly positive probability measure; the two conditions are equivalent.

Note that, for all $\lambda \in \Lambda$,

$$\frac{1}{\lambda' 1^S} = \rho + 1.$$

For $\lambda \in \Lambda$, define

$$\nu(\lambda) = \lambda(\rho + 1);$$

note that $\nu(\lambda)$ is a strictly positive probability measure on the states of nature. From the nonarbitrage condition, it follows that

$$E_{\nu(\lambda)} r_i = \nu(\lambda)' r_i = (\rho+1)\frac{\lambda' d_i}{q' y_i} - 1 = (\rho+1)\frac{\lambda' D(p) y_i}{\lambda' D(p) y_i} - 1 = \rho.$$

Let

$$\mathfrak{N} = \{\nu : \nu' R = 1^A \rho\}$$

be the set of probability measures on the states of nature compatible with the martingale property.

For $\nu \in \mathfrak{N}$, define

$$\lambda(\nu) = \nu \frac{1}{\rho + 1};$$

note that $\lambda(\nu) \gg 0$. From the martingale property, it follows that

$$\lambda(\nu)' d_i = \lambda(\nu)' q_i (r_i + 1) = q_i \left(\frac{\rho}{\rho+1} + \frac{1}{\rho+1} \right) = q_i.$$

4 Nonarbitrage and empirical properties

The testing of asset pricing theories is based on the actual realization of payoffs and prices. We use this as the point of departure and assume that the empirical probability measure is directly observable. This is just the frequency function

$$\pi = (\ldots, \pi(s), \ldots),$$

which we assume to be strictly positive.

Any vector $x = (\ldots, x(s), \ldots)$ can be viewed as a random variable, whose probability distribution is fully described by any probability measure on the set of states of nature, in particular π. We consider empirical properties – that is, properties of random variables endowed with the empirical measure. Clearly, the return of an asset is such a random variable. Define expectations with respect to the empirical measure to write

$$\mu_i = Er_i,$$

$$\sigma_i^2 = \operatorname{var}(r_i) = E(r_i - \mu_i)^2,$$

$$\sigma_{i,j} = \operatorname{cov}(r_i, r_j) = E(r_i - \mu_i)(r_j - \mu_j),$$

as expectations, variances, and covariances.

The nonarbitrage condition imposes a restriction on the prices of attainable assets: these prices equal the expectation of payoffs, with respect to the measure ν; this measure need not equal the empirical one. In addition, when the asset market is incomplete, ν is not even unique. It is then not clear that the nonarbitrage restriction has any empirical counterpart. We derive here the empirical implications of the nonarbitrage restrictions. Clearly, this is a useful exercise only when the ν is distinct from π.

Generically,

$$\pi \notin \mathfrak{N},$$

even when individuals agree that π defines the probability of occurrence of the states of nature and maximize expected utility.

The following lemma restates the nonarbitrage condition in terms of the empirical measure.

Lemma 1. *Asset prices satisfy the nonarbitrage condition if and only if there exists a bounded random variable v with*

$$v < Ev + 1,$$

such that, for every attainable asset i,

$$\mu_i - \rho = \operatorname{cov}(v, r_i).$$

Proof: Suppose asset prices satisfy the nonarbitrage condition. This implies that they satisfy the martingale property with respect to any probability measure $\nu \in \mathfrak{N}$. For any constant k, define

$$v(k, \nu) = 1^S k + \Pi^{-1}\nu,$$

where

$$\Pi = \operatorname{diag}(\ldots, \pi(s), \ldots).$$

Note that $v < k = Ev + 1$; it is bounded since π is strictly positive. It follows that

$$\text{cov}(v, r_i) = Evr_i - (k-1)\mu_i = \mu_i - \rho.$$

Suppose such a random variable v exists. Define

$$\nu(v) = \Pi(1^S(1+Ev) - v).$$

Evidently, ν is a strictly positive probability measure on the states of nature. Since

$$E_\nu r_i = \mu_i - \text{cov}(v, r_i) = \rho,$$

asset prices satisfy the martingale property with respect to ν and hence do not allow for arbitrage. □

Clearly, the random variable $v = v(k, \nu)$ is not uniquely defined; we need to specify k and, more importantly, $\nu \in \mathfrak{N}$. As we show in what follows, there is a unique v^* that is the payoff of an attainable asset; as a result, there is a unique portfolio of that asset that generates returns colinear with v^*. This portfolio is fully specified by the empirical characteristics of returns.

4.1 *Pricing and the benchmark portfolio*

We use some simplifying notation in the derivations; this should also make the correspondence with existing literature on asset pricing transparent.

The portfolio with state-independent payoff coincides with asset $a = 1$:

$$\bar{y} = (1, 0, \ldots, 0).$$

Portfolios are

$$y = (y_1, y_2) = (y_1, y_2, \ldots, y_A).$$

The matrix of returns of marketed assets is

$$R = (r_1, R_2) = (r_1, r_2, \ldots, r_A).$$

The return on a portfolio is

$$r(y) = Ry = r_1 y_1 + R_2 y_2.$$

For $a = 2, \ldots, A$, the returns r_a are nondegenerate random variables. Let

$$\mu = E(r_2, \ldots, r_A) = R_2' \pi$$

be the vector of expectations and

$$\Sigma = E(r_2 - \mu_2, \ldots, r_A - \mu_A)(r_2 - \mu_2, \ldots, r_A - \mu_A)' = R_2' \Pi R_2 - \mu\mu'$$

be the variance-covariance matrix that is square, symmetric, of dimension $A-1$, and strictly positive definite.

Proposition 2. *The benchmark portfolio*

$$y^* = (1-(1^{A-1})'\Sigma^{-1}(\mu-\rho 1^{A-1}), \Sigma^{-1}(\mu-\rho 1^{A-1}))$$

with return

$$r^* = r_1 + (R_2 - r_1(1^{A-1})')\Sigma^{-1}(\mu-\rho 1^{A-1})$$

is the unique portfolio with the property that, for every attainable asset i,

$$\mu_i - \rho = \operatorname{cov}(r^*, r_i).$$

Proof: From Lemma 1, the benchmark property holds for

$$v(k,\nu) = 1^S k - \Pi^{-1}\nu$$

for any constant k, and any strictly positive measure such that

$$R_2'\nu = 1^{A-1}\rho$$

and

$$1^{S'}\nu = 1.$$

Let

$$\theta = \Sigma^{-1}(\mu - \rho 1^{A-1}).$$

Define

$$k^* = 1 + \rho(1-\theta' 1^{A-1}) + \mu'\theta;$$

and

$$\nu^* = \Pi(1^S k^* - r^*) = \Pi(1^S + (1^S\mu' - R_2)\theta).$$

By construction,

$$r^* = 1^S k^* = \Pi^{-1}\nu^*.$$

Since

$$R_2'\pi = R_2'\Pi 1^S = \mu,$$

by direct substitution,

$$R_2'\nu^* = 1^{A-1}\rho,$$

and

$$1^{S'}\nu^* = 1.$$

Hence, y^* has the benchmark property.

Suppose any other portfolio $y = (1-(1^{A-1})'y_2, y_2)$ has the benchmark property. Suppose that $y_2 = \theta + e$. Then

$$\begin{aligned}\operatorname{cov}(r(y), r_i) &= \operatorname{cov}(r^*(b), r_i) + \operatorname{cov}(R_2 e, r_i)\\ &= \mu_i - \rho + \operatorname{cov}(R_2 e, r_i),\end{aligned}$$

whenever r_i is attainable. The benchmark property requires that

$$\operatorname{cov}(R_2 e, r_i) = 0$$

for each attainable asset. Now, the portfolio $y_e = (1 - e'1^{A-1}, e)$ is attainable and has return $r(y_e) = R_2' e$, so that

$$\operatorname{cov}(r(y_e), r(y_e)) = e'\Sigma e = 0,$$

whenever y is a benchmark portfolio. Since Σ is positive definite, this can hold if and only if $e = 0$. □

By construction, the benchmark portfolio selects the unique Arrow prices compatible with the payoffs of the marketed assets such that

$$\lambda^* \in [\Pi D] = [\Pi R].$$

4.2 *The Capital Asset Pricing Model*

The Capital Asset Pricing Model specifies a relationship between the excess returns of attainable assets and their covariances with the return to a portfolio, the market portfolio.

Corollary 1. *Let a constant, $m \neq 0$, index the market portfolio:*

$$r_m = (1-m) r_1 + m r^*.$$

The Capital Asset Pricing Model holds with respect to r_m as the return to the market portfolio: for every attainable asset,

$$\mu_i - \rho = \beta_i (\mu_m - \rho),$$

where

$$\beta_i = \frac{\operatorname{cov}(r_m, r_i)}{\operatorname{var}(r_m)}.$$

Proof: For $m \neq 0$,

$$\operatorname{cov}(r_m, r_i) = m \operatorname{cov}(r^*, r_i) = m(\mu_i - \rho).$$

Further,

$$\operatorname{var}(r_m) = m^2 \operatorname{var}(r^*) = m^2 (Er^* - \rho) = m(Er_m - \rho).$$

The result follows from Proposition 2 by substitution. □

A one-parameter family of portfolios serves as market portfolios for the pricing of assets. Each of these is a portfolio of asset $a=1$ and the benchmark asset. The indexing parameter m characterizes the trade-off between mean excess return and variance in the return of the market:

$$m=\frac{\operatorname{var}(r_m)}{Er_m-\rho}.$$

Evidently, $Er_m-\rho$ is positive if and only if $m>0$. Since

$$m^2=\frac{\operatorname{var}(r_m)}{\theta'\Sigma\theta},$$

the family of market returns r_m have the property that

$$\frac{(Er_m-\rho)^2}{\operatorname{var}(r_m)}=\theta'\Sigma\theta.$$

For $m>0$, this defines a monotonically increasing and linear relation between the excess returns of market portfolios and their standard deviations; the locus of expected excess returns and standard deviations of market portfolios coincides with the efficient frontier.

Of course, generically, the market portfolio so specified is different from the aggregate market portfolio or the aggregate consumption of individuals.

5 Pricing nonattainable assets

A nonattainable asset i can be priced if and only if, for $h=1,\ldots,H$,

$$d_i'\gamma^h(2)=\gamma^h(1)q_i;$$

otherwise it cannot be priced.

Evidently, every asset, not necessarily attainable, can be priced if and only if the asset market is effectively complete; then

$$q_i=d_i'\gamma.$$

For simplicity, we suppose that there is only one commodity: $L=1$; also, that commodity prices are

$$p=(p(1),p(2))=(p(1),\ldots,p(2,s),\ldots)=(1,\ldots,1,\ldots)$$

and

$$D=B.$$

This is not essential, but simplifies the argument.

Consider the following restrictive assumptions on the utility functions and initial endowments of individuals and on the asset structure.

For $h=1,\ldots,H$, the utility function is intertemporally separable:

$$u^h = u^h(1) + u^h(2).$$

Over second-period consumption, the utility function satisfies the expected utility hypothesis with respect to the empirical measure over states of nature; locally, at the solution to the individual optimization problem, the cardinal utility index is state-independent and quadratic:

$$u^h(2) = E\alpha^h x(2) - (1/2)x(2)^2.$$

For $h=1,\ldots,H$, the initial endowment of second-period commodities lies in the span of the matrix of asset payoffs:

$$w^h(2) \in [B].$$

There exists a riskless asset: for some portfolio of marketed assets,

$$B\bar{y} = 1^S.$$

Lemma 2. *Under the restrictive assumptions on the utility functions and the initial endowments of individuals and on the asset structure, the asset market is effectively complete and 2-fund separation obtains: for* $h=1,\ldots,H$,

$$w^h(2) + By^h \in [1^S, B(B'\Pi B)^{-1}q]$$

(Cass and Stiglitz, 1970).

Proof: For $h=1,\ldots,H$, from the first-order conditions for individual optimization in the second-period commodity markets,

$$\Pi(1^S\alpha^h - w^h(2) - By^h) = \gamma^h(2);$$

thus,

$$\gamma^h(2) \in [\Pi B].$$

Then from the first-order conditions for optimization in the first-period asset market,

$$\gamma^h(2) = \Pi B(B'\Pi B)^{-1} q \gamma^h(1);$$

hence, the asset market is effectively complete. Finally, by substitution,

$$w^h(2) + By^h = 1^S\alpha^h - B(B'\Pi B)^{-1} q\gamma^h(1). \qquad \square$$

Evidently, for $h=1,\ldots,H$, the return to the consumption portfolio of individual h is

$$r^h = \frac{1}{(w^h(2)+By^h)'\gamma} w^h(2) + By^h - 1^S.$$

Proposition 3. *Under the restrictive assumptions on the utility functions and initial endowments of individuals and on the asset structure, for every asset, not necessarily attainable,*

$$\mu_i - \rho = \text{cov}(r^*, r_i).$$

Proof: It suffices to show that, for $h=1,\ldots,H$,

$$\frac{1}{\gamma^h(1)}\gamma^h(2) = \lambda^*.$$

But this is evident, since the Arrow prices selected by the benchmark return are the unique Arrow prices such that

$$\lambda^* \in [\Pi B],$$

and, from the proof of Lemma 2, for $h=1,\ldots,H$,

$$\frac{1}{\gamma^h(1)}\gamma^h(2) \in [\Pi B]. \qquad \square$$

The return to the aggregate consumption portfolio is

$$r^A = \frac{1}{(w^A + By^A)'\gamma}(w^A + By^A) - 1^S,$$

where

$$w^A = \sum_h w^h$$

and

$$y^A = \sum_h y^h.$$

Corollary 2 (Geanakoplos and Shubik, 1989). *The Capital Asset Pricing Model holds with respect to r^A, the return to the aggregate consumption portfolio: for every asset, not necessarily attainable,*

$$\mu_i - \rho = \beta_i(\mu^A - \rho)$$

where

$$\beta_i = \frac{\text{cov}(r^A, r_i)}{\text{var}(r^A)}.$$

Proof: Evidently,

$$\lambda^* = \frac{1}{\sum_h \gamma^h(1)} \sum_h \gamma^h(2).$$

From the first-order conditions for individual optimization in the second-period commodity markets and in the first-period asset market, it follows then that

$$\lambda^* = \frac{1+\rho}{\pi'(1^S\alpha-(w+By))}\Pi(1^S\alpha-(w+By)),$$

where

$$\alpha = \sum_h \alpha^h.$$

Since

$$r^* = 1^S k^* - \Pi^{-1}\nu^* = 1^S k^* - \frac{1}{1+\rho}\Pi^{-1}\lambda^*,$$

it follows that

$$r^* \in [r_1, r^A].$$

The result then follows from Proposition 3. □

Evidently, the Capital Asset Pricing Model holds for any nondegenerate return spanned by the return to the risk-free asset and the return to the aggregate consumption portfolio.

Generically, the restrictive assumptions on the utility functions and initial endowments of individuals and on the asset structure do not hold; more importantly, the asset market is not effectively complete. We analyze the properties of "approximate pricing" of nonattainable assets in such a situation.

Let r_i, r_j be the returns of any two assets, not necessarily attainable. We define the distance between the returns as

$$\delta(r_i, r_j) = (r_i - r_j)'\Pi(r_i - r_j) = E(r_i - r_j)^2.$$

The distance δ is the weighted Euclidean metric with weights corresponding to the empirical probabilities; alternatively, it is the empirical mean-squared error.

For any asset i, with return r_i, not necessarily attainable, we define the portfolio

$$\hat{y}_i = \arg\min \delta(r_i, r(y))$$

and the return

$$\hat{r}_i = r(\hat{y}_i) = r_1(1-(1^{A-1})'y_{i,2}) + R_2 y_{i,2}.$$

Evidently, $\hat{y}_i$ is the portfolio of marketed assets that approximates the return of the asset i most closely: we call this the projection portfolio of the asset i and the return of the projection portfolio the projection return. It is straightforward that $r_i = \hat{r}_i$ if and only if the asset i is attainable.

Lemma 3. *Let m be a market portfolio. For any asset, not necessarily attainable,*

$$\beta_i = \frac{\operatorname{cov}(r_m, r_i)}{\operatorname{var}(r_m)} = \frac{E\hat{r}_i - \rho}{Er_m - \rho}.$$

Proof: Since $\hat{r}_i$ is attainable, it follows from Corollary 1 that

$$\hat{\beta}_i = \frac{\operatorname{cov}(r_m, \hat{r}_i)}{\operatorname{var}(r_m)} = \frac{E\hat{r}_i - \rho}{Er_m - \rho};$$

we need to show that

$$\operatorname{cov}(r_m, r_i - \hat{r}_i) = 0.$$

But this is evident, since by definition $\operatorname{cov}(r_m, r_i - \hat{r}_i) = \delta(r_i - \hat{r}_i, r_m)$, and by construction, the quantity $e_i = r_i - \hat{r}_i$ is orthogonal to r_a, $a = 1, \ldots, A$ and r_m is in the span $[r_1, R]$. □

This result establishes that approximately pricing a nonattainable asset at its expected payoff with a correction for covariance with the benchmark return is equivalent to pricing the projection portfolios of the asset. We refer to this price as the projection of an asset.

We provide an example of projection pricing in an economy with two assets: a risk-free bond and a risky asset. We compute the projection portfolio in closed form and use it to find the projection price of an option. An option on the risky asset, which has a truncated payoff, is not in the span of marketed assets. In order to derive restrictions on prices, we specify the example in terms of asset payoffs and prices.

Consider an economy with two marketed assets, $A = 2$. Asset $a = 1$ is a riskless bond with payoff $d_1 = 1^S$. Asset $a = 2$ is a risky asset, with payoff d.

Prices for the two marketed assets are q_1 and q_2, respectively. Asset prices satisfy the nonarbitrage restriction whenever Arrow prices $\lambda \gg 0$ satisfy $\lambda' 1^S = q_1$ and $\lambda' d = q_2$.

The expectation and variance of the payoff of the risky asset in terms of the empirical measure are $\bar{d}$ and σ^2, respectively.

Consider any asset, not necessarily attainable, with payoff d_i. The projection of d_i on the span of $[1^S, d]$ in the weighted Euclidean norm is

$$\hat{d}_i = (Ed_i - \beta_i) + \beta_i d,$$

where

$$\beta_i = \frac{\operatorname{cov}(d, d_i)}{\sigma^2}.$$

It follows that the projection price is

$$q_i = q_1(Ed_i - \beta_i \bar{d}) + \beta_i q_2.$$

Clearly, if d_i is uncorrelated with d, its projection price is equal to the present value of the expected payoff.

A call option with exercise price c is a secondary asset with payoff $d_i = (d-c)^+$. In order to price this asset by projection, we need to compute explicitly Ed_i, and $\text{cov}(d_i, d)$, which are functions of the truncated means and variances of d. Let

$$S_c = \{s \in \mathbb{S} : d(s) > c\}$$

and

$$\pi_c = \sum_{s \in S_c} \pi(s) = \text{Prob}(d > c).$$

Define

$$\bar{d}_c = E_{S_c}(d) = \frac{\sum_{s \in S_c} \pi(s) d(s)}{\pi_c}$$

and

$$\sigma_c^2 = \text{var}_{S_c}(d) = \frac{\sum_{s \in S_c} \pi(s) d^2(s)}{\pi_c} - (\bar{d}_c)^2$$

as the truncated mean and variance of d. By substitution, we obtain

$$Ed_i = \pi_c \bar{d}_c$$

as the expected payoff of the option, while its covariance with d is

$$\text{cov}(d_i, d) = \pi_c(\sigma_c^2 + (\bar{d}_c - \bar{d})(\bar{d}_c - c)).$$

It follows that the projection price of the option is equal to

$$q_i = \pi_c(\bar{d}_c q_1 + \beta_i(q_2 - \bar{d} q_1)),$$

where

$$\beta_i = \frac{\sigma_c^2 + (\bar{d}_c - \bar{d})(\bar{d}_c - c)}{\sigma^2}.$$

It remains to characterize the properties of the projection price as an approximate price when the asset market is not effectively complete.

6 Conclusions

In this chapter, we investigated the properties of asset prices when the asset market is possibly incomplete. Of particular interest are observable properties, which we interpret as the properties of asset returns with respect to their empirical distribution.

We showed that, irrespective of the possible incompleteness of the asset market, all attainable assets are priced by their covariance with a unique portfolio of marketed assets. This portfolio, called the benchmark portfolio, can be explicitly characterized as a function of the empirical means and variances of the returns. The empirical interest of this formulation comes because this construct is based on observations of asset returns alone, without reference to the utility functions and initial endowments of individuals, which are not observable.

We also demonstrated that the benchmark pricing rule can be used to price nonattainable assets. This amounts to finding the value of the projection portfolio. This is the portfolio of marketed assets whose return best approximates that of the nonattainable asset, distance being measured by the mean-squared error, or, equivalently, by the weighted Euclidean metric. This pricing rule is, generically, only approximate. It is exact under the restrictive conditions on the utility functions and the initial endowments of individuals and on the asset structure that imply that the asset market is effectively complete and 2-fund separation.

Projection pricing may be understood as the pricing of a large number of assets by a smaller number of factors; the two factors that are used to price all assets are the risk-free return and the benchmark return. This is precisely the theme of Arbitrage Pricing Theory (Ross, 1976). Our results suggest that this class of pricing rules are valid under restrictive conditions that entail, among others, that the asset market is effectively complete.

The valuation of investment projects by firms is a bothersome problem in the theory of production with incomplete markets. Since projection pricing yields a determinate valuation rule for all such projects, it is worth examining the implications of the implied decision criterion for firms.

Notation

- $\gg$, $>$, $\geq$: vector inequalities. For $a=(\ldots,a_k,\ldots)$ and $b=(\ldots,b_k,\ldots)$, $a\gg b$ if and only if $a_k>b_k$ for all k; $a>b$ if and only if $a_k\geq b_k$ for all k, with some strict inequality; $a\geq b$ if and only if $a_k\geq b_k$ for all k. The terms strictly positive, positive, and nonnegative refer to $\gg 0$, >0, and ≥ 0, respectively; for scalars, the terms strictly positive and positive coincide.
- $'$: the transpose. All vectors are column vectors; in the text, vectors are written as row vectors.
- [ ]: the space spanned by a collection of vectors; also by the columns of a matrix.

- $\perp$: the orthogonal complement.
- $\mathcal{E}^K$: the Euclidean space of dimension K.

REFERENCES

Arrow, K. J. 1953. "Le Rôle des Valeurs Boursieres pour la Repartition la Meillieure des Risques." *Econometrie* 11: 41-7.

Bewley, T. F. 1980. "The Martingale Property of Asset Prices," mimeo.

Cass, D., and J. Stiglitz. 1970. "The Structure of Investor Preferences and Asset Returns and Separability in Portfolio Allocation: A Contribution to the Pure Theory of Mutual Funds." *Journal of Economic Theory* 2: 122-60.

Drèze, J. H. 1971. "Market Allocation Under Uncertainty." *European Economic Review* 2: 133-65.

Geanakoplos, J. D., and H. M. Polemarchakis. 1986. "Existence, Regularity and Constrained Suboptimality of Competitive Allocations when the Asset Market is Incomplete." In *Uncertainty, Information and Communication: Essays in Honor of K. J. Arrow,* Vol. III, W. P. Heller, R. M. Starr, and D. Starrett, Eds. New York: Cambridge University Press, pp. 65-96.

1990. "Optimality and Observability." *Journal of Mathematical Economics* 19: 153-66.

Geanakoplos, J. D., and M. Shubik. 1990. "The Capital Asset Pricing Model as a General Equilibrium with Incomplete Markets." *Geneva Papers on Risk and Insurance* 15: 55-72.

Harrison, J. M., and D. Kreps. 1979. "Martingales and Arbitrage in Multiperiod Securities Markets." *Journal of Economic Theory* 20: 381-408.

Lintner, J. 1965. "The Valuation of Risky Assets and the Selection of Risky Investments in Stock Portfolios and Capital Budgets." *Review of Economics and Statistics* 47: 13-37.

Lucas, R. E. 1978. "Asset Prices in an Exchange Economy." *Econometrica* 46: 1429-45.

Mossin, J. 1966. "Equilibrium in a Capital Asset Market." *Econometrica* 35: 768-83.

Ross, S. 1976. "Arbitrage Theory of Capital Asset Pricing." *Journal of Economic Theory* 13: 341-60.

1978. "A Simple Approach to the Valuation of Risky Streams." *Journal of Business* 51: 453-75.

Sharpe, W. 1964. "Capital Asset Prices: A Theory of Market Equilibrium Under Conditions of Risk." *Journal of Finance* 19: 425-42.

Treynor, J. 1961. "Towards a Theory of the Market Value of Risky Assets," mimeo.

CHAPTER 3

The nonneutrality of money in a production economy with nominal assets

Michael Magill and Martine Quinzii

1 Introduction

Recent work on the theory of incomplete markets (see Magill and Shafer, 1991) can be viewed as an attempt to broaden the scope and applicability of standard general equilibrium theory by introducing a structure of markets, contracts, and constraints on agent participation which conforms more closely with that observed in the real world. The key idea is that once we recognize that we live in a world in which time and uncertainty enter in an essential way, we must acknowledge that the system of markets is incomplete.

Drèze (1974) was one of the first to extend the traditional Arrow-Debreu theory to the framework of incomplete markets, following the earlier lead of Diamond (1967). He recognized the importance of differences in agents' rates of substitution for the single most significant type of firm ownership structure - the shareholder-owned firm (Drèze, 1987, ch. 15, 16). He emphasized the inevitably controversial role of a firm that seeks to make decisions in the typically conflicting interests of its three sets of clienteles - its shareholders, its employees, and the consumers in the marketplace (Drèze, 1989). These contributions have greatly increased our understanding of the central role played by shareholder-owned corporations in a modern economy.

Although the subsequent literature on incomplete markets has emphasized the relationship between the *real* and *financial* markets, there has

This chapter was presented at the Conference in honor of Jacques Drèze, "Equilibrium Theory and its Applications," CORE, University of Louvain-La-Neuve, Belgium, June 9 and 10, 1989. It was in part written in the hospitable environment of the Laboratoire d'Econometrie de l'Ecole Polytechnique. We are grateful to participants in the 1989 IMSSS Summer Workshop at Stanford University for helpful comments. Research support from the Deutsche Forschungsgemeinschaft, G. W. Leibnitz Forderpreis during BoWo 89 and from National Science Foundation Grant SES-8911877 is gratefully acknowledged.

not been sufficient recognition of the far-reaching changes that arise once *money* is explicitly introduced. In a modern economy, money is primarily used as a medium of exchange: its presence permits the introduction of *nominal contracts,* which are promises to deliver amounts of money in future states. In an economy with money, price levels are influenced by monetary policy: If agents exchange nominal assets then their opportunity sets are altered by changes in price levels. Thus, in an economy with money and nominal contracts, monetary changes have real effects.

The problem of introducing money into a model with incomplete markets has been studied for the case of an *exchange* economy by Magill and Quinzii (1991). Our object here is to extend the analysis to the case of a *production* economy. After laying out the assumptions of a *smooth* production economy (Section 2), we introduce the system of spot and financial markets (equity and bonds) and show how money circulates through these markets, performing its role as a medium of exchange (Section 3). Since we allow firms as well as consumers to trade on the financial markets, some clarification is required to obtain a well-defined objective function for each firm: the present value of profit for each firm is obtained by using the average present value vector of the firm's *original* shareholders. We stress that at the present time, no definitive criterion for the firm has been discovered for this class of equilibrium models. There are a number of plausible criteria, and this one is chosen among these because it simplifies the qualitative analysis of the effects of changes in monetary policy.

After introducing the concept of a *monetary equilibrium* (Section 4), we explain a simplification relative to the earlier exchange analysis of Magill and Quinzii (1991): We restrict the qualitative analysis to those equilibria in which money is used solely as a medium of exchange, the *positive nominal interest-rate equilibria.* For those parameter values for which agents are induced to use money as a store of value in competition with the other financial assets, the induced changes in the velocity of circulation of money greatly complicate the analysis in Section 6. We thus confine our analysis to parameter values leading to the positive interest-rate case. We analyze monetary equilibria by reducing them to an equivalent *reduced-form* concept of equilibrium (Section 5). This enables us to establish generic existence of monetary equilibria by a straightforward application of the powerful fixed-point theorem of Husseini, Lasry, and Magill (1990) (see also Hirsch, Magill, and Mas-Colell, 1990 for a geometric proof of the theorem).

Section 6 contains the basic qualitative analysis of the effects of changes in monetary policy. We distinguish between *anticipated* and *unanticipated* monetary changes. We say that a monetary change has *real effects* if it alters a given equilibrium allocation, that is, if it alters either the consumption plan of at least one agent or the production plan of at least one firm or both; we say that it has *production effects* if it alters the production plan of at least one firm. We show that if the asset markets are complete, then anticipated monetary changes have no real effects (Theorem 2). However, if the asset markets are incomplete and if the number of agents (I) exceeds the number of nominal assets ($K \geq 1$), then generically there is a subspace Λ such that all nontrivial anticipated marginal monetary changes chosen from this subspace have real effects. Since the dimension of Λ is at least $S-(J+K)$ (where S is the number of states at date 1 and J is the number of firms), there are always some local monetary changes that have real effects. To be sure that there are production effects, we need an additional assumption that ensures that the initial ownership of firms is not too diffused among consumers (Theorem 3). Unanticipated monetary changes always have real effects; under the assumption of nondiffused initial ownership, there are production effects provided the induced income effects do not cancel (Theorem 4).

This chapter should be viewed as a preliminary general equilibrium study of the way the presence of nominal assets and contracts enables monetary policy to have real effects by altering price levels and, hence, the purchasing power of nominal asset returns. The analysis can thus be viewed as a generalization of the *real balance effect,* which has played such a central role in macroeconomics (see, for example, Tobin, 1980, ch. 1). The analysis of this chapter has been confined to the case of nominal assets in zero net supply: The results thus depend crucially on the general equilibrium analysis of income effects, an analysis that is typically ignored in the macroeconomic literature.

2 The production economy

We consider the simplest production economy with time and uncertainty. The economy consists of a finite number of consumers ($i=1,\ldots,I$) and firms ($j=1,\ldots,J$) and a finite number of goods ($h=1,\ldots,H$). There are two time periods ($t=0,1$) and one of S states of nature ($s=1,\ldots,S$) occurs at date 1. For convenience, we call date $t=0$, state $s=0$, so that in total there are $S+1$ states.

Since there are H goods available in each state ($s=0,1,\ldots,S$) the *commodity space* is $\mathbb{R}^n$, with $n=H(S+1)$. Each consumer i ($i=1,\ldots,I$) has an *initial endowment* of the H goods in each state $w^i=(w_0^i, w_1^i,\ldots, w_S^i)$. The preference ordering of agent i is represented by a *utility function:*

$$u^i: \mathbb{R}^n_+ \to \mathbb{R}, \quad i=1,\ldots,I$$

defined over *consumption bundles* $x^i=(x_0^i, x_1^i,\ldots, x_S^i)$ lying in the nonnegative orthant $\mathbb{R}^n_+$, which satisfies the following:

Assumption A (Preferences). (1) $u^i: \mathbb{R}^n_+ \to \mathbb{R}$ *is continuous on* $\mathbb{R}^n_+$ *and* $\mathcal{C}^2$ *on* $\mathbb{R}^n_{++}$. (2) *If* $U^i(\xi) = \{x \in \mathbb{R}^n_+ \mid u^i(x) \geq u^i(\xi)\}$, *then* $\overline{U^i(\xi)} \subset \mathbb{R}^n_{++}$, $\forall \xi \in \mathbb{R}^n_{++}$. (3) *For each* $x \in \mathbb{R}^n_{++}$, $Du^i(x) \in \mathbb{R}^n_{++}$ *and* $h^T D^2 u^i(x) h < 0$ *for all* $h \neq 0$ *such that* $Du^i(x)h = 0$.

Production in the economy is carried out by the J firms $(j = 1, \ldots, J)$, each characterized by a production set $Y^j \subset \mathbb{R}^n$. The managers of firm j choose a production plan $y^j \in Y^j$, where $y^j = (y^j_0, y^j_1, \ldots, y^j_S)$, and $y^j_s = (y^j_{s1}, \ldots, y^j_{sH})$ with $y_{sh} < 0$ (> 0), indicating that good h is used in state s as an input (is produced in state s as an output). In order to obtain a smooth supply function for firm j, we assume that the *boundary* ∂Y^j of Y^j is a smooth submanifold of a subspace $E^j \subset \mathbb{R}^n$. The production sets are assumed to satisfy the following conditions.

Assumption B (Production sets). (1) $Y^j \subset \mathbb{R}^n$ *is closed, convex and* $\mathbb{R}^n_- \subset Y^j$. (2) $(\Sigma^I_{i=1} w^i + \Sigma^J_{j=1} Y^j) \cap \mathbb{R}^n_+$ *is compact.* (3) Y^j *is a full dimensional submanifold of* $E^j \subset \mathbb{R}^n$, *whose boundary* ∂Y^j *is a* $\mathcal{C}^2$ *manifold with strictly positive Gaussian curvature at each point.*

Since we use genericity arguments, we need a way of *parametrizing* the decision of agents. We parametrize the decisions of consumers by the vector of initial endowments $\omega = (w^1, \ldots, w^I) \in \mathbb{R}^{nI}_+$ of the I consumers. To parametrize the production activity of firms, we assume that the production of each firm consists of two components, the *endogenously* chosen $y^j \in Y^j$ and an exogenously given vector of outputs $\eta^j \in \mathbb{R}^n_+$, so that the total production of firm j is $y^j + \eta^j$. We call η^j the *initial endowment* vector of firm j and let $\eta = (\eta^1, \ldots, \eta^J)$. To obtain genericity results, we parametrize the decisions of consumers and producers by the initial endowment vector

$$(\omega, \eta) \in \Omega \subset \mathbb{R}^{nI}_+ \times \mathbb{R}^{nJ}_+.$$

If we choose utility functions $u = (u^1, \ldots, u^I)$, production sets $Y = (Y^1, \ldots, Y^J)$, and an initial endowment vector $(\omega, \eta) \in \Omega$, then we obtain an economy $\mathcal{E}(u, Y; \omega, \eta)$. The assumptions made on the set Ω depend on whether the economy is being viewed as an *exchange* economy - in which case, we can set $\Omega = \mathbb{R}^{nI}_{++} \times \{0\}$ - or as a *production* economy - in which case, the goods with which consumers are initially endowed are typically different from those produced by firms. Thus, we made the following assumption.

Assumption C (Initial endowments). (a) (ω, η) *lie in an open subset* $\Omega \subset \mathbb{R}^{nI}_{++}$ *or* (b) $\Sigma^I_{i=1} w^i + \Sigma^J_{j=1} \eta^j \in \mathbb{R}^n_{++}$ *and* $w^i_{s1} > 0$, $s = 1, \ldots, S$ *for* $i = 1, \ldots, I$.

3 Markets, transactions, and money

Our object is to study the allocation of resources obtained when we adjoin to the economy $\mathcal{E}(u, Y; \omega, \eta)$ a market structure consisting of *n spot markets* and *J+K asset markets.* It is convenient to begin by describing the financial assets: These are basically of two kinds, the *J securities* of the firms and *K nominal* assets (bonds). At date 0, the ownership of firm j is distributed among a set of *initial shareholders,* with z_0^{ij} denoting the proportion of firm j owned by consumer i, where $z_0^{ij} \geq 0$ for all i, j and $\sum_{i=1}^{I} z_0^{ij} = 1$. Agent i receives the proportion z_0^{ij} of the dividends D_0^j of firm j at date 0, where D_0^j is measured in francs (the unit of account of the medium of exchange). The securities of firm j are then traded on a *stock market.* The market price of firm j is q_j (francs) and full ownership of firm j conveys the right to the dividend stream $D_1^j = (D_1^j, \ldots, D_S^j)$ at date 1. We assume that both consumers and firms can trade on the equity market for firm j $(j = 1, \ldots, J)$. Let z^{ij} denote the proportion of firm j purchased (sold if $z^{ij} < 0$) by consumer i and let $\xi^{j'j}$ denote the proportion purchased by firm j'. Clearly, market clearing will require $\sum_{i=1}^{I} z^{ij} + \sum_{j'=1}^{J} \xi^{j'j} = 1$, $j = 1, \ldots, J$.

At date 0, consumer i inherits an ownership of z_0^{ik} units of nominal asset k: To simplify the later analysis, we assume that firms initial holdings of bonds are zero ($\xi_0^{jk} = 0$, $j = 1, \ldots, J$). The bond holdings are in zero net supply ($\sum_{i=1}^{I} z_0^{ik} = 0$). Asset k gives consumer i the right to receive $N_0^k z_0^{ik}$ francs at date 0. These one-period contracts are then traded on a *bond market.* For the price q_k, an agent receives the right to the income stream $N_1^k = (N_1^k, \ldots, N_s^k)$ (francs) at date 1. We let $z^{ik}(\xi^{jk})$ denote the number of units bought (sold if $z^{ik} < 0$ $(\xi^{jk} < 0)$) by consumer i (firm j). Each nominal asset is in *zero net supply,* so that market clearing requires $\sum_{i=1}^{I} z^{ik} + \sum_{j=1}^{J} \xi^{jk} = 0$, $k = J+1, \ldots, J+K$.

In addition to these financial assets, there is another financial instrument, *fiat money,* which serves as the medium of exchange and defines the unit of account (*francs*) for all transactions on markets. While in a *barter* economy, goods can be exchanged for goods directly, in a *monetary* economy, a good is always exchanged for money and this money is then used to purchase other commodities. We use the procedure introduced in Magill and Quinzii (1991) to describe the way in which money circulates in the economy. The transactions activities of each period ($s = 0, 1, \ldots, S$) are decomposed into transactions in three separate subperiods (s_1, s_2, s_3). At date 0, in the first subperiod 0_1, consumers and firms sell their initial endowments

$$(\omega_0, \eta_0) = (w_0^1, \ldots, w_0^I, \eta_0^1, \ldots, \eta_0^J) \tag{1}$$

to a central exchange. They thus receive the amounts of fiat money

$$(m_0^1, \ldots, m_0^I, \tilde{m}_0^1, \ldots, \tilde{m}_0^J),$$

where $m_0^i = p_0 w_0^i$, and $\tilde{m}_0^j = p_0 \eta_0^j$, $p_0 = (p_{01}, \ldots, p_{0H})$, denoting the vector of *spot prices* at date 0. In the second subperiod 0_2, armed with the money balances acquired in subperiod 0_1, agents proceed to the financial markets. Consumers and firms receive (make) dividend payments implied by their *initial portfolios*

$$(z_0, \xi_0) = (z_0^1, \ldots, z_0^I, \xi_0^1, \ldots, \xi_0^J). \tag{2}$$

To simplify the analysis, we assume $\xi_0 = 0$ so that firms have no initial holdings of financial assets. Consumers and firms then purchase *new portfolios* in the stock and bond markets

$$(z, \xi) = (z^1, \ldots, z^I, \xi^1, \ldots, \xi^J), \tag{2'}$$

where z^i and ξ^j lie in $\mathbb{R}^{J+K}$. All transactions on the financial markets are made with fiat money. The full amount of the money balances acquired in the subperiods 0_1 and 0_2 will be used for purchasing commodities in subperiod 0_3, *provided agents do not have an incentive to use money as a store of value*[1] from date 0 to date 1. Although this circumstance is of considerable interest, in this chapter, we concentrate on the simpler case where money is used purely as a medium of exchange. A sufficient condition for this is that money be dominated by some financial asset as a method for transferring purchasing power between date 0 and date 1. This can be ensured in two steps as follows. The first step consists in assuming that all agents (consumers and firms) have access to riskless borrowing and lending. For convenience, we introduce the full set of conditions imposed on the bond matrix N_1 as follows.

Assumption D (Bond matrix). *The bond matrix N_1 satisfies* (i)

$$\operatorname{rank} N_1 = K,$$

(ii) *the first column of N_1 is the riskless bond*

$$N_1^1 = (N_1^1, \ldots, N_S^1) = (1, \ldots, 1).$$

The price q_1 of the riskless bond is related to the *riskless nominal rate of interest* r_1 by the equation $q_1 = 1/(1+r_1)$. *If $r_1 > 0$, no agent will use money as a store of value between dates* 0 *and* 1. The second step consists in restricting attention to those parameter values of the economy

[1] Clearly, money is always used as a store of value between the subperiods 0_1 and 0_3 – but this is qualitatively different from its use in storing value between dates 0 and 1, where it competes in the portfolio role with other financial assets: This case has been studied in some detail for an exchange economy in Magill and Quinzii (1991).

(explained in what follows) for which each monetary equilibrium has a positive nominal rate of interest, $r_1 > 0$.

Under these assumptions, all the money balances acquired in the subperiods 0_1 and 0_2 are used by consumers and firms to purchase commodities

$$(x_0, y_0) = (x_0^1, \dots, x_0^I, y_0^1, \dots, y_0^J) \tag{3}$$

from the central exchange and the total amount of money

$$M_0 = \sum_{i=1}^{I} m_0^i + \sum_{j=1}^{J} \tilde{m}_0^j \tag{4}$$

injected into the economy by the central exchange in subperiod 0_1 is returned to it in subperiod 0_3.

Transactions in each state s at date 1 are similarly divided into transactions in three separate subperiods (s_1, s_2, s_3). In the first subperiod s_1, consumers and firms sell the commodities

$$(w_s, y_s + \eta_s) = (w_s^1, \dots, w_s^I, y_s^1 + \eta_s^1, \dots, y_s^J + \eta_s^J) \tag{5}$$

to the central exchange. They thus receive the amounts of fiat money

$$(m_s^1, \dots, m_s^I, \tilde{m}_s^1, \dots, \tilde{m}_s^J),$$

where $m_s^i = p_s w_s^i$, and $\tilde{m}_s^j = p_s(y_s^j + \eta_s^j)$, $p_s = (p_{s1}, \dots, p_{sH})$, denoting the vector of *spot prices* in state s. In the second subperiod s_2, consumers and firms receive (make) the dividend payments implied by their contractual commitments (z, ξ) in (2′) at date 0. In the final subperiod s_3, consumers use the money balances at their disposal to purchase the goods

$$x_s = (x_s^1, \dots, x_s^I) \tag{6}$$

from the central exchange. Since no money is transferred from date 0, the total amount of money returned to the central exchange in subperiod s_3 coincides with the amount of money

$$M_s = \sum_{i=1}^{I} m_s^i + \sum_{j=1}^{J} \tilde{m}_s^j \tag{7}$$

that it injects into the economy in subperiod s_1. Figure 1 gives a schematic breakdown of the transactions and money flows involved in (1)–(7).

We assume that the vector of money supplies (the *monetary policy*)

$$M = (M_0, M_1, \dots, M_S) \in \mathfrak{M} = \mathbb{R}_{++}^{S+1}$$

(where $\mathfrak{M}$ is the *monetary policy space*) is exogenously determined by the government. Just as the decisions of consumers and firms are parametrized by the initial endowment vector $(\omega, \eta) \in \Omega$, so the action of the government can be viewed as being parametrized by the monetary policy M. Thus, the triple

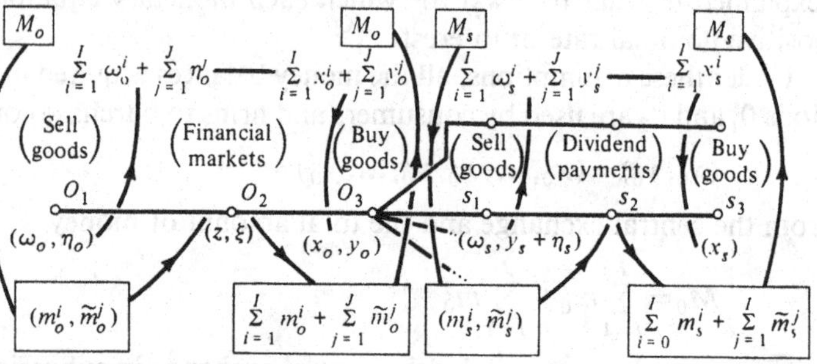

Figure 1. Transactions and money flows.

$$(\omega, \eta, M) \in \Omega \times \mathfrak{M}$$

constitutes the basic set of parameters for the economy.

4 Monetary equilibrium

To make precise our concept of a monetary equilibrium, we need to define the opportunity sets, objectives, and resulting actions of consumers and firms. Consider, first, the consumers. Let $z_0^i = (z_0'^i, z_0''^i) \in \mathbb{R}^J \times \mathbb{R}^K$ and $z^i = (z'^i, z''^i) \in \mathbb{R}^J \times \mathbb{R}^K$ denote the *initial* (inherited) and *new* (posttrade) portfolios of stocks and bonds held by consumer i and let

$$q = (q', q'') = (q_1, \ldots, q_J, q_{J+1}, \ldots, q_{J+K}),$$

$$(D_s, N_s) = (D_s^1, \ldots, D_s^J, N_s^1, \ldots, N_s^K), \quad s = 0, 1, \ldots, S,$$

denote the vector of stock and bond prices and their vectors of dividend payments across the states, measured in francs. Then the previous transactions flows lead to the following budget equations for consumer i:

$$\begin{aligned} p_0 x_0^i &= p_0 w_0^i + (q' + D_0, N_0) z_0^i - q z^i, && \text{(i)} \\ p_s x_s^i &= p_s w_s^i + (D_s, N_s) z^i, \quad s = 1, \ldots, S. && \text{(ii)} \end{aligned} \tag{8}$$

For $x^i \in \mathbb{R}^{H(S+1)}$ and $p \in \mathbb{R}^{H(S+1)}$ define the *box product*

$$p \,\square\, x^i = (p_0 x_0^i, p_1 x_1^i, \ldots, p_S x_S^i)$$

and let $e_0 = (1, 0, \ldots, 0) \in \mathbb{R}^{S+1}$. If we let $W_0 = (q' + D_0, N_0)$,

$$W = \begin{bmatrix} -q' & -q'' \\ D_1 & N_1 \end{bmatrix} = \begin{bmatrix} -q_1 & \cdots & -q_J & -q_{J+1} & \cdots & -q_{J+K} \\ D_1^1 & \cdots & D_1^J & N_1^1 & \cdots & N_1^K \\ \vdots & & \vdots & \vdots & \ddots & \vdots \\ D_S^1 & \cdots & D_S^J & N_S^1 & \cdots & N_S^K \end{bmatrix} \tag{9}$$

denote the financial asset *returns matrices,* then the budget set of consumer i can be written as $(i=1,\dots,I)$

$$B^i(p,q,D,N,\omega,\eta)=\{x^i\in \mathbb{R}^n_+ \mid \exists z^i\in \mathbb{R}^{J+K} \text{ such that } p\,\square\,(x^i-w^i)=W_0 z^i_0 e_0+Wz^i\}. \qquad (10)$$

Define the *subspace of income transfers* in $\mathbb{R}^{S+1}$ generated by the columns of the matrix W

$$\langle W\rangle=\{\tau\in \mathbb{R}^{S+1} \mid \exists z\in \mathbb{R}^{J+K} \text{ such that } \tau=Wz\}$$

and the *orthogonal (dual) subspace of present-value vectors* (state prices)

$$\langle W\rangle^{\perp}=\{\beta\in \mathbb{R}^{S+1} \mid \beta W=0\}.$$

A variant of the Minkowski–Farkas lemma asserts that

$$\textit{either} \quad \langle W\rangle\cap(\mathbb{R}^{S+1}_+\backslash 0)\neq\emptyset \quad \textit{or} \quad \langle W\rangle^{\perp}\cap\mathbb{R}^{S+1}_{++}\neq\emptyset. \qquad (11)$$

It is easy to see that *consumer i's maximum problem*

$$\max_{x^i\in B^i(p,q,D,N,\omega,\eta)} u^i(x^i), \quad i=1,\dots,I, \qquad (12)$$

has a solution if and only if $\langle W\rangle\cap(\mathbb{R}^{S+1}_+\backslash 0)=\emptyset$. This is just the *no-arbitrage* condition, which by (11) is equivalent to the existence of a vector of state prices $\beta\in\langle W\rangle^{\perp}\cap\mathbb{R}^{S+1}_{++}$, which can be written in the *normalized* present value form $\beta=(1,\beta_1)$ and satisfies

$$\beta W=0. \qquad (13)$$

Let $\lambda^i=(\lambda^i_0,\lambda^i_1,\dots,\lambda^i_S)\in\mathbb{R}^{S+1}_{++}$ denote the Lagrange multipliers induced by the $S+1$ budget constraints in (12) and let

$$\pi^i=(1,\pi^i_1,\dots,\pi^i_S)=(1,\lambda^i_1/\lambda^i_0,\dots,\lambda^i_S/\lambda^i_0), \quad i=1,\dots,I,$$

denote the *normalized* multipliers. We call π^i the *present-value vector* of consumer i since π^i_S denotes the value to consumer i at date 0 of a contract that promises to pay one franc in state s. From the first-order conditions for the choice of portfolio z^i in (12)

$$\pi^i W=0, \quad i=1,\dots,I. \qquad (14)$$

Thus, the first-order conditions imply that $\pi^i\in\langle W\rangle^{\perp}\cap\mathbb{R}^{S+1}_{++}$.

Given production and portfolio decisions

$$(y,\xi)=(y^1,\dots,y^J,\xi^1,\dots,\xi^J)$$

for the firms and market prices (p,q), the dividends of the firms are defined by the relations $(j=1,\dots,J)$

$$\begin{aligned} D^j_0&=p_0(y^j_0+\eta^j_0)-q\xi^j, && \text{(i)}\\ D^j_s&=p_s(y^j_s+\eta^j_s)+(Ds,Ns)\xi^j, \quad s=1,\dots,S. && \text{(ii)} \end{aligned} \qquad (15)$$

As Duffie and Shafer (1986) first observed, in order that equations (15) lead to well-defined dividends for the firms, the matrix

$$I-\xi'=\begin{bmatrix} 1-\xi^{11} & -\xi^{21} & \cdots & -\xi^{J1} \\ -\xi^{12} & 1-\xi^{22} & \cdots & -\xi^{J2} \\ \vdots & \vdots & \ddots & \vdots \\ -\xi^{1J} & -\xi^{2J} & \cdots & 1-\xi^{J2} \end{bmatrix} \tag{16}$$

must be invertible, ξ' being the $J\times J$ matrix of *interfirm shareholdings.* When this condition is satisfied, the $S\times J$ matrix of date 1 dividends can be written as

$$D_1=[p_1\square(y_1+\eta_1)+N_1\xi''][1-\xi']^{-1}, \tag{17}$$

where

$$\xi''=\begin{bmatrix} \xi^{1,J+1} & \cdots & \xi^{J,J+1} \\ \vdots & \ddots & \vdots \\ \xi^{1,J+K} & \cdots & \xi^{J,J+K} \end{bmatrix}$$

is the $K\times J$ matrix of *firm bondholdings.* To obtain an objective function for each firm, it suffices to introduce a vector of state prices

$$\beta^j=(1,\beta_1^j,\ldots,\beta_S^j)\in\mathbb{R}_{++}^{S+1}, \quad j=1,\ldots,J, \tag{18}$$

which translates the stream of dividends into a present value at date 0. Recall the asset-returns matrix $W=W(q,D_1,N_1)$ defined in (9). Using (15) and (18) leads to the following expression for the present value of firm j's dividends

$$\beta^jD^j=\beta^j(p\square(y^j+\eta^j))+\beta^jW(q,D_1,N_1)\xi^j, \quad j=1,\ldots,J.$$

Thus, firm j's profit-maximizing problem

$$\max_{(y^j,\xi^j)\in Y^j\times\mathbb{R}^{J+K}} \beta^j\cdot D^j, \quad j=1,\ldots,J,$$

has a solution only if β^j *satisfies the orthogonality condition* $\beta^jW=0$, *which is equivalent to*

$$\beta^j\in\langle W\rangle^{\perp}\cap\mathbb{R}_{++}^{S+1}, \quad j=1,\ldots,J,$$

so that

$$\beta^j\cdot D^j=\beta^j\cdot(p\square(y^j+\eta^j)). \tag{19}$$

If the firm's maximum problem is to have a solution, then the present value of its profit can only depend on its production decision (y^j) *and must not be influenced by its choice of financial policy* (ξ^j). This irrelevance of ξ^j for the firms profit is the first part of the Modigliani–Miller theorem.

The problem of selecting a discount vector β^j for firm j thus reduces to selecting a present-value vector which in some sense represents the collective interests of the firm's owners - namely, its *shareholders*. It was Drèze (1974) who first proposed a criterion of this kind with

$$\beta^j = \sum_{i=1}^{I} z^{ij}\pi^i \quad (\text{for } z^{ij} \geq 0), \quad j=1,\ldots,J,$$

being the average present-value vector of the *new* shareholders ($z^{ij} \geq 0$) of firm j. Although this criterion has substantial *normative* appeal (see Geanakoplos et al., 1990), adopting it would make our subsequent comparative static analysis very complex. We could employ the elegant refinement of this criterion subsequently introduced by Drèze (1985) by which in essence only a subgroup of the largest shareholders has a dominant say in the firms decisions - a criterion with great *descriptive* appeal - but this criterion also makes comparative static analysis difficult. We are thus led to adopt the other natural candidate criterion introduced by Grossman and Hart (1979) by which

$$\beta^j = \sum_{i=1}^{I} z_0^{ij}\pi^i, \quad j=1,\ldots,J,$$

is the average present-value vector of the firm's *original* shareholders (z_0^{ij}). To prove that monetary changes have production effects, we will also require that the original ownership of the firms is not too diffused among the set of consumers. Even though the technical difficulties of working with the Drèze criterion are substantially greater, it is our belief that the qualitative results that we obtain do not depend on the particular criterion that we have adopted.

We are now in a position to define the concept of a monetary equilibrium which forms the basis for the analysis that follows.

Definition 1. *A* monetary equilibrium *for the economy* $\mathcal{E}(u, Y, N, \omega, \eta, M)$ *is a pair of actions and prices* $((\bar{x}, \bar{z}), (\bar{y}, \bar{\xi}); (\bar{p}, \bar{q}, \bar{\pi}))$ *such that*

(i) $(\bar{x}^i, \bar{z}^i, \bar{\pi}^i)$, $i=1,\ldots,I$, *satisfy*

$$\bar{x}^i = \underset{x^i \in B^i(\bar{p}, \bar{q}, \bar{D}, N, \omega, \eta)}{\arg\max} \; u^i(x^i), \qquad \bar{p} \,\square\, (\bar{x}^i - w^i) = W_0 z_0^i e_0 + \bar{W}\bar{z}^i.$$

$\bar{\pi}^i$ *is the present-value vector of agent i and* $(\bar{W}, \bar{D})$ *are defined by* (9), (15) (i), *and* (17).

(ii) $(\bar{y}^j, \bar{\xi}^j)$, $j=1,\ldots,J$, *satisfy*

$$\bar{y}^j = \underset{y^j \in Y^j}{\arg\max}\; \bar{\beta}^j \cdot (\bar{p} \,\square\, y^j), \qquad \bar{\beta}^j = \sum_{i=1}^{I} z_0^{ij}\bar{\pi}^i$$

and the matrix $(I - \bar{\xi}')$ *in* (16) *is invertible.*

(iii) $\sum_{i=1}^{I}(\bar{x}^i - w^i) = \sum_{j=1}^{J} \bar{y}^j + \eta^j.$

(iv) $\sum_{i=1}^{I} \bar{z}'^i + \sum_{j=1}^{J} \xi'^j = e, \qquad e = (1, \dots, 1) \in \mathbb{R}^J,$

$\sum_{i=1}^{I} \bar{z}''^i + \sum_{j=1}^{J} \xi''^j = 0.$

(v) $\bar{p}_0\left(\sum_{i=1}^{I} w_0^i + \sum_{j=1}^{J} \eta_0^j\right) = M_0,$

$\bar{p}_s\left(\sum_{i=1}^{I} w_s^i + \sum_{j=1}^{J} (y_s^j + \eta_s^j)\right) = M_s, \quad s = 1, \dots, S.$

We say that the equilibrium has a positive nominal interest rate *if* $q_1 < 1$. *If* $\text{rank}[D_1, N_1] = \rho$, *we say that the equilibrium has* rank ρ.

Remark 1. A positive nominal interest-rate equilibrium will not exist for all parameter values $(\omega, \eta, M) \in \Omega \times \mathfrak{M}$. For a given production economy $\mathcal{E}(u, Y; \omega, \eta)$, if the money supplies at date 1, M_s $(s = 1, \dots, S)$, are sufficiently small relative to M_0, then the marginal utility of a franc at date 1 $(\sum_{s=1}^{S} \lambda_s^i)$ is greater than the marginal utility of a franc at date 0 (λ_0^i)

$$\sum_{s=1}^{S} \lambda_s^i > \lambda_0^i \Leftrightarrow \sum_{s=1}^{S} \pi_s^i > 1$$

and consumers will respond by carrying forward part of their date 0 money balances for use at date 1. But then the quantity of money exchanged for goods is not the same at subperiods 0_1 and 0_3 although the total quantity of goods exchanged remains unchanged. Thus, the prices at which agents sell their initial endowment to the central exchange at 0_1 must differ from the prices to which they buy their consumption bundles at 0_3. The budget constraint is then different from the one given in (i) of Definition 1 and the previous concept of a monetary equilibrium does not apply.

Since the money supplies M that lead to positive interest-rate equilibria depend upon the data of the economy $\mathcal{E}(u, Y; \omega, \eta)$ in a complex way, it is difficult to analyze monetary equilibria if we restrict attention to positive interest-rate equilibria from the start. We are thus led to extend the concept of a monetary equilibrium to include *negative* interest-rate equilibria $(q_1 > 1)$. We will show that with this extended concept, a monetary equilibrium exists for a generic subset of $\Omega \times \mathfrak{M}$. Furthermore, such equilibria are locally finite and smooth functions of the parameters (ω, η, M). Once these results have been obtained, it is straightforward to find the positive interest-rate equilibria and to carry out the basic qualitative analysis of the effects of changes in monetary policy.

Remark 2. It is clear that if agents can carry money from one period to the next, the interest rate cannot become negative. However, the negative nominal interest-rate equilibria can be given an economic interpretation if we assume that *separate currencies* are issued for use at dates 0 and 1 and that the date 0 currency is not legal tender for transactions at date 1. Although there are circumstances under which such an interpretation may be of interest, it does not deal with the important issue of extending the concept of equilibrium so as to allow agents to hoard part of their money balances for use at date 1. Such an extension has been given by Magill and Quinzii (1991) for the case of an exchange economy: A similar analysis for the case of a production economy becomes complex – especially if we are to obtain interesting comparative statics results. We have, therefore, chosen to concentrate on the more tractable positive nominal interest-rate equilibria.

5 Analysis via reduced form and pseudoequilibrium

The first step is to establish that monetary equilibria exist. This, however, is not a trivial problem since the budget sets, (10), do not vary continuously with the spot prices. We will show that the existence proof of Husseini, Lasry, and Magill (HLM) (1990) for an *exchange economy* with incomplete financial assets, consisting solely of real assets (equity and futures contracts), can be extended to a *production economy* in which there are both real and nominal assets in addition to money. To do this, we will apply the fixed-point theorem of HLM.

To carry out the existence proof and also for the subsequent comparative static analysis, it is convenient to introduce the concept of a *reduced-form equilibrium* and the associated concept of a *pseudoequilibrium*. These are essentially two types of *constrained* Arrow–Debreu equilibria in which asset trades and asset prices are eliminated by using the no-arbitrage condition (13). The $J+K$ asset prices q are replaced by a vector of state prices $\beta=(1,\beta_1)\in\mathbb{R}^{S+1}_{++}$ in such a way that the map $q\mapsto\beta$ is one to one. A pseudoequilibrium has the additional property that the date 1 subspace of income transfers achievable by trading in the assets is replaced by a surrogate $J+K$ dimensional subspace of income transfers.

5.1 *Derivation of reduced-form equilibrium*

This concept is derived as follows. Substituting (13) written as

$$q'=\beta_1 D_1,\qquad q''=\beta_1 N_1 \tag{20}$$

into the date 0 budget equation (8) (i) gives

$$p_0(x_0^i - w_0^i) = \beta D z_0'^i + N_0 z_0''^i - \beta_1[D_1, N_1]z^i$$
$$= \beta\cdot[p\square(y+\eta)]z_0'^i + N_0 z_0''^i - \beta_1(p_1\square(x_1^i - w_1^i))$$

in view of (19) and (8) (ii). Let

$$\gamma_0^i(p,\beta,y,\eta) = \beta\cdot(p\square(y+\eta))z_0'^i + N_0 z_0''^i$$

denote the *initial financial wealth* of consumer i, then the date 0 budget equation becomes

$$\beta\cdot(p\square(x^i - w^i)) = \gamma_0^i(p,\beta,y,\eta). \tag{21}$$

Substituting D_1 in (17) into the date 1 equation 8 (ii) gives

$$p_1\square(x_1^i - w_1^i) = [p_1\square(y_1+\eta_1), N_1]\gamma^i, \tag{22}$$

where $\gamma^i = (\gamma'^i, \gamma''^i) = ([1-\xi']^{-1}z'^i, \xi''[1-\xi']^{-1}z'^i + z''^i)$.

Thus, each consumer has access to any date 1 *income transfers lying in the subspace of* $\mathbb{R}^S$

$$\langle p_1\square(y_1+\eta_1), N_1\rangle$$

regardless of the financial policies $\xi = (\xi', \xi'') \in \mathbb{R}^J \times \mathbb{R}^K$ *chosen by the firms.* In other words, since consumers and firms have access to the same financial markets, consumers can undo any financial policy chosen by the firms. The assertion that the budget sets are uninfluenced by firms choices of financial policies constitutes the second part of the Modigliani–Miller theorem (see DeMarzo, 1987).

Let $V = [D_1, N_1]$. If $\dim\langle V\rangle < S$, we say that the (asset) markets are *incomplete.* It is clear that the dimension of the set of no-arbitrage vectors satisfies

$$\dim\{\beta \in \mathbb{R}_{++}^{S+1} \mid \beta_1 V = q\} = S - \dim\langle V\rangle.$$

Despite this multiplicity of no-arbitrage vectors, we can make the transformation $q \mapsto \beta = (1, \beta_1)$ one-to-one by selecting a *particular* no-arbitrage vector – any other choice of no-arbitrage β will then generate the same budget sets for the agents. In particular, by (14) the present-value vector $\pi^i = (1, \pi_1^i)$ of any consumer is a no-arbitrage vector. Thus, we may select $\beta = \pi^1$. This choice of β is equivalent to eliminating the date 1 constraints (22) for consumer 1. Thus, if we introduce the date 0 *present-value prices*

$$P = \beta\square p, \tag{23}$$

then the budget set of consumer 1 becomes

$$\mathbb{B}^1(P,y;\omega,\eta)=\{x^1\in\mathbb{R}^n_+ \mid P(x^1-w^1)=\gamma^1_0(P,y,\eta)\}. \tag{24}$$

If we define the diagonal matrix

$$[\beta_1]=\begin{bmatrix}\beta_1 & \cdots & 0\\ \vdots & \ddots & \vdots\\ 0 & \cdots & \beta_S\end{bmatrix}$$

and the ρ-dimensional subspace of $\mathbb{R}^S$ $(K\le\rho\le J+K)$

$$L=\langle P_1\square(y_1+\eta_1),\,[\beta_1]N_1\rangle, \tag{25}$$

then the budget sets of consumers $i=2,\dots,I$ can be written as

$$\mathbb{B}^i(P,y,L;\omega,\eta)=\left\{x^i\in\mathbb{R}^n_+ \,\middle|\, \begin{matrix}P(x^i-w^i)=\gamma^i_0(P,y,\eta)\\ P_1\square(x^i_1-w^i_1)\in L\end{matrix}\right\}. \tag{26}$$

Let $G^\rho(\mathbb{R}^S)$ denote the *Grassmanian manifold* of *ρ-dimensional subspaces of* $\mathbb{R}^S$. Any $L\in G^\rho(\mathbb{R}^S)$ can be represented by a system of equations. More precisely for any $L\in G^\rho(\mathbb{R}^S)$, there is a permutation $\sigma\in\Sigma_{1,\dots,S}$ (the set of permutations of $1,\dots,S$) and a $\rho\times(S-\rho)$ matrix $A_\sigma(L)$ such that

$$L=\{v\in\mathbb{R}^S \mid [I\,|\,A_\sigma(L)]E_\sigma v=0\},$$

where E_σ is the permutation matrix induced by σ. Although there are several permutations $\sigma\in\Sigma_{1,\dots,S}$ that can be chosen, for any *given* permutation σ, the matrix $A_\sigma(L)$ is unique. (For a discussion of the problem of representing $G^\rho(\mathbb{R}^S)$, see, for example, Duffie and Shafer, 1985.) Thus, if we define

$$[P_1]=\begin{bmatrix}P_1^T & 0 & \cdots & 0\\ 0 & P_2^T & \cdots & 0\\ \vdots & \vdots & \ddots & \vdots\\ 0 & 0 & \cdots & P_S^T\end{bmatrix},\qquad Q_\sigma(L)=[I\,|\,A_\sigma(L)]E_\sigma$$

$$\Phi_\sigma(P,L)=\left[\begin{array}{c|ccc}P_0^T & P_1^T & \cdots & P_S^T\\ \hline 0 & & Q_\sigma(L)[P_1] & \end{array}\right]. \tag{27}$$

Then the budget set (26) can be written as

$$\mathbb{B}^i(P,L,y,\omega,\eta)=\left\{x^i\in\mathbb{R}^n_+ \,\middle|\, \Phi_\sigma(P,L)(x^i-w^i)=\begin{bmatrix}\gamma^i_0(P,y,\eta)\\ 0\end{bmatrix}\right\}, \tag{28}$$

where L is given by (25). The change in the representation of the budget set from (10) to (28) leads to a change in the associated Lagrange multipliers from $\pi^i\in\mathbb{R}^{S+1}_{++}$ to $\mu^i_\sigma=(\mu^i_{\sigma 0},\dots,\mu^i_{\sigma,S-\rho})\in\mathbb{R}^{S-\rho+1}$. To express the objective functions of the firms, we must be able to recover the π^i vectors in the new variables. This can be done by noting that the first-order conditions under the two representations lead to the same consumption bundle x^i so that

$$\lambda_0^i \pi^i \square p = D_{x^i} u^i = \mu_\sigma^i \Phi_\sigma(P, L).$$

Since $\lambda_0^i = \mu_{\sigma 0}^i$, if we define the *normalized* multiplier

$$\nu_\sigma^i = (1, \nu_{\sigma 1}^i, \ldots, \nu_{\sigma, S-\rho}^i) = \left(1, \frac{\mu_{\sigma 1}^i}{\mu_{\sigma 0}^i}, \ldots, \frac{\mu_{\sigma, S-\rho}^i}{\mu_{\sigma 0}^i}\right),$$

then $\pi^i \square p = \nu_\sigma^i(P, y, L)\Phi_\sigma(P, L)$. Thus, even though the terms ν_σ^i and Φ_σ separately depend on the permutation σ (i.e., the representation of L) chosen, the product $\nu_\sigma^i \Phi_\sigma$ is independent of σ and depends only on L. Thus, we can write

$$\pi^i \square p = (\nu^i \Phi)(P, y, L).$$

For the purpose of writing the objective of the firms, agent 1 can be treated symmetrically with the other agents with the convention that $\mu^1 = (\mu_0^1, 0, \ldots, 0)$ and $\nu^1 = (1, 0, \ldots, 0)$. Let $\nu = (\nu^1, \ldots, \nu^I)$. Then the previous transformations have reduced the study of a monetary equilibrium to the study of the following analytically more tractable concept of equilibrium.

Definition 2. *A* reduced-form (RF) equilibrium *of rank ρ ($K \le \rho \le J+K$) for the economy $\mathcal{E}$ is a pair of actions and prices*

$$((\bar{x}, \bar{y}), (\bar{P}, \bar{L}, \bar{\beta}, \bar{\nu})) \in \mathbb{R}_+^{nI} \times \mathbb{R}^{nJ} \times \mathbb{R}_{++}^n \times G^\rho(\mathbb{R}^S) \times \mathbb{R}_{++}^{S+1} \times \mathbb{R}^{(S-\rho+1)I},$$

such that

(i) $(\bar{x}^i, \bar{\nu}^i)$, $i = 1, \ldots, I$, *satisfy*

$$\bar{x}^i = \underset{x^i \in \mathbb{B}^i(\bar{P}, \bar{y}, \bar{L}; \omega, \eta)}{\arg\max} u^i(x^i), \quad i = 1, \ldots, I,$$

with multipliers $\bar{\nu}^i$, $i = 1, \ldots, I$,

where $\mathbb{B}^1$ *is defined by* (24) *and* $\mathbb{B}^i$ *is defined by* (28), $i = 2, \ldots, I$.

(ii) $\bar{y}^j$, $j = 1, \ldots, J$, *satisfy*

$$\bar{y}^j = \underset{y^j \in Y^j}{\arg\max} \sum_{i=1}^I z_0^{ij} (\bar{\nu}^i \Phi)(\bar{P}, \bar{y}, \bar{L}) \cdot y^j, \quad j = 1, \ldots, J.$$

(iii) $\sum_{i=1}^I (\bar{x}^i - w^i) = \sum_{j=1}^J (\bar{y}^j + \eta^j)$.

(iv) $\langle \bar{P}_1 \square (\bar{y}_1 + \eta_1), [\bar{\beta}_1] N_1 \rangle = \bar{L}$.

(v) $\bar{P}_0 \left(\sum_{i=1}^I w_0^i + \sum_{j=1}^J \eta_0^j \right) = M_0$,

$$\bar{P}_s\left(\sum_{i=1}^{I} w_s^i + \sum_{j=1}^{J}(\bar{y}_s^j + \eta_s^j)\right) = \bar{\beta}_s M_s, \quad s=1,\ldots,S.$$

We say that a reduced-form equilibrium has a positive nominal interest rate *if* $\sum_{s=1}^{S} \bar{\beta}_s < 1$, *where* $\bar{\beta} = (1, \bar{\beta}_1)$.

This analysis has established part (i) of the following proposition; part (ii) is left to the reader.

Proposition 1. (i) *If* $((\bar{x}, \bar{z}), (\bar{y}, \bar{\xi}); (\bar{p}, \bar{q}, \bar{\pi}))$ *is a (positive interest rate) monetary equilibrium of rank* ρ *then there exist* $(\bar{\beta}, \bar{L}, \bar{\nu})$ *such that* $((\bar{x}, \bar{y}), (\bar{\beta} \square \bar{p}, \bar{L}, \bar{\beta}, \bar{\nu}))$ *is a (positive interest rate) reduced-form equilibrium of rank* ρ. (ii) *If* $((\bar{x}, \bar{y}), (\bar{P}, \bar{L}, \bar{\beta}, \bar{\nu}))$ *is a (positive interest rate) reduced-form equilibrium of rank* ρ *then there exist* $((\bar{z}, \bar{\xi}), (\bar{p}, \bar{q}, \bar{\pi}))$ *with* $\bar{\beta} \square \bar{p} = \bar{P}$, $\bar{q} = \bar{\beta}_1[\bar{p}_1 \square (\bar{y}_1 + \eta_1), N_1]$ *such that* $((\bar{x}, \bar{z}), (\bar{y}, \bar{\xi}); (\bar{p}, \bar{q}, \bar{\pi}))$ *is a (positive interest rate) monetary equilibrium of rank* ρ.

5.2 *Existence of equilibrium*

To establish the existence of a reduced-form equilibrium of rank $\rho = J+K$, we need to relax the requirement of equality in Definition 2 (iv): We want the dimension of the subspaces L to remain unchanged so that L can be parametrized by $G^{\rho}(\mathbb{R}^S)$, while allowing for the fact that the dimension of $\langle P_1 \square (y_1 + \eta_1), [\beta_1] N_1 \rangle$ will change as the prices P and production plans y change. This leads to the following concept.

Definition 3. *A* pseudoequilibrium *for the economy* $\mathcal{E}$ *is a reduced-form equilibrium of rank* $J+K$ *in which Definition 2* (iv) *is replaced by*

(iv)′ $\langle \bar{P}_1 \square (\bar{y}_1 + \eta_1), [\bar{\beta}_1] N_1 \rangle \subset \bar{L}$.

We need one more restriction on the model in order to be sure of having an equilibrium. If the initial level of indebtedness of agent i is excessive relative to his initial resources then he may not be able to afford any positive consumption bundle: In this case, the budget set $\mathbb{B}^i$ is empty and his demand function is not well-defined. Let

$$\hat{\gamma}_0^i(\omega, \eta, M) = \min\left\{P_0 w_0^i \;\middle|\; P_0 \in \mathbb{R}_+^H, P_0\left(\sum_{i=1}^{I} w_0^i + \sum_{j=1}^{J} \eta_0^j\right) = M_0\right\},$$

$i = 1, \ldots, I.$

Assumption E (Initial indebtedness). $N_0 z_0''^i > -\hat{\gamma}_0^i(\omega, \eta, M)$, $i = 1, \ldots, I$.

A set $A \subset \Omega$ is said to be *generic* if its complement is a closed set of measure zero in Ω.

Theorem 1 (Existence and smoothness). *Under Assumptions A to E, there exists a generic set* $\Gamma \subset \Omega \times \mathfrak{M}$ *such that for all* $(\omega, \eta, M) \in \Gamma$ (i) *there exists a reduced-form equilibrium of rank* $J+K$; (ii) *there is at most a finite number of reduced-form equilibria of rank* $J+K$*, each of which is locally a smooth function of the parameters* (ω, η, M).

Proof: We first establish the following lemma.

Lemma 1. *Under the hypotheses of Theorem 1, there exists a pseudo-equilibrium for all* $(\omega, \eta, M) \in \Omega \times \mathfrak{M}$.

Proof: The idea is to construct appropriate maps so that the fixed-point theorem of HLM (1990) can be applied. The maps that handle the *production* side of the economy are borrowed from the existence proof for an economy with increasing returns by Beato and Mas-Colell (1985).

Step 1 (Truncated sets). Let $X^i = \mathbb{R}^n_+$ denote the consumption set of agent i $(i = 1, \ldots, I)$. Assumption B implies that the set of *feasible* allocations

$$\mathfrak{F} = \left\{ (x, y) \in \prod_{i=1}^{I} X^i \times \prod_{j=1}^{J} Y^j \;\middle|\; \sum_{i=1}^{I} (x^i - w^i) \leq \sum_{j=1}^{J} (y^j + \eta^j) \right\}$$

is compact. Let $\hat{X}^i$ denote the projection of $\mathfrak{F}$ on X^i and let $\hat{Y}^j$ denote the projection of $\mathfrak{F}$ on Y^j. For each firm, we modify the production set $Y^j \to \tilde{Y}^j$ in such a way that $\tilde{Y}^j$ coincides with Y^j on $\hat{Y}^j$ and production plans in $\tilde{Y}^j$ involving large amounts of inputs are inefficient (no additional output with additional inputs). To simplify the analysis, we consider first the case where the subspace E^j in Assumption B(3) satisfies $E^j = \mathbb{R}^n$. $\tilde{Y}^j$ is then constructed as follows. Pick $\hat{a}^j \in \mathbb{R}^n_{++}$ such that $\hat{Y}^j \subset \mathbb{R}^n_+ - \hat{a}^j$. Then choose $a^j \gg \hat{a}^j$ and construct $\tilde{Y}^j$ (see Figure 2) such that $\partial \tilde{Y}^j$ is smooth and

$$y^j \in \tilde{Y}^j \Leftrightarrow y^j \in Y^j \quad \text{for all } y^j \in \mathbb{R}^n_+ - \hat{a}^j,$$
$$y^j \in \tilde{Y}^j \Leftrightarrow y^j \in (Y^j \cap (\mathbb{R}^n_+ - a^j)) - \mathbb{R}^n_+ \quad \text{for all } y^j \in (\mathbb{R}^n_+ - a^j)^c.$$

Let $\tilde{X}^i$ be a compact convex subset of $\mathbb{R}^n_+$ such that $\tilde{X}^i \subset \hat{X}^i$, $i = 1, \ldots, I$, and let

$$\tilde{\mathfrak{F}} = \left\{ (x, y) \in \prod_{i=1}^{I} \tilde{X}^i \times \prod_{j=1}^{J} \tilde{Y}^j \;\middle|\; \sum_{i=1}^{I} (x^i - w^i) \leq \sum_{j=1}^{J} (y^j + \eta^j) \right\};$$

then $\tilde{\mathfrak{F}} = \mathfrak{F}$. Let $\mathcal{E}$ and $\tilde{\mathcal{E}}$ denote the economies with consumption and production sets $(X^1, \ldots, X^I, Y^1, \ldots, Y^J)$ and $(\tilde{X}^1, \ldots, \tilde{X}^I, \tilde{Y}^1, \ldots, \tilde{Y}^J)$, re-

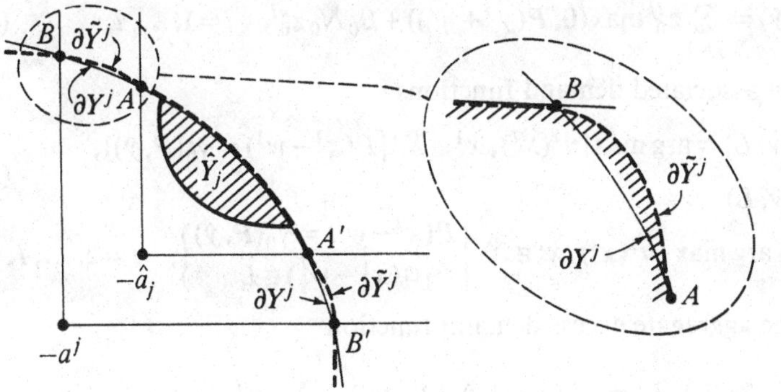

Figure 2. The smooth truncation $\tilde{Y}^j$ of Y^j.

spectively. Then, since agents maximize over convex sets the equilibria of $\mathcal{E}$ and $\tilde{\mathcal{E}}$ coincide.

Step 2 (Maps). Let $\Delta = \{v \in \mathbb{R}^n_+ \mid \sum_{j=1}^n v_j = 1\}$ denote the $n-1$ dimensional simplex. We will construct a pair of continuous functions (ϕ, ψ)

$$\begin{aligned} &\phi: \Delta^{J+1} \times G^{J+K}(\mathbb{R}^S) \to \Delta^{J+1}, \\ &\psi: \Delta^{J+1} \times G^{J+K}(\mathbb{R}^S) \to \mathbb{R}^{(J+K)S}, \end{aligned} \tag{29}$$

and apply the fixed-point theorem of HLM (1990, Theorem A) by which, if $(P, \hat{y}, L)$ is a typical element of $\Delta \times \Delta^J \times G^{J+K}(\mathbb{R}^S)$, then there exists $(P^*, \hat{y}^*, L^*) \in \Delta^{J+1} \times G^{J+K}(\mathbb{R}^S)$ such that

$$\phi(P^*, \hat{y}^*, L^*) = (P^*, \hat{y}^*), \quad \langle \psi(P^*, \hat{y}^*, L^*) \rangle \subset L^*. \tag{30}$$

By the assumption of free disposal, the boundary $\partial\tilde{Y}^j \cap (\mathbb{R}^n_+ - a^j)$ of $\tilde{Y}^J \cap (\mathbb{R}^n_+ - a^j)$ is homeomorphic to the simplex Δ under the homeomorphism

$$\alpha_j: \partial\tilde{Y}^j \cap (\mathbb{R}^n_+ - a^j) \to \Delta, \quad \alpha_j = \frac{y^j + a^j}{\sum_{s,h}(y^j_{sh} + a^j_{sh})}, \quad j = 1, \ldots, J,$$

and the *unit normal* map (i.e., $\sum_{s,h} n^j_{sh} = 1$)

$$n^j: \partial\tilde{Y}^j \cap (\mathbb{R}^n_+ - a^j) \to \Delta, \quad j = 1, \ldots, J,$$

is well-defined. In the analysis that follows, let $y^j = \alpha_j^{-1}(\hat{y}^j)$. If we let

$$\beta_0(P) = \frac{P_0(\sum_{i=1}^I w^i_0 + \sum_{j=1}^J \eta^j_0)}{M_0}$$

and define the modified date 0 revenue functions

$$\tilde{\gamma}_0^i(P,\hat{y}) = \sum_{j=1}^{J} z_0^{ij} \max(0, P(y^j+\eta^j)) + \beta_0 N_0 z_0^{\prime\prime i}, \quad i=1,\ldots,I, \tag{31}$$

and the associated demand functions

$$\begin{aligned} f^1(P,\hat{y},L) &= \arg\max\{u^1(x^1), x^1 \in \tilde{X}^1 \mid P(x^1-w^1) = \tilde{\gamma}_0^1(P,\hat{y})\}, \\ f^i(P,\hat{y},L) & \\ &= \arg\max\left\{u^1(x^i), x^i \in \tilde{X}^i \,\middle|\, \begin{matrix} P(x^i-w^i) = \tilde{\gamma}_0^i(P,\hat{y}) \\ P_1 \square (x_1^i - w_1^i) \in L \end{matrix}\right\}, \quad i=2,\ldots,I, \end{aligned} \tag{32}$$

then the aggregate excess demand function

$$Z(P,\hat{y},L) = \sum_{i=1}^{I} (f^i(P,\hat{y},L)-w^i) - \sum_{j=1}^{J} (y^j+\eta^j)$$

satisfies Walras Law $PZ(P,\hat{y},L)=0$ whenever $P(y^j+\eta^j) \geq 0$, $j=1,\ldots,J$. Furthermore, the truncation $\hat{X}^1$ can be made sufficiently large so that $P_{sh}=0$ implies $Z_{sh}>0$ for all $s=0,\ldots,S$, $h=1,\ldots,H$. Let $\beta(P,\hat{y}) = (\beta_0(P), \beta_1(P,\hat{y}),\ldots,\beta_S(P,\hat{y}))$, where

$$\beta_s(P,\hat{y}) = \frac{P_s(\sum_{i=1}^{I} w_s^i + \sum_{j=1}^{J}(y_s^j+\eta_s^j))}{M_s}, \quad s=1,\ldots,S, \tag{33}$$

and let

$$b^j(P,\hat{y},L) = \frac{\sum_{i=1}^{I} z_0^{ij}(\nu^i\Phi)(P,y,L)}{\sum_{i=1}^{I} z_0^{ij} \sum_{s,h}(\nu^i\Phi)_{sh}(P,y,L)}, \quad j=1,\ldots,J,$$

denote the vector of present-value prices of firm j, normalized to lie in the simplex, $\Phi(P,L)$ being given by (27) (for an appropriate choice of σ) and $\nu^i = \nu_\sigma^i(P,\hat{y},L)$ being the normalized multiplier induced by consumer i's maximum problem (32). Then the maps $(\phi,\psi) = (\phi^0,\phi^1,\ldots,\phi^J,\psi)$ in (29) are defined as follows, for $s=0,1,\ldots,S$, $h=1,\ldots,H$:

$$\phi_{sh}^0(P,\hat{y},L) = \frac{(P_{sh}+\max(0,Z_{sh}(P,\hat{y},L)))}{1+\sum_{s,h}\max(0,Z_{sh}(P,\hat{y},L))},$$

$$\phi_{sh}^j(P,\hat{y},L) = \frac{(\hat{y}_{sh}^j+\max(0,b_{sh}^j(P,\hat{y},L)-n_{sh}^j(y^j))}{1+\sum_{s,h}\max(0,b_{sh}^j(P,\hat{y},L)-n_{sh}^j(y^j))},$$

$$\psi(P,\hat{y},L) = [P_1\square(y_1+\eta_1), [\beta_1(P,\hat{y})]N_1].$$

Step 3 (The fixed point is an equilibrium). Let $(P^*,\hat{y}^*,L^*)$ denote the fixed point defined by (30). We will show that $((\bar{x},\bar{y}),(\bar{P},\bar{L},\bar{\beta},\bar{\nu}))$ defined by

$$\bar{x} = (f^1(P^*,L^*,\hat{y}^*),\ldots,f^I(P^*,L^*,\hat{y}^*)), \quad \bar{y} = \alpha^{-1}(\hat{y}^*),$$

$$\bar{P} = \frac{P^*}{\beta_0(P^*)}, \qquad \bar{L} = L^*, \qquad \bar{\beta} = \frac{\beta(P^*,\hat{y}^*)}{\beta_0}, \qquad \bar{\nu} = \nu^*,$$

is a pseudoequilibrium. $\phi^{j*}=\hat{y}^{j*} \Rightarrow b^{j*}=n^{j*} \Rightarrow$ firm j maximizes profit under the prices $\Sigma_{i=1}^{I} z_0^{ij}(\nu^{i*}\Phi^*)=\beta_0^* \Sigma_{i=1}^{I} z_0^{ij}(\bar{\nu}^i\bar{\Phi})$. Since $\eta^j \geq 0 \Rightarrow \Sigma_{i=1}^{I} z_0^{ij}(\bar{\nu}^{i*}\Phi^*)(y^{j*}+\eta^j) \geq 0$. $\langle\psi^*\rangle \subset L^* \Rightarrow Q_\sigma(L^*)[P_1](y_1^*+\eta_1)=0 \Rightarrow 0 \leq \Sigma z_0^{ij}(\nu^{i*}\Phi^*)(y^{j*}+\eta^j)=P^*(y^{j*}+\eta^j)$. $P^* \gg 0$ since $P_{sh}^*=0 \Rightarrow Z_{sh}^*>0$. $\phi_{sh}^{0*}=P_{sh}^* \Rightarrow \max(0, Z_{sh}^*)=0 \Rightarrow Z_{sh}^* \leq 0$. Since $\Sigma_{s,h} P_{sh}^* Z_{sh}^*=0 \Rightarrow Z_{sh}^*=0$, $\forall s, h$. Finally, equations (33) and $\bar{P}=P^*/\beta_0(P^*)$ ensure that the monetary equations in Definition 2(v) hold and that the budget sets in (32) coincide with those in (24) and (28). □

The proof of Theorem 1 is completed by establishing the following lemma.

Lemma 2. *Under the hypotheses of Theorem 1:* (i) *there exists a generic set* $\Gamma' \subset \Omega \times \mathfrak{M}$ *such that for all* $(\omega, \eta, M) \in \Gamma'$, *there are at most a finite number of pseudoequilibria and each pseudoequilibrium is locally a smooth function of the parameters* (ω, η, M); (ii) *there exists a generic set* $\Gamma \subset \Gamma'$ *such that for all* $(\omega, \eta, M) \in \Gamma$ *every pseudoequilibrium is a reduced-form equilibrium of rank* $J+K$.

Proof: The ideas behind the proofs of (i) and (ii) are simple. To show (i), we show that a pseudoequilibrium can be written as a solution of a system of equations in which the number of equations equals the number of unknowns. To prove (ii), we show that generically there are no pseudoequilibria of rank $\rho < J+K$. When the condition $\text{rank}[P_1 \square (y_1+\eta_1), [\beta_1]N_1] < J+K$ is expressed as a system of equations and added to the equations of a pseudoequilibrium, we obtain a system with *more* equations than unknowns, which generically has no solution. To prove (i) and (ii) *without perturbing the nominal returns matrix* N_1, we must be careful to express precisely that we work with the subset of $G^{J+K}(\mathbb{R}^S)$ *consisting of subspaces L that contain* $\langle\beta_1 N_1\rangle$ (see Step 1 of the proof that is completed in the Appendix).

6 Effects of changes in monetary policy

In this section, we study the way changes in monetary policy affect the equilibrium allocation $(\bar{x}, \bar{y})$. In macroeconomics, a distinction is made between *anticipated* and *unanticipated* changes in monetary policy. If agents inherit no initial holdings of bonds $(z_0''=0)$, then they are free to adapt their portfolios to any change in M. In this case, we say that the agents can *anticipate* monetary changes. If the agents inherit initial holdings of bonds $(z_0'' \neq 0)$, then these initial portfolios cannot be adapted to changes in the date 0 monetary policy. In this case, we say that date 0 monetary changes are *unanticipated.* We want to analyze the effect of anticipated and unanticipated monetary changes on positive interest-rate equilibria.

6.1 *Positive interest-rate parameters*

In the previous section, we have shown that there is a generic set $\Gamma \subset \Omega \times \mathfrak{M}$ such that monetary equilibria of rank $J+K$ exist for all parameter values $(\omega, \eta, M) \in \Gamma$ and all such equilibria are locally smooth functions of the parameters. *Let $\hat{\Gamma} \subset \Gamma$ denote the subset of parameters for which all equilibria have a positive nominal interest rate.* Note that if (P, y, L, β_1) is a reduced-form equilibrium price for the parameter value (ω, η, M), then $(P, y, L, \beta_1/\alpha)$ is a reduced-form equilibrium price for the parameter value (ω, η, M') with $M' = (M_0, \alpha M_1)$ for $\alpha \neq 0$: If the money supply is doubled in each state s $(s \geq 1)$, then the value of a contract promising one franc at date 1 is halved. Thus, a sufficient (proportional) increase in the money supply at date 1 will always force the nominal interest rate to be positive. Consider the correspondence $\gamma : \Gamma \to \Gamma$ defined by

$$\gamma(\omega, \eta, M) = \{(\omega, \eta, M_0, \alpha M_1) \mid \alpha > \alpha^*(\omega, \eta, M)\},$$

where $\alpha^*(\omega, \eta, M) = \max\{\sum_{s=1}^{S} \beta_s \mid (P, y, L, \beta) \text{ is an RF equilibrium for } (\omega, \eta, M)\}$. Then $\hat{\Gamma} = \gamma(\Gamma)$.

6.2 *Anticipated monetary changes*

Consider a regular parameter value $(\bar{\omega}, \bar{\eta}, \bar{M}) \in \hat{\Gamma}$ and an associated equilibrium "price" $(\bar{P}, \bar{y}, \bar{L}, \bar{\beta})$. Since at an equilibrium of rank $J+K$,

$$\bar{L} = \langle \bar{P}_1 \square (\bar{y}_1 + \eta_1), [\bar{\beta}_1] N_1 \rangle,$$

the variables $(\bar{P}, \bar{y}, \bar{\beta})$ determine completely the equilibrium. For equilibria with parameter values in $\hat{\Gamma}$, we can thus view

$$\mathcal{P} = \mathbb{R}^n_{++} \times \mathbb{R}^{nJ} \times \mathbb{R}^S_{++}$$

as the space of "prices." By Theorem 1(ii), we know that there exists a neighborhood $\mathfrak{N}_{(\bar{\omega}, \bar{\eta}, \bar{M})} \subset \hat{\Gamma}$ and a function $g : \mathfrak{N}_{(\bar{\omega}, \bar{\eta}, \bar{M})} \to \mathcal{P}$ that gives the equilibrium prices (P, y, β) for each $(\omega, \eta, M) \in \mathfrak{N}_{(\bar{\omega}, \bar{\eta}, \bar{M})}$. Since the comparative static analysis is confined to local changes in M, we consider the neighborhood

$$\mathfrak{N}_{\bar{M}} = \{M \in \mathfrak{M} \mid (\bar{\omega}, \bar{\eta}, M) \in \mathfrak{N}_{(\bar{\omega}, \bar{\eta}, \bar{M})}\}.$$

Let $g(\bar{\omega}, \bar{\eta}, M) = (P(M), y(M), \beta(M))$ and let $f(g(\bar{\omega}, \bar{\eta}, M), \bar{\omega}, \bar{\eta}) = x(M)$, where $f = (f^1, \ldots, f^I)$ is the vector of demand functions $f^i : \mathcal{P} \times \Omega \to \mathbb{R}^n$ in Definition 2(i).

Theorem 2 (Neutrality of money). *Let Assumptions A to E hold, let* $z_0''=0$, *and let* $(\bar{\omega},\bar{\eta},\bar{M})\in\hat{\Gamma}$.

(i) *For all* $M=(\alpha\bar{M}_0,\alpha'\bar{M}_1)\in\mathfrak{M}_{\bar{M}}$ *with* $\alpha>0,\ \alpha'>0$,

$$(x(M),y(M))=(x(\bar{M}),y(\bar{M})). \tag{34}$$

(ii) *If* $J+K=S$, *then* (34) *holds for all* $M\in\mathfrak{M}_{\bar{M}}$.

Proof: (i) It is easy to check in Definition 2(i) to (v) that

$$(P(M),y(M),\beta(M))=(\alpha P(\bar{M}),y(\bar{M}),(\alpha/\alpha')\beta(\bar{M}))$$

and $x(M)=x(\bar{M})$. (ii) follows because each agent's budget set (26) reduces to the Arrow-Debreu budget set with shareholdings $(z_0'^i)$, and each firm's objective function reduces to Py^j since $\nu\Phi=P$. □

Remark 3. In Theorem 2(i), when $\alpha=\alpha'\neq 1$, spot prices p change by the factor α, but the nominal interest rate r_1 is unchanged. When $\alpha>1$, $\alpha'=1$, date 0 spot prices increase and the nominal interest rate falls; when $\alpha=1$, $\alpha'>1$, date 1 spot prices increase and the nominal interest rate increases. These are nominal changes that do not affect consumption or production decisions.

Theorem 2 points out that there are certain monetary changes that have no real effects. To take the analysis further, we restrict ourselves to the study of marginal changes at the equilibrium under consideration. By Theorem 1, the equilibrium allocation map

$$(x,y):\mathfrak{M}_{\bar{M}}\to\mathbb{R}^{nI}\times\mathbb{R}^{nJ}$$

is differentiable at $\bar{M}$ and we let

$$(D_{\bar{M}}x,D_{\bar{M}}y):\mathbb{R}^{S+1}\to\mathbb{R}^{nI}\times\mathbb{R}^{nJ}$$

denote the derivative map. We say that a monetary change $dM\in\mathbb{R}^{S-1}$ has *real effects* if $(dx,dy)=(D_{\bar{M}}x,D_{\bar{M}}y)dM\neq 0$; we say that it has *production effects* if $dy=(D_{\bar{M}}y)dM\neq 0$. To describe precisely the marginal monetary changes that have real effects (which amounts to describing $\ker D_{\bar{M}}(x,y)$) requires a more precise knowledge of the structure of the bond matrix N_1. *Without adding any further conditions on* N_1, *we can, however, give a lower bound on the number of linearly independent directions in which monetary changes dM have real effects.* As we will see in the case where the riskless bond is the only nominal asset ($K=1$), this bound is exact. We will need an assumption regarding the distribution of ownership of firms amongst consumers to show that monetary changes have production effects. To this end, let $\mathcal{I}'=\{i\mid z_0^{ij}>0 \text{ for some } j\in\{1,\dots,J\}\}$ and let $I'=\#\mathcal{I}'$ (the number of agents in $\mathcal{I}'$).

Theorem 3 (Real effects of anticipated monetary changes). *Let Assumptions A to E hold and let $z_0''=0$.*

(i) *If* (a) $J+K<S$, (b) $K<I$, *then there exists a generic set* $\hat{\Gamma}^* \subset \hat{\Gamma}$ *such that if* $(\bar{\omega}, \bar{\eta}, \bar{M}) \in \hat{\Gamma}^*$, *there is a subspace* $\Lambda \subset \mathbb{R}^{S-1}$ *with* $\dim \Lambda \geq S-J-K$ *for which*

$$(dx, dy) = (D_{\bar{M}} x, D_{\bar{M}} y) dM \neq 0, \quad \forall dM \in \Lambda \backslash \{0\}.$$

(ii) *If* (a) $J+K<S$, (b) $K<I' \leq J$, (c) $(z_0'^i,\ i \in \mathcal{I}')$ *are linearly independent,* (d) $E^j = \mathbb{R}^n$, $j=1,\dots,J$, *then* (i) *holds with* $dy \neq 0$.

Proof: (i) Let $\bar{L} = \langle \bar{P}_1 \square (\bar{y}_1 + \bar{\eta}_1), [\bar{\beta}_1] N_1 \rangle$ and pick $d\beta_1 \in \bar{L}^\perp$. Consider the change dM such that $dM_0 = 0$, $dM_s/\bar{M}_s = -d\bar{\beta}_s/\bar{\beta}_s$, $s=1,\dots,S$. We show that $(dx, dy) = (D_{\bar{M}} x, D_{\bar{M}} y) dM \neq 0$. Suppose not. Then differentiating the first-order condition for agent 1 gives $dx^{1T} D^2 u^1 = d\lambda_0^1 \bar{P} + \bar{\lambda}_0^1 dP$, and since $dx^1 = 0$, $dP = -(d\lambda_0^1/\bar{\lambda}_0^1)\bar{P}$. From the date 0 monetary equation, $d(P_0(\sum_{i=1}^I \bar{w}_0^i + \sum_{j=1}^J \bar{\eta}_0^j)) = dM_0 = 0 \Rightarrow dP = 0$. From the date s monetary equation, since $dy = 0$ and $dP_s = 0$, $0 = d(\beta_s M_s) = \bar{\beta}_s dM_s + d\beta_s \bar{M}_s$; thus $d\beta_s = d\bar{\beta}_s$, $s=1,\dots,S$. Since $d\beta_1 \in \bar{L}^\perp$, $[\bar{\beta}_1 + d\beta_1] N_1^1 = \bar{\beta}_1 + d\beta_1 \notin \bar{L}$; thus

$$\langle \bar{P}_1 \square (\bar{y}_1 + \eta_1), [\bar{\beta}_1 + d\beta_1] N_1 \rangle \neq \bar{L}. \tag{35}$$

Since $dy_1 = 0$, $dP_1 = 0$, and $dx_1 = 0$,

$$\bar{P}_1 \square (\bar{x}_1^i - \bar{w}_1^i) \in \langle \bar{P}_1 \square (\bar{y}_1 + \bar{\eta}_1), [\bar{\beta}_1 + d\beta_1] N_1 \rangle, \quad i = 2, \dots, J+1. \tag{36}$$

Lemma 3, which follows, implies that (35) contradicts (36). This argument holds for all $dM \in \Lambda'$ defined by

$$\Lambda' = \left\{ dM \,\middle|\, dM_0 = 0,\ dM_1 = -\left[\frac{\bar{M}_1}{\bar{\beta}_1}\right] d\beta_1,\ d\beta_1 \in \bar{L}^\perp \right\}, \tag{37}$$

where

$$\left[\frac{\bar{M}_1}{\bar{\beta}_1}\right] = \begin{bmatrix} \bar{M}_1/\bar{\beta}_1 & & 0 \\ & \ddots & \\ 0 & & \bar{M}_S/\bar{\beta}_S \end{bmatrix}$$

so that $\Lambda' \cap \ker D_{\bar{M}}(x,y) = \{0\}$. Thus, there exists a subspace Λ'' such that

$$\ker D_{\bar{M}}(x,y) \oplus \Lambda' \oplus \Lambda'' = \mathbb{R}^{S+1}.$$

Since $\dim \bar{L}^\perp = S - (J+K)$, it follows that $\Lambda = \Lambda' \oplus \Lambda''$ satisfies $\dim \Lambda \geq S-(J+K)$ and the proof of (i) is complete.

Lemma 3. *If* $I > K$, *then there exists a generic set* $\hat{\Gamma}^* \subset \hat{\Gamma}$ *such that if* $((\bar{x}, \bar{y}), (\bar{P}, \bar{y}, \bar{\beta}))$ *is a reduced-form equilibrium for* $(\bar{\omega}, \bar{\eta}, \bar{M}) \in \hat{\Gamma}^*$, *then*

$\bar{L} = \langle \bar{P}_1 \square (\bar{x}_1^{i_1} - \bar{w}_1^{i_1}), \ldots, \bar{P}_1 \square (\bar{x}_1^{i_K} - \bar{w}_1^{i_K}), \bar{P}_1 \square (\bar{y}_1^1 + \bar{\eta}_1^1), \ldots, \bar{P}_1 \square (y_1^J + \bar{\eta}_1^J) \rangle$
for every K-element subset $\{i_1, \ldots, i_K\}$ *of* $\{1, \ldots, I\}$.

Proof: See the Appendix.

(ii) Consider $dM \in \Lambda'$ defined by (37) and suppose $dy = 0$. Let $n^j : \partial Y^j \to \Delta$ denote the unit normal map for the boundary ∂Y^j of firm j's production set. By the first-order conditions for profit maximization, there exists $\alpha_j \neq 0$ such that $\alpha_j n^j(\bar{y}^j) = \sum_{i=1}^I z_0^{ij}(\bar{\nu}^i \Phi)$. Differentiating and using $dy^j = 0$ gives $d\alpha_j n^j(\bar{y}^j) = \sum_{i=1}^I z_0^{ij}(d\nu^i \bar{\Phi} + \bar{\nu}^i d\Phi)$ and since $\bar{\nu}^i = (1, \bar{\nu}_1^i, \ldots, \bar{\nu}_{S-(J+K)}^i)$ and $\sum_{i=1}^I z_0^{ij} = 1$, the date 0 component implies $dP_0 = d\alpha_j n^j(\bar{y}^j) = (d\alpha_j/\alpha_j)\bar{P}_0$. Since $\bar{P}_0(\sum_{i=1}^I w_0^i + \sum_{j=1}^J \eta_0^j) = \bar{M}_0$ and $dM_0 = 0$, $dP_0 = 0 \Rightarrow d\alpha_j = 0$, $j = 1, \ldots, J$, so that $\sum_{i=1}^I z_0^{ij}(d\nu^i \bar{\Phi} + \bar{\nu}^i d\Phi) = 0$, $j = 1, \ldots, J$. Assumption (c) in (ii) then implies

$$d\nu^i \bar{\Phi} + \bar{\nu}^i d\Phi = 0, \quad \forall i \in \mathcal{I}'. \tag{38}$$

Without loss of generality, we may assume agent 1 satisfies $z_0'^1 \neq 0$ $(1 \in \mathcal{I}')$. Since $\bar{\nu}^1 = (1, 0, \ldots, 0)$, (38) implies $dP = 0$. Differentiating the first-order conditions for agent i $D_{\bar{x}^i} u^i = \bar{\mu}^i \bar{\Phi}$ (where $D_{\bar{x}^i} u^i$ is viewed as a row vector) gives

$$dx^{iT} D_{\bar{x}^i}^2 u^i = d\mu^i \bar{\Phi} + \bar{\mu}^i d\Phi, \quad \forall i \in \mathcal{I}'.$$

Since $\nu^i = \mu^i/\mu_0^i$, $d\mu^i = d\mu_0^i \nu^i + \mu_0^i d\nu^i$. By (38),

$$dx^{iT} D_{\bar{x}^i}^2 u^i = d\mu_0^i \bar{\nu}^i \bar{\Phi}, \quad \forall i \in \mathcal{I}'.$$

Differentiating the budget constraint

$$\Phi(\bar{x}^i - \bar{w}^i) = \begin{bmatrix} \bar{\gamma}_0^i \\ 0 \end{bmatrix}, \quad \forall i \in \mathcal{I}', \tag{39}$$

gives $\bar{\Phi} dx^i = -d\Phi(\bar{x}^i - \bar{w}^i)$, since $dP_0 = 0$, $dy = 0 \Rightarrow d\gamma_0^i = 0$. Thus, by (38), (39) and $d\nu_0^i = 0$,

$$\nu^i \bar{\Phi} dx^i = -\bar{\nu}^i d\Phi(\bar{x}^i - \bar{w}^i) = d\nu^i \bar{\Phi}(\bar{x}^i - \bar{w}^i) = 0, \quad \forall i \in \mathcal{I}'.$$

Thus, $\forall i \in \mathcal{I}'$, $\bar{\nu}^i \bar{\Phi} dx^i = 0 \Rightarrow D_{\bar{x}^i} u^i dx^i = 0$, and $dx^{iT} D_{\bar{x}^i}^2 u^i dx^i = 0$. From Assumption A(3), we conclude $dx^i = 0$, $i \in \mathcal{I}'$. Since $I' > K$, applying the argument in (i) previously completes the proof. □

Remark 4. If the riskless bond is the only nominal asset $(K = 1)$, then it is clear from the proof of (i) that

$$\ker(D_{\bar{M}}(x, y)) = \tilde{\Lambda} = \left\{ dM \;\middle|\; dM_1 = -\begin{bmatrix} \bar{M}_1 \\ \bar{\beta}_1 \end{bmatrix} d\beta_1, d\beta_1 \in \bar{L} \right\}$$

so that there are exactly $J+K+1$ directions of change dM that do not affect the equilibrium allocation. If there are other bonds ($K \geq 2$), then $\ker(D_{\bar{M}}(x,y))$ can be a strict subspace of $\bar{\Lambda}$, since $d\beta_1 \in \bar{L}$ does not imply $[d\beta_1]N^k \in \bar{L}$ for $k \geq 2$. If we are prepared to view the bond returns $N^2,\ldots,N^K$ as being "drawn at random," then a result of Geanakoplos and Mas-Colell (1989, Theorem 2) implies that *generically in* $(\omega, \eta, N^2, \ldots, N^K)$,

$$\ker(D_{\bar{M}}(x,y)) = \{dM \mid dM_1 = \alpha \bar{M}_1, \alpha \in \mathbb{R}\}$$

so that all marginal changes differing from those given in Theorem 2(i) *have real effects.* It can be argued, however, that using genericity with respect to $N^2,\ldots,N^K$ is a somewhat implausible economic assumption since it implies in particular that each bond has a different return in each state.

6.3 *Unanticipated monetary changes*

When agents have initial holdings of nominal assets, the conditions under which monetary policy is neutral can be stated as follows.

Theorem 2′ (Neutrality of money). *Let Assumptions A to E hold and let* $(\bar{\omega}, \bar{\eta}, \bar{M}) \in \hat{\Gamma}$.

(i) *For all* $M = (\bar{M}_0, \alpha' \bar{M}_1) \in \mathfrak{N}_{\bar{M}}$ *with* $\alpha' > 0$,

$$(x(M), y(M)) = (x(\bar{M}), y(\bar{M})). \tag{40}$$

(ii) *If* $J+K=S$, *then* (40) *holds for all* $M \in \mathfrak{N}_{\bar{M}}$ *with* $M_0 = \bar{M}_0$.

Thus, date 1 monetary changes that were neutral in previous Section 6.2 remain neutral. Date 0 monetary changes are not, however, neutral, as we will now show. Since the effect of a change in M_0 depends fundamentally on *income effects,* we need the extension of the *Slutsky analysis* of consumer demand to the case of incomplete markets. This can be obtained as follows.

Slutsky analysis. Consider the first-order conditions for an agent with a budget set given by (28)

$$D_{x^i} u^i = \mu^i \Phi, \qquad \Phi(x^i - w^i) = \begin{bmatrix} \gamma_0^i \\ 0 \end{bmatrix}.$$

Differentiating gives ($i = ,\ldots, I$)

$$J^i \begin{bmatrix} dx^i \\ d\mu^{iT} \end{bmatrix} = \begin{bmatrix} d\Phi^T \mu^{iT} \\ d\Phi(x^i - w^i) - \begin{bmatrix} d\gamma_0^i \\ 0 \end{bmatrix} \end{bmatrix} \quad \text{where } J^i = \begin{bmatrix} D^2_{x^i} u^i & -\Phi^T \\ -\Phi & 0 \end{bmatrix}. \tag{41}$$

It can be shown that J^i is invertible. Writing the inverse in block form similar to that used for J^i gives

$$[J^i]^{-1} = \begin{bmatrix} A_1^i & A_2^i \\ A_2^{iT} & A_3^i \end{bmatrix},$$

where A_1^i is $n \times n$ and A_2^i is $n \times (S+1)$. The following properties analogous to those in standard consumer demand theory are readily derived (see Balasko and Cass, 1991):

(i) *The Slutsky matrix* A_1^i *is symmetric,* rank $A_1^i = n-(S+1-(J+K))$ *and*

$$\ker A_1^i = \langle \Phi^T \rangle.$$

(ii) *The matrix of income effects satisfies* $-\Phi A_2^i = I_{S+1-(J+K)}$.

Since $[J^i]^{-1}$ exists, solving from (41) gives

$$dx^i = A_1^i d\Phi^T \mu^{iT} + A_2^i d\Phi(x^i - w^i) - A_2^{i0} d\gamma_0^i, \tag{42}$$

where A_2^{i0}, the first column of A_2^i, gives the effect on consumption of a change $d\gamma_0^i$ in the present value of consumer i's wealth.

Theorem 4 (Real effects of unanticipated monetary changes). *Let Assumptions A to E hold and let* $(\bar{\omega}, \bar{\eta}, \bar{M}) \in \hat{\Gamma}$.

(i) *If* $z_0'' \neq 0$, *then*

$$(dx, dy) = (D_{\bar{M}} x, D_{\bar{M}} y) dM \neq 0, \quad \forall dM = (dM_0, 0) \neq 0.$$

(ii) *If* (a) $\sum_{i=1}^{I} (N_0 z_0''^i) A_2^{i0} \neq 0$, (b) $K < I' \leq J$, (c) $(z_0'^i,\ i \in \mathcal{I}')$ *are linearly independent,* (d) $E^j = \mathbb{R}^n$, $j = 1, \ldots, J$, *then* (i) *holds with* $dy \neq 0$.

Proof: (i) As in the proof of Theorem 3(i), $dx^1 = 0$ implies dP is proportional to $\bar{P}$. Differentiating the date 0 monetary equation gives $dP = (dM_0/\bar{M}_0)\bar{P}$ and differentiating the date s monetary equation gives $d\beta_s = (dM_0/\bar{M}_0)\bar{\beta}_s$, $s = 1, \ldots, S$. Thus, the subspace $\bar{L}$ and, hence, the matrix $\bar{Q}$ in (27) does not change $\Rightarrow d\Phi = (dM_0/\bar{M}_0)\bar{\Phi}$. Since

$$d\gamma_0^i = \frac{dM_0}{\bar{M}_0} (\bar{P} \square (\bar{y} + \bar{\eta})) z_0'^i$$

and

$$(d\Phi(\bar{x}^i - \bar{w}^i))_0 = \frac{dM_0}{\bar{M}_0} (\bar{P} \square (\bar{y} + \bar{\eta})) z_0'^i + N_0 z_0''^i,$$

and since by property (i) of $[J^i]^{-1}$, $\ker A_1^i = \langle \bar{\Phi}^T \rangle$, (40) implies

$$dx^i = \frac{dM_0}{\bar{M}_0}(N_0 z_0''^i)A_2^{i0}, \quad i=1,\ldots,I. \tag{43}$$

Since $A_2^{i0} \neq 0$ by property (ii) of $[J^i]^{-1}$, $dx=0$ contradicts $z_0'' \neq 0$.

(ii) Suppose $dy=0$. By the first-order conditions for profit maximization, there exists $\alpha_j \neq 0$ such that $\alpha_j n^j(\bar{y}^j) = \Sigma_{i=1}^I z_0^{ij}(\bar{v}^i\bar{\Phi})$. Differentiating gives

$$\sum_{i=1}^I z_0^{ij}(dv^i\bar{\Phi} + \bar{v}^i d\Phi) = d\alpha_j n^j(\bar{y}^j) = \frac{d\alpha_j}{\alpha_j}\sum_{i=1}^I z_0^{ij}(\bar{v}^i\bar{\Phi}).$$

The date 0 component implies $dP_0 = (d\alpha_j/\alpha_j)\bar{P}_0$ and the date 0 monetary equation then implies $d\alpha_j/\alpha_j = dM_0/\bar{M}_0$ so that

$$\sum_{i=1}^I z_0^{ij}\left(\bar{v}^i d\Phi + \left(dv^i - \frac{dM_0}{\bar{M}_0}\bar{v}^i\right)\bar{\Phi}\right) = 0, \quad j=1,\ldots,J.$$

It follows from (c) that $\bar{v}^i d\Phi + (dv^i - (dM_0/\bar{M}_0)\bar{v}^i)\bar{\Phi} = 0$, $\forall i \in \mathcal{I}'$. Since there is no loss of generality in assuming that agent 1 lies in $\mathcal{I}' \Rightarrow dP = (dM_0/\bar{M}_0)\bar{P}$. But then $dy=0$ implies $0 = \Sigma_{j=1}^J dy^j = \Sigma_{i=1}^I dx^i$, which in view of (43) and the hypothesis in (ii)(a),

$$\sum_{i=1}^I dx^i = \frac{dM_0}{\bar{M}_0}\sum_{i=1}^I (N_0 z_0''^i)A_2^{i0} \neq 0,$$

leads to a contradiction. □

Remark 5. In view of Theorem 2′(i), the monetary change $dM = (dM_0, 0)$ is equivalent to the monetary change $dM = (dM_0, (dM_0/\bar{M}_0)\bar{M}_1)$: *a local proportional change in all the money supplies has the same real effects as a local change in the date 0 money supply alone.*

Remark 6. There is a well-known case where condition (ii)(a) cannot hold. When the consumer side of the economy can be represented by a single consumer, that is, when all agents have identical homothetic preferences (an example frequently used in macroeconomics), then $A_2^{i0} = A_2^0$, $i=1,\ldots,I$, so that $\Sigma_{i=1}^I z_0''^i = 0$ implies $\Sigma_{i=1}^I (N_0 z_0''^i)A_2^0 = 0$. This example is not robust, however, to a slight perturbation in the utility functions of the agents. More generally, if we add a suitable finite dimensional perturbation $\delta = (\delta^1,\ldots,\delta^I)$ of the utility functions $u = (u^1,\ldots,u^I)$ to the basic parameters (ω, η, M), then it can be shown (along the lines of Geanakoplos and Polemarchakis, 1986) that generically in $(\omega, \eta, \delta, M)$, condition (ii)(a) holds. *Thus, generically, an unanticipated monetary change has production effects.*

Appendix

Proof of Lemma 2: We break the proofs of (i) and (ii) into a sequence of steps.

Step 1. To simplify notation, we drop the subscript and let $\beta_1 = \beta$ and $N_1 = N$. We show that *for fixed* (β, N), *the subset of the Grassmanian* $G^{J+K}(\mathbb{R}^S)$ *defined by*

$$G_{\beta N}^{J+K}(\mathbb{R}^S) = \{L \in G^{J+K}(\mathbb{R}^S) \mid L \supset \langle [\beta] N \rangle\}$$

is diffeomorphic to $G^J(\mathbb{R}^{S-K})$.

Let $\{e^1, \ldots, e^S\}$ denote the standard basis of $\mathbb{R}^S$, and let $\{N^1, \ldots, N^K, N^{K+1}, \ldots, N^S\}$ be another basis for $\mathbb{R}^S$, where $N^1, \ldots, N^K$ are the K columns of N and $N^{K+1}, \ldots, N^S$ are $S-K$ vectors of $\mathbb{R}^S$ that span $\langle N \rangle^\perp$. Let $N^\perp = [N^{K+1} \ldots N^S]$ denote the associated $S \times (S-K)$ matrix. It is clear that for any $\beta \in \mathbb{R}^S_{++}$, the columns of the matrix $[[\beta]N, [\beta]^{-1}N^\perp]$ form a basis for $\mathbb{R}^S$, since $\langle [\beta]^{-1} N^\perp \rangle = \langle [\beta] N \rangle^\perp$. For each $L \in G_{\beta N}^{J+K}(\mathbb{R}^S)$, there exists a unique J-dimensional subspace $\tilde{l}$ in $\langle [\beta] N \rangle^\perp$ such that

$$L = \langle [\beta] N \rangle \oplus \tilde{l}.$$

Let $\theta: \mathbb{R}^{S-K} \to \langle [\beta]^{-1} N^\perp \rangle$ denote the isomorphism that sends the standard basis of $\mathbb{R}^{S-K}$ onto the basis $\{[\beta]^{-1}N^{K+1}, \ldots, [\beta]^{-1}N^S\}$; then θ induces a diffeomorphism $\tau: G^J(\mathbb{R}^{S-K}) \to G^J(\langle [\beta]^{-1} N^\perp \rangle)$. Thus, there exists $l \in G^J(\mathbb{R}^{S-K})$ such that $\tau(l) = \tilde{l}$. By the standard representation of $G^J(\mathbb{R}^{S-K})$, there exists a permutation $\sigma' \in \Sigma_{K+1,\ldots,S}$ (the set of permutations of $K+1, \ldots, S$) and a unique matrix $A' = A_{\sigma'}(l) \in \mathbb{R}^{(S-K-J)J}$ such that

$$\tilde{l} = \{v \in \langle [\beta]^{-1} N^\perp \rangle \mid [I \mid A'] E_{\sigma'}[v] = 0\},$$

where I is the $(S-K-J) \times (S-K-J)$ identity matrix, $E_{\sigma'}$ is the permutation matrix for σ', and the vectors v are written $v = \sum_{i=1}^{S-K} \nu_{K+i} [\beta]^{-1} N^{K+i}$ with $[v] = (\nu_{K+1}, \ldots, \nu_S)$. Whenever $\{M_1, \ldots, M_{S-K-J}\}$ is a basis for the subspace of $\langle [\beta] N \rangle^\perp$, orthogonal to $\tilde{l}$, then $\{M_1, \ldots, M_{S-K-J}\}$ is a basis for $L^\perp$ in $\mathbb{R}^S$ (see Figure 3).

Thus, if we write

$$\begin{array}{c} \\ M_1 \\ \vdots \\ M_{S-K-J} \end{array} \begin{array}{c} \begin{array}{ccccccc} [\beta]N^1 & \cdots & [\beta]N^K & [\beta]^{-1}N^{K+1} & & \cdots & [\beta]^{-1}N^S \end{array} \\ \left[\begin{array}{ccc|c} 0 & \cdots & 0 & \\ \vdots & \ddots & \vdots & [I \mid A'_{\sigma'}] E_{\sigma'} \\ 0 & \cdots & 0 & \end{array} \right] \end{array},$$

then L can be represented as

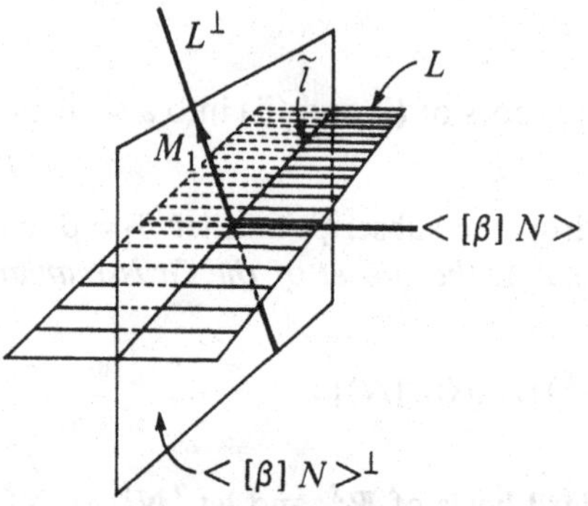

Figure 3. Geometry of subspaces ($S=3$, $K=J=1$).

$$L = \{v \in \mathbb{R}^S \mid [0 \mid [I \mid A'_{\sigma'}] E_{\sigma'}][v]_{\beta N} = 0\}, \tag{A.1}$$

where $[v]_{\beta N}$ denotes the coordinates of v in the basis $\{[\beta]N^1, \ldots, [\beta]N^K, [\beta]^{-1}N^{K+1}, \ldots, [\beta]^{-1}N^S\}$. Thus, if we let

$$B(\beta, N) = [[\beta]N, [\beta]^{-1}N^{\perp}]^{-1} \tag{A.2}$$

denote the matrix for the change of basis, then L can be written as

$$L = \{v \in \mathbb{R}^S \mid Q_{\sigma'} v = 0\} \tag{A.3}$$

where

$$Q_{\sigma'} = [0 \mid [I \mid A'_{\sigma'}] E_{\sigma'}] B(\beta, N) \tag{A.4}$$

Step 2. Let $f^i(P, y, L; \omega, \eta)$, $i = 1, \ldots, I$, denote the consumer *demand* functions induced by Definition 2(i) and let $g^j(P, y, L; \omega, \eta)$, $j = 1, \ldots, J$, denote the producer *supply* functions induced by Definition 2(ii). To express all pseudoequilibria as solutions of a system of equations, we consider for each permutation $\sigma' \in \Sigma_{K+1,\ldots,S}$ a system of equations

$$F_{\sigma'}(P, y, A', \beta_1; \omega, \eta, M) = 0,$$

where the unknowns are the "prices" (P, y, A', β_1) that lie in the *price space*

$$\mathcal{P} = \mathbb{R}^n_{++} \times \mathbb{R}^{nJ} \times \mathbb{R}^{J(S-K-J)} \times \mathbb{R}^S_{++}$$

and the parameters (ω, η, M) lie in the parameter $\Omega \times \mathfrak{M}$. The functions

$$F_{\sigma'}: \mathcal{P} \times \Omega \times \mathfrak{M} \to \mathbb{R}^{n-1} \times \mathbb{R}^{nJ} \times \mathbb{R}^{S+1} \times \mathbb{R}^{J(S-K-J)}$$

are defined by

$$\begin{aligned}
&\sum_{i=1}^{I}(\hat{f}^i(P,y,L(\beta_1,A');\omega,\eta)-\hat{w}^i)-\sum_{j=1}^{J}(\hat{y}^j+\hat{\eta}^j)=0, && \text{(i)}\\
&g^j(P,y,L(\beta_1,A');\omega,\eta)-y^j=0,\quad j=1,\dots,J, && \text{(ii)}\\
&P_0\Big(\sum_{i=1}^{I}w_0^i+\sum_{j=1}^{J}\eta_0^j\Big)-M_0=0, && \text{(iii)} \qquad \text{(A.5)}\\
&P_S\Big(\sum_{i=1}^{I}w_s^i+\sum_{j=1}^{J}(y_s^j+\eta_s^j)\Big)-\beta_s M_s=0,\quad s=1,\dots,S, && \text{(iv)}\\
&Q_{\sigma'}(\beta_1,A')P_1\square(y_1^j+\eta_1^j)=0,\quad j=1,\dots,J, && \text{(v)}
\end{aligned}$$

where $L(\beta_1,A')$ and $Q_{\sigma'}(\beta_1,A')$ are defined by (A.3) and (A.4) and $\hat{f}^i$ is the truncated demand function obtained from f^i by omitting the demand for good 1 in state 0. The proof that

$$\operatorname{rank}(D_{\omega,\eta,M}F_{\sigma'})=n-1+nJ+S+1+J(S-K-J)$$

is straightforward and left to the reader. A standard argument based on Sard's Theorem proves that there exists a generic set $\Gamma'\subset\Omega\times\mathfrak{M}$ such that for each $(\omega,\eta,M)\in\Gamma'$, there is at most a finite number of pseudoequilibria, each of which is locally a smooth function of the parameters. This completes the proof of (i).

Step 3. We show that for a generic set $\Gamma''\subset\Gamma'$, all pseudoequilibria satisfy $\operatorname{rank}[P_1\square(y_1+\eta_1)]=J$. If the rank is less than J, then there exist $(\alpha_1,\dots,\alpha_J)\in\mathbb{S}^{J-1}$ (the $J-1$ dimensional sphere) such that

$$\begin{aligned}
\sum_{j=1}^{J}\alpha_j P_1\square(y_1^j+\eta_1^j)=0 &\Leftrightarrow \sum_{j=1}^{J}\alpha_j B(\beta,N)P_1\square(y_1^j+\eta_1^j)=0\\
&\Leftrightarrow \sum_{j=1}^{J}\alpha_j[P_1\square(y_1^j+\eta_1^j)]_{\beta N}=0.
\end{aligned}$$

Let $\sigma'=$ identity, so that $E_{\sigma'}=I$. For a vector $v\in\mathbb{R}^S$, make the decomposition $[v]_{\beta N}=[v]_a,[v]_b,[v]_c$ (viewed as a column vector) so as to be conformable with the matrix $[0\,|\,[I\,|\,A']]$ in (A.1). If a pseudoequilibrium is such that $\operatorname{rank}[P_1\square(y_1^j+\eta_1^j)]<J$, then the system of equations

$$F_{\sigma'}(P,y,A',\beta_1;\omega,\eta,M)=0, \qquad \text{(A.5)}$$

$$\sum_{j=1}^{J}\alpha_j[P_1\square(y_1^j+\eta_1^j)]_c=0 \qquad \text{(A.6)}$$

in the unknowns (P,y,A',β_1,α) must have a solution. Since equations (A.6) introduce more equations (J) than new unknowns ($J-1$), the overall system, equations (A.5) and (A.6), generically has no solution if each equation in (A.6) can be locally controlled without affecting the others. To control equation k in (A.6), we pick a vector $v \in \mathbb{R}^S$ such that $[v]_a = 0$, $[v]_c = (0,\dots,1,\dots,0)$ (1 in the kth component) and $[v]_b$ such that $[0 \,|\, [I \,|\, A']][v]_{\beta N} = 0$. For some j, $\alpha_j \neq 0$. Pick $d\eta_1^j$ such that $B(P_1 \square d\eta_1^j) = [v]_{\beta N}$ and $d\eta_0^j$ such that $P \cdot d\eta^j = 0$. If we let $dw^1 = -d\eta^j$, then all the equations except for the kth equation in (A.6) are unchanged. When σ' is not the identity, the decomposition of $[v]_{\beta N}$ is made conformably with σ'. By running over all the permutations $\sigma' \in \Sigma_{K+1,\dots,S}$ and applying the standard transversality argument in each case, we obtain the desired set Γ''.

Step 4. We show that for a generic set $\Gamma \subset \Gamma''$, all pseudoequilibria satisfy $\langle P_1 \square (y_1 + \eta_1) \rangle \cap \langle \beta_1 N_1 \rangle = \{0\} \Leftrightarrow P_1 \square (y_1^j + \eta_1^j) \notin \langle \beta_1 N_1 \rangle$, $j = 1,\dots,J$. If at a pseudoequilibrium, $P_1 \square (y_1^j + \eta_1^j) \in \langle \beta_1 N_1 \rangle$ for some j, then the system of equations

$$F_{\sigma'}(P, y, A', \beta_1; \omega, \eta, M) = 0, \tag{A.5}$$

$$[P_1 \square (y_1^j + \eta_1^j)]_b = 0, \tag{A.7}$$

$$[P_1 \square (y_1^j + \eta_1^j)]_c = 0 \tag{A.8}$$

has a solution for some $\sigma' \in \Sigma_{K+1,\dots,S}$. Since (A.7) and (A.8) introduce new equations but no new unknowns, the system, equations (A.5), (A.7), and (A.8), generically has no solution if one of the equations in (A.7) or (A.8) can be locally controlled without perturbing (A.5). This is straightforward to show. A standard transversality argument then leads to the desired generic set Γ. □

Proof of Lemma 3: Since $\bar{P}_1 \square (\bar{x}_1^i - \bar{w}_1^i) \in \bar{L}$, there exist $\bar{z}^i = (\bar{z}'^i, \bar{z}''^i)$ such that for $i = 1,\dots,I$,

$$\bar{P}_1 \square (\bar{x}_1^i - \bar{w}_1^i) = [\bar{P}_1 \square (\bar{y}_1 + \bar{\eta}_1)]\bar{z}'^i + [[\bar{\beta}_1]N_1]\bar{z}''^i. \tag{A.9}$$

Let $(i_1,\dots,i_K)$ denote a K-element subset of $\{1,\dots,I\}$, let $[\bar{z}']_K$ and $[\bar{z}'']_K$ denote the induced $J \times K$ and $K \times K$ matrices, respectively, of portfolio holdings, and let $[\bar{P}_1 \square (\bar{x}_1 - \bar{w}_1)]_K$ denote the $S \times K$ matrix of excess expenditures for these K agents; then (A.9) implies

$$[\bar{P}_1 \square (\bar{x}_1 - \bar{w}_1)]_K - [\bar{P}_1 \square (\bar{y}_1 + \bar{\eta}_1)][\bar{z}']_K = [[\beta_1]N_1][\bar{z}'']_K.$$

It remains to prove the existence of a generic set $\hat{\Gamma}^* \subset \hat{\Gamma}$ such that $[\bar{z}'']_K$ is invertible for every K-element subset of $\{1,\dots,I\}$. Suppose that for some K-element subset $\operatorname{rank}[\bar{z}'']_K < K$, then there exists $\alpha \in S^{K-1}$ such that the system of equations

$$F_{\sigma'}(P, y, A', \beta_1; \omega, \eta, M) = 0, \tag{A.5}$$

$$\sum_{i=i_1}^{i_K} \alpha_i z''^i = 0 \tag{A.10}$$

in the unknowns $(P, y, A', \beta_1, \alpha)$ must have a solution. Again, since equations (A.10) introduce more equations (K) than unknowns $(K-1)$, the overall system, equations (A.5) and (A.10), generically has no solution if each of the equations in (A.10) can be locally controlled without affecting the others. To control equation k in (A.10), let i_1 be such that $\alpha_{i_1} \neq 0$. To induce a one-unit change in agent i_1's demand for nominal asset k, $dz''^{i_1} = (0, \ldots, 1, \ldots, 0)$, consider a change $dw_s^{i_1}$ such that $\bar{P}_s dw_s^{i_1} = -\beta_s N_s dz''^{i_1}$, $s = 1, \ldots, S$, $\bar{P}_0 dw_0^{i_1} + \sum_{s=1}^{S} \bar{P}_s dw_s^{i_1} = 0$. Choose a new agent $i_{K+1} \notin \{i_1, \ldots, i_K\}$ and set $dw^{i_{K+1}} = -dw^{i_1}$ to restore the equation of equilibrium (A.5). □

REFERENCES

Balasko, Y., and D. Cass. 1989. "The Structure of Financial Equilibrium with Exogenous Yields: The Case of Incomplete Markets." *Econometrica* 57: 135–62.

1991. "Regular Demand with Several Budget Constraints." Forthcoming in *Equilibrium and Dynamics, Essays in Honor of David Gale,* M. Majumdar, Ed. London: Macmillan.

Beato, P., and A. Mas-Colell. 1985. "On Marginal Cost Pricing with Given Tax-Subsidy Rules." *Journal of Economic Theory* 37: 356–65.

DeMarzo, P. 1987. "An Extension of the Modigliani–Miller Theorem to Stochastic Economies with Incomplete Markets." *Journal of Economic Theory* 45: 353–69.

Diamond, P. 1967. "The Role of a Stock Market in a General Equilibrium Model with Technological Uncertainty." *American Economic Review* 57: 759–76.

Drèze, J. 1974. "Investment Under Private Ownership: Optimality, Equilibrium and Stability." In *Allocation Under Uncertainty: Equilibrium and Optimality,* J. Drèze, Ed. New York: Wiley, pp. 261–96.

1985. "(Uncertainty and) the Firm in General Equilibrium Theory." *Economic Journal* 95 (Supplement: Conference Papers): 1–20.

1987. *Essays on Economic Decisions under Uncertainty.* Cambridge: Cambridge University Press.

1989. *Labour Management, Contracts and Capital Markets* (Jahnsson Lectures). New York: Blackwell.

Duffie, D., and W. Shafer. 1985. "Equilibrium in Incomplete Markets I: A Basic Model of Generic Existence." *Journal of Mathematical Economics* 14: 285–300.

1986. "Equilibrium and the Role of the Firm in Incomplete Markets." Research Paper 915, Graduate School of Business, Stanford University.

Geanakoplos, J., M. J. P. Magill, M. Quinzii, and J. Drèze. 1990. "Generic Inefficiency of Stock Market Equilibrium When Markets are Incomplete." *Journal of Mathematical Economics* 19: 113–52.

Geanakoplos, J., and A. Mas-Colell. 1989. "Real Indeterminacy with Financial Assets." *Journal of Economic Theory* 47: 22–38.

Geanakoplos, J., and H. Polemarchakis. 1986. "Existence, Regularity, and Constrained Suboptimality of Competitive Portfolio Allocations When the Asset Market is Incomplete." In *Uncertainty, Information and Communication, Essays in Honor of Kenneth J. Arrow,* Vol. III, W. P. Heller, R. M. Starr, and D. A. Starrett, Eds. New York: Cambridge University Press, pp. 65–95.

Grossman, S. J., and O. Hart. 1979. "A Theory of Competitive Equilibrium in Stock Market Economies." *Econometrica* 47: 293–330.

Hahn, F. H. 1983. *Money and Inflation.* Cambridge, MA: The MIT Press.

Hirsch, M. D., M. Magill, and A. Mas-Colell. 1990. "A Geometric Approach to a Class of Equilibrium Existence Theorems." *Journal of Mathematical Economics* 19: 95–106.

Husseini, S. Y., J. M. Lasry, and M. J. P. Magill. 1990. "Existence of Equilibrium with Incomplete Markets." *Journal of Mathematical Economics* 19: 39–67.

Magill, M. J. P., and M. Quinzii. 1991. "Real Effects of Money in General Equilibrium." Forthcoming in *Journal of Mathematical Economics.*

Magill, M. J. P., and W. J. Shafer. 1991. "Incomplete Markets." In *The Handbook of Mathematical Economics,* Vol. IV, W. Hildenbrand and H. Sonnenschein, Eds. Amsterdam: North-Holland, in press.

Modigliani, F. 1977. "The Monetarist Controversy or Should We Forsake Stabilisation Policies." *American Economic Review* 67: 1–19.

Modigliani, F., and M. Miller. 1958. "The Cost of Capital, Corporation Finance, and the Theory of Investment." *American Economic Review* 48: 261–97.

Tobin, J. 1980. *Asset Accumulation and Economic Activity* (Jahnsson Lectures). Chicago: University of Chicago Press.

CHAPTER 4

General equilibrium theory with increasing returns: The existence problem

Jean-Marc Bonnisseau and Bernard Cornet

1 Introduction

Recent papers have been considering the existence problem of equilibria in an economy that may exhibit increasing returns to scale or more general types of nonconvexities in the production sector. This includes the work by Beato (1979, 1982), Beato and Mas-Colell (1985); Bonnisseau (1988a, 1988b); Bonnisseau and Cornet (1988, 1990a, 1990c); Brown and Heal (1982); Brown et al. (1986); Cornet (1990); Dierker, Guesnerie, and Neuefeind (1985); Kamiya (1988b); Mantel (1979); and Vohra (1988).

In these papers, the firms are assumed to follow general pricing rules, which formalize various standard behavioral rules encountered in the economic literature: profit maximizing, average cost, marginal cost pricing, etc. The treatment of the existence problem in the case of marginal cost pricing (cf. Bonnisseau and Cornet, 1990a, 1990c) is, however, fundamentally different from the case of other behavioral rules; it also involves more sophisticated mathematical techniques from differential topology.

The purpose of this chapter is to propose a unified treatment of the existence problem. We will also provide extensions of the previous papers by weakening the so-called survival assumption, which is the key assumption in this type of model. Our approach will also follow Debreu (1956), Gale (1955), and Nikaido (1956) by proving first an abstract result that generalizes theirs and then applying the abstract result to prove the existence of equilibria as in Debreu (1959).

The chapter is organized as follows. In the next section, we state our main existence result (Theorem 3), which generalizes the fundamental result of Debreu, Gale, and Nikaido. In Section 3, we give some consequences of this result to the existence of equilibria (Theorem 4). Finally, in Section 4, we give the proof of Theorem 3.

2 Statement of the main result

Let[1] $X, Y_1, Y_2, \ldots, Y_n$ be $n+1$ subsets of R^l and let S be the simplex of R^l defined by $S = \{p \in R^l_+ \mid \sum_{h=1}^l p_h = 1\}$. Let z be a correspondence from $S \times \prod_{j=1}^n \partial Y_j$ to R^l and let φ be a correspondence from $S \times \prod_{j=1}^n \partial Y_j$ to S^n, the n-fold Cartesian product of S.

In the following, e denotes the vector of R^l with every coordinate equal to 1. For every real number $t \geq 0$, we define the set A_t as follows:

$$A_t = \left\{ (y_j) \in \prod_{j=1}^n \partial Y_j \;\middle|\; \sum_{j=1}^n y_j + te \in X \right\}.$$

We define the set of production equilibria, denoted PE, and the set of attainable production equilibria, denoted APE, as follows:

$$\mathrm{PE} = \left\{ (p, (y_j)) \in S \times \prod_{j=1}^n \partial Y_j \;\middle|\; (p, \ldots, p) \in \varphi(p, (y_j)) \right\},$$

$$\mathrm{APE} = \left\{ (p, (y_j)) \in \mathrm{PE} \;\middle|\; \sum_{j=1}^n y_j \in X \right\}.$$

We now recall the definition of Clarke's normal and tangent cones (see Clarke, 1975, 1983). Firstly, a perpendicular vector to Y_j at $y_j^* \in \mathrm{cl}\, Y_j$ is an element in the set:

$$\perp_{Y_j}(y_j^*) \overset{\text{def}}{=} \{ p \in R^l \mid \exists \rho \in R, \forall y_j \in Y_j : p \cdot y_j^* \geq p \cdot y_j - \rho \| y_j^* - y_j \|^2 \}.$$

Then, Clarke's normal cone to Y_j at y_j^*, denoted $N_{Y_j}(y_j^*)$, is the closed convex hull of the set:

$$\{ p \in R^l \mid \exists (y_j^\nu) \subset \mathrm{cl}\, Y_j, (y_j^\nu) \to y_j^*, \exists (p^\nu) \subset R^l, (p^\nu) \to p \text{ and } p^\nu \in \perp_{Y_j}(y_j^\nu) \forall \nu \}.$$

Clarke's tangent cone $T_{Y_j}(y_j^*)$ to Y_j at y_j^* is then defined as the negative polar cone of the normal cone. In the following, we let NC be the correspondence from $S \times \prod_{j=1}^n \partial Y_j$ to S^n defined by:

$$\mathrm{NC}(p, (y_j)) = [N_{Y_1}(y_1) \cap S] \times [N_{Y_2}(y_2) \cap S] \times \cdots \times [N_{Y_n}(y_n) \cap S].$$

We now posit the following assumptions:

[1] If $x = (x_h)$, $y = (y_h)$ are vectors in R^l, we let $x \cdot y = \sum_{h=1}^l x_h y_h$ be the scalar product of R^l, and $\|x\| = (x \cdot x)^{1/2}$ be the Euclidean norm. The notation $x \geq y$ (resp., $x \gg y$) means $x_h \geq y_h$ (resp., $x_h > y_h$) for all h; we let $R^l_+ = \{x \in R^l \mid x \geq 0\}$ and $R^l_{++} = \{x \in R^l \mid x \gg 0\}$. We denote by $[x]_+$ the vector in R^l with coordinates $\max\{0, x_h\}$ and by e the vector in R^l with every coordinate equal to 1. For $A \subset R^l$, we denote by $\mathrm{cl}\, A$, $\mathrm{int}\, A$, ∂A, and $\mathrm{co}\, A$, respectively, the closure, the interior, the boundary, and the convex hull of A, and for $B \subset R^l$, and real numbers λ, μ, we let $\lambda A + \mu B = \{\lambda a + \mu b \mid a \in A, b \in B\}$. If A is non-empty, and $x \in R^l$, we let $d_A(x) = \inf\{\|x - a\| \mid a \in A\}$, $\inf x \cdot A = \inf\{x \cdot a \mid a \in A\}$, $\sup x \cdot A = \sup\{x \cdot a \mid a \in A\}$, and for $r \geq 0$, $B(A, r) = \{x \in R^l \mid d_A(x) \leq r\}$.

Assumption P. *For every j, Y_j is non-empty, closed and $Y_j - R^l_+ \subset Y_j$.*

Assumption B. *For every $t \geq 0$, the set A_t is bounded.*

Assumption C_0. *X is non-empty, closed, convex and $X + R^l_+ \subset X$.*

Assumption WSA. *For every $(p,(y_j)) \in PE$, and for every $t \geq 0$, if $\sum_{j=1}^n y_j + te \in X$, then $p\cdot(\sum_{j=1}^n y_j) + t > \inf p\cdot X$.*

Assumption ED. (i) *z is an upper hemicontinuous correspondence with non-empty, convex, compact values;* (ii) *for every $(p,(y_j)) \in APE$, then $z(p,(y_j)) + \{\sum_{j=1}^n y_j\} \subset X$ and* $\sup p\cdot z(p,(y_j)) \leq 0$.

Assumption PR. *φ is an upper hemicontinuous correspondence with non-empty, convex, compact values.*

Assumption WBL. *There exists a real number $t_0 \geq 0$, for every $t \geq t_0$, for every $(p,(y_j)) \in S \times A_t$, for every $(q_j) \in \varphi(p,(y_j))$, $p\cdot(\sum_{j=1}^n y_j + te) =$* $\inf p\cdot X$ *implies $\sum_{j=1}^n q_j \cdot y_j \geq p\cdot \sum_{j=1}^n y_j$.*

We now state the first result of this chapter. This result is the generalization of the Debreu–Gale–Nikaido's Lemma, which allows us in the next section to deduce the existence of an equilibrium in economies with non-convex production sets.

Theorem 1. *Under Assumptions P, B, C_0, WSA, and ED, and if φ satisfies Assumptions PR and WBL, or if $\varphi = NC$, then there exists $(p^*,(y_j^*)) \in S \times \prod_{j=1}^n \partial Y_j$ satisfying:*

(a) $\sum_{j=1}^n y_j^* \in X$;
(b) $(p^*,\ldots,p^*) \in \varphi(p^*,(y_j^*))$;
(c) $z(p^*,(y_j^*)) \cap -R_+e \neq \emptyset$.

Remark 1. The assumptions of Theorem 1 are motivated by the applications to the existence of equilibria in economies with increasing returns (cf. Section 3). The sets Y_j represent the production sets, the correspondence φ represents the pricing rule, and the correspondence z represents an abstract excess demand correspondence.

Remark 2. Part (i) of Assumption ED(i) can be weakened by supposing that the property of z holds only on the set APE (using an extension result of Cellina). The second condition (ii) of Assumption ED is the analogue of Walras' Law in the Arrow–Debreu environment. It is a consequence of the fact that the wealth of the economy is distributed among the consumers of the economy.

Remark 3. We notice that the correspondence NC verifies Assumption PR if Assumption P holds but does not verify Assumption WBL, in general. When $\varphi = \text{NC}$, the proof of Theorem 1 crucially uses the relationship between φ and the geometry of the sets Y_j. More precisely, Assumptions P, B, C_0 and WSA imply that the set $A_0 = \{(y_j) \in \prod_{j=1}^n \partial Y_j \mid \sum_{j=1}^n y_j \in X\}$ is an absolute retract of a ball (see also Cornet 1988, Kamiya 1988a).

Remark 4. In Bonnisseau and Cornet (1988), it is assumed that the correspondence φ verifies the following assumption:

Assumption BL. *There exists a real number α such that, for every $(p, (y_j)) \in S \times \prod_{j=1}^n \partial Y_j$, for every $(q_j) \in \varphi(p, (y_j))$, $\sum_{j=1}^n q_j \cdot y_j \geq \alpha$.*

Assumption BL is stronger than Assumption WBL. Indeed, if φ verifies Assumption BL, let $t_0 \geq \sup\{q \cdot x_0 \mid q \in S\} - \alpha$, where x_0 is any fixed element of X. Then, for every $t \geq t_0$, for every $(p, (y_j)) \in S \times A_t$, for every $(q_j) \in \varphi(p, (y_j))$, if $p \cdot (\sum_{j=1}^n y_j + te) = \inf p \cdot X$, one has $\sum_{j=1}^n q_j \cdot y_j \geq \alpha \geq \sup\{q \cdot x_0 \mid q \in S\} - t_0 \geq \sup\{q \cdot x_0 \mid q \in S\} - t \geq \inf p \cdot X - t = p \cdot (\sum_{j=1}^n y_j)$; hence, φ verifies Assumption WBL.

Remark 5. Conditions (a) and (b) of Theorem 1 are only saying that $(p^*, (y_j^*))$ belongs to the set APE. This explains why, in Assumption ED, it is sufficient to assume that the properties of z holds only on APE (cf. Remark 2).

Finally, we notice that condition (c) of Theorem 1 is stronger than saying that

$$z(p^*, (y_j^*)) \cap -R_+^l \neq \emptyset,$$

since $-R_+ e \subset -R_+^l$ and $-R_+ e \neq R_+^l$. This allows us in the next section to prove the existence of equilibria instead of free-disposal equilibria.

We now deduce from Theorem 1 the classical result of Debreu (1956), Gale (1955), and Nikaido (1956).

Theorem 2. *Let z be an upper hemicontinuous correspondence from S to R^l with non-empty, convex, compact values that satisfy* $\sup p \cdot z(p) \leq 0$ *for every $p \in S$. Then there exists $p^* \in S$ satisfying:*

$$z(p^*) \cap -R_+^l \neq \emptyset.$$

Proof: Since S is compact and the correspondence z is upper hemicontinuous with compact values, there exists a real number $a<0$ such that $z(p)\subset\{ae\}+R^l_+$ for every $p\in S$. Let $X=\{ae\}+R^l_+$, let $Y_1=-R^l_+$, let ζ be the correspondence from $S\times\partial Y_1$ to R^l defined by $\zeta(p,y_1)=z(p)-y_1$, and let φ be the correspondence from $S\times\partial Y_1$ to S defined by $\varphi(p,y_1)=N_{Y_1}(y_1)\cap S$.

One easily checks that Assumptions P, B, C_0, WSA, and ED are satisfied by X, Y_1, ζ, and φ, recalling that $(p,y_1)\in S\times\partial Y_1$ and $p\in\varphi(p,y_1)$ imply that $p\cdot y_1=0$. Consequently, from Theorem 1, there exists $(p^*,y_1^*)\in S\times\partial Y_1$ such that $\zeta(p^*,y_1^*)\cap -R_+e\neq\emptyset$. This implies that $z(p^*)\cap[\{y_1^*\}-R_+e]\neq\emptyset$; hence, $z(p^*)\cap -R^l_+\neq\emptyset$ since $\{y_1^*\}-R_+e\subset -R^l_+$. □

We now state a generalization of Theorem 1 in which we remove the assumption that X is convex. We first need to weaken the previous assumptions:

Assumption WC$_0$. *X is non-empty, closed, and $X+R^l_+\subset X$.*

Assumption WSA′. *For every $(p,(y_j))\in PE$, for every $t\geq 0$,*

$$\sum_{j=1}^n y_j+te\in\partial X, \quad \textit{implies } p\notin -N_X\left(\sum_{j=1}^n y_j+te\right).$$

Assumption WED. (i) *z is an upper hemicontinuous correspondence with non-empty, convex, compact values;* (ii) *for every $(p,(y_j))\in APE$, then*

$$z(p,(y_j))\subset T_X\left(\sum_{j=1}^n y_j\right) \quad \textit{and} \quad \sup p\cdot z(p,(y_j))\leq 0.$$

Assumption WBL′. *There exists a real number $t_0\geq 0$, for every $t\geq t_0$, for every $(p,(y_j))\in S\times A_t$, for every $(q_j)\in\varphi(p,(y_j))$,*

$$p\in -N_X\left(\sum_{j=1}^n y_j+te\right) \quad \textit{implies} \quad \sum_{j=1}^n q_j\cdot y_j\geq p\cdot\sum_{j=1}^n y_j.$$

Theorem 3. *Under Assumptions P, B, WC$_0$, WSA′, WED, and if φ satisfies Assumptions PR and WBL′ or if $\varphi=NC$, then there exists $(p^*,(y_j^*))\in S\times\prod_{j=1}^n\partial Y_j$ satisfying:*

(a) $\sum_{j=1}^n y_j^*\in X$;
(b) $(p^*,\ldots,p^*)\in\varphi(p^*,(y_j^*))$;
(c) $z(p^*,(y_j^*))\cap -R_+e\neq\emptyset$.

Remark 6. Assumptions WSA′, WED, and WBL′ coincide, respectively, with Assumptions WSA, ED, and WBL when X is convex, recalling in this case that

$$N_X(x)=\{p\in R^l \mid p\cdot x\geq p\cdot x' \text{ for all } x'\in X\}, \quad \text{and}$$
$$T_X(x)=\text{cl}\{\lambda(y-x)\mid y\in X, \lambda\geq 0\}.$$

3 Existence of equilibria

We consider an economy with positive numbers l of commodities, m of consumers, and n of producers. We let ω in R^l be the vector of total initial endowments. The technological possibilities of the jth producer $(j=1,\dots,n)$ are represented by a subset Y_j of R^l. We denote by $X_i\subset R^l$ the set of possible consumption plans of the ith consumer $(i=1,\dots,m)$. The tastes of this consumer are described by a complete, reflexive, transitive, binary preference relation $\preccurlyeq_i$ on the consumption set X_i. The wealth of the ith consumer, denoted by $r_i(p,(y_j))$, is defined by a function $r_i: R^l_+\times\prod_{j=1}^n \partial Y_j\to R$, which depends upon the price vector p and the production plans y_j. This abstract wealth structure clearly encompasses the case of a private ownership economy for which $r_i(p,(y_j))=p\cdot\omega_i+\sum_{j=1}^n \theta_{ij}p\cdot y_j$, where the θ_{ij} $(i=1,\dots,m;\ j=1,\dots,n)$ are given real numbers satisfying $\theta_{ij}\geq 0$ for every i,j and $\sum_{i=1}^m \theta_{ij}=1$ for every j, and where $\omega_i\in R^l$ is the initial endowment of the ith consumer and satisfies $\sum_{i=1}^m \omega_i=\omega$.

We now define the behavior of the producer. We assume that the producers follow a pricing rule φ that is a correspondence from $S\times\prod_{j=1}^n \partial Y_j$ to S^n (the n-fold Cartesian product of S). The production sector of the economy is at equilibrium for the price vector p and the production plans $y_j\in\partial Y_j$ $(j=1,\dots,n)$ if $(p,\dots,p)\in\varphi(p,(y_j))$.

Definition 1. *An equilibrium of the economy* $\mathcal{E}=((X_i,\preccurlyeq_i,r_i),(Y_j),\varphi,\omega)$ *is an element* $((x_i^*),(y_j^*),p^*)$ *in* $R^{lm}\times R^{ln}\times R^l$ *satisfying:*

(a) *for every* i, x_i^* *is a greatest element for* $\preccurlyeq_i$ *in* $\{x_i\in X_i\mid p^*\cdot x_i\leq r_i(p^*,(y_j^*))\}$;
(b) $(y_j^*)\in\prod_{j=1}^n \partial Y_j$ *and* $(p^*,\dots,p^*)\in\varphi(p^*,(y_j^*))$;
(c) $\sum_{i=1}^m x_i^*=\sum_{j=1}^n y_j^*+\omega$.

This definition is taken from Bonnisseau and Cornet (1988). It generalizes the notion of a Walras equilibrium by replacing the profit-maximization behavior of the producers by the condition that the producers follow a general pricing rule φ.

When $\varphi = NC$, that is,

$$\varphi(p, (y_j)) = \prod_{j=1}^{n} [N_{Y_j}(y_j) \cap S],$$

an equilibrium is called a marginal pricing equilibrium following the terminology of Bonnisseau and Cornet (1990c).

Before stating our existence result, we introduce some notation. We let

$$X = \sum_{i=1}^{m} X_i + R_+^l - \omega,$$

so that, for every $t \geq 0$, the sets A_t, PE, and APE can be equivalently defined as follows:

$$A_t = \left\{ (y_j) \in \prod_{j=1}^{n} \partial Y_j \;\middle|\; \exists x \in \sum_{i=1}^{m} X_i : \sum_{j=1}^{n} y_j + \omega + te \geq x \right\},$$

$$\mathrm{PE} = \left\{ (p, (y_j)) \in S \times \prod_{j=1}^{n} \partial Y_j \;\middle|\; (p, \ldots, p) \in \varphi(p, (y_j)) \right\},$$

$$\mathrm{APE} = \left\{ (p, (y_j)) \in \mathrm{PE} \;\middle|\; \exists x \in \sum_{i=1}^{m} X_i : \sum_{j=1}^{n} y_j + \omega \geq x \right\}.$$

Theorem 4. *The economy $\mathcal{E} = ((X_i, \preccurlyeq_i, r_i), (y_j), \varphi, \omega)$ has an equilibrium if Assumptions P, B, and WSA are satisfied, if φ satisfies Assumptions PR and WBL or $\varphi = NC$ and if:*

Assumption C. *For every i, X_i is non-empty, closed, convex, and the binary preference relation $\preccurlyeq_i$ is complete, transitive, reflexive, continuous, convex, and nonsatiated.*[2] *The set $\{(x_i) \in \prod_{i=1}^{m} X_i \mid \exists y \in \sum_{j=1}^{n} Y_j : \sum_{i=1}^{m} x_i \leq y + \omega\}$ is bounded.*

Assumption R. *For every i,* (i) *the function $r_i : R_+^l \times \prod_{j=1}^{n} \partial Y_j \to R$ is continuous and satisfies $\sum_{i=1}^{m} r_i(p, (y_j)) = p \cdot \omega + \sum_{j=1}^{n} p \cdot y_j$;* (ii) *for every $(p, (y_j)) \in APE$, $r_i(p, (y_j)) > \inf p \cdot X_i$.*

Remark 7. Theorem 4 generalizes the existence results of Bonnisseau and Cornet (1988, 1990c). In the case of the marginal pricing equilibrium, we simply remove the fact that the consumption sets are bounded below and the fact that the preferences of the consumers are locally nonsatiated.

In the case of general pricing rules, we weaken in addition our previous version of the survival assumption and the bounded-losses assumption.

[2] That is, for every $x_i \in X_i$, the set $\{x \in X_i \mid x \preccurlyeq_i x_i\}$ is closed, the set $\{x \in X_i \mid x_i \preccurlyeq_i x\}$ is closed and convex, and there exists $x \in X_i$ such that $x_i \prec x$.

Indeed, in Bonnisseau and Cornet (1988) we were assuming the following "survival assumption":

Assumption SA. *$(p,(y_j)) \in PE$ implies $p \cdot (\Sigma_{j=1}^{n} y_j) \geq \inf p \cdot X$.*

This is clearly stronger than Assumption WSA and we were assuming Assumption BL presented in Remark 4, which is stronger than Assumption WBL (cf. Remark 4).

One remarks that the economy of the example of Beato and Mas-Colell (1985) verifies Assumptions WSA and WBL although it does not satisfy Assumptions SA and BL. Consequently, one can deduce the existence of an equilibrium in this economy by using Theorem 4 in the case of general pricing rules; this gives a simpler proof than the one suggested in Bonnisseau and Cornet (1990c). Nevertheless, the marginal pricing rule with $X = R^l_+$, and with the following production set Y does not verify Assumption WBL.

$$Y = \{(y_1, y_2) \in R^2 \mid y_1 \leq 0, y_2 \leq E(y_1)\},$$

denoting by $E(y)$, the integer part of the real number y. Consequently, in general, one cannot deduce the theorem on the existence of marginal pricing equilibria from the theorem on the existence of equilibria with general pricing rule.

Proof of Theorem 4: We denote by $\hat{X}_i$, the attainable set of the ith consumer $(i = 1, \ldots, m)$. From Assumptions C and B, the set $\hat{X}_i$ is compact. Consequently, from Assumption C, for every $i = 1, \ldots, m$, there exists $x_i^0 \in X_i$ such that $x \prec_i x_i^0$ for every $x \in \hat{X}_i$. For every integer k, we let $K^k = \{x \in R^l \mid -ke \leq x \leq ke\}$ and for every $i = 1, \ldots, m$, we let $X_i^k = X_i \cap K^k$.

We now claim that there exists an integer k_0 large enough so that, for every $k \geq k_0$, for every i, $x_i^0 \in X_i^k$, $\hat{X}_i \subset \operatorname{int} K^k$, and for every $(p,(y_j)) \in$ APE, $r_i(p,(y_j)) > \inf p \cdot X_i^k$. Indeed, if it is not true, there exists a sequence $(k^\nu, i^\nu, p^\nu, (y_j^\nu)) \in N \times \{1, \ldots, m\} \times \text{APE}$ such that $k^\nu \to +\infty$, and $r_{i^\nu}(p^\nu, (y_j^\nu)) \leq \inf p^\nu \cdot X_{i^\nu}^{k^\nu}$. Without any loss of generality, we can assume that the sequence (i^ν) is constant, say, equal to some i, and that the sequence $(p^\nu, (y_j^\nu))$ converges to some element $(\bar{p}, (\bar{y}_j)) \in \text{APE}$. Since $r_i(\bar{p}, (\bar{y}_j)) > \inf \bar{p} \cdot X_i$, there exists $x_i \in X_i$ such that $r_i(\bar{p}, (\bar{y}_j)) > \bar{p} \cdot x_i$. For ν large enough, $x_i \in X_i^{k^\nu}$; hence, $p^\nu \cdot x_i \geq \inf p^\nu \cdot X_i^{k^\nu} \geq r_i(p^\nu, (y_j^\nu))$. Consequently, $\bar{p} \cdot x_i = \lim_\nu p^\nu \cdot x_i \geq \lim_\nu r_i(p^\nu, (y_j^\nu)) = r_i(\bar{p}, (\bar{y}_j)) > \bar{p} \cdot x_i$, which is impossible. Hence, the claim is proved. □

For every $k \geq k_0$, we define the correspondences β_i^k, ξ_i^k, ψ_i^k, and f_i^k from $S \times R$ to X_i^k as follows:

$$\beta_i^k(p,w_i)=\{x_i\in X_i^k \mid p\cdot x_i\le w_i\};$$

$$\xi_i^k(p,w_i)=\{x_i\in\beta_i^k(p,w_i)\mid x\preccurlyeq_i x_i \text{ for every } x\in\beta_i^k(p,w_i)\};$$

$$\psi_i^k(p,w_i)=\{x_i\in\xi_i^k(p,w_i)\mid p\cdot x_i=\max p\cdot\xi_i^k(p,w_i)\};$$

$$f_i^k(p,w_i)=\begin{cases}\psi_i^k(p,w_i) & \text{if } w_i>\inf p\cdot X_i^k;\\ \{x_i\in X_i^k\mid p\cdot x_i=\inf p\cdot X_i^k\} & \text{if } w_i\le\inf p\cdot X_i^k.\end{cases}$$

The definition of these correspondences is taken in Debreu (1962). From Lemmas 1 and 2 of Debreu (1962), the correspondence f_i^k is upper hemicontinuous with non-empty, convex, compact values. We now define the correspondence z^k from $S\times\prod_{j=1}^n\partial Y_j$ to R^l as follows:

$$z^k(p,(y_j))=\sum_{i=1}^m f_i^k(p,r_i(p,(y_j)))-\left\{\sum_{j=1}^n y_j+\omega\right\}.$$

We now check that $X, Y_1,\ldots,Y_n, z^k$, and φ satisfy the assumptions of Theorem 1. It is straightforward for Assumptions P, B, C_0, and WSA. Assumption ED is satisfied since

$$z^k(p,(y_j))+\left\{\sum_{j=1}^n y_j\right\}=\sum_{i=1}^m f_i^k(p,r_i(p,(y_j)))-\{\omega\}\subset\sum_{i=1}^m X_i^k-\{\omega\}\subset X.$$

Furthermore, if $(p,(y_j))\in\text{APE}$, $f_i^k(p,r_i(p,(y_j))=\psi_i^k(p,r_i(p,(y_j));$ hence, $\sup p\cdot(\sum_{i=1}^m f_i^k(p,r_i(p,(y_j)))\le\sum_{i=1}^m r_i(p,(y_j))=p\cdot(\sum_{j=1}^n y_j+\omega)$; consequently, $\sup p\cdot z^k(p,(y_j))\le 0$. Finally, one easily checks that either φ satisfies Assumptions PR and WBL or $\varphi=\text{NC}$.

Consequently, from Theorem 1, for every $k\ge k_0$, there exists

$$(p^k,(y_j^k))\in S\times\prod_{j=1}^n\partial Y_j$$

satisfying $\sum_{j=1}^n y_j^k\in X$, $(p^k,\ldots,p^k)\in\varphi(p^k,(y_j^k))$ and $z^k(p^k,(y_j^k))\cap -R_+e\neq\emptyset$. From the definition of z^k, there exists $(x_i^k)\in\prod_{i=1}^m X_i^k$ and $\rho^k\in R_+$ such that $x_i^k\in f_i^k(p^k,r_i(p^k,(y_j^k)))$ and $\sum_{i=1}^m x_i^k=\sum_{j=1}^n y_j^k+\omega-\rho^k e$. The sequence $((x_i^k),(y_j^k),p^k)$ remains in the compact set $\prod_{i=1}^m\hat{X}_i\times A_0\times S$. Consequently, without any loss of generality, we can assume that the sequence $((x_i^k),(y_j^k),p^k)$ converges to some element $((x_i^*),(y_j^*),p^*)$.

We end the proof by showing that $((x_i^*),(y_j^*),p^*)$ is an equilibrium of the economy $\mathcal{E}$. From the compactness of the set APE, one deduces that $(p^*,(y_j^*))\in\text{APE}$. We now check that $\sum_{i=1}^m x_i^*=\sum_{j=1}^n y_j^*+\omega$. For this, we prove that $p^k\cdot x_i^k\ge r_i^k\overset{\text{def}}{=}r_i(p^k,(y_j^k))$. Since $(p^k,(y_j^k))\in\text{APE}$, one gets $r_i^k>\inf p^k\cdot X_i^k$; hence, $x_i^k\in\psi_i(p^k,r_i^k)$. Let us assume, by contraposition, that $p^k\cdot x_i^k<r_i^k$. Recalling that $x_i^0\in X_i^k$ and that $x_i^k<_i x_i^0$, one deduces that $p^k\cdot x_i^0>r_i^k$ from the fact that $x_i^k\in\xi_i^k(p^k,r_i^k)$. Consequently, for $t\in(0,1)$ well chosen, $x_i^t\overset{\text{def}}{=}tx_i^0+(1-t)x_i^k$ belongs to X_i^k and verifies $p^k\cdot x_i^t=$

$r_i^k > p^k \cdot x_i^k$. Furthermore, from Assumption C, $x_i' \succcurlyeq_i x_i^k$, which contradicts the fact that $x_i^k \in \psi_i^k(p^k, r_i^k)$. Consequently, $p^k \cdot x_i^k \geq r_i^k$. We now remark that $0 \leq \rho^k = p^k \cdot (\Sigma_{j=1}^n y_j^k + \omega - \Sigma_{i=1}^m x_i^k) \leq \Sigma_{i=1}^m (r_i^k - p^k \cdot x_i^k) \leq 0$. Hence, $\rho^k = 0$, $r_i^k = p^k \cdot x_i^k$ for every i, and $\Sigma_{i=1}^m x_i^k = \Sigma_{j=1}^n y_j^k + \omega$. At the limit, when $k \to \infty$, one gets $\Sigma_{i=1}^m x_i^* = \Sigma_{j=1}^n y_j^* + \omega$.

We end the proof by showing that $((x_i^*), (y_j^*), p^*)$ satisfies condition (a) of Definition 1. If it is not true, there exists $x_i \in X_i$ verifying $p^* \cdot x_i \leq r_i^* \overset{\text{def}}{=} r_i(p^*, (y_j^*))$ and such that $x_i \succ_i x_i^*$. Clearly, from the continuity of $\preccurlyeq_i$ and since $r_i^* > \inf p^* \cdot X_i$, there exists $x_i' \in X_i$ verifying $p^* \cdot x_i' < r_i^*$ and $x_i' \succ_i x_i^*$. Consequently, for k large enough, $p^k \cdot x_i' < r_i^k$, $x_i' \succ_i x_i^k$, and $x_i' \in X_i^k$. This contradicts the fact that $x_i^k \in \psi_i^k(p^k, r_i^k) \subset \xi_i^k(p^k, r_i^k)$ and ends the proof of Theorem 4. □

4 Proof of Theorem 3

We first recall several results that will be used in what follows. We let $Y_0 = -X$. Under the assumptions of Theorem 3, each of the sets $\partial Y_0, \partial Y_1, \ldots, \partial Y_n$ is homeomorphic to the Euclidean space $e^\perp \overset{\text{def}}{=} \{s \in R^l \mid s \cdot e = 0\}$. More precisely, for every $s \in e^\perp$, for every $j = 0, \ldots, n$, there exists a unique real number $\lambda_j(s)$ such that $s - \lambda_j(s) e \in \partial Y_j$; the function $\lambda_j : e^\perp \to R$ is Lipchitzian and the mapping $\Lambda_j : s \to s - \lambda_j(s) e$ is a homeomorphism from $e^\perp$ onto ∂Y_j (cf. Lemma 5.1 of Bonnisseau and Cornet, 1988). Consequently, the mapping $\Lambda : (e^\perp)^n \to \Pi_{j=1}^n \partial Y_j$ defined by $\Lambda(s) = (\Lambda_1(s_1), \ldots, \Lambda_n(s_n))$ for $s = (s_1, \ldots, s_n)$ is also a homeomorphism. We also remark that for every $t \geq 0$,

$$M_t \overset{\text{def}}{=} \Lambda^{-1}(A_t) = \left\{ s \in (e^\perp)^n \;\middle|\; \sum_{j=1}^n \Lambda_j(s_j) + te \in X \right\} = \{ s \in (e^\perp)^n \mid \theta(s) \leq t \},$$

where θ is the function from $(e^\perp)^n$ to R defined by

$$\theta(s) = \sum_{j=1}^n \lambda_j(s_j) + \lambda_0\left(-\sum_{j=1}^n s_j \right).$$

Finally, we recall that the generalized gradient $\partial \lambda_j(s_j)$ of λ_j at s_j is given by

$$\partial \lambda_j(s_j) = N_{Y_j}(\Lambda_j(s_j)) \cap S - \left\{ \frac{1}{l} e \right\}$$

(cf. Lemma 4.2 and the proof of Lemma 4.1 in Bonnisseau and Cornet 1990c). Consequently,

$$\partial \theta(s) \subset \Delta(s) \overset{\text{def}}{=} \left\{ (p_1 - p, \ldots, p_n - p) \;\middle|\; \begin{array}{l} p \in -N_X(-\Lambda_0(-\Sigma_{j=1}^n s_j)) \cap S \\ (p_j) \in \mathrm{NC}(p, (\Lambda(s))) \end{array} \right\}$$

In the following, we denote by $\mathrm{proj}_{e^\perp}$ the orthogonal projection onto $e^\perp$, by π the projection mapping from R^l onto S, and we define the mapping proj_X from R^l to X as follows:

$$\mathrm{proj}_X(y) = \mathrm{proj}_{e^\perp} y + \max\left\{\lambda_0(-\mathrm{proj}_{e^\perp} y), \frac{y \cdot e}{l}\right\} e.$$

We notice that $\mathrm{proj}_X(y) = y$ if $y \in X$ and that $\mathrm{proj}_X(y) - y \in R_+ e$. We now come to the proof of Theorem 3.

4.1 *Part I*

The first part is devoted to the construction of an auxiliary correspondence. Before, we fix a real number $\alpha > 0$ and we let

$$S_\alpha = \left\{ p \in R^l \,\middle|\, \sum_{h=1}^{l} p_h = 1, \text{ and } p_h \geq -\alpha \text{ for every } h = 1, \ldots, l \right\}.$$

We define the set U by

$$U = \left\{ (p, (y_j)) \in S_\alpha \times \prod_{j=1}^{n} \partial Y_j \,\middle|\, p \notin -N_X\left(\mathrm{proj}_X\left(\sum_{j=1}^{n} y_j\right)\right) \right\}.$$

From the properties of the normal cone and the continuity of the mapping proj_X, U is an open subset of $S_\alpha \times \prod_{j=1}^n \partial Y_j$ (for its relative topology), which contains the set PE by Assumption WSA′. Consequently, using the fact that the set APE is compact, there exists $\epsilon_0 > 0$ such that for every $\epsilon \in (0, \epsilon_0)$, $B(\mathrm{APE}, \epsilon) \subset U$ and for every $(p, (y_j)) \in B(\mathrm{APE}, \epsilon)$, p belongs to the relative interior of S_α. For every $\epsilon \in (0, \epsilon_0)$, there exists a continuous mapping τ^ϵ from $S_\alpha \times \prod_{j=1}^n \partial Y_j$ to $[0,1]$ verifying $\tau^\epsilon(p, (y_j)) = 1$ if $(p, (y_j)) \in \mathrm{APE}$ and $\tau^\epsilon(p, (y_j)) = 0$ if $(p, (y_j)) \notin B(\mathrm{APE}, \epsilon)$.

We now define the correspondence Φ from $S_\alpha \times \prod_{j=1}^n \partial Y_j$ to R^l as follows:

$$\Phi(p, (y_j)) = \mathrm{int}\, T_X\left(\mathrm{proj}_X\left(\sum_{j=1}^{n} y_j\right)\right) \cap \{u \in R^l \mid p \cdot u < 0\} \cap \mathrm{int}\, B(0,1).$$

Clearly, Φ is an open correspondence[3] with convex values and $\Phi(p, (y_j))$ is non-empty on U. Consequently, there exists a continuous mapping ψ from U to R^l, which is a selection of Φ, that is, such that $\psi(p, (y_j)) \in \Phi(p, (y_j))$ for every $(p, (y_j)) \in U$. We now define the correspondence ζ from $S_\alpha \times \prod_{j=1}^n \partial Y_j$ to R^l as follows:

$$\zeta(p, (y_j)) = \begin{cases} \{\psi(p, (y_j))\} & \text{if } (p, (y_j)) \in U, \\ B(0,1) & \text{if } (p, (y_j)) \notin U. \end{cases}$$

[3] That is, for every $v \in R^l$, the set $\{(p, (y_j)) \in S_\alpha \times \prod_{j=1}^n \partial Y_j \mid v \in \Phi(p, (y_j))\}$ is open.

Clearly, ζ is an upper hemicontinuous correspondence with non-empty, convex, compact values. We end this part by defining the correspondence z^ϵ for every $\epsilon \in (0, \epsilon_0)$ as follows:

$$z^\epsilon(p,(y_j)) = \tau^\epsilon(p,(y_j))z(\pi(p),(y_j)) + (1-\tau^\epsilon(p,(y_j)))\zeta(p,(y_j)).$$

Clearly, z^ϵ is an upper hemicontinuous correspondence with non-empty, convex, compact values, which satisfies the following properties:

$$z^\epsilon(p,(y_j)) = z(p,(y_j)) \quad \text{if } (p,(y_j)) \in \text{APE},$$

$$z^\epsilon(p,(y_j)) = \{\psi(p,(y_j))\} \quad \text{if } (p,(y_j)) \in U \backslash B(\text{APE}, \epsilon).$$

4.2 *Part II*

We claim that for every $\epsilon \in (0, \epsilon_0)$, there exist $(p^\epsilon, (y_j^\epsilon)) \in B(\text{APE}, \epsilon)$ and $x^\epsilon \in z^\epsilon(p^\epsilon, (y_j^\epsilon))$ such that $x^\epsilon \in Re$. Furthermore, if $\sum_{j=1}^n y_j^\epsilon \in \text{int } X$, then $(p^\epsilon, (y_j^\epsilon)) \in \text{APE}$.

In the proof of this assertion, we will distinguish the case of a general correspondence φ and the case where $\varphi = \text{NC}$.

4.3 *Part IIa (General pricing rule)*

We choose a non-empty ball B in $(e^\perp)^n$ of center 0 such that $M_{t_0} \subset \text{int } B$, where t_0 is the real number given by Assumption WBL′.

We now remark that the properties of z^ϵ imply that there exists a non-empty, convex, compact subset K of R^l such that $z^\epsilon(p, \Lambda(s)) \subset K$ for every $(p,s) \in S_\alpha \times B$.

We now define the correspondence F from $K \times B \times S_\alpha \times S^n$ to itself as follows:

$$F(x,s,p,(p_j)) = \prod_{\nu=1}^{4} F_\nu(x,s,p,(p_j)),$$

where

$$F_1(x,s,p,(p_j)) = z^\epsilon(p, \Lambda(s));$$

$$F_2(x,s,p,(p_j)) = \left\{\sigma \in B \;\middle|\; \sum_{j=1}^{n} (p-p_j)\cdot(\sigma_j - \sigma_j') \geq 0 \text{ for every } (\sigma_j') \in B\right\};$$

$$F_3(x,s,p,(p_j)) = \{q \in S_\alpha \mid (q-q')\cdot x \geq 0 \text{ for every } q' \in S_\alpha\};$$

$$F_4(x,s,p,(p_j)) = \varphi(\pi(p), \Lambda(s)).$$

The correspondence F is upper hemicontinuous with non-empty, convex, compact values from Assumption PR, from the properties of z^ϵ, and from the maximum theorem (in Berge, 1966). Consequently, by Kakutani's Theorem, there exists a fixed point $(x^\epsilon, s^\epsilon, p^\epsilon, (p_j^\epsilon))$ of F that satisfies:

$$\sum_{j=1}^{n}(p^{\epsilon}-p_j^{\epsilon})\cdot s_j^{\epsilon} \geq \sum_{j=1}^{n}(p^{\epsilon}-p_j^{\epsilon})\cdot s_j \quad \text{for every } (s_j)\in B, \tag{1}$$

$$p^{\epsilon}\cdot x^{\epsilon} \geq q\cdot x^{\epsilon} \quad \text{for every } q\in S_{\alpha}, \tag{2}$$

$$(p_j^{\epsilon})\in\varphi(\pi(p^{\epsilon}),\Lambda(s^{\epsilon})). \tag{3}$$

The following claims will show that $(p^{\epsilon},(y_j^{\epsilon}))\in B(\text{APE},\epsilon)$, where $y_j^{\epsilon}=\Lambda_j(s_j^{\epsilon})$, $j=1,\dots,n$, and that $x^{\epsilon}\in z^{\epsilon}(p^{\epsilon},(y_j^{\epsilon}))\cap Re$. Furthermore, if $\sum_{j=1}^{n} y_j^{\epsilon}\in X$, then $(p^{\epsilon},(y_j^{\epsilon}))\in \text{APE}$.

Claim 1a. $(p^{\epsilon},(y_j^{\epsilon}))\in U$.

Proof: Assume that $(p^{\epsilon},(y_j^{\epsilon}))\notin U$. Then $p^{\epsilon}\in -N_X(\text{proj}_X(\sum_{j=1}^{n} y_j^{\epsilon}))\subset S$ and $(p^{\epsilon},(y_j^{\epsilon}))\notin \text{PE}$ (recalling that $\text{PE}\subset U$). From (3), one deduces that $(p^{\epsilon}-p_1^{\epsilon},\dots,p^{\epsilon}-p_n^{\epsilon})$ is a nonzero vector of $(e^{\perp})^n$; hence, (1) implies that $s^{\epsilon}\in\partial B$. From our choice of B, one then deduces that $(y_j^{\epsilon})\notin M_{t_0}$; hence, $\pi_X(\sum_{j=1}^{n} y_j^{\epsilon})=\sum_{j=1}^{n} y_j^{\epsilon}+te$ with $t\geq t_0$.

We now remark that for $\rho>0$ small enough,

$$s=\rho(p^{\epsilon}-p_1^{\epsilon},\dots,p^{\epsilon}-p_n^{\epsilon})\in B.$$

Consequently, by (1), one gets

$$\sum_{j=1}^{n}(p^{\epsilon}-p_j^{\epsilon})\cdot s_j^{\epsilon}\geq\sum_{j=1}^{n}(p^{\epsilon}-p_j^{\epsilon})\cdot s_j=\rho\sum_{j=1}^{n}(p^{\epsilon}-p_j^{\epsilon})\cdot(p^{\epsilon}-p_j^{\epsilon})>0.$$

Hence,

$$\begin{aligned}\sum_{j=1}^{n} p^{\epsilon}\cdot y_j^{\epsilon} &= \sum_{j=1}^{n} p^{\epsilon}\cdot s_j^{\epsilon}-\sum_{j=1}^{n}\lambda_j(s_j^{\epsilon})\\ &> \sum_{j=1}^{n} p_j^{\epsilon}\cdot s_j^{\epsilon}-\sum_{j=1}^{n}\lambda_j(s_j^{\epsilon})=\sum_{j=1}^{n} p_j^{\epsilon}\cdot y_j^{\epsilon}.\end{aligned}$$

But this inequality contradicts Assumption WBL′ since

$$p^{\epsilon}\in -N_X\left(\pi_X\left(\sum_{j=1}^{n} y_j^{\epsilon}\right)\right)$$

and $(p_j^{\epsilon})\in\varphi(p^{\epsilon},(y_j^{\epsilon}))$ from (3), recalling that $p^{\epsilon}\in S$. □

Claim 2a. *If* $\sum_{j=1}^{n} y_j^{\epsilon}\in X$, $(p^{\epsilon},(y_j^{\epsilon}))\in APE$; *otherwise* $(p^{\epsilon},(y_j^{\epsilon}))\in B(\text{APE},\epsilon)$.

Proof: Let us first suppose that $\sum_{j=1}^{n} y_j^{\epsilon}\in X$. Then $s^{\epsilon}\in M_0\subset M_{t_0}\subset \text{int } B$, and thus (1) implies that $p^{\epsilon}=p_j^{\epsilon}$ for every j, which together with (3) implies that $(p^{\epsilon},\dots,p^{\epsilon})\in\varphi(p^{\epsilon},(y_j^{\epsilon}))$, which means that $(p^{\epsilon},(y_j^{\epsilon}))\in \text{APE}$.

We now suppose that $\sum_{j=1}^n y_j^\epsilon \notin X$ and we prove the claim by contraposition. If $(p^\epsilon, (y_j^\epsilon)) \notin B(\text{APE}, \epsilon)$, from the definition of z^ϵ, $x^\epsilon \in \zeta(p^\epsilon, (y_j^\epsilon))$. But from Claim 1a, $(p^\epsilon, (y_j^\epsilon)) \in U$; hence, $\zeta(p^\epsilon, (y_j^\epsilon)) = \{\psi(p^\epsilon, (y_j^\epsilon))\}$. Since $\psi(p^\epsilon, (y_j^\epsilon)) \in \Phi(p^\epsilon, (y_j^\epsilon))$, $p^\epsilon \cdot x^\epsilon < 0$ and $x^\epsilon \in \text{int}\, T_X(\text{proj}_X(\sum_{j=1}^n y_j^\epsilon))$. From (2), for every $q \in S_\alpha$, $q \cdot x^\epsilon < 0$; hence, x^ϵ belongs to the interior of the polar cone of S_α, which is included is $-R^l_{++}$. But

$$-R^l_{++} \cap \text{int}\, T_X\left(\text{proj}_X\left(\sum_{j=1}^n y_j^\epsilon\right)\right) = \emptyset$$

since $\text{proj}_X(\sum_{j=1}^n y_j^\epsilon) \subset \partial X$ and $X + R^l_+ = X$. This contradicts the fact that $x^\epsilon \in -R^l_{++} \cap \text{int}\, T_X(\text{proj}_X(\sum_{j=1}^n y_j^\epsilon))$. □

Claim 3a. $x^\epsilon \in z^\epsilon(p^\epsilon, (y_j^\epsilon)) \cap Re$.

Proof: From our choice of ϵ_0 and Claim 2a, p^ϵ belongs to the relative interior of S_α. Hence, (2) implies that x^ϵ is in the orthogonal space of the affine space spanned by S_α, which is equivalent to saying that $x^\epsilon \in Re$. □

4.4 *Part IIb (Marginal pricing)*

We choose a non-empty closed ball B in $(e^\perp)^n$ such that $M_0 \subset \text{int}\, B$. We now claim that there exists a continuous mapping ρ from B to M_0, which satisfies:

(i) $\rho(s) = s$ for every $s \in M_0$;
(ii) $\rho(s) \in \text{int}\, M_0$ implies $s \in M_0$;
(iii) there exists $\eta > 0$ such that for every $s \in M_\eta$, for every $\delta \in \Delta(\rho(s))$, one has $0 \le (s - \rho(s)) \cdot \delta$.

This is a consequence of the following deformation lemma (see Bonnisseau and Cornet 1990b, 1990c).

Theorem 5. *Let E be a finite dimensional Euclidean space, let a and b be real numbers such that $a > b$, let $\theta: E \to R$ be a locally Lipchitzian function, and let Δ be a correspondence from E to E. We assume that* (i) *the set $M_b = \{s \in E \mid \theta(s) \le b\}$ is compact and non-empty;* (ii) *Δ is an upper-hemicontinuous correspondence with non-empty, convex, compact values and $\partial\theta(s) \subset \Delta(s)$ for all $s \in E$;* (iii) *$0 \notin \Delta(s)$ if $a \le \theta(s) \le b$.*

(a) *Then, there exists a continuous mapping ρ from M_b to M_a such that $\rho(s) = s$ if $s \in M_a$ and $\rho(s) \in \text{int}\, M_a$ implies $s \in M_a$.*
(b) *There exists a real number $\eta \in (0, b-a)$ such that for all $s \in E$, $a \le \theta(s) \le a + \eta$, one has*

$$0 \le (s - \rho(s)) \cdot \delta \quad \textit{for all } \delta \in \Delta(\rho(s)).$$

Indeed, it suffices to apply this theorem with $E=(e^{\perp})^n$, $a=0$, $b=\max\{\theta(s)\mid s\in B\}$, θ and Δ as they are defined in the beginning of the proof. We remark that for every $t\geq 0$, the set $M_t=\{s\in(e^{\perp})^n\mid\theta(s)\leq t\}$ is compact from Assumption B and $0\notin\Delta(s)$ if $\theta(s)\geq 0$ from Assumption WSA′. Hence, the mapping θ and the correspondence $\Delta(\cdot)$ satisfy the assumptions of the previous deformation lemma.

We now choose a real number $\gamma>0$ small enough such that for every $(p,s)\in S_\alpha\times M_0$, for every $(p_j)\in S^n$, $s-\gamma(p_1-p,\dots,p_n-p)\in M_\eta\cap B$.

We now remark that there exists a non-empty, convex, compact subset K of R^l such that for every $(p,s)\in S_\alpha\times M_0$, $z^\epsilon(p,\Lambda(s))\subset K$ since z^ϵ is upper hemicontinuous with non-empty, convex, compact values.

We now define the correspondence F from $K\times B\times S_\alpha$ to itself by

$$F(x,s,p)=\prod_{\nu=1}^{3}F_\nu(x,s,p),$$

$$F_1(x,s,p)=z^\epsilon(p,\Lambda(\rho(s))),$$

$$F_2(x,s,p)=\{\rho(s)-\gamma(p_1-p,\dots,p_n-p)\mid(p_j)\in\mathrm{NC}(\pi(p),(\Lambda(\rho(s))\},$$

$$F_3(x,s,p)=\{q\in S_\alpha\mid(q-q')\cdot s\geq 0\text{ for every }q'\in S_\alpha\}.$$

The correspondence F is upper hemicontinuous with non-empty, convex, compact values; this is a consequence of the continuity of the mapping $\gg$and ρ, of the properties of z^ϵ, of the maximum theorem (Berge 1966), and of the properties of the correspondence NC. Consequently, by Kakutani's Theorem, there exists a fixed point $(x^\epsilon,s^\epsilon,p^\epsilon)$ in $K\times B\times S_\alpha$ of the correspondence F. That is, if we let $y_j^\epsilon=\Lambda_j(\rho_j(s^\epsilon))$ $(j=1,\dots,n)$, there exists $p_j^\epsilon\in R^l$ $(j=1,\dots,n)$ such that

$$x^\epsilon\in z^\epsilon(p^\epsilon,(y_j^\epsilon)),\tag{4}$$

$$s^\epsilon=\rho(s^\epsilon)-\gamma(p_1^\epsilon-p^\epsilon,\dots,p_n^\epsilon-p^\epsilon),\tag{5}$$

$$(p_j^\epsilon)\in\mathrm{NC}(\pi(p^\epsilon),(y_j^\epsilon)),\tag{6}$$

$$p^\epsilon\cdot x^\epsilon\geq q\cdot x^\epsilon\quad\text{for every }q\in S_\alpha.\tag{7}$$

The following claims will show that $(p^\epsilon,(y_j^\epsilon))\in B(\mathrm{APE},\epsilon)$ and that $x^\epsilon\in RE$. Furthermore, if $\sum_{j=1}^n y_j^\epsilon\in\operatorname{int}X$, then $(p^\epsilon,(y_j^\epsilon))\in\mathrm{APE}$.

Claim 1b. $(p^\epsilon,(y_j^\epsilon)\in U$.

Proof: If $s^\epsilon\in M_0$, then $s^\epsilon=\rho(s^\epsilon)$, and (5) and (6) imply that $(p^\epsilon,\dots,p^\epsilon)\in\mathrm{NC}(p^\epsilon,(y_j^\epsilon))$; hence, $(p^\epsilon,(y_j^\epsilon))\in\mathrm{APE}\subset U$.

If $s^\epsilon\notin M_0$, let us suppose that $(p^\epsilon,(y_j^\epsilon))\notin U$. $\rho(s^\epsilon)\in M_0$; hence, $\sum_{j=1}^n y_j^\epsilon\in X$; consequently, $\pi_X(\sum_{j=1}^n y_j^\epsilon)=\sum_{j=1}^n y_j^\epsilon$, and, from the definition of U, $p^\epsilon\in -N_X(\sum_{j=1}^n y_j^\epsilon)$. From the definition of Δ and from

(6), $(p_1^\epsilon - p^\epsilon, \ldots, p_n^\epsilon - p^\epsilon) \in \Delta(\rho(s^\epsilon))$. From our choice of γ and from the property (iii) satisfied by ρ, one deduces that $0 \leq (s^\epsilon - \rho(s^\epsilon)) \cdot (p_1^\epsilon - p^\epsilon, \ldots, p_n^\epsilon - p^\epsilon) = -\gamma \sum_{j=1}^n \|p_j^\epsilon - p^\epsilon\|^2$. Consequently, $p^\epsilon = p_j^\epsilon$ for every j; hence, (5) and (6) imply that $(p^\epsilon, (y_j^\epsilon)) \in \text{PE} \subset U$, which contradicts the fact that $(p^\epsilon, (y_j^\epsilon)) \notin U$. □

Claim 2b. *If* $\sum_{j=1}^n y_j^\epsilon \in \text{int}\, X$, $(p^\epsilon, (y_j^\epsilon)) \in APE$; *otherwise* $(p^\epsilon, (y_j^\epsilon)) \in B(\text{APE}, \epsilon)$.

Proof: If $\sum_{j=1}^n y_j^\epsilon \in \text{int}\, X$, $\rho(s^\epsilon) \in \text{int}\, M_0$, hence, from the property (ii) of ρ, $s^\epsilon \in M_0$ and $s^\epsilon = \rho(s^\epsilon)$. Then (5) and (6) imply that $(p^\epsilon, (y_j^\epsilon)) \in \text{APE}$.

Let us assume, by contraposition, that $(p^\epsilon, (y_j^\epsilon)) \notin B(\text{APE}, \epsilon)$. Then, from the definition of z^ϵ, from (4), and from Claim 1b, $x^\epsilon = \psi(p^\epsilon, (y_j^\epsilon))$. Consequently, $x^\epsilon \in \text{int}\, T_X(\sum_{j=1}^n y_j^\epsilon)$, and $p^\epsilon \cdot x^\epsilon < 0$. From (7), for every $q \in S_\alpha$, $q \cdot x^\epsilon < 0$, hence x^ϵ belongs to the interior of the polar cone of S_α which is included in $-R_{++}^l$. Consequently $T_X(\sum_{j=1}^n y_j^\epsilon) = R^l$ since $R_+^l \subset T_X(\sum_{j=1}^n y_j^\epsilon)$ and $x^\epsilon \in T_X(\sum_{j=1}^n y_j^\epsilon) \cap -R_{++}^l$. This implies that $\sum_{j=1}^n y_j^\epsilon \in \text{int}\, X$.

The first part of the proof of the claim implies that, in that case, $(p^\epsilon, (y_j^\epsilon)) \in \text{APE}$, which contradicts $(p^\epsilon, (y_j^\epsilon)) \notin B(\text{APE}, \epsilon)$.

Claim 3b. $x^\epsilon \in Re$.

Proof: It is similar to the proof of Claim 3a. □

4.5 *Part III*

We now end the proof with a limit argument. From Part II and the definition of z^ϵ in Part I, we know that, for every $\epsilon \in (0, \epsilon_0)$, there exists $(p^\epsilon, (y_j^\epsilon), x^\epsilon, t^\epsilon, u^\epsilon) \in S_\alpha \times \prod_{j=1}^n \partial Y_j \times Re \times [0,1] \times R^l$ satisfying

$$(p^\epsilon, (y_j^\epsilon)) \in B(\text{APE}, \epsilon),$$

$$x^\epsilon = t^\epsilon u^\epsilon + (1 - t^\epsilon)\psi(p^\epsilon, (y_j^\epsilon)),$$

$$u^\epsilon \in z(\pi(p^\epsilon), (y_j^\epsilon)).$$

Furthermore, if $(\epsilon, (y_j^\epsilon))$ satisfies $\sum_{j=1}^n y_j^\epsilon \in \text{int}\, X$, then $(p^\epsilon, (y_j^\epsilon)) \in$ APE; hence, from the definition of τ^ϵ, $t^\epsilon = 1$.

Recalling that, for every $\epsilon \in (0, \epsilon_0)$, $B(\text{APE}, \epsilon) \subset \text{cl}\, B(\text{APE}, \epsilon_0)$, which is compact, one deduces that there exists a sequence $(\epsilon_\nu) \subset (0, \epsilon_0)$ converging to 0 such that the sequence $(p^{\epsilon_\nu}, (y_j^{\epsilon_\nu}), x^{\epsilon_\nu}, t^{\epsilon_\nu}, u^{\epsilon_\nu})$ converges to some element $(p^*, (y_j^*), x^*, t^*, u^*)$ of $S_\alpha \times \prod_{j=1}^n \partial Y_j \times Re \times [0,1] \times R^l$.

Clearly, $(p^*, (y_j^*))$ belongs to APE; hence, $p^* \in S$. From the upper hemicontinuity of z and the continuity of ψ, one gets

$$u^* \in z(p^*, (y_j^*)),$$
$$x^* = t^* u^* + (1-t^*)\psi(p^*, (y_j^*)).$$

We now distinguish two cases. Firstly, if $\sum_{j=1}^n y_j^* \in \operatorname{int} X$, then, for ν large enough, $\sum_{j=1}^n y_j^{\epsilon_\nu} \in \operatorname{int} X$, which implies $t^{\epsilon_\nu} = 1$. Consequently, $x^* = u^* \in z(p^*, (y_j^*))$. From Assumption WED, one has $p^* \cdot x^* \leq 0$, which together with $x^* \in Re$ implies $x^* \in -R_+ e$. Hence, $(p^*, (y_j^*))$ satisfies the conclusion of Theorem 3.

Secondly, if $\sum_{j=1}^n y_j^* \in \partial X$, we first show that $p^* \cdot x^* \leq 0$. Indeed, from Assumption WED, $p^* \cdot u^* \leq 0$ and from the definition of ψ, $p^* \cdot \psi(p^*, (y_j^*)) \leq 0$, which clearly implies that $p^* \cdot x^* \leq 0$. Consequently, since $x^* \in Re$ and $p^* \in S$, $x^* \in -R_+ e$. We now end the proof by showing that $x^* = u^*$, that is, $t^* = 1$. If it is not true, from Assumption WED and the definition of ψ, one deduces that x^* is a convex combination of two points in $T_X(\sum_{j=1}^n y_j^*)$, one of which is in the interior of $T_X(\sum_{j=1}^n y_j^*)$. Consequently, $x^* \in \operatorname{int} T_X(\sum_{j=1}^n y_j^*)$, which contradicts that $x^* \in -R_+ e$ (recalling that $X + R_+^l = X$ and $\sum_{j=1}^n y_j^* \in \partial X$). Consequently, $t^* = 1$, $x^* \in z(p^*, (y_j^*)) \cap -R_+ e$, which shows that $(p^*, (y_j^*))$ satisfies the conclusion of Theorem 3. □

REFERENCES

Beato, P. 1979. "Marginal Cost Pricing and Increasing Returns." Ph.D. dissertation, University of Minnesota, Minneapolis.

1982. "The Existence of Marginal Cost Pricing Equilibria with Increasing Returns." *The Quarterly Journal of Economics* 389, 669–88.

Beato, P., and A. Mas-Colell. 1985. "On Marginal Cost Pricing with Given Tax-Subsidy Rules." *Journal of Economic Theory* 37: 356–65.

Berge, C. 1966. *Espaces topologiques: Fonctions multivoques.* Paris: Dunod.

Bonnisseau, J. M. 1988a. "On Two Existence Results of Equilibria in Economies With Increasing Returns." *Journal of Mathematical Economics* 17: 193–207.

1988b. "A Remark on the Existence of Equilibria in Economies With Increasing Returns." CORE Discussion Paper 8814, Université Catholique de Louvain, Belgium.

Bonnisseau, J. M., and B. Cornet. 1988. "Existence of Equilibrium when Firms Follow Bounded Losses Pricing Rules." *Journal of Mathematical Economics* 17: 119–47.

1990a. "Existence of Marginal Cost Pricing Equilibria in an Economy with Several Nonconvex Firms." *Econometrica* 58: 661–82.

1990b. "Fixed-Point Theorems and Morse's Lemma for Lipschitzian Functions." *Journal of Mathematical Analysis and Applications* 146: 318–32.

1990c. "Existence of Marginal Cost Pricing Equilibria: The Nonsmooth Case." *International Economic Review* 31: 685–708.

Brown, D. J., and G. M. Heal. 1982. "Existence, Local Uniqueness and Optimality of a Marginal Cost Pricing Equilibrium with Increasing Returns." Social Science Working Paper 415, California Institute of Technology, Pasadena.

Brown, D. J., G. Heal, Ali M. Khan, and R. Vohra. 1986. "On a General Existence Theorem for Marginal Cost Pricing Equilibria." *Journal of Economic Theory* 38: 371-9.

Clarke, F. 1975. "Generalized Gradients and Applications." *Transactions of the American Mathematical Society* 205: 247-62.

1983. *Optimization and Nonsmooth Analysis.* New York: Wiley.

Cornet, B. 1988. "Topological Properties of the Set of Attainable Productions Plans in a Nonconvex Production Economy." *Journal of Mathematical Economics* 17: 275-92.

1990. "Existence of Equilibria in Economies With Increasing Returns." In *Contributions to Operations Research and Economics: The Twentieth Anniversary of C.O.R.E.* Cambridge, MA: The MIT Press.

Debreu, G. 1956. "Market Equilibrium." *Proceedings of the National Academy of Sciences of the U.S.A.* 42: 876-8.

1959. *Theory of Value.* New York: Wiley.

1962. "New Concepts and Techniques for Equilibrium Analysis." *International Economic Review* 3: 257-73.

Dierker, E., R. Guesnerie, and W. Neuefeind. 1985. "General Equilibrium Where Some Firms Follow Special Pricing Rules." *Econometrica* 53: 1369-93.

Gale, D. 1955. "The Law of Supply and Demand." *Mathematica Scandinavica* 3: 155-69.

Kamiya, K. 1988a. "On the Survival Assumption in Marginal Cost Pricing." *Journal of Mathematical Economics* 17: 261-73.

1988b. "Existence and Uniqueness of Equilibria with Increasing Returns." *Journal of Mathematical Economics* 17: 149-78.

Mantel, R. 1979. "Equilibrio con rendimiento crecientes a escala." *Anales de la Asociation Argentina de Economia Politica* 1: 271-83.

Nikaido, H. 1956. "On the Classical Multilateral Exchange Problem." *Metroeconomica* 8: 135-45.

Vohra, R. 1988. "On the Existence of Equilibria in Economies with Increasing Returns." *Journal of Mathematical Economics* 17: 179-92.

CHAPTER 5

Increasing returns and new developments in the theory of growth

Paul Romer

With the publication of *The Wealth of Nations,* Adam Smith put two propositions at the center of economic theory. The first was that competition allocates the preexisting stock of productive inputs in a way that is wealth maximizing. The second was that an endogenous process of accumulation and investment was the fundamental force that led to increases in the stock of these inputs, and, therefore, to growth in income and wealth. In the developments leading up to the acceptance of the neoclassical growth model in the late 1950s and early 1960s, economists moved away from Smith's second proposition, not so much because they were convinced that it was wrong, but rather because it was difficult to reconcile with the theoretical apparatus of competitive equilibrium theory that had evolved to capture the first proposition.

In the last decade, a new round of growth models has rehabilitated the idea that endogenous accumulation causes growth. Economists now have a clearer understanding of how endogenous accumulation can be reconciled with the existence of decentralized markets, and the focus has turned to identifying the fundamental factor that is accumulated (physical capital? human capital? knowledge or technology?) and the market mechanism that supports this process of accumulation.

Concurrent with the evolution in the substantive issues considered by growth theory, the set of technical models under consideration has expanded. Until recently, perfect competition, with its assumptions of both price-taking behavior and perfect markets, was the only equilibrium concept used in models of growth. We now have several models that preserve

This chapter was presented at the Conference on Equilibrium Theory and Applications held at CORE in Brussels on June 1989, and benefited from the comments of the participants. Comments from Paul David and two referees are also gratefully acknowledged. This work was supported by the National Science Foundation Grants #SES 8821943 and BNS87-00864 and a Sloan Foundation Fellowship, and is part of the NBER's research programs in Economic Fluctuations and Growth.

price-taking behavior but allow for market imperfections like external effects or distorting taxes. More importantly, a class of dynamic-equilibrium growth models that allow for departures from price taking is emerging.

Before turning in the second section to a description of the recent crop of models of growth, this chapter begins with a brief and admittedly impressionistic description of the early developments in growth theory from Smith down to Solow. The point of this discussion is not to provide a carefully documented history of thought, but rather to add a longer-run perspective to the implicit questions that are raised by this review: Why did economists of the 1960s and 1970s devote so much theoretical and empirical attention to a model of growth in which calendar time was the most important explanatory variable? And what explains the abandonment of exogenous technological change as a foundation of growth theory in the last 10 years?

The answer suggested here is that the assumption that markets were perfectly competitive dictated the assumption that technological change was exogenous. Given the state of economic theory 30 years ago, this assumption generated theoretical insights that more than compensated for the limitations that it imposed on the analysis of growth. But based on the theoretical progress that this framework made possible, it is now possible to go beyond it and bring technological change at the aggregate level back into the realm of economic analysis.

1 Introduction and historical background

A complete history of economic thought concerning long-run growth would track many influences that were internal to the evolution of economics as a discipline and many others that impinged from outside, a task that is far beyond the scope of this chapter. This review emphasizes just one internal influence, the effect exerted by technical difficulty when economic arguments are formalized in mathematical terms. In the 180 years following the publication of *The Wealth of Nations,* economists steadily improved their understanding of perfect competition and of the associated mathematical notion of convexity. As they did, the logic of their arguments led them to sacrifice the study of endogenous accumulation in exchange for a coherent and operational view of how an entire economy functions.

The nadir for growth based on endogenous accumulation was reached with the publication in 1956 of Robert Solow's and Trevor Swan's demonstration that changes in the savings rate, and implicitly in government policy variables, have no lasting effect on the rate of growth of output per worker. These papers were part of a much larger movement within economics toward the use of fully specified mathematical models of the economy as a whole. In applications to international trade and to growth, these models were highly aggregative and very simple, but they nonetheless were explicit general equilibrium models. Marshallian partial equilibrium analysis had allowed monopoly pricing and markets with nonconvexities to co-exist on roughly equal theoretical grounds with price-taking competition in markets that were convex. Technically more difficult general equilibrium models, however, were developed almost entirely within the simplest available mathematical framework, that of price-taking competition within perfect markets.

Convexity plays a central role in both abstract and applied general equilibrium analysis. At the abstract level, it is crucial in general proofs of the existence of an equilibrium and of the second welfare theorem. In applied work, the second welfare theorem permits all of the tools of optimization theory to be used in the calculation of equilibria. In particular, the shadow prices or multipliers associated with constrained optimization problems have immediate interpretations as market prices, an observation that has been particularly valuable in the calculation of dynamic equilibria.

The power of convexity and perfect competition was nowhere more evident than in growth theory. One of the most natural assumptions that one could ask about growth and accumulation is what effect a 1% increase in the rate of growth of capital would have on the rate of growth of output. Without the assumption of perfect competition, this kind of question can only be addressed by empirical work that is certain to be plagued by the problem of simultaneity that arises in all aggregate level analysis. But as Solow (1957) showed so clearly, if one merely assumes that prices are determined in perfectly competitive markets, the answer to this question can be found by calculating the division of national income between capital and labor.

This observation brought with it the related finding that growth in the stock of capital and in the labor force was not sufficient to account for growth in output. The natural explanation for this finding was that technological change must account for part of the unexplained growth. Had the United States managed to achieve in the 1860s the same value of capital per worker as that attained in the 1960s, it seemed totally implausible that output per worker would have been as high as it was in the 1960s. Something else about production in 1960 was manifestly different.

Growth accounting made it possible to explicitly calculate the unexplained residual and to offer explicit empirical evidence at the level of the economy as a whole that technological change was of fundamental importance for economic growth. The paradox, however, was that the competitive theory that generated the evidence was inconsistent with any explanation of how technological change could arise as the result of the self-interested actions of individual economic actors. By definition, all of national output had to be paid as returns to capital and labor; none remained as possible compensation for technological innovations. Hence, there was no way to connect this aggregate level analysis with historical studies of invention and diffusion of new technologies or with microlevel analysis of effects of private sector research and development. The assumptions of convexity and perfect competition placed the accumulation of new technologies at the center of the growth process and simultaneously denied the possibility that economic analysis could have anything to say about this process.

The tension between Smith's two propositions about competition and accumulation was most clearly evident in the growth models of the late 1950s, but it had been uncovered long before. Stimulated by increases in food prices and land rents associated with the war with France, Malthus and Ricardo developed the notion of diminishing returns to a particular factor of production, labor, as its quantity increased relative to the quantities of other factors like land. Once the logic of diminishing returns associated with changing factor proportions was clear, it was evident that it would apply equally well to changes in the proportion of capital relative to the stock of labor. This put limits on the potential for capital accumulation to generate increases in income per capita.

By the end of the classical period of economic thought, dated, for example, by the publication of John Stuart Mill's *Principles of Political Economy,* the notion of a steady-state level of income determined by diminishing returns was firmly embedded in economics. Economics was forever after the dismal science. Mill allowed for the possibility that the steady state might move over time in response to changes in our understanding of the physical world, but he argued that the details of the process of technological improvement were beyond the scope of economics. Thus, even by the middle of the nineteenth century, all of the elements of the neoclassical theory of growth could be discerned: diminishing returns that limited the scope for capital accumulation and exogenous changes in our understanding of the physical world that could act to raise the returns to capital accumulation.

Ultimately, mainstream economists accepted the logic of this argument and placed exogenous technological change at the center of models of growth. But they did so half-heartedly. Policy pronouncements by economists often seemed closer to those suggested by Smith than by the accepted model. Since the time of Smith, economists have never ceased proselytizing for higher levels of savings and investment.

Because they found the conclusions of this kind of theory unattractive, many economists tried to extend it in ways that would retain for savings and accumulation a significant role in the growth process without giving up the features that made the theory so powerful. The most influential of these attempts can be attributed to Alfred Marshall (1890). He squarely faced the tension between the diminishing returns implied by competitive analysis and the steady improvement in income per capita that belied the gloomy forecasts of Malthus and Ricardo. To explain the observed growth, Marshall disputed the presence of diminishing returns to accumulation, and supposed instead that increasing returns might be present. To reconcile increasing returns that were internal to a firm with the existence of decentralized markets with many firms, Marshall relied on his famous but unpersuasive analogy with trees (1890, Chapter XIII, Book IV): Firms, like trees, grow big, but then they die and new ones come along.

From the point of view of theoretical acceptance, his more successful innovation was the introduction of the notion of an externality. This made possible the notion of external increasing returns that manifest themselves at the level of the industry or economy, even though returns at the level of the firm are not increasing. Because firms were small and could still be assumed to be price takers, the notion of an industry supply curve could still be used; but because the supply curve might slope down, increases in demand, arising, for example, from population growth, could lead to falling prices and increases in individual welfare. The beauty of external increasing returns was that it preserved much of the apparatus of economic theory (e.g., supply and demand curves that summarize the actions of price-taking agents) while at the same time departing from the convexity assumptions that seemed inimical to a complete understanding of growth.

The lasting success of external increasing returns would not seem to be due to any direct empirical evidence concerning their presence. Marshall's description of internal increasing returns was far more extensive and persuasive than his description of external increasing returns. In one of the exchanges in the "cost controversies" of the 1920s, Frank Knight (1924) claimed that Frank Graham's use of a trade model with external increasing returns was inappropriate because no one had been able to cite a convincing example of an industry with external increasing returns and price-taking competition, an assertion that Graham was not able to rebut. Except for Marshall's suggestion that trade knowledge that cannot be kept secret is an important source of external effects in production (1890, Chapter XI, Book IV), no convincing example of a productive externality has been put forth. And as noted in Section 2.4, which follows, introducing knowledge explicitly into models of growth poses other problems, so even this route offers little hope of saving price-taking behavior. Questions about their empirical relevance notwithstanding, external increasing returns persisted as an important theoretical device in the static theory of international trade, and have recently reemerged in the theory of growth and in macroeconomic theory.

The other main approach to growth theory can be traced to Frank Knight's thesis advisor, Allyn Young, but its roots go back to Marshall and even Smith. Young (1928) articulated the view that introduction of new goods was the crucial driving force in economic growth and argued that the potential for new goods is necessary to understand Smith's emphasis on a role for the extent of the market. Larger markets permit more specialization, not so much in the sense that workers focus their time on a narrower set of tasks, but rather because larger markets support the provision of a larger set of specialized inputs in consumption and production. Like Marshall, Young called the beneficial effects arising from the introduction of a new good a positive external effect. Consequently, he tried to describe a model of growth driven by aggregate increasing returns that were external to individual firms.

From a modern point of view, the analogy with external effects is suggestive but ultimately misleading. It is true that the introduction of new goods and a role for the extent of the market seem to be fundamentally inconsistent with perfect competition, but the channel whereby an increase in the size of the market increases the utility of consumers and the production possibilities of firms is quite different from the channel emphasized in standard discussions of external effects in production or consumption. A natural way to conceive of the introduction of new goods is to suppose that there is some fixed cost associated with their introduction. Once the aggregate demand for the good is large enough, the stream of profit that can be extracted by a firm that introduces the good will be large enough to offset the initial fixed cost.

There is a sense in which this kind of process can lead to something that resembles an externality. Consider the case where the contemplated new good is an intermediate input in production, so its demand curve is simply a marginal productivity schedule. A firm that contemplated supplying the new good but that is incapable of price discrimination will value the new good in terms of the monopoly revenue that it can generate. The social value of the new good is this term plus the area under the derived demand curve. This divergence between the perceived private value of a new good and its social value is analogous to the divergence that would be present if there were productive externalities. The difference between this divergence and one introduced by a technological externality in production or consumption is that it arises because of the nature of pricing. It is a function of the market mechanism, not of physical quantities used in production or consumption, and it is precisely the nature of the market and the nature of equilibrium that must be the focus of attention, not the specification of preferences and the technology.

The tools for undertaking the analysis of this kind of market and equilibrium were introduced by another of Allyn Young's students, Edward Chamberlain (1933), and independently by Joan Robinson (1933). These tools have only begun to be used for aggregate analysis of issues in trade and growth. It is sometimes supposed that an ideological predisposition against government intervention explains the preference that economists demonstrate for models with perfect competition, but this does not explain why they should prefer models with externalities to ones with imperfect competition. A far more likely determinant of modeling strategy is technical difficulty. Perfect competition is the first-pass model for many questions simply because it is the easiest model to describe and understand. Allowing for external effects in the next pass removes the presumption in favor of optimality, but preserves price-taking behavior. The formal tools used in the analysis remain largely the same. Imperfect competition is naturally a last resort because it forces a more drastic change in the formal analysis of equilibrium and is associated with a much higher level of analytical difficulty than competition with external effects.

Until the specification of the additively separable functional form for preferences over many goods (Dixit and Stiglitz, 1977), an aggregate analysis of a model with monopolistic competition was completely infeasible. With the interpretation of this functional as a production functional depending on a large number of intermediate inputs instead of a preference functional (Ethier, 1982), a dynamic aggregate analysis of a model with imperfect competition comparable to the Solow–Swan analysis of the competitive model can now be undertaken.

After Young's article was published in 1928 (back to back with Frank Ramsey's famous paper on optimal savings, 1928), the depression of the 1930s focused attention on problems other than long-run growth. Monopolistic competition became embroiled in controversies concerning industrial organization, and its aggregate implications were not explored. In contrast, the general equilibrium analysis of competition progressed rapidly. Their qualms about exogenous technological change notwithstanding, economists adopted the neoclassical model with its assumption of perfect competition, and made no sustained attempt to put forth an alternative. Nicholas Kaldor and Joan Robinson waged a form of guerrilla warfare against the neoclassical model, and they invoked Young's name, among others, in support of their cause. But they offered no tractable alternative model.

In an attempt to capture some of the effects emphasized by Kaldor, Kenneth Arrow (1962b) described a growth model that allowed for external increasing returns in the Marshallian tradition. But neither this model nor its very clear elaboration by Eytan Sheshinski (1967) generated the prediction that higher savings rates would lead to higher growth rates, except perhaps in a borderline case. Nor did these models consider explicit research and development, patents, or inventive activity. The main prediction was that an exogenously higher rate of population growth led to a higher rate of growth of income per capita. Since accumulation, either in the form of physical capital or in the form of new ideas, was not a determinant of the growth rate in these models, they may not have offered a very attractive alternative to the neoclassical model for someone concerned with the role of endogenous accumulation in generating growth. Perhaps for this reason, the direction suggested by these models was not pursued by others.

Because the substantive implications of the model of exogenous technological change are so implausible, its unchallenged supremacy during the 1960s and 1970s can be rationalized only on methodological grounds. Its fundamental premise implies that private firms do not devote valuable resources to activities like research and development and that the rate of growth in an economy would be unchanged if patents and other forms of intellectual property rights were abolished. If we judge from the way the model was used, it seems clear that no one took these implications seriously. The exogeneity of technological change was apparently intended as a provisional assumption that would be relaxed as soon as theoretical developments permitted.

But even early on, it was evident that making technological change endogenous would force fundamental changes in the structure of the model. Kenneth Arrow (1962a), Karl Shell (1966, 1967, 1973), William Nordhaus (1969), Robert Wilson (1975), Richard Nelson and Sidney Winter (1982), and no doubt many others, pointed to the difficulty that competition poses for understanding activities like research and development. The basic point is that expenditures on these activities do not contribute to the marginal cost of producing the new goods that result. They are the fixed costs necessary to introduce a good. Once they have been incurred, they have nothing to do with manufacturing, which most plausibly takes place according to a constant returns to scale technology using conventional inputs like capital and labor. If the equilibrium price of a good must be equal to its marginal cost of production, then firms that spend resources on invention or research and development will not break even. They will have no way to recoup the initial expenditures. One of the advantages of the

Solow model is that it made this point so clearly. If output takes the form $Y=F(K,AL)$ or $Y=AF(K,L)$ for a production function F that is homogeneous of degree 1, then as noted in the beginning of this section, the total value of output is paid as compensation to labor and capital. Nothing is left to pay for increases in A.

Despite the apparent importance of corporate research and development and of private inventive activity, and despite the attention economists paid to them in microlevel analyses, few attempts were made to give these variables a realistic role in a model of growth, Karl Shell's 1973 paper being a notable exception that apparently received little attention. Economists seemed to accept the Solow–Swan attempt to defer consideration of the problem more and more as a final solution, and less and less as a provisional step in the analysis. Because a competitive equilibrium provides no way to compensate resources used in the activities that lead to improvements in the technology, all such resources are assumed not to get compensation. Technology is simply assumed to grow nonetheless.

2 Recent models

When external increasing returns were reintroduced into growth models in the early 1980s, attention focused first on how to sustain growth without introducing exogenous technological change. Subsequent work has broadened the horizon to include questions about international comparisons of growth, the spatial location of economic activity, and a more fundamental discussion of ideas and knowledge as economic goods.

To organize the discussion of the recent models, it is useful to describe several different reasons that have been suggested for why a model of growth must allow for some departure from the usual convexity assumptions (convexity in the sense of sets, not of functions). Four main questions can be identified:

1. Do fixed factors of production drive growth rates to zero in a model with a convex technology?
2. Can a convex technology explain the time trend in observed growth rates?
3. Is a convex technology consistent with the patterns of international trade, factor movements, and growth rates?
4. Can research and development and patents be incorporated in a convex model?

These questions, together with models designed to address them, are discussed in the next four sections.

2.1 *Fixed factors*

My interest in growth began with my Ph.D. thesis (Romer, 1983), results from which were published in 1986. I asserted that the answer to each of the first three questions listed above was negative: (1) A convex model cannot generate growth if there are fixed factors of production. (2) A convex model cannot explain the time trend of growth rates. (3) A convex model cannot explain international differences in levels and rates of growth of income.

The logic behind the first of these three assertions is simple, and is correct as far as it goes, but it requires two important qualifications noted in what follows. Suppose that growth is determined by an accumulation equation of the form

$$\dot{K} = F(K, X) - C, \tag{1}$$

where K denotes a factor like capital that can be accumulated on a per-capita basis, C denotes aggregate consumption, and X represents a factor like land or labor that is assumed to be in fixed supply per capita. The maximum feasible path for K as a function of time is given as the solution to

$$\dot{K}_{max}(t) = F(K_{max}(t), X). \tag{2}$$

Suppose that F is concave, hence, that it can be no more than homogeneous of degree 1. Then dividing by $K_{max}(t)$ gives

$$\frac{\dot{K}_{max}}{K_{max}} \leq F\left(1, \frac{X}{K_{max}}\right). \tag{3}$$

Suppose further that the fixed factor X is "essential" in the sense that $F(K, X) = 0$ if $X = 0$. Then as K_{max} goes to infinity, X/K_{max} goes to zero, which implies that $\dot{K}_{max}/K_{max}$ must also go to zero. From this observation, it follows that any feasible monotonic path for K (and, hence, also for output) will have a growth rate that asymptotically approaches 0.

Consideration of feasibility alone suggests that constant exponential growth is not possible in a convex model that has an essential fixed factor in the accumulation equation. Adding the possibility that savings rates may decrease with reductions in the rate of return will only reinforce the arguments for slowing growth. These are the kinds of arguments that concerned the classical economists and led to the focus on the steady state.

To address this concern, my model allowed for the possibility that the aggregate production function for an economy as a whole, $F(K, X)$, could exhibit nondiminishing marginal productivity of K; for example, it could take the form $K^{\alpha}X^{\beta}$, where $\alpha \geq 1$. It follows that F cannot be concave. The variable K was assumed to represent a composite of physical capital and knowledge, and the knowledge component was assumed to generate external effects or spillovers. Thus, the model relied on Marshallian external increasing returns to preserve price taking. For a small firm using inputs k and x when the aggregate stock of knowledge and capital is K, output could take the form

$$y = K^{\varphi}k^{\nu}x^{\beta}, \quad \text{where } \nu+\beta \leq 1, \quad \text{but } \varphi+\nu=\alpha \geq 1. \tag{4}$$

(Section 2.4 returns to the important questions that are swept under the rug here by tying knowledge to capital and failing to give it a separate existence.)

The next, and very influential, contribution to the recent work on growth was a paper by Robert Lucas (1988, a version of which circulated in 1985). Lucas's model introduced increasing returns and external effects for reasons associated with the third question, the one concerned with international comparisons. (These issues are treated in Section 2.3, which follows.) It did not rely on increasing returns to generate persistent growth, a point that was most fully developed by Sergio Rebelo (1988). Lucas's paper built on a framework introduced by Hirofumi Uzawa (1965), and, as Rebelo showed, a convex version of this model is perfectly capable of generating constant exponential growth even in the presence of essential fixed factors of production. All that is needed is that there be one technology for accumulating a capital good that does not depend on any fixed factors.

Suppose, for example, that net output $Y = G(K, H_1, T)$ is a function of capital K, the portion H_1 of total human capital that is devoted to the production of final output, and land T, which is a fixed factor of production. Suppose that capital is produced from foregone consumption,

$$\dot{K} = Y - C = G(K, H_1, T) - C. \tag{5}$$

Suppose that total human capital H grows in proportion to the fraction of human capital that is devoted to education:

$$\dot{H} = \mu(H - H_1). \tag{6}$$

What is crucial here is that although the equation for $\dot{K}$ has a fixed factor in it, the equation for $\dot{H}$ does not. If a constant fraction of human capital $(H-H_1)/H$ is devoted to education, H can grow at a constant exponential rate. If, for example, G takes the log-linear form $G(K, H_1, T) = K^{\alpha}H_1^{1-\alpha-\beta}T^{\beta}$, and H grows at the rate g, output can grow at the rate $(1-\alpha-\beta)g$ even if no capital accumulation takes place. In fact, capital can grow at the same exponential rate as output, which implies that growth in output can take place forever at the rate $[(1-\alpha-\beta)/(1-\alpha)]g$. Thus, the argument outlined before, suggesting that essential fixed factors in a convex production technology must cause growth to come to a halt, must be qualified. This is true only if the fixed factors are present in all of the fundamental accumulation equations for the economy.

A further point was emphasized by Lawrence Jones and Rodolfo Manuelli (1990). They note that fixed factors can arise even in the fundamental accumulation sector for an economy as long as these factors are not essential. For example, suppose that the function $F(K,X)$ used in equations (1) to (3) takes the constant elasticity of substitution form

$$F(K,X)=[\alpha K^{\rho}+(1-\alpha)X^{\rho}]^{1/\rho}. \tag{7}$$

If the substitution parameter ρ lies in the range $(0,1]$ so K and X are good substitutes, then neither K nor X is essential for production. Asymptotically, as K goes to ∞ for fixed X, F approaches a function that is linear in K, and constant exponential growth is feasible. It is true, as the classical authors suggested, that an increase in the ratio of K to X is associated with a fall in the marginal product of K. But a monotonically falling marginal product does not imply that the marginal product converges to 0. The marginal product goes to 0 only in the case where the fixed factor is essential.

The claim that a convex model will not generate persistent growth is true only if one believes that there is an essential fixed factor in all of the accumulation equations in the model. A convex aggregate technology is consistent with the assertions (a) that constant exponential growth is feasible, and (b) that a fixed factor of production like land is present, provided that the fixed factor is not essential or does not enter into one of the fundamental accumulation equations of the model.

Economists were aware of this kind of result during the 1950s and 1960s. Part of the reason that exogenous technological change was adopted instead of a model based on equation (7) is that the shares of capital and labor in total income change slowly over time. Moreover, to the extent that a trend could be observed, the share of capital was falling. This observation rules out the simple interpretation that K in equation (7) represents physical capital, for this functional form implies that a growing share of total income is paid to capital. The one result that has been clear ever since is that a convex model based on physical capital accumulation alone does not fit the facts. As Jones and Manuelli suggest, for an explanation based on an equation like (7) to fit, the variable K must be interpreted to stand for an aggregate of both physical capital and human capital, with X representing something like unskilled physical labor. In this case, the measured share of capital in total income does correspond to the share of the variable K in the model. It is possible that the income

Table 1.[a]

Leading country	Time period	Average annual labor productivity growth rate (%)
Netherlands	1700–85	−0.07
United Kingdom	1785–1820	0.5
United Kingdom	1820–90	1.4
United States	1890–1970	2.3

[a] Data are taken from Maddison, 1982. For each time period, the country cited is the world leader in the level of output per man-hour.

share of human capital plus physical capital has indeed been increasing over time.

As a logical matter, the possibility that the marginal product of capital is bounded away from zero suggests a way to preserve models of growth based on a convex technology and perfect competition. (It still leaves empirical difficulties such as explaining the presence of a growth accounting residual.) Nonconvexities are not logically essential for explaining persistent growth, but the formulation based on human capital accumulation contains the seeds of another idea that is ultimately hostile to convexity and perfect competition. It relies on a notion of human capital that can grow without bound when measured on a per-capita basis. As such, it differs in a crucial way from the usual notion of human capital as measured by labor economists in years of schooling or experience in the labor force. This new kind of human capital can be passed down from one individual to the next, or from one generation to the next. The possibility of transmission suggests that human capital defined in this way must contain something like scientific ideas, or the stock of knowledge, or the level of the technology, that has an existence outside of any individual. As Arrow, Shell, Nordhaus, Wilson, and others have pointed out, and as Section 2.4 argues once again, the presence of this type of good poses a serious problem for convexity and competition.

2.2 *Time trends in growth rates*

One piece of evidence that distinguishes between convex models like those proposed by Rebelo (1990) and Jones and Manuelli (1990) and models with some form of increasing marginal productivity as in my 1986 paper is the fact that, viewed over a long horizon, growth rates have been increasing. Table 1 reproduces a table from my paper on long-run trends. It reports productivity growth rates estimated by Angus Maddison (1982) for the country that is estimated to have the highest level of productivity in each of four different epochs.

A simple calculation shows why earlier growth rates must have been smaller than the recent values. The productivity growth rate of 2.3% per year reported for the United States in the most recent period implies that output per hour worked doubles every 30 years. If we use the cross-sectional estimates of income per capita prepared by Robert Summers and Alan Heston (1988), a rough guess of a borderline subsistence level is something like 1/20 or 1/30 of current GDP per capita in the United States. In 1890, output per hour worked stood at something like 1/10 its current value. Because hours worked per capita fell over the last century, the level of income per capita in the United States or the UK was slightly higher, roughly 1/8 its current value. Starting from this value for per-capita income, it is possible to project backward a productivity growth rate of 2.3% per year and infer the level of per-capita income in earlier eras. By going back in time from 1890, this calculation would imply that income in even the most advanced countries was at or below the borderline of subsistence only 200 years ago. If hours worked stayed at the high levels observed at the end of the nineteenth century, output per capita in 1830 would have been 1/32 of its current value. Even if one makes the implausible allowance that hours worked per capita were four times higher in earlier eras than they were in 1890, one buys only an additional 60 years of survival back into the eighteenth century.

A labor productivity growth rate of 2.3% per year has not been sustained in the United States in the years since 1970, but even higher productivity growth rates have been observed in countries in Western Europe and in Japan, countries that may soon overtake the United States in productivity. Thus, from the point of view of the world as a whole, there is not yet good reason to be convinced that growth is finally slowing down.

Convex models like those of Rebelo and of Jones and Manuelli predict that rates of return to the basic input that is accumulated are nonincreasing as accumulation takes place. In the kind of model considered by Rebelo, where there are no fixed factors in the essential accumulation sector, rates of return are constant. In the model of Jones and Manuelli, with inessential fixed factors, rates of return fall. If accumulation responds positively to rates of return, these models cannot by themselves explain the time trend of growth rates.

Models with some underlying form of increasing returns suggest the possibility that rates of return could be increasing as accumulation takes place. My paper (Romer, 1986) shows how this can lead to rates of growth that increase over time in one particular example. A simpler and more appealing example is given by Danyang Xie (in press). More generally, such models can generate the possibility that appreciable growth does not start until some minimal level of output and stocks of productive factors has been achieved.

If all of the explanatory power is forced onto the technology, this kind of evidence weighs in favor of departures from the standard convexity assumptions. An alternative view, however, would be to place some of the weight on institutional factors that are taken as exogenously given. Legal and social institutions conducive to the accumulation of private property have evolved dramatically over the course of recorded history. Improvements in these institutions would lead to increased accumulation even if raw rates of return were constant or falling over time.

Changes in institutions, therefore, can solve the problem of explaining the time trend in growth rates, but they do so by exchanging exogenous technological change for exogenous institutional change. Making institutional change exogenous allows economists to conduct a provisional analysis that focuses on issues they understand relatively well and sets aside ones they do not; but, ultimately, one would like to be able to explain the evolution of institutions as well. It seems quite plausible that increasing rates of return and increasing opportunities for private investment and accumulation caused the evolution of institutions that supported these activities. After all, it is not true that early economies were incapable of accumulating large amounts of physical capital. What is striking about investments like those in pyramids, raised field systems, cathedrals, and possibly even flood control and irrigation systems is both the size of the social investment involved and the relatively low rate of return it generated. If large unexploited investment opportunities were present in early times, it is hard to understand why they were not pursued.

Even if one agrees in principle with an ambitious program for explaining institutional change and understanding growth in a broad historical context, the concerns raised here may seem far removed from the issues encountered by someone who looks at postwar time series in developed economies or who worries about current policy issues. For this reason, it is unlikely that long-run trends will be decisive in the debate over the theoretical foundations of growth theory. If these trends were the only basis of support for models that depart from the usual convexity assumptions, it seems likely that those convexity assumptions would continue to be maintained in most aggregative models.

2.3 *International evidence*

The last two sections argue, first, that persistent growth may make perfect competition seem less attractive as the equilibrium concept for modeling growth, but it does not rule it out on purely logical grounds; and, second, that the long-run evidence on trends in growth rates presents more of a challenge, but is unlikely to be a decisive factor in the choice of models. International data on levels of income, growth rates, and factor movements and the problems they pose for convex models are likely to be much more influential in shaping the approach that aggregate models adopt. There is, of course, a separate and older line of attack on perfect competition as the foundation of static trade theory generated by the perception that convex technologies combined with differences in factor endowments are not sufficient to explain the patterns of trade that are observed (see, for example, Helpman and Krugman, 1985). The discussion here will focus on only the issues most closely related to growth.

The difficulty presented by the neoclassical model of growth in a world where nations have different levels of income is that it seems to imply persistent unexploited profit opportunities. If the exogenous technology is treated as something that is freely available to all firms in a particular economy, then it would seem natural to assume that it is available to all firms in the world as well, leaving only differences in the capital labor ratio to explain differences in income. But the required differences in the capital labor ratio are so large that the implied differences in the marginal productivity of capital are impossibly large. Since the share of capital in total income is judged to be on the order of 0.33, the many countries identified by Summers and Heston that have income per capita that is 1/10 that in the United States would have to have a capital labor ratio that is smaller by a factor of 10^3. The marginal product of capital would have to be larger by a factor of 10^2. Productivity differentials of this size are very hard to reconcile with the observed patterns of investment and rates of return.

As a result, most applications of the neoclassical model to a cross section of countries allow the level as well as the rate of growth of the technology to differ across countries. This explains the cross-country variation by making it a premise of the theory, ruling out any opportunity for the theory to comment on the sources of the cross-country variation. It also seems to leave intact large profit opportunities. If the technology is 10 times more advanced in one country than another, there should be large returns to anyone who can cause the advanced technology to be used in the less-advanced country. If technology has the kind of public good character attributed to it in the neoclassical model, it should not be hard to put it to use somewhere else in the world.

Both my paper (Romer, 1986) and Lucas's (1988) use increasing returns to overturn the usual presumption in favor of convergence and profit opportunities implicit in a convex model. My paper uses the framework outlined in previous equation (4). If total output in country i takes the form $F(K_i, X_i) = K_i^{\alpha} X_i^{\beta}$ with $\alpha \geq 1$, then the marginal product of additional investment will be highest, not lowest, in the country that is most advanced. By using the specification in equation (4), this will be true of both private and social returns. Even if the spillover benefits of the knowledge implicit in K are assumed to extend to foreign countries, the most advanced country will still have the highest marginal productivity as long as the external effects are stronger in the home country than in the foreign country. With this kind of specification, it is no surprise that accumulation can be larger in the more advanced country and that resources could even flow from the less-developed country to the advanced country (a result that is shown explicitly for an example).

The difficulty with this analysis is that it ties knowledge and capital too tightly together. Lucas (1988) sharpens the analysis by effectively splitting the aggregate variable K into two parts. (His paper actually contains two models. The discussion here pertains to the first of them.) One part, call it P, corresponds to physical capital and has no external effects associated with it. (This is not Lucas's notation.) The other, H, represents human capital. As in the model described before, Lucas's model assumes that output increases more than proportionally with increases in P and H taken together. It also invokes the notion of external effects that are local in extent to decentralize this technology in a price-taking equilibrium. Thus, output for a firm depends on its own stock of human capital, h, and an economywide value H. If P and H moved together in lockstep, the model would be mathematically very similar to my model. The key differences are that the two factors P and H can be varied separately and that of the two, only P is internationally mobile. This assumption about factor mobility implies that rates of return on physical capital will be equated across countries, but returns to human capital need not be.

Suppose that output as a function of P and H can be written as

$$Y = P^{\eta} H^{\theta} h^{\delta}, \quad \text{with } \eta + \delta = 1,\ 0 < \theta.$$

The sum $\eta + \theta + \delta > 1$ is analogous to the exponent α in the argument in Section 2.1; it is the exponent that describes the behavior of the marginal productivity of human and physical capital when it expands along a ray in P–H space. If one of two countries had more of both P and H but these countries had identical ratios of P to H, the fact that this exponent is greater than 1 implies that the marginal product of both P and H will be higher in the more-developed country than in the less-developed country. For H, this statement is true of both the social and private marginal products. If P is free to move between countries, the ratio of P to H must increase in the developed country and decrease in the less-developed country for the private marginal product of P in the two countries to be brought into equality. This increase in the ratio of P to H reduces the differential in the marginal productivity of physical capital, but raises the differential in the marginal products of human capital H that is assumed not to be mobile. Thus, increasing returns can explain why capital mobility is not sufficient to remove pressures for migration. A person living in a less-developed country could earn more by moving to the more-developed one.

If both physical capital and human capital were mobile in this model, they could both migrate to the developed country as they do in the example discussed in my paper. If, as in that example, there are other factors of production like land that are not mobile, these resources need not shift to the new location all at once, and some positive amount will always stay behind. If we relabel the developed region a city and the less-developed region the countryside, this description seems to account fairly well for the process of urbanization that is observed within nations, where both P and H are, in fact, mobile. Thus, the international evidence on potential migration flows and wage differences and the national evidence on urbanization are strongly suggestive of increasing returns of some kind. (For a discussion of urbanization and increasing returns, see Abdel-Raman and Fujita, 1990.)

The kind of model considered by Rebelo or Jones and Manuelli, which relies on constant returns to scale in production, can explain international differences in the level of income. If the increasing returns are dropped from Lucas's model, so that the exponents η, θ, and δ sum to 1, free mobility of capital will equalize the ratio of physical capital to human capital in each country. Whether or not there are external effects (i.e., whether or not δ is equal to 0), large differences in income per capita could result from large differences in endowments of both physical capital and human capital. A country with income per capita equal to 1/10 that in the United States could have stocks of P and H per capita that are 1/10 as large as the comparable values in the United States. Thus, a typical worker transported from the less-developed country would still be 10 times less productive than the average worker in the advanced country and would still earn 10 times less even after moving.

This kind of model cannot explain the apparently large pressures for migration flows for people of all skill levels from less-developed countries to developed countries. Moreover, it offers no explanation for the extreme concentration of resources in specific geographical locations. It does, however, have the advantage that it avoids the necessity of invoking the ephemeral externalities that the models with increasing returns rely on so heavily.

I think that this criticism, essentially the same as Knight's criticism of Graham, represents a serious challenge for both the model from my thesis and Lucas's (1988) model. Spillovers seem to be inherently tied to forms of knowledge that can exist outside of any person, the same kinds of knowledge that seem to be crucial to the notion that human capital can be passed down from one generation to the next and can, therefore, grow without bound. One way to think of both my model and Lucas's model is that they allow for this special kind of knowledge but assume that it is produced only as a side effect of other activities, investment in physical capital or investment in schooling, respectively. The next section considers the possibility that knowledge is produced intentionally, not as a side effect.

2.4 *Abstract knowledge*

The modern definition of a public good identifies two distinct attributes of a good: rivalry and excludability (Cornes and Sandler, 1986; Starrett, 1988). These attributes are usually applied to consumption goods, but they are equally relevant for inputs in production, especially for an input like knowledge. A good is rivalrous if its use by one person or firm precludes its use by another. Rivalry is a feature of the physical properties of the good and the technology for using it. A good is excludable if the producer of the good can keep others from being able to take advantage of it without consent. Excludability depends on both the technology and the legal system. The notion of a purely excludable or nonexcludable good, or of a purely rival or nonrival good, is an idealization. Most goods fall in between the extremes, but usually close enough to one extreme or the other that the terms can be used without qualification.

Conventional economic goods are said to be both rivalrous and excludable. Public goods are both nonrivalrous and nonexcludable. For growth theory, the interesting intermediate case is a good that is nonrivalrous but at least partially excludable. For example, the music contained on a record album is a nonrivalrous input in the production of entertainment services; it can be copied and used as many times as desired. Under the legal system prevailing in the United States, it is also at least partially excludable; it is illegal to copy the music and resell it.

The feature of abstract knowledge that has attracted the most attention is that it is not excludable, or is at best partially excludable. There are many well-known examples of discoveries that seem to have generated large spillover effects, that is, large benefits for people who did not have to pay for them. When researchers at IBM developed the technology for magnetic disk drives, or when biologists at Genentech developed the recombinant

DNA techniques needed to create bacteria that could produce human insulin, hundreds of other firms learned valuable information that they could exploit.

It is clear that private markets cannot provide goods that are completely nonexcludable. The natural solution to nonexcludability is to use the legal system to strengthen property rights. For example, in fisheries, the government can allocate rights to catch a fixed number of fish. If this number is set correctly, no other intervention is called for. Competitive markets can be relied on to do the rest. By analogy, one might hope (incorrectly) that an extensive patent system that removed problems of excludability would let ideas trade in competitive markets just like other goods. Patents can support private markets for ideas, but they cannot support competitive markets. They do not change the fact that ideas are nonrival. By its very definition, a nonrival input is one that has no opportunity cost. When a firm uses a mechanical drawing for a disk drive or a list of instructions for manipulating DNA, it does not inhibit any other firm from using them at the same time. For the cost of a photocopy, it is technologically feasible for anyone else to use them as well.

A replication argument immediately indicates the problem this poses for competitive equilibrium theory. Let Z be a nonrival input in production, say, a mechanical drawing for a disk drive, and let X be a comprehensive list of all the rival inputs (machines, structures, trained production workers, supervisors, managers, etc.) used in producing the physical units of the drive. Let $G(Z, X)$ denote the services, measured in megabytes of storage, that are produced each year from inputs X using design Z. The input Z could be measured as the cost of producing the particular design. By neglecting integer constraints, replication implies that G must be at least homogeneous of degree 1 in the rival inputs X alone. Output could be doubled merely by doubling all of them and replicating all productive activities. If Z has productive value as well (that is, if devoting additional resources to the design effort could have yielded more megabytes of storage from the same inputs X), then $G(\cdot,\cdot)$ cannot be concave. For integer values of λ greater than 1,

$$G(\lambda Z, \lambda X) > G(Z, \lambda X) = \lambda G(Z, X).$$

Because of this nonconvexity, competitive prices are not feasible. If all of the components of X were paid their marginal value product, then by Euler's Theorem, payments to them would exhaust the value of output. There is nothing left to pay for the cost of producing the design. From the point of view of marginal cost pricing, if output is homogeneous of degree 1 in rival inputs, then marginal cost is simply the constant unit cost. If firms charge a price equal to marginal cost, they would not recover the initial expenditure on the nonrival design input.

A common response to this observation is to assume that $G(Z, X)$ is not homogeneous of degree 1 in the rivalrous inputs X. Then Z can be compensated out of the quasirents. Although the formal properties of my 1986 model strongly resembled those of the learning-by-doing model described by Arrow (1962b), I tried to use this kind of formulation to avoid the implication that all knowledge was discovered by accident. This now seems to me to be no more than a finesse of the basic issue here. As appealing as the assumption is at a technical level, it flies in the face of everything we know about the physical world. It has to be true that it is possible to double output by doubling all of the rivalrous inputs used in production. Arguments that try to deny this ultimately fall back to the position that it is not possible to double some of the rivalrous inputs (e.g., the special managerial skill of an owner or supervisor), or that it takes time or is costly to double all of these inputs. These observations have no logical bearing on the thought experiment that asks what would happen to total output if one could double the rival inputs. This thought experiment reveals the presence of an underlying nonconvexity, and this poses an unavoidable threat to price-taking competition.

(There is a technical issue here. It is sometimes suggested that adding costs of adjustment can convexify a model that is not convex. In fact, doing so does not remove the nonconvexity, but to make the point rigorously forces one to put the analysis in terms of sets of dynamic paths in a function space. Suppose that $F(X)$ is a function that has a portion that is not concave, and suppose the theorist adds a cost-of-adjustment term that depends on $\dot{X}$, the rate of change of X. To check for convexity of the technology, one must consider the set of feasible paths for inputs $X(t)$ and outputs $Y(t)$, and verify whether this is a convex set in a function space. No matter how convex a cost function like $H(\dot{X})$ is, if $F(X)$ has a portion that is not concave, then the set of paths

$$\{Y, X: Y(t) \leq F(X(t)) - H(\dot{X}(t))\}$$

will not be a convex set.)

What partial equilibrium theory identifies as quasirents arising from upward-sloping marginal-cost curves are really forms of compensation for rival inputs that have not been explicitly specified and are held fixed. By the underlying replication argument, the true cost function in terms of all rival inputs must exhibit constant cost. McKenzie (1959) is particularly clear about this, and refers to the input that is typically left out as the "entrepreneurial factor." If there are nonrival inputs as well, then there must be a departure from homogeneity of degree 1. As a result, it is not possible to pay each input a return equal to its marginal productivity. If Marshallian quasirents are used to compensate research and development, then some other rival factor of production is being undercompensated. One of the decisive advantages of the kind of general equilibrium formulation used in growth theory is that it forces one to take account of this kind of overall adding-up restriction.

The problem, then, is how to compensate for the production of ideas in a general equilibrium model. The neoclassical model assumes that they are not compensated at all. Formally, my 1986 model assumes that they are compensated out of quasirents. An alternative interpretation of this model, one that removes the reliance on quasirents, is that ideas are not compensated, but arise as a side effect of the production of capital as described by Arrow (1962b). Lucas (1988) also relies on ideas as the nonrival good that is capable of generating the spillovers he identifies and that cause a nonconvexity. In effect, his model assumes that these ideas are produced as a side effect of schooling.

None of these models gives a very satisfactory description of private-sector research and development or any indication of how changes in patent protection might affect the aggregate rate of growth. In subsequent work (Romer, 1987a, 1987b, 1990), I abandoned price taking to be able to address these issues. Specifically, firms are assumed to produce knowledge that is used in the production of a new good. The operative analogy is that knowledge is like a design. Each firm is assumed to have a patent on the design that lasts forever, so no other firm can produce the good. As in the models of Avinash Dixit and Joseph Stiglitz (1977) or Ken Judd (1985), it is assumed that there is a large number of firms, each of which produces a distinct good. The equilibrium is one of monopolistic competition with zero profit. My models (Romer, 1987a, 1987b, 1990) follow the static model in Ethier (1982) and assume that the many different goods are producer inputs. In this setting, growth takes place because of the continual introduction of new goods, as Allyn Young suggested.

The idea that market power is essential to innovation should not be controversial. The widely acknowledged purpose of a patent or copyright is precisely to provide a monopoly on the use of a nonrival input for some period of time. The monopoly rents compensate for the cost of generating the input. These models of growth assume that the creation of new nonrival inputs lies at the heart of growth, and that the problem of compensating these kinds of inputs is pervasive. Suggestions of this kind can be found in the later writings of Joseph Schumpeter (1942).

Models where new ideas are associated with the design of new goods have the theoretical side effect of suggesting why international trade might be important in fostering growth. The basic intuition is that with trade, it is no longer necessary for each country to reinvent the wheel. Two units of research effort can be used to produce two designs for the wheel in two closed economies, or they can be used to design the wheel in one country and to design a harness in the other. Harnesses can then be traded for wheels. This kind of specialization results in a kind of trade that looks superficially like trade based on comparative advantage; countries that are good at producing wheels export them and countries that are good at producing harnesses export them. It is, however, a form of endogenously acquired comparative advantage, not one that is the result of differences in resource endowments.

The key result from my 1990 model is not only that trade avoids redundancy in research effort, but also that total worldwide research effort will increase when two closed economies open for trade, and growth will speed up. This dynamic effect is special to the growth model, and it would not have been predicted by a simple static trade model. Qualifications to this result have been suggested by Grossman and Helpman (1989a). If consumption goods are country-specific and one country is assumed to be better at research than the other, then it is possible that free trade tends to cause too much research to be done in the less-capable country. Trade restrictions that reallocate research effort from the country that is less capable of doing research to the country that is better at it could actually lead to faster growth.

Nevertheless, the general conclusion that emerges from this kind of analysis is that if nonrival goods can be used over and over again and the introduction of new nonrival goods is central to growth, then more open trade can have a pure scale effect that lets the fruits of research be exploited more broadly and speeds up growth. When increased trade is considered between two symmetric countries, only the scale effect operates, and the presumption is that the growth effect will be present. Increases in the extent of trade between countries that differ in factor endowments or the available technology will have other effects on the incentive to do research, the kinds of effects that arise in any multisector model. In some cases, these effects can overwhelm the growth-enhancing scale effects.

There are many open questions about the details of models like this. My models (Romer, 1987a, 1987b, 1990) and one of the models used by Grossman and Helpman (1990) assume that new ideas are always associated with new goods. More recent models by Aghion and Howitt (1990) and Grossman and Helpman (1989b) assume instead that new ideas can pertain to production techniques or quality attributes of existing goods. All of these models assume that there is a continuum of firms, each of which has some amount of market power because they sell distinct goods. This assumption avoids the many ambiguities introduced when there is strategic behavior among a small group of firms. At some point, this assumption, itself made purely for technical reasons, will have to be weakened. (Future economists may well ask why it was that economists of the 1980s and 1990s studied models of growth in which there was no strategic behavior, much as this paper starts by asking why it was the economists studied models of growth with exogenous technological change.) For now, it seems that there is much to be learned from growth models that do not emphasize strategic behavior. We are only beginning to understand general equilibrium dynamic models with monopolistic competition and are far from a consensus about how to go about studying comparable models with small numbers of agents and complicated forms of strategic behavior.

In any generalization, the basic elements identified so far should persist. If ideas are recognized as nonrival inputs, then firms must recover research-and-development expenses by charging a price for new goods that is higher than the marginal cost of production, and there will exist a form of increasing returns at the level of the economy as a whole.

3 Conclusion

Classified on methodological grounds, there are now four main types of models of growth:

1. Models that have no technological change and no increasing returns, and that support growth through accumulation of human capital.
2. Models that allow for technological change but make it exogenous.
3. Models that treat ideas as nonrival inputs and recognize the resulting nonconvexity but that use Marshallian external increasing returns to support an equilibrium with price taking for rival inputs.
4. Models with ideas that go one step further, departing from price-taking behavior and assuming instead some form of monopolistic competition.

These models differ in how they handle ideas. The first type of model treats an idea as a good that is intangible but otherwise conventional. Ideas are assumed to be both rivalrous and excludable. The operative analogy is that they are like an education for an individual.

The second, third, and fourth models treat ideas as nonrival inputs in production. All three, therefore, imply some form of increasing returns when ideas are included in the set of inputs. The neoclassical model (number 2) and the spillover models (3) both assume that ideas are purely nonexcludable, and hence earn no compensation. In the neoclassical model, ideas continue to arrive for reasons that are outside of the model. In the spillover models, ideas arise as side effects of other activities, in one case, from physical capital investment, in another, from acquiring education. These models of side effects or learning by doing rely critically on the assumption that ideas are completely nonexcludable, for, as Partha Dasgupta and Joseph Stiglitz (1988) have emphasized, even partial excludability will lead to a failure of price-taking competition in a setting with increasing returns to scale. Because of this complete non-excludability, these models cannot capture the intentional production of ideas.

Only the fourth model, which drops the assumption of price taking, can allow for the possibility that ideas are partially or completely excludable. As a result, only this class of models can accommodate patents and intentional research and development.

As noted earlier, there is some empirical evidence that is supportive of the presence of increasing returns. Trends in growth rates, as well as patterns of spatial location of economic activity and of international trade and factor movements, are easier to understand in a model that is not convex than in one that is. Ultimately, however, the factor that is most likely to move the profession toward acceptance of models with increasing returns and even departures from price taking is the incongruity between what economists actually believe and what their models of growth predict. A very large majority of economists believe that private-sector research-and-development expenditure is an important determinant of long-run potential for growth and that the presence or absence of intellectual property rights is important as well. Discussions of the economics of the firm or the industry typically reflect this belief. It is only in formal models of growth for the economy as a whole that these effects have been absent.

The central thesis of this chapter is that this incongruity reflects the technical constraints economists faced when they first tried to formulate dynamic equilibrium models, and that theory has advanced to the point that these constraints can now be relaxed. In particular, we now have tractable methods for studying dynamic equilibrium models with price taking and spillovers, and more important, we are beginning to develop experience with a range of tractable dynamic models of monopolistic competition.

This is not to say that the insight gained from the other types of models is irrelevant. On the contrary, all of the effects identified in each of the other models should be present in a more complicated model with imperfect competition. Human capital as acquired in school is of enormous importance for growth, especially if it is a complement to the production and use of new ideas. The neoclassical model made the fundamental contribution of showing that a nonrival good – knowledge or technology – has to be taken seriously within models of growth. Models with spillovers that focus on the effects of increasing returns at the level of society as a whole demonstrate effects that will still be present if the equilibrium is one with monopolistic competition instead of price taking with spillovers.

Nor does the development of a richer class of models imply that all models of growth need to try to address all possible issues at once. For explaining cross-country variation in income and growth rates, it may be sufficient to ignore the mechanisms that generate new ideas in the few developed countries and to concentrate instead on variables like schooling and human-capital formulation that seem most important for the use of these ideas in less developed countries. (See, for example, King and Rebelo, 1990.) Or to study the interaction between the rate of growth of income and individual fertility decisions, it may be sufficient to use a very simple model of the technology, for example, one in which output is linear in the stock of human capital. (See Becker, Murphy, and Tamura, 1990.) Similarly, many of the dynamic effects identified in models of increasing returns with spillovers are harder to derive in models with monopolistic competition, but the qualitative results in the two types of models are very much the same. In many cases, it will still be appropriate to use models that use external effects to preserve price-taking behavior for purely technical reasons. The difference now is that this should be recognized as a shortcut. Theorists must at least consider the robustness of any conclusions reached to extensions that allow for departures from price taking.

The net effect for growth theory is that there is a whole range of new questions that has only just begun to be explored, and an associated set of new modeling techniques. Compared to the neoclassical model, the analysis in these extended frameworks will be somewhat harder and the conclusions somewhat less clear-cut, but these drawbacks should be more than offset by the richness of the issues that can be addressed in the theory of aggregate growth.

REFERENCES

Abdel-Raman, H., and M. Fujita. 1990. "Product Variety, Marshallian Externalities, and City Size." *Journal of Regional Science* 30: 165–83.

Aghion, P., and P. Howitt. 1990. "A Model of Growth Through Creative Destruction." NBER working paper No. 3223, Cambridge, MA.

Arrow, K. G. 1962a. "Economic Welfare and the Allocation of Resources For Invention." In *The Rate and Direction of Inventive Activity.* Princeton: NBER and Princeton University Press, pp. 609–25.

1962b. "The Economic Implications of Learning by Doing." *Review of Economic Studies* 29: 155–73.

Becker, G., K. Murphy, and R. Tamura. 1990. "Economic Growth, Human Capital, and Population Growth." *Journal of Political Economy* 98: S12–137.

Chamberlain, E. 1933. *The Theory of Monopolistic Competition.* Cambridge, MA: Harvard University Press.

Cornes, R., and T. Sandler. 1986. *The Theory of Externalities, Public Goods, and Club Goods.* Cambridge: Cambridge University Press.
Dasgupta, P., and J. Stiglitz. 1988. "Learning-By-Doing, Market Structure and Industrial and Trade Policies." *Oxford Economic Papers* 40: 246–68.
Dixit, A., and J. Stiglitz. 1977. "Monopolistic Competition and Optimum Product Diversity." *American Economic Review* 76: 297–308.
Ethier, W. J. 1982. "National and International Returns to Scale in the Modern Theory of International Trade." *American Economic Review* 72: 389–405.
Grossman, G., and E. Helpman. 1989. "Quality Ladders in the Theory of Growth." NBER working paper No. 3099, Cambridge, MA.
1990. "Comparative Advantage and Long-Run Growth. *American Economic Review* 80: 796–815.
Helpman, E., and P. Krugman. 1985. *Market Structure and Foreign Trade.* Cambridge, MA: The MIT Press.
Jones, L., and R. Manuelli. 1990. "A Convex Model of Equilibrium Growth." NBER working paper No. 3241, Cambridge, MA.
Judd, K. L. 1985. "On the Performance of Patents." *Econometrica* 53: 567–85.
King, R., and S. Rebelo. 1990. "Public Policy and Economic Growth." *Journal of Political Economy* 98: S126–50.
Knight, F. 1924. "Some Fallacies in the Interpretation of Social Cost." *Quarterly Journal of Economics* 30: 582–606.
Lucas, R. E., Jr. 1988. "On the Mechanics of Economic Development." *Journal of Monetary Economics* 22: 3–42.
Maddison, A. 1982. *Phases of Capitalist Development.* Oxford: Oxford University Press.
Marshall, A. 1890. *Principles of Economics.* London: Macmillan.
McKenzie, L. 1959. "On the Existence of General Equilibrium for a Competitive Market." *Econometrica* 27: 54–71.
Nelson, R., and S. Winter. 1982. *An Evolutionary Theory of Economic Change.* Cambridge, MA: Harvard University Press.
Nordhaus, W. 1969. *Invention, Growth, and Welfare: A Theoretical Treatment of Technological Change.* Cambridge, MA: The MIT Press.
Ramsey, F. 1928. "A Mathematical Theory of Savings." *Economic Journal* 38: 543–59.
Rebelo, S. 1990. "Long Run Policy Analysis and Long Run Growth." NBER working paper No. 3325, Cambridge, MA.
Robinson, J. 1933. *The Economics of Imperfect Competition.* London: Macmillan.
Romer, P. M. 1983. "Dynamic Competitive Equilibria with Externalities, Increasing Returns and Unbounded Growth." Unpublished Ph.D. thesis, University of Chicago.
1986. "Increasing Returns and Long-Run Growth." *Journal of Political Economy* 94: 1002–37.
1987a. "Crazy Explanations for the Productivity Slowdown." In *NBER Macroeconomics Annual,* S. Fischer, Ed. Cambridge, MA: The MIT Press, pp. 163–201.
1987b. "Growth Based on Increasing Returns Due to Specialization." *American Economic Review* 77: 56–62.
1990. "Endogenous Technological Change." *Journal of Political Economy* 98: S71–103.

Schumpeter, J. 1942. *Capitalism, Socialism, and Democracy.* New York: Harper Brothers.

Shell, K. 1966. "Toward a Theory of Inventive Activity and Capital Accumulation." *American Economic Review* 56: 62–8.

1967. "A Model of Inventive Activity and Capital Accumulation." In *Essays in the Theory of Optimal Economic Growth,* K. Shell, Ed. Cambridge, MA: The MIT Press.

1973. "Inventive Activity, Industrial Organization and Economic Activity." In *Models of Economic Growth,* J. A. Mirrlees and N. H. Stern, Eds. London: Macmillan.

Sheshinski, E. 1967. "Optimal Accumulation with Learning by Doing." In *Essays in the Theory of Optimal Economic Growth,* K. Shell, Ed. Cambridge, MA: The MIT Press.

Solow, R. M. 1956. "A Contribution to the Theory of Economic Growth." *Quarterly Journal of Economics* 70: 65–94.

1957. "Technical Change and the Aggregate Production Function." *Review of Economics and Statistics* 39: 312–20.

Starrett, D. 1988. *Foundations of Public Economics.* Cambridge: Cambridge University Press.

Summers, R., and A. Heston. 1988. "A New Set of International Comparisons of Real Product and Prices: Estimates for 130 Countries, 1950–1985." *Review of Income and Wealth* 34: 1–26.

Swan, T. 1956. "Economic Growth and Capital Accumulation." *The Economic Record* 32: 334–61.

Uzawa, H. 1965. "Optimum Technical Change in an Aggregative Model of Economic Growth." *International Economic Review* 6: 18–31.

Wilson, R. 1975. "Informational Economies of Scale." *Bell Journal of Economics* 6: 184–95.

Xie, D. In press. "Increasing Returns and Increasing Rates of Growth." *Journal of Political Economy.*

Young, A. A. 1928. "Increasing Returns and Economic Progress." *Economic Journal* 38: 527–42.

CHAPTER 6

Stability of cycles with adaptive learning rules

Roger Guesnerie and Michael Woodford

1 Introduction

This chapter considers the problem of stability of learning procedures in a dynamical system that is one-dimensional and one-step forward-looking. Such dynamical systems have often been studied in the economic literature when, for example, they are associated with simple versions of the overlapping generations model.

In this chapter, and this is its main specificity, attention is focused on a simple category of learning rules, that is, adaptive learning rules. With such learning rules, which have been introduced in the early literature on learning, expectations are revised according to the gap between previous expectations and realizations. The rules depend on a single parameter α, which describes how quickly expectations react to present conditions. The coefficient α then reflects the relative weight of present observations and of an aggregate index of past observations.

The study of this simple class of learning rules had two main purposes.

First, interest in simple learning rules has remained vivid in the recent literature (see, e.g., the least squares learning of Marcet and Sargent, 1989). In this chapter, by focusing attention on a simple class of adaptive rules, for which the trade-off between present and (aggregate) past observations can be parametrized, one can expect both to exhibit more precise results and to develop intuition that cannot be grasped through the complexity of more general learning procedures.

Second, the present study is intended to be a first step toward a study of learning stability where sunspot equilibria rather than purely periodic equilibria are considered. Results on this subject have been obtained by Mike Woodford (1990). The adaptive learning procedures considered here, which later will be compared to the ones analyzed in Woodford's article,

We thank J. M. Grandmont and G. Laroque for very helpful comments.

provide a potentially more general setting that is well-designed to test the robustness of previous results.

The study proceeds as follows:

- Section 2 presents the model.
- In Section 3, we first exhibit a necessary condition for learning stability and then a sufficient condition. The latter result is reminiscent of the results obtained by Grandmont and Laroque (1986, 1988) for general, but not directly comparable, learning rules in a similar setting.
- In Section 4, we exploit fully the possibilities offered by the specific structure under scrutiny and we exhibit a necessary and sufficient condition for learning stability.

2 The model

We are considering a one-dimensional one-step forward-looking dynamical system. The dynamics of the system are governed by

$$p_t = \varphi(p^e_{t+1}). \tag{1}$$

The level of the state variable today, p_t, depends on the expected level of the state variable tomorrow, p^e_{t+1} (expectations are point expectations commonly held by all actors in the system). Many dynamic models of the economic literature can be studied under the reduced form (1). In particular, in simple versions of the overlapping generations model, p_t can be identified with the money price level at period t, and p^e_{t+1} is the expected price level for period $t+1$. (See Chiappori and Guesnerie, 1989.)

It is useful to recall some classical definitions.

- A *perfect foresight equilibrium* consists of a sequence $\{p_t\}$ such that

  $$p_t = \varphi(p_{t+1}). \tag{1'}$$

- A *steady-state equilibrium* is associated with $\bar{p}$ such that

  $$\bar{p} = \varphi(\bar{p}).$$

- A *periodic equilibrium* of order k consists of $\bar{p}_1, \ldots, \bar{p}_k$ such that

  $$\bar{p}_1 = \varphi(\bar{p}_2), \ldots, \bar{p}_{k-1} = \varphi(\bar{p}_k), \quad \bar{p}_k = \varphi(\bar{p}_1). \tag{2}$$

  Equivalently, if one denotes φ^k the kth iterate of φ, then

  $$\bar{p}_l = \varphi^k(\bar{p}_l), \quad l = 1, \ldots, k. \tag{3}$$

An important issue in the study of stationary equilibria (steady-state or periodic equilibria) is whether they are determinate or indeterminate. A stationary equilibrium is determinate if there is no perfect foresight equilibrium (in the sense of the previous definition (1′)) that is close (for some adequate topology on the space of infinite sequences) to the stationary equilibrium. (See Woodford, 1984, for a comprehensive discussion of the concept.)

Determinacy normally obtains whenever there exists *no* other perfect foresight equilibrium $\{p_t\}$ that converges to the stationary equilibrium under consideration. This latter fact is itself a consequence of local asymptotic stability of the equilibrium with respect to φ (or φ^k).

When the function φ of the reduced form (1) is differentiable, then the following criteria for asymptotic stability (and then for determinacy) are well known.

- A steady-state $\bar{p}$ is *determinate* if $|\varphi'|<1$, where φ' is the derivative of φ at $\bar{p}$.
- A periodic equilibrium $(\bar{p}_1, \ldots, \bar{p}_k)$ is *determinate* if

  $$|\varphi_1' \times \varphi_2' \times \cdots \times \varphi_k'|<1,$$

  where $\varphi_1', \varphi_2', \ldots, \varphi_k'$ are the derivatives of φ, respectively, at $\bar{p}_1$, $\bar{p}_2, \ldots, \bar{p}_k$.

Equivalently, the criterion says that the absolute value of the derivative of φ^k at (any) $\bar{p}_l$ is smaller than 1.

We are now going to provide another interpretation of the previous conditions for determinacy.

Normalize p on $[0,1]$ and consider ψ^1 a vector field on $[0,1]$: $\psi^1 : p \to p-\varphi(p)$.

The Poincaré–Hopf index of the vector field ψ^1 in $\bar{p}$ is $+1$ iff the derivative of ψ^1 is positive iff $\varphi'<1$.

Note that if the vector field is "pointing outward" – as it typically is in standard economic specifications reducible to form (1) – a Poincaré–Hopf index (from now on PH index) of -1 would signal other zeros of ψ and then other steady states. On the contrary, a PH index of $+1$ does not "signal" other steady states.

In the general case, consider ψ^k a vector field on $[0,1]^k$:

$$\psi^k : (p_1, p_2, \ldots, p_k) \to (p_1-\varphi(p_2), p_2-\varphi(p_3), \ldots, p_k-\varphi(p_1)).$$

The PH index of the vector field ψ^k at $(\bar{p}_1, \bar{p}_2, \ldots, \bar{p}_k)$, a zero of ψ^k, is $+1$ iff the determinant of the Jacobian matrix associated with ψ^k at $(\bar{p}_1, \bar{p}_2, \ldots, \bar{p}_k)$ is positive. In fact, the value of the determinant is easily computed and equals $1-\varphi_1' \cdots \varphi_k'$. Hence the PH index is $+1$ iff $\varphi_1' \cdots \varphi_k' < 1$.

From now on, we denote $\varphi_1', \ldots, \varphi_k'$ as ν^k. We should recall

$$\text{the PH index of } \psi^k \text{ is } +1 \Leftrightarrow \nu^k < 1. \tag{4}$$

Note that, as in the one-dimensional case, if the vector field ψ^k points outward, a PH index of -1 in one zero of the vector field signals the existence of other zeros.

Let us now come to the learning dynamics we are going to consider. It is described by

$$p_{t+1}^e = \alpha p_{t+1-k} + (1-\alpha) p_{t+1-k}^e, \quad \alpha \in [0,1]. \tag{5}$$

The price expected at time $t+1$ is a convex combination of the *actual* and *expected* prices k periods before. The learning rule can be rewritten as a function of past observations alone. Putting

$$p_{nk+l}^e = \alpha p_{(n-1)k+l} + \alpha(1-\alpha) p_{(n-2)k+l} + \alpha(1-\alpha)^2 p_{(n-3)k+1} + \cdots$$
$$l = 1, \ldots, k. \tag{5'}$$

We note here that the rule does not belong to the class of finite memory learning rules considered by Grandmont and Laroque (1986, 1988). However, adapting previous definitions of these authors, the rule would detect cycles of order k: If a cycle $\bar{p}_1, \ldots, \bar{p}_k$ repeats itself an infinity of times before time t, agents will forecast a new cycle from time t on. Note, nevertheless, that there is no sense in which the rule detects cycles of period $2k$.

The rule is an adaptation of learning rules that are standard in the case of a steady state to the case where agents do not rule out the possibility of occurrence of periodic equilibria of period k. In some basic sense, this rule is ad hoc, as any other learning rule. It has the merit of simplicity and also can be justified by agents' beliefs, which, although they fall short of being "fully rational," are "reasonable." For example, agents believe that the process generating prices is (potentially) periodic with period k, so that prices are drawn from the same distribution every kth period, whereas the distributions drawn from in any k successive periods need have no connections with one another. Given this belief, agents attempt separately to estimate $\bar{p}_1$, the average of p_t in any period where $t = nk+1$, $\bar{p}_2$ the average value of p_t in any period where $t = nk+2$, and so on. The estimate of $\bar{p}_1$ is updated each time a new observation occurs in a period where $t = nk+1$, using an "adaptive expectations" formula of the type used by Cagan, Nerlove, and others. The weighting of periods made explicit in (5′) does not treat present and past symmetrically. It can be justified by a belief that permanent changes in the true value of $\bar{p}_1$ occur occasionally so that more recent observations are of greatest value in helping to estimate the current value. With such beliefs, the size of α that makes sense depends upon one's belief about how frequently the permanent changes occur and how large the variance of such changes, relative to the variance in the prices drawn from the distribution when $\bar{p}_1$ is fixed.

The learning dynamics of the system obtains from the superposition of the equilibrium rule (1) and the learning rule (5):

$$p_t = \varphi(p_{t+1}^e), \tag{1}$$

$$p_{t+1}^e = \alpha p_{t+1-k} + (1-\alpha)p_{t+1-k}^e. \tag{5}$$

Consider a periodic solution of order k of equations (2) $(\bar{p}_1, \ldots, \bar{p}_k)$. Then $p_t = \bar{p}_{t\,(\mathrm{mod}\,k)}$, $p_t^e = \bar{p}_{t\,(\mathrm{mod}\,k)}$ is also a periodic solution of equations (1) and (5). The central question of this chapter can now be precisely formulated: Under which conditions is such a periodic equilibrium locally stable under the learning dynamics, (1) and (5)?

In order to answer the question, let us eliminate expectations from (1) and (5) and let us focus attention on the dynamics of actual prices. Combining (1) and (5) yields:

$$p_t = \varphi[\alpha p_{t+1-k} + (1-\alpha)\varphi^{-1}(p_{t-k})]. \tag{6}$$

Adding

$$\begin{aligned} p_{t-1} &= p_{t-1}, \\ &\vdots \\ p_{t+1-k} &= p_{t+1-k}, \end{aligned}$$

we can write

$$\begin{pmatrix} p_t \\ \vdots \\ p_{t+1-k} \end{pmatrix} = \Phi \begin{pmatrix} p_{t-1} \\ \vdots \\ p_{t-k} \end{pmatrix}.$$

Hence, the evolution of actual prices is associated with a dynamical system in the space $\mathbb{R}^k$. It is easy to check that a periodic equilibrium $(\bar{p}_k, \ldots, \bar{p}_1)$ of order k (solution of (2)) is also a fixed point of the kth iterate of the map Φ (we denote it Φ^k). Local stability of the learning dynamics depends upon the stability of Φ^k and, hence, on the eigenvalues of the Jacobian matrix of Φ^k at the fixed point. The next section is devoted to the study of the latter question.

3 Preliminary results

Let $(\bar{p}_k, \ldots, \bar{p}_1)$ be a periodic equilibrium of order k and let $D(\Phi^k)$ be the Jacobian of the kth iterate of the map Φ just defined before in equations (6'). Lemma 1 gives an explicit form of $D(\Phi^k)$.

Lemma 1. *For $k \geq 3$,*

$$D(\Phi^k) = \begin{bmatrix} 1-\alpha & 0 & 0 & \cdots & \alpha^2\varphi_1'\varphi_k' & \alpha(1-\alpha)\varphi_1' \\ \alpha\varphi_2' & 1-\alpha & 0 & \cdots & 0 & 0 \\ 0 & \alpha\varphi_3' & 1-\alpha & \cdots & 0 & 0 \\ & & & & \alpha\varphi_k' & 1-\alpha \end{bmatrix},$$

where $\varphi_1', \ldots, \varphi_k'$ are the derivatives of φ at $\bar{p}_1, \ldots, \bar{p}_k$. Also

$$D(\Phi^2) = \begin{pmatrix} 1-\alpha+\alpha^2\varphi_1'\varphi_2' & \alpha(1-\alpha)\varphi_1' \\ \alpha\varphi_2' & 1-\alpha \end{pmatrix},$$

$$D(\Phi) = \left(\frac{1-\alpha}{1-\varphi'\alpha}\right).$$

Proof: We have

$$\begin{pmatrix} \bar{p}_k \\ \vdots \\ \bar{p}_1 \end{pmatrix} = \Phi \times \Phi \cdots \Phi \begin{pmatrix} \bar{p}_k \\ \vdots \\ \bar{p}_1 \end{pmatrix}.$$

Let $D\Phi_j$ be the derivative $D\Phi$ evaluated at

$$\begin{bmatrix} \bar{p}_{j-2(\text{mod}\,k)} \\ \vdots \\ \bar{p}_{j-(k+1)(\text{mod}\,k)} \end{bmatrix}.$$

Then $D\Phi^k = D\Phi_1 \times D\Phi_2 \cdots D\Phi_k$. Note that

$$D\Phi_j = \begin{bmatrix} 0 & - & - & 0 & \alpha\varphi_j' & 1-\alpha \\ & & I_{k-1} & & & 0 \end{bmatrix},$$

where $\varphi_j' = \varphi'(\bar{p}_j)$.

Let us proceed by induction (for $k \geq 3$) and assume that the product of the first p terms, for any $1 \leq p \leq k-2$, is

$$\begin{bmatrix} 0 & - & - & 0 & \alpha\varphi_1' & 1-\alpha & 0 & - & 0 \\ & & & & 0 & \alpha\varphi_2' & 1-\alpha & & \vert \\ & & & & 0 & \ddots & \ddots & \ddots & \vert \\ & & & & & & \ddots & \ddots & 0 \\ & & & & & & & \alpha\varphi_p' & 1-\alpha \\ & & I_{k-p} & & & & & 0 & 0 \\ & & & & & & & & 0 \end{bmatrix}.$$

One then shows that the product of the $p+1$ terms is

$$\begin{bmatrix} 0 & \cdots & 0 & \alpha\varphi_1' & 1-\alpha & 0 & \cdots & 0 \\ & & & 0 & \alpha\varphi_2' & 1-\alpha & & 0 \\ & & & & \ddots & \ddots & \ddots & \vdots \\ & & & & & \alpha\varphi_{p+1}' & & 1-\alpha \\ & & & & & & 0 & 0 \\ I_{k-p-1} & & & & \cdots & & & \end{bmatrix}.$$

The last iteration consists in the multiplication of

$$\begin{bmatrix} \alpha\varphi_1' & 1-\alpha & 0 & \cdots & \cdots & 0 \\ 0 & \alpha\varphi_2' & 1-\alpha & & & \vdots \\ \vdots & & \ddots & \ddots & & \vdots \\ 0 & & & \alpha\varphi_{k-1}' & & 1-\alpha \\ 1 & 0 & \cdots & \cdots & 0 & 0 \end{bmatrix} \begin{bmatrix} 0 & \cdots & \cdots & 0 & \alpha\varphi_k' & 1-\alpha \\ 1 & \ddots & & & 0 & 0 \\ \vdots & & \ddots & & \ddots & \\ \vdots & & & \ddots & & \ddots \\ 0 & \cdots & \cdots & \cdots & 1 & 0 \end{bmatrix}.$$

The cases where $k=2$ and $k=1$ are treated directly. The conclusion follows. □

Lemma 2 exhibits the "characteristic polynomial" of $D(\Phi^k)$.

Lemma 2. *The zeros of the characteristic polynomial associated with $J(\Phi^k)$ are the zeros of*

$$P(\lambda) = (\lambda-(1-\alpha))^k - \lambda\alpha^k\nu^k,$$

where ν^k is defined (as before) by $\nu^k = \varphi_1' \cdots \varphi_k'$.

Proof: The characteristic polynomial is defined by

$$\det(D(\Phi^k) - \lambda I) = 0.$$

Developing (for example) with respect to the first line yields (for $k \geq 3$)

$$(1-\alpha-\lambda)^k + (-1)^k(1-\alpha-\lambda)\alpha^k\nu^k + (-1)^{k+1}(1-\alpha)\alpha^k\nu^k,$$

that is,

$$(1-\alpha-\lambda)^k + (-1)^{k+1}\lambda\alpha^k\nu^k,$$

the zeros of which are the same as those of

$$P(\lambda) = (\lambda-(1-\alpha))^k - \lambda\alpha^k\nu^k.$$

The same result obtains for $k=2,1$. □

It should be noted here that the characteristic polynomial and hence the eigenvalues of $D\Phi^k$ depend upon the parameter of the learning rule (α), and upon the characteristics of the original dynamical systems only through ν^k.

Let us recall that, as shown in Section 2:

$$|\nu^k|<1 \Leftrightarrow \text{determinacy of the system (1')},$$

$$\nu^k<1 \Leftrightarrow \text{the PH index of the mapping } \psi^k \text{ is } +1.$$

A necessary (Proposition 1) and a sufficient (Proposition 2) condition for stability can be stated as follows:

Proposition 1. *A* necessary *condition for local stability is that $\nu^k<1$, that is, that the PH index of the k-period cycle, defined with respect to the map ψ^k, is $+1$.*

Proof: A necessary condition for stability is that

$$\text{Sign } P(\lambda=1)=\text{Sign } P(\lambda=+\infty).$$

But Sign $P(\lambda=+\infty)$ is positive and Sign $P(\lambda=1)$ is the sign of $1-\nu^k$. The conclusion follows. □

Proposition 2. *A* sufficient *condition for local stability is that $|\nu^k|<1$, that is, that perfect foresight dynamics be determinate near the period k cycle.*

Proof: We must show that $|\nu^k|<1$ implies that $P(\lambda)=0$ cannot have a solution outside the unit circle.

We will show that

$$|\lambda-(1-\alpha)|^k=|\lambda||\alpha^k\nu| \tag{7}$$

is impossible whenever $|\lambda|\geq 1$.

Let us put $|\lambda|=1+\epsilon$, $\epsilon\geq 0$,

$$|\lambda-(1-\alpha)|\geq|\lambda|-1-\alpha=\epsilon+\alpha,$$

and

$$|\lambda-1-\alpha|^k\geq(\epsilon+\alpha)^k.$$

If the equation $(\epsilon+\alpha)^k=(1+\epsilon)\alpha^k|\nu^k|$ has no solution for $\epsilon>0$, then (7) has no solution for $|\lambda|\geq 1$.

Let us consider the curves $y=(\epsilon+\alpha)^k$ and $y=(1+\epsilon)\alpha^k|\nu^k|$ depicted in Figure 1. Considering the diagram and the convexity of x^k, one concludes that the two curves will have no intersection point for $\epsilon>0$ whenever $|\nu^k|$

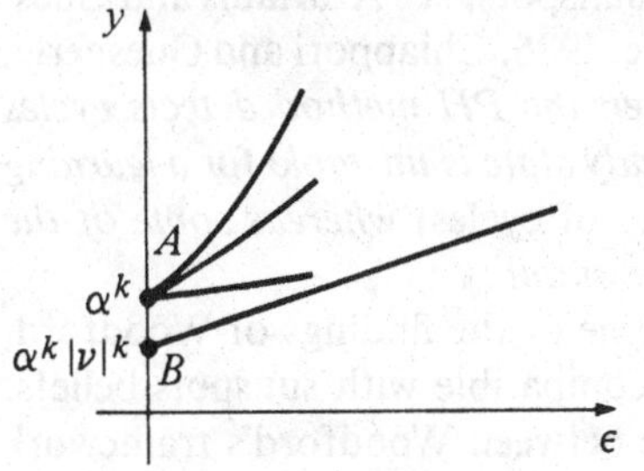

Figure 1.

is smaller than 1 and the slope of the curve at A is larger than the slope of the line. This latter inequality, $k\alpha^{k-1} > \alpha^k|\nu^k|$, holds when $|\nu^k| < 1$. □

Let us comment briefly on the results:

The sufficient condition given in Proposition 2 is remarkably simple and the statement speaks for itself. The fact that determinacy of the dynamic system and convergence of the learning dynamics have a relationship is intuitively plausible. For example, in the limit case, where the weight of the past in the formulation of expectations vanishes ($\alpha = 1$), the learning dynamics reduces to $p_t = \varphi(p_{t+1-k})$ and its local stability is equivalent to the fact that $|\nu^k| < 1$, that is, equivalent to determinacy. This equivalence ceases to hold when $\alpha \neq 1$, but it is remarkable that determinacy remains a sufficient condition for stability whatever α.

In the literature, the role of ν^k for local stability has been ascertained for learning rules with finite memory but with more general functional forms. In fact, an extension of the proposition in Grandmont and Laroque to general learning rules with finite memory would imply our Proposition 2 as a particular case. (We leave it to the reader to check precisely this assertion.) We do not know whether such extensions are true, but they are intuitively plausible.

Proposition 1 is also extremely simple. One of its consequences is not so transparent and deserves some comments. Consider the vector field ψ^k. Assume that the system under consideration has a unique steady state and assume that the PH index of ψ^k in this steady state is -1. Then if the vector field points outward, the fact that the PH index in the steady state is -1 implies that the vector field has other zeros and these zeros are necessarily truly periodic equilibria. Note that two of these zeros, at least, have necessarily an index of $+1$ and satisfy the necessary condition for local stability of any α-learning rule. In this case, we would say that the Poincaré–Hopf method "detects cycles" (in the economic literature, the PH method has mainly been used to detect sunspots; see Azariadis and Guesnerie, 1982, 1986; Spear, 1984; Guesnerie, 1986; Chiappori and Guesnerie, 1989). The remarkable fact is that *when the PH method detects cycles* from a given steady state, *the given steady state is unstable for a learning process* (which considers the possibility of cycles) *whereas some of the detected cycles are good candidates for stability.*

The latter result is reminiscent of some of the findings of Woodford, who considers learning rules that are compatible with sunspots beliefs. There is no immediate correspondence between Woodford's framework and ours. However, our problems become quite similar when, on the one hand, the sunspot matrices tend to cycle matrices in Woodford's model and, on the other hand, $\alpha \to 0$ in our model. Indeed, the findings on the stability of equilibria detected by PH methods drawn from Proposition 2 and from Woodford's results, in the limit case just sketched, do coincide.

4 Necessary and sufficient conditions for stability

Both Propositions 1 and 2 are, in fact, special cases of the following more general characterization:

Theorem 1. *Given $k \geq 2$ and $0 < \alpha < 1$, there exists a critical value $\nu^*(k, \alpha)$ such that a k cycle will be locally stable under the learning dynamics if and only if $\nu^*(k, \alpha) < \nu^k < 1$. Furthermore, for all k and α, $-\infty < \nu^*(k, \alpha) < -1$.*

Proof of this requires that we first establish some preliminary lemmas.

From now on, we denote ν^k by ν (dropping the upper index). A lower index will be used sometimes for denoting specific values of ν. Recall that (ignoring nongeneric cases) a k cycle is locally stable if and only if all k roots of the polynomial

$$[\lambda - (1-\alpha)]^k = \alpha^k \nu \lambda \tag{7}$$

have modulus less than 1. From this, it is obvious that, for a given k and α, stability depends only upon the value of ν. Accordingly, we wish to study how the set of roots of (7) changes as we vary ν. Let us define $B(k, \alpha)$ as the set of negative *bifurcation values* for ν, given k and α, that is, as the set of values $\nu < 0$ for which there exists a (possibly complex) λ with $|\lambda| = 1$ that satisfies (7). Only at such a value of ν can the number of roots with modulus less than 1 change. We need only consider negative bifurcation values, since Propositions 1 and 2 have already established that all k roots have modulus less than 1 for all $-1 < \nu < 1$, whereas less than k roots have this property for all $\nu > 1$.

Lemma 3. *If k is even, $B(k,\alpha)$ is a set of $k/2$ distinct values. Let $k \geq 2$ and $0 < \alpha < 1$. Then*

$$-\left(\frac{2-\alpha}{\alpha}\right)^k = \nu_{k/2} < \cdots < \nu_2 < \nu_1 < -1.$$

At each of the higher values, ν_1 through $\nu_{k/2-1}$, there is a complex pair of roots of (7) *with $|\lambda| = 1$. At $\nu_{k/2}$, there is a real root $\lambda = -1$. If k is odd, $B(k,\alpha)$ is a set of $(k-1)/2$ distinct values,*

$$-\left(\frac{2-\alpha}{\alpha}\right)^k < \nu_{(k-1)/2} < \cdots < \nu_2 < \nu_1 < -1$$

at each of which there is a complex pair of roots with $|\lambda| = 1$.

Proof: If $|\lambda| = 1$, we can write $\lambda = e^{i\theta}$ for some $-\pi < \theta \leq \pi$. Then $\nu \in B(k,\alpha)$ if and only if the equation

$$[e^{i\theta} - (1-\alpha)]^k = \alpha^k \nu e^{i\theta} \tag{8}$$

has a solution $-\pi < \theta \leq \pi$. Let us also adopt the notation

$$[e^{i\theta} - (1-\alpha)] = x e^{i\phi}, \quad -\pi < \phi \leq \pi.$$

This defines two continuous functions, $x(\theta,\alpha)$ and $\phi(\theta,\alpha)$, on the domain $-\pi < \theta \leq \pi$. For future reference, it should be noted that these functions are defined by

$$x(\theta,\alpha) = [2(1-\alpha)(1-\cos\theta) + \alpha^2]^{1/2}, \tag{9}$$

$$\tan\phi(\theta,\alpha) = \frac{\sin\theta}{\cos\theta - (1-\alpha)}, \tag{10}$$

where the solution to (10) is selected from the interval $0 \leq \phi < \pi$ for $0 \leq \theta < \pi$, from the interval $-\pi < \phi \leq \pi$ for $-\pi < \theta \leq 0$, and the solution is chosen to be $\phi = \pi$ in the case $\theta = \pi$. (Under these selection rules, $\phi(\theta,\alpha)$ is a smooth function of both arguments, even though the right-hand side of (10) is discontinuous.) By adopting this change of variable, (8) is equivalent to

$$x(\theta,\alpha)^k = -\alpha^k \nu, \tag{11}$$

$$k\phi(\theta,\alpha) = \theta + \pi (\text{mod } 2\pi). \tag{12}$$

(In deriving (11) and (12), we are restricting attention to the case $\nu < 0$.)

Now for each θ that solves (12), there exists a unique $\nu < 0$ that solves (11), because $x(\theta,\alpha) > 0$ for all values of its arguments. Hence, the set $B(k,\alpha)$ can be identified with the set of angles $-\pi < \theta \leq \pi$ that solves (12). We turn to a consideration of the solutions of (12).

It should be noted that (10) implies that the function $\phi(\theta,\alpha)$ has the following properties:

$$\phi(-\theta,\alpha)=-\phi(\theta,\alpha), \tag{13}$$

$$\theta\leq\phi(\theta,\alpha)<\theta+\frac{\pi}{2}, \quad \text{for } 0\leq\theta\leq\pi, \tag{14}$$

$$\theta-\frac{\pi}{2}<\phi(\theta,\alpha)\leq\theta, \quad \text{for } -\pi\leq\theta\leq 0, \tag{15}$$

$$\lim_{\theta\to-\pi}\phi(\theta,\alpha)=-\pi, \qquad \phi(0,\alpha)=0, \qquad \phi(\pi,\alpha)=\pi, \tag{16}$$

$$\frac{1}{2-\alpha}\leq\phi_\theta(\theta,\alpha)\leq\frac{1}{\alpha}, \tag{17}$$

$$\lim_{\theta\to-\pi}\phi_\theta(\theta,\alpha)=\frac{1}{2-\alpha}, \quad \phi_\theta(0,\alpha)=\frac{1}{\alpha}, \quad \phi_\theta(\pi,\alpha)=\frac{1}{2-\alpha}, \tag{18}$$

$$\phi_{\theta\theta}(\theta,\alpha)<0, \quad \text{for } 0\leq\theta\leq\pi, \tag{19}$$

$$\phi_{\theta\theta}(\theta,\alpha)>0, \quad \text{for } -\pi\leq\theta\leq 0. \tag{20}$$

(The general shape of the function $\phi(\theta,\alpha)$ as a function of θ is indicated in Figure 2.)

Now for $k\geq 2$, the left-hand side of (12) is a monotonically increasing function on the interval $[-\pi,\pi]$, taking values from $-k\pi$ to $k\pi$, with a slope always greater than 1, since

$$k\phi_\theta\geq\frac{k}{2-\alpha}>1,$$

from (17). The right-hand side of (12) consists of a family of parallel straight lines of slope 1. If k is even, the line $\theta+(k-1)\pi$ intersects the curve $k\phi(\theta,\alpha)$ at $\theta=\pi$, and is above it everywhere on the interval $(-\pi,\pi)$, whereas the line $\theta-(k-1)\pi$ intersects the curve $k\phi(\theta,\alpha)$ at $\theta=-\pi$, and is below it everywhere on the interval $(-\pi,\pi)$. (See Figure 1.) It follows that each of the lines $\theta+(2n-1)\pi$, $(4-k)/2\leq n\leq k/2$, intersects the curve $k\phi(\theta,\alpha)$ at exactly one point in the interval $[-\pi,\pi]$. Let the point of intersection of the line $\theta+(2n-1)\pi$ be denoted θ_s, where $s=n+k/2-1$. One obtains a sequence of $k-1$ intersection points $-\pi<\theta_1<\theta_2<\cdots<\theta_{k-1}=\pi$, with the further property that $\theta_{k-1-s}=-\theta_s$.

Similarly, if k is odd, the curve $k\phi(\theta,\alpha)$ lies between the lines $\theta+(k-2)\pi$ and $\theta+k\pi$ at $\theta=\pi$, and between the lines $\theta-k\pi$ and $\theta-(k-2)\pi$ at $\theta=-\pi$. It follows that each of the lines $\theta+(2n-1)\pi$, $(3-k)/2\leq n\leq(k-1)/2$, intersects the curve at exactly one point in $(-\pi,\pi)$. Let the point of intersection of the line $\theta+(2n-1)\pi$ be denoted θ_s, where, in this

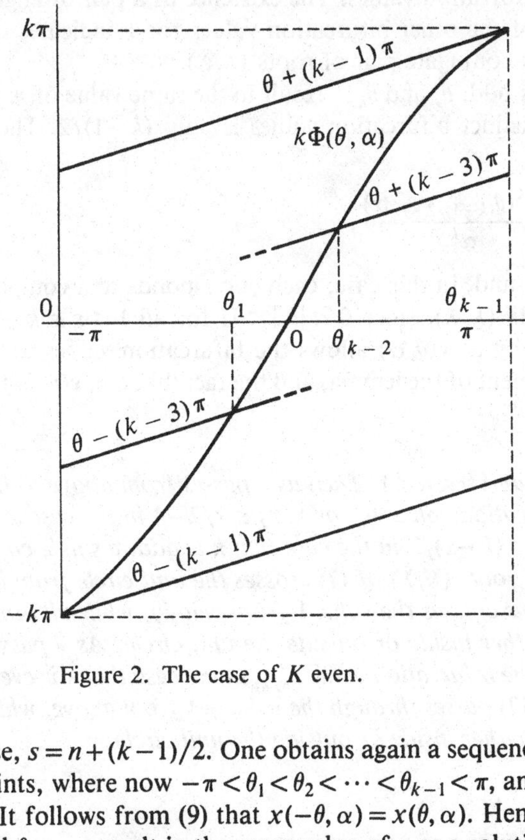

Figure 2. The case of K even.

case, $s = n + (k-1)/2$. One obtains again a sequence of $k-1$ intersection points, where now $-\pi < \theta_1 < \theta_2 < \cdots < \theta_{k-1} < \pi$, and $\theta_{k-s} = -\theta_s$.

It follows from (9) that $x(-\theta, \alpha) = x(\theta, \alpha)$. Hence, when k is even, θ_s and θ_{k-1-s} result in the same value of ν as a solution to (11). Hence, the number of distinct bifurcation values in the set $B(k, \alpha)$ is only $k/2$. Let these values be denoted ν_j, $j = 1, \ldots, k/2$, where

$$\nu_j(k, \alpha) = \frac{-x^k(\theta_{k/2+j-1}, \alpha)}{\alpha^k}.$$

Because $x(\theta, \alpha)$ is a monotonically increasing function of θ, for $0 \le \theta \le \pi$, the bifurcation values can be ordered as indicated in the statement of the lemma, and $\theta_{k-1} = \pi$ implies that $\nu_{k/2} = -((2-\alpha)/\alpha)^k$. Furthermore, (9) implies that for all $0 < |\theta| < \pi$, so that $((2-\alpha)/\alpha)^k < \nu_j < -1$,

$$\alpha < x(\theta, \alpha) < 2 - \alpha \quad \text{for } 1 \le j \le \frac{k}{2} - 1.$$

Finally, $\theta_{k-1} = \pi$ implies the existence of a root $\lambda = e^{i\pi} = -1$ corresponding to $\nu_{k/2}$, whereas $0 < |\theta_s| < \pi$ for $s \ne k-1$ implies that $\lambda = e^{i\theta}$ is complex at each of the other bifurcation values. The existence of a pair of angles $(\theta_s, \theta_{k-1-s})$ for each of the other bifurcation values for ν indicates the existence of a complex conjugate pair of roots $(\lambda, \bar{\lambda})$.

Similarly, when k is odd, θ_s and θ_{k-s} result in the same value of ν, so that the number of distinct bifurcation values is only $(k-1)/2$. These values are given by

$$\nu_j(k,\alpha) = \frac{-x^k(\theta_{(k-1)/2+j}, \alpha)}{\alpha^k},$$

for $j = 1, \ldots, (k-1)/2$, and, in this case, each corresponds to a complex conjugate pair of roots $(\lambda, \bar{\lambda})$, since $0 < |\theta_s| < \Pi$ for all $1 \leq s \leq k-1$. Again, the monotonicity at $x(\theta, \alpha)$ allows the bifurcation values to be ordered as in the statement of the lemma, and the fact that $\alpha < x(\theta_s, \alpha) < 2-\alpha$ implies the bounds. □

Lemma 4. *Let $k \geq 2$ and $0 < \alpha < 1$. Then as ν passes from above to below the negative bifurcation value ν_j, for $1 \leq j \leq k/2-1$ in the case that k is even, or for $1 \leq j \leq (k-1)/2$ in the case that k is odd, a single complex conjugate pair of roots $(\lambda, \bar{\lambda})$ of* (7) *crosses the unit circle from inside (i.e., their modulus crosses the value* 1 *from below), while all other roots of* (7) *remain either inside or outside the unit circle. As ν passes from above to below the bifurcation value $\nu_{k/2}$, in the case that k is even, a single real root λ of* (7) *passes through the value* -1 *from above, while all other roots remain either inside or outside the unit circle.*

Proof: See Appendix A.

Proof of Theorem 1: Proposition 2 has already established that not all roots of (7) have modulus less than 1 if $\nu > 1$, and Proposition 1 has already established that all k roots have modulus less than 1 if $-1 < \nu < 1$. Since by Lemma 1, no bifurcation values occur betwen ν_1 and -1, all k roots must have modulus less than 1 for all $\nu_1 < \nu < 1$. From Lemma 2, it follows furthermore that there are exactly $k-2$ roots with modulus less than 1 for all $\nu_2 < \nu < \nu_1$, exactly $k-4$ such roots for all $\nu_3 < \nu < \nu_2$, and so on, until, if k is odd, there is exactly one such root for all $-\infty < \nu < \nu_{(k-1)/2}$; or, if k is even, exactly two such roots for all $-\infty < \nu < \nu_{k/2}$. Hence, whether k is odd or even, all k roots have a modulus less than 1 if and only if $\nu_1 < \nu < 1$, and the theorem follows given the identification

$$\nu^*(k,\alpha) = \nu_1(k,\alpha).$$

Note that whether k is odd or even,

$$\nu^*(k,\alpha)=\frac{-x(\theta^*(k,\alpha);\alpha)^k}{\alpha^k}, \tag{21}$$

where $\theta^*(k,\alpha)$ is the unique solution to

$$k\phi(\theta,\alpha)=\theta+\pi \tag{22}$$

in the interval $-\pi<\theta\leq\pi$. □

A few remarks are in order relating to the result just obtained. First of all, it will be observed that the assumption $k\geq 2$ is required in the proof of both Lemmas 1 and 2. In fact, the theorem is not true in the case $k=1$, that is, the case of steady-state equilibrium. In that case, it is easily seen that (7) has one solution,

$$\lambda=\frac{1-\alpha}{1-\alpha\nu}.$$

The stability condition is $|\lambda|<1$, which is true if $\nu<1$ *or* if $\nu>((2-\alpha)/\alpha)$. Hence, when $k=1$, unlike any of the cases $k\geq 2$, the region of stability for ν is not a single connected interval; it has neither a lower nor an upper bound, and, in particular, 1 is not the upper bound.

It is also worth commenting briefly upon what happens when a k-cycle loses stability due to ν being moved outside the region of stability defined in the theorem. Specifically, consider a smooth one-parameter family of economies, indexed by a parameter μ, with an equilibrium condition

$$p_t=\varphi(p_{t+1}^e,\mu).$$

Suppose that $(\bar{p}_1(\mu),\ldots,\bar{p}_k(\mu))$ describes a smooth family of equilibrium k-cycles, one for each value of μ in some interval, and consider how $\nu(\mu)$, evaluated at this particular k-cycle, varies as μ varies.

At a value of μ such that $\nu(\mu)=1$, (7) has a root $\lambda=1$, and as a result, the derivative condition

$$\mathrm{Det}[D\Phi^k-I]\neq 0,$$

needed in order to use the inverse function theorem to prove that the fixed point of the map $\Phi^k(\mu)$ is locally unique, fails when $\nu(\mu)=1$. Typically (although this depends upon higher derivative conditions that we do not discuss here), there will be another family of k-cycles (fixed points of $\Phi^k(\mu)$) that intersects the family under investigation at that particular value of μ. In this case, the loss of stability of the family of k-cycles under investigation as $\nu(\mu)$ goes above 1 for that family may coincide with the existence of one or more nearby k-cycles that are stable (because for them $\nu<1$) for the same values of μ.

In the case of a value of μ such that $\nu(\mu)=\nu^*(k,\alpha)$, more complicated bifurcations are possible. When $k=2$, as $\nu(\mu)$ passes through the value $\nu^*(2,\alpha)$, a root of (7) passes through the value -1. In such a case, one typically (again depending upon some higher derivatives) has a *flip bifurcation,* in which a cycle of period $2k$ (of the learning dynamics) comes into existence for μ on one side or the other of the critical value. It is possible that as the k-cycle loses stability, a stable nearby $2k$-cycle comes into existence, to which the learning dynamics are attracted instead. Since we have assumed a learning rule that is consistent with all cycles of period k, but not with cycles of period $2k$, the $2k$ cycle of the *learning* dynamics will not generally correspond to a $2k$ cycle of the *perfect foresight* dynamics. When $k>2$, as $\nu(\mu)$ passes through the value $\nu^*(k,\alpha)$, a complex conjugate pair of roots passes through the unit circle. In such a case, one typically has a discrete-time *Hopf bifurcation,* in which an invariant circle of the learning dynamics comes into existence. It is possible that as the k cycle loses stability, the learning dynamics are attracted instead to quasi-periodic motion on a nearby invariant circle. Again, this will not generally involve expectations becoming correct even asymptotically.

The following result indicates how the speed of adjustment of the learning rule affects the size of the region of stability for a k cycle:

Proposition 3. *Given $k\geq 2$, the critical value $\nu^*(k,\alpha)$ is a continuous monotonically increasing function of α, with limiting values*

$$\lim_{\alpha\to 0}\nu^*(k,\alpha)=-\left(\cos\frac{\pi}{k}\right)^{-k},$$

$$\lim_{\alpha\to 0}\nu^*(k,\alpha)=-1.$$

Proof: See Appendix B.

It is also of some interest to consider how $\nu^*(k,\alpha)$ is affected by variation in k, for given α. It is clear from (22), together with the fact that $k\phi_\theta>1$, that increasing k causes $\theta^*(k,\alpha)$ to decrease. From (9), it is then obvious that $X^*(k,\alpha)$ (as defined in Appendix B) falls as well. It is not, however, clear from (21) how $\nu^*(k,\alpha)$ changes. If $X^*(k,\alpha)$ did not fall, the change in the exponents in (21) would make $\nu^*(k,\alpha)$ lower, since $X^*(k,\alpha)>\alpha$. On the other hand, if the exponents did not change, the decrease in $X^*(k,\alpha)$ would make $\nu^*(k,\alpha)$ higher. The ultimate effect on $\nu^*(k,\alpha)$ depends upon which of these two effects is larger, and we have not been able to reach any general conclusion about this. However, it is at least possible to describe generally what must happen in the limit of very large k:

Proposition 4. *For given* $0<\alpha<1$, $\nu^*(k,\alpha)$ *approaches* -1 *as k is made arbitrarily large. Furthermore, the rate of convergence is given by the expression*

$$\nu^*(k,\alpha) = -1 - \frac{(1-\alpha)\pi^2}{2k} + O(k^{-2}).$$

Proof: See Appendix C.

5 Conclusion

The results of Section 4 have provided a characterization of the conditions of learning stability. The description of the areas of stability, in terms of the underlying parameters of the system, could still be slightly refined. But on the whole, the program announced in the introduction has been completed in a way that seems reasonable.

Appendix A: Proof of Lemma 4

In order to determine how the roots of (7) vary with ν in a neighborhood of a bifurcation value, we must differentiate (7) at such a value of ν and near some root λ. We obtain

$$\frac{d\lambda}{d\nu} = \frac{\alpha^k \lambda}{k[\lambda-(1-\alpha)]^{k-1} - \alpha^k \nu}, \tag{A.1}$$

where the right-hand side is evaluated at the particular root λ whose motion we wish to consider. Let (21) be evaluated at a bifurcation value ν_j and at a root such that $|\lambda|=1$. We are interested in the sign of

$$\begin{aligned}\frac{1}{|\lambda|}\frac{d|\lambda|}{d\nu} &= \mathrm{Re}\left[\frac{1}{\lambda}\frac{d\lambda}{d\nu}\right]\\ &= \mathrm{Re}\left[\frac{\alpha^k}{k[\lambda-(1-\alpha)]^{k-1}-\alpha^k\nu}\right]\\ &= \mathrm{Re}\left[\frac{\alpha^k}{kx^{k-1}e^{i(k-1)\phi}+x^k}\right],\end{aligned}$$

where we use (A.1), and in the final line, we again use the notation introduced in (9) and (10) for the case of a root with $|\lambda|=1$, as well as equation (11). It follows that

$$\begin{aligned}\mathrm{sign}\,\frac{d|\lambda|}{d\nu} &= \mathrm{sign}\,\mathrm{Re}[kx^{k-1}e^{i(k-1)\phi}+x^k]\\ &= \mathrm{sign}[k\cos(k-1)\phi + x]\\ &= \mathrm{sign}[k\cos(\theta+\pi-\phi)+x]\end{aligned}$$

$$= \text{sign}[x - k\cos(\phi - \theta)]$$

using (12).

Equations (9) and (10) imply that

$$\cos(\phi - \theta) = \frac{1 - (1-\alpha)\cos\theta}{x}. \tag{A.2}$$

Equation (9) also implies that

$$\begin{aligned} x^2 &= 1 + (1-\alpha)^2 - 2(1-\alpha)\cos\theta \\ &< 2[1 - (1-\alpha)\cos\theta] \\ &= 2\cos(\phi - \theta) \end{aligned}$$

using (22), so that

$$\cos(\phi - \theta) > \frac{x}{2} \geq \frac{x}{k}$$

given that $k \geq 2$. This implies $d|\lambda|/d\nu < 0$, so that the modulus of the eigenvalue crosses 1 from below as ν crosses the bifurcation value from above. The remaining details of the statement of the lemma then follow from Lemma 1. □

Appendix B: Proof of Proposition 3

The continuity, and indeed differentiability, of $\nu^*(k, \alpha)$ in α follows immediately from its implicit definition by (21) and (22). In determining how it varies with α, we consider separately the cases $k = 2$ and $k \geq 3$.

If $k = 2$, $\theta^*(2, \alpha) = \pi$ for all α. It follows from (9) and (23) that

$$\nu^*(2, \alpha) = -\left(\frac{2-\alpha}{\alpha}\right)^2.$$

This is a monotonically increasing function, and has the limits indicated in the statement of the proposition. (Note that $\cos(\pi/2) = 0$.)

If $k \geq 3$, we cannot solve for $\theta^*(k, \alpha)$ in closed form. However, differentiation of (22) implies that

$$\frac{\partial\theta^*}{\partial\alpha} = \frac{k\sin\theta^*}{(k-2)[1-(1-\alpha)\cos\theta^*] + \alpha(2-\alpha)}. \tag{B.1}$$

Now it follows from (16) that

$$k\phi(0, \alpha) = 0 < \pi = 0 + \pi,$$

while it follows from (4) that

$$k\phi(\text{arc}\cos(1-\alpha), \alpha) = \frac{k\pi}{2} \geq \frac{3\pi}{2} > \text{arc}\cos(1-\alpha) + \pi$$

given $k \geq 3$. Hence, the solution to (22) must lie in the interval

$$0 < \theta^*(k, \alpha) < \arccos(1-\alpha). \tag{B.2}$$

This implies that $\sin\theta^* > 0$, so that (B.1) implies that $\partial\theta^*/\partial\alpha > 0$. Defining $X^*(k, \alpha) = x(\theta^*(k, \alpha), \alpha)$, we can differentiate (9) to obtain

$$\frac{\partial X^*}{\partial \alpha} = \frac{1}{X^*}\left\{\frac{(1-\alpha)k\sin^2\theta^*}{(k-2)[1-(1-\alpha)\cos\theta^*]+\alpha(2-\alpha)} + [\cos\theta^* - (1-\alpha)]\right\}. \tag{B.3}$$

The first term inside the braces is positive as just noted, and the second term is also positive because of (B.2). Hence, (B.3) implies that

$$\frac{\partial X^*}{\partial \alpha} > 0.$$

Finally, differentiation of (21) yields

$$\frac{\partial \nu^*}{\partial \alpha} = \frac{K\nu^*}{\alpha}\left[\frac{\alpha}{X^*}\frac{\partial X^*}{\partial \alpha} - 1\right]. \tag{B.4}$$

Hence, the sign of $\partial\nu^*/\partial\alpha$ depends upon the sign of $(\alpha/X^*)(\partial X^*/\partial\alpha)$. Using (B.3), we obtain

$$\begin{aligned}
\frac{\alpha}{X^*}\frac{\partial X^*}{\partial \alpha}
&= \frac{\alpha}{(X^*)^2}\left\{\frac{(1-\alpha)k\sin^2\theta^*}{(k-2)[1-(1-\alpha)\cos\theta^*]+\alpha(2-\alpha)} + [\cos\theta^* - (1-\alpha)]\right\} \\
&= \frac{\alpha}{[\cos\theta^* - (1-\alpha)]^2 + \sin^2\theta^*} \\
&\quad \times \left\{\frac{[(k-1)\cos\theta^* + (1-\alpha)][\cos\theta^* - (1-\alpha)]^2 + \sin^2\theta^*}{(k-1)([\cos\theta^* - (1-\alpha)]^2 + \sin^2\theta^*) + k(1-\alpha)[\cos\theta^* - (1-\alpha)]}\right\} \\
&= \frac{\alpha[(k-1)\cos\theta^* + (1-\alpha)]}{(k-1)\{[\cos\theta^* - (1-\alpha)]^2 + \sin^2\theta^*\} + k(1-\alpha)[\cos\theta^* - (1-\alpha)]} \\
&= \frac{\alpha(k-\alpha) - \alpha(k-1)(1-\cos\theta)}{\alpha(k-\alpha) + (1-\alpha)(k-2)(1-\cos\theta)} < 1,
\end{aligned}$$

where we have used (9) in the third and fourth lines. Comparing this with (B.4), and recalling that $\nu^* < 0$, we see that $\partial\nu^*/\partial\alpha > 0$, as stated in the proposition.

We turn to the evaluation of the limiting values for $\nu^*(k, \alpha)$. Consider, first, the limit as $\alpha \to 1$. Equation (9) implies that

$$\lim_{\alpha \to 1} X^*(k, \alpha) = 1,$$

so that (21) implies

$$\lim_{\alpha \to 1} \nu^*(k, \alpha) = -1.$$

The limit as $\alpha \to 0$ is not so easily evaluated. The bounds in (26) imply that

$$\lim_{\alpha \to 0} \theta^*(k, \alpha) = 0,$$

so that (9) implies

$$\lim_{\alpha \to 0} X^*(k, \alpha) = 0.$$

But this cannot be substituted into (21) to yield a determinate limit, since both numerator and denominator approach zero. However, the limit can be easily evaluated in another way. Consider how the roots of (7) vary as α approaches zero. It is evident that all k roots approach 1 as $\alpha \to 0$. Furthermore, each root approaches 1 as

$$\lambda(\alpha) = 1 + \alpha\mu + O(\alpha^2),$$

where μ is a corresponding root of the equation

$$(\mu+1)^k = \nu. \tag{B.5}$$

The modulus $|\lambda(\alpha)|$ approaches 1 from below if and only if $\operatorname{Re}\mu < 0$. Hence, all roots of (7) have a modulus less than 1 as α is made very close to zero if and only if ν is such that all k roots of (29) have a negative real part. But in the case that $\nu < 0$, the roots of (29) are

$$\mu_j = -1 + |\nu|^{1/k} e^{\frac{i\pi(2j-1)}{k}}$$

for $j = 1, \ldots, k$. Hence,

$$\operatorname{Re}\mu_j = -1 + |\nu|^{1/k} \cos\left((2j-1)\frac{\pi}{k}\right).$$

The largest such value is the one corresponding to $j = 1$ (or equivalently to $j = k$), so that a necessary and sufficient condition for $\operatorname{Re}\mu_j < 0$ for all j is that

$$-1 + |\nu|^{1/k} \cos\left(\frac{\pi}{k}\right) < 0$$

or, equivalently, that

$$|\nu|<\left(\cos\frac{\pi}{k}\right)^{-k},$$

which is to say that

$$\nu>-\left(\cos\frac{\pi}{k}\right)^{-k}.$$

Hence, this must be the limiting value of $\nu^*(k,\alpha)$ as α approaches zero. □

Appendix C: Proof of Proposition 4

It is easily verified from (9), (18), and (22) that $\theta^*(k,\alpha)$, $X^*(k,\alpha)$, and $\nu^*(k,\alpha)$ are well defined (even if not meaningful) for nonintegral values of k, and that these functions so interpreted are continuous, and indeed differentiable, functions of k. Let us consider these quantities as functions of k^{-1}, as k^{-1} approaches zero.

It is evident from (22) that

$$\lim_{k^{-1}\to 0}\theta^*(k,\alpha)=0,$$

$$\lim_{k^{-1}\to 0}k\phi(\theta^*,\alpha)=\pi.$$

Furthermore, differentiation of (22) yields

$$\frac{\partial\theta^*}{\partial k^{-1}}=\frac{k\phi(\theta^*,\alpha)}{\phi_\theta(\theta^*,\alpha)-k^{-1}}$$

and then, since

$$\lim_{k^{-1}\to 0}\phi_\theta(\theta^*,\alpha)=\phi_\theta(0,\alpha)=\frac{1}{\alpha},$$

we obtain

$$\lim_{k^{-1}\to 0}\frac{\partial\theta^*}{\partial k^{-1}}=\alpha\pi. \tag{C.1}$$

Equation (9) implies

$$\lim_{k^{-1}\to 0}X^*(k,\alpha)=x(0,\alpha)=\alpha,$$

while differentiation of (9) yields

$$\frac{\partial}{\partial k^{-1}}[\log X^*(k,\alpha)]=\frac{(1-\alpha)\sin\theta^*}{X^{*2}}\frac{\partial\theta^*}{\partial k^{-1}} \tag{C.2}$$

so that

$$\lim_{k^{-1}\to 0}\frac{\partial}{\partial k^{-1}}[\log X^*(k,\alpha)]=0.$$

Finally, (21) implies

$$\lim_{k^{-1}\to 0} [\log(-\nu^*(k,\alpha))] = \lim_{k^{-1}\to 0} k\left[\log \frac{X^*(k,\alpha)}{\alpha}\right]$$
$$= \lim_{k^{-1}\to 0} \frac{\partial}{\partial k^{-1}}[\log X^*(k,\alpha)] = 0,$$

where we use l'Hospital's rule in the second line, so that

$$\lim_{k^{-1}\to 0} -\nu^*(k,\alpha) = -1$$

as stated in the proposition. Furthermore, differentiation of (23) yields

$$\lim_{k^{-1}\to 0} \frac{\partial \nu^*}{\partial k^{-1}} = \lim_{k^{-1}\to 0} \nu^* \frac{\partial}{\partial k^{-1}}\left[k \log \frac{X^*(k,\alpha)}{\alpha}\right]$$
$$= \lim_{k^{-1}\to 0} \frac{\partial}{\partial k^{-1}}\left[k \log \frac{X^*(k,\alpha)}{\alpha}\right].$$

Now

$$\lim_{k^{-1}\to 0} \frac{\partial}{\partial k^{-1}}\left[k \log \frac{X^*(k,\alpha)}{\alpha}\right]$$
$$= \lim_{k^{-1}\to 0} \left\{-k^2 \log \frac{X^*(k,\alpha)}{\alpha} + k\frac{\partial}{\partial k^{-1}}\left[\log \frac{X^*(k,\alpha)}{\alpha}\right]\right\}$$
$$= -\lim_{k^{-1}\to 0} \frac{\partial}{\partial k^{-1}}\left[k \log \frac{X^*(k,\alpha)}{\alpha}\right] + \lim_{k^{-1}\to 0} k\frac{\partial}{\partial k^{-1}}\left[\log \frac{X^*(k,\alpha)}{\alpha}\right]$$

using l'Hospital's rule, so that

$$\lim_{k^{-1}\to 0} \frac{\partial}{\partial k^{-1}}\left[k \log \frac{X^*(k,\alpha)}{\alpha}\right] = \frac{1}{2} \lim_{k^{-1}\to 0} k\frac{\partial}{\partial k^{-1}}\left[\log \frac{X^*(k,\alpha)}{\alpha}\right]$$
$$= \lim_{k^{-1}\to 0}\left[\frac{(1-\alpha)k \sin\theta^*(k,\alpha)}{2X^*(k,\alpha)^2} \frac{\partial \theta^*}{\partial k^{-1}}\right]$$
$$= \frac{1-\alpha}{2\alpha} \lim_{k^{-1}\to 0} k \sin\theta^*(k,\alpha)$$

using (31) and (32). Finally, using l'Hospital's rule again,

$$\lim_{k^{-1}\to 0} k \sin\theta^*(k,\alpha) = \lim_{k^{-1}\to 0} \frac{\partial}{\partial k^{-1}}[\sin\theta^*(k,\alpha)]$$
$$= \lim_{k^{-1}\to 0}\left[\cos\theta^*(k,\alpha)\frac{\partial \theta^*}{\partial k^{-1}}\right]$$
$$= \alpha\pi$$

due to (32). Hence, we obtain

$$\lim_{k^{-1}\to 0} \frac{\partial \nu^*}{\partial k^{-1}} = \lim_{k^{-1}\to 0} \frac{\partial}{\partial k^{-1}} \left[k \log \frac{X^*(k,\alpha)}{\alpha} \right] = \frac{(1-\alpha)\pi^2}{2}.$$

This implies that $\nu^*(k,\alpha)$ approaches -1 at the rate stated in the proposition. □

REFERENCES

Azariadis, C., and R. Guesnerie. 1982. "Prophéties créatrices et persistance des théories." *Revue Economique* 33: 787–806.

1986. "Sunspots and Cycles." *Review of Economic Studies* 53: 725–36.

Chiappori, P. A., and R. Guesnerie. 1989. "On Stationary Sunspot Equilibria of Order *k*." In *Economic Complexity: Chaos, Bubbles and Nonlinearity,* W. A. Barnett, S. Geweke, and K. Shell, Eds. Cambridge: Cambridge University Press, pp. 21–44.

1990. "Sunspot Equilibria in Sequential Market Models." Forthcoming in *Handbook of Mathematical Economy,* W. Hildenbrand and H. Sonnenschein, Eds.

Grandmont, J. M., and G. Laroque. 1986. "Stability of Cycles and Expectations." *Journal of Economic Theory* 40: 138–51.

1988. "Stability, Expectations and Predetermined Variables." IMSSS Economic Series, Stanford.

Guesnerie, R. 1986. "Stationary Sunspot Equilibria in an *n*-Commodity World." *Journal of Economic Theory* 40(1): 103–27.

Spear, S. 1984. "Sufficient Conditions for the Existence of Sunspot Equilibria." *Journal of Economic Theory* 35: 360–70.

Woodford, M. 1984. "Indeterminacy of Equilibrium in the Overlapping Generations Model." Mimeo, Columbia University, New York.

1990. "Learning to Believe in Sunspots." *Econometrica* 58: 277–307.

CHAPTER 7

Sunspot equilibrium as a game-theoretical solution concept

Françoise Forges

1 Introduction

It has now become usual to refer to *perfectly correlated extraneous signals,* namely, public signals that do not affect the agents' payoffs, as "sunspots"[1] (see, for instance, the survey of Shell, 1987). The analogy with game-theoretical concepts has been acknowledged, for instance, in Maskin and Tirole (1987), Peck and Shell (1988), and Forges (1986, 1988).

The effects of such signals before the beginning of a (strategic form) game is to convexify the set of Nash equilibrium payoffs. If the model is enriched by allowing the players to observe private extraneous signals (private information on the sunspots) before the beginning of the game, a more interesting solution concept is achieved: the (strategic form) *correlated equilibrium* (Aumann, 1974, 1987). This concept can obviously be used in multistage games, but in these, it is tempting to add extraneous signals before every stage of the game, which yields the *extensive form* correlated equilibrium (Forges, 1986). This concept generalizes Aumann's correlated equilibrium and allows thus for private signals as well. Here, we will consider a variant: the *"extensive form publicly correlated equilibrium,"* where a public signal can be observed before every stage of the game. In dynamic games, the simple observation of a public signal at every stage may have nontrivial effects (see, e.g., Myerson, 1986). In specific contexts like infinitely repeated games with complete information, "extensive form publicly correlated equilibria" are essentially equivalent to Nash equilibria (see Fudenberg and Maskin, 1986).

This chapter was prepared for "Equilibrium Theory and Applications: A Conference in Honor of J. Drèze," the Sixth Symposium in Economic Theory and Econometrics, Louvain-la-Neuve, Belgium, June 9-10, 1989.

[1] An early reference to sunspot in this sense is Cass and Shell (1983). The terminology is an allusion to the work of Jevons (1884).

The common approach to the previous equilibrium concepts is to define them as a Nash equilibrium of an appropriate extension of the underlying game. Since the new equilibria must be interpreted as solutions to the given game, it is crucial to preserve this given game as much as possible. The structure added to the game must be independent of it so that the original game may be played according to its rules. Extraneous signals *before the beginning* of the game are legitimate from this point of view since the rules are strictly followed once the game starts. The same would not hold for signals affecting the payoffs, for instance.

Extraneous signals at every stage of a multistage game require a wider interpretation of the original description of the game. Still, the actions to be taken by the players, the way in which the payoffs depend on actions and information, etc., are not modified and the extraneous signals structure is fully independent of the original game. But the players must be able to perceive something of the outside world, which was not modeled initially.

Apart from some specific examples (e.g., Maskin and Tirole, 1987; Aumann, Peck, and Shell, 1988; see also Azariadis and Guesnerie, 1982, where it is suggested that some agents could believe in sunspots and others, in "moonspots"), the economic literature, where the sunspot equilibrium was introduced (Cass and Shell, 1983), has focused on perfectly correlated extraneous signals. These are described exactly as in the game-theoretical models. However, in the competitive context, an interesting new perspective is often added: Once sunspots become available, *contingent claims markets* (with delivery contingent on the state of sunspot) can be open. The - extrinsic - states of sunspot are just treated as intrinsic states of nature in the Arrow–Debreu model. In particular, one can adopt the equivalent model introduced by Arrow (1953) with a securities market taking place before observing the sunspots. Cass and Shell (1983) showed that sunspots do not modify the competitive equilibria of a standard Arrow–Debreu economy, but they also exhibited a context where "sunspots do matter." A model with this property, in which sunspot equilibria have been extensively studied, is the so-called *overlapping generations model* (see, e.g., Azariadis, 1981; Azariadis and Guesnerie, 1982).

Both mathematical economics and game theory have thus developed solution concepts using extraneous signals. A natural question arises: What is the relationship between the two frameworks? The main motivation for studying this question is to look for a "Cournotian foundation of sunspot equilibrium," as it has now become classical for the competitive equilibrium (in the way initiated by Shapley and Shubik, 1977; see the survey of Mas-Colell, 1982). Such an approach could be strengthened by recent interpretations of the correlated equilibrium (see Aumann, 1987).

Obviously, interesting results would concern games converging to limit economies where sunspots do matter, like overlapping generations models. In these, the concept of sunspot equilibrium does not necessarily go along with the opening of contingent claims markets (see, e.g., Azariadis and Guesnerie, 1982); in this case, with the appropriate game-theoretical framework, sunspot equilibria can be seen as extensive form (publicly) correlated equilibria. To study the effect of adding securities markets once sunspots become observable, Peck and Shell (1988) (henceforth referred to as P-S) have considered sunspot equilibria in a specific class of "market games" (a variant of the model introduced by Shapley and Shubik, 1977, closely related to the one studied in Dubey, Mas-Colell, and Shubik, 1980, and Mas-Colell, 1982).[2] Imperfectly competitive economies seem indeed quite appropriate to compare sunspot and correlated equilibria. Aumann's definition can be applied in a market game as in any other game: a *correlated* equilibrium is a Nash equilibrium of an extension of the market game where before trading on the spot market, each player can observe a private extraneous signal. A correlated equilibrium consists thus of an extraneous signals structure independent of the market game and a Nash equilibrium of the extended game obtained by adding this structure to the market game.

The notion of *sunspot* equilibrium, especially in the imperfectly competitive context, is not so well defined. P-S proceed by constructing a "securities game" from the given market game. They fix a perfectly correlated extraneous signals structure, consisting of s possible states of sunspot, with a given probability distribution. Before observing this public signal, the players are allowed to trade Arrow securities. In the imperfectly competitive context, this market itself is conceived as a Shapley-Shubik market game, with s trading posts. The securities game is described as follows: First, the players trade on this securities market; no player gets any information on the moves (bids, offers) of his opponent; then, one of the s states of sunspot is observed by all the players; finally, the players trade on the initial commodities market. The payoff function in the securities game differs from the original one, not only by taking into account the money transfers from the securities market, but also by involving a punishment for violation of the budget constraints on this market. The punishment consists of confiscating all initial endowments in the original market game, which results in a mixture of the extraneous structure and the given game. The securities game is thus obtained from deep

[2] Articles like Aumann, Peck, and Shell (1988) and Maskin and Tirole (1987) are also attempts to relate sunspot equilibria and correlated equilibria, by introducing imperfectly correlated extraneous signals in economic examples. Unlike these papers, we reserve the terminology "sunspot" for public signals, according to the economic tradition.

modifications in the original one. As observed in Shell (1987), the construction requires that the extraneous structure "becomes part of the rules of the game," with the consequence that the original game is, in fact, not played at all.

Observe that in this approach, if the signals structure changes, the securities game also changes; there is a family of such games. Speaking of "the" securities game is not meaningful, unless the expression is followed by "associated with the given signals structure." Observe also that the apparent three-stage dynamics of the securities game (securities market–sunspot–commodities market) is partly lost by the fact that the players do not get any information on the first stage and thus have no possibility to react to the past actions. Introducing such a possibility would, however, allow scenarios of "threats and punishments" and this would yield solutions that do not correspond to the motivation for sunspot equilibria.

Many other definitions of sunspot equilibrium in market games are conceivable. First, a variety of models of "noncooperative general exchange" are available (see the survey of Mas-Colell, 1982; more recent references are, e.g., Amir et al., 1990; Sahi and Yao, 1989). Second, as observed by Peck and Shell (1989), a contingent claims market for commodities could be considered instead of a securities market (Peck and Shell, 1989, argue – in a specific model – that the results of Arrow, 1953, do not hold in the noncompetitive context). The latter approach is appropriate to define sunspot equilibria unambiguously in *any* market game. This will be useful in the sequel to compare different models.

The goal of our analysis is to shed some light on the relationships between sunspot and correlated equilibria. Let us start with a preliminary remark. We want to solve a given game Γ by different solution concepts, each of them corresponding to a family of extensions of Γ, with different strategy spaces. The only general way to compare the solution concepts is through their set of expected payoffs (i.e., in utility space). More precisely, to a solution concept defined as a Nash equilibrium of a certain form of extension of the game, we associate the set of all Nash equilibrium payoffs that can be achieved in some such extension (we thus consider all possible extensions of the given form and all Nash equilibrium payoffs of every extended game). Following this approach, let $C(\Gamma)$, $EPC(\Gamma)$, and $S(\Gamma)$ denote, respectively, the strategic form (i.e., Aumann) correlated, the extensive form publicly correlated, and the sunspot equilibrium[3] payoffs of Γ (the second set is meaningful if Γ is a multistage game and the last one if Γ is a market game).

[3] From now on, "equilibrium" should always be understood to mean "pure strategies equilibrium."

The spontaneous answer concerning the *link* between sunspot and correlated equilibria is that the two concepts are completely different, since the first one allows for transfers across states of nature and the second may involve partially correlated signals. Obviously, this conceptual argument does not suffice to conclude that in a game G_0, where the two solution concepts make sense (typically, a market game), $C(G_0) \neq S(G_0)$! A "miracle" may happen, especially in situations where the set of equilibrium payoffs are "large." In P-S, an *example* is exhibited of a sunspot equilibrium payoff that could not be the payoff of a correlated equilibrium *with exactly the same signals structure* as the sunspot equilibrium. However, the same payoff can also be achieved at a *Nash equilibrium*. To show this, we characterize all Nash equilibria in a simple class of market games (this is done in the appendix). Section 2.4 contains two examples. In the second one,[4] $C(G_0)$ is *strictly included* in $S(G_0)$. The contribution of this example is however weakened by its extreme degeneracy. The first example consists of a sunspot equilibrium with two states of sunspot: *s* (sunspot) and *ns* (no sunspot); money is transferred from one state to the other in such a way that the allocation of player 1 (resp. 2) when no sunspot (resp. sunspot) occurs is *not individually rational* in the original game (i.e., has a lower utility than the initial endowment). Hence, neither the *s*-state allocation, nor the *ns*-state allocation could be Nash or correlated equilibrium allocations. In particular, a correlated equilibrium with two possible public signals *s* and *ns* and the same allocation as the sunspot equilibrium is not conceivable. However, as in the P-S example, the associated sunspot equilibrium *payoff* is a *Nash equilibrium payoff*. The lesson from the first example is thus that comparisons of equilibrium concepts in terms of scenarios and in terms of payoffs may not yield the same answer. Both examples illustrate how the sunspot equilibrium - with contingent transfers - differs from the correlated equilibrium, so that without specific assumptions, one should not hope that $S(G_0) \subseteq C(G_0)$.

In Section 3, we point out a conceptual relationship between the correlated equilibrium and the sunspot equilibrium, which does not rely on some mysterious phenomenon in payoff space, but enlightens the properties of these solution concepts. We show that the sunspot equilibrium payoffs of a market game G_0 are closely related to the extensive form publicly correlated equilibrium payoffs of a slight modification G of G_0, where money transfers are possible. The result is easier to state if G_0 is modeled as in Amir et al. (1990) and sunspot equilibria are defined through contingent claims market for commodities (but an analog holds in the model used in P-S; this version is presented in Section 3). We construct

[4] I am indebted to J. Peck for his suggestion.

from G_0 a two-stage game G that does not modify G_0 too much, in particular, such that the sets of Nash equilibrium payoffs of G and G_0 coincide: $N(G)=N(G_0)$. We establish that if there are at least three players, $S(G_0)$ coincides with $EPC(G)$ – namely, the set of extensive form publicly correlated equilibrium payoffs of G. $S(G_0)=EPC(G)$ means that all sunspot equilibrium payoffs of G_0 associated with different scenarios of transfers can be achieved as particular correlated equilibrium payoffs of a variant (G) of G_0. This suggests that the sunspot equilibrium can really be treated as a game-theoretical solution concept once the basic game to be studied is modeled properly (as G, instead of G_0).

2 Sunspot and correlated equilibria

2.1 *Perfectly correlated extraneous signals*

Fix an n-person game Γ. *Extraneous* signals are signals that can be observed by the players of Γ, but are completely independent of the game. In particular, they have no effect on the payoffs in Γ. They are *perfectly correlated* if they are identical for all players. More precisely, a perfectly correlated extraneous signals structure consists of r states of signal $1, \ldots, s, \ldots, r$ of respective probability $\pi_1, \ldots, \pi_s, \ldots, \pi_r$.

Given the two distinct independent structures (the game Γ to be played according to well-defined rules and the extraneous signals), one can construct a new game, extending Γ, by letting the players of Γ observe a signal s chosen according to π at some point of Γ.

Adding extraneous signals modifies the original game Γ and is not legitimate if the rules of Γ are taken in a strict sense. The weakest extension consists of allowing the players to observe extraneous signals before the beginning of Γ (i.e., only the strategic form of Γ is considered). Then, even if the players can base their behavior in Γ on extraneous signals, once Γ has begun, its rules are strictly followed.

Let us define $N(\Gamma)$ as the set of all (pure) Nash equilibrium payoffs of Γ and $PC(\Gamma)$ as the set of all (pure) Nash equilibrium payoffs that can be achieved in an extension of Γ, where perfectly correlated extraneous signals can be observed before the beginning of Γ. $PC(\Gamma)$ is referred to as the set of (strategic form) publicly correlated equilibrium payoffs of Γ. $N(\Gamma)$ and $PC(\Gamma)$ (as well as all sets of equilibrium payoffs considered through the chapter) are subsets of $\mathbb{R}^n$. In the extended game, a pure strategy for player h tells how to act on each possible signal s ($s=1, \ldots, r$) and the payoff associated with n-tuples of such strategies is the expected payoff with respect to π. It is well known that

$PC(\Gamma) = \text{Conv}\, N(\Gamma),$

where "Conv" denotes the convexification of a set.

The effect of extraneous signals is thus rather trivial. More interesting phenomena can arise if Γ is a multistage game and extraneous signals can be observed during the course of the game (see Forges, 1986; this is illustrated in Section 3). This requires to interpret the rules of the game in a wider sense than before. Still, the signals structure remains independent of the game structure. Let us define $PC_i(\Gamma)$ in a similar way as $PC(\Gamma)$ with extraneous signals observed (only) just before stage i of Γ ($i = 1, 2, \ldots$). Let $EPC(\Gamma)$ be the set of all (pure) Nash equilibrium payoffs that can be achieved in an extension of Γ, where perfectly correlated extraneous signals can be observed before every stage of Γ. The extended game is thus obtained by adding to Γ a device selecting a public signal before every stage.[5] In an analogous way as in Forges (1986), $EPC(\Gamma)$ can be called the set of "extensive form publicly correlated equilibrium" payoffs of Γ.

Apart from some exceptions, the "sunspots" of the economic literature are perfectly correlated extraneous signals. As we will see, they are associated with wider extensions of the game than the ones considered before.

2.2 *Partially correlated extraneous signals*

Before coming to the extensions used to define sunspot equilibria, let us generalize the previous structure by allowing different players to observe different correlated signals. Define $C(\Gamma)$ in the same way as $PC(\Gamma)$, with partially correlated signals instead of perfectly correlated ones. $C(\Gamma)$ is the set of strategic form correlated equilibrium payoffs of Γ introduced in Aumann (1974) and further developed in Aumann (1987). A set of extensive form correlated equilibrium payoffs can be defined in the same way (see Forges, 1986).

Let us illustrate some of the notions in an example.

Example

Consider the following version of "chicken," where each player has two possible actions: "fight" or "retreat":

	F	R
F	$-2, -2$	$2, -1$
R	$-1, 2$	$1, 1$

[5] Without loss of generality, lotteries preceding different stages may be assumed independent (see Section 3).

This game has two (pure) Nash equilibria: (F, R) and (R, F), with respective payoff $(2, -1), (-1, 2)$ $(\in N)$. If before playing the game, both players can observe whether there is a sunspot or not (this event occurring with probability $\frac{1}{2}$), the following strategies form an equilibrium: player 1 (resp. 2) fights (resp. retreats) if he sees a sunspot and retreats (resp. fights) otherwise. The associated expected payoff is $(\frac{1}{2}, \frac{1}{2})$ $(\in PC = \text{Conv}\, N)$.

Suppose now player 1 can only observe whether there is a sunspot or not (which occurs again with probability $\frac{1}{2}$) and player 2 can only observe whether there is a "moonspot" (which also happens with probability $\frac{1}{2}$). Sunspots and moonspots are independent. The following strategies are in equilibrium: player 1 (resp. 2) fights if he sees a sunspot (resp. a moonspot) and retreats otherwise. The associated expected payoff is $(0, 0)$ $(\in C$; this payoff is, in fact, a mixed Nash equilibrium payoff).

Finally, suppose there are three levels of sunspot activity: high, medium, and low, arising with equal probability $\frac{1}{3}$, and that player 1 (resp. 2) can only distinguish high (resp. low) activity from the other two levels; the tools they use to look at the sunspots have a different sensitivity. Then the following strategies are in equilibrium: player 1 (resp. 2) fights if he sees high (resp. low) activity and retreats otherwise. The associated expected payoff is $(\frac{2}{3}, \frac{2}{3})$ $(\in C$; this payoff does not belong to the convex hull of Nash equilibrium payoffs, even if mixed strategies are allowed).

An important feature of the previous approach is that the original game Γ and the extraneous signal structures are always well-separated. As already observed, this seems a basic requirement if one wants to consider equilibria of an extension of Γ as solutions for Γ itself: The original game has to be played according to its rules at some point. One can admit that the players enter the game with some extraneous information or that they are not completely disconnected from the outside world while they are playing. This does not change the actions to be taken in Γ nor their effect on the payoffs. By preserving carefully the game Γ, one can define properly new sets of solutions for Γ by varying the extraneous signal structures.

2.3 *Transfers and sunspot equilibria*

As recalled in the introduction, the idea behind the sunspot equilibrium introduced by Cass and Shell (1983) is that if perfectly correlated extraneous signals are observable, contingent claims markets can be open before the observation of sunspots. In P-S, a notion of sunspot equilibrium for market games is developed by constructing a market game for Arrow securities. As already pointed out, this is a substantial step toward a game-theoretical notion of sunspot equilibrium. Still, a sunspot equilibrium is conceived as a Nash equilibrium of another market game, with different rules than the original ones.

Let us describe briefly the basic *market games* (the model is adapted from Dubey, Mas-Colell, and Shubik, 1980; and Mas-Colell, 1982; see P-S for details). Each player h $(h=1,\dots,n)$ is endowed with a quantity $\omega_h^j>0$ of commodity j $(j=1,\dots,l)$ and $\omega_h^m\geq 0$ of money. His actions consist of bids $b_h^j\geq 0$ and offers q_h^j, $0\leq q_h^j\leq \omega_h^j$, $j=1,\dots,l$, so that his set Σ_h^c of actions is

$$\Sigma_h^c=\mathbb{R}_+^l\times\prod_{j=1}^{l}[0,\omega_h^j].$$

q_h^j is interpreted as the quantity of commodity of j that player h is offering for sale; b_h^j represents his demand for commodity j, expressed as the amount of money he is ready to devote to purchasing commodity j. Money is just a means of transaction; there is no utility for it. Given b_h^j, q_h^j, $j=1,\dots,l$, $h=1,\dots,n$, let us set

$$p^j=\frac{\Sigma_h b_h^j}{\Sigma_h q_h^j}I\Big(\sum_h q_h^j>0\Big), \tag{1}$$

$$t_h^j=\Big(\frac{b_h^j}{p^j}-q_h^j\Big)I(p^j>0), \tag{2}$$

where I is the "indicator" function, p^j corresponds to the unit price of commodity j, and t_h^j to the net transfer to player h in commodity j. These can take place if each player satisfies his budget constraint. A bankrupt player is severely punished: His whole endowment is confiscated.[6] This yields the following outcome function (with values in $\mathbb{R}_+^l$):

$$x_h^j(\omega_h^m,\sigma^c)=(\omega_h^j+t_h^j)I\Big(\sum_{j=1}^{l}p^jt_h^j\leq\omega_h^m\Big),\quad j=1,\dots,l, \tag{3}$$

where

$$\sigma^c=(b,q)=(b_h,q_h)_{1\leq h\leq n},$$

$$\sigma_h^c=(b_h,q_h)=(b_h^j,q_h^j)_{1\leq j\leq l}.$$

The description is completed by utility functions[7] $u_h:\mathbb{R}_+^l\to\mathbb{R}$. The game is referred to as $G_0(\omega^m)$.

In P-S presentation, $\omega^m=0$ (let us denote the game as G_0 in this case). The previous formulation becomes useful once transfers can be made before the beginning of the game.

[6] As pointed out in the introduction, other market games are conceivable; see what follows.

[7] Standard assumptions (u_h concave, increasing, etc.) can be made, following the results to be proved.

For $\omega^m = 0$, the market game G_0 has a trivial equilibrium, where no player is active on any market ($b_h^j = q_h^j = 0$, $\forall j, h$). The corresponding payoff to player h is $u_h(\omega_h)$. This is also his individual rationality level: By being inactive, player h's opponents prevent him from getting more than $u_h(\omega_h)$. Player h can also guarantee $u_h(\omega_h)$ to himself by playing $b_h = q_h = 0$.

If the utility functions u_h are strictly increasing, the games $G_0(\omega^m)$ have a strict *monotonicity* property. Let σ_{-h}^c be an $(n-1)$-tuple of strategies (different from the status quo) for the opponents of player h and let σ_h^c be a best reply of player h in $G_0(\omega^m)$. If σ_{-h}^c remains fixed, player h can do better with a higher initial fortune $\tilde{\omega}_h^m > \omega_h^m$: there exists $\tilde{\sigma}_h^c$ such that

$$u_h(x_h(\tilde{\omega}_h^m, \tilde{\sigma}_h^c, \sigma_{-h}^c)) > u_h(x_h(\omega_h^m, \sigma^c)).$$

This is easily checked. Since σ_{-h}^c is not the status quo, assume there is activity on commodity market 1: $\sum_{k \neq h} q_1^k > 0$. Because σ_h^c is a best reply, $\sum_j p^j t_h^j \leq \omega_h^m$. If the initial budget of player h is increased from ω_h^m to $\tilde{\omega}_h^m$, player h can increase his bid at commodity market 1 from b_h^1 to $b_h^1 + \beta_h^1$, without violating his budget constraint, by choosing

$$\beta_h^1 \leq (\tilde{\omega}_h^m - \omega_h^m) \frac{\sum_k q_k^1}{\sum_{k \neq h} q_h^1}.$$

This increases player h's net transfer in commodity 1 and thus his utility.

Suppose that before playing G_0, the players can observe a public extraneous signal, that is, a state of sunspot, and that before that, they can trade on a *securities market,* which yields a net money transfer $t_h^m(s)$ to player h if state s occurs.

Suppose r states of sunspots $s = 1, \ldots, r$ can occur, with respective probability $\pi_1, \ldots, \pi_r$. Consider a market game like the one described before, with as many commodities as states of sunspot, commodity s consisting of state-s money, that is, money that can only be used if state s occurs. No player is endowed with any commodity s: purchases of securities will have to be financed by sales of securities. Let $b_h^m(s)$ be player h's bid (in current money) and $q_h^m(s)$ be his offer (in state-s money) at security market s ($s = 1, \ldots, r$). Let σ_h^m be the action of player h ($\sigma_h^m \in \mathbb{R}_+^{2r}$):

$$\sigma_h^m = (b_h^m(s), q_h^m(s))_{1 \leq s \leq r},$$

$$\sigma^m = (\sigma_h^m)_{1 \leq h \leq n}.$$

As in (1) and (2), let $p^m(s)$ be the price of one unit of state-s money (in current money) and $t_h^m(s)$ be the net transfer of player h in state-s money. The budget constraint of player h is

$$\sum_{s=1}^{r} p^m(s)t_h^m(s) \leq 0. \tag{4}$$

According to P-S definition, a *sunspot equilibrium* for G_0, with r states of sunspot $s=1,\ldots,r$ of respective probability π_s is a Nash equilibrium $(b,q)=(b_h^m(s), q_h^m(s); b_h^j(s), q_h^j(s): 1 \leq s \leq r, 1 \leq j \leq l, 1 \leq h \leq n)$ of the market game constituted by the securities market game together with the original market game, with payoff function

$$v_h(b,q) = \sum_{s=1}^{r} \pi_s u_h(x_h(s;b,q)), \quad h=1,\ldots,n,$$

where

$$x_h^j(s;b,q) = (\omega_h^j + t_h^j(s)) I\left(\sum_{j=1}^{l} p^j(s)t_h^j(s) \leq t_h^m(s)\right)$$
$$\times I\left(\sum_{s=1}^{r} p^m(s)t_h^m(s) \leq 0\right), \tag{5}$$

which is easily derived from (3) and the description of the securities market. Observe that failure to satisfy a budget constraint on the securities market or the commodities market is punished similarly by confiscation of all initial endowments, which assumes *interaction* between the different structures.

Let $S(G_0)$ be the set of *sunspot equilibrium payoffs* of G_0 (obtained by varying the extraneous signals structures and the equilibrium strategies in the corresponding modified games).

Remark 1. If sunspot equilibria are to be interpreted as solutions to the given game G_0, it is important to preserve G_0 as much as possible. The previous definition is not satisfactory in this respect since it modifies the payoff function of G_0; it entails playing a different game, obtained by combining the original one and the securities market. Obviously, one could not take account of transfers contingent on the states of sunspot without modifying the payoff function somehow. But one would like to adopt a presentation of sunspot equilibria where the players come to play the original game with some extraneous money in their pocket, in the same way as they come with some extraneous signal in their mind in the context of correlated equilibria. For instance, all transfers can be cancelled as soon as one agent violates his budget constraint (4). Then, for each state s of sunspot, a game of the same form is played, namely, $G_0(\omega^m(s))$, where $\omega^m(s) = t^m(s)$ if (4) is satisfied *for every h*, 0 otherwise. The drawback of this approach is that it will likely enlarge the set of sunspot equilibrium payoffs. In the new scenario, deviations of an agent leading to the violation of the budget constraint of another are prevented by the threat of a zero transfer. Such deviations have no consequence in the original context.[8] Nevertheless, the set of sunspot equilibrium payoffs does not change with weaker punishments than in (5), namely, by setting $\omega_h^m(s) = t_h^m(s)$ if (4) is satisfied (for h), 0 otherwise and playing $G_0(\omega^m(s))$ if s occurs. Such formulations, with a game $G_0(\omega^m(s))$ of the same class, indexed by a parameter ("initial fortune of the players"), can be useful to generalize the sunspot equilibrium solution concept to a purely game-theoretical context.

Remark 2. It could be tempting to adopt a definition of sunspot equilibrium related with extensions of G_0, where the players would get information from the securities market (at least their own transfer) and where violation of a budget constraint by one player might affect the others (so as to avoid extraneous support). This would likely enlarge $S(G_0)$.

Remark 3. As suggested in Peck and Shell (1989), sunspot equilibria in market games can also be defined directly through *contingent claims markets for commodities:* r states of sunspot lead to $l.r$ commodities (j,s), $j=1,\dots,l$, $s=1,\dots,r$, interpreted as contracts for delivery of good j if state s occurs. A sunspot equilibrium of G_0 is then defined as a Nash equilibrium of the market game similar to G_0, with $l.r$ commodities, initial endowments $\omega_h(j,s) = \omega_h^j$, $s=1,\dots,r$, and utility functions v_h. This definition is certainly legitimate in view of the economic tradition. The advantage of this approach is that it yields a clean *definition of sunspot equilibrium in any* market game, including the recent models of Amir et al. (1990) and Sahi and Yao (1989).

Remark 4. The last remark can be useful because some models of market games may be more tractable than others to establish given properties. For instance, as a first step toward a "canonical representation" (see Forges, 1986) of sunspot equilibria or simply to get a more elegant result in Section 3, one would like to prove that $S(G_0)$ is *convex*. This is easy if G_0 is a market game in the sense of Amir et al. (1987), consisting of $l(l-1)$ trading posts (i,j), $i,j=1,\dots,l$, where commodities i and j can be exchanged for each other. Consider two sunspot equilibria, with r and r' states, respectively; the first one consists of $l.r$ markets and the second of $l.r'$ *different* markets. A single sunspot equilibrium can be constructed from a lottery over the two given equilibria, in the obvious way: $l(r+r')$ markets are open, but each player just keeps using the same strategy so that the lr (resp. lr') goods of the first (resp. second) equilibrium are traded for each other. In other words, all markets $[(i,s),(j,s')]$ with

[8] More can be said in the case of two agents.

$1 \le s \le r$ and $1 \le s' \le r'$ are closed. Recall that in the noncompetitive context, a market is closed as soon as no player is active on it and a single player cannot gain in bidding at a market where his opponents are inactive. The argument showing that $S(G_0)$ is convex does not work for market games with fiat money like the P-S model (independently of the definitions of sunspot equilibrium, with securities or with contingent commodities). In trying to merge two sunspot equilibria as before, one faces the problem of possible interaction between market (i,s) and (j,s').

2.4 *Examples*

We start with a market game similar to the one in P-S:

$$n = l = 2, \qquad \omega_1 = (7,63), \qquad \omega_2 = (63,7),$$
$$u_h(x^1,x^2) = \log x^1 + \log x^2, \quad h = 1,2.$$

Let us describe a sunspot equilibrium for this game, with two states of sunspots ("s" – sunspot; "ns" – no sunspot), of probability $\frac{1}{2}$. When a sunspot occurs, only commodity 1 market is open. (In this imperfectly competitive context, a market is open if the players are active on it and closed otherwise. As soon as one player does not participate at a market, bidding on that market is worthless for the other.) Player 2 sells 3 units of commodity 1 to player 1, who finances this purchase with 3 units of "sunspot money" acquired on the securities market, in exchange of 3 units of "no sunspot money." The situation where no sunspot is observed is described in a symmetric way. The strategies and allocations of commodities are as follows:

$$b_1^m(s) = 6 = b_2^m(ns), \qquad b_2^m(s) = 3 = b_1^m(ns),$$
$$q_1^m(s) = 3 = q_2^m(ns), \qquad q_2^m(s) = 6 = q_1^m(ns),$$

so that $p^m(s) = 1 = p^m(ns)$ and $t_1^m(s) = -t_2^m(s) = 3 = -t_1^m(ns) = t_2^m(ns)$;

$$b_1^1(s) = 10 = b_2^2(ns), \qquad b_2^1(s) = 60 = b_1^2(ns),$$
$$q_1^1(s) = 7 = q_2^2(ns), \qquad q_2^1(s) = 63 = q_1^2(ns),$$

while all other bids and offers are zero. Hence, $p^1(s) = 1 = p^2(ns)$, $t_1^1(s) = -t_2^1(s) = 3 = -t_1^2(ns) = t_2^2(ns)$. The computation to check that this is indeed a sunspot equilibrium can be found in the appendix (Section A.2). The corresponding allocation of commodities is

$$(x_1^1(s), x_1^2(s)) = (10,63), \qquad (x_2^1(s), x_2^2(s)) = (60,7),$$
$$(x_1^1(ns), x_1^2(ns)) = (7,60), \qquad (x_2^1(ns), x_2^2(ns)) = (63,10),$$

with the associated payoffs

$$u_1 = \tfrac{1}{2}(\log 10 + \log 63 + \log 7 + \log 60) = u_2.$$

The main feature of this example is that in the original game, the allocation of commodities (7, 60) (resp. (60, 7)) when a sunspot (resp. no sunspot) occurs would *not* be *individually rational* for player 1 (resp. 2). The transfers thus modify the original game in a substantial way: they change the individual rationality levels of the players.

Without transfers across the states of nature, a phenomenon like before could never arise at an equilibrium. In particular, the previous *scenario* does not correspond to a correlated equilibrium. More precisely, given the perfectly correlated signals, this scenario does not consist of a lottery over Nash equilibria.

Nevertheless, the corresponding expected *payoff* belongs to Conv $N(G_0)$ and thus to $C(G_0)$. Indeed, it can be checked that (10, 60) and (60, 10) can be achieved as Nash equilibrium allocations (see Section A.1 of the appendix). u_1 and u_2 are thus also the payoffs obtained by "convexifying" between this equilibrium and the status quo, (7, 63) and (63, 7). Moreover, one can even check that (u_1, u_2) belongs to $N(G_0)$, that is, is simply a *Nash* equilibrium payoff (see Section A.2 of the appendix).

This last pattern is shared by the P-S example: the corresponding expected payoff also belongs to $N(G_0)$ (this can be checked exactly as before). But in P-S, the allocations associated with the two different states are all individually rational.

Remark 5. An interesting question concerns an intermediate means of comparison between sunspot and correlated equilibria in this example: Is there a correlated equilibrium with asymmetric information and a partition $\{S_s, S_{ns}\}$ of the states (pairs of extraneous signals) of positive probability such that the allocation at each state in S_s (resp. S_{ns}) is the s-state (resp. ns-state) allocation of the sunspot equilibrium? (The new aspect is that s and ns are not observed directly by the agents.) Although some elements of (negative) answer are available, to my knowledge, the question is not completely solved.

Let us turn to a second example, even more caricatural than the previous one (the underlying economy is degenerate):

$$n = l = 2, \qquad \omega_1 = (0, 1), \qquad \omega_2 = (1, 0),$$
$$u_h(x_1, x_2) = [\min(x_1, x_2)],$$

where $[x]$ denotes the integer part of x. The two goods can thus be interpreted as left and right gloves. The only pair of *feasible* payoffs is (0, 0), so that

$$N(G_0) = C(G_0) = \{(0,0)\}.$$

The intuitive reason is that player 1 (say) can only acquire good 1 in exchange of some amount of good 2. However,

$$(\tfrac{1}{2}, \tfrac{1}{2}) \in S(G_0).$$

Transfers contingent on the states of sunspots will allow the agents to exchange a "left glove if sunspot" against a "right glove if no sunspot." Consider the same signals structure and the same market structure as in the previous example; the trivial strategies ($b_1^m(s) = q_1^m(ns) = b_2^m(ns) = q_2^m(s) = b_1^1(s) = q_1^2(ns) = b_2^2(ns) = q_2^1(s) = 1$, the other bids and offers are 0) form an equilibrium. The allocation of player 1 (resp. 2) is $(1,1)$ when a (resp. no) sunspot is observed.

This example may be too degenerate to provide a final answer to the question of the possible inclusion of $S(G_0)$ in $C(G_0)$. It illustrates at least that the contingent transfers modify completely the achievable outcomes, which does not arise in the context of correlated equilibria.

Remark 6. Similar examples can be constructed in the context of the model described at the end of Section 2.3.

3 A way of viewing sunspot equilibria as correlated equilibria

The possibility of transfers involved in the sunspot equilibrium makes it difficult to get $S(G_0)$ as the set of solutions to G_0 associated with a known game-theoretical concept based on extraneous signals. Here we show that this becomes possible if G_0 is first modified slightly (this is made precise in what follows) into a game G. In most of the section, G_0 is the P-S market game described in Section 2.3. At the end, we show that the result takes a stronger form in another context.

3.1 *Extended game G*

As G_0, G has n players. For most further results, it will be assumed that $n \geq 3$. G is played in two stages.

Stage 1 consists of a securities market. There are countably many potential markets 1, 2, ... Each player can be active in finitely many markets, that is, each player h chooses $(b_h^m(i), q_h^m(i)) \in \mathbb{R}_+^2$ for $i = 1, \ldots, r_h$ (r_h is thus the largest index of market where player h is active).[9] No information is given on the choices made by other players.

[9] Obviously, player h can set $b_h^m(i) = q_h^m(i) = 0$ for as many i's as he wants.

At *Stage 2,* each player h decides which securities market $z_h \in \{1, 2, \ldots, r_h\}$ is effective and chooses an action $\sigma_h^c \in \Sigma_h^c$, that is, makes a decision in $\{1, 2, \ldots, r_h\} \times \Sigma_h^c$ (recall Section 2.3).

To describe the payoffs in G, let us set

$$\sigma_h^m = (b_h^m(i), q_h^m(i))_{1 \le i \le r_h},$$
$$\sigma^m = (\sigma_h^m)_{1 \le h \le n},$$
$$z = (z_h)_{1 \le h \le n},$$

let us define $\bar{z}$ $(= \bar{z}(z))$ as the security market chosen by most players if such a majority emerges, $\bar{z} = 1$ otherwise, and set $r = \max r_h$. The following outcome to player h is associated with the n-tuple (σ^m, z, σ^c) of actions in G:

$$y_h^j(\sigma^m, z, \sigma^c) = (\omega_h^j + t_h^j) I\left(\sum_{j=1}^{l} p^j t_h^j \le t_h^m(\bar{z})\right) I\left(\sum_{i=1}^{r} p^m(i) t_h^m(i) \le 0\right).$$

Payoffs are evaluated as before, using u_h (see (5)).

Observe that in G, there is no move of nature, no signal of any kind. Stage 1 can be interpreted as follows: Before making decisions in the basic game G_0, the players have the possibility of realizing transfers, using a securities market, exactly as in the previous section, except that the number of markets is not fixed. A security market is open as soon as some agents are active in that market. Obviously, transfers can only occur if there are at least two agents active on the same market. To avoid the problem of threats, as in Section 2, we do not allow the players to observe the actions of their opponents on the securities market so that they cannot react to these actions at Stage 2. To figure out how G is played, one can think that, at Stage 1, the players transmit simultaneously their bids and offers to a broker, a central agency operating the securities market. Later on, at Stage 2, possibly after having observed some extraneous event (but not necessarily; this is not modeled in G), each player tells the broker which security market is effective, that is, which transfer is due to him. To decide on an actual state $\bar{z}$ from the reports of the players, the broker uses majority rule if possible; otherwise, he decides on state 1; he distributes the transfers $t_h^m(\bar{z})$ if they are feasible. To complete the scenario of G, $G_0(t^m(\bar{z}))$ is essentially played at Stage 2, that is, the payoff of player h when (σ^m, z, σ^c) is played is the payoff resulting from σ^c and an initial fortune of $t_h^m(\bar{z})$. G is the combination of two distinct parts: a general institution to trade securities, independent of the particular set of states that can occur (σ^m, z and the resulting transfers $t^m(\bar{z})$); and the game G_0.

One realizes easily that without extraneous signals between Stage 1 and Stage 2, the security market is useless, that is, G amounts to G_0. This is formalized in the next section. Once sunspots are added between Stage 1 and Stage 2, one may expect to get equilibria equivalent to sunspot equilibria. This is established in Section 3.3. As already announced, the advantage of the new formulation, that is, of the game G, is that the security market is modeled independently of the extraneous signals so that one can obtain the different sunspot equilibria of G_0 by varying only the extraneous signals added between Stage 1 and Stage 2.

3.2 *Nash equilibria in G*

The simple idea behind the result is that without extraneous uncertainty, there is no need for insurance.

Proposition 1. $N(G)=N(G_0)$.

Proof: $N(G_0)\subseteq N(G)$ is quite obvious. Let σ^c be a Nash equilibrium of G_0. Complete it with $b_h^m=q_h^m=0$, $z_h=1$, $h=1,\dots,n$ (in particular, no activity on the security market).

To prove that conversely $N(G)\subseteq N(G_0)$, let (σ^m, z, σ^c) be an equilibrium of G. Let us show that necessarily $t_h^m(\bar{z})=0$, $h=1,\dots,n$ (hence, σ^c must be a Nash equilibrium of the original game G_0, where each player has no initial budget – $\omega^m=0$ – and this determines the payoff). If $t_h^m(\bar{z})\neq 0$ for some h, then $t_h^m(\bar{z})<0$ for some h. By monotonicity (see Section 2.3), player h could increase his payoff by being inactive on the securities market (so as to get a zero transfer) and modifying his action σ_h^c at Stage 2. □

Remark 7. We get immediately that

$$PC(G)=\text{Conv}\,N(G_0).$$

3.3 *Correlated equilibria in G*

Recall that $S(G_0)$ is the set of all sunspot equilibrium payoffs of G_0 and that $EPC(G)$ is the set of all extensive form publicly correlated equilibrium payoffs of G. From now on, we assume $n\geq 3$. We will establish an analog of the above for sunspot equilibria:

Proposition 2. $EPC(G)=\text{Conv}\,S(G_0)$.

The result can be divided into two parts:

$$PC_2(G)=S(G_0) \quad \text{and} \quad EPC(G)=\text{Conv}\,PC_2(G).$$

Recall that $PC_2(G)$ is the set of all equilibrium payoffs that can be achieved in an extension of G, where the players observe the same extraneous signal between Stage 1 and Stage 2. We start with the first part.

Lemma 1. $PC_2(G) = S(G_0)$.

Proof: Take a payoff y in $S(G_0)$. Let $\{1, \ldots, r\}$, $(\pi_1, \ldots, \pi_r)$, (σ^m, σ^c) be, respectively, the associated set of states of sunspot, probability distribution over this set, and equilibrium strategies (following the definition of Section 2.3). To show that $y \in PC_2(G)$, we must extend G by adding signals just before Stage 2 and construct an equilibrium of the extended game with payoff y. Once they observe a signal before Stage 2, the players may choose their actions z, σ^c as a function of this signal. Let the signals before Stage 2 be exactly as the sunspots; let the strategy of player h be $r_h = r$ and $\sigma_h^m(s)$, $s = 1, \ldots, r$, as in the sunspot equilibrium, at Stage 1 and $z_h(s) = s$, $\sigma_h^c(s)$ if s is observed, at Stage 2.

If all the opponents of player h report s when s is observed before Stage 2, $\bar{z}(s) = s$ whatever player h does and deviation there is useless. The sunspot equilibrium conditions show that no other deviation can be profitable.

Now let $y \in PC_2(G)$. Let us specify an extension of G by k possible common signals $s = 1, \ldots, k$ of respective probability $\pi(s)$ and equilibrium strategies r_h, σ_h^m, z_h, σ_h^c, $h = 1, \ldots, n$, yielding the payoff y in the extended game. Keep the extraneous signals structure.

A sunspot equilibrium $(\hat{\sigma}^m, \hat{\sigma}^c)$ with payoff y can be constructed by taking $\hat{\sigma}^c = \sigma^c$ and $\hat{\sigma}^m(s) = \sigma^m(\bar{z}(s))$. Observe that if s is not "effective" (i.e., of the form $\bar{z}(\lambda)$ for some λ), then $t_h^m(s) = 0$ $(h = 1, \ldots, n)$. Otherwise, let h be such that $t_h^m(s) > 0$. Let us show that player h can gain in deviating in the context of $PC_2(G)$. Let him choose $\tilde{b}_h^m(s) = \tilde{q}_h^m(s) = 0$ (instead of $b_h^m(s), q_h^m(s)$) and increase $b_h^m(s')$ to $\tilde{b}_h^m(s') = b_h^m(s') + \beta_h^m$ in order to get $\tilde{t}_h^m(s') > t_h^m(s')$ for an effective state s'; this can be done in such a way that

$$\tilde{p}^m(s')\tilde{t}_h^m(s') \leq p^m(s')t_h^m(s') + p^m(s)t_h^m(s),$$

that is, without violating the securities market budget constraint (one can proceed as for showing that market games satisfy monotonicity). Player h becomes richer in state s' and by monotonicity, he can increase his payoff in that state. □

We come to the second result. Observe that $PC_2(G)$ is not necessarily *convex* (as a trivial example, suppose the game of the example of Section 2.2 is played at Stage 1 and that payoffs at Stage 2 are always 0, the final payoff being the sum of the stage payoffs).

Lemma 2. *For any two-stage game G, $EPC(G) = \text{Conv}\, PC_2(G)$.*

Proof: Obviously, only that $EPC(G) \subseteq PC_2(G)$ has to be proved. First, observe that every equilibrium payoff in $EPC(G)$ can be realized by means of a device selecting the signal before Stage 1 independently of the signal before Stage 2. If the signals before the second stage, say, in S_2, are chosen according to $\pi(\cdot \mid s_1)$ for every signal $s_1 \in S_1$ preceding Stage 1, one modifies the device by taking new signals before Stage 2, consisting of $|S_1|$-tuples of the form $(s_2(s_1))_{s_1 \in S_1}$ with the $s_2(s_1)$'s chosen independently of each other, according to $\pi(s_2 \mid s_1)$. The players having perfect recall, they can identify the useful component of the vector of signals at Stage 2.

Thus, $EPC(G)$ is the union over all possible devices d_1 and d_2 acting, respectively, before Stage 1 and Stage 2 of the sets of Nash equilibrium payoffs of the extended games $G_{d_1+d_2}$ obtained by adding such devices d_1 and d_2 to G. Fix d_2 and vary d_1: we get the convexification of the Nash equilibrium payoffs of G_{d_2}: $EPC(G) = \bigcup_{d_2} \text{Conv}\, N(G_{d_2})$. Consequently, $EPC(G) \subseteq \text{Conv} \bigcup_{d_2} N(G_{d_2}) = \text{Conv}\, PC_2(G)$. □

The relationship between the different sets of equilibrium payoffs can be summarized as follows:

$$
\begin{aligned}
N(G_0) &= N(G) \subseteq \text{Conv}\, N(G_0) \\
&= \text{Conv}\, N(G) = PC(G) \subseteq S(G_0) \subseteq \text{Conv}\, S(G_0) = EPC(G).
\end{aligned}
$$

Remark 8. If $S(G_0)$ is convex, the result becomes $S(G_0) = EPC(G)$. As observed at the end of Section 2.3 (Remark 4), such a property is easily obtained if G_0 is modeled as in Amir et al. (1990) and sunspot equilibria are defined by means of contingent markets for commodities.

4 Concluding remarks

The previous sections are an attempt to clarify the relationships between sunspot equilibria and game-theoretical solution concepts. In the context of market games G_0, we have a (rather degenerate) example of a payoff in $S(G_0) \setminus C(G_0)$. We did not address the question of the inclusion of $C(G_0)$ in $S(G_0)$. The concepts involve different scenarios, since Aumann's correlated equilibrium relies on asymmetric signals that are not modeled in the sunspot equilibrium. Elements of the answer are given in Aumann, Peck, and Shell (1988) and Maskin and Tirole (1987), but these examples pertain to the competitive context.

In this chapter, we tried to argue that it might be easier to compare sunspot equilibria with *extensive form* correlated equilibria, rather than with strategic form correlated equilibria. The previous approach is convincing in this respect in market games G_0, where it is established that $S(G_0)$ is a *convex* set. Sunspot equilibria without "additional" contingent claims market in overlapping generations models (as considered by Azariadis and Guesnerie, 1982) could also provide an appropriate framework to develop this idea. It could take a precise form in a dynamic market game with n "young" players at each stage $t=1,2,\ldots$, alive until the next period, in which they become "old" (there are thus n young and n old players at each stage). Each young player is endowed with one unit of time, which he can devote to leisure and production of a commodity; this is the only decision to be made. The commodity is consumed by the old players, who finance their purchases with the money earned when young. Suppose that at stage t, each old player h possesses an amount ω_h^t of money ($h=1,\ldots,n$) and each young player k decides to produce q_k^t ($k=1,\ldots,n$); the unit price of the commodity can be formed naively as

$$p_t=\frac{\sum_h \omega_h^t}{\sum_k q_k^t}$$

and depends only on the strategy of the young players at stage t. Obviously, if there are many players, individual effects become negligible. The consumption of old player h is

$$x_h^t=\frac{\omega_h^t}{p_t}.$$

Hence, the payoff of player k, young at stage t, may be evaluated as $u(q_k^t, x_k^{t+1})$ with x_k^{t+1} computed from $\omega_k^{t+1}=p_t q_k^t$ and p_{t+1}. If he cannot influence prices, player h's problem is to choose q_k^t to maximize $u(q_k^t, p_t q_k^t/p_{t+1})$. It is thus not difficult to associate a market game with an overlapping generations model; with this formulation, sunspot equilibria are just extensive form publicly[10] correlated equilibria. Once sunspots are observable before each stage t, young players can condition their decision on the state of sunspot, so that the prices depend on the state of sunspots. At a Nash equilibrium of the extended game, where sunspots are observed before every stage, each player takes the others' strategy as given and thus anticipates the effect of sunspots on prices. It could be worthwhile to investigate this model or more sophisticated versions of it by studying the extensive form correlated equilibria of versions with finitely many players (thus influencing prices) and by replicating the players to get results on the limit economy.

[10] Most often, but not always; recall the "moonspots" of Azariadis and Guesnerie (1982).

Appendix

A.1 *Necessary and sufficient conditions for Nash equilibrium transfers*

We consider market games of the form of Section 2.4, namely, with two agents, two commodities, initial endowments (ω^1, ω^2), (ω^2, ω^1) for agent 1 and agent 2, respectively, and utility functions

$$u_h(x^1, x^2) = \log x^1 + \log x^2, \quad h = 1, 2.$$

Let b_h^j, q_h^j ($j = 1, 2$; $h = 1, 2$) be given bids and offers. As in (2) and (3), the corresponding prices and net transfers are

$$p_j = \frac{b_1^j + b_2^j}{q_1^j + q_2^j},$$

$$t_1^1 = \frac{b_1^1}{p_1} - q_1^1 = q_2^1 - \frac{b_2^1}{p_1} = -t_2^1 = t^1, \tag{A.1}$$

$$t_1^2 = \frac{b_1^2}{p_2} - q_1^2 = q_2^2 - \frac{b_2^2}{p_2} = -t_2^2 = -t^2,$$

where the last equalities are definitions of t^1 and t^2, respectively. Observe that the definition of p_1 and p_2 can be recovered from (A.1). We now show that t^1, t^2 *are Nash equilibrium transfers if and only if either*

$$0 \le t^i \le \omega^2, \quad \text{if } \omega^1 < \omega^2, \quad i = 1, 2,$$

or

$$-\omega^1 \le t^i \le 0, \quad \text{if } \omega^2 < \omega^1,$$

and

$$\frac{\omega^2 t^i(\omega^1 + t^i)}{\omega^2 - t^i} \le \frac{\omega^1 t^j(\omega^2 - t^j)}{\omega^1 + t^j}, \quad i, j = 1, 2_{i \ne j}. \tag{A.2}$$

Proof: Observe that player 1's budget constraint

$$p_1 t_1^1 + p_2 t_1^2 \le 0$$

can be written as

$$b_2^1 - q_2^1 p_1 + b_2^2 - q_2^2 p_2 \le 0,$$

which depends on player 1's strategy through the prices only. A similar expression can obviously be obtained for player 2.

Set

$$L_1 = \log(\omega^1 + t^1) + \log(\omega^2 - t^2) - \lambda(q_2^1 p_1 + q_2^2 p_2),$$
$$L_2 = \log(\omega^2 - t^1) + \log(\omega^1 - t^2) - \mu(q_1^1 p_1 + q_1^2 p_2).$$

Following (A.1), t^1 and t^2 can be expressed as functions of p_1, p_2 and player 2's strategy. Player 1's maximization problem thus can be solved by taking the derivative of L_1 with respect to p_1 and p_2; similarly for player 2.

t^1 and t^2 are Nash equilibrium transfers if and only if there exist b_h^j, q_h^j $(j=1,2;\ h=1,2)$, λ, μ such that

$$\frac{\partial L_i}{\partial p_j}=0, \quad i,j=1,2, \tag{A.3}$$

$$p_1t^1-p_2t^2=0, \tag{A.4}$$

$$\lambda>0, \qquad \mu>0, \qquad b_h^j\geq 0, \quad j,h=1,2,$$

$$0\leq\frac{q_1^1}{q_2^2}\leq\omega^1, \qquad 0\leq\frac{q_2^1}{q_1^2}\leq\omega^2,$$

$$x_h^j\geq 0, \ j,h=1,2, \quad \text{namely,}\ \omega^1+t^j\geq 0,$$
$$\omega^2-t^j\geq 0, \ j=1,2.$$

Equations (A.2) give the b_h^j's as functions of λ, μ, p_1, p_2, ω^1, ω^2, x_h^j; the constraints $b_h^j\geq 0$ are then satisfied as soon as the others are. Substituting the b_h^j's and x_h^j's in (A.1) yields the q_h^j's as functions of t^j, λ, μ, ω^j ($j=1,2$). Since the b_h^j's and p_j's will be determined up to a positive multiplicative constant, (A.4) yields $p_1=|t^2|$, $p_2=|t^1|$. We have come to: t^1, t^2 are Nash equilibrium transfers if and only if

$$\omega^1+t^j\geq 0, \quad \omega^2-t^j\geq 0, \quad j=1,2,$$

and either $t^1, t^2\geq 0$ and $\exists\lambda,\mu>0$ such that

$$0\leq\frac{t^1}{\mu t^2(\omega^2-t^1)-1}\leq\omega^1,$$

$$0\leq\frac{t^2}{1-\mu t^1(\omega^1+t^2)}\leq\omega^2,$$

$$0\leq\frac{t^1}{1-\lambda t^2(\omega^1+t^1)}\leq\omega^1,$$

$$0\leq\frac{t^2}{\lambda t^1(\omega^2-t^2)-1}\leq\omega^2,$$

or $t^1, t^2\leq 0$ and $\exists\lambda,\mu$ such that similar inequalities (obtained by setting $p^1=-t^2$, $p^2=-t^1$, the ones before corresponding to the case $p^1=t^2$, $p^2=t^1$). The result is immediately deduced from this; one notices that the first (resp. second) set of inequalities (A.2) is contradictory for $\omega^1>\omega^2$ (resp. $\omega^1<\omega^2$).

Remark A.1. To check that (u_1, u_2) is a pair of Nash equilibrium payoffs of the preceding market game, one can solve

$$\log(\omega^1+t^1)+\log(\omega^2-t^2)=u_1,$$

$$\log(\omega^2-t^1)+\log(\omega^1+t^2)=u_2,$$

for t^1, t^2 and use the previous conditions. The system can be rewritten as

$$\frac{c_1}{\omega^1+t^1}+\frac{c_2}{\omega^2-t^1}=\omega^1+\omega^2,$$

$$\frac{c_1}{\omega^2-t^2}+\frac{c_2}{\omega^1+t^2}=\omega^1+\omega^2,$$

where $c_j=e^{u_j}$.

A.2 *Computation of the first example of Section 2.4*

Player 1's problem is to maximize

$$\log[7+t_1^1(s)]+\log[63+t_1^2(ns)]$$

under the constraints

$$p^m(s)t_1^m(s)+p^m(ns)t_1^m(ns)\le 0,$$

$$p_s t_1^1(s)\le t_1^m(s),$$

$$p_{ns}t_1^2(ns)\le t_2^m(ns),$$

where p_s (resp. p_{ns}) is the unit price of commodity 1 (resp. 2) if state s (resp. ns) occurs. As in (A.1), all expressions can be rewritten in terms of player 2's strategy and prices, which gives

$$\max\left(\log\left(1-\frac{6}{7p_s}\right)+\log\left(1-\frac{1}{7p_{ns}}\right)\right)$$

subject to

$$6p^m(s)+3p^m(ns)-9\le 0,$$

$$63p_s+\frac{3}{p^m(s)}-66\le 0,$$

$$7p_{ns}+\frac{6}{p^m(ns)}-13\le 0,$$

which is solved by $p^m(s)=p^m(ns)=p_s=p_{ns}=1$.

Using the previous remark, one can check that the payoff (u_1, u_2) associated with this example is a Nash equilibrium payoff: the transfers satisfy

$t^1 = t^2 = t$ and t is one of the solutions of $t^2 - 56t + 73.3928 = 0$ ($t =$ 1.3428).

REFERENCES

Amir, R., S. Sahi, M. Shubik, and S. Yao. 1990. "A Strategic Market Game with Complete Markets." *Journal of Economic Theory* 51(1): 126–43.

Arrow, K. 1953. "Le rôle des valeurs boursières pour la répartition la meilleure des risques." Econométrie, Colloques Internationaux du CNRS, Paris, 40, 41–7; English translation: 1964. "The Role of Securities in the Optimal Allocation of Risk Bearing." *Review of Economic Studies* 31: 91–6.

Aumann, R. 1974. "Subjectivity and Correlation in Randomized Strategies." *Journal of Mathematical Economics* 1(1): 67–96.

1987. "Correlated Equilibrium as an Expression of Bayesian Rationality." *Econometrica* 55(1): 1–18.

Aumann, R., J. Peck, and K. Shell. 1988. "Asymmetric Information and Sunspot Equilibria: A Family of Simple Examples." CAE Working Paper 88-34, Cornell University, Ithaca, NY.

Azariadis, C. 1981. "Self-Fulfilling Prophecies." *Journal of Economic Theory* 25(3): 380–96.

Azariadis, C., and R. Guesnerie. 1982. "Prophéties créatrices et persistance des théories." *Revue Economique* 33: 787–806.

Cass, D., and K. Shell. 1983. "Do Sunspots Matter?" *Journal of Political Economy* 91(2): 193–227.

Dubey, P., A. Mas-Colell, and M. Shubik. 1980. "Efficiency Properties of Strategic Market Games: An Axiomatic Approach." *Journal of Economic Theory,* Symposium Issue, 339–63.

Forges, F. 1986. "An Approach to Communication Equilibria." *Econometrica* 54(6): 1375–85.

1988. "Can Sunspots Replace a Mediator?" *Journal of Mathematical Economics* 17: 347–68.

Fudenberg, D., and E. Maskin. 1986. "The Folk Theorem in Repeated Games with Discounting or with Incomplete Information." *Econometrica* 54: 533–54.

Jevons, W. 1884. *Investigations in Currency and Finance.* London: Macmillan.

Mas-Colell, A. 1982. "The Cournotian Foundations of Walrasian Equilibrium Theory: An Exposition of Recent Theory." In *Advances in Economic Theory,* W. Hildenbrand, Ed. Cambridge: Cambridge University Press, pp. 183–224.

Maskin, E., and J. Tirole. 1987. "Correlated Equilibria and Sunspots." *Journal of Economic Theory* 43(2): 364–73.

Myerson, R. 1986. "Multistage Games with Communication." *Econometrica* 54(2): 323–58.

Peck, J., and K. Shell. 1988. "Market Uncertainty: Correlated Equilibrium and Sunspot Equilibrium in Imperfectly Competitive Economies." CAE Working Paper 88-22, Cornell University, Ithaca, NY.

1989. "On the Nonequivalence of the Arrow-Securities Game and the Contingent Commodities Game." In *Economic Complexity: Chaos, Sunspots, Bubbles, and Nonlinearity,* W. A. Barnett, J. Geweke, and K. Shell, Eds. Cambridge: Cambridge University Press, Pt. I, Chap. 4, pp. 61–85.

Sahi, S., and S. Yao. 1989. "The Noncooperative Equilibria of a Trading Economy with Complete Markets and Consistent Prices." *Journal of Mathematical Economics* 18: 325–46.

Shapley, L., and M. Shubik. 1977. "Trade Using One Commodity as a Means of Payment." *Journal of Political Economy* 85(5): 937–68.

Shell, K. 1987. "Sunspot Equilibrium." In *The New Palgrave Dictionary of Economics,* Vol. 4, J. Eatwell, M. Milgate, and P. Newmann, Eds. London: Macmillan, pp. 549–51.

CHAPTER 8

Provision of quality and power of incentive schemes in regulated industries

Jean-Jacques Laffont and Jean Tirole

1 Introduction

An unregulated monopolist may have two incentives to provide quality: the "sales incentive" and the "reputation incentive." When quality is observed by consumers before purchasing (search good), a reduction in quality reduces sales, and thus revenue as the monopoly price exceeds marginal cost. In contrast, when quality is observed by consumers only after purchasing (experience good), the monopolist has no incentive to supply quality unless consumers may repeat their purchase in the future. The provision of quality is then linked with the monopolist's desire to keep its reputation and preserve future profits.

In this chapter, we investigate whether similar incentives to provide quality exist in a regulated environment. Before doing so, it is useful to distinguish between *observable* and *verifiable* quality. Quality is usually observable by consumers either before or after consumption. Quality is furthermore verifiable if its level can be (costlessly) described ex ante in a contract and ascertained ex post by a court. When quality is verifiable, the regulator can impose a quality target to the regulated firm or more generally reward or punish the firm directly as a function of the level of quality. For instance, a regulatory commission may dictate the heating value of gas or may punish an electric utility on the basis of the number and intensity of outages. Formally, the regulation of verifiable quality is analogous to the regulation of a multiproduct firm, as the level of quality on a given product may be treated as the quantity of another, fictitious product.[1]

Research support from the Taussig visiting professorship at Harvard University, the Guggenheim Foundation, the Pew Charitable Trust/Ford Foundation ENS Program, the Center for Energy Policy Research at MIT, the National Science Foundation, and the French Commissariat Général du Plan is gratefully acknowledged.

[1] See Sappington (1983) and Laffont and Tirole (1990) for information-based theories of the regulation of a multiproduct firm with and without cost regulation.

This chapter is concerned with observable but *unverifiable* quality. The effectiveness of a new weapons system, the quality of broadcasting by a regulated television station, the level of services enjoyed by a railroad passenger, and the probability of a core meltdown at a nuclear plant are hard to quantify and include in a formal contract. As Kahn (1988, p. 22) argues:

> But it is far more true of quality of service than of price that the primary responsibility remains with the supplying company instead of with the regulatory agency, and that the agencies, in turn, have devoted much more attention to the latter than to the former. The reasons for this are fairly clear. Service standards are often much more difficult to specify by the promulgation of rules.

When quality is unverifiable, the regulator must recreate the incentives of an unregulated firm to provide quality without throwing away the benefits of regulation. First, it must reward the regulated firm on the basis of sales. Second, the threat of nonrenewal of the regulatory license, of second sourcing, or of deregulation makes the regulated firm concerned about its reputation as supplier of quality.

The focus of our analysis is the relationship between quality concern and power of optimal incentive schemes. An incentive scheme is high- (low-) powered if the firm bears a high (low) fraction of its realized costs. Thus, a fixed-price contract is very high-powered, and a cost-plus contract is very low-powered.

The link between quality and the power of incentive schemes has been much discussed. For instance, there has been a concern that "incentive regulation" (understand: high-powered incentive schemes) conflicts with the safe operation of nuclear power plants by forcing management to hurry work, take shortcuts, and delay safety investments. There have been accounts that the switch to a high-powered incentive scheme for British Telecom (price caps) after its privatization produced a poor record on the quality front (Vickers and Yarrow, 1988, p. 228).[2]

Similarly, Kahn (1988, I, p. 24) contends that, under cost-of-service regulation (a very low-powered incentive scheme), in the matter of quality "far more than in the matter of price, the interest of the monopolist on the one hand and the consumer on the other are more nearly coincident than in conflict." Kahn's intuition is that the regulated monopolist does not suffer from incurring monetary costs to enhance quality because these costs are paid by consumers through direct charges. This intuition is incomplete. First, some components of quality involve nonmonetary

[2] It is not surprising that the dissatisfaction with the quality performance subsequently led to costly development and monitoring of quality indices to be included in the incentive schemes.

costs. Second, and more importantly, under pure cost-of-service regulation, the regulated firm does not gain from providing costly services either, so that a low perceived cost of supplying quality does not imply a high incentive to supply quality.[3] Last, in the context of military procurement, Scherer (1964, pp. 165–6) has suggested that

> There is reason to believe that the use of fixed-price contracts would not greatly reduce the emphasis placed on quality in weapons development projects, although it might affect certain marginal tradeoff decisions with only a minor expected impact on future sales.

To give formal arguments to assess the relevance of these perceptions, we introduce two related natural monopoly models of an experience and of a search good. Whether the power of regulatory contracts decreases when quality becomes more desirable depends crucially on whether contractual incentives can be based on sales (on top of cost) or not, that is, on whether the regulated firm supplies a search or an experience good. In our two-period model of an experience good, the regulator purchases a fixed amount from the regulated firm. Because quality is ex ante unverifiable, the regulator has no alternative than to accept the product. The supplier's incentive to provide quality is then the reputation incentive, that is, the possibility of losing future sales. In contrast, our static search good model has the firm sell to consumers who observe quality before purchasing. The former model is best thought of as a procurement model, and the latter as a regulation model, although other interpretations are possible (in particular, some regulated products are experience goods).

In the case of an *experience good,* we argue that incentives to supply quality and those to reduce cost are inherently in conflict. The regulator has a single instrument – the cost reimbursement rule – to provide both types of incentives. High-powered incentive schemes induce cost reduction but increase the firm's perceived cost of providing quality. This *crowding-out effect* implies that the more important quality is, the lower the power of an optimal incentive scheme. We also show that when the firm becomes more concerned about the future, its perceived cost of supplying quality decreases, which induces the regulator to offer more powerful incentive schemes. We thus find Scherer's suggestion quite perceptive.

[3] In practice, one does not observe pure cost-of-service regulation. Due to the regulatory lag, the regulated firm is, like an unregulated monopolist, the residual claimant for the revenue it generates and costs it incurs between rate reviews (the differences being that the prices are fixed and that the regulated monopolist is concerned about the ratchet effect); thus, actual cost-of-service incentive schemes are not as low-powered as one might believe. We will not try to study (variants of) cost-of-service regulation, but will rather focus on optimal regulation. See Joskow and Rose (1989) for empirical evidence on the level of services under cost-of-service regulation.

In the case of a *search good,* the crowding-out effect is latent but has no influence on the power of incentive schemes. In our model, the regulator can separate the two incentive problems because it has two instruments: cost-reimbursement rule and sales incentives. The incentive to provide quality is provided through a reward based on a quality index, which is the level of sales corrected by the price charged by the firm. As in the case of an experience good, the cost-reducing activity is encouraged through the cost-reimbursement rule, which is now freed from the concern of providing the right quality incentives. This dichotomy does not, however, imply that an increase in the desirability of quality has no effect on the power of incentive schemes; it has an indirect effect because higher services may increase or decrease the optimal level of output, which in turn changes the value of reducing marginal cost and thus affects the regulator's arbitrage between incentives and rent extraction.

Before proceeding, we should comment on the possibility of having (search) goods whose quality is observable by consumers but is not verifiable by regulators. We have in mind the case of a TV station or of a railroad, whose services are hard to measure objectively and yet are relatively well-perceived by the consumers. It is important, however, to realize that regulators can in practice resort to user panels. For instance, a wide range of consumer-satisfaction variables in telecommunications services has been collected in the states of New York and Florida (percentage call completions, consumer trouble reports, missed repair appointments, accuracy of billing, operator response time, etc.; see, e.g., Noam, 1989). Very generally, regulators face a trade-off between developing costly quality performance measures and giving the firm monetary incentives of the sort described in the search good section of this chapter (or using both methods).

Although there exists a vast literature on the provision of quality by an unregulated monopoly,[4] surprisingly little theoretical research has been devoted to this issue in a regulated environment. Besanko, Donnenfeld, and White (1987) assume that the monopolist offers a range of verifiable qualities to discriminate among consumers with different tastes for quality (à la Mussa and Rosen, 1978) and investigate the effect of imposing minimum quality standards or price ceilings (see also Laffont, 1987). Closer to our chapter is the work of Lewis and Sappington (1988a), who examine both verifiable and unverifiable quality. Sales depend on a demand parameter, price and quality. When quality is unverifiable, Lewis and Sappington assume that the regulator monitors prices (but not cost, quantity, or quality) and operates transfers to the firm. To give incentives to provide quality, the regulator allows prices in excess of the (known) marginal

[4] See, e.g., Tirole (1988, Chap. 2 and 3).

cost. A higher markup above marginal cost raises the dead-weight loss due to pricing but also raises quality. Lewis and Sappington show that the rent derived by the firm from its private information about the demand parameter is higher when quality is verifiable than when it is not. Our work differs from theirs in that, among other things, we allow cost observation and focus on the effect of quality concerns on the power of incentive schemes.

The chapter is organized as follows. Section 2 develops a single product, static model of sales incentive. The regulator observes the total cost, price, and output of a natural monopoly. The regulator's imperfect knowledge of the production technology and of the demand function makes the problems of inducing cost-reducing activities and provision of quality/services nontrivial. Services are monetary or nonmonetary; monetary services enter total cost but cannot be disentangled from other costs, that is, cannot be recovered from the aggregate accounting data. Section 3 solves for the optimal incentive scheme. Section 4 shows that the optimum can be implemented by a scheme that is linear in both realized cost and a quality index that is computed from price and sales data. Section 5 links variations in the quality concern and the slope (power) of incentive schemes. Section 6 discusses reputation incentives. It develops a model of an experience good in which a quality choice has permanent effects. The observation of quality today reveals information about future quality. This model is one of moral hazard (unverifiable intertemporal choice of quality). In contrast, many models of reputation in the industrial organization literature have assumed that the firm can be "born" a high- or low-quality producer, and can, at a cost, masquerade as a high-quality producer if it is a low-quality producer. Appendix B stages a variant of the reputation models of Kreps and Wilson (1982), Milgrom and Roberts (1982), and Holmström (1982) in a regulatory context and obtains results similar to those in the moral-hazard model. Section 7 concludes the chapter and suggests some desirable extensions.

PART A: SEARCH GOODS

2 The model

We consider a natural monopoly producing a single commodity in quantity q with observable but unverifiable quality/services s. Before describing the model, we briefly discuss the methodology. We assume that the firm's cost increases with output and with the level of services, decreases with the cost-reducing activity e, and depends on some privately known technological parameter $\beta: C = C(q, s, e, \beta)$. On the demand side, we assume that the regulator does not perfectly know the demand curve; otherwise he would be able to infer the exact level of services provided by the firm from the price and output data; we thus posit an inverse demand function $p = P(q, s, \theta)$, where P decreases with q and increases with s, and θ is a demand parameter that is known by the firm only. Our model is thus one of two-dimensional moral hazard (e and s) and especially two-dimensional adverse selection (β and θ). In order to obtain a closed-form solution, we specialize it to *linear* cost and demand functions, which enable us to reduce the problem to a one-dimensional adverse selection one.

Quantity and quality are *net complements* if an increase in quality raises the net marginal willingness to pay, that is, the difference between price and marginal cost: $\partial^2(S^g - C)/\partial s \partial q = \partial(p - C_q)/\partial s > 0$. As we will see, the effect of quality concerns on the power of incentive schemes depends on whether quantity and quality are net complements or net substitutes.

Let us now describe the model in more detail.

The (variable) cost function is

$$C = (\beta + s - e)q, \tag{1}$$

where β in $[\underline{\beta}, \bar{\beta}]$ is an intrinsic cost parameter known only to the firm, and e is the firm's cost-reducing activity or effort and is also unobservable by the regulator. Note that (1) assumes that the cost of providing quality is monetary. The remark that follows shows that a relabeling of variables allows the cost of providing quality to be nonmonetary. Note also that a scale effect is built into the cost function. The higher the production level, the more valuable is effort.

The cost C is verifiable and, by accounting convention, borne by the regulator. Similarly, we assume without loss of generality that the regulator receives directly the payment pq made by the consumers in exchange for the good, where p is the good's price. After paying C and receiving pq, the regulator pays a net transfer t to the firm (that will depend on observable and verifiable variables C, p, q).

By letting $\psi(e)$ (with $\psi' > 0$, $\psi'' > 0$, $\psi''' \geq 0$)[5] denote the firm's disutility of effort, the firm's utility or rent is

$$U = t - \psi(e). \tag{2}$$

Consumers observe the quality before purchasing the (search) good and derive from the consumption of the commodity a gross surplus:

$$S^g(q, s, \theta) = (A + ks - h\theta)q - \frac{B}{2}q^2 - \frac{(ks - h\theta)^2}{2}, \tag{3}$$

[5] The technical assumption $\psi''' \geq 0$ ensures that stochastic mechanisms are not optimal.

where A, B, h, and k are known positive constants, and θ in $[\underline{\theta}, \bar{\theta}]$ is a demand parameter.[6]

The inverse demand curve is then

$$p = \frac{\partial S^g}{\partial q} = A + ks - h\theta - Bq. \tag{4}$$

Quantity and quality are net complements if $k > 1$ and net substitutes if $k < 1$. We will, of course, focus on parameters that put the problem in the relevant range ($\partial S^g/\partial q > 0$, $\partial S^g/\partial s > 0$).

Let $1+\lambda > 1$ be the social cost of public funds.[7] The consumers'/taxpayers' net surplus is

$$S^n = (A + ks - h\theta)q - \frac{B}{2}q^2 - \frac{(ks-h\theta)^2}{2} - pq - (1+\lambda)(C - pq + t). \tag{5}$$

Equation (5) includes the taxes needed by the regulator to finance the firm. From (4), (5) can be rewritten:

$$S^n = (A + ks - h\theta)q - \frac{B}{2}q^2 - \frac{(ks-h\theta)^2}{2}$$
$$+ \lambda(A + ks - h\theta - Bq)q - (1+\lambda)(C+t). \tag{6}$$

Remark. As mentioned before, our model covers the case of a non-monetary cost of providing quality. Suppose that the accounting cost is $C = (\beta - \tilde{e})q$, where $\tilde{e}$ is the effort to reduce cost. Suppose further that the firm exerts a second type of effort s that provides services to consumers s per unit of output. Then the disutility of effort is $\psi(\tilde{e}+s)$. By letting $e \equiv \tilde{e}+s$, the accounting cost becomes $C = (\beta + s - e)q$ and the disutility of effort is $\psi(e)$. This remark shows vividly that cost-reducing activities ($\tilde{e}$) and the provision of services (s) are *substitutes:* an increase in services raises the marginal disutility $\psi'(\tilde{e}+s)$ of exerting effort to reduce cost.

Under *complete information,* a utilitarian regulator maximizes the sum of consumer and producer surpluses under the constraint that the firm be willing to participate:

6 Note that S^g differs from 0 at $q = 0$. One can think of S^g as a local approximation in the relevant range. Or one might allow services to affect consumers even in the absence of consumption. The reader should be aware that the Spencian comparison between the marginal willingness to pay for quality of the marginal and the average consumers under regulated monopoly requires that S^g be equal to zero at $q = 0$.

7 λ is strictly positive because distortive taxes are used to raise public funds. When $\lambda = 0$, transfers from consumers to the firm are costless and incentive problems can be solved at no cost to society.

$$\underset{\{q,s,e\}}{\text{Max}}\left\{W=(1+\lambda)(A+ks-h\theta)q-B\left(\frac{1}{2}+\lambda\right)q^2-\frac{(ks-h\theta)^2}{2}\right.$$
$$\left.-(1+\lambda)((\beta+s-e)q+t)+t-\psi(e)\right\}, \tag{7}$$

subject to

$$t-\psi(e)\geq 0, \tag{8}$$

where (8) normalizes the firm's reservation utility to be zero. For B large enough, the program $\{(7),(8)\}$ is concave and its (interior) maximum is characterized by the first-order conditions:

$$(1+\lambda)p-\lambda Bq=(1+\lambda)(\beta+s-e), \tag{9}$$

$$(1+\lambda)kq-k(ks-h\theta)=(1+\lambda)q, \tag{10}$$

$$\psi'(e)=q, \tag{11}$$

$$t=\psi(e). \tag{12}$$

Equation (9) equates the marginal social utility of the commodity (composed of the marginal utility of the commodity to consumers S_q^n and the financial marginal gain $(d/dq)(\lambda pq)$ to its marginal social cost $((1+\lambda)C_q)$. Similarly, (10) equates the marginal social utility of service quality to its marginal social cost. Equation (11) equates the marginal disutility of effort $\psi'(e)$ to its marginal utility q. And (12) says that no rent is left to the firm.

Equations (9) and (10) are most easily interpreted in the following forms:

$$\frac{p-C_q}{p}=\frac{\lambda}{1+\lambda}\frac{1}{\eta}, \quad \text{where } \eta\equiv\frac{p}{Bq}, \tag{9'}$$

$$\frac{\partial S^g}{\partial s}+\lambda\frac{\partial p}{\partial s}q=(1+\lambda)\frac{\partial C}{\partial s}. \tag{10'}$$

The Lerner index – or price-marginal cost ratio – is equal to a Ramsey index (a number between 0 and 1) times the inverse of the elasticity of demand. And the optimal level of services equates the marginal gross surplus plus the shadow cost of public funds times the increase in revenue to the social marginal cost of quality.

For the record, it is worth comparing the regulated level of quality with that chosen by an unregulated monopoly. Because the cost and demand functions are linear in services, the monopoly solution is "bang-bang." Quality is either zero if quantity and quality are net substitutes or maximal (if an upper bound on quality exists) if quantity and quality are net complements. As in Spence (1975), an unregulated monopolist may over- or undersupply quality for a given quantity.

3 Optimal regulation under asymmetric information

We now assume that the regulator faces a multidimensional asymmetry of information. He knows neither β nor θ and cannot observe e and s. However, he observes C, p, and q. Faced with this informational gap, the regulator is assumed to behave as a Bayesian statistician who maximizes expected social welfare and has a prior distribution F_1 on $\beta \in [\underline{\beta}, \bar{\beta}]$ and a prior distribution F_2 on $\theta \in [\underline{\theta}, \bar{\theta}]$. The firm knows β and θ before contracting.

The regulator knows that consumers equate their marginal utility of the commodity to the price, hence

$$p = A + ks - h\theta - Bq. \tag{13}$$

By using the observability of p and q, it is possible to eliminate the unobservable service quality level s in the consumers' gross valuation of the commodity, which becomes

$$S^g(p,q) = \frac{B}{2}q^2 + pq - \frac{1}{2}(p - A + Bq)^2. \tag{14}$$

Similarly, the cost function becomes

$$C = \left(\beta + \frac{h\theta}{k} - e\right)q + q\left(\frac{p - A + Bq}{k}\right). \tag{15}$$

Note that β and θ enter the cost function only through the linear combination $\gamma \equiv \beta + (h/k)\theta$. This feature, which also holds for the firm's and regulator's objective functions (see what follows), reduces the model to a single-dimensional adverse-selection problem, and will enable us to obtain a closed-form solution.[8]

Consider now the firm's objective function (recalling our accounting convention that the regulator pays the cost and receives the revenue):

$$U = t - \psi(e) = t - \psi\left(\gamma + \frac{p - A + Bq}{k} - \frac{C}{q}\right). \tag{16}$$

The regulator wishes to maximize expected social welfare under the incentive and individual rationality constraints of the firm. From the

[8] A more general formulation of the consumers' tastes would lead to a truly two-dimensional adverse-selection problem. The qualitative results would be similar, but the technical analysis would be greatly complicated (see Laffont, Maskin, and Rochet, 1987, for example).

revelation principle, we can restrict the problem of control of the firm to the analysis of direct and truthful revelation mechanisms.

For simplicity, we assume that the cumulative distribution function $F(\cdot)$ of γ on $[\underline{\gamma},\bar{\gamma}]=[\underline{\beta}+(h/k)\underline{\theta},\bar{\beta}+(h/k)\bar{\theta}]$ (the convolution of F_1 and F_2) satisfies the monotone hazard rate property: $d(F(\gamma)/f(\gamma))/d\gamma>0$. Appendix A1 derives sufficient conditions on the primitive distributions F_1 and F_2 for this to hold. This assumption avoids bunching without significant loss for the economics of the problem. The firm is faced with a revelation mechanism $\{t(\gamma),c(\gamma),p(\gamma),q(\gamma)\}$ that specifies for each announced value of γ a net transfer to the firm, $t(\gamma)$; an average cost to realize, $c(\gamma)$; a price to charge, $p(\gamma)$; and a quantity to sell, $q(\gamma)$. Truth telling is caused by the first- and second-order conditions of incentive compatibility (see Appendix A2):

$$\dot{t}=\left(\frac{\dot{p}+B\dot{q}}{k}-\dot{\left(\frac{C}{q}\right)}\right)\psi', \tag{17}$$

$$\frac{\dot{p}+B\dot{q}}{k}-\dot{\left(\frac{C}{q}\right)}\leq 0, \tag{18}$$

where $\dot{t}\equiv dt/d\gamma$, etc.

By using (13) to substitute out quality, the social welfare function (7) can be written:

$$W=\frac{B}{2}q^2+(1+\lambda)pq-\frac{1}{2}(p-A+Bq)^2$$
$$-(1+\lambda)\left((\gamma-e)q+q\left(\frac{p-A+Bq}{k}\right)+\psi(e)\right)-\lambda U. \tag{19}$$

The regulator maximizes the expected social welfare function under the incentive compatibility conditions {(17), (18)} and the individual rationality constraint of the firm:

$$U(\gamma)\geq 0 \quad \text{for any } \gamma.^9 \tag{20}$$

The maximization program is, using U as a state variable,

$$\text{Max}\int_{\underline{\gamma}}^{\bar{\gamma}}\Big\{\frac{B}{2}q^2+(1+\lambda)pq-\frac{1}{2}(p-A+Bq)^2$$
$$-(1+\lambda)\left[(\gamma-e)q+q\left(\frac{p-A+Bq}{k}\right)+\psi(e)\right]-\lambda U\Big\}\,dF(\gamma) \tag{21}$$

subject to

$$\dot{U}(\gamma)=-\psi'(e), \tag{22}$$

[9] We implicitly assume here that it is worth producing for any γ in $[\underline{\gamma},\bar{\gamma}]$.

$$\dot{e}-1 \leq 0, \tag{23}$$

$$U(\bar{\gamma}) \geq 0. \tag{24}$$

Equation (22) is another version of the first-order incentive compatibility constraint (17). Moreover, because $U(\gamma)$ is decreasing, the IR constraint (20) reduces to the boundary condition (24). From Appendix A2, (23) is a rewriting of the second-order condition (18). We ignore it in a first step and later check that it is indeed satisfied by the solution of the subconstrained program. For A and B large enough, the program is concave and the optimum is characterized by its first-order conditions (see Appendix A3). Let $\mu(\gamma)$ denote the Pontryagin multiplier associated with (22) and H the Hamiltonian associated with the program {(21), (22), (24)}. From the Pontryagin principle, we have

$$\dot{\mu}(\gamma) = -\frac{\partial H}{\partial U} = \lambda. \tag{25}$$

From the transversality condition and (25), we derive

$$\mu(\gamma) = \lambda F(\gamma). \tag{26}$$

Maximizing the Hamiltonian with respect to q, p, and e, we get, after some algebraic manipulations:

$$(1+\lambda)p - \lambda Bq = (1+\lambda)\left(\gamma - e + \frac{p-A+Bq}{k}\right), \tag{27}$$

$$(1+\lambda)kq - k(p-A+Bq) = (1+\lambda)q, \tag{28}$$

$$\psi'(e) = q - \frac{\lambda}{1+\lambda}\frac{F(\gamma)}{f(\gamma)}\psi''(e). \tag{29}$$

Equations (27) and (28), which correspond to the maximizations with respect to q and p, coincide with (9) and (10). That is, for a given effort e, the price, quantity, and quality are the same as under complete information about the technology and demand parameter. This result is reminiscent of (although not implied by) the incentives–pricing dichotomy result for multiproduct firms obtained in Laffont and Tirole (1990). Appendix A4 derives a more general class of cost functions for which the dichotomy holds in this quality problem.

To extract part of the firm's rent, the effort is distorted downward for a given output level [compare (29) and (11)], except when $\gamma = \underline{\gamma}$.

Appendix A3 shows that for the solution to {(27), (28), (29)}, $\dot{p}(\gamma) > 0$, $\dot{q}(\gamma) < 0$, and $\dot{e}(\gamma) < 0$. In particular, the neglected second-order condition for the firm $(1-\dot{e}(\gamma) \geq 0)$ is satisfied.

Next, we compare the levels of quality under complete and incomplete information about β and θ:

Proposition 1. *The level of quality is lower under incomplete information than under complete information if and only if quantity and quality are net complements.*

Proof: See Appendix A5.

Incomplete information makes rent extraction difficult and reduces the power of incentive schemes, that is, leads to a decrease in effort. This raises marginal cost and reduces output. If quantity and quality are net complements, lower services are desirable; and conversely for net substitutes. Note that asymmetric information lowers quality exactly when the regulated monopolist oversupplies quality.

To conclude this section, for a search good, sales are an indicator of quality in the same way cost is an indicator of effort (and quality). The regulation of quality and effort under asymmetric information is, therefore, in the spirit of the regulation of a multiproduct firm (see Laffont and Tirole, 1990).

4 Implementation of the optimal regulatory mechanism

For each announcement of the firm's technological parameter and of the consumers' taste parameter, the regulator imposes a level of average cost to achieve, a quantity to produce, and a market price to charge. An appropriate net transfer $t(\gamma)$ is offered to induce truthful behavior.

This transfer can be reinterpreted as follows. Let

$$z \equiv \frac{C}{q} - \frac{p-A+Bq}{k}.$$

Then, the first-order incentive compatibility condition is (see Appendix A2)

$$\frac{dt}{d\gamma} + \psi'(\gamma - z)\frac{dz}{d\gamma} = 0 \tag{30}$$

or

$$\frac{dt}{dz} = -\psi'(\gamma - z) < 0. \tag{31}$$

Differentiating (31), we obtain

$$\frac{d^2t}{dz^2} = -\psi''(\gamma - z)\left(\frac{1}{dz/d\gamma} - 1\right). \tag{32}$$

From the second-order condition, $dz/d\gamma \geq 0$ and $1 - dz/d\gamma = de/d\gamma < 0$ from Appendix A3. Therefore, $d^2t/dz^2 > 0$, that is, the transfer as a function of z is a convex and decreasing function (see Figure 1).

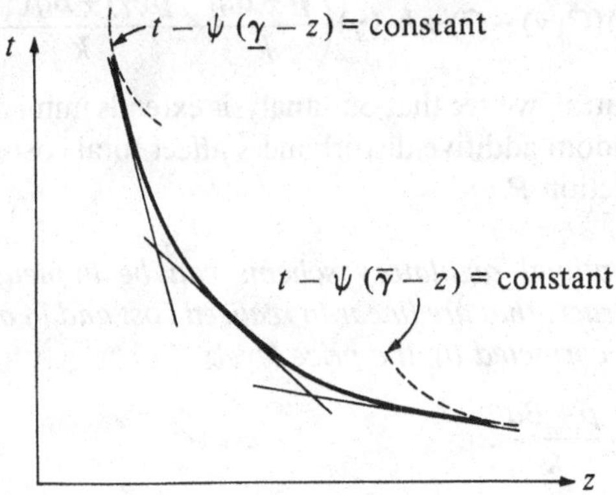

Figure 1.

As in Laffont and Tirole (1986), the convex nonlinear transfer function $t(z)$ can be replaced by a menu of linear contracts:

$$t(z,\gamma) = a(\gamma) + b(\gamma)(z(\gamma) - z),$$

where $z(\gamma)$ is the announced value of $C/q - (p - A + Bq)/k$, and z is the observed ex post value. The transfer is therefore a function of a performance index that subtracts from the realized average cost an approximation of the service quality inferred from market data. In other words, the firm is offered a choice in a menu of linear contracts and is rewarded or penalized according to deviations from an index aggregating cost data and service quality data inferred from observation of market price and quantity and from a priori knowledge of the demand function.

The coefficient $b(\gamma)$ sharing the overrun in the performance index is $\psi'(e^*(\gamma))$, where $e^*(\gamma)$ is the solution of the regulator's optimization program. Indeed,

$$\operatorname*{Max}_{\{e,\tilde{\gamma}\}} \left\{ a(\tilde{\gamma}) + \psi'(e^*(\tilde{\gamma}))(z(\tilde{\gamma}) - \gamma + e) - \psi(e) \right\}$$

implies $\psi'(e^*(\tilde{\gamma})) = \psi'(e)$, and therefore $e = e^*(\tilde{\gamma})$ and

$$\dot{a}(\tilde{\gamma}) + \psi''\dot{e}^*(\tilde{\gamma})(z(\tilde{\gamma}) - z) + \psi'(e^*(\tilde{\gamma}))\dot{z}(\tilde{\gamma}) = 0.$$

If $a(\cdot)$ is chosen so that $\dot{a}(\gamma) + \psi'(e^*(\gamma))\dot{z}(\gamma) = 0$ for any γ or $\dot{a}(\gamma) = \dot{t}(\gamma)$, then $\tilde{\gamma} = \gamma$.

Alternatively, the menu of linear contracts can be decomposed into a linear sharing of total costs overruns with a coefficient $b_1(\gamma) = \psi'(e^*(\gamma))/q^*(\gamma)$ and a linear sharing of overruns in the service quality index with a coefficient $b_2(\gamma) = \psi'(e^*(\gamma))$ or

$$t=a(\gamma)+b_1(\gamma)(C(\gamma)-C)+b_2(\gamma)\left(\frac{p+Bq}{k}-\frac{p(\gamma)+Bq(\gamma)}{k}\right).$$

Since the firm is risk-neutral, we see that our analysis extends immediately to the case in which random additive disturbances affect total cost C and the inverse demand function P.

Proposition 2. *The optimal regulatory scheme can be implemented through a menu of contracts that are linear in realized cost and in a quality index equal to sales corrected by the price level:*

$$t=\tilde{a}-b_1C+b_2\frac{p+Bq}{k}.$$

Clearly, the parameters characterizing the power of the incentive schemes, $b_1(\gamma)=\psi'(e(\gamma))/q(\gamma)$ and $b_2(\gamma)=q(\gamma)b_1(\gamma)$, are related. If we study the comparative statics of these coefficients with respect to a parameter x, we have

$$\frac{d}{dx}\left(\frac{\psi'(e)}{q}\right)=\frac{\psi''\dot{e}_x q-\psi'\dot{q}_x}{q^2}.$$

From

$$\psi'(e)=q-\frac{\lambda}{1+\lambda}\frac{F}{f}\psi''(e),\qquad \dot{q}_x=\left(\psi''+\frac{\lambda}{1+\lambda}\frac{F}{f}\psi'''\right)\dot{e}_x,$$

and

$$\frac{d}{dx}\left(\frac{\psi'(e)}{q}\right)=\dot{e}_x\frac{\lambda}{1+\lambda}\frac{F}{f}[\psi''^2-\psi'\psi'''].$$

The comparative statics of $b_2(\gamma)=\psi'(e^*(\gamma))$ is the same as the comparative statics of $e^*(\gamma)$; the comparative statics of $b_1(\gamma)$ is identical as long as ψ''' is not too large, which we will assume in Section 5 (of course, no such assumption is needed if one studies the slope of the incentive schemes with respect to marginal cost). Note that b_1 and b_2 are then positively correlated over the sample of types.

5 Concern for quality and the power of incentive schemes

This section studies the effects of an increase in the consumers' marginal surplus from quality ($\partial S^g/\partial s$) and of an increase in the marginal cost of supplying quality ($\partial C/\partial s$) on the power of incentive schemes. For a clean analysis of these effects, the change must not affect the structure of information, in particular, the information revealed by the demand data about the level of quality or by the cost data about the cost-reducing effort. The three changes we consider yield identical results (their proofs are provided in Appendix A6).

Suppose, first, that the consumers' gross surplus S^g is replaced by $\tilde{S}^g = S^g + l(ks - h\theta, \nu)$, where $l_{11} < 0$ and $l_{12} > 0$ (ν is a parameter indexing the marginal gross surplus with respect to quality).[10] Note that a change in ν does not affect the inverse demand curve and therefore does not change the information revealed by q and p about s. The first-order conditions (27) to (29) are unchanged except that $(\partial l/\partial s)[B-(1+\lambda)/k]$ and $(\partial l/\partial s)(1/k)$ must be added to (27) and (28), respectively. Differentiating (27) to (29) totally with respect to ν yields Proposition 3.

Proposition 3. *An increase in the concern for quality (in the sense of an increase in ν) raises the power of incentive schemes if quantity and quality are net complements and lowers the power of incentive schemes if they are net substitutes.*

Next, let us consider an increase in the marginal cost of quality. To keep the structure of information constant, we transform the cost function into $\tilde{C} \equiv C + m(ks - h\theta, \rho)$, where $m_{11} > 0$ and $m_{12} > 0$ (an increase in ρ corresponds to an increase in marginal cost; the structure of information is kept unchanged because the term $ks - h\theta$ is equal to $p - A + Bq$ and is therefore verifiable).

Proposition 4. *An increase in the marginal cost of supplying quality (in the sense of an increase in ρ) lowers the power of incentive schemes if quantity and quality are net complements and raises the power of incentive schemes if they are net substitutes.*

Last, let us consider an increase in k, keeping h/k constant. The point of keeping h/k constant is to leave the asymmetry of information unaffected: When facing demand parameter θ, the firm can claim that the demand parameter is $\hat{\theta}$ by choosing services $s(\hat{\theta})$ satisfying $ks - h\theta = ks(\hat{\theta}) - h\hat{\theta}$ without being detected through the demand data p and q. Thus, the "concealment set" is invariant.

Proposition 5. *An increase in k, keeping h/k constant, raises the power of incentive schemes if quantity and quality are net complements and lowers the power of incentive schemes if they are net substitutes.*

10 Subscripts here denote partial derivatives.

Proposition 5 admits several interpretations. First, an increase in k corresponds to an increase in the marginal willingness to pay for the good p if and only if $k>1$. To see this, note that $\partial p/\partial k \propto ks - h\theta = (1+\lambda)(k-1)q/k$ from (28). Proposition 5 thus says that increases in the marginal willingness to pay for the good tilt the optimal contracts toward a fixed-price contract for all k.[11]

Second,

$$\operatorname{sign}\left(\frac{\partial^2 S^g}{\partial k \partial s}\bigg|_{h/k=\text{constant}}\right) = \operatorname{sign}\left(1-2(1+\lambda)\left(\frac{k-1}{k}\right)\right),$$

(using (28)). Proposition 5 shows that an increase in the marginal valuation for quality ($\partial S^g/\partial s$) has an ambiguous effect on the power of incentive schemes: For $k<1$, an increase in the marginal valuation for quality lowers the power of incentive schemes. For $k>1$, but "not too large," it raises the power of incentive schemes.

The intuitions for all these propositions are similar. An increase in the concern for quality (or a decrease in the marginal cost of supplying quality) makes higher quality socially desirable. If quality and quantity are net complements, higher quantity is also socially more desirable. Effort then becomes more effective since it affects more units of the product. To encourage effort, more powerful incentive schemes are used.

PART B: EXPERIENCE GOODS

6 Reputation incentive

In some industries, the sales incentive is limited either because the quantity purchased is fixed or inelastic (for example, the good is an experience good) or because the buyer is the regulator himself, as in the case in procurement, or both. Suppose that the buyer (regulator) buys a fixed amount from the firm. The firm's main incentive to provide quality is then the threat of jeopardizing future trading opportunities with the buyer rather than current ones. In general terms, one can think of two mechanisms that link current quality and future sales. First, the buyer may develop a reputation for punishing the agent, for instance, by not trading with him, when the latter has supplied low quality in the past. This mechanism is likely to be particularly powerful when the buyer oversees many agents and thus has a good opportunity to develop such a reputation. Second, and closer to the industrial organization tradition, the buyer may infer information about the profitability of future trade from the observation of current quality. We focus on this second mechanism.

[11] This result is similar to the one obtained when unverifiable quality is not an issue (see Laffont and Tirole, 1986).

The industrial organization literature has identified two informational reasons why a buyer may find future trade undesirable after observing poor quality. On the one hand, the quality of the product supplied by the seller may have permanent characteristics, that is, the seller commits long-term investments that affect the quality level over several periods. On the other hand, the intertemporal link may be human capital rather than technological investment. The seller then signals his competence or diligence through today's choice of quality and conveys information about tomorrow's future quality even though he will manufacture a possibly brand-new product using new machines. In this section, we focus on a permanent and unverifiable choice of technology. Appendix B develops a model of reputation for being a high-quality producer. The two models yield similar results. We emphasize the new insights added by the new model in the appendix.

For the seller to care about future trade, it must be the case that this trade creates a rent. This rent can be an informational rent, but other types of rents (due, for instance, to bargaining power of the seller, or to the necessity for the buyer to offer an "efficiency wage" scheme to create incentives) are consistent with the model. So in our model, complete information about period 2 destroys the possibility of creating incentives for quality provision in period 1.

The model has two periods, $\tau = 1, 2$. In period 1, the seller (regulated firm) produces one unit of the good for the buyer (regulator), at cost:

$$C_1 = \beta_1 - e_1 + s, \tag{33}$$

where C_1 is the first-period verifiable cost, β_1 an efficiency parameter, e_1 the firm's effort to reduce the first-period cost, and s the level of "care." As in the sales incentive model of Sections 2 through 5, s is formalized as a monetary cost, but alternatively can be interpreted as a nonmonetary cost. The variables β_1, e_1, and s are private information to the firm; the regulator has a prior cumulative distribution $F(\beta_1)$ on $[\underline{\beta}_1, \bar{\beta}_1]$ with density $f(\beta_1)$ that satisfies the monotone "hazard rate" property $(d/d\beta_1)[F(\beta_1)/f(\beta_1)] \geq 0$. Effort e_1 involves disutility $\psi(e_1)$ (with $\psi' > 0$, $\psi'' > 0$, $\psi''' \geq 0$). With probability $\pi(s) \in [0, 1]$, the product "works" and yields a gross social surplus S_1; with probability $(1 - \pi(s))$, the product is defective and yields gross social surplus 0. We will say that the firm produces a high- or low-quality item, respectively. We assume that $\pi' > 0$, $\pi'' < 0$; as well as $\pi'(0) = +\infty$ (in order to avoid a corner solution at $s = 0$) and $\pi''' \leq 0$ (which is a sufficient condition for the regulator's program to be concave). Whether the product works or is defective is observed at the end of period 1 by the regulator, but is not verifiable by a court, so that the regulatory contract cannot be contingent on the quality outcome.

Parties have a discount factor $\delta > 0$ between the two periods. To obtain the simplest model, we assume that the firm's second-period product is defective if and only if the first-period product is defective (i.e., the first- and second-period quality outcomes are both determined by the first-period level of care and are perfectly correlated; as is easily seen, what matters for the results is that a higher s in period 1 raises the expected quality level in period 2). Our assumption implies that the firm won't be asked to produce in period 2 if its product is defective in period 1; in this case, the second-period social welfare and firm's rent are normalized to be zero. Let $\bar{U}_2 > 0$ and $\bar{W}_2 > 0$ denote the second-period expected rent for the firm and expected social welfare, respectively. For simplicity, we assume that $\bar{U}_2$ and $\bar{W}_2$ are independent of β_1.[12]

Let $s(\beta_1)$ and $e_1(\beta_1)$ denote the firm's first-period care and effort levels functions, $U_1(\beta_1)$ denote the firm's first-period rent, and $U(\beta_1) \equiv U_1(\beta_1) + \delta \bar{U}_2 \pi(s(\beta_1))$ denote the firm's intertemporal rent. Note that a firm with type β_1 can always duplicate the cost and probability of high quality of a firm with type $(\beta_1 - d\beta_1)$ by choosing levels $s(\beta_1 - d\beta_1)$ and $e_1(\beta_1 - d\beta_1)$ so that the incentive compatibility constraint for effort is

$$\dot{U}(\beta_1) = -\psi'(e_1(\beta_1)). \tag{34}$$

Next, consider the firm's choice of care. Suppose that it raises the level of care by 1. To reach the same cost, the firm must increase its effort by 1. At the margin, such changes do not affect the firm's rent. The incentive compatibility constraint with respect to effort is thus

$$\delta \pi'(s) \bar{U}_2 - \psi'(e_1) = 0. \tag{35}$$

Next, suppose that the firm cannot produce in period 2 if it hasn't produced (and thus invested) in period 1. The individual rationality constraint says that the firm must obtain at least its reservation utility, which we normalize at zero: for all β_1:

$$U_1(\beta_1) + \delta \bar{U}_2 \pi(s(\beta_1)) \geq 0. \tag{36}$$

As usual, the individual rationality constraint is binding at $\beta_1 = \bar{\beta}_1$ only:[13]

[12] To give an example: suppose that

(a) the firm produces one unit of the same good or a related good in period 2 at cost $C_2 = \beta_2 - e_2$, where $\beta_2 \in [\underline{\beta}_2, \bar{\beta}_2]$ is the second-period efficiency parameter, is uncorrelated with β_1 and is learned (by the firm only) between the two periods (β_2 might reflect the new input costs);

(b) the second-period gross surplus is equal to S_2 (possibly equal to S_1) if the firm has produced a high-quality item in period 1, and zero otherwise; and

(c) the regulator offers the second-period contract at the beginning of period 2 (no commitment).

In this simple example, $\bar{U}_2$ and $\bar{W}_2$ are computed as in Laffont and Tirole (1986). Furthermore, if S_2 is sufficiently large relative to $\bar{\beta}_2$, $\bar{U}_2$ is independent of S_2.

[13] This results from equation (34).

$$U_1(\bar{\beta}_1)+\delta\bar{U}_2\pi(s(\bar{\beta}_1))=0. \tag{37}$$

Note that type $\bar{\beta}_1$ "buys in," that is, he is willing to trade a negative first-period rent for an expected second-period rent.[14] Expected social welfare can then be written:

$$\int_{\underline{\beta}_1}^{\bar{\beta}_1}[\pi(s)(S_1+\delta\bar{W}_2)-(1+\lambda)(\beta_1-e_1+s+\psi(e_1)) \\ -\lambda(U(\beta_1)-\delta\pi(s)\bar{U}_2)]f(\beta_1)\,d\beta_1. \tag{38}$$

The regulator maximizes (38) subject to (34), (35), and (37). Let $\mu(\beta_1)$ and $\nu(\beta_1)f(\beta_1)$ denote the multipliers of constraints (34) and (35), respectively. The Hamiltonian is

$$\mathcal{H}=[\pi(s)(S_1+\delta\bar{W}_2)-(1+\lambda)(\beta_1-e_1+s+\psi(e_1))-\lambda U+\lambda\delta\bar{U}_2\pi(s)]f \\ -\mu\psi'(e_1)+\nu f[\delta\pi'(s)\bar{U}_2-\psi'(e_1)]. \tag{39}$$

We have

$$\dot{\mu}\equiv\frac{d\mu}{d\beta_1}=-\frac{\partial\mathcal{H}}{\partial U}=\lambda f. \tag{40}$$

Because $\underline{\beta}_1$ is a free boundary and $F(\underline{\beta}_1)=0$, we thus obtain

$$\mu(\beta_1)=\lambda F(\beta_1). \tag{41}$$

Taking the derivatives of $\mathcal{H}$ with respect to the control variables e_1 and s yields

$$\psi'(e_1)=1-\frac{\lambda}{1+\lambda}\frac{F(\beta_1)}{f(\beta_1)}\psi''(e_1)-\frac{\nu}{1+\lambda}\psi''(e_1), \tag{42}$$

$$\pi'(s)(S_1+\delta\bar{W}_2+\lambda\delta\bar{U}_2)-(1+\lambda)+\nu\delta\pi''(s)\bar{U}_2=0. \tag{43}$$

Equation (42) tells us that the need to give incentives for care induces the regulator to alter the power of the incentive contract (term $[\nu/(1+\lambda)]\psi''(e_1)$). Whether incentives are more or less powerful than when quality s is verifiable (i.e., whether $\nu \gtreqless 0$) is ambiguous. On the one hand, the firm does not internalize the externality of an increase in quality on the welfare of the rest of society ($S_1+\delta\bar{W}_2+\lambda\delta\bar{U}_2>\delta\bar{U}_2$). This externality calls for a subsidization of investments in quality, that is, for a decrease in the power of the incentive scheme. On the other hand, incomplete information about technology already yields low-powered incentives; because its investment is subsidized, the firm has an incentive to overinvest in quality. (When S_1 is small (or δ is large) and the firm captures a high fraction of future rents, the second effect dominates; for small asymmetries of information, that is, F/f small, the firm's contract when quality is verifiable is close to a fixed-price contract and the first effect dominates.) While the effect of the nonverifiability of quality on the power

[14] Such "buy-in" phenomena are typical of noncommitment models, in which firms trade off current losses and future rents. See, e.g., Riordan and Sappington (1989).

of the schemes is ambiguous, the effect of a change in the desirability of quality is unambiguous (as shown in Proposition 6).

As we will see in the proof of the next proposition, the second-order conditions for maximization are satisfied. The solution $\{e_1(\beta_1), s(\beta_1), \nu(\beta_1)\}$ is thus given by (35), (42), and (43). We now derive the comparative statics results using the interpretation of the optimal incentive scheme as a menu of linear contracts (see Appendix A7).

Proposition 6. *Optimal cost-reimbursement rules are linear. The first-period contract tends toward a cost-plus contract (the slope of the incentive scheme decreases for all β_1) when*

(a) *the discount factor δ decreases;*
(b) *(if $\partial \bar{W}_2/\partial S_1 \geq 0$ and $\partial \bar{U}_2/\partial S_1 = 0$; see footnote 14 for an example) the social value of quality S_1 increases.*

Proof: See Appendix A8.

Thus, when quality becomes very important, the firm must be given a low-powered incentive scheme to supply more care [result (b)].[15] This illustrates the crowding-out effect, according to which care and effort are substitutes, so that the production of more quality is obtained at the expense of cost-reducing activities. Last, result (a) formalizes the reputation argument. Far-sighted firms can be given high-powered incentive schemes.

7 Concluding remarks

We have analyzed the circumstances under which quality concerns call for low-powered incentive schemes. For an experience good, the lack of informational value of the current sale indicator makes the cost-reimbursement rule the only instrument to achieve the conflicting goals of quality provision and cost reduction. A high concern for quality leads to low-powered incentive schemes. We have also argued that steeper incentive schemes are optimal if the supplier is sufficiently eager to preserve his reputation. For a search good, there is no "crowding-out effect" as direct sales incentives can be provided. There is, however, a new "scale effect" of quality concern on the power of incentive schemes; a high concern for quality leads to low-powered incentive schemes if and only if quantity and quality are net substitutes.

This chapter has considered the important polar cases of a search good with scale effects (in which a higher output makes cost reduction more valuable) and of an experience good without scale effect (for which output was taken as given). Understanding the crowding-out and the scale

[15] A similar conclusion was arrived at independently by Holmström and Milgrom (1990).

Table 1. *Effect of an increase in the marginal social value of quality on the power of incentive schemes*

	Search good	Experience good
Effort reduces marginal cost	+ if q and s net complements − if q and s net substitutes	Ambiguous
Effort reduces fixed cost	0	−

effects makes it easy to extend the theory to cover the other two polar cases. Consider, first, a search good and assume that the cost-reducing activity affects the fixed cost rather than the marginal cost: $C = cq + \beta - e + s$.[16] When quality becomes more desirable, output changes,[17] but the optimal effort is unaffected. Because direct sales incentives can be given and because there is no scale effect, the power of incentive schemes is independent of the demand for quality. Second, consider an experience good with variable scale such that (a) an (observable) increase in quality raises the demand for the good and (b) the effort reduces the marginal cost. For such a good, a higher valuation for quality leads to an increase in quality, which raises demand for the good and creates a scale effect that may offset the crowding-out effect. Thus, we have Table 1.

We should also note that scale effects can take other forms than the one obtained in this chapter. If the two moral hazard variables s and e interact in the cost function ($\partial^2 C/\partial s \partial e \neq 0$), an increase in the demand for quality has a direct effect on effort, not only an indirect one through the complementarity or substitutability of quality and output. While ruling out this interaction is a good working hypothesis, one can think of situations in which effort produces a new technology that reduces the marginal cost of providing services ($\partial^2 C/\partial s \partial e < 0$). We conjecture that in such situations, there is a new scale effect that leads to high-powered incentive schemes when the demand for quality is high.

Our theory may also shed some light on the behavior of more complex regulatory hierarchies, for instance, ones in which regulators have other objectives than maximizing welfare. For instance, suppose that the regulator derives perks from the supplier's delivering high-quality products. That is, the regulator values quality more than the public at large. The

16 This technology is chosen to keep the adverse selection one-dimensional and yield a closed-form solution. The analysis follows the lines of Section 3, and is left to the reader.

17 For the previous cost function, output increases, because quantity and quality are net complements as long as they are gross complements.

regulator will then lobby in favor of low-powered incentive schemes if the good is an experience good. Our theory thus offers a clue as to why Department of Defense officials who value quality highly sometimes manage to transform fixed-price contracts into cost-plus contracts.[18]

Last, the distinction between verifiable and unverifiable quality is extreme. More generally, one would want to allow quality to be verifiable at a cost. It would be worthwhile to analyze the relationship between expenses to monitor quality, quality and reputation concerns, and power of incentive schemes.

Appendix A1

Let $\gamma = \beta + (h/k)\theta$ and assume for notational simplicity that $h = k$. It is reasonable in this problem to assume that the distributions of β and θ, $F_1(\cdot)$ and $F_2(\cdot)$, are independent. Then

$$F(\gamma) \equiv \text{Prob}(\tilde{\gamma} \le \gamma) = \int_{-\infty}^{+\infty} \text{Prob}(\theta \le \tilde{\theta} \le \theta + d\theta)\,\text{Prob}(\beta \le \gamma - \theta)$$

$$= \int_{-\infty}^{+\infty} f_2(\theta) F_1(\gamma - \theta)\, d\theta,$$

$$f(\gamma) = \int_{-\infty}^{+\infty} f_2(\theta) f_1(\gamma - \theta)\, d\theta,$$

and

$$\frac{d}{d\gamma}\left(\frac{F(\gamma)}{f(\gamma)}\right) = 1 - \frac{\int_{-\infty}^{+\infty} f_2(\theta) F_1(\gamma-\theta)\, d\theta \int_{-\infty}^{+\infty} f_2(\theta) f_1'(\gamma - \theta)\, d\theta}{\left(\int_{-\infty}^{+\infty} f_2(\theta) f_1(\gamma - \theta)\, d\theta\right)^2}$$

In particular, if β is uniformly distributed (or, by symmetry, if θ is uniformly distributed), $(d/d\gamma)[F(\gamma)/f(\gamma)] = 1 > 0$.

More generally, if one of the densities is nonincreasing ($f_1' \le 0$ or $f_2' \le 0$), $F(\cdot)$ satisfies the monotone hazard-rate condition.

Appendix A2

The firm is faced with the relevation mechanism $t(\tilde{\gamma})$, $p(\tilde{\gamma})$, $q(\tilde{\gamma})$, and $(C/q)(\tilde{\gamma})$. For simplicity, we assume that the mechanism is differentiable (see Guesnerie and Laffont, 1984, for a proof of this). The firm chooses the announcement $\tilde{\gamma}$, which maximizes its objective function, that is, solves

$$\underset{\tilde{\gamma}}{\text{Max}}\left\{ t(\tilde{\gamma}) - \psi\left(\gamma + \frac{p(\tilde{\gamma}) - A + Bq(\tilde{\gamma})}{k} - \frac{C}{q}(\tilde{\gamma})\right)\right\}$$

$$\Leftrightarrow \underset{\tilde{\gamma}}{\text{Max}}\{t(\tilde{\gamma}) - \psi(\gamma - z(\tilde{\gamma}))\}, \tag{A.1}$$

[18] See also Scherer (1964, pp. 33–4, 236–9). DOD officials are well-known to favor performance over cost. They often feel that fixed-price contracts encourage contractors to make "uneconomic" reliability trade-offs and make them reluctant to make design improvements.

where

$$z(\tilde{\gamma}) \equiv \frac{C}{q}(\tilde{\gamma}) - \frac{p(\tilde{\gamma}) - A + Bq(\tilde{\gamma})}{k}.$$

The first-order condition of incentive compatibility is

$$\dot{t}(\gamma) + \psi'(\gamma - z(\gamma))\dot{z}(\gamma) = 0, \tag{A.2}$$

and the second-order condition is

$$\dot{z}(\gamma) \geq 0. \tag{A.3}$$

Equations (A.2) and (A.3) constitute necessary and sufficient conditions for incentive compatibility (see Guesnerie and Laffont, 1984).

Note that $z(\gamma) = \gamma - e(\gamma)$. So the second-order condition can be rewritten:

$$\dot{e} - 1 \leq 0. \tag{A.4}$$

Appendix A3

The regulator maximizes H with respect to $\{q, p, e\}$. The matrix of second derivatives of H with respect to these variables is (divided by f)

$$\begin{bmatrix} B - B^2 - \dfrac{2(1+\lambda)B}{k} & (1+\lambda) - B - \dfrac{1+\lambda}{k} & 1+\lambda \\ (1+\lambda) - B - \dfrac{1+\lambda}{k} & -1 & 0 \\ 1+\lambda & 0 & -(1+\lambda)\psi'' - \dfrac{\lambda F \psi'''}{f} \end{bmatrix}.$$

[This matrix differs from the Jacobian of equations (27) through (29) in that (28) was used to obtain equation (27).] For the submatrix in $\{q, p\}$ to be semidefinite negative, it must be the case that

$$B > 1 - \frac{2(1+\lambda)}{k} \tag{A.5}$$

and

$$B(1+2\lambda) > (1+\lambda)^2\left(1 - \frac{1}{k}\right)^2. \tag{A.6}$$

The determinant is

$$\Delta = -(1+\lambda)q\Delta_1 + (1+\lambda)^2,$$

where Δ_1 is the determinant of the submatrix in $\{q, p\}$. Or

$$\Delta < 0 \Leftrightarrow q\Delta_1 > 1 + \lambda.$$

Solving (27) and (28), we get

$$\Delta_1 q = (1+\lambda)(A - (\gamma - e)).$$

To sum up, sufficient conditions for the second-order conditions to be satisfied are

$$A > \underline{\gamma} + 1,$$

$$B > \text{Max}\left\{1 - \frac{2(1+\lambda)}{k}, \frac{(1+\lambda)^2}{1+2\lambda}\left(1 - \frac{1}{k}\right)^2\right\}.$$

Moreover, the solution obtained in Section 3 is valid if the second-order incentive constraint $\dot{e} \leq 1$ is satisfied by the solution of the previous first-order equations.

Differentiating (27), (28), and (29), we obtain

$$-\left(\lambda + \frac{1+\lambda}{k}\right)B\dot{q} + (1+\lambda)\left(1 - \frac{1}{k}\right)\dot{p} + (1+\lambda)\dot{e} = 1 + \lambda, \quad \text{(A.7)}$$

$$((1+\lambda)(k-1) - Bk)\dot{q} - k\dot{p} = 0, \quad \text{(A.8)}$$

$$\dot{q} - \left(\psi''(e) + \frac{\lambda}{1+\lambda}\frac{F(\gamma)}{f(\gamma)}\psi'''(e)\right)\dot{e} = \frac{\lambda}{1+\lambda}\psi''(e)\frac{d}{d\gamma}\left(\frac{F(\gamma)}{f(\gamma)}\right). \quad \text{(A.9)}$$

Hence,

$$\dot{p} = \frac{1}{\Delta}((1+\lambda)(k-1) - Bk)(1+\lambda)$$
$$\times\left[\psi''(e) + \frac{\lambda}{1+\lambda}\frac{F(\gamma)}{f(\gamma)}\psi'''(e) + \frac{\lambda}{1+\lambda}\psi''(e)\frac{d}{d\gamma}\left(\frac{F(\gamma)}{f(\gamma)}\right)\right],$$

where Δ is the determinant of the system, which is negative since we are at a maximum. Since $\psi'' > 0$, $\psi''' \geq 0$ and $(d/d\gamma)[F(\gamma)/f(\gamma)] > 0$, $\dot{p} > 0$ for $B > (1+\lambda)(k-1)/k$, which, if $B > 1$, is automatically satisfied in the relevant range: (28) implies that $\partial S^g/\partial s = kq(1-(1+\lambda)(1-1/k)) > 0$. From (A.8), $\dot{q} < 0$; and from (A.9), $\dot{e} < 0$. In that case, the second-order condition of incentive compatibility is satisfied.

Appendix A4

The dichotomy result between optimal pricing and quality in optimal incentive schemes obtained in Section 3 can be generalized as follows.

Let $\tilde{C}(\beta, e, q, s)$ denote a general cost function and let $s = \xi(\theta, q, p)$ be obtained by inverting the demand function $q = D(p, s, \theta)$.

The derived cost function is

$$C(\beta, \theta, e, q, p) = \tilde{C}(\beta, e, q, \xi(\theta, q, p)).$$

Let $e = E(\beta, \theta, C, q, p)$ be the solution of

$$C(\beta, \theta, e, q, p) = C.$$

The problem is here genuinely two-dimensional. The first-order incentive constraints can be written

$$U_\beta = -\psi'(e)E_\beta,$$
$$U_\theta = -\psi'(e)E_\theta,$$
$$U_{\beta\theta} = U_{\theta\beta},$$

where subscripts denote partial derivatives.

A sufficient condition for the dichotomy result is[19]

$$\frac{\partial E_\beta}{\partial q} = \frac{\partial E_\beta}{\partial p} = \frac{\partial E_\theta}{\partial q} = \frac{\partial E_\theta}{\partial p} = 0,$$

which requires (from Leontief's theorem) that there exists $\Lambda(\cdot,\cdot)$ and $\Gamma(\cdot,\cdot)$ such that

$$C = C(\Lambda(\beta, e), \Gamma(\theta, e), p, q),$$

a special case of which is

$$C = C(\Phi(\beta, \theta, e), p, q).$$

In our example, we have $\Phi(\beta, \theta, e) = \beta + h\theta/k - e$.

Appendix A5

Since the equations defining quality and price are the same as under complete information (dichotomy result), the comparison between complete and incomplete information can be easily obtained by observing that incomplete information gives a lower level of effort conditionally on the level of production (equation (29)). This decrease of effort itself leads, from (27) and (28), to a decrease of q (reinforcing the initial decrease of effort, which is therefore an unconditional decrease of effort) and to an increase in p.

For any γ, let us call (de) an infinitesimal decrease in effort. Differentiating (27) and (28) yields

$$k\frac{ds}{de} = \frac{dp}{de} + B\frac{dq}{de} = (1+\lambda)\left(1 - \frac{1}{k}\right)\frac{dq}{de}.$$

The conclusion follows because e and q are lower under incomplete information from the first- and second-order conditions.

Appendix A6

Proof of Propositions 3, 4, and 5: We offer a single proof to the three propositions. After substituting for the shadow price of (22) (see (26)), the Hamiltonian becomes

[19] If these conditions hold, the derivatives of the Hamiltonian with respect to p and q involve no terms associated with the incentive constraints and therefore with asymmetric information.

$$H=\frac{B}{2}q^2+(1+\lambda)pq-\frac{1}{2}(p-A+Bq)^2+l(p-A+Bq,\nu)$$
$$-(1+\lambda)\left[(\gamma-e)q+q\left(\frac{p-A+Bq}{k}\right)+m(p-A+Bq,\rho)+\psi(e)\right]$$
$$-\lambda\frac{F}{f}\psi'(e). \tag{A.10}$$

Letting $\Delta<0$ denote the determinant of the Jacobian with respect to the control variables $\{q,p,e\}$, we have

$$\frac{de}{dx}=-\frac{1}{\Delta}\begin{vmatrix}\frac{\partial^2 H}{\partial q^2} & \frac{\partial^2 H}{\partial q\partial p} & \frac{\partial^2 H}{\partial q\partial x}\\ \frac{\partial^2 H}{\partial q\partial p} & \frac{\partial^2 H}{\partial p^2} & \frac{\partial^2 H}{\partial p\partial x}\\ \frac{\partial^2 H}{\partial e\partial q} & \frac{\partial^2 H}{\partial e\partial p} & \frac{\partial^2 H}{\partial e\partial x}\end{vmatrix} \tag{A.11}$$

for $x=\nu$, ρ, and k.

But $\partial^2 H/\partial e\partial q=1+\lambda$, $\partial^2 H/\partial e\partial p=0$, and $\partial^2 H/\partial e\partial x=0$ for $x=\nu$, ρ, and k. Hence,

$$\operatorname{sign}\left(\frac{de}{dx}\right)=\operatorname{sign}\begin{vmatrix}\frac{\partial^2 H}{\partial q\partial p} & \frac{\partial^2 H}{\partial q\partial x}\\ \frac{\partial^2 H}{\partial p^2} & \frac{\partial^2 H}{\partial p\partial x}\end{vmatrix}. \tag{A.12}$$

The propositions follow from

$$\frac{\partial^2 H}{\partial q\partial p}=(1+\lambda)\left(1-\frac{1}{k}\right)-B(1+m_{11}(1+\lambda)-l_{11}),$$
$$\frac{\partial^2 H}{\partial p^2}=-(1+m_{11}(1+\lambda)-l_{11}),$$
$$\frac{\partial^2 H}{\partial q\partial \nu}=Bl_{12}=B\frac{\partial^2 H}{\partial p\partial \nu};\qquad \frac{\partial^2 H}{\partial q\partial \rho}=-Bm_{12}=B\frac{\partial^2 H}{\partial p\partial \rho},$$
$$\frac{\partial^2 H}{\partial q\partial k}=\frac{1+\lambda}{k^2}(p-A+2Bq);\qquad \frac{\partial^2 H}{\partial p\partial k}=\frac{1+\lambda}{k^2}q.$$

(To obtain Proposition 5, use (28) to substitute $p-A+Bq$.)

Appendix A7. The linearity of contracts

From Laffont and Tirole (1986), we know that we can decentralize a nonlinear contract with a menu of linear contracts if the transfer $t(C_1)$ is convex. From the first-order conditions of incentive compatibility,

$$\frac{dt}{d\beta_1}+\psi'(e_1)\frac{dC_1}{d\beta_1}=0 \quad \text{with} \quad \frac{dC_1}{d\beta_1}\geq 0$$

from second-order incentive compatibility conditions. Hence,

$$\frac{dt}{dC_1}=-\psi'(e_1) \quad \text{and} \quad \frac{d^2t}{dC_1^2}=-\psi''\dot{e}_1\frac{1}{dC_1/d\beta_1}.$$

$t(C_1)$ is convex iff $\dot{e}_1<0$. Differentiating the first-order conditions, we get

$$\dot{e}_1=\frac{-(\delta\pi''\bar{U}_2)^2\frac{\lambda}{1+\lambda}\psi''\frac{d}{d\beta_1}\frac{F(\beta_1)}{f(\beta_1)}}{\left[(\delta\pi''\bar{U}_2)^2\left((1+\lambda)\psi''+\lambda\frac{F(\beta_1)}{f(\beta_1)}\psi'''+\nu\psi'''\right)-(S_1+\delta\bar{W}_2)(\pi''+\nu\delta\pi'''\bar{U}_2)(\psi'')^2\right]}$$

$$<0.$$

Appendix A8

Proof of Proposition 6: Differentiating (42), (43), and (35) totally yields

$$\left[\psi''+\left(\frac{\lambda}{1+\lambda}\frac{F}{f}+\frac{\nu}{1+\lambda}\right)\psi'''\right]de_1=-\frac{\psi''}{1+\lambda}d\nu, \tag{A.13}$$

$$\left[\pi''(S_1+\delta\bar{W}_2+\lambda\delta\bar{U}_2)+\nu\delta\bar{U}_2\pi'''\right]ds+\left[\pi'+\delta\frac{\partial\bar{W}_2}{\partial S_1}\right]dS_1$$
$$+[\nu\pi''\bar{U}_2+\pi'\bar{W}_2+\lambda\bar{U}_2\pi']d\delta+\delta\pi''\bar{U}_2d\nu=0, \tag{A.14}$$

$$\psi''de_1=(\pi'\bar{U}_2)d\delta+(\delta\bar{U}_2\pi'')ds. \tag{A.15}$$

Substituting,

$$\text{sign}\left(\frac{\partial e_1}{\partial S_1}\right)=\text{sign}\left(-\left(\pi'+\delta\frac{\partial\bar{W}_2}{\partial S_1}\right)\right)<0, \tag{A.16}$$

$$\text{sign}\left(\frac{\partial e_1}{\partial\delta}\right)=\text{sign}(-\pi''\pi'\bar{U}_2S_1-\delta\nu\bar{U}_2^2\pi'''\pi'+\delta\bar{U}_2^2(\pi'')^2\nu)>0, \tag{A.17}$$

using (43), $\psi''' \geq 0$ and $\pi''' \leq 0$. Furthermore, it is easily seen that the assumptions $\psi''' \geq 0$ and $\pi''' \leq 0$ guarantee that the second-order conditions are satisfied.

Appendix B. Quality, asymmetric information, and reputation

We consider a two-period model in which the firm is, with probability x, a high-quality producer, that is, generates a social surplus S^H when producing. With probability $1-x$, it is a low-quality producer, that is, generates a social surplus $S^L < S^H$, unless it puts some effort $s > 0$, in which case, the social surplus is S^H.

To avoid signaling issues that would complicate the analysis, we assume the firm does not know in period 1 if it is a high- or a low-quality producer. [Thus, the model is closer to Holmström's (1982) than to Kreps and Wilson's (1982) and Milgrom and Roberts' (1982).] Moreover, quality cannot be contracted upon. At the end of period 1, if production occurs, the regulator discovers the quality level.

In period 1, the firm has a cost function

$$C_1 = \beta_1 - e,$$

where β_1 is known to and C_1 observed by the regulator, and e_1 is a cost-reducing effort. Total effort for the firm is $e_1 = e$ or $e_1 = e + s$ when the firm is putting the extra effort s to make sure that first-period quality is high. Let t_1 be the transfer given to the firm in period 1.

The regulator cannot commit for period 2. In period 2, the firm has a cost parameter $\beta_2 \in [\underline{\beta}, \bar{\beta}]$ with a (common knowledge) distribution $F(\cdot)$ and a cost function

$$C_2 = \beta_2 - e_2.$$

β_2 will be learned by the firm at the beginning of date 2. Therefore, at that time, we will be in a one-period adverse-selection problem (Laffont and Tirole, 1986).

For any expected social surplus S in period 2, second-period welfare is

$$W^*(S) = \int_{\underline{\beta}}^{\bar{\beta}} \{S - (1+\lambda)(\psi(e^*(\beta_2)) + \beta_2 - e^*(\beta_2)) - \lambda U^*(\beta_2)\} \, dF(\beta_2),$$

where (according to Laffont and Tirole, 1986)

$$\psi'(e^*(\beta_2)) = 1 - \frac{\lambda}{1+\lambda} \frac{F(\beta_2)}{f(\beta_2)} \psi''(e^*(\beta_2)),$$

$$U^*(\beta_2) = \int_{\beta_2}^{\bar{\beta}} \psi'(e^*(\tilde{\beta}_2)) \, d\tilde{\beta}_2.$$

Let t^*, C^*, and U^* be the expected transfer, cost, and rent, respectively, in this optimal second-period mechanism.

To limit the analysis to the most interesting cases, we postulate the following.

Assumption 1. *If* $S = xS^H + (1-x)S^L$, *then* $W^*(S) > 0$ *for any* $F(\cdot)$ *on* $[\underline{\beta}, \bar{\beta}]$. *If* $S = S^L$, *then* $W^*(S) < 0$ *for any* $F(\cdot)$ *on* $[\underline{\beta}, \bar{\beta}]$.

Assumption 1 means that for an expected quality defined by the prior, it is worth realizing the project. However, if the firm is known to be a low-quality firm, it is not worth doing it, even if attention is restricted to the best types (close to $\underline{\beta}$). Assumption 1 requires that $(\bar{\beta} - \underline{\beta})$ not be "too large."

Assumption 2.

$$s < \frac{(1-\delta)(1-x)}{1+\lambda}(S^H - S^L).$$

Assumption 2 means that the extra effort needed to upgrade quality is not too high compared to the social gain $(S^H - S^L)$. Without this assumpsumption, it is never optimal to induce upgrading of quality in the first period.

Two policies must be considered. In policy A, s is not induced, and in policy B, s is induced (inducing randomization by the firm is never optimal).

Policy A

Social welfare is

$$W = xS^H + (1-x)S^L - (1+\lambda)(\beta_1 - e_1 + t_1) + \delta x(S^H - (1+\lambda)(t^* + C^*)) + U,$$

where U is the firm's intertemporal rent, and we use the fact that in period 2, the regulator knows whether he is facing a high-quality firm.

Social welfare must be maximized under the individual rationality (IR) and incentive compatibility (IC) constraints.

If the firm does not produce in period 1, the regulator learns nothing and the firm can expect a rent U^* in period 2. Accordingly, the IR constraint takes the form:

$$t_1 - \psi(e_1) + \delta x U^* \geq \delta U^*. \qquad (\text{IR}_\text{A})$$

The IC constraint is

$$t_1 - \psi(e_1) + \delta x U^* \geq t_1 - \psi(e_1 + s) + \delta U^*. \qquad (\text{IC}_\text{A})$$

In regime I, (IC_A) is not binding and therefore

$$\psi'(e_1)=1 \quad \text{or} \quad e_1=e^*,$$
$$t_1=\psi(e_1)+\delta(1-x)U^*,$$
$$U=\delta U^*.$$

(IC_A) can be rewritten with $\tilde{\Phi}(e)\equiv\psi(e+s)-\psi(e)$,

$$\tilde{\Phi}(e_1)\geq\delta(1-x)U^* \quad \text{or} \quad \delta\leq\delta_1,$$

where $\tilde{\Phi}(e^*)\equiv\delta_1(1-x)U^*$.

In regime II, (IC_A) is binding, and effort is defined by

$$\tilde{\Phi}(e(\delta))=\delta(1-x)U^*,$$

with $de/d\delta>0$ and $e(\delta)>e^*$. Welfare is then

$$W^{\text{I}}=xS^H+(1-x)S^L-(1+\lambda)(\beta_1-e^*+\psi(e^*)) +\delta xW^*(S^H)-\lambda(1-x)\delta U^*,$$
$$W^{\text{II}}=xS^H+(1-x)S^L-(1+\lambda)(\beta_1-e^*(\delta)+\psi(e^*(\delta))) +\delta xW^*(S^H)-\lambda(1-x)\delta U^*.$$

$W^{\text{I}}\geq W^{\text{II}}$, but regime I is not feasible for $\delta>\delta_1$.

Policy B

Social welfare is now

$$W=S^H-(1+\lambda)(\beta_1-(e_1-s)+t_1) +\delta[S^H-(1-x)(S^H-S^L)-(1+\lambda)(t^*+C^*)]+U$$

with the constraints

$$t_1-\psi(e_1)+\delta U^*\geq\delta U^*, \tag{IR_B}$$
$$t_1-\psi(e_1)+\delta U^*\geq t_1-\psi(e_1-s)+\delta xU^*. \tag{IC_B}$$

In regime III, (IC_B) is not binding, and $e_1=e^*$, $t_1=\psi(e_1)$.

Regime III prevails as long as

$$\tilde{\Phi}(e_1-s)=\psi(e_1)-\psi(e_1-s)\leq\delta(1-x)U^*$$

or $\delta>\delta_0$ with $\delta_1>\delta_0$.

If $\delta<\delta_0$, (IC_B) is binding and e_1 is defined by

$$\tilde{\Phi}(e_1-s)=\delta(1-x)U^*$$

or $e_1=e(\delta)+s$ with $s+e(\delta)<e^*$ (regime IV).

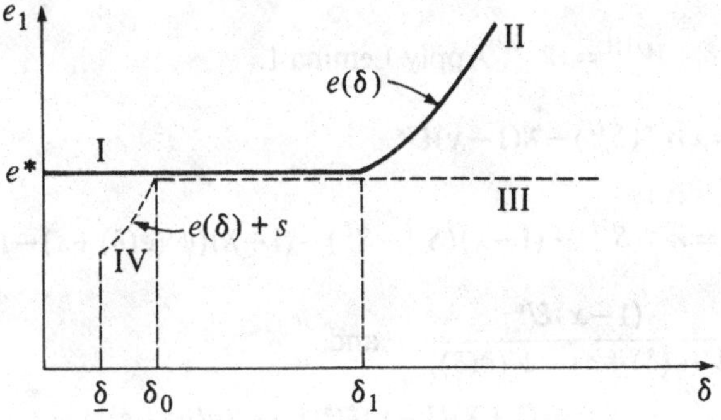

Figure 2.

For $\delta \leq \underline{\delta}$ defined by $s = e(\underline{\delta})$, it is *not possible* to induce quality. Welfares are

$$W^{\text{III}} = S^H - (1+\lambda)(\beta_1 - e^* + s + \psi(e^*)) + \delta(W^*(S^H) - (1-x)(S^H - S^L)),$$

$$W^{\text{IV}} = S^H - (1+\lambda)(\beta_1 - e(\delta) + \psi(e(\delta)+s)) + \delta(W^*(S^H) - (1-x)(S^H - S^L)).$$

Effort levels are summarized in Figure 2.

Lemma 1. $W^{\text{III}} > W^{\text{I}}$.

Proof:

$$W^{\text{III}} - W^{\text{I}} = (1-\delta)(1-x)(S^H - S^L) - (1+\lambda)s + (1-x)\delta(S^H - (1+\lambda)E(\psi(e^*(\beta_2)) + \beta_2 - e^*(\beta_2)))).$$

The sum of the first two terms is positive in view of Appendix A2 and the third term is positive in view of Appendix A1. □

As $W^{\text{II}} < W^{\text{I}}$, regime III is optimal for $\delta \geq \delta_0$. For $\delta < \underline{\delta}$, regime I is clearly optimal.

Lemma 2.

(a) *There exists $\hat{\delta} \in [\underline{\delta}, \delta_0)$ such that for $\delta > \hat{\delta}$, the optimum is to induce quality and*

$$e_1 = e(\delta) + s < e^* \quad \text{if } \hat{\delta} < \delta \leq \delta_0,$$
$$= e^* \quad \text{if } \delta > \delta_0.$$

(b) *If $S^H - S^L < \lambda U^*$, for $\delta < \hat{\delta}$, the optimum is not to induce quality and $e_1 = e^*$.*

Proof:

(a) At $\delta=\delta_0$, $W^{\text{III}}=W^{\text{IV}}$. Apply Lemma 1.

(b) $$\frac{dW^{\text{I}}}{d\delta}=xW^*(S^H)-\lambda(1-x)U^*,$$

$$\frac{dW^{\text{IV}}}{d\delta}=W^*(S^H)-(1-x)(S^H-S^L)-(1+\lambda)(\psi'(e(\delta)+s)-1)\frac{de}{d\delta},$$

$$\frac{de}{d\delta}=\frac{(1-x)U^*}{\psi'(e(\delta)+s)-\psi'(e(\delta))},\quad \text{and}$$

$$\frac{dW^{\text{IV}}}{d\delta}=W^*(S^H)+\frac{(1+\lambda)(1-x)U^*(1-\psi'(e(\delta)+s))}{\psi'(e(\delta)+s)-\psi'(e(\delta))}-(1-x)(S^H-S^L).$$

If $S^H-S^L<\lambda U^*$, $dW^{\text{IV}}/d\delta>dW^{\text{I}}/d\delta$, hence the result. □

Thus, we get the following.

Proposition 7.

(a) *Incentives are higher when one does not want to induce quality.*
(b) *Conditional on inducing quality, the incentive scheme becomes more high-powered when δ increases.*

Proof:

(a) This follows because $e_1\le e^*$ when quality is induced.
(b) This follows from $de/d\delta>0$. □

The results are thus very similar to those of the moral hazard model of Section 6. A difference is that incentives are not monotonic in the discount factor. For a low discount factor, an extremely low-powered incentive scheme is needed for the firm to exert *s*. The loss of incentive to reduce cost is too costly, which yields a corner solution: Because the firm is not induced to provide quality and β_1 is common knowledge, the first-period contract is a fixed-price contract. But as long as the discount factor is sufficiently high to make it worthwile to induce quality, incentives to reduce cost increase with the discount factor.

REFERENCES

Besanko, D., S. Donnenfeld, and L. White. 1987. "Monopoly and Quality Distortion: Effects and Remedies." *Quarterly Journal of Economics* 102: 743–68.

Guesnerie, R., and J.-J. Laffont. 1984. "A Complete Solution to a Class of Principal-Agent Problems with an Application to the Control of a Self-Managed Firm." *Journal of Public Economics* 25: 329–69.

Holmström, B. 1982. "Managerial Incentive Problems: A Dynamic Perspective." In *Essays in Economics and Management in Honor of Lars Wahlbeck,* Helsinki: Swedish School of Economics.

Holmström, B., and P. Milgrom. 1990. "Multi-Task Principal Agent Analysis: Incentive Contracts, Asset Ownership and Job Design." Mimeo, Yale University, New Haven.

Joskow, P., and N. Rose. 1989. "The Effects of Economic Regulation." In *Handbook of Industrial Organization,* Vol. 2, R. Schmalensee and R. Willig, Eds. Amsterdam: North-Holland, pp. 1449–1506.

Kahn, A. 1988. *The Economics of Regulation: Principles and Institutions.* Cambridge, MA: The MIT Press.

Kreps, D., and R. Wilson. 1982. "Reputation and Imperfect Information." *Journal of Economic Theory* 27: 253–79.

Laffont, J.-J. 1987. "Optimal Taxation of a Nonlinear Pricing Monopolist." *Journal of Public Economics* 33: 137–55.

Laffont, J.-J., E. Maskin, and J.-C. Rochet. 1987. "Optimal Nonlinear Pricing with Two-Dimensional Characteristics." In *Information, Incentives and Economic Mechanisms,* T. Groves, R. Radner, and S. Reiter, Eds. Minneapolis: University of Minnesota Press, Chap. 8.

Laffont, J.-J., and J. Tirole. 1986. "Using Cost Observation to Regulate Firms." *Journal of Political Economy* 94: 614–41.

1990. "The Regulation of Multiproduct Firms, I: Theory." *Journal of Public Economics* 43: 1–66.

Lewis, T., and D. Sappington. 1988a. "Monitoring Quality Provision in Regulated Markets." Discussion Paper, University of California at Davis and Bellcore.

1988b. "Regulating a Monopolist with Unknown Demand." *American Economic Review* 78: 986–98.

Milgrom, P., and J. Roberts. 1982. "Predation, Reputation and Entry Deterrence." *Journal of Economic Theory* 27: 280–312.

Mussa, M., and S. Rosen. 1978. "Monopoly and Product Quality." *Journal of Economic Theory* 23: 301–17.

Noam, E. 1989. "The Quality of Regulation in Regulating Quality: A Proposal for an Integrated Incentive Approach to Telephone Service Performance." Albany, NY: New York State Public Service Commission.

Riordan, M., and D. Sappington. 1989. "Second Sourcing." *Rand Journal of Economics* 20: 41–58.

Sappington, D. 1983. "Optimal Regulation of a Multiproduct Monopoly with Unknown Technological Capabilities." *Bell Journal of Economics* 14: 453–63.

Scherer, F. 1964. *The Weapons Acquisition Process: Economic Incentives.* Cambridge, MA: Graduate School of Business Administration, Harvard University.

Spence, A. M. 1975. "Monopoly, Quality and Regulation." *Bell Journal of Economics* 6: 417–29.

Tirole, J. 1988. *The Theory of Industrial Organization.* Cambridge, MA: The MIT Press.

Vickers, J., and G. Yarrow. 1988. *Privatization: An Economic Analysis.* Cambridge, MA: The MIT Press.

PART III

Equilibrium and dynamics

CHAPTER 9

Stability of a Keynesian adjustment process

Jacques H. Drèze

1 Introduction

1.1

In this chapter, I study the stability of an adjustment process on prices and quantities that converges in finitely many steps to an equilibrium admitting excess supply of (some) factors of production. The finite convergence results because the leading adjustments are finite, and the equilibrium concept allows for ϵ-discrepancies between transacted *input* levels and those required by technology. The excess supply of factors of production at the equilibrium is associated with downward rigidities of nominal factor prices. Such an equilibrium is a special case of the so-called "supply-constrained equilibria" studied by Dehez and Drèze (1984), following a seminal contribution of van der Laan (1980). These rigidities are best understood as reflecting noncompetitive supply behavior by owners of the production factors. (Here the supply of factors by individual households is modeled as totally inelastic to prices, whose downward rigidity may be viewed as a form of collective income protection.)

The modeling of the economy embodies a distinction between primary inputs and other commodities. The leading adjustments concern the prices and quantities of primary inputs; quantity adjustments reflect the profit-seeking decisions of producers (firms) and price increases take place under the pressure of excess demand. Thus, the quantity adjustments are decentralized firm by firm, and the price adjustments are decentralized market by market.

A tâtonnement process is studied first to clear the ground on a simpler case. My main interest, however, goes to a nontâtonnement process, with production and consumption activities carried out in continuous time out

Helpful suggestions from Paul Champsaur, Pierre Dehez, Henry Tulkens, and Gerd Weinrich are gratefully acknowledged.

of equilibrium. Feasibility of these activities is ensured by inventories, and it is shown that bounded inventory levels are sufficient for feasibility.

To establish finite convergence of a simple decentralized nontâtonnement adjustment process, with ongoing production and consumption, is a major step toward realism. The equilibrium concept also has claims to realism. The empirical record clearly supports the view that nonstorable factors of production, in particular labor and the services of capital, are not fully used all the time; see Figure 1 for European data, 1973–89. It thus seems meaningful to study the stability properties of equilibria with that property. (The ϵ-feature I regard as entirely innocuous; some might claim that it adds to realism; to me, it is a convenience, neither more nor less.)

Of course, a price has to be paid for these results, in the form of assumptions. These come at three distinct levels.

1. Most basic are the behavioral assumptions about consumers and producers. Consumers are, as usual, price takers and preference maximimizers. They hold endowments of the primary factors of production and supply these inelastically – an assumption that is not quite realistic for (female) labor services, but could be relaxed. Producers are modeled implicitly as setting prices of commodities through a markup on production costs (where the markup rates may reflect perceived demand elasticities or fixed costs); their demand for factors is derived from their input needs to meet the demand for commodities at these prices. As suggested in Section 1.2, these behavioral assumptions seem consistent with empirical findings. I regard them as specific, but not particularly restrictive.

2. A major difficulty arising in nontâtonnement processes with ongoing production and consumption concerns the modeling of expectations and intertemporal optimization under uncertainty. That difficulty is completely eschewed here, to concentrate on stability. Both firms and consumers are assumed to hold static-deterministic expectations, that is, to anticipate that prices and quantity constraints observed today will continue to prevail forever after. That assumption is very crude, and motivated exclusively by the understandable desire to split difficulties. It is accompanied by an assumption of stationary preferences for consumers and by an equally crude assumption about inventory decisions by firms. I regard these (standard) assumptions as very strong, but provisional.

3. At a third level, I will introduce two assumptions – one on technology and the other on consumer preferences – that are clearly restrictive, but are needed for my stability proofs. The assumption on technology combines the absence of joint production with constant returns. This permits choosing input coefficients on the basis of input prices alone, without

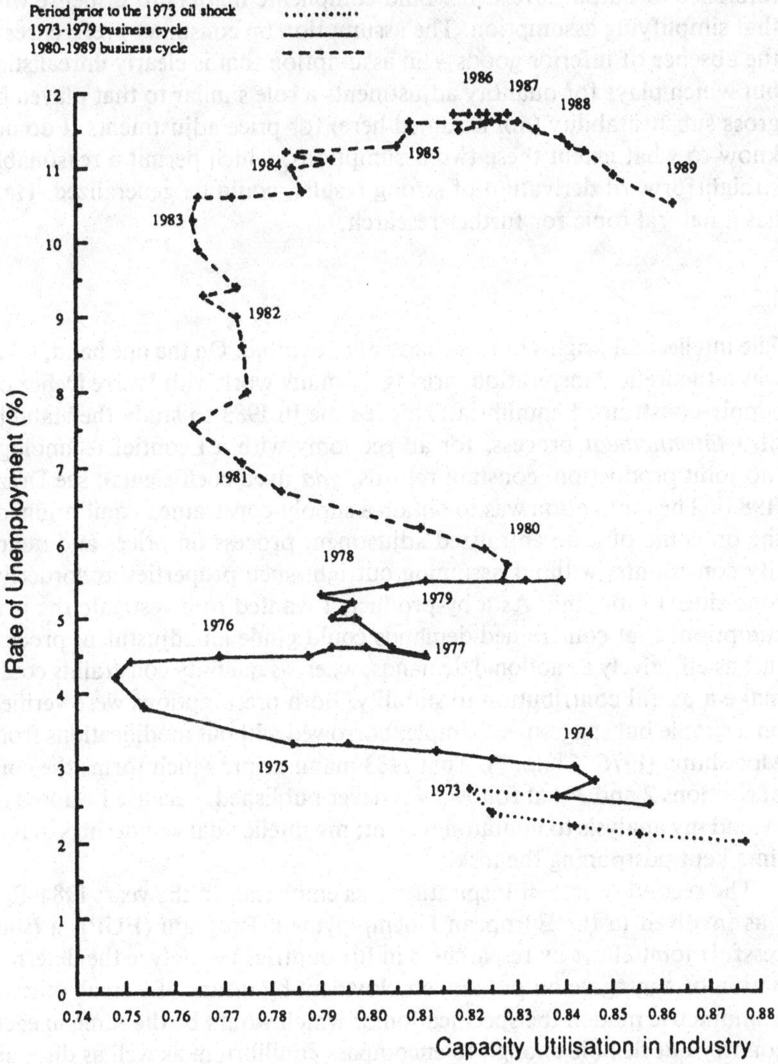

Figure 1. Rate of unemployment and capacity utilization in industry in the European Community. Quarterly observations are shown, with the years marked against the first quarter. *Source: European Economy.*

reference to output levels. It would complicate matters to dispense with that simplifying assumption. The assumption on consumer preferences is the absence of inferior goods - an assumption that is clearly unrealistic,[1] but which plays for quantity adjustments a role similar to that played by gross substitutability (not assumed here) for price adjustments. I do not know to what extent these two assumptions, which permit a reasonably straightforward derivation of strong results, could be generalized. Here lies a natural topic for further research.

1.2

The intellectual origins of this chapter are twofold. On the one hand, there was a theoretical inspiration, arising from my work with Pierre Dehez on supply-constrained equilibria. This led me in 1983 to study the stability of a *tâtonnement* process, for an economy with a Leontief technology (no joint production, constant returns, *and* fixed coefficients); see Drèze (1983). The motivation was to obtain a supply-constrained equilibrium as the outcome of a decentralized adjustment process on prices and quantity constraints, without assuming outright such properties as "orderly" (one-sided) rationing. As a by-product, I wanted to investigate the presumptions that constrained demands could guide an adjustment process just as effectively as notional demands, whereas quantity constraints could make a useful contribution to stability. Both presumptions were verified on a simple but suggestive example, borrowed without modifications from Morishima (1976, Chap. 7). That 1983 manuscript, which forms the core of Sections 2 and 3 that follow, was never published, because I wanted to extend my analysis to nontâtonnement; my intellectual wanderings in real time kept postponing the task.

The second source of inspiration was empirical. In the years 1984–9, I was involved in the European Unemployment Program (EUP), a (successful) joint effort by researchers in 10 countries to analyze the determination of aggregate output and employment by means of a small macroeconometric model, the specification of which would be the same in each country but flexible enough to encompass equilibrium as well as disequilibrium situations; see Drèze et al. (1991). That methodology led to the verification of a number of empirical regularities, in which I recognized interesting similitudes with the structure of Morishima's model. These regularities include econometric results compatible with the following specifications: (1) pricing at average cost plus a markup; (2) no rationing of

[1] See, however, Section 8.5.

final demand; (3) downward rigidity of nominal wages; (4) persistent unemployment; and (5) CES-Leontief technology with constant returns (see Drèze and Bean, 1990).

These findings provided the motivation to extend my earlier analysis in two directions, namely: a more general technology encompassing the CES-Leontief specification (general convex production sets, subject only to the twin restrictions of constant returns and absence of joint production); and nontâtonnement. These extensions are included in the present chapter. In the process of carrying out the extensions, I also realized that my 1983 stability proof could be simplified significantly.

The chapter is divided in two parts. Part I presents the tâtonnement process corresponding to Morishima's model (Sections 2 and 3), with a simple illustration for the Barro and Grossman (1971)–Malinvaud (1977) Macroeconomic Model (Section 4) and the extension to variable input coefficients (Section 5). Part II presents the extension to nontâtonnement (Sections 6 and 7). Some comments and concluding remarks are offered in Section 8.

PART I: TÂTONNEMENT

2 The economy and the process

2.1

The tâtonnement process studied in Part I may be viewed as a formalization of the system described in Morishima (1976, Chap. 7), and summarized as follows by the author:

> The Keynesian system we have described . . . has the following system of transmission between its parts. First, suppose that prices of factors of production are given arbitrarily or historically. The prices of products are determined so that they satisfy the equation: prices = costs + normal profits. Now all prices are given, and therefore the income of workers and capitalists per unit of product is determined, and we can determine the remaining unknowns, l individual outputs, by the equations of the theory of effective demand, . . . since we take the gross investment in capital goods as given. Outputs thus determined decide the demand for labor and the services of capital goods. When these demands do not exceed the existing quantities of capital goods and the supplies of various kinds of labor corresponding to given prices and wages, then there is no excess demand for producer goods. Therefore, . . . prices are stationary because of the downward rigidity of wages and the prices of capital services, and we have an underemployment equilibrium accompanied by idle capital or unemployment. . . .
>
> In contrast to this, if excess demand exists for capital services or for labor, the prices of producer goods will change. . . . The change spreads in turn to product

prices, the outputs of each good and the excess demands for the producer goods, and then back once again to the point of departure, namely the prices of producer goods. The process of price adjustment is repeated until full-employment equilibrium or underemployment equilibrium is eventually established.

The structure of the economy is summarized in the upper half of Table 1.

There are $1+m+n$ commodities. Commodity 0 is "money", commodities $1, \ldots, m$ are inputs, commodities $m+1, \ldots, m+n$ are consumer goods. The price of money is equal to 1. The prices of inputs are denoted $p \in R^m$, and the prices of outputs are denoted $q \in R^n$.

An $m \times n$ technology matrix A describes the net input requirements for producing consumer goods. Thus, A_{kj} is the quantity of input k consumed per unit of consumer good j. It is a net quantity, in the sense that intermediate commodities are not recognized explicitly but instead are represented by their own input requirements. This assumes that the economy is "productive" (no A_{kj} is infinite). Inputs are of three types: labor services, natural resources (land, minerals, etc.) and "machines". The availability of inputs is fixed in the short run and is the only limiting factor in the production of consumer goods.[2]

There are N consumers indexed $i=1, \ldots, N$. Consumer i initially holds a positive quantity of money m_0^i and a nonnegative vector of input endowments $z^i \in R^m$. Typically, each consumer will supply one type of labor services, up to a maximal amount corresponding to his or her endowment. Ownership of natural resources and "machines" is shared among consumers, possibly reflecting their fixed ownership fractions in firms controlling these inputs.

The (nominal) prices of inputs are initially set at given levels $p(0)$ and are eventually adjusted *upward* along the process in response to excess demand; they are never adjusted downward. At these prices, consumers supply their total endowments z^i. Excess supply of an input is accompanied by quantity rationing. I denote by $\zeta_k^i(t)$ the upper bound on the net sales of input k by consumer i at stage t of the process. By construction, $z_k^i \geq \zeta_k^i(t) \geq 0$. (Under an alternative interpretation, the ζ^i's denote

[2] It is suggestive, although not necessary, to think about each consumer good as being produced on a specific "machine", the capacity of which sets an upper limit to the production of that good. In this interpretation, a "machine" is typically a shop or plant (e.g., a weaving plant with many looms, rather than a single loom). All the facilities that permit production of a given consumer good with the same unit requirements in labor and natural resources may thus be lumped into a single "machine". When the input requirements differ, variable coefficients and diminishing returns fit into the linear technology – but at the cost of handling perfect substitutes in consumption, hence demand correspondences.

Table 1.

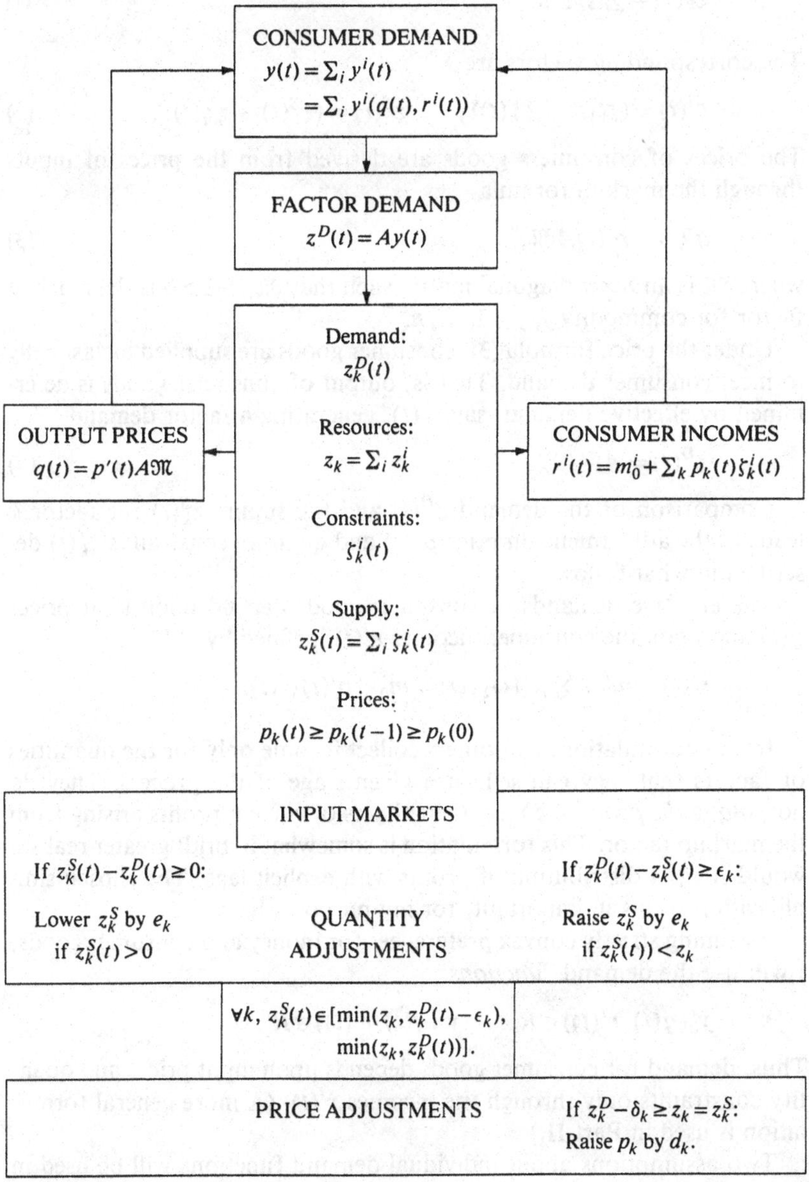
CONSUMER DEMAND
$y(t) = \Sigma_i y^i(t)$
$= \Sigma_i y^i(q(t), r^i(t))$
FACTOR DEMAND
$z^D(t) = Ay(t)$
Demand:
$z_k^D(t)$
Resources:
$z_k = \Sigma_i z_k^i$
Constraints:
$\zeta_k^i(t)$
Supply:
$z_k^S(t) = \Sigma_i \zeta_k^i(t)$
Prices:
$p_k(t) \geq p_k(t-1) \geq p_k(0)$
INPUT MARKETS
OUTPUT PRICES
$q(t) = p'(t)A\mathfrak{M}$
CONSUMER INCOMES
$r^i(t) = m_0^i + \Sigma_k p_k(t)\zeta_k^i(t)$
If $z_k^S(t) - z_k^D(t) \geq 0$:
Lower z_k^S by e_k
if $z_k^S(t) > 0$
QUANTITY
ADJUSTMENTS
If $z_k^D(t) - z_k^S(t) \geq \epsilon_k$:
Raise z_k^S by e_k
if $z_k^S(t)) < z_k$
$\forall k,\ z_k^S(t) \in [\min(z_k, z_k^D(t) - \epsilon_k),$
$\min(z_k, z_k^D(t))]$.
PRICE ADJUSTMENTS
If $z_k^D - \delta_k \geq z_k = z_k^S$:
Raise p_k by d_k.

input levels for which household i has contracted with the production sector.) I also define the *effective aggregate supply* of inputs by

$$z_k^S(t) = \sum_i \zeta_k^i(t). \tag{1}$$

The corresponding vectors are

$$\zeta^i(t) = (\zeta_1^i(t) \cdots \zeta_m^i(t))', \qquad z^S(t) = (z_1^S(t) \cdots z_m^S(t))'. \tag{2}$$

The prices of consumers goods are derived from the prices of inputs through the markup formula

$$q'(t) = p'(t)A\mathfrak{M}, \tag{3}$$

where $\mathfrak{M}$ is an $n \times n$ diagonal matrix such that $\mathfrak{M}_{jj} - 1 \geq 0$ is the markup factor for commodity j, $j = 1, \ldots, n$.

Under the price formula (3), consumer goods are supplied inelastically to meet consumer demand. That is, output of consumer goods is determined by effective demand, say, $y(t)$, generating a factor demand

$$z^D(t) = Ay(t). \tag{4}$$

Comparison of the demand $z_k^D(t)$ and the supply $z_k^S(t)$ for factor k leads to the adjustments in price $p_k(t)$ and quantity constraints $\zeta_k^i(t)$ described in what follows.

The effective demands of consumer goods depend upon their prices $q(t)$ and upon the consumer incomes $r^i(t)$, defined by

$$r^i(t) = m_0^i + \sum_k p_k(t)\zeta_k^i(t) = m_0^i + p'(t)\zeta^i(t). \tag{5}$$

In this formulation, consumers collect income only for the quantities of factors that they can sell, at a given stage of the process. They do not, *along the process,* collect their shares of current profits arising from the markup factor. This formulation is somewhat hybrid; greater realism would suggest distribution of profits with explicit lags. The chosen simplification seems unimportant, for my purposes here.

Assuming strictly convex preferences for money and consumer goods, I will use the demand *functions*

$$y_0^i(q(t), r^i(t)) \in R, \qquad y^i(q(t), r^i(t)) \in R^n.$$

Thus, demand for consumer goods depends upon input prices and quantity constraints only through the incomes $r^i(t)$. (A more general formulation is used in Part II.)

Two assumptions about individual demand functions will be used in what follows.

Assumption NI. *For all i, for all q,* r^i *and* $\hat{r}^i \geq r^i$: $y^i(q, \hat{r}^i) \geq y^i(q, r^i)$.

Assumption MPC. *For each i, there exists* $\gamma^i > 0$ *(independent of q and* r^i*) such that, for all q,* r^i *and* $\hat{r}^i \geq r^i$: $y_0^i(q, \hat{r}^i) \geq y_0^i(q, r^i) + \gamma^i(\hat{r}^i - r^i)$.

Assumption NI (Noninferiority) rules out inferior goods, which is very unfortunate, since there is nothing pathological about such goods (see, however, Section 8.5). Assumption MPC (Marginal Propensity to Consume) states that the marginal propensity to spend is bounded away from unity.

The description of the economy is now complete, and may be summarized as follows (see also Table 1):

1. Given a vector of input prices $p(t)$ and a matrix of quantity constraints $[\zeta_k^i(t)]$, individual incomes are defined by

$$r^i(t) = m_0^i + \sum_k p_k(t)\zeta_k^i(t) = m_0^i + p'(t)\zeta^i(t), \tag{5}$$

and prices for consumer goods are defined by

$$q(t) = p'(t)A\mathfrak{M}. \tag{3}$$

2. Demand for consumer goods is defined by

$$y(t) = \sum_i y^i(t) = \sum_i y^i(q(t), r^i(t)); \tag{6}$$

that demand implies a demand for inputs

$$z^D(t) = Ay(t). \tag{4}$$

2.2

Upon comparing the demand vector for inputs $z^D(t)$ with the supply vector $z^S(t) = \sum_i \zeta^i(t)$, adjustments in prices and quantity constraints can be defined. I will consider a *hierarchical process,* under which *prices are adjusted only after all justified adjustments in quantity constraints have been realized;* in other words, quantities move faster than prices, in agreement with the Clower–Leijonhufvud reappraisal of Keynesian economics.[3]

The process is *discrete*. For each input k, there is a quantity unit e_k, of which all initial endowments are treated as integer multiples. Quantity

[3] "In the Keynesian macrosystem the Marshallian ranking of price- and quantity-adjustment speeds is reversed: in the shortest period flow quantities are freely variable, but one or more prices are given, and the admissible range of variation for the rest of the prices is thereby limited" (Leijonhufvud, 1968, p. 52).

constraints $\zeta_k^i(t)$ are adjusted by discrete steps of fixed, constant size e_k. And there is a price unit d_k. Prices $p_k(t)$ are similarly adjusted by discrete steps of fixed, constant size d_k.

The adjustment rules involve *thresholds*. No adjustment in input levels, hence in quantity constraints, takes place unless the excess demand or supply for an input, $|z_k^D(t)-z_k^S(t)|$, reaches some a priori given minimal level ϵ_k (at least one quantity unit, possibly more). And no adjustment in price takes place unless the excess *demand* for an input, $z_k^D(t)-z_k^S(t)$, is at least equal to some a priori given minimal level δ_k ($\geq \epsilon_k$).

This approach has two consequences. First, it leads to a finite convergence theorem, under rather weak assumptions. Second, it leads only to an *approximate equilibrium,* where a small discrepancy between supply and demand (at most δ_k) is tolerated.

The idea that prices are not adjusted unless demand exceeds supply by at least some given (but arbitrarily small) δ_k is definitely appealing, considering the fixed costs of changing prices. An arbitrarily small discrepancy between supply and demand of an *input* seems tolerable, as it can be absorbed by a commensurate adjustment in productivity, product quality, or inventories.[4] In my definition of equilibrium, the discrepancy is of arbitrary sign. In the adjustment process, I assume that firms always get rid of excess inputs, and rely on productivity or inventory adjustments to achieve feasibility. That formulation is geared to the nontâtonnement analysis, where it is technically more convenient and logically more congruent with the notion that excess demand for final commodities is absorbed by inventories.

Definition 1. *An* ϵ-equilibrium with excess supply *consists of a vector of input prices* $p\in R^m$, *a matrix of quantity constraints* $[\zeta_k^i]\in R^{Nm}$, *a vector of inputs* $z^D\in R^m$, *a vector of outputs* $y\in R^n$, *a vector of prices* $q\in R^n$ *with* $q'=p'A\mathfrak{M}$, *and an N-tuple of vectors* $(y_0^i, y^i)\in R\times R^n$ *such that:*

(i) (z^D, y) *maximizes* $q'y-p'z^D$ *subject to* $z^D\geq Ay$, $y\leq \Sigma_i y^i$;
(ii) (y_0^i, y^i) *maximizes i's preferences, subject to* $y_0^i+q'y^i\leq m_0^i+p'\zeta^i$;
(iii) $[0]\leq[\zeta_k^i]\leq[z_k^i]$, $\Sigma_i y^i\leq y$;
(iv) *for all* $k=1,\dots,m$, $|z_k^D-\Sigma_i\zeta_k^i|\leq\epsilon$.

[4] Note that, if profits are defined as $\pi=q'y-p'\Sigma_i\zeta^i$, so that any discrepancy between supply and demand of inputs is absorbed by the production sector, then automatically $\Sigma_i y_0^i+\pi=\Sigma_i m_0^i$ in equilibrium. Indeed,

$$\sum_i y_0^i+\pi=\sum_i(r^i-q'y^i)+\pi=\sum_i(m_0^i+p'\zeta^i)-q'y+q'y-p'\sum_i\zeta^i=\sum_i m_0^i,$$

which corresponds to Walras' law in this model.

Description of the process P

The process is defined in terms of the sequence $(p(t), [\zeta_k^i(t)])$, $t = 0, 1, \ldots$. The other parameters are at all stages defined through (3)-(6).

(P i) *Initiation*

Initial input prices $p(0)$ are historically given, with $p_k(0) > 0$ for all k.

Initial quantity constraints are historically set at $\zeta_k^i(0)$, an integer multiple of e_k, with $z_k^i \geq \zeta_k^i(0) \geq 0$ for all i and k.

(P ii) *General step: Adjustment of a quantity constraint*

At stage t, a single quantity constraint is adjusted, provided there exists an input k for which such an adjustment is justified. (The order in which markets are visited is immaterial.)

Two situations are distinguished:

(a) $z_k^S(t) - z_k^D(t) > 0$.

Then necessarily $z_k^S(t) > 0$, and there exists i such that $\zeta_k^i(t) > 0$. For some (any) such i, set

$$\zeta_k^i(t+1) = \zeta_k^i(t) - e_k. \tag{7}$$

(That is, the constraint on net sales of input k by consumer i is lowered by one unit e_k. Because $\zeta_k^i(t)$ results from the operation of the process, starting from an integer multiple of e_k, $\zeta_k^i(t) > 0$ implies $\zeta_k^i(t+1) \geq 0$.)

(b) $z_k^D(t) - z_k^S(t) \geq \epsilon_k$ with $z_k^S(t) < z_k$.

Then necessarily there exists i such that $\zeta_k^i(t) < z_k^i$. For some (any) such i, set

$$\zeta_k^i(t+1) = \zeta_k^i(t) + e_k. \tag{8}$$

(That is, the constraint on net sales of input k by consumer i is raised by one unit e_k. Because both $\zeta_k^i(t)$ and z_k^i are integer multiples of e_k, $\zeta_k^i(t) < z_k^i$ implies $\zeta_k^i(t+1) \leq z_k^i$.)

(P iii) *General step: Adjustment of a price*

If, at stage t, no adjustment of quantity constraints is justified, then it must be the case that, for all k,

$$z_k^S(t) \in [\min(z_k, z_k^D(t) - \epsilon_k), \min(z_k, z_k^D(t))], \quad z_k^S(t) \leq z_k^D(t). \tag{9}$$

If there exists k such that $z_k^D(t) - \delta_k \geq z_k^S(t) = z_k$, set

$$p_k(t+1) = p_k(t) + d_k. \tag{10}$$

(That is, if input k is in excess demand by at least δ_k, with no binding constraints on net sales, the price of that input is raised by a fixed amount d_k.)

(P iv) *Termination*

If, for all k, (9) holds with $z_k^D(t) < z_k + \delta_k$, the process terminates.

A state of the economy when the process terminates is an *ε-equilibrium with excess supply,* where

$$\epsilon \leq \max_k \delta_k, \tag{11}$$

an arbitrarily small quantity.

Indeed, conditions (i)–(iii) in the previous definition are always satisfied along process P. Condition (iv) is satisfied when the process terminates, since (9) implies $z_k^S(t) - z_k^D(t) \leq 0$ and (P iv) implies $z_k^S(t) - z_k^D(t) > -\delta_k$, so that $|z_k^D(t) - z_k^S(t)| \leq \delta_k$ as desired.

3 Stability

The proof of the stability theorem that follows rests upon the following lemma, which establishes that *all prices are bounded along the process P.*

Lemma 1. *Under process P, for all k, for all t,*

$$p_k(t) \leq \max\left(\frac{\sum_i m_0^i}{\delta_k} + d_k, p_k(0)\right) \stackrel{\text{def}}{=} \bar{p}_k.$$

Proof: From the definition of the process, $p_k(t+1) = p_k(t)$ unless

$$z_l^D(t) - z_l^S(t) \geq 0 \quad \text{for all } l, \qquad z_k^D(t) - z_k^S(t) \geq \delta_k. \tag{12}$$

Moreover,

$$\begin{aligned}
\sum_l p_l(t) z_l^D(t) &= \sum_l p_l(t) \sum_{j=1}^n A_{lj} y_j(t) && \text{by (4)} \\
&= \sum_{j=1}^n \frac{1}{\mu_{jj}} q_j(t) y_j(t) \leq \sum_{j=1}^n q_j(t) y_j(t) && \text{by (3)} \\
&= \sum_i (r^i(t) - y_0^i(t)) && \text{by (6)} \\
&= \sum_i \left[\sum_l p_l(t) \zeta_l^i(t) + m_0^i - y_0^i(t)\right] && \text{by (5)} \\
&= \sum_l p_l(t) z_l^S(t) + \sum_i (m_0^i - y_0^i(t)).
\end{aligned}$$

Thus,

$$\sum_{\substack{l=1\\l\neq k}}^{m} p_l(t)[z_l^D(t)-z_l^S(t)]+p_k(t)[z_k^D(t)-z_k^S(t)]\leq \sum_i (m_0^i-y_0^i(t)).$$

If $p_k(t+1)>p_k(t)$, then

$$\delta_k p_k(t)\leq p_k(t)[z_k^D(t)-z_k^S(t)]\leq \sum_i (m_0^i-y_0^i(t))-\sum_{\substack{l=1\\l\neq k}}^{m} p_l(t)[z_l^D(t)-z_l^S(t)]$$
$$\leq \sum_i m_0^i,$$

where the last inequalities follow from (12) and $y_0^i(t)\geq 0$. Thus, $p_k(t+1)$ will not rise above $p_k(t)$ unless $p_k(t)\leq(\sum_i m_0^i)/\delta_k$, which proves the lemma. □

The logic of the previous proof is straightforward. If the demand for input k exceeds its supply by the finite amount δ_k, *and no input is in excess supply,* then even with zero markup, the value of aggregate demand must exceed the revenue from the sale of factors by at least $\delta_k p_k(t)$; that discrepancy must be financed from initial money holdings, so that $\delta_k p_k(t)\leq \sum_i m_0^i(t)$.

The lemma has a very important implication, namely, that *only a finite bounded number of price adjustments can occur under process P.* Indeed, each such adjustment calls for increasing some price p_k by the constant finite amount d_k, and each p_k has a finite upper bound $\bar{p}_k$. In order to establish finite convergence of the process, it will thus suffice to establish that only a finite, *uniformly* bounded number of quantity adjustments can take place between two price adjustments. The overall process will thus consist of a bounded number of uniformly bounded numbers of steps, that is, of a bounded number of steps.

Theorem 1. *Under Assumptions NI and MPC, provided for all $k=1,\dots,m$, e_k is small enough ($e_k\leq\frac{1}{2}\epsilon_k$), the process P is stable, and converges in a bounded number of steps to an ϵ-equilibrium with excess supply.*

Proof: We only need to prove that at most a finite uniformly bounded number of quantity adjustments can take place between two price adjustments. Let p denote the price vector resulting from either initiation or some price adjustment, and let $t+1$ denote a general quantity-adjustment step. The process P is best viewed, over the set of quantity-adjustment steps between two successive price adjustments, as associating with $(p,[\zeta_k^i(t)])\in R^m\times R^{Nm}$ the set of solutions $(p,[\zeta_k^i(t+1)])\in R^m\times R^{Nm}$ compatible with the description of the process. This is a finite set, with elements generated by alternative choices of k or i, where alternative choices exist. Hence, it is closed, and compact because the solutions are bounded: $z_k^i \geq \zeta_k^i(t) \geq 0$ for all i, k, and t. The proof is a simplified version of the proof of Theorem 6.2 in Champsaur, Drèze, and Henry (1977, pp. 290–1), using the Lyapunov function

$$L(t) = \sum_{l=1}^{m} p_l \max[z_l^D(t) - \epsilon_l - z_l^S(t), z_l^S(t) - z_l^D(t)]$$
$$\leq \sum_{l=1}^{m} p_l \max[z_l^D(t), z_l^S(t)]. \tag{13}$$

That function is uniformly bounded above, because p_l is bounded (by $\bar{p}_l$ in the lemma), $z_l^S(t) \leq \sum_i z_l^i$ and $p_l z_l^D(t) \leq \sum_j p_j z_j^D(t) \leq \sum_j p_j \sum_i z_j^i + \sum_i m_0^i$ as verified in the proof of the lemma. In addition, $L(t) \geq -\sum_{l=1}^m p_l \epsilon_l \geq -\sum_{l=1}^m \bar{p}_l \epsilon_l$. Hence, $L(t)$ is uniformly bounded, both above and below. The proof consists in showing that there exists a positive constant $c = \min_{k=1,\dots,m} c_k$, *bounded away from zero,* such that $L(t) - L(t+1) \geq c$, unless no further quantity adjustment is possible at $(t+1)$. The two possibilities corresponding to (P ii)(a) and (P ii)(b) are considered successively.

Case (P ii)(a)

In this case, for all $l = 1, \dots, m$, $p_l(t+1) = p_l(t) = p_l$, so that $q(t+1) = q(t)$ as well. Also, for all $h = 1, \dots, N$, $h \neq i$, $\zeta^h(t+1) = \zeta^h(t)$, so that $r^h(t+1) = r^h(t)$ and $y^h(t+1) = y^h(q(t), r^h(t)) = y^h(t)$. For all $l = 1, \dots, m$, $l \neq k$, $\zeta_l^i(t+1) = \zeta_l^i(t)$, so $z_l^S(t+1) = z_l^S(t)$. On the other hand, $\zeta_k^i(t+1) = \zeta_k^i(t) - e_k$, so that $z_k^S(t+1) = z_k^S(t) - e_k$. Finally,

$$r^i(t+1) = r^i(t) + p_k[\zeta_k^i(t+1) - \zeta_k^i(t)] = r^i(t) - e_k p_k < r^i(t).$$

In view of Assumption NI, $y^i(t+1) = y^i(q(t), r^i(t+1)) \leq y^i(q(t), r^i(t)) = y^i(t)$, so that $y(t+1) \leq y(t)$ and $z^D(t+1) \leq z^D(t)$.

For all $l = 1, \dots, m$, $l \neq k$,

$$\max[z_l^D(t+1) - \epsilon_l - z_l^S(t+1), z_l^S(t+1) - z_l^D(t+1)]$$
$$= \max[z_l^D(t+1) - \epsilon_l - z_l^S(t), z_l^S(t) - z_l^D(t+1)]$$
$$\leq z_l^D(t) - z_l^D(t+1) + \max[z_l^D(t) - \epsilon_l - z_l^S(t), z_l^S(t) - z_l^D(t)].$$

Also, $z_k^D(t+1) \leq z_k^D(t) < z_k^S(t) = z_k^S(t+1) + e_k$, and for e_k small enough ($e_k \leq \frac{1}{2}\epsilon_k$),

$$z_k^D(t+1) - \epsilon_k - z_k^S(t+1)$$
$$= z_k^D(t+1) - \epsilon_k - z_k^S(t) + e_k$$
$$\leq z_k^D(t+1) - e_k - z_k^S(t) \leq z_k^D(t) - e_k - z_k^S(t) < -e_k$$
$$< z_k^S(t) - e_k - z_k^D(t) = z_k^S(t+1) - z_k^D(t) \leq z_k^S(t+1) - z_k^D(t+1),$$

so that

$$\begin{aligned}&\max[z_k^P(t+1)-\epsilon_k-z_k^S(t+1),\, z_k^S(t+1)-z_k^P(t+1)]\\&\quad=z_k^S(t+1)-z_k^D(t+1)\\&\quad=z_k^S(t)-z_k^P(t)-e_k+z_k^D(t)-z_k^P(t+1)\\&\quad=\max[z_k^P(t)-\epsilon_k-z_k^S(t),\, z_k^S(t)-z_k^P(t)]+z_k^P(t)-z_k^P(t+1)-e_k.\end{aligned}$$

Consequently,

$$L(t+1)-L(t)\le\sum_{l=1}^{m}p_l[z_l^P(t)-z_l^P(t+1)]-e_kp_k.$$

Furthermore,

$$z_l^P(t)-z_l^P(t+1)=\sum_{j=1}^{n}A_{lj}[y_j^i(t)-y_j^i(t+1)]\quad\text{and}\quad\sum_{l=1}^{m}p_lA_{lj}=\frac{1}{\mu_{jj}}q_j,$$

so that

$$\begin{aligned}\sum_{l=1}^{m}p_l[z_l^P(t)-z_l^P(t+1)]&=\sum_j\frac{1}{\mu_{jj}}q_j(t)[y_j^i(t)-y_j^i(t+1)]\\&\le\sum_j q_j(t)[y_j^i(t)-y_j^i(t+1)]\\&=[r^i(t)-y_0^i(t)-r^i(t+1)+y_0^i(t+1)]\\&=[e_kp_k+y_0^i(t+1)-y_0^i(t)]\le e_kp_k(1-\gamma^i),\end{aligned}$$

where the last inequality follows from Assumption MPC. Hence,

$$L(t+1)-L(t)\le e_kp_k(1-\gamma^i-1)\le -e_kp_k\gamma^i\le -c_k<0,$$

where the existence of $c_k>0$ follows from $p_k\ge p_k(0)>0$.

Case (P ii)(b)

This case is entirely symmetrical to the previous one, and the same reasoning applies, with $\zeta_k^i(t+1)=\zeta_k^i(t)+e_k$, $r^i(t+1)=r^i(t)+e_kp_k$, and $z^D(t+1)\ge z^D(t)$.

For all $l=1,\ldots,m$, $l\ne k$, we have $z_l^S(t+1)=z_l^S(t)$ and

$$\begin{aligned}&\max[z_l^P(t+1)-\epsilon_l-z_l^S(t+1),\, z_l^S(t+1)-z_l^P(t+1)]\\&\quad\le\max[z_l^P(t+1)-\epsilon_l-z_l^S(t),\, z_l^S(t)-z_l^P(t)]\\&\quad\le z_l^P(t+1)-z_l^P(t)+\max[z_l^D-\epsilon_l-z_l^S(t),\, z_l^S(t)-z_l^D(t)].\end{aligned}$$

Also, for $e_k\le\epsilon_k/2$,

$$\begin{aligned}z_k^D(t+1)-\epsilon_k-z_k^S(t+1)&\ge z_k^D(t)-\epsilon_k-z_k^S(t)-e_k\ge -e_k\ge e_k-\epsilon_k\\&\ge z_k^S(t)+e_k-z_k^D(t)\ge z_k^S(t+1)-z_k^D(t+1),\end{aligned}$$

so that

$$\max[z_k^D(t+1)-\epsilon_k-z_k^S(t+1), z_k^S(t+1)-z_k^D(t+1)]$$
$$=z_k^D(t+1)-\epsilon_k-z_k^S(t+1)=z_k^D(t+1)-z_k^D(t)-e_k+z_k^D(t)-\epsilon_k-z_k^S(t)$$
$$=z_k^D(t+1)-z_k^D(t)-e_k+\max[z_k^D(t)-\epsilon_k-z_k^S(t), z_k^S(t)-z_k^D(t)].$$

By the reasoning of the previous case,

$$\sum_{l=1}^{m} p_l[z_l^D(t+1)-z_l^D(t)] \leq r^i(t+1)-y_0^i(t+1)-r^i(t)+y_0^i(t)$$
$$\leq e_k p_k(1-\gamma^i),$$
$$L(t+1)-L(t) \leq -e_k p_k \gamma^i \leq -c_k < 0.$$

Combining the two cases, and writing c for $\min_k c_k$, we have shown that $L(t+1)-L(t) \leq -c < 0$ unless (9) holds and no further quantity adjustment is possible. Since $L(t)$ is uniformly bounded above and below for all t, only a finite number of successive quantity adjustments is possible. The condition $e_k p_k(t)\gamma^i \geq c_k > 0$ may be imposed in the form $e_k p_k(t)\gamma^i \geq e_k p_k(0)\gamma^i \geq c_k > 0$, so that c_k is independent of the stage of the process, and the number of successive quantity adjustments is uniformly bounded, as desired. □

The logic of the second part of the proof is again straightforward. Each quantity adjustment on z_k^S reduces the absolute money value of excess demand for input k by $e_k p_k(t)$ at unchanged demand for commodities, and affects only the disposable income of a single consumer by that same amount. By MPC, the money value of effective demand for commodities will adjust by at most $(1-\gamma^i)e_k p_k(t)$, leaving a positively bounded margin of $e_k p_k(t)\gamma^i \geq c$ by which the absolute money value of excess demand for inputs must fall.

4 Illustration

The so-called "three goods economy" dear to macrotheorists has money, a single input labor ($m=1$), and a single produced commodity ($n=1$). In the specification of Malinvaud (1977), the N consumers are identical. At a given money wage $p(t)$ and commodity price $q(t)=p(t)a\mu$, the economy is conveniently described by Figure 2. The horizontal axis corresponds to labor, and the vertical axis to the commodity. The ray OA describes the Leontief technology. Let each household supply a single unit of labor – the e_k of Section 2 being here renormalized to unity; hence, its labor-supply constraint (ζ_k^i) can take two values: 0 or 1. To these two values

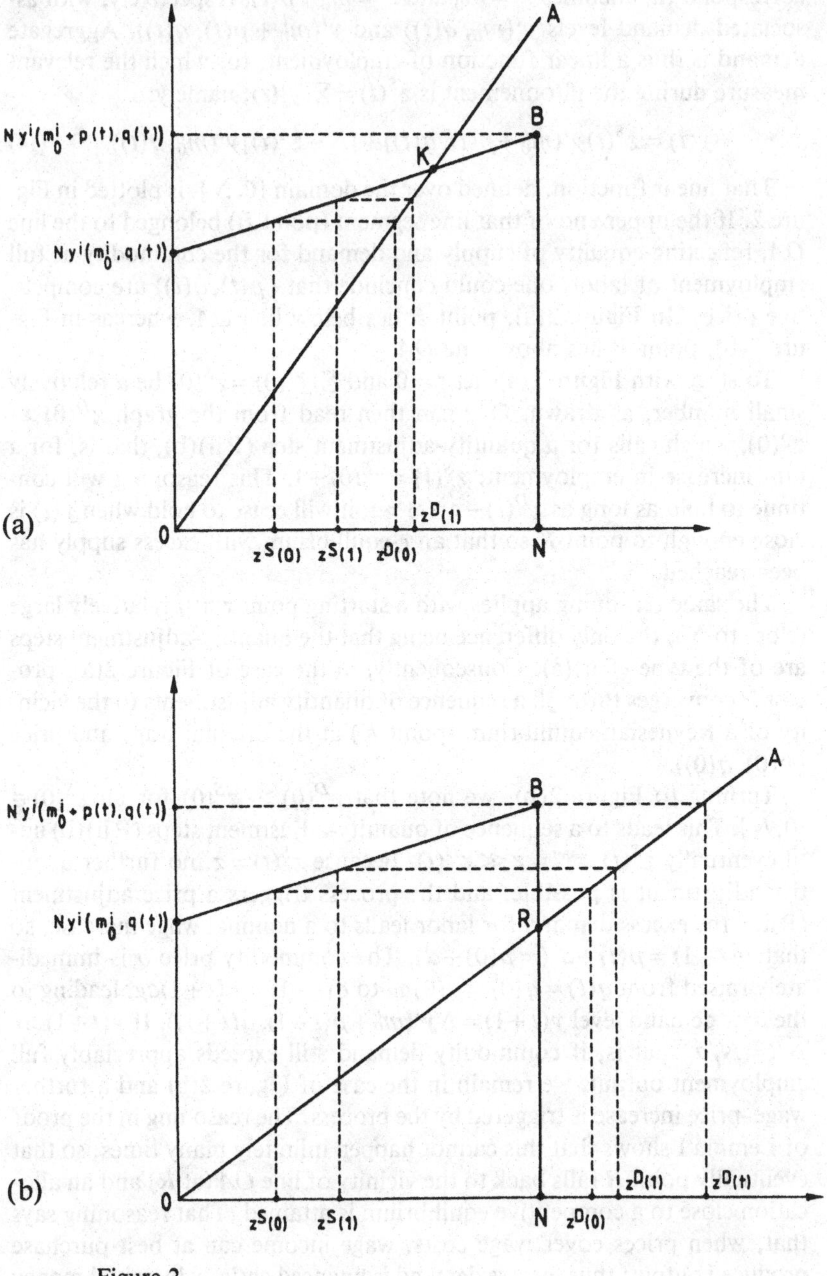
A
B
K
$Ny^i(m_0^i + p(t), q(t))$
$Ny^i(m_0^i, q(t))$
(a)
0
$z^{S}(0)$
$z^{S}(1)$
$z^{D}(0)$
$z^{D}(1)$
N
A
B
R
$Ny^i(m_0^i + p(t), q(t))$
$Ny^i(m_0^i, q(t))$
(b)
0
$z^{S}(0)$
$z^{S}(1)$
N
$z^{D}(0)$
$z^{D}(1)$
$z^{D}(t)$

Figure 2.

correspond the incomes $r^i = m_0^i$ and $r^i = m_0^i + p(t)$, respectively, with associated demand levels $y^i(m_0^i, q(t))$ and $y^i(m_0^i + p(t), q(t))$. Aggregate demand is thus a linear function of employment, for which the relevant measure during the tâtonnement is $z^S(t) = \Sigma_i \zeta^i(t)$; namely:

$$y(t) = z^S(t) y^i(m_0^i + p(t), q(t)) + [N - z^S(t)] y^i(m_0^i, q(t)). \tag{14}$$

That linear function, defined over the domain $[0, N]$, is plotted in Figure 2. If the upper end of that line segment (point B) belonged to the line OA, reflecting equality of supply and demand for the commodity at full employment of labor, one could conclude that $(p(t), q(t))$ are competitive prices. In Figure 2(a), point B lies below line OA, whereas in Figure 2(b), point B lies above line OA.

To start with Figure 2(a), let $t = 0$ and $\Sigma_i \zeta^i(0) = z^S(0)$ be a relatively small number, as drawn. One can then read from the graph $z^D(0) \gg z^S(0)$, which calls for a quantity-adjustment step (P ii)(b), that is, for a unit increase in employment: $z^S(1) = z^S(0) + 1$. This reasoning will continue to hold as long as $z^D(t) - z^S(t) > \epsilon$; it will cease to hold when $y(t)$ is close enough to point K so that an ϵ-equilibrium with excess supply has been reached.

The same reasoning applies with a starting point $z^S(0)$ relatively large (close to N), the only difference being that the quantity-adjustment steps are of the type (P ii)(a). Consequently, in the case of Figure 2(a), process P converges through a sequence of quantity adjustments to the vicinity of a Keynesian equilibrium (point K) at the original wage and price $(p(0), q(0))$.

Turning to Figure 2(b), we note that $z^D(0) \gg z^S(0)$ for all $z^S(0) \in [0, N]$. This leads to a sequence of quantity-adjustment steps (P ii)(b) until eventually $z^S(t) = N = z \ll z^D(t)$. Because $z^S(t) = z$, no further quantity adjustment is possible, and the process triggers a price adjustment (P iii): the excess demand for labor leads to a nominal wage increase, so that $p(t+1) = p(t) + d$ $(= p(0) + d)$. The commodity price q is immediately raised from $q(t) = q(0) = p(0) a\mu$ to $q(t+1) = p(t+1) a\mu$, leading to the new demand level $y(t+1) = N y^i(m_0^i + p(t+1), q(t+1))$. If $y(t+1) \gg \overline{NR} = N/a$, that is, if commodity demand still exceeds appreciably full employment output, we remain in the case of Figure 2(b) and a further wage–price increase is triggered by the process. The reasoning in the proof of Lemma 1 shows that this cannot happen infinitely many times, so that eventually point B falls back to the vicinity of line OA (at R) and an allocation close to a competitive equilibrium is attained. That reasoning says that, when prices cover wage costs, wage income can at best purchase produced output; thus, excess demand is financed entirely by initial money holdings, and must become negligible as the price level keeps rising. (That compelling argument does not assert that excess demand falls *monotonically* - only that it falls *eventually.*) Thus, in the case of Figure 2(b), process P converges, through a sequence of quantity adjustments followed by a sequence of wage-price increases, to the vicinity of a competitive equilibrium.

A further complication arises when existing equipment permits employing only $M<N$ workers. In order to fit that complication into process P, one must treat equipment as another input, with a price (rent) that will rise under the pressure of excess demand, eventually bringing the economy to the vicinity of a point with a clearing commodity market and unemployment - at the original wage and at a commodity price inflated by the rent on capital equipment.[5] Details are left to the reader.

5 Variable coefficients

The description of the technology in the model of Sections 2 and 3 is very specific. The a priori distinction between primary inputs and final commodities is perhaps acceptable at the economywide level. But the Leontief technology is extreme. The standard approach in general equilibrium economics would introduce a convex aggregate production set Y, then rewrite condition (i) in the definition of an ϵ-equilibrium as

$$(z^D, y) \text{ maximizes } q'y - p'z^D \quad \text{subject to } (z^D, y) \in Y, \; y \leq \sum_i y^i. \tag{i*}$$

The Leontief specification says that "$(z^D, y) \in Y$ if and only if $z^D \geq Ay$", where A is a given matrix.

There is no difficulty in extending the definition of process P to a general specification of the technology. For instance, one could define $z^D(t)$ at each step through cost minimization at given input prices and output levels:

$$(z^D, y) \text{ minimizes } p'(t)z^D(t) \quad \text{subject to } (z^D(t), y(t)) \in Y. \tag{15}$$

It would be interesting to know whether the extended process converges. My conjecture is that it would - possibly under some mild conditions, but the technique of the proof would be more complicated. Short of having investigated the matter, I can at least give an example of a variable coefficients technology under which the extended process has the same properties as the original process, namely, a convex technology with constant returns and no joint production.

[5] In the standard terminology of equilibria with quantity rationing, the process terminates at the intersection of the Keynesian and classical regimes - as suggested in Keynes' *General Theory.*

In that case, the aggregate production set Y is the sum of n distinct production sets Y^j, one for each commodity $j=1,\dots,n$, and Y^j is a convex cone with vertex zero (constant returns), such that, for all $(z^D, y) \in Y^j$, $y_l = 0$, $l = 1,\dots,n$, $l \neq j$ (no joint production). The important implication of such a technology, for my purposes, is that *technological choices are fully determined by input prices and do not depend upon output levels*. If either cuts of Y^j in z^D space for given y_j are strictly convex, or an appropriate selection is made when (15) has multiple solutions,[6] then *we are back to the Leontief technology as long as input prices do not change*.

For process P, this means that we can work with the Leontief specification along sequences of quantity adjustment steps (P ii), and update the input–output matrix at (within) price adjustment steps (P iii) only. Consequently, the proof of Theorem 1 remains valid without modification. This establishes the following corollary.

Corollary 1. *If the Leontief technology of Section 2 is extended to a general convex technology with constant returns and no joint production, Theorem 1 still holds, wording unchanged.*

Some econometricians – including Sneessens and Drèze (1986) or Drèze and Bean (1990) – would argue that technical coefficients are revised infrequently anyhow; accordingly a more realistic extension of process P would retain the hierarchical structure, and introduce revisions of technical coefficients only when the process terminates. This would lead us to consider a sequence of processes, each of which converges in finitely many steps, with technical coefficients for the νth process minimizing cost for the input prices and output levels at the termination of process $\nu-1$. I would again conjecture that convergence of such a sequence would follow from mild conditions.

PART II: NONTÂTONNEMENT

6 A nontâtonnement process

6.1

It is not difficult to suggest a guiding principle toward one extension of Theorem 1 to a nontâtonnement process, with production and consumption activities carried out in continuous time out of equilibrium. Suppose that firms hold inventories of consumer goods, out of which consumer demand can be satisfied *temporarily* when it exceeds production. Such an assumption is not as general as one would like, because it rules out

[6] For instance, minimize $|z^D(t) - z^D(t-1)|$.

nonstorable commodities, like electricity, opera seats, and labor services (which are occasionally subject to demand rationing). This is an exploratory chapter, and storable commodities will do. If consumer demand is never rationed, and the production sector is still treated as an aggregate, then activities "out of equilibrium" differ from activities "at equilibrium" (of the process) in a single respect, namely, that the quantities of inputs stipulated by the process may differ from those needed to satisfy demand. That households may experience excess supply of inputs, along the process, is not a novel feature, since that possibility is already accepted at equilibrium. But firms realize their input demands at equilibrium, whereas that may not be possible out of equilibrium. Still, excess demand for some inputs should not prevent firms from making use of whatever production possibilities they have, in order to satisfy at least partially the demand for their outputs, while drawing *temporarily* on inventories for the balance. And hoarding some inputs *temporarily* is commonplace, when firms adjust progressively to a demand shortfall or are prevented from using some input k because the complementary input l is in short supply. Modeling production activities out of equilibrium is a natural task, as those who have worked on dynamic planning of production, inventories, and work force know.

A key word in my tale so far is "temporarily". Clearly, inventory depletion cannot go on forever, nor will firms hoard factors of production forever. Regarding the first point, adjustment in either production levels or prices (to choke off demand) should be fast enough that the drain on inventories comes to a halt before the warehouse or the shelves are empty.[7] A reasonable assignment for nontâtonnement stability analysis is thus to investigate *sufficient conditions* on the adjustment process under which *a form of equilibrium is reached, in real time, before reasonable levels of initial inventories are depleted.* This is where the finite convergence property established in Theorem 1 pays off! If that property can be extended to a nontâtonnement framework, with production and consumption activities out of equilibrium, then it will suffice to show that the amount of inventory depletion between two steps of the process is uniformly bounded; one will then conclude that bounded initial inventories are sufficient to guarantee feasibility of the nontâtonnement process. That is precisely the approach followed here, and the nature of the result established by Theorem 2.

The second point - namely, that hoarding of factors of production should also be temporary - has two aspects. One aspect concerns the optimizing behavior of firms with respect to hiring and firing of inputs given

[7] This property is *assumed,* not demonstrated, in the imaginative, and rather unique, analysis of nontâtonnement stability by Fisher (1983).

their anticipations regarding input prices and product demand. This is a topic in the difficult area of stochastic optimization. Another aspect concerns the drain on liquidities associated with temporary hoarding of factors of production. Bankruptcies present genuine modeling difficulties. Again, these can be avoided if initial cash holdings plus proceeds from the sale of inventories suffice to finance factor hoardings out of equilibrium.

In this chapter, stochastic optimization will be bypassed altogether, through assumptions on (static and deterministic) expectations. And the idea that quantities move faster than prices will be carried to the extreme, so that disequilibrium during the real time devoted to quantity adjustments (hiring and firing of primary factors of production) will not have destabilizing consequences. (This is explained in Section 6.5.) Under these conditions, the key to the stability analysis will still be provided by a lemma establishing that input prices are bounded above, so that finitely many upward price adjustments need be considered.

6.2

In reality, firms make decisions about prices and input levels at arbitrary points in time, whereas production and consumption activities are carried out as continuous flows. I will model the nontâtonnement counterpart of the adjustment process introduced in Part I in terms of *rates of flow per unit of calendar time* of input uses, incomes, consumption, and production; and in terms of *steps of the process,* that is, adjustments of prices or input flows, occurring at *finitely spaced points of calendar time.* It is natural to think of these steps as taking place in quick succession, and to ignore the variations of the rates of flow (of consumption or production) inside the short intervals separating two steps. Accordingly, *the points in calendar time corresponding to the steps of the process are also the decision points for the agents.* Stock variables - like money or inventories - are then easily updated (integrals of flows are obtained as the product of a constant rate of flow by the length of a time span).

The basic notation for Part II consists in using the integers $\ldots, t, t+1, \ldots$ to number the steps of the process; and in using the symbol $\tau(t)$ to denote the span of calendar time separating steps t and $t+1$, with the natural normalization $\tau(t) \leq 1$. Furthermore, the symbols z, ζ, and y, used with appropriate indices in Part I to denote the supply and demand of inputs or commodities, retain the same definitions; they are now interpreted as rates of flow per unit of calendar time. Production and consumption decisions concern these rates of flow. Equilibrium requires equality (up to ϵ, insofar as inputs are concerned) of the demand *rates* and supply *rates.*

6.3

Insofar as consumers are concerned, I will now use *stationary demand functions* with three arguments: $m^i(t)$, $p'(t)\zeta^i(t)$, and $q(t)$. Thus, the income $r^i(t) = m_0^i + p'(t)\zeta^i(t)$ of (5) is split into two components: a stock of money balances $m^i(t)$, and a flow of income $p'(t)\zeta^i(t)$ from the sale of inputs. The reason for separating out these two components is, of course, that the intertemporal budget constraint recognizes the repetitive nature of the income flow associated with the input sales. I will assume that the endowments of inputs are perpetual flows at the constant rates $[z_k^i]$, and that consumers hold *static point expectations* about p, q, and ζ^i.[8] Thus, after observing $p(t)$, $q(t)$, and $\zeta^i(t)$, household i expects $p(t') = p(t)$, $q(t') = q(t)$, and $\zeta^i(t') = \zeta^i(t)$ for all $t' > t$; and it solves the problem of optimally allocating its resources – consisting of the stock $m^i(t)$ and the perpetual constant flow $p'(t)\zeta^i(t)$ – to consumption over time. The solution of that problem is an infinite sequence of flows of consumption per unit of calendar time, the first component of which, to be denoted $y^i(t)$, is implemented. Because $\tau(t) \leq 1$, a new step of the process will take place before the unit of calendar time covered by $y^i(t)$ is exhausted; at that point, the household will observe $p(t+1)$, $q(t+1)$, and $\zeta^i(t+1)$ and will choose $y^i(t+1)$ in the same way. The stationarity of the demand functions says that, if $m^i(t+1) = m^i(t)$, $p'(t+1)\zeta^i(t+1) = p'(t)\zeta^i(t)$, and $q(t+1) = q(t)$, then $y^i(t+1) = y^i(t)$.

Money balances are defined recursively by

$$m^i(t+1) = m^i(t) + \tau(t)[p'(t)\zeta^i(t) - q'(t)y^i(t)] \geq 0. \tag{16}$$

That is, money balances are updated by the flow of receipts minus expenditures since the previous step and they are not allowed to become negative. With static expectations and stationary demand functions, households typically plan to deplete gradually their money balances; in that case, $m^i(t+1) < m^i(t)$ and, when $p'(t+1)\zeta^i(t+1) = p'(t)\zeta^i(t)$ and $q'(t+1) = q(t)$, then $y^i(t+1) < y^i(t)$.

At the date of step t of the process, the rate of consumption flow per unit of calendar time chosen by household i is thus

$$y^i(t) = y^i(m^i(t), p'(t)\zeta^i(t), q(t)) \in R^n. \tag{17}$$

It satisfies suitable extensions of Assumptions NI and MPC, namely:

Assumption NI′. *For all i, for all q, m^i, $p'\zeta^i$, and $\hat{m}^i \geq m^i$, $\hat{p}'\hat{\zeta}^i \geq p'\zeta^i$:*

[8] If consumers are infinitely lived and have stationary additive consumption tastes (so that past consumption is irrelevant to current decisions), the stationarity of demand should follow; I have not investigated that question in detail.

$$y^i(\hat{m}^i, \hat{p}'\hat{\zeta}^i, q) \geq y^i(m^i, p'\zeta^i, q).$$

Assumption MPC′. *For each i, there exist* $\beta^i > 0$ *and* $\gamma^i > 0$ *(independent of* q, m^i, *and* $p'\zeta^i$*) such that, for all* q, m^i, $p'\zeta^i$, *and* $\hat{m}^i \geq m^i$, $\hat{p}'\hat{\zeta}^i \geq p'\zeta^i$:

$$\hat{p}'\hat{\zeta}^i - q'y^i(\hat{m}^i, \hat{p}'\hat{\zeta}^i, q) \geq p'\zeta^i - q'y^i(m, p'\zeta^i, q) + \gamma^i(\hat{m}^i - m^i) + \beta^i(\hat{p}'\hat{\zeta}^i - p'\zeta^i).$$

6.4

In the nontâtonnement process, it is suggestive to think about the ζ's as *levels of contracts between consumers and producers*. This is most transparent for labor services: $\zeta_k^i(t)$ measures the flow of labor service k for which household i is engaged in a labor contract at the date of step t. To say that $\zeta_k^i(t+1) = \zeta^i(t) + (-)e_k$ is to say that employment of household i goes up (down) by e_k, that is, by one elementary unit of labor type k. Similarly, if good k is a plot of land owned by household i, then $\zeta_k^i \leq z_k^i$ is the acreage rented out at the date of step t. In a more contrived way, perhaps: if good k is an oil refinery belonging to a firm in which household i holds a fraction z_k^i of the shares, and if the refinery operates at 60% of capacity, earning an imputed rent equal to 60% of p_k, then $\zeta_k^i = 0.6z_k^i$ is the *share* of the rent p_k accruing to household i.

The behavior of producers (or "implicit firms") at the date of step t will then be defined by the solution of the following problem, where $\hat{y}(t)$ denotes the flow of production at that date:

$$\max_{\hat{y}(t)} q'(t)\hat{y}(t) \quad \text{subject to} \quad \hat{y}(t) \leq y(t) = \sum_i y^i(t), \qquad A\hat{y}(t) \leq \sum_i \zeta^i(t), \tag{18}$$

where $q'(t) = p'(t)A\mathfrak{M}$ as per (3). This formulation reflects revenue-maximizing production decisions under two constraints: production should not exceed demand $y(t)$, and production cannot use more inputs than currently under contract. (By treating the cost of inputs as given by the extant contracts, revenue maximization is equivalent to profit maximization.)

The first constraint is introduced as a shortcut, to eschew the more complex issue of inventory accumulation, that should be faced in a further elaboration of the model introduced here. (It is indeed inelegant to assume that firms withdraw from inventories to fill the gap between sales and production, but never replenish inventories during the time span covered by the adjustment process; the saving grace is, of course, the finiteness of that time span, established in Theorem 2, which follows.) The second constraint is transparent. Note, however, the implicit efficiency in the use of inputs. Because production is here modeled in aggregate terms, it will not be the case that some inputs are idle in one firm while another firm has to forego profitable production due to lack of the same inputs. There would be no difficulty whatever, and some gain of realism, in treating subsets of commodities as the outputs of different firms, say, $f=1,\ldots,F$, and denoting by $\zeta^i_{kf}(t)$ the amount of input k sold by household i to firm f at t.

As another related shortcut, I will assume that firms hire (fire) inputs when the quantity contracted is inferior (superior) to the level *needed to meet final effective demand* $y(t)$. In that way, step (P ii) of process P is kept unchanged. This formulation remains somewhat unsatisfactory, because it implies, for instance, that an airline will react to an increase in demand by hiring pilots and stewards, even though its planes are used to capacity. Under a more realistic formulation, these quantity adjustments should depend upon information regarding the *potential* availability of *all* inputs, $\Sigma_i(z^i-\zeta^i)$. (Thus, the airline might hire personnel if it knows that there exist idle planes for sale or hire.) It should be possible to develop such an approach.

I will introduce a simplification that reduces drastically the extent to which firms keep under contract (and remunerate) idle inputs. The simplification consists in carrying to the limit the idea (introduced in Section 2.2) that quantity adjustments are faster than price adjustments. A natural way to implement that idea consists in imposing that the span of calendar time separating a quantity adjustment from the previous step is much shorter than the corresponding span separating a price adjustment from the previous step. Since the latter time span is finite, the limit of "much shorter" is zero, and I will assume that *stocks do not change* (the integral of the flows vanishes) *between a quantity adjustment and the previous step of the process*. That is, I will suppress the calendar time required to make quantity adjustments; only between successive price adjustments will there elapse sufficient time to justify updating stocks. (Boundedness of all rates of flow is not an issue.)

An important implication of this specification is that, provided the finite convergence properties are preserved, conditions (9) will hold all the time, except for a set of measure zero (the finite set of time spans, themselves each of measure zero, preceding quantity adjustments). Accordingly, the quantities of inputs hired by firms will never exceed those needed to satisfy commodity demand, except over a set of measure zero in calendar time. This does not mean that firms never retain idle inputs. But the reason for idleness will then be always the same (except again over the null set just defined), namely, that *other* inputs are not currently available. Inputs in excess of the requirements associated with commodity demand are assumed to be "fired" instantaneously. (Similarly, inputs corresponding to these requirements are "hired" instantaneously, *if available* in idle supply.) This is a major simplification, which could eventually be relaxed in an attempt at greater realism.

Under that specification, the receipts of firms from the sale of commodities always cover their outlays for payment of inputs, when $\mathcal{M}-I \geq [0]$. This is because the quantities of inputs contracted do not exceed the requirements corresponding to the sales: given that output prices cover (possibly with a margin) input costs, sales receipts cover outlays for inputs. It does not follow that the margin exceeds the value of inventory depletion; only that the net cash flows are nonnegative, outside of the null set. Liquidity is thus never an issue for the firms (for the production sector). Moreover, *the stock of money held by households is nonincreasing over calendar time.* Indeed, net cash flows of households and producers sum to zero and the set of measure zero in calendar time does not affect money stocks.

7 Stability

7.1

Putting together the elements introduced in Section 6, we may describe the state of the economy at the time of step t by the triple $(p(t), \zeta^i(t), m^i(t))_{i=1,\dots,N}$. From these variables, we may successively compute:

(i) output prices $q(t)$, via (3),
(ii) demand for consumer goods, via (17),
(iii) demand for inputs, via (4).

The evolution of the economy is governed by the process P′, defined in terms of the sequences $(p(t), \zeta^i(t), m^i(t))$, $t = 0, 1.2, \dots$, and of conditions (3), (4), (16), and (17).

Description of process P′

(P′i) *Initiation*

Initial input prices $p(0) > 0$, quantity constraints $[\zeta_k^i(0)]$, $[z_k^i] \geq [\zeta_k^i(0)] \geq [0]$, and money stocks $m^i(0) > 0$ are historically given.

(P′ii) *General step: Adjustment of a quantity constraint*

Such a step is carried out if there exists k such that either

$$z_k^S(t) - z_k^D(t) > 0 \tag{19}$$

or

$$z_k^D(t) - z_k^S(t) \geq \epsilon_k \quad \text{with } z_k^S(t) < z_k. \tag{20}$$

Then let $p(t+1) = p(t)$, $\tau(t) = 0$, and $m^i(t+1) = m^i(t)$ for all i. Two situations are distinguished:

(a) If some (any) k is such that (19) holds, then necessarily $z_k^S(t) > 0$ and there exists i such that $\zeta_k^i(t) > 0$. For some (any) such i, set

$$\zeta_k^i(t+1) = \zeta_k^i(t) - e_k. \tag{7}$$

Then

$$y^i(t+1) = y^i(m^i(t), p'(t)\zeta^i(t) - p_k(t)e_k, q(t))$$

and, for all $h \neq i$,

$$y^h(t+1) = y^h(t) = y^h(m^i(t), p'(t)\zeta^h(t), q(t)).$$

(b) If some (any) k is such that (20) holds, then necessarily there exists i such that $\zeta_k^i(t) < z_k^i$. For some (any) such i, set

$$\zeta_k^i(t+1) = \zeta_k^i(t) + e_k. \tag{8}$$

Then

$$y^i(t+1) = y^i(m^i(t), p'(t)\zeta^i(t) + p_k(t)e_k, q(t))$$

and, for all $h \neq i$,

$$y^h(t+1) = y^h(t) = y^h(m^h(t), p'(t)\zeta^h(t), q(t)).$$

(P′iii) *General step: Adjustment of a price*

Such a step is carried out if there exists no k for which either (19) or (20) holds. It must then be the case that, for all k,

$$z_k^S(t) \in [\min(z_k, z_k^D(t) - \epsilon_k), \min(z_k, z_k^D(t))], \quad z_k^S(t) \leq z_k^D(t). \tag{9}$$

If there exists k such that $z_k^D(t) - \delta_k \geq z_k^S(t) = z_k$, set

$$p_k(t+1) = p_k(t) + d_k; \tag{21}$$

for all $j \neq k$, set $p_j(t+1) = p_j(t)$; and set $[\zeta^i(t+1)] = [\zeta^i(t)]$. Also, for some $1 \geq \tau(t) > 0$, let

$$m^i(t+1) = m^i(t) + \tau(t)[p'(t)\zeta^i(t) - q'(t)y^i(t)], \tag{16}$$

$$y^i(t+1) = y^i(m^i(t+1), p'(t)\zeta^i(t) + d_k\zeta_k^i(t), q(t+1)), \tag{17}$$

where $q_j(t+1) = q_j(t) + A_{kj}d_k$.

(P′iv) *Termination*

If for all k, (9) holds with $z_k^D(t) < z_k + \delta_k$, the process terminates.

Definition 2. *An* ϵ-equilibrium with excess supply *consists of a state* (p, ζ^i, m^i), *a vector of inputs* $z^D \in R^m$, *a vector of outputs* $\hat{y} \in R^n$, *a vector of prices* $q \in R^n$ *with* $q' = p'A\mathfrak{M}$, *and an N-tuple of vectors* $y^i \in R^n$ *such that*

(i) $(z^D, \hat{y})$ *maximizes* $q'\hat{y} - p'z^D$ *subject to* $z^D \geq A\hat{y}$, $\hat{y} \leq \Sigma_i y^i$;
(ii) $y^i = y^i(m^i, p'\zeta^i, q)$;
(iii) $0 \leq \zeta^i \leq z^i$, $\Sigma_i y^i \leq \hat{y}$;
(iv) *for all* $k = 1, \ldots, m$, $|z_k^D - \Sigma_i \zeta_k^i| \leq \epsilon$.

As before, a state of the economy where the process terminates defines an ϵ-equilibrium with excess supply, where ϵ satisfies (11). The equilibrium is defined by the terminal values of (p, ζ^i, m^i) together with $\hat{y} = \Sigma_i y^i$, $z^D = A\hat{y}$, $q' = p'A\mathfrak{M}$ and $y^i = y^i(m^i, p'\zeta^{i'}, q)$. These values satisfy conditions (i)–(iii) in the definition. Equation (9) and (P′iv) still imply that condition (iv) holds as well.

7.2

The proof of stability, Theorem 2 (which follows), rests upon the analogue of Lemma 1, proved here in two easy steps.

Lemma 2. *Under process P′, for all* $t = 0, 1, 2, \ldots$,

$$\sum_i m^i(t+1) \leq \sum_i m^i(t) \leq \sum_i m^i(0).$$

Proof: From the definition of the process, $\tau(t) = 0$ unless $z_l^S(t) \leq z_l^D(t)$ for all l. Thus, $\tau(t) > 0$ implies

$$p'(t)z^S(t) \leq p'(t)z^D(t) = p'(t)Ay(t) \leq p'(t)A\mathfrak{M}y(t) = q'(t)y(t). \quad (22)$$

Consequently, for all t:

$$\tau(t)[p'(t)z^S(t) - q'(t)y(t)] \leq 0. \quad (23)$$

By aggregating (16) over i, then using (23):

$$\sum_i m^i(t+1) = \sum_i m^i(t) + \tau(t)[p'(t)z^S(t) - q'(t)y(t)] \leq \sum_i m^i(t), \quad (24)$$

which proves the lemma. □

Lemma 3. *Under process P′, for all k, for all t,*

$$p_k(t) \leq \max\left(\frac{\sum_i m^i(0)}{\delta_k} + d_k, p_k(0)\right) \stackrel{\text{def}}{=} \bar{p}_k.$$

Proof: From the definition of the process, $p_k(t+1) = p_k(t)$ unless $z_l^S(t) \leq z_l^D(t)$ for all l; and $p'(t)z^D(t) \leq q'(t)y(t)$ by (22). The condition $m^i(t+1) \geq 0$ for all $\tau(t) \in [0,1]$ implies – see (16) with $\tau(t) = 1$ – that

$$q'(t)y^i(t) \leq m^i(t) + p'(t)\zeta^i(t). \tag{25}$$

By summing over i, and using (22) and then Lemma 2:

$$\begin{aligned} p'(t)z^D(t) &\leq \sum_i m^i(t) + p'(t)z^S(t) \\ &\leq \sum_i m^i(0) + p'(t)z^S(t). \end{aligned} \tag{26}$$

Proceeding as in the proof of Lemma 1,

$$\begin{aligned} \delta_k p_k(t) &\leq p_k(t)[z_k^D(t) - z_k^S(t)] \\ &\leq \sum_i m^i(0) - \sum_{l \neq k} p_l(t)[z_l^D(t) - z_l^S(t)] \leq \sum_i m^i(0), \end{aligned}$$

and the proof of the lemma follows. □

Theorem 2. *Under Assumptions NI′ and MPC′, provided for all $k = 1, \ldots, m$, e_k is small enough ($e_k \leq \frac{1}{2}\epsilon_k$) and provided initial inventories are high enough (meaning at least equal to a finite lower bound related to the data of the economy), the process P′ is feasible, is stable, and converges in a bounded number of steps to an ε-equilibrium with excess supply.*

Proof: The proof is entirely parallel to that of Theorem 1.

It follows from Lemma 3 that the number of price adjustments is bounded. Let *their* number be $T \leq \bar{T}$ and number them $\theta = 1, \ldots, T$. Also, because the quantity adjustments are treated as instantaneous, the aggregate withdrawals from inventories are given by

$$\sum_{\theta=1}^{T} \tau(\theta)[y(\theta) - \hat{y}(\theta)] \leq \sum_{\theta=1}^{T} [y(\theta) - \hat{y}(\theta)] \leq \sum_{\theta=1}^{T} y(\theta). \tag{27}$$

For each θ, $y(\theta)$ is a uniformly bounded quantity, because

$$\begin{aligned} q'(\theta)y(\theta) &\leq \sum_i m^i(\theta) + p'(\theta)z^S(\theta) \\ &\leq \sum_i m^i(0) + \bar{p}'z, \end{aligned} \tag{28}$$

and $q'(\theta)$ is bounded below by $q'(0)=p'(0)A\mathfrak{M}>0$. This establishes the boundedness of the initial inventory levels that are required in order for process P′ to be feasible at all steps (without any need for quantity rationing of consumer demand).

To complete the proof, there remains only to verify that the number of quantity-adjustment steps (P′ii) between any pair of price-adjustment steps (P′iii) is uniformly bounded. The reasoning used in the proof of Theorem 1 to establish that property is readily extended to the present case. Indeed, if t denotes a price-adjustment step and $p(t+\nu)=p(t)$, $\nu>0$, then $t+\nu$ is a general quantity-adjustment step, and $\tau(t+\nu)=0$. For all $\nu>1$, it follows that $m^i(t+\nu)=m^i(t+\nu-1)$. We may accordingly use that property in the proof (adding the single step corresponding to $\nu=1$ does not affect the boundedness property). We may then repeat the reasoning in the proof of Theorem 1, substituting $m^i(t+1)$ for $m^i(0)$ and $p'(t)\zeta^i(t+\nu)$ for $r^i(t)$. In the discussion of case (P ii)(a), the equality $r^i(t+1)=r^i(t)-e_kp_k$ is then replaced by

$$p'(t)\zeta^i(t+\nu+1)=p'(t)\zeta^i(t+\nu)-e_kp_k; \tag{29}$$

and Assumption NI′ implies $y^i(t+\nu+1)\le y^i(t+\nu)$. The discussion of that case then proceeds without modification, until Assumption MPC is used. That specific step is now replaced by

$$\begin{aligned}\sum_l p_l[z_l^P(t+\nu)-z_l^P(t+\nu+1)] &\le \sum_j q_j(t)[y_j^i(t+\nu)-y_j^i(t+\nu+1)]\\ &\le e_kp_k(1-\beta^i),\end{aligned} \tag{30}$$

where the last inequality follows directly from MPC′ and (29). Similar remarks apply to the discussion of case (P ii)(b), and the proof of Theorem 2 is complete. □

8 Comments and conclusions

8.1 *Summary*

In broadest outline, this chapter gives content to a very simple idea: If nominal prices are downward rigid, and if they are prevented by some nominal rigidity from rising indefinitely, then price dynamics are apt to converge. A realistic feature of this chapter, inspired by the work of Morishima (1976), is to trace back all downward price rigidities to primary factors of production. As for the upper bound on inflation, it comes from the combination of a nonvanishing demand for, and an exogenous stock of, nominal balances. These two aspects deserve some discussion, provided in Sections 8.2 and 8.3.

The downward price rigidities impose an equilibrium concept allowing for excess supply. Some claim to the realism of such a concept was made in the introduction. At any rate, it is a necessary corollary to price rigidities. Still, I discuss in Section 8.4 the two main avenues toward a competitive equilibrium, namely, price flexibility and fiscal expansion.

These specifications contribute some novel features to stability analysis. They have enabled me to prove stability of a tâtonnement process from the minimal assumption of noninferiority (further discussed in Section 8.5); then to define a rather realistic nontâtonnement process, and to prove its feasibility and stability under a reasonable condition on inventory holdings.

The nontâtonnement process allows for production and consumption activities out of equilibrium. But I do not take here the crucial step of modeling explicitly the uncertainty surrounding future prices and quantity constraints, then the stochastic optimization problems faced by consumers and producers. That step deserves priority on the research agenda. It is related to the issue of money demand, taken up in Section 8.2.

The specific formulation of the processes P and P′, the assumptions, and the methods of proof used in this chapter are quite crude. No doubt, the presentation could be improved substantially through further technical work. One comment in that direction is offered in Section 8.6.

8.2 *Temporary equilibrium and money demand*

The uncertainty about future prices (and quantity constraints) is modeled explicitly in the theory of temporary equilibrium - see Grandmont (1974, 1977) - where much attention has been given to the conditions (on expectations) under which inflation remains bounded. Clearly, that is the proper way to study price dynamics, but it is a hard way.

The notion that money supply has something to do with inflation is familiar to many. But it needs to be spelled out in microeconomic models of price making, of which one example is offered here.

Assumption MPC, putting a floor to money demand, is rather crude and should be generalized, both by deriving money demand explicitly from consumer behavior, and by including assets and their prices (e.g., interest rate) in the analysis.

An intriguing question is whether the supply of money or direct controls on the prices of primary inputs are the only conceivable instruments to check inflation in models of the type studied here (in models with downwards price rigidities and markup pricing).

8.3 *Downward price rigidities*

Why some prices remain downward rigid in the face of excess supply is an intriguing question, revived in particular by the persistence of European unemployment.

In the case of labor services, the protection by trade unions of workers' incomes is undoubtedly an important element of the answer. The extent to which that protection should be regarded as inefficient use of monopoly power, or as a second-best efficient arrangement in the absence of contingent or forward markets for jobs, remains to be ascertained; see Gollier (1988), Drèze (1989), and Drèze and Gollier (1989) for a theoretical second-best analysis.

The issue concerns other inputs as well, in particular plant and equipment. When excess capacity prevails, the prices of commodities (e.g., automobiles) are not automatically geared to short-run marginal cost. This is probably a mixture once again of monopolistic profit maximization and of second-best efficient arrangements under incomplete markets. Price fluctuations are costly for consumers, and are apt to generate erratic patterns of intertemporal substitution, compounding the difficulty of investment decisions under incomplete markets. Our understanding of these issues is still limited: the combination of nonconvex technology, monopolistic competition, and incomplete markets remains forbidding.

One clear-cut difference between labor on the one hand and plant or equipment on the other is the ease with which excess physical capacities can be eliminated through scrapping and postponement of investment, whereas excess demand for physical capacities can be eliminated through investment. There lies probably the reason for the differences in the evolution of unemployment and excess capacities in Figure 1.

In the model presented here, physical capacities are treated as primary inputs. It would be natural to put an upper bound on their real prices, reflecting the cost of additional investment; and to introduce a scrapping or investment postponement feature, to eliminate progressively the excess capacities. The model would gain in realism, probably at little technical complication. And the role of wages in explaining downward price rigidities would stand out all the more sharply.

8.4 *Toward competitive equilibria*

The quantity-adjustment steps of Process P or P′ bring about "orderly" (one-sided) rationing; the price-adjustment steps eliminate all forms of excess demand. What sort of additional steps could eliminate the excess supplies?

Price flexibility is a first answer – even though I have just argued that some form of downward rigidity makes sense. Since the process is governed by input prices, it seems plausible that an assumption of gross substitutability for inputs would pave the way to convergence of a process with flexible prices toward competitive equilibria. And most econometricians would find the substitutability assumption for inputs quite acceptable. Eventually this issue should be investigated.

It is appropriate to remind ourselves, at this point, that Keynes regarded wage flexibility as the hard way, and thought that demand stimulation through monetary policy provided an easier way. (On pp. 267–9 of *The General Theory,* he argues that "it can only be a foolish . . . an unjust . . . an inexperienced person who would prefer a flexible wage policy to a flexible money policy.") The model of the present chapter lends itself to study of the effect of increasing the money balances of the households, which amounts to a fiscal expansion through income transfers, with accommodating money supply.

It is easy to construct examples where no finite amount of fiscal expansion will eliminate excess supplies altogether. (Thus, if two inputs are always used in the ratio 1 to 2, but are supplied inelastically in the ratio 1 to 1, so that the competitive price of the first is zero; then a competitive equilibrium could only be obtained in the limit, with *infinite* fiscal expansion cum inflation.[9]) But it is also easy to think about assumptions under which fiscal policy would be effective. (Some degree of input substitutability would help.) A serious attack on these problems again requires explicit treatment of the uncertainties associated with fiscal policy (whether it will ultimately be financed by taxes or monetized, for instance). So I must refer back to Section 8.2.

8.5 *The noninferiority assumption*

Of all the undesirable assumptions used in this chapter, none is more *blatantly* unrealistic than absence of inferior goods (NI). That assumption is used only once, in the proof of Theorem 1, to show that lower (higher) household incomes lead to lower (higher) demand for *all primary inputs.* In that sense, the relevant assumption is one of "noninferior factors" – and is perhaps less blatantly unrealistic. Still, if potatoes are an inferior good, and a plot of land is good only for growing potatoes, we have an instance of "inferior factor". I have accordingly used Assumption

[9] More technically: at full use of the second input, fiscal expansion would create excess demand, hence, an increase in the price of that input, passed into output prices; but the price of the first input (in excess supply) remains fixed, so that its relative (real) price tends to zero as fiscal expansion keeps feeding inflation.

NI, because I could not think of any other primitive assumption ruling out inferior factors.

It is plausible that further research may permit weakening even the "noninferior factors" assumption; perhaps I have convinced myself too quickly that it was a natural requirement for the problem at hand. Otherwise, it would be a matter of empirical research to discover how significant the problem is.[10]

8.6 *Farewell*

As intimated before, I regard the basic idea of this chapter as sound and useful, but the formulation as technically crude. In particular, the technical formulation is more extreme than common sense and casual empiricism would suggest. Thus, not all output prices are set by producers as a markup on costs; not all primary inputs have downward rigid prices; increases in input prices are apt to be passed into output prices only if they are viewed as permanent; and so on. I can only hope that the crude formulation does not obliterate the useful ideas.

Among the improvements that seem easiest to achieve, I should mention first explicit disaggregation of production into the activities of a number of producers, each endowed with its own production set, hiring its own factors, setting its own prices, and possibly distributing its profits. Readers are invited to interpret the chapter as if that improvement had already been achieved – it would have, had more time been available.

Also, suppressing altogether the calendar time needed for quantity adjustments, and the redistribution of profits during the time span covered by the process, are convenient simplifications that do not seem essential.

The lasting usefulness of the contribution attempted in this chapter is apt to stand or fall on the realism of widespread downward factor price rigidities and widespread markup pricing of produced commodities. And the major challenge to all *students* of price dynamics remains that of *modeling* nondeterministic expectations and stochastic sequential decision making by consumers and firms.

REFERENCES

Barro, R., and H. Grossman. 1971. "A General Disequilibrium Model of Income and Employment." *American Economic Review* 61: 82–93.

Champsaur, P., J. H. Drèze, and C. Henry. 1977. "Stability Theorems with Economic Applications." *Econometrica* 45: 273–94.

10 The more relevant empirical question is probably whether some broad types of labor (like unskilled physical labor) are inferior factors.

Dehez, P., and J. H. Drèze. 1984. "On Supply-Constrained Equilibria." *Journal of Economic Theory* 33: 172–82.

Drèze, J. H. 1983. "Stability of a Keynesian Adjustment Process." Mimeo, CORE, Université Catholique de Louvain, Louvain-la-Neuve, Belgium.

1989. "L'arbitrage entre équité et efficacité en matière d'emploi et de salaires." 8ème Congrès des Economistes de Langue Française, Commission 6, Chap. 4; also reprinted in *Recherches Economiques de Louvain* 55: 1–31.

Drèze, J. H., and C. Bean. 1990. "European Employment: Lessons from a Multi-country Econometric Study." *Swedish Journal of Economics* 92: 135–65.

Drèze, J. H., C. Bean, J. P. Lambert, F. Mehta, and H. Sneessens, Eds. 1991. *Europe's Unemployment Problem.* Cambridge, MA: The MIT Press.

Drèze, J. H., and C. Gollier. 1989. "Risk-Sharing in the Labour Market." Mimeo, CORE, Université Catholique de Louvain, Louvain-la-Neuve, Belgium.

Fisher, F. M. 1983. *Disequilibrium Foundations of Equilibrium Economics.* Cambridge: Cambridge University Press.

Gollier, C. 1988. *Intergenerational Risk-Sharing and Unemployment.* Unpublished Ph.D. dissertation, Université Catholique de Louvain, Belgium.

Grandmont, J. M. 1974. "On the Short-Run Equilibrium in a Monetary Economy." In *Allocation under Uncertainty: Equilibrium and Optimality,* J. H. Drèze, Ed. New York: Macmillan, pp. 213–28.

1977. "Temporary General Equilibrium Theory." *Econometrica* 45: 535–72.

Leijonhufvud, A. 1968. *On Keynesian Economics and the Economics of Keynes.* New York: Oxford University Press.

Malinvaud, E. 1977. *The Theory of Unemployment Reconsidered.* Oxford: Blackwell.

Morishima, M. 1976. *The Economic Theory of Modern Society.* Cambridge: Cambridge University Press.

Sneessens, H., and J. H. Drèze. 1986. "A Discussion of Belgian Unemployment, Combining Traditional Concepts and Disequilibrium Econometrics." *Economica* 53: 89–119.

van der Laan, G. 1980. "Equilibrium under Rigid Prices with Compensation for the Consumers." *International Economic Review* 21: 63–74.

CHAPTER 10

Capacity adjustments in a competitive industry

Jean J. Gabszewicz and Philippe Michel

1 Introduction

In this chapter, we study an adjustment process of the productive capacities for firms operating in a competitive industry. Our basic assumption is that firms adjust their capacity at each period so as to reduce the total cost of current production. This type of investment behavior is well-known in macroeconomics since it underlies the neoclassical theory of the accelerator (see, e.g., Jorgenson, 1963): It is this assumption that sustains the definition of the accelerator in the macroeconomic investment equations. Here we examine the microeconomic implications of this investment behavior on the capacity adjustments of firms, when it is combined with a simultaneous adjustment of output market price at equilibrium. We perform this analysis in the context of a competitive market, and show that this combined process generates a sequence of short-run market equilibria that converges to the long-run equilibrium in which capacities of firms are optimally adjusted to their production level. The adjustment process we consider is inspired by the microeconomic distinction between short- and long-run cost curves: while in the short run, variable factors can be freely adapted to meet an immediate production requirement, today's decisions, which concern the amount of productive capacity, reveal their effects in the future only, with some time lag on current productive decisions. Accordingly, today production is constrained to be operated with an equipment inherited from the past, and nothing can prevent a priori this equipment to be ill-adapted to the current required production level. In particular, according to running factor prices, this production level could have been realized with more capital and less variable factors, or vice versa. Then the level of production capacity should be revised according to some criterion, so as to prepare future production to be realized under lower cost conditions.

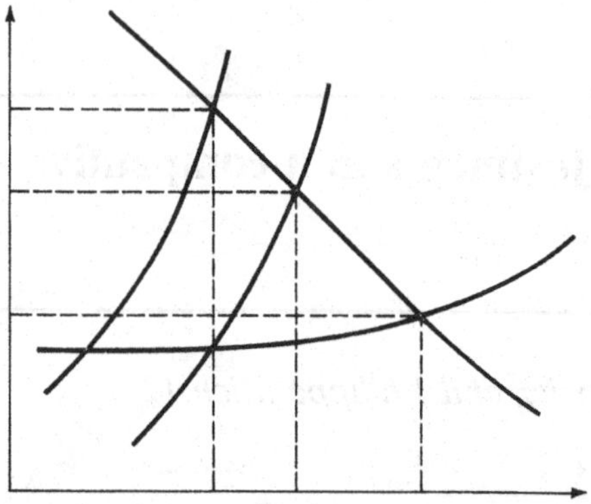

Figure 1.

We assume in this chapter that the competitive firms operating in the industry with a capacity inherited from period $t-1$ adjust this capacity at period t so as to reduce the cost of current production. Endowed at period $t+1$ with this adjusted amount of capital, their supply function in this period is itself derived from this new productive capacity level, entailing on the market an adjustment of price and output to their resulting equilibrium values. The question we ask is whether this process leads the industry to the efficient steady state where the equipment of each firm is optimally adapted to its repeated contribution to the output level of the industry.

To illustrate the time path of economic variables through the described process, let us consider an industry whose productive sector is represented by an aggregate production function $Y=F(K,L)$, where K denotes the amount of equipment, and L the labor force. Suppose that the equipment available in period t has been chosen in period $t-1$ and becomes active in period t. Then the short-run cost function $C(K(t-1),Y)$ is obtained in period t by using the minimum quantity of labor, given $K(t-1)$, to produce Y. The long-run cost function $\Gamma(Y)$ corresponds to the optimal choice of both capital and labor, given the factor prices, to produce an amount Y of output. Suppose that, at each period, the output market is competitive, so that the quantity sold by the productive sector is such that its short-run marginal cost equals price. Using Figure 1, we can easily represent the equilibrium on this market at period t.

DD' represents the demand curve for the good and S_tS_t' represents the (short-run) supply curve in period t, which coincides, since the market is competitive, with the short-run marginal cost curve $(\partial/\partial Y)C(K(t-1),Y)$ of the productive sector endowed with an amount of capital $K(t-1)$; the pair $(p^*(t), Y^*(t))$ is the market equilibrium at period t. As for the curve $d\Gamma/dY$, it represents the long-run marginal cost. Clearly, at period t, the productive sector is undercapacitied to produce the amount $Y^*(t)$. The capital–labor ratio is underadapted to the observed level of economic activity, and there is a clear incentive to increase capacity so as to reduce the cost of producing $Y^*(t)$. Assuming that the new capacity $K(t)$ is chosen so as to minimize the cost of producing $Y^*(t)$, a new short-run marginal cost curve $(\partial/\partial Y)C(K(t), Y)$ obtains in period $t+1$ represented in Figure 1 by the curve $S_{t+1}S'_{t+1}$. The pair $(p^*(t+1), Y^*(t+1))$ is the market equilibrium at period $t+1$. Eventually, successive capital adjustments will lead to the steady state $(\hat{Y}, \hat{p})$, where the installed equipment, price, and output are identically renewed from period to period.

In the following, we study the global stability of a process that constitutes a generalized disaggregated version of the previous example. The industry consists of n firms i, $i = 1, \dots, n$, whose technologies exhibit nonincreasing returns to scale. At period t, firm i chooses its output level $y_i(t)$ so as to maximize current profits, given the equipment $k_i(t-1)$ inherited from period $t-1$. The output price at period t obtains from the equality of supply and demand, leading firm i to supply a quantity $y_i^*(t)$ at equilibrium. Finally, firm i adjusts its capacity at period t at some level $k_i(t)$ *that reduces the productive costs of current output* $y_i^*(t)$: $k_i(t)$ is the level of equipment available for production at period $t+1$. Our main result consists in showing that the resulting time paths of capacities, production levels, and price all converge to the long-run steady-state equilibrium. The model is introduced in Section 2. In this section, we examine also the problems of existence and uniqueness of the short-run and long-run market equilibrium. The adjustment process and an example are studied in Section 3. The global stability of the process is analyzed in Section 4 under the assumption that firms' technologies exhibit strictly decreasing returns to scale. Section 5 considers the case of constant returns to scale. Finally, the assumptions of our analysis are discussed and compared with alternative formulations in a brief concluding section.

2 The model and some preliminary results

We study an industry embodying *n firms*. The market *demand function* for the product, which we denote by $p(y)$, where y represents aggregate output, is continuous and nonincreasing. To simplify the study, we will assume that there exists $\bar{y}$ such that $p(\bar{y}) = 0$, and that the integral $\int_0^y p(u)\,du$ is defined for all $y > 0$. For each firm i, $i = 1, \dots, n$, its total cost function $C_i(k, y)$, where k denotes the amount of capital and y the firm's output level, satisfies the following assumptions:

(i) C_i is differentiable and strictly convex;
(ii) $(\partial/\partial y)C_i(k,y) \geq 0$;
(iii) for each y, $\lim_{k\to\infty} C_i(k,y) = +\infty$ and $\partial C_i(k,y)/\partial k \geq 0$.

Given an n-tuple of *capital endowments* $K \overset{\text{def}}{=} (k_1,\dots,k_i,\dots,k_n)$, an n-dimensional vector $Y^* \overset{\text{def}}{=} (y_1^*,\dots,y_i^*,\dots,y_n^*)$ is a *short-run market equilibrium* (SRME) if, for each firm i, y_i^* maximizes with respect to y_i:

$$\Pi_i(y_i,k_i) \overset{\text{def}}{=} p^* y_i - C_i(k_i,y_i)$$

with $p^* = p(y^*)$ and $y^* = \sum_{i=1}^n y_i^*$. We will alternatively denote by $Y^*(K)$ an SRME corresponding to the vector of capital endowments K. A pair $(\hat{K},\hat{Y})$, with $\hat{K} = (\hat{k}_1,\dots,\hat{k}_i,\dots,\hat{k}_n)$ and $\hat{Y} = (\hat{y}_1,\dots,\hat{y}_i,\dots,\hat{y}_n)$, is a *long-run market equilibrium* (LRME) if, for each firm i:

(i) $\hat{y}_i$ solves $\max_{y_i} \hat{p}\cdot y_i - C_i(\hat{k}_i,y_i)$;
(ii) $\hat{k}_i$ solves $\max_{k_i} \hat{p}\cdot \hat{y}_i - C_i(k_i,\hat{y}_i)$;

with $\hat{p} = p(\hat{y})$ and $\hat{y} = \sum_{i=1}^n \hat{y}_i$.

Thus an SRME is an n-tuple of output levels y_i^* such that, given the capital endowment of each firm i, y_i^* maximizes its short-run profits at the price that clears the output market. An LRME is a short-run market equilibrium resulting from that n-tuple of capital endowments that, for each firm, minimizes the cost of producing the corresponding output. Accordingly, at an LRME, we have $\hat{Y} = Y^*(\hat{K})$. Finally, given an n-tuple of capital endowments K and an n-tuple of output levels Y, we define *the consumers' surplus function* $S(K,Y)$ by

$$S(K,Y) = \int_0^{\sum_{i=1}^n y_i} p(u)\,du - \sum_{i=1}^n C_i(k_i,y_i).$$

Notice that, by assumption (i) on $C_i(k,y)$, $S(K,Y)$ is a strictly concave function of (K,Y) as the difference between a concave and strictly convex function. By the same assumption again, the necessary conditions

$$p^* - \frac{\partial}{\partial y}C_i(k_i,y_i^*) \leq 0 \quad\text{and}\quad p^* - \frac{\partial}{\partial y}C_i(k_i,y_i^*) = 0$$
$$\text{if } y_i^* > 0,\ i = 1,\dots,n,$$

are also sufficient and must be satisfied at an SRME Y^*. Since $S(k,y)$ is strictly concave, the same first-order conditions are also necessary and sufficient whenever S is maximized with respect to Y for a given n-tuple K of capital endowments. Consequently, $Y^*(K)$ is an SRME for an n-tuple of capital endowments K if and only if Y^* maximizes $S(K,Y)$ for the same n-tuple K. This remark allows us to prove:

Proposition 1. *For each K, there exists a unique SRME $Y^*(K)$. Furthermore, $Y^*(K)$ is a continuous function of K.*

Proof: Existence follows from the fact that the production vector Y belongs to the compact set $[0, \bar{y}]^n$.

Uniqueness follows immediately from the strict concavity of S and the previous remark. Because $S(K, Y)$ is a continuous function of K, the strict concavity of S implies that $Y^*(K)$ is itself a continuous function of K. □

Now consider an LRME $(\hat{Y}, \hat{K})$. Since $\hat{Y} = Y^*(\hat{K})$, $\hat{Y}$ maximizes $S(\bar{K}, Y)$ with respect to Y. On the other hand, at an LRME, we know that $\hat{k}_i$ solves, for each i, $\min_{k_i} C_i(k_i, \hat{y}_i)$. Accordingly, the necessary and sufficient conditions satisfied at a vector $\hat{K} = (\hat{k}_1, \ldots, \hat{k}_i, \ldots, \hat{k}_n)$ corresponding to an LRME are the same as those that must be satisfied at the solution of the problem $\max_K S(K, \hat{Y})$. It follows that $(\hat{Y}, \hat{K})$ is an LRME if and only if $\hat{Y}$ and $\hat{K}$ are the global maxima of $S(K, Y)$.

Proposition 2. *There exists a unique LRME.*

Proof: The strict concavity of S immediately implies the uniqueness of the LRME. Furthermore, by the previous remark, the existence of an LRME follows from the existence of a global maximum of S with respect to (K, Y). This global maximum obtains for finite values of K and Y, since Y belongs to the set $[0, \bar{y}]^n$ and since, by assumption (iii), $S(K, Y)$ tends to $-\infty$ as any k_i tends to $+\infty$. □

Proposition 2 guarantees that the consumers' surplus $S(K, Y)$ reaches its maximum at a unique pair $(\hat{K}, \hat{Y})$, which is the unique long-run market equilibrium.

Remark 1. The assumptions made on the demand function (zero price at a finite level of production $\bar{y}$ and convergence of the integral $\int_0^y p(u)\,du$) can be relaxed. First, in the definition of $S(K, Y)$, we can replace in the integral the lower bound zero by some fixed positive level: the partial derivatives of $S(K, Y)$ are unchanged. Second, in the case $\bar{y} = +\infty$, the existence of the SRME and of the LRME is obtained when the maximum of $S(K, Y)$ is reached for finite values of the variables. For this to be the case, it is sufficient that S tends to $-\infty$ as one of the variables tends to $+\infty$. This property holds in the example considered in what follows.

3 A dynamic adjustment process for productive capacities

To adapt the dynamics considered in our introductory section to the model we have just described, we proceed as follows. At period t, firm i has a capital endowment $k_i(t-1)$ inherited from period $t-1$; it chooses its output level so as to maximize short-run profits $\Pi_i(y_i, k_i(t-1))$ at the output price $p^*(t)$ that clears the market. Accordingly, firm i's output level $y_i^*(t)$ corresponds to the short-run market equilibrium $Y^*(K(t-1)) = Y^*(t) = (y_1^*(t), \ldots, y_i^*(t), \ldots, y_n^*(t))$ associated with the vector of capital endowments $K(t-1) = (k_1(t-1), \ldots, k_n(t-1))$. On the other hand, the capital endowment of firm i is supposed to be adjusted at period t *so as to reduce the cost of existing capacity in the production of* $y_i^*(t)$. To this end, we assume that, for each firm i, there exists a continuous function $h_i(k_i, y_i)$ – the *cost-reducing function* – verifying the property:

$$\text{for all } (k_i, y_i), \quad C_i(h_i(k_i, y_i), y_i) \le C_i(k_i, y_i), \quad \text{and}$$
$$C_i(h_i(k_i, y_i), y_i) < C_i(k_i, y_i) \quad \text{whenever} \quad C_i(k_i, y_i) > \min_k C_i(k, y_i).$$

Thus, the cost function h_i indicates, for each pair (k_i, y_i), the new equipment $h_i(k_i, y_i)$ the firm decides to invest (disinvest) so as to reduce the cost of using capacity k_i for producing the output level y_i. Furthermore, this reduction must be strict whenever the capacity k_i is not exactly adjusted to the production y_i.

By applying the function h_i to the pair $(k_i(t-1), y_i^*(t))$, the capital endowment of firm i decided in period t is equal to

$$k_i(t) = h_i(k_i(t-1), y_i^*(t)), \quad i = 1, \ldots, n,$$

which generates a new vector of capital endowments:

$$K(t) = (h_1(k_1(t-1), y_1^*(t)), \ldots, h_i(k_i(t-1), y_i^*(t)), \ldots, h_n(k_n(t-1), y_n^*(t)).$$

Taking into account the fact that $Y^*(t) = Y^*(K(t-1))$, we finally obtain the system of difference equations:

$$K(t) = F(K(t-1)), \tag{1}$$

where $F_i(K(t-1)) = h_i(k_i(t-1), y_i^*(K(t-1)))$.

A particular simple form for the cost-reducing function h_i consists in assuming that, given y_i, firm i adjusts its capacity so as to produce y_i at the lowest possible cost, that is,

$$C_i(h_i(y_i), y_i) = \min_k C_i(k, y_i);$$

(in that case, we denote h_i by h_i^*). It is also possible to consider that firms only proceed to a *partial* adjustment in the direction of the equipment optimal for the production of y_i; for instance, h_i can be defined as

$$h_i(k_i, y_i) = \lambda_i h_i^*(y_i) + (1 - \lambda_i)k_i, \quad 0 < \lambda_i < 1, \tag{2}$$

in which case the existing amount of capital k_i is partially combined with the optimal one $(h_i^*(y_i))$. Finally, we notice that the previous formulation may take into account the existence of irreversibility constraints entailing investments that compensate the physical depreciation of capital. This constraint writes as $h_i(k_i, y_i) \geq (1-\mu)k_i$, $0<\mu<1$.

To illustrate the dynamic process we have just defined, let us consider the following example with a single firm, whose production function is of the Cobb–Douglas type, that is,

$$y = k^{\alpha} l^{\beta}, \quad \alpha>0, \ \beta>0, \ \alpha+\beta\leq 1,$$

where k (resp. l) denotes the amount of capital (resp. labor).

The market demand function $p(y)$ is defined by

$$p(y) = y^{-\epsilon}, \quad \epsilon>0.$$

If r and w denote, respectively, the price of capital and the wage rate, the total cost function of the firm is

$$C(k,y) = rk + wk^{-\alpha/\beta} y^{1/\beta}.$$

The SRME is obtained by solving the equation $p(y) = (\partial/\partial y)C(k,y)$, that is,

$$y^{-\epsilon} = \frac{w}{\beta} k^{-\alpha/\beta} \cdot y^{1/(\beta-1)},$$

so that

$$y^*(k) = ak^{\alpha/(1-\beta+\beta\epsilon)} \tag{3}$$

with $a = (\beta/w)^{\beta/(1-\beta+\beta\epsilon)}$.

To analyze the dynamics in this example, we will assume that the cost-reducing function h is defined by (2). The optimal equipment to produce y, that is, $h^*(y)$, is obtained by solving

$$\frac{\partial}{\partial k} C(k,y) = 0,$$

that is,

$$k = h^*(y) = \left(\frac{\alpha w}{\beta r}\right)^{\beta/(\alpha+\beta)} \cdot y^{1/(\alpha+\beta)},$$

so that, applying (2), we obtain

$$h(k,y) = \lambda \left(\frac{\alpha w}{\beta r}\right)^{\beta/(\alpha+\beta)} \cdot y^{1/(\alpha+\beta)} + (1-\lambda)k,$$

or, in the dynamic formulation,

$$k(t) = h(k(t-1), y^*(k(t-1))) = \lambda h^*(y^*(k(t-1))) + (1-\lambda)k(t-1).$$

Taking (3) into account, we get

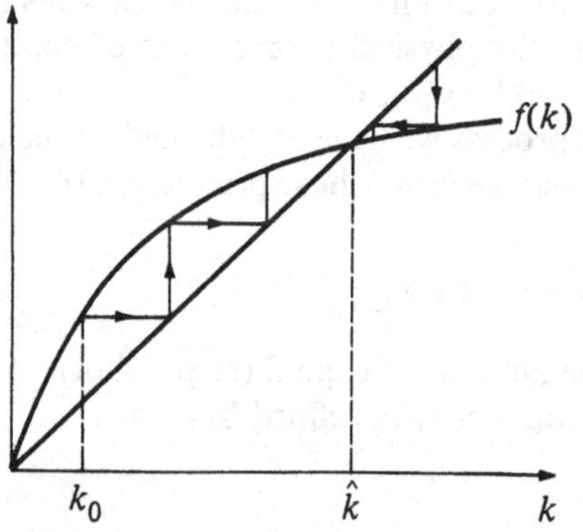

Figure 2.

$$k(t)=\lambda bk(t-1)^{\gamma}+(1-\lambda)k(t-1), \tag{4}$$

with $b=(\alpha w/\beta r)^{\beta/(\alpha+\beta)}\cdot a^{1/(\alpha+\beta)}$ and $\gamma=\alpha/(\alpha+\beta)(1-\beta+\beta\epsilon)$.

Notice that $0<\gamma<1$, since $\alpha\leq(\alpha+\beta)(1-\beta)=\alpha+\beta(1-\alpha-\beta)$. Define $f(k)$ by

$$f(k)=\lambda bk^{\gamma}+(1-\lambda)k.$$

The function f is monotone increasing and satisfies

$$f(k)\gtreqless k\Leftrightarrow k\lesseqgtr\hat{k},$$

with $\hat{k}=b^{1/(1-\gamma)}$. It follows that the LRME

$$(\hat{k},\hat{y})=(b^{1/(1-\gamma)},\alpha(b^{1/(1-\gamma)})^{\alpha/(1-\beta+\beta\epsilon)})$$

is globally stable for the difference equation defined by (4).

Figure 2 describes the time path of capacity adjustments in this example.

It is interesting to notice that the property of global stability holds in this example with $\alpha+\beta<1$ as well as with $\alpha+\beta=1$. In the first case, the firm's technology exhibits strictly decreasing returns to scale, whereas in the second, returns to scale are constant. As we will see in Section 5, the latter case must be treated more carefully when there is more than one firm in the industry.

4 Stability analysis: The case of strictly decreasing returns to scale

In this section, we analyze the global stability of the process defined by (1) when firms' technologies exhibit strictly decreasing returns to scale. In that case, we know from Proposition 2 that there exists a unique LRME $(\hat{K}, \hat{Y})$. Let us define the function v by

$$v(K) = S(K, Y^*(K)),$$

that is, $v(K)$ equals the consumers' surplus corresponding to the SRME $Y^*(K)$ associated with the vector of capital endowments K.

Lemma 1. *For all* K,

(i) $v(F(K)) \geq v(K)$; *and*
(ii) $v(F(K)) = v(K) \Rightarrow F(K) = K = \hat{K}$.

Proof: First, it is clear that

$$v(F(K)) = S(F(K), Y^*(F(K))) \geq S(F(K), Y^*(K)),$$

since $S(F(K), Y)$ reaches its maximum with respect to Y at $Y^*(F(K))$. Furthermore, by definition of F and the functions h_i, we have also that $S(F(K), Y^*(K)) \geq S(K, Y^*(K)) = v(K)$, which implies $v(F(K)) \geq v(K)$, that is, (i).

To prove (ii), we notice that the cost-reducing functions h_i strictly decrease costs as long as the capacities are not optimally adjusted to current production. Consequently, the equality $v(F(K)) = v(K)$ implies $F(K) = K$. Since the equality $F(K) = K$ means that the vector of capital endowments is optimally adjusted to the SRME $Y^*(K)$, it follows that $(K, Y^*(K))$ is an LRME. Finally, the uniqueness of the LRME implies that $K = \hat{K}$. Thus we have shown that $v(F(K)) = v(K) \Rightarrow F(K) = K$ and $K = \hat{K}$, which completes the proof of the lemma. □

Let us come back to the adjustment process defined by (1). To the sequence $\{K(t)\} = \{F(K(t-1))\}$, we may associate the sequence of consumers' surpluses $\{v(t)\}$ defined by

$$v(t) = S(K(t-1), Y^*(t)). \tag{5}$$

Now we prove the following theorem.

Theorem 1. *The sequence* $\{K(t)\}$ *defined by* (1) *converges asymptotically to the vector of capital endowments* $\hat{K}$ *corresponding to the LRME* $(\hat{K}, \hat{Y})$.

Proof: Property (i) of the lemma implies that the sequence $\{v(t)\}$ defined by (1) is monotone nondecreasing. This sequence is bounded by the maximum of the consumers' surplus function $S(\hat{K}, \hat{Y}) \overset{\text{def}}{=} \hat{v}$. Thus, it converges to some limit $\bar{v} \leq \hat{v}$. Consider the sequence $\{K(t)\}$ defined by (1) and let $\bar{K}$ be a limit point of this sequence. There exists a subsequence $K(\alpha(t))$ that converges to $\bar{K}$ and, by continuity of v, we have

$$\bar{K} = \lim_{t\to\infty} K(\alpha(t)) \quad \text{and} \quad \bar{v} = \lim_{t\to\infty} v(\alpha(t+1)) = v(\bar{K}).$$

By continuity of F and v, it also follows that

$$F(\bar{K}) = \lim_{t\to\infty} F(K(\alpha(t)) = \lim_{t\to\infty} K(\alpha(t)+1)$$

and

$$v(F(\bar{K})) = \lim_{t\to\infty} v(\alpha(t)+2) = \bar{v}.$$

The equality $v(F(\bar{K})) = v(\bar{K})$ implies $\bar{K} = \hat{K}$: any converging subsequence of the bounded sequence $\{K(t)\}$ converges to $\hat{K}$, which implies that $\{K(t)\}$ converges to $\hat{K}$. □

Two remarks are in order. First, we have shown that the function $\hat{v} - v(K)$ is a Lyapounov function for the system of difference equations defined by (1). Thus we obtain also the Lyapounov stability of this process: For any preassigned neighborhood of $\hat{K}$, if the sequence $\{K(t)\}$ is initiated sufficiently close to $\hat{K}$, all of its terms remain within this preassigned neighborhood. On Lyapounov stability of difference equations systems, the reader may refer to Brock and Scheinkman (1975) or Michel (1984, Chap. 32). On the other hand, the proof of convergence relies heavily on the existence and uniqueness of short-run and long-run equilibria, which, in turn, follow from the assumption of strict convexity of C_i (assumption (i)). It is clear, however, that the whole proof of convergence would go through with *convex* functions C_i, as long as short-run and long-run equilibria are *unique*. We will use this property in the next section, which constitutes the case of constant returns to scale.

5 Stability analysis: The case of constant returns to scale

In this section, we allow some firms to be characterized by technologies obeying constant returns to scale, and thus having linear long-run cost functions. More precisely, we will assume now that, for a subset I of firms, the total cost function $C_i(k,y)$, $i \in I$, is homogeneous of degree 1, but strictly convex separately with respect to k and y: returns to scale are constant, whereas the marginal product of each factor is strictly decreasing. As for the firms $i \notin I$, we keep this assumption that total cost functions $C_i(k,y)$ are strictly convex with respect to (k,y).

The study of the short-run market equilibria presented in Section 2 remains unchanged: Due to the assumption of strictly decreasing marginal products, the consumers' surplus function $S(K,Y)$ is strictly concave for any fixed vector of capital endowments K. Accordingly, for any n-tuple $K=(k_1,\dots,k_i,\dots,k_n)$, there exists a unique SRME $Y^*(K)$. On the other hand, the surplus function $S(K,Y)$ is no longer *strictly* concave so that there could exist more than a unique global maximum and, thus, more than a unique LRME. For each firm i, define $\Gamma_i(y)$ by

$$\Gamma_i(y)=\min_k C_i(k,y);$$

Γ_i is the long-run cost function of firm i. Since the marginal product of capital is strictly decreasing in each firm i, there exists for each y a unique value of k, say, $k_i(y)$, that solves $\min_k C_i(k,y)$. On the other hand, define $M(Y)$ by

$$M(Y)\stackrel{\text{def}}{=}\max_K S(K,Y)=\int_0^{\sum_{i=1}^n y_i} p(u)\,du-\sum_{i=1}^n \Gamma_i(y_i).$$

The uniqueness of the LRME is implied by the uniqueness of $\hat{Y}$, the solution to the problem $\max_Y M(Y)$; indeed, assuming that $\hat{Y}$ is unique, the LRME $(\hat{K},\hat{Y})$ defined by

$$\hat{Y}=(\hat{y}_1,\dots,\hat{y}_i,\dots,\hat{y}_n)\quad\text{and}\quad \hat{K}=(k_1(\hat{y}_1),\dots,k_n(\hat{y}_n))$$

is also unique. Notice that, for $i\in I$, the long-run cost function Γ_i is linear: We will denote by γ_i the scalar for which $\Gamma_i(y_i)=\gamma_i y_i$.

Proposition 1. *If the market demand function $p(y)$ is strictly decreasing, and if there exists one most efficient firm, that is, if there exists a unique index $\bar{\imath}$, $\bar{\imath}\in I$, such that, for all $i\in I$, $i\neq\bar{\imath}$,*

$$\gamma_{\bar{\imath}}=\min_{i\in I}\{\gamma_i\}<\gamma_i,$$

then the LRME $(\hat{K},\hat{Y})$ is unique, and, for all $i\in I$, $i\neq\bar{\imath}$, $\hat{y}_i=0$.

Proof: Let $\hat{Y}=(\hat{y}_1,\dots,\hat{y}_i,\dots,\hat{y}_n)$ be the production levels associated to an LRME (not necessarily unique). The first-order conditions, for firms $i\in I$, are, at the solution $\hat{Y}$ to the problem $\max_Y M(Y)$,

$$\hat{p}\le\gamma_i$$

and

$$\hat{p}=\gamma_i\quad\text{if }\hat{y}_i>0,$$

with $\hat{p}=p(\sum_{i=1}^n \hat{y}_i)$. Since, for all $i\in I$, $i\neq\bar{\imath}$, $\gamma_{\bar{\imath}}\ge\hat{p}$, we must have

$$\forall i\in I,\ i\neq\bar{\imath},\quad \gamma_i>\hat{p},$$

so that $\hat{y}_i=0$ for all $i\neq\bar{\imath}$, $i\in I$. Thus, we have

$$\max_Y S(K,Y)=\int_0^{y_{\bar{\imath}}+\sum_{i\notin I}y_i} p(u)\,du-\gamma_{\bar{\imath}}y_{\bar{\imath}}-\sum_{i\notin I}\Gamma_i(y_i).$$

The function

$$\int_0^{y_T+\Sigma_{i\notin I} y_i} p(u)\,du-\gamma_T y_T-\sum_{i\notin I}\Gamma_i(y_i)$$

is strictly concave as a function of y_T: indeed, the function $p(y)$ is strictly decreasing and, for $i\notin I$, $-\Gamma_i(y_i)$ is strictly concave. Accordingly, this function is strictly concave in all of its arguments, which implies the uniqueness of $\hat{Y}$. Since, for each i, $k_i(y)$ is also unique, $(\hat{K},\hat{Y})$ is the unique LRME. □

At the last remark of Section 4, we have stressed the fact that the proof of Theorem 1 can be applied to firms with convex functions insofar as the LRME is unique. Consequently, we have the following theorem.

Theorem 2. *Under the assumption of Proposition 1, the sequence* $\{K(t)\}$ *defined by* (1) *converges asymptotically to the vector of capital endowments* $\hat{K}$ *corresponding to the unique LRME* $(\hat{K},\hat{Y})$.

Under constant returns to scale, it may well happen that several firms have identical long-run cost functions so that the function $M(Y)$ does depend only on the *sum* of output levels corresponding to these firms. Since any arbitrary assessment of this sum among these firms leads to the same value of M, it is not surprising that constant returns to scale combined with identical firms lead to a multiplicity of long-run market equilibria. The assumption underlying Proposition 1 precisely excludes this difficulty. Notwithstanding, if *all* firms exhibiting constant returns to scale would be identical with all respects (cost functions, cost-reducing functions, initial capital endowments), they would remain identical through the whole process, so that this process would again converge to the LRME for which the production levels of these firms are all equal.

6 Conclusion

In this chapter, we have proposed an adjustment process of productive capacities of firms operating in a competitive industry. This process is driven by the assumption that firms adjust their equipment at each period so as to reduce the productive costs of current output, while the short-run output price clears the market. Whatever the initial conditions about the capital endowments of firms, the process converges to the long-run market equilibrium, the steady state at which capacities are optimally adapted to the repeated level of economic activity. Thus, this process has remarkable stability properties, when compared to alternative dynamic formulations of capacity adjustments, like those based on naive expectations about the current setting price (the "Cobweb" model). The method used to prove the convergence of the process relies on the fact that the consumers' surplus is always increasing along its trajectory: The consumers' surplus function thus serves as a Lyapounov function in the proof of convergence.

The expectations of firms are admittedly naive along the process since their investment decisions are driven by the observed output, and not by rational anticipations based on the causalities through which the economic magnitudes are determined. Nevertheless, the firms we consider behave competitively so that, in any case, they are assumed to be naive about the market mechanism that determines the output price. Accordingly, they cannot anticipate the future levels of output they will have to produce and, a fortiori, the optimal investments' trajectory needed to meet these production requirements. Furthermore, we feel that, in spite of its simplicity, the adjustment process we have considered incorporates an important ingredient of the observed behavior of firms. More precisely, it seems that when the current capital–labor ratio is ill-adapted to current production, firms tend to adjust this ratio in the "right" direction: more capital and less labor if equipment is insufficient for current production, and vice versa in case of overcapacity. This is exactly the behavioral assumption underlying our model. Similar myopic behavior has been assumed for describing the evolution of firms from short-run to long-run equilibrium in the context of a differentiated product market; see Sonnenschein (1981, 1982) and Artzner, Simon, and Sonnenschein (1988).

This chapter is closely related to an earlier piece of work (Gabszewicz and Quinzii, 1986), in which a similar process was analyzed. Nevertheless, there are significant differences between the two approaches. First of all, it is assumed there that the productive sector is aggregated and has production possibilities described by a Cobb–Douglas production function with constant returns to scale. Furthermore, the investment decisions of this aggregated productive sector are assumed to be guided by the specific cost-reducing function h_i^* applied to current output. On the other hand, the analysis in Gabszewicz and Quinzii (1986) takes into account the effects of the adjustment process in the output market on market prices for the productive factors. It is clear, indeed, that in their endeavor to adjust optimally the level of productive factors to the observed output level, firms modify in each period their demand for these productive factors and, accordingly, factor prices may well fluctuate if they adjust instantaneously at their equilibrium values. Such "general equilibrium" effects are not analyzed here: The industry we consider is assumed to be sufficiently "small," so that the input decisions of the firms in the industry do not affect significantly their factor prices and, thus, their cost conditions, which are assumed to remain invariant through the process.

This chapter could be extended in various directions. A first extension would consist in combining the approach considered in the earlier work referred before with the case of a disaggregated industry, as in the present chapter, by taking into account the consequence on input prices of the adjustment process in the output market. It would also be natural to consider a similar adjustment process in the case of interrelated output markets, with several goods that are substitutes. Finally, we have assumed here that the market demand function $p(y)$ remains invariant through time. It would be interesting to let the demand function be time-dependent, either obeying a trend, or fluctuations with alternating periods of booms and recessions. Most probably, the process would then generate more elaborate trajectories with possible oscillations along a long-run equilibrium cycle. All these topics are beyond the scope of the present analysis, but constitute a fruitful territory for further research.

REFERENCES

Artzner, P., C. Simon, and H. Sonnenschein. 1988. "Convergence of Myopic Firms to Long-Run Equilibria via the Method of Characteristics." Mimeo.

Brock, W., and J. Scheinkman. 1975. "Some Results of Global Asymptotic Stability of Difference Equations." *Journal of Economic Theory* 10: 265–8.

Gabszewicz, J. J., and M. Quinzii. 1986. "The Dynamics of Capacity Adjustments in a Competitive Economy." *European Economic Review* 30: 729–45.

Jorgenson, D. 1963. "Capital Theory and Investment Theory." *American Economic Review* 53(2): 247–59.

Michel, P. 1984. *Cours de Mathématiques pour Economistes.* Paris: Economica.

Sonnenschein, H. 1981. "Price Dynamics and the Disappearance of Short Run Profits: An Example." *Journal of Mathematical Economics* 8: 201–4.

1982. "Price Dynamics Based on the Adjustment of Firms." *American Economic Review* 72: 1088–96.

CHAPTER 11

Economic dynamics with learning: Some instability examples

Jean-Michel Grandmont and Guy Laroque

A long-standing issue in the theory of temporary equilibrium dynamics is to assess the stability of long-run steady states when traders employ prespecified learning rules (Fuchs, 1976, 1977a, 1977b, 1979a, 1979b; Fuchs and Laroque, 1976). There has been a renewed interest in the topic in recent years. Several authors have studied the stability of self-fulfilling expectations equilibria - stationary states, deterministic cycles, or finite Markov sunspot equilibria - in simple overlapping generations models (Tillman, 1983, 1985; Grandmont, 1985; Grandmont and Laroque, 1986, 1990; Benassy and Blad, 1989; Guesnerie and Woodford, 1989; Woodford, 1990). Other researchers have analyzed convergence to self-fulfilling expectations in stochastic linear or nonlinear macroeconomic models (De Canio, 1979; Bray, 1982, 1983; Frydman, 1982; Wickens, 1982; Champsaur, 1983; Gourieroux, Laffont, and Monfort, 1983; Bray and Savin, 1986; Fourgeaud, Gourieroux, and Pradel, 1986; Marcet and Sargent, 1988, 1989; Calvo, 1988; Kurz, 1989). The issue has also surfaced in game theory: After an early study by Shapley (1964), researchers have been investigating convergence to particular equilibria in repeated games, when players revise adaptively their expectations and/or their strategies over time (Crawford, 1974, 1983, 1985, 1988; Jordan, 1986; Fudenberg and Kreps, 1988; Canning, 1989). The hope underlying part of the research program is apparently (see, e.g., Lucas, 1986) that stability criteria in plausible dynamics with learning could be useful to reduce the embarrassing multiplicity of long-run (deterministic or stochastic) equilibria that

This paper was prepared for the conference in honor of Jacques Drèze, "General Equilibrium Theory and Applications," CORE, University Catholiqué de Louvain, Belgium, June 1989. We are grateful to Jean-Pascal Benassy, Truman Bewley, John Geanakoplos, Christian Gourieroux, Mordecai Kurz, Martine Quinzii, and Herbert Scarf for their helpful comments and suggestions.

occurs generally in "rational" expectations dynamic socioeconomic systems (see Evans, 1983, 1985, 1989; Evans and Honkapohja, 1989, for instance, for an extensive use of stability criteria as a selection device in linear macroeconomic models).

This chapter is a progress report on our ongoing study of temporary equilibrium dynamics with adaptive learning. We analyze the local stability of a stationary state, within the framework of a simple deterministic example. Our preliminary findings suggest that if traders are prepared, when trying to learn the dynamic laws of their environment, to extrapolate a sufficiently large set of past growth rates, then the stationary state will be actually unstable (Section 1). It should be emphasized that, our formulation being nonlinear, local instability does *not* imply that the actual dynamics will be globally explosive: As the system is pulled away from the steady state, nonlinearities become important, and they may keep the trajectories bounded. If instability of this sort were to be a general phenomenon, as we believe it is, it would suggest that adaptive learning may be an important source of endogenous fluctuations, and a possible explanation of the complexity and the volatility of quite a few observed economic time series: Even though the economic system would have been orderly and simple, had the traders been able to coordinate their expectations through some central mechanism so as to achieve a "rational" expectations equilibrium, *decentralized* adaptive learning might generate endogenously complex nonlinear trajectories, along which forecasting errors would never vanish.

Our findings suggest also that convergence results can be indeed obtained in theoretical models, but only at the cost of imposing assumptions that restrict, often quite narrowly, the kind of regularities that traders are able to recognize in past data, and to extrapolate into the future, when forming their expectations. We illustrate this point in Section 2 by showing how such restrictive assumptions indeed explain some convergence results that can be found in the recent literature on least squares learning, such as those of Marcet and Sargent (1989). As these authors state in the formal presentation of their model, they get convergence results by forcing all traders' beliefs to lie in a small enough, prespecified neighborhood of a "well-behaved" rational expectations equilibrium. Such a procedure is generally innocuous when the rational expectations equilibrium is unique, as in the examples selected by Marcet and Sargent (1989, Section 4), for the prespecified neighborhood may then often be chosen as the whole domain of definition of the model. The restriction runs counter to the spirit of the whole inquiry, however, when there are multiple rational expectations equilibria. For it means that all traders try not only to learn the dynamic laws of the system, but also to coordinate their expectations schemes so as to *control* (stabilize) it collectively, by ignoring systematically all observations indicating that the system is leaving the immediate vicinity of the prespecified target equilibrium. The example we consider in Section 2 involves multiple equilibria, and we show that if the traders use *unrestricted* least squares schemes, the system diverges for an open set of initial conditions. This instability result is in effect closely related to previous findings by Champsaur (1983, Appendix); Gourieroux, Laffont, and Monfort (1983); and Benassy and Blad (1989).

1 Differentiable expectation functions

We consider the simple case that we began to analyze in a previous report (Grandmont and Laroque, 1990, Section 2), where the state variable at each date is a real number, the traders plan one period ahead, and where there is only one lag in the system. We abstract from all sources of uncertainty, and assume that the trader's forecasts are subjectively certain (we would get the same formulation if expectations were probability distributions, but traders were risk-neutral). We suppose that there are many individual traders, each of whom has a negligible impact on the whole system. Each trader observes current and past states, but has no direct information on the other traders' current and past forecasts. To simplify notation, we assume that all traders' forecasts are identical, but that each individual believes that the others' forecasts may be different (otherwise, he could easily infer the others' forecasts from his, and learning the dynamics of the system would become more or less a trivial matter).

Specifically, the dependence of the current equilibrium state x_t on the past state x_{t-1}, and on current forecasts of the future state ${}_tx^e_{t+1}$, is described by the *temporary equilibrium relation:*

$$T(x_{t-1}, x_t, {}_tx^e_{t+1}) = 0. \tag{1}$$

Our analysis is local, that is, near a stationary state that we may, without loss of generality, take as $x = 0$. So we assume that $T(0,0,0) = 0$, and that the temporary equilibrium map T is well-defined and continuously differentiable when its arguments are small enough. An equation like (1) would arise, for instance, as a market-clearing condition in simple versions of the overlapping generations model, or in infinite horizon models with (binding) cash-in-advance constraints.

The temporary equilibrium map T summarizes the "structural" characteristics of the system. The other central ingredient of the model is the description of how the traders forecast the future at any moment, as a function of their observations on current and past states:

$${}_tx^e_{t+1} = \psi(x_t, \ldots, x_{t-L}). \tag{2}$$

The forecasting rule, or *expectation function* ψ, summarizes how people extract information from past data. It is general enough to encompass the particular case where traders revise in each period, in the light of past observations, their beliefs about the dynamic laws of the system and then use their updated beliefs to form their expectations. An important assumption embodied in (2) is that traders have a fixed (but possibly very large) memory lag L: observations in the far distant past have a negligible impact on current forecasts.[1] We postulate that the traders' expectation formation is regular enough, so that ψ is well-defined and continuously differentiable at least for all sequences $(x_t, \ldots, x_{t-L})$ that lie near the stationary state.

The *actual temporary equilibrium dynamics* are obtained by replacing forecasts in (1) by their expression in (2):

$$T(x_{t-1}, x_t, \psi(x_t, \ldots, x_{t-L})) = 0. \tag{3}$$

This determines in principle the current temporary equilibrium state x_t, given past history $(x_{t-1}, \ldots, x_{t-L})$. We will assume either that the traders know beforehand the value of the stationary state (in which case $\psi(0, \ldots, 0) = 0$), or that, if they don't know it, they are prepared to extrapolate constant sequences (in which case $\psi(x, \ldots, x) = x$, at least for all x sufficiently near 0). In either case, $x = 0$ is a stationary solution of (3). We require that the partial derivative of its left-hand side with respect to x_t, evaluated at the stationary state, differs from 0. Then it follows from the implicit function theorem that (3) can be solved uniquely for x_t near $x = 0$, given past history. The resulting difference equation

$$x_t = W_{\mathrm{loc}}(x_{t-1}, \ldots, x_{t-L}) \tag{4}$$

is then well-defined, continuously differentiable in the immediate vicinity of the stationary state. The issue is to analyze its stability in relation to the local properties of the functions T and ψ.

1.1 *Locally self-fulfilling expectation functions*

Perfect foresight is a particular case of the foregoing general formulation if we are willing to admit that all present and future traders know a priori the structure of the system and that they can coordinate their forecasts,

[1] A convenient consequence of this assumption is that the dynamical systems we will deal with are time-independent. Analyzing what happens when traders accumulate data over time should be the topic of further research. It would be interesting, in particular, to study if the formulation in the text is, for L large, a good approximation of the case where traders use time-dependent expectation functions of the form ${}_t x_{t+1}^e = \psi_t(x_t, \ldots, x_0; \bar{x}_{-1}, \ldots, \bar{x}_{-L})$, where $\bar{x}_{-1}, \ldots, \bar{x}_{-L}$ are given but arbitrary initial conditions, when the functions ψ_t do not change much eventually (in a sense to be made precise), as t goes to $+\infty$.

by choosing collectively a "correct" expectation function. Under perfect foresight, sequences of temporary equilibria will have to satisfy the recurrence equation obtained by replacing forecasts ${}_t x^e_{t+1}$ in (1) with the actual value x_{t+1}:

$$T(x_{t-1}, x_t, x_{t+1}) = 0. \tag{5}$$

We denote by a, b_0, and b_1 the partial derivatives of T with respect to x_{t+1}, x_t, and x_{t-1}, respectively, evaluated at the stationary state, and we assume that *expectations matter,* that is, $a \neq 0$. In that case, again from the implicit function theorem, (5) can be solved uniquely for x_{t+1} near 0, and we denote the resulting (local) recurrence equation by

$$x_{t+1} = F_{\text{loc}}(x_t, x_{t-1}). \tag{6}$$

Suppose now that all traders know beforehand the structure of the system, and hence the exact form of equation (6), at least near 0, and that they are able to coordinate their forecasts by choosing collectively the following expectation function:

$${}_t x^e_{t+1} = F_{\text{loc}}(F_{\text{loc}}(x_{t-1}, x_{t-2}), x_{t-1}). \tag{7}$$

That is, the forecast is obtained, given x_{t-1} and x_{t-2}, by "iterating twice" the recurrence equation defined by F_{loc}. Replacing forecasts by the previous expression in (1) yields an equation of the form (3), which can be solved uniquely for x_t near the stationary state, given x_{t-1} and x_{t-2}, provided that $b_0 \neq 0$. It is readily verified that the resulting local temporary equilibrium dynamics (4) coincides then with $x_t = F_{\text{loc}}(x_{t-1}, x_{t-2})$ for every x_{t-1} and x_{t-2} sufficiently near the origin.[2] The expectation function (7) is indeed locally self-fulfilling.

There are typically other locally self-fulfilling expectation functions when the "eigenvalues" of the perfect foresight recurrence equation (5) or (6) are real. The characteristic polynomial corresponding to (5) is

$$Q_F(z) \equiv az^2 + b_0 z + b_1 = 0. \tag{8}$$

Since $a \neq 0$, it has two roots, λ_1 and λ_2. If they are real and different from ± 1, there exists for each eigenvalue λ_k a unique locally invariant surface

[2] Equation (3) becomes in that case $T(x_{t-1}, x_t, F_{\text{loc}}(F_{\text{loc}}(x_{t-1}, x_{t-2}), x_{t-1})) = 0$, which can be solved uniquely for x_t near 0 if $b_0 \neq 0$. The solution is bound to coincide locally with $x_t = F_{\text{loc}}(x_{t-1}, x_{t-2})$ since, by definition of F_{loc}, $T(x_{t-1}, x_t, F_{\text{loc}}(x_t, x_{t-1})) \equiv 0$ for every x_t and x_{t-1} near 0, and thus for $x_t = F_{\text{loc}}(x_{t-1}, x_{t-2})$. Note the importance, when selecting a self-fulfilling expectation function, of satisfying the requirement that (3) can be solved for x_t. For instance, the forecasting rule ${}_t x^e_{t+1} = F_{\text{loc}}(x_t, x_{t-1})$ would *not* work, because (3) would become the identity $T(x_{t-1}, x_t, F_{\text{loc}}(x_t, x_{t-1})) \equiv 0$: For every x_{t-1} near 0, *every* small enough value of x_t could qualify as a temporary equilibrium state. No meaningful dynamics could be defined.

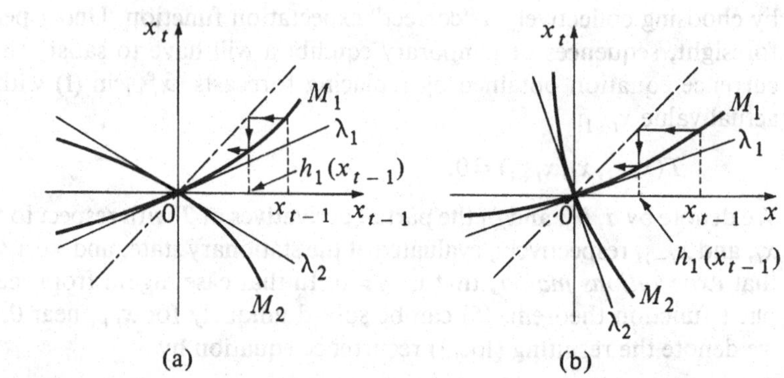

Figure 1.

(manifold) M_k that is tangent to the eigenvector $x_{t-1}=1$, $x_t=\lambda_k$, as shown in the plane in Figure 1. The manifold M_k is, near 0, the graph of some continuously differentiable function, say, $x_t=h_k(x_{t-1})$, with $h_k(0)=0$ and $h_k'(0)=\lambda_k$. The local invariance of the manifold means that the dynamics generated by (6), applied to initial conditions (x_t, x_{t-1}) such that $x_t= h_k(x_{t-1})$, yields then $x_{t+1}=h_k(x_t)$ for every small enough x_{t-1}. Suppose now that the traders know exactly the structure of the system, and that they are able to coordinate their forecasts by focusing on a single root λ_k and by choosing collectively the (local) expectation function obtained by iterating h_k twice:

$$ {}_tx^e_{t+1}=h_k(h_k(x_{t-1})). \tag{9}$$

In this case, too, replacing forecasts in (1) by their expression in (9) yields a recurrence relation of the form (3), which can be solved uniquely for x_t near 0 provided that $b_0\neq 0$. The corresponding temporary equilibrium dynamics (4) coincide then locally with $x_t=h_k(x_{t-1})$.[3] The resulting trajectories lie on the invariant manifold M_k for any initial condition x_{t-1} near 0. They converge to $x=0$ if $|\lambda_k|<1$ and diverge if $|\lambda_k|>1$. Figure 1(a) describes a case where the two roots are real and stable. Then the two expectation functions (9) for $k=1,2$, as well as the forecasting rule (7), are locally self-fulfilling and generate convergent temporary equilibrium sequences. Figure 1(b) describes the case of a *saddle point* in the perfect

[3] Equation (3) becomes, in that case, $T(x_{t-1}, x_t, h_k(h_k(x_{t-1})))=0$, which can be solved uniquely for x_t near 0 if $b_0\neq 0$. The solution is bound to coincide locally with $x_t= h_k(x_{t-1})$, since the invariance of the manifold M_k means

$$T(x_{t-1}, h_k(x_{t-1}), h_k(h_k(x_{t-1})))\equiv 0$$

for every small x_{t-1}.

foresight dynamics ($|\lambda_1|<1<|\lambda_2|$). If all (present and future) traders choose collectively the expectation function (9) corresponding to λ_1, the resulting temporary equilibrium trajectories will "jump" on the stable manifold M_1 for any initial condition x_{t-1} near 0, and will converge to the stationary state.

The locally self-fulfilling forecasting rules (7) or (9) can be supported by a variety of underlying beliefs. They can be generated from the belief that there exist direct intertemporal links between the state variables x_t at different dates, as was implicitly assumed in the foregoing discussion. They are also compatible with beliefs that the endogenous states x_t are functions of well-chosen (exogenous) variables s_t. The expectation function (9), for instance, can be supported by the belief that $x_t = f(s_t)$, where $f(0)=0$ and f is invertible near 0, whenever the exogenous variable obeys the difference equation $s_t = g(s_{t-1})$, with $g = f^{-1} \circ h_k \circ f$.[4]

1.2 *Dynamics with learning*

The assumptions underlying perfect foresight are too extreme to be met, short of a mythical auctioneer who would coordinate the choice of a common self-fulfilling expectation function by all present and future traders. In a decentralized setup, individual traders will not know for sure the dynamic laws of their environment, and will try to learn these laws by extracting regularities from past data and by extrapolating them into the future.

We summarize a trader's mental process by the time-independent expectation function (2), where ψ satisfies $\psi(0,\ldots,0)=0$ and is well-defined and continuously differentiable in a small neighborhood of 0. As noted earlier, this formulation is compatible with a specification where a trader has a set of a priori beliefs (models) about the dynamics of his environment, indexed, for instance, by a vector of unknown parameters. The trader would revise in each period his estimate of the unknown parameters, in view of past data, by using statistical techniques, and would use the model corresponding to the new estimates to form expectations (see Grandmont, 1977, Section 2.4). An example of learning of this sort, which in fact yields a linear time-independent expectation function, is the case where a trader's set of a priori beliefs is represented by the class of models

[4] The preceding discussion should help dispose of a common error, which claims that perfect foresight or rational expectations are "forward looking," whereas "backward looking" forecasts formed as functions of past observations are "irrational." This is wrong: In *all* cases, whether forecasts are self-fulfilling or not, expectations *must* be formulated as functions of past information if one wishes to be able to describe the evolution of the model as a recursive dynamical system in calendar time.

$x_t = s_t'\beta + u_t$. Here β is an n-dimensional column vector of unknown parameters, u_t is a sequence of i.i.d. random variables with zero mean and constant variance, and s_t is an n-dimensional column vector of deterministic exogenous variables, the evolution of which summarizes the "prior guesses" of the traders about the growth rates and cyclical patterns he thinks he is likely to face. For instance, if he wants to detect a trend with a constant growth rate r, he will include among the exogenous variables the time series $(1+r)^t$. To detect a cyclical pattern of period $2\pi/\alpha$ around such a trend, the two time series $(1+r)^t \cos \alpha t$ and $(1+r)^t \sin \alpha t$ will appear among the regressors. More generally, let the exogenous variables obey the difference equation $s_t = Cs_{t-1}$, where the eigenvalues of C (assumed to be nonzero and distinct) represent the trends and frequencies that the traders wish to track down. The trader's OLS estimates of β at date t, as a function of the observations made at dates $t, \ldots, t-L$, is then

$$\beta_t = R_t^{-1} \sum_0^L s_{t-j} x_{t-j}, \quad \text{with } R_t = \sum_0^L s_{t-j} s_{t-j}' \tag{10}$$

(we assume, without loss of generality, that R_t is invertible). The corresponding forecasting rule is

$${}_t x_{t+1}^e = s_{t+1}' \beta_t = s_{t+1}' R_t^{-1} \sum_0^L s_{t-j} x_{t-j}. \tag{11}$$

It is easy to verify that (11) yields a linear forecasting rule,

$${}_t x_{t+1}^e = \sum_0^L c_j x_{t-j},$$

where the coefficients are actually independent of time. It is a property of least squares that any realization of the endogenous variables that is a linear combination of the variables in s_t will give an exact fit. Therefore, the polynomial corresponding to the expectation function (11), that is, $z^{L+1} - \sum_0^L c_j z^{L-j} = 0$, inherits all eigenvalues of the matrix C. This property is preserved if one uses generalized least squares when the variance of the error term u_t changes over time: only the other roots of the polynomial depend upon the particular assumptions made on the disturbance terms and the choice of the estimation procedure.

One can proceed similarly in the general case. Consider the characteristic polynomial corresponding to the expectation function (2):

$$Q_\psi(z) \equiv z^{L+1} - \sum_0^L c_j z^{L-j} = 0, \tag{12}$$

where c_j is the partial derivative of ψ with respect to x_{t-j}, evaluated at the stationary state. If the traders are prepared to extrapolate constant sequences, that is, $\psi(x, \ldots, x) = x$ for all small x, then $\mu = 1$ is a root of

(12). If the trader extrapolates sequences that have period k, then all kth roots of unity are solutions of (12) (Grandmont and Laroque, 1986, 1990). More generally, the $L+1$ eigenvalues of ψ (solutions of (12)) describe the local regularities that the traders are able to recognize in, and extrapolate from, past history near the stationary state.

Given the forecasting rule ψ, the actual temporary equilibrium dynamics with learning is described implicitly by

$$T(x_{t-1}, x_t, \psi(x_t, \dots, x_{t+L})) = 0. \tag{13}$$

We assume that the partial derivative of this expression, with respect to x_t, does not vanish, that is, $b_0 + ac_0 \neq 0$. Then (13) can be solved uniquely for x_t near 0, to yield a local difference equation of the form

$$x_t = W_{\text{loc}}(x_{t-1}, \dots, x_{t-L}).$$

Stability or instability of the stationary state in this local dynamics will be generically governed by the roots of the characteristic polynomial associated to (13):

$$Q_W(z) \equiv b_1 z^{L-1} + b_0 z^L + a \sum_0^L c_j z^{L-j} = 0. \tag{14}$$

If all roots of (14) have modulus less than 1, the stationary state is locally stable. But as soon as one root of (14) has modulus greater than 1, the stationary state is unstable: For all initial conditions $(x_{t-1}, \dots, x_{t-L})$ near 0, except perhaps for a set that has Lebesgue measure 0, the trajectories generated by the dynamics with learning (13) are pulled away from the stationary state.

The distribution, in the complex plane, of the eigenvalues of ψ reflects in some sense the prior beliefs of the traders about the kind of local regularities (growth, fluctuations) they think they are more or less likely to experience. If the storage memory L is large, for instance, the roots of (12) can be distributed in the complex plane so as to approximate closely any distribution with a continuous density, which we may interpret as the traders' "prior." The following proposition is an example of a result that we believe is general: If the traders do not exclude a priori that the system might be locally divergent, that is, if the distribution of the characteristic roots of the expectation function ψ puts some positive (but perhaps very small) weight on eigenvalues that have modulus greater than 1, then the actual temporary equilibrium dynamics with learning will be locally unstable.

Proposition 1. *Assume that expectations matter, that is, $a \neq 0$, and that $b_0 + ac_0 \neq 0$, so that the actual temporary equilibrium dynamics with learning is well-defined near the stationary state.*

Let λ_k, $k=1,2$, be the two roots of the perfect foresight characteristic polynomial Q_F defined in (8). *Assume that the characteristic polynomial Q_ψ associated to the expectation function has two real roots, $\mu_1 \geq 1$ and $\mu_2 \leq -1$, and that if the perfect foresight roots λ_k are real, they belong to the open interval (μ_2, μ_1), for $k=1,2$.*

Then the characteristic polynomial Q_W associated to the actual dynamics with learning has real root r that satisfies either $r > \mu_1 \geq 1$ or $r < \mu_2 \leq -1$.

Proof: By adding and subtracting az^{L+1} to (14), one gets

$$Q_W(z) \equiv z^{L-1} Q_F(z) - aQ_\psi(z).$$

$Q_W(z)$ is a polynomial of degree L, and the coefficient of its term of degree L is $b_0 + ac_0$. On the other hand, $z^{L-1}Q_F(z)$ is a polynomial of degree $L+1$, the coefficient of the term of highest degree being a. Suppose first that $b_0 + ac_0$ and a have opposite signs. This means that $-b_0/a$, that is, the sum of the two perfect foresight roots $\lambda_1 + \lambda_2$, is larger than c_0, that is, the sum of all roots of Q_ψ. Then

$$\begin{aligned}(b_0+ac_0)Q_W(\mu_1) &= \mu_1^{L-1}(b_0+ac_0)Q_F(\mu_1)\\ &= \mu_1^{L-1}(b_0+ac_0)a(\mu_1-\lambda_1)(\mu_1-\lambda_2) < 0.\end{aligned}$$

But $(b_0+ac_0)Q_W(r)$ is real and tends to $+\infty$ when r is real and goes to $+\infty$. So, in this case, Q_W has a real root $r > \mu_1$.

Consider now the other case, where $b_0 + ac_0$ and a have the same sign. Here the sum of all eigenvalues of ψ, that is, c_0, exceeds the sum of the two perfect foresight roots, that is, $-b_0/a = \lambda_1 + \lambda_2$. Then

$$\begin{aligned}(-1)^L(b_0+ac_0)Q_W(\mu_2) &= (-1)^L \mu_2^{L-1}(b_0+ac_0)Q_F(\mu_2)\\ &= -|\mu_2|^{L-1}(b_0+ac_0)a(\mu_2-\lambda_1)(\mu_2-\lambda_2) < 0.\end{aligned}$$

But $(-1)^L(b_0+ac_0)Q_W(r)$ is real and tends to $+\infty$ when r is real and goes to $-\infty$. So, in this case, Q_W has a real root $r < \mu_2$. □

It should be noted that the proposition involves a joint condition on the eigenvalues of the perfect foresight polynomial Q_F and of the expectation function polynomial Q_ψ.[5] In order to get some insight into this condition, consider an expectation function ψ having at least two real roots $\mu_1 \geq 1$ and $\mu_2 \leq -1$. Let us also fix the parameters b_0 and b_1 describing the

[5] If one assumes $\mu_1 = 1$ and $\mu_2 = -1$ in the proposition, one gets that the stationary state is locally stable in the actual temporary equilibrium dynamics only if it is a saddle point in the perfect foresight dynamics ($|\lambda_1| < 1 < |\lambda_2|$), provided that no root of Q_W has modulus 1. This result was obtained in our previous paper (1990, Section 2). It was also shown there that the converse is true if (and in general only if) the linear approximation of the forecasting rule, that is, ${}_tx^e_{t+1} = \sum_0^L c_j x_{t-j}$, has the form ${}_tx^e_{t+1} = x_{t-1}$.

local influence of x_t and x_{t-1} on the temporary equilibrium map T, but let the parameter $a \neq 0$ summarizing the local impact of forecasts vary. Since $Q_F(z) \equiv az^2 + b_0 z + b_1$, the eigenvalues of the perfect foresight dynamics move with a according to $\lambda_1 + \lambda_2 = -b_0/a$ and $\lambda_1\lambda_2 = b_1/a$. If a goes to 0, then one of the roots, say, λ_1, converges to $-b_1/b_0$, while λ_2 has a modulus that tends to $+\infty$ (we assume $b_0 \neq 0$ for the sake of this argument). In view of (14), the polynomial Q_W will behave ultimately as $z^{L-1}(b_1 + b_0 z)$. Therefore, if the influence of expectations is small, Q_W has $L-1$ roots close to 0, and the remaining one is approximately equal to λ_1. If we assume $|b_0| \neq |b_1|$, the actual temporary equilibrium dynamics will be stable if and only if λ_1 has modulus less than 1. The eigenvalues of the forecasting rule then have a negligible impact, as one should have expected. If we look at the other extreme case in which expectations matter a lot ($|a|$ is large), the actual dynamics become unstable. Indeed, if $|a|$ goes to $+\infty$, the perfect foresight roots λ_1 and λ_2 both tend to 0. Thus, one has ultimately $\mu_2 < \lambda_k < \mu_1$ whenever λ_1 and λ_2 are real, and one can apply the proposition. When the parameter a takes on intermediate values, the picture is not so clear. Nevertheless, a possible interpretation of the proposition is that, given an expectation function with at least two real roots $\mu_1 \geq 1$ and $\mu_2 \leq -1$, and given the parameters b_0 and b_1, the actual temporary equilibrium dynamics will be unstable provided that the influence of expectations is significant enough.

Alternatively, one may consider a fixed economic system, or rather a family of temporary equilibrium relations T such that the corresponding perfect foresight roots λ_1 and λ_2 belong to a given bounded set K in the complex plane. This is equivalent to the condition that the family of ratios $-b_0/a = \lambda_1 + \lambda_2$ and $b_1/a = \lambda_1\lambda_2$ be bounded (loosely speaking, the "relative" importance of expectations is uniformly bounded away from 0 across the family). Let us consider now an expectation function ψ corresponding to a very large memory capacity L. The distribution of the $L+1$ characteristic roots of Q_ψ over the complex plane may be interpreted as the traders' prior beliefs about the kind of growth rates and cyclical patterns they may face. If the traders' assign a positive (but perhaps very small) relative weight to the possibility that the system might experience high inflation or deflation rates, one may expect that, for a large L, the forecasting rule ψ would have two real roots $\mu_1 \geq 1$ and $\mu_2 \leq -1$ such that $\mu_2 < \lambda_k < \mu_1$ for all real roots in the bounded set K. For such an expectation function, the proposition would apply for *every* member of the family of temporary equilibrium maps T under consideration.[6]

[6] Note the importance of the condition that the set K of perfect foresight roots λ_1 and λ_2 be bounded for the validity of this argument. If K were unbounded, one could have a case where b_0 and b_1 are fixed and a arbitrarily small. The behavior of the actual temporary equilibrium dynamics would then be unclear when L is large and $|a|$ is small.

2 Least squares regressions on endogenous variables

In Section 1, we focused on a case where the traders' learning process was regular enough to be representable by a *continuously differentiable* expectation function. We saw that such a situation could arise if traders used least squares regression to discover some possible relations between exogenous and endogenous variables. We showed that if the traders are ready to detect a large enough range of past growth rates of the state variable, then at least one of the characteristic roots of the local dynamics with learning has a modulus greater than 1. The dynamics with learning are then locally divergent for an open set of initial condition $(x_{t-1},\ldots,x_{t-L})$ near the stationary state, and, in fact, the set of such initial conditions generating locally convergent paths is "exceptional," that is, has Lebesgue measure 0.

We look now at a less pleasant case in which the traders' expectations are formed by means of direct regressions of the endogenous state variable on its lagged values. The corresponding estimation rule and expectation function then involve quite disagreeable discontinuities. Our previous instability result will nevertheless carry over to the present case: If the traders are prepared to extrapolate arbitrary rates of growth from the past, the system is still locally divergent for an open set of initial conditions.

Unstability of self-fulfilling expectations is then a robust phenomenon. As a corollary, one may get convergence to self-fulfilling expectations in that sort of model, but only by restricting narrowly the range of regularities (here, the growth rates of the state variable) that traders are able to recognize in, and extrapolate from, past data. We will see that such ad hoc restrictions underlie, in fact, the convergence results that can be found in the recent literature on least squares learning, such as those of Marcet and Sargent (1989).

Because of the lack of regularity of the expectation function, the study of the nonlinear case is quite difficult. Therefore, we directly consider a linear temporary equilibrium relation:

$$b_1x_{t-1}+b_0x_t+a({}_tx^e_{t+1})=0, \tag{15}$$

where we assume $a\neq 0$ and $b_0\neq 0$. This specification is to be interpreted as a grand "magnification" of what happens near the stationary state in the nonlinear case (1). In particular, divergence to infinity in the linear approximation only means that the system is pulled away from the immediate vicinity of the stationary state in the nonlinear case. We will assume in this section that the corresponding perfect foresight characteristic roots λ_1 and λ_2 are both real, with λ_1 being the root of smallest modulus.

As for the traders' expectations formation, we assume that the set of "models" of the world the traders have in their minds are of the form

$$x_t = \beta x_{t-1}, \tag{16}$$

where β is an arbitrary (unknown) real number (adding a disturbance term u_t to (16), where the u_t's are i.i.d. with zero mean and constant variance, would not change any of what follows). This formulation implicitly assumes that the traders know the value of the stationary state $x = 0$, and that they try to predict growth rates, out of the stationary trajectory, in order to improve their forecasts. One might suppose more generally that the agents do not know the stationary state, and try to learn it by adding a constant term in (16), as in the differentiable case of Section 1. The treatment of this more general situation is much more difficult and is beyond the scope of this chapter.

For any "model" β, traders would form expectations at date t according to the forecasting rule ${}_tx^e_{t+1} = \beta^2 x_{t-1}$, which is obtained by iterating (16) twice. The corresponding actual temporary equilibrium dynamics would then be found by replacing forecasts in (15) by this value, which yields

$$x_t = -b_0^{-1}(b_1 + \beta^2 a)x_{t-1} \equiv \Omega(\beta)x_{t-1}. \tag{17}$$

The expectation function ${}_tx^e_{t+1} = \beta^2 x_{t-1}$ is self-fulfilling for any x_{t-1} if and only if (16) and (17) coincide or, equivalently, if and only if β is a fixed point of the map $\beta \to \Omega(\beta)$. This map describes the relation between the traders' beliefs, as parameterized by β, and the parameter $\Omega(\beta)$ characterizing the corresponding actual temporary equilibrium dynamics. The fixed points of that map represent self-fulfilling expectation functions, and they are equal to the two perfect foresight roots λ_k. Therefore, there are two self-fulfilling expectation functions here, and they are in effect linear approximations of the locally self-fulfilling forecasting rules (9) that we discussed for the nonlinear case in Section 1. The graph of $\Omega(\beta)$ is represented in Figure 2 when the parameters a and b_0 have opposite signs, for later reference. The case where they have the same sign is obtained qualitatively from Figure 2 through a symmetry with respect to the horizontal axis.

Since, in a decentralized setup, traders do not know a priori the true structure of the system, they will try to learn it by extracting regularities from past data. We assume that each trader estimates the model (16), at the outset of each period t, through OLS on the past data $x_{t-1}, \ldots, x_{t-L}$. Not taking into account the current state in the estimation will allow us to avoid inconvenient simultaneity problems, where x_t and β_t would influence each other at date t (Marcet and Sargent, 1989, use a similar device in most of their paper). This gives the estimate

$$\beta_t = \begin{cases} (\Sigma_2^L x_{t-j}^2)^{-1} \Sigma_2^L x_{t-j+1} x_{t-j} & \text{if } \Sigma_2^L x_{t-j}^2 \neq 0, \\ \text{indeterminate} & \text{otherwise.} \end{cases} \tag{18}$$

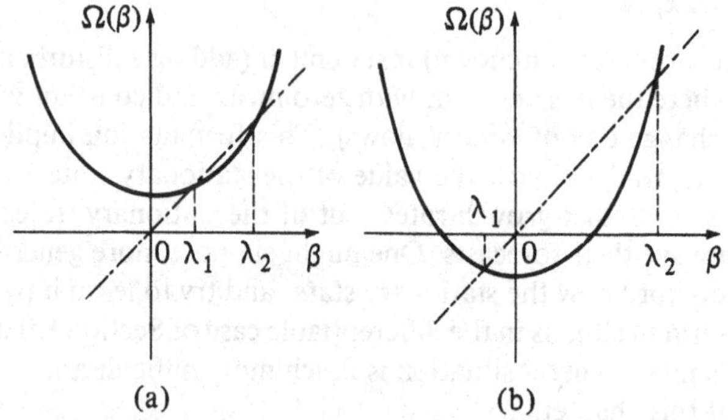

Figure 2. (a) $\lambda_1+\lambda_2=-b_0/a>0$, $\lambda_1\lambda_2=b_1/a>0$.
(b) $\lambda_1+\lambda_2=-b_0/a>0$, $\lambda_1\lambda_2=b_1/a<0$.

The estimate β_t is, of course, indeterminate when $x_{t-j}=0$ for $j=2,\ldots,L$, since it is defined as 0/0. The corresponding forecasting rule is

$$_tx^e_{t+1}=\beta_t^2x_{t-1}, \quad \beta_t \text{ given by (18).} \tag{19}$$

This yields a forecasting rule that looks like $_tx^e_{t+1}=\psi(x_{t-1},\ldots,x_{t-L})$, as in the general structure of Section 1. The important difference is that ψ is here a well-defined function only out of the stationary state, that is, only when $x_{t-j}\neq 0$ for some $j=1,\ldots,L$ (the expectation function is then smooth). But β_t and ψ are highly discontinuous at the point that interests us most: These quantities can converge to any limit, or diverge to infinity, according to how $(x_{t-1},\ldots,x_{t-L})$ approaches $(0,\ldots,0)$. This unpleasant feature will typically occur when least squares estimation techniques are used if the set of regressors includes endogenous variables.

The actual temporary equilibrium dynamics corresponding to the forecasting rule (19) is obtained here as in Section 1 by inserting this expression into (15):

$$x_t=\Omega(\beta_t)x_{t-1}, \quad \beta_t \text{ given by (18).} \tag{20}$$

This relation looks like $x_t=W_{\text{loc}}(x_{t-1},\ldots,x_{t-L})$ of Section 1. Here again, however, it determines the current state as a smooth function of past states only when $x_{t-j}\neq 0$ for some $j=1,\ldots,L$. The dynamical system (20) is undefined and quite discontinuous at the stationary state. Yet one can still ask whether sequences of states x_t starting out of the stationary state do, or do not, converge to it. One can also ask whether the corresponding sequences of estimates β_t defined through (18) do, or do not, converge to self-fulfilling expectations, that is, to one of the perfect foresight characteristic roots λ_k.

Since the model of Section 1 and the present one have the same general structure (up to the discontinuity at the origin), one may wonder whether the kind of regularities that the traders are prepared to extract from past data should play a significant role. An important feature of the OLS estimate (18) is that if past data were generated by $x_{t-j+1} = rx_{t-j}$, with $x_{t-L} \neq 0$, then $\beta_t = r$. Thus, the forecasting rule (19) satisfies

$$r^{L+1}x = \psi(r^L x, \ldots, rx, x), \quad \text{all } r, \text{ all } x \neq 0. \tag{21}$$

Every real number r is an "eigenvalue" of ψ! (The price we must pay for that is, of course, the essential discontinuity at the origin.) Hence, there are two "eigenvalues" of ψ, that is, $r_1 \geq 1$ and $r_2 \leq -1$, such that $r_2 < \lambda_k < r_1$. If our analysis of the differentiable case has any relevance to the case at hand, then we should expect the dynamical system (20) to be unstable. The proposition that follows states that this is indeed the case: The system *always* diverges for an open set of initial conditions. If we had differentiability, that would be the end of the story, for the system would then diverge for almost all initial conditions. But the present specification is discontinuous, and all sorts of exotic phenomena can happen. The second part of the proposition states that, under some conditions, there may also exist another open set of initial conditions for which trajectories x_t in the state space converge to the stationary state, whereas the corresponding sequences of estimates β_t converge to the perfect foresight characteristic root λ_1 having the smallest modulus ($|\lambda_1| < |\lambda_2|$).

The intuition behind this result can be seen directly in Figure 2 in the simple case where $L = 2$ and where $\lambda_2 > 0$. In such a case, the least squares formula (18) yields $\beta_t = x_{t-1}/x_{t-2}$ whenever $x_{t-2} \neq 0$. If, in addition, $x_{t-1} \neq 0$, (20) gives

$$\beta_{t+1} = \frac{x_t}{x_{t-1}} = \Omega(\beta_t).$$

Provided that $x_t \neq 0$ for all t, one can first analyze the dynamics of the estimates through $\beta_{t+1} = \Omega(\beta_t)$, and then deduce from it the behavior of the trajectory followed by the temporary equilibrium states through $x_t = \beta_{t+1}x_{t-1}$. From Figure 2, if the initial conditions $x_{-1} \neq 0$ and $x_{-2} \neq 0$ are such that $\beta_0 = x_{-1}/x_{-2} > \lambda_2$, then β_t diverges to $+\infty$ and, therefore, $|x_t|$ as well. If the initial growth rate is too large, the stationary state is unstable. On the other hand, if $|\Omega'(\beta)|$ is less than 1 at $\beta = \lambda_1$, the dynamics of the estimate β_t is locally convergent near λ_1. It follows that, if $|\lambda_1|$ is smaller than 1, the sequences of temporary equilibria x_t starting with an initial growth rate close to λ_1 converge toward the stationary state $x = 0$, where the estimates β_t tend to the rational expectations equilibrium λ_1.

Proposition 2. *Assume that $a \neq 0$, $b_0 \neq 0$, and that the two perfect foresight roots are real, with $|\lambda_2| \geq |\lambda_1|$ (since $\lambda_1 + \lambda_2 = -b_0/a$, this implies that $\lambda_2 \neq 0$). We also assume that the initial conditions at $t=0$, that is, $x_{-1}, \ldots, x_{-L}$, are all different from 0.*

(1) Let the initial conditions be such that the ratios $x_{-1}/x_{-2}, \ldots, x_{-L+1}/x_{-L}$ have all the same sign as λ_2, and a modulus greater than $|\lambda_2|$. Then for every $t \geq 0$, the temporary equilibrium states defined by (20) are such that $x_t \neq 0$. The sequences $|x_t|$, $|x_t/x_{t-1}|$, and $|\beta_t|$ all diverge to $+\infty$.

(2) Assume that $|\lambda_2| > |\lambda_1| > 0$, and that the derivative of the map $\beta \to \Omega(\beta) = -b_0^{-1}(b_1 + \beta^2 a)$, evaluated at $\beta = \lambda_1$, has a modulus less than 1, that is, $2|\lambda_1| < |\lambda_1 + \lambda_2|$. Let the initial conditions be such that

$$\left|\frac{x_{-1}}{x_{-2}} - \lambda_1\right| \leq \epsilon, \ldots, \left|\frac{x_{-L+1}}{x_{-L}} - \lambda_1\right| \leq \epsilon,$$

where $\epsilon > 0$ is small enough. Then the temporary equilibrium states satisfy $x_t \neq 0$ for all $t \geq 0$. The growth rates x_t/x_{t-1} and the estimates β_t tend to the perfect foresight characteristic root λ_1. The sequence $|x_t|$ goes to 0 if $|\lambda_1| < 1$ and diverges to $+\infty$ if $|\lambda_1| > 1$.

Proof: Remark, first, that when all $x_t \neq 0$, the ratios $y_t = x_t/x_{t-1}$ are well-defined. The estimates β_t are then given by

$$\beta_t = \left(\sum_2^L x_{t-j}^2 y_{t-j+1}\right) \Big/ \left(\sum_2^L x_{t-j}^2\right), \tag{22}$$

while (20) becomes $y_t = \Omega(\beta_t)$.

(1) We will prove the statements in the case where $\lambda_2 > 0$, which is represented in Figure 2. The case $\lambda_2 < 0$ is dealt with by a simple rewording of the proof.

By assumption, the initial (gross) rates of growth $y_{-1}, \ldots, y_{-L+1}$ are all greater than λ_2. Let $\eta > \lambda_2$ be the minimum of these initial growth rates and let $\alpha = \Omega(\eta) - \eta > 0$. Since $\Omega(\beta) - \beta$ is an increasing function of $\beta > \lambda_2$ (see Figure 2), one has $\Omega(\beta) \geq \beta + \alpha$ for every $\beta \geq \eta$.

From (22), β_0 is a convex combination of all past rates of growth, with positive weights. Hence, $\beta_0 \geq \eta$, and $y_0 = \Omega(\beta_0) \geq \beta_0 + \alpha \geq \eta + \alpha$, in which case $x_0 \neq 0$. If η_0 is the minimum of $y_0, \ldots, y_{-L+2}$, one gets $\eta_0 \geq \eta$. Proceeding by induction on t, one finds that the sequence of temporary equilibrium states is such that $x_t \neq 0$ for all $t \geq 0$, and that

$$y_t = \Omega(\beta_t) \geq \beta_t + \alpha \geq \eta_{t-1} + \alpha,$$

where η_{t-1} is the minimum of $y_{t-1}, \ldots, y_{t-L+1}$. The sequence η_t is then nondecreasing, bounded below by $\eta > \lambda_2$. Furthermore, $\eta_{t+h} \geq \eta_t + \alpha$ for

$h \geq L$. Hence, the sequence η_t diverges to $+\infty$. This implies that the sequence y_t and β_t are also bounded below by η and diverge to $+\infty$. The sequence $|x_t| = |y_t||x_{t-1}|$ is then bound to diverge to $+\infty$, too.

(2) Assume now that $0 < |\lambda_1| < |\lambda_2|$, and that $|\Omega'(\lambda_1)| < 1$. Consider the interval I of all β such that $|\beta - \lambda_1| \leq \epsilon$. Choose $\epsilon > 0$ small enough to guarantee that 0 does not belong to I, and that $|\Omega'(\beta)| \leq k < 1$ for some k, for all β in I (ϵ must be at least smaller than the minimum of $|\lambda_1|$ and of $|\lambda_2 - \lambda_1|$).

Let the initial conditions be such that the growth rates $y_{-1}, \ldots, y_{-L+1}$ belong to I. Let $\gamma \leq \epsilon$ be the maximum of $|y_{-1} - \lambda_1|, \ldots, |y_{-L+1} - \lambda_1|$. In view of (22), $\beta_0 - \lambda_1$ is a convex combination of $y_{-1} - \lambda_1, \ldots, y_{-L+1} - \lambda_1$, with positive weights. Thus, $|\beta_0 - \lambda_1| \leq \gamma$. Therefore,

$$|y_0 - \lambda_1| = |\Omega(\beta_0) - \lambda_1| \leq k|\beta_0 - \lambda_1| \leq k\gamma.$$

Hence, y_0 belongs to I, in which case $x_0 \neq 0$. If γ_0 is the maximum of $|y_0 - \lambda_1|, \ldots, |y_{-L+2} - \lambda_1|$, then $\gamma_0 \leq \gamma$. Proceeding by induction on t, one finds that the temporary equilibrium states satisfy $x_t \neq 0$ for all $t \geq 0$, and that

$$|y_t - \lambda_1| \leq k|\beta_t - \lambda_1| \leq k\gamma_{t-1},$$

where γ_{t-1} is the maximum of $|y_{t-1} - \lambda_1|, \ldots, |y_{t-L+1} - \lambda_1|$. The sequence $\gamma_t \geq 0$ is then nonincreasing, bounded above by $\gamma \leq \epsilon$. Furthermore, $\gamma_{t+h} \leq k\gamma_t$ for $h \geq L$. Thus, the sequence γ_t tends to 0. This implies that the sequence $|y_t - \lambda_1|$ and $|\beta_t - \lambda_1|$ are bounded above by ϵ and converge to 0. The sequence $|x_t| = |y_t||x_{t-1}|$ tends to 0 if $|\lambda_1| < 1$ and diverges to $+\infty$ if $|\lambda_1| > 1$. □

In the proof, we only used an elementary property of the OLS estimation technique (18): The estimate β_t is a convex combination of the past gross rates of growth $y_{t-j+1} = x_{t-j+1}/x_{t-j}$, for $j = 2, \ldots, L$, whenever those rates are well-defined (see (22)). Therefore, we have in fact proved the following.

Corollary 1. *The conclusions of Proposition 2 are still valid if at each date t, the estimate β_t is a convex combination of the past growth rates $y_{t-1} = x_{t-1}/x_{t-2}, \ldots, y_{t-L+1} = x_{t-L+1}/x_{t-L}$ provided that those rates are finite. That is, whenever $x_{t-j} \neq 0$ for $j = 1, \ldots, L$,*

$$\beta_t = \sum_2^L \gamma_{tj} y_{t-j+1}, \quad \gamma_{tj} \geq 0, \quad \sum_2^L \gamma_{tj} = 1, \tag{23}$$

where the weights γ_{tj} are well-defined (but possibly discontinuous and time-dependent) functions of $x_{t-1} \neq 0, \ldots, x_{t-L} \neq 0$.

A particular case of this specification arises when traders employ a weighted least squares estimation technique, in which the observations x_{t-j} are weighted at time t by the given numbers $\alpha_{tj} \geq 0$ for $j = 2, \ldots, L$, with $\Sigma_j \alpha_{tj} > 0$, according to the rule

$$\beta_t = \begin{cases} (\Sigma_2^L \alpha_{tj} x_{t-j+1} x_{t-j}) / (\Sigma_2^L \alpha_{tj} x_{t-j}^2) & \text{if } \Sigma_2^L \alpha_{tj} x_{t-j}^2 \neq 0, \\ \text{indeterminate} & \text{otherwise.} \end{cases} \tag{24}$$

A formulation of this sort appears, for instance, in Marcet and Sargent (1988, 1989). They assume, in a general linear multidimensional stochastic model, that a vector of unknown parameters is estimated at each date through recursive weighted least squares on the past (vector) states, say $x_{t-1}, \ldots, x_0, x_{-1}, \ldots, x_{-L}$, the observations x_{t-j} being weighted at time t by the given number $\alpha_{tj} = \alpha_{t-j} > 0$.

Proposition 2 and its corollary show that if the traders are ready to extrapolate a weighted average of the growth rates that prevailed in the past, and if we draw at random the initial conditions $x_{-1}, \ldots, x_{-L}$, then the system will diverge with a positive probability. To simplify matters, consider the case in which $\lambda_2 > 0$, as in Figure 2. If the initial growth rates happen to be all greater than λ_2, then the estimates β_t will all exceed λ_2 and go to $+\infty$. This will also be true of the actual growth rates $x_t / x_{t-1} = \Omega(\beta_t)$, as they will always exceed the estimated growth rates β_t in such a case. As noted earlier, the linear specification considered here is only an approximation of what would happen in the immediate vicinity of the stationary state $x_t = 0$ in a more general nonlinear model. Hence, the "explosive" behavior we get here should not be interpreted literally: It *only* means that, in the nonlinear case, the trajectories x_t in the state space are *locally* unstable.

This instability property still holds if we require the traders' estimates to be bounded. Consider again the case where $\lambda_2 > 0$, as in Figure 2, and let us modify the estimation rule by saying that at each date, β_t is the minimum of the expression (18) or (23), and of some arbitrarily given upper bound $\mu_1 > \lambda_2$. By a simple adaptation of the proof of Proposition 2, it is easy to see that if the initial conditions $x_1, \ldots, x_{-L}$ are such that the initial growth rates all exceed λ_2, then the estimated growth rates β_t will tend to μ_1, whereas the actual growth rates $x_t / x_{t-1} = \Omega(\beta_t)$ will go to $\Omega(\mu_1) > \mu_1$. Self-fulfilling expectations are unstable. The temporary equilibrium states x_t will diverge accordingly to $+\infty$ if $\Omega(\mu_1) > 1$ and converge to 0 if $\Omega(\mu_1) < 1$. The case where $\lambda_2 < 0$ yields similar results if we set a negative lower bound for the estimates β_t equal to $\mu_2 < \lambda_2$.[7]

[7] The lack of convergence of the estimates and of the growth rates is also preserved in the case of a memory that increases over time. Let us assume that β_t is estimated through

We get here instability for reasons similar to those that were discussed in Section 1 for the differentiable case. We have in both cases multiple self-fulfilling expectation functions, as characterized by the two finite (real) perfect foresight roots λ_1 and λ_2. The set of the "eigenvalues" of the expectation function induced by the estimation rule (18) or (23) ("eigenvalues" in the loose sense of (21)) is the whole interval $[\mu_2, \mu_1]$, if we require the estimates to be bounded above by μ_1 and below by μ_2. Then, if the traders are ready to extrapolate a large range of growth rates from the past, so that $\mu_1 \geq 1$, $\mu_2 \leq -1$, and $\mu_2 < \lambda_k < \mu_1$ for $k = 1, 2$, we get instability for an open set of initial conditions. The similarity with Proposition 1 is obvious.[8] *The existence of multiple self-fulfilling expectation functions λ_1 and λ_2 is clearly essential for these findings.* If there were only one such equilibrium, the root of largest modulus $|\lambda_2|$ would be infinite, which would mean that the parameter *a* describing the influence of expectations vanishes, and none of our instability arguments would go through.[9]

The novelty here, which is due to the discontinuity at the stationary state, is exemplified by the second part of Proposition 2: The system can diverge for an open set of initial conditions and converge for another open set of initial states. Consider the case where $|\lambda_2| > |\lambda_1| > 0$ and where the map $\beta \to \Omega(\beta)$ is contracting near λ_1, that is, $|\Omega'(\lambda_1)| < 1$. Then if the

recursive OLS on the past states $x_{t-1}, \ldots, x_0, x_{-1}, \ldots, x_{-L}$. Or, more generally, assume that when each of these states is different from 0, β_t is a weighted average of the corresponding growth rates $y_{t-1}, \ldots, y_0, y_{-1}, \ldots, y_{-L+1}$ (as in Corollary 1, but with a variable memory). Consider again the case where $\lambda_2 > 0$, as in Figure 2, and assume that the initial conditions are such that the minimum η of $y_{-1}, \ldots, y_{-L+1}$ is greater than λ_2. It is immediate to see that in such a case, for every $t \geq 0$, one gets $x_t \neq 0$, $y_t = \Omega(\beta_t) > \beta_t \geq \eta$. The actual behavior of x_t, y_t, and β_t will depend upon the particular estimation technique under consideration. But it is clear that the estimates β_t and the actual growth rates y_t cannot tend to either λ_2 or λ_1: self-fulfilling expectations are unstable. The case where $\lambda_2 < 0$ is dealt with similarly.

8 The parallel with Proposition 1 is still true if we consider the case where the two perfect foresight roots are *nonreal*. For instance, the case where the two nonreal roots have a positive real part corresponds to an analogue of Figure 2 (since then $\lambda_1 + \lambda_2 = -b_0/a > 0$), in which the graph of $\Omega(\beta)$ would lie strictly above the broken 45° line. In that case, there is clearly an $\alpha > 0$ such that $\Omega(\beta) \geq \beta + \alpha$ for every β. By a simple rewording of the proof of Proposition 2, if the initial conditions $x_{-1} \neq 0, \ldots, x_{-L} \neq 0$ are such that the initial growth rates are all positive, then the estimates β_t tend to $\mu_1 \geq 1$, whereas the actual growth rates $x_t/x_{t-1} = \Omega(\beta_t)$ tend to $\Omega(\mu_1) > \mu_1$. Again, one gets divergence. The case where the two perfect foresight roots are nonreal and have a negative real part ($\lambda_1 + \lambda_2 < 0$) is dealt with similarly. Thus, if $\mu_1 \geq 1$ and $\mu_2 \leq -1$, and if the two perfect foresight roots are nonreal, the system diverges for an open set of initial conditions, as in Proposition 1.

9 These conclusions should not be changed in a significant way if the analysis is extended to a linear stochastic framework. It seems indeed implausible that the addition of white noise to the linear temporary equilibrium relation (15) can make the system stable in a meaningful sense when its deterministic part is unstable, as shown here.

initial states $x_{-1}, \ldots, x_{-L}$ are such that the corresponding growth rates are all clustered near λ_1, one gets convergence to rational expectations: The estimated and actual growth rates β_t and x_t/x_{t-1} both tend to λ_1. The temporary equilibrium states x_t will go to 0 if $|\lambda_1|<1$ and diverge if $|\lambda_1|>1$. In view of the first part of the proposition, obviously, one can get divergence when the initial growth rates are clustered near λ_2 (the explanation is that the map Ω is expanding there, i.e., $\Omega'(\lambda_2)\geq 1$, with strict inequality if and only if $\lambda_1 \neq \lambda_2$; see Figure 2). As for λ_1, one has always $\Omega'(\lambda_1)<1$ when $|\lambda_1|<|\lambda_2|$, so the sufficient contracting condition $|\Omega'(\lambda_1)|<1$ is, in fact, equivalent to $\Omega'(\lambda_1)>-1$. We claim that the condition is *necessary* in the following sense.

Corollary 2. *Assume* $\Omega'(\lambda_1)\neq -1$. *Then the stability property stated in part* (2) *of Proposition 2 is true for every member of the class of learning processes specified in* (23) *for a given* $L\geq 2$ *if and only if* $|\Omega'(\lambda_1)|<1$.

Proof: The "if" part is in fact part (2) of Proposition 2. We have only to prove the converse part, namely, that if $\Omega'(\lambda_1)<-1$, then there exists a member of the class of learning processes (23) for which the property is not true.

Consider the special class of estimators defined by (24), where the α_{tj}'s are independent of t, that is, $\alpha_{tj}=\alpha_j\geq 0$, and assume without loss of generality that $\alpha_L>0$. The OLS (18) is obtained when $\alpha_j=1$ for all j. Assume now that $x_{t-j}\neq 0$ for $j=2, \ldots, L$. The growth rates $y_{t-j+1}=x_{t-j+1}/x_{t-j}$ are then finite for those j, and one can express each x_{t-j} as a function of previous growth rates and of x_{t-L}, through the formula

$$x_{t-j}=(y_{t-j}\cdots y_{t-L+1})x_{t-L}.$$

When replacing each x_{t-j} by this expression in (24), with $\alpha_{tj}=\alpha_j$, we see that the factors x_{t-L}^2 in the numerator and the denominator cancel each other. We are left with an expression giving the estimate β_t as a time-independent function of $y_{t-1}\neq 0, \ldots, y_{t-L+1}\neq 0$ alone:

$$\beta_t = g(y_{t-1}, \ldots, y_{t-L+1}). \tag{25}$$

If, in addition, $x_{t-1}\neq 0$, then the growth rate $y_t=x_t/x_{t-1}=\Omega(\beta_t)$ is well-defined and we get

$$y_t=\Omega(g(y_{t-1}, \ldots, y_{t-L+1}))\equiv f(y_{t-1}, \ldots, y_{t-L+1}). \tag{26}$$

Equations (25) and (26) describe the evolution of the estimates and the growth rates in our original dynamical system if none of the x_t's vanishes along the trajectory. These equations depend, of course, on the particular coefficients α_j that have been chosen. The function g (and, thus, f) we obtained through this procedure is, in fact, well-defined and continuously differentiable *everywhere*.

An important property of the class of estimators considered here is that traders extrapolate constant rates of growth, that is, $y \equiv g(y, \ldots, y)$. It follows that the stationary solutions of (26) are the fixed points of the map Ω, that is, λ_1 and λ_2. Now, assume $0 < |\lambda_1| < |\lambda_2|$, and consider the characteristic polynomial of (26) at the stationary solution λ_1:

$$Q_f(z) = z^{L-1} - \Omega'(\lambda_1) \sum_{1}^{L-1} g_j z^{L-1-j}, \tag{27}$$

where g_j is the partial derivative of g with respect to y_{t-j}, evaluated at the constant sequence $(\lambda_1, \ldots, \lambda_1)$. If all roots of (27) have a modulus less than 1, the stability property stated in part (2) of Proposition 2 is true for the particular estimator under consideration, as characterized by the given coefficients α_j. If one of the roots of the polynomial has a modulus greater than 1, this stability property is false. Consider now the case where $\alpha_j = 1$ when j is odd, and $\alpha_j = 0$ when j is even: The estimate β_t is a convex combination of all y_{t-j} for j odd. This implies that $g(y_1, y_2, y_1, y_2, \ldots) \equiv y_1$. It follows from this assumption that $\Sigma_1^{L-1}(-1)^j g_j = -1$. In that case,

$$(-1)^{L-1} Q_f(-1) = 1 + \Omega'(\lambda_1),$$

which is negative when $\Omega'(\lambda_1) < -1$. Since $(-1)^{L-1} Q_f(r)$ is real and tends to $+\infty$ when r is real and goes to $-\infty$, Q_f has a real root less than -1. Thus, if $\Omega'(\lambda_1) < -1$, the stability property stated in part (2) of Proposition 2 is false when $\alpha_j = 1$ for j odd and $\alpha_j = 0$ for j even. □

An important outcome of the present analysis is that one should not expect to get dynamic stability for (almost) all initial conditions in a socio-economic model with learning unless the range of regularities - of growth rates, in particular - that traders are ready to extrapolate from the past is narrowly restricted. A prominent example of a restriction of this sort is provided by the class of learning schemes put forward by Marcet and Sargent (1988, 1989). As noted earlier, these authors consider a general linear multidimensional stochastic model with learning through recursive least squares. When transposed to our simpler one-dimensional deterministic framework with a bounded memory L, their learning schemes are particular cases of (24), and thus of (23). If that were all, then we would get divergence for an open set of initial conditions, as our study showed. The *essential* restriction that drives Marcet and Sargent's stability results exploits the property stated in part (2) of Proposition 2. They assume, in effect, that all traders already have at the start a fairly good knowledge of their environment, in particular of the region where the perfect foresight root of smallest modulus (i.e., λ_1) approximately lies. Then all present and future traders coordinate their expectations so as not only to learn the precise value of λ_1, but also to collectively stabilize the system. Specifically, they agree that if the estimator β_t they get from (24) and (23) falls within ϵ of the target root λ_1, with $\delta > 0$ small enough, they will use it as their actual estimate β_t^* to form expectations. If, however, the outcome of the estimation procedure falls outside this prespecified neighborhood, all traders will deliberately ignore it and set their actual estimate β_t^* equal to an arbitrary growth rate $\bar{\beta}_t$ that lies near the target root λ_1. What is going to happen then should be clear if we remark that the actual temporary equilibrium growth rates x_t/x_{t-1} are given by $\Omega(\beta_t^*)$: If one waits long enough, one is back to the case described in part (2) of Proposition 2, and indeed one gets convergence.

Corollary 3 (Marcet and Sargent, 1989). *Assume that* $0 < |\lambda_1| < |\lambda_2|$, $|\Omega'(\lambda_1)| < 1$, *and let* $\epsilon > 0$. *Assume that the traders' estimates at date t, that is,* β_t^*, *are formed in the following way whenever* $x_{t-1} \neq 0, \ldots, x_{t-L} \neq 0$. *Let* β_t *be the estimator* (23) *where the weighting function* γ_{tj} *are given. Then*

$$\beta_t^* = \begin{cases} \beta_t & \text{when } |\beta_t - \lambda_1| \leq \epsilon, \\ \text{arbitrary in } [\lambda_1 - \epsilon, \lambda_1 + \epsilon] & \text{when } |\beta_t - \lambda_1| > \epsilon. \end{cases} \tag{28}$$

Then if $\epsilon > 0$ *is small enough, for any initial conditions* $x_{-1} \neq 0, \ldots, x_{-L} \neq 0$, *the temporary equilibrium states satisfy* $x_t \neq 0$ *for all* $t \geq 0$. *The estimates* β_t^* *and the actual growth rates* x_t/x_{t-1} *converge to* λ_1. *The sequence* $|x_t|$ *goes to 0 when* $|\lambda_1| < 1$ *and to* $+\infty$ *when* $|\lambda_1| > 1$.

Proof: Choose $\epsilon > 0$, as in the proof of part (2) of Proposition 2, small enough to ensure that $\beta \neq 0$ and $|\Omega'(\beta)| \leq k$ for some $k < 1$ whenever $|\beta - \lambda| \leq \epsilon$. The actual growth rates will then satisfy

$$\left| \frac{x_t}{x_{t-1}} - \lambda_1 \right| = |\Omega(\beta_t^*) - \lambda_1| \leq k|\beta_t^* - \lambda_1| < \epsilon$$

whenever $x_{t-1} \neq 0, \ldots, x_{t-L} \neq 0$. This implies that $x_t \neq 0$ for all $t \geq 0$ and that $\beta_t^* = \beta_t$ for $t \geq L-1$. From $t = L-1$ onwards, the proof of part (2) of Proposition 2 applies, which shows the result. □

The restriction involved in Corollary 3 seems justified if we are willing to consider a central *planner* who has some good but imperfect a priori information on the structure of the environment, wants to learn precisely the value of the root λ_1, and wishes at the same time to *control* the system by preventing it from going away from the targeted equilibrium (the techniques used by Marcet and Sargent are indeed borrowed from the engineering control literature; see Ljung and Söderström, 1983). However, the restriction runs counter to the spirit of the whole inquiry in a decentralized framework (as here), short of a mythical auctioneer who would be able to coordinate all present and future traders' expectation schemes. In our model, each individual trader is in a sense a "free rider," as his own influence on the whole market is negligible. Without central coordination of expectations, it is then in each trader's best interest to try to guess where the market is going, and thus to be ready to extrapolate a large range of regularities (e.g., growth rates) from past data, irrespective of whether these data display convergent or divergent tendencies. We have shown that in such circumstances, one should expect the actual dynamics of the system to diverge for an open set of initial conditions.

Remark 1. The claim that the actual dynamics with learning may be divergent when there are multiple self-fulfilling expectations equilibria is not new: it can be found in Gourieroux, Laffont, and Monfort (1983), where time-dependent adaptive (but not least squares) learning schemes are studied. Champsaur (1983, Appendix), in an interesting paper that did not receive the attention it deserves, had argued that OLS might lead to unstable temporary equilibrium dynamics with learning in a linear stochastic model, the structure of which is quite close to ours.

Benassy and Blad (1989) have an example of instability that is also fairly close to ours. When transposed to the linear framework of the present section, their example corresponds to a temporary equilibrium relation (15) with $b_1 = 0$; hence $\lambda_1 = 0$ and $\lambda_2 = -b_0/a < 1$. In this brief description of how their work fits into our framework, we will stick nevertheless to the general formulation where λ_1 and λ_2 are real but arbitrary, with $b_0 \neq 0$ and $a \neq 0$. The "models" of the world the traders have in their minds are of the form $x_t = \beta_1 x_{t-1} + \beta_2 x_{t-2}$. In the text, in fact, we made the assumption $\beta_2 = 0$. Benassy and Blad's specification, when transposed to the present framework, amounts to imposing the restriction $\beta_1 = 0$. Given that restriction, if the traders use a given parameter β_2 through time, then their forecasts are defined by

$$_t x^e_{t+1} = \beta_2 x_{t-1}, \tag{29}$$

which leads to the actual temporary equilibrium dynamics:

$$x_t = -b_0^{-1}(b_1 + a\beta_2)x_{t-1} \equiv H(\beta_2)x_{t-1}. \tag{30}$$

The parameter β_2 corresponds to self-fulfilling expectations if and only if the value of x_{t+1} obtained by iterating (30) twice coincides with the forecast (29) for every x_{t-1}. This means that $[H(\beta_2)]^2 = \beta_2$, and it is easy to see that this second-degree equation yields the two perfect foresight solutions $\beta_2 = \lambda_1^2$ and $\beta_2 = \lambda_2^2$.

Benassy and Blad assume essentially that the traders' estimate at date t is $\beta_{2t} = x_{t-1}/x_{t-3}$ when $x_{t-3} \neq 0$, and that β_{2t} is indeterminate otherwise: this is, in fact, the OLS estimator of the model $x_t = \beta_2 x_{t-2}$ on the observations x_{t-1}, x_{t-2}, and x_{t-3}. The actual temporary equilibrium dynamics with learning is then governed by (30), with $\beta_2 = \beta_{2t}$, as just described. It follows immediately that along a sequence of temporary equilibrium states such that $x_t \neq 0$, the growth rates $y_t = x_t/x_{t-1}$ obey the second-order difference equation

$$y_t = -b_0^{-1}(b_1 + a y_{t-1} y_{t-2}), \tag{31}$$

since $\beta_{2t} = y_{t-1} y_{t-2}$. Equation (31) has two stationary solutions that are given by $y = \Omega(y)$, and thus by $y = \lambda_1$ and $y = \lambda_2$. Benassy and Blad consider the specification $\lambda_1 = 0$ and show that the other root $\lambda_2 \neq 0$ is unstable.[10] This can be seen directly here. Indeed, in that case, (31) reduces to $y_t = y_{t-1} y_{t-2}/\lambda_2$. When, for instance, $\lambda_2 > 0$, one has $y_t > \lambda_2$ whenever $y_{t-1} > \lambda_2$ and $y_{t-2} > \lambda_2$. The variables $w_t = \log(y_t/\lambda_2) > 0$ then form a divergent Fibonacci sequence, since (31) becomes in that case $w_t = w_{t-1} + w_{t-2}$. Thus, if the initial conditions $x_{-1} \neq 0$, $x_{-2} \neq 0$, and $x_{-3} \neq 0$ are such that the initial growth rates y_{-1} and y_{-2} all exceed λ_2, the temporary equilibrium states in the dynamics with learning are such that $x_t \neq 0$ for all $t \geq 0$, and the estimates β_{2t}, the actual growth rates y_t, as well as $|x_t|$, all diverge to $+\infty$. A similar result holds when $\lambda_2 < 0$.

As a matter of fact, one can verify that the results of Proposition 2 are still valid in the present framework when the perfect foresight roots λ_1 and λ_2 are real and arbitrary, in the general case where the estimate β_{2t} at date t is a weighted average – in the same spirit as in (23) – of the products of past growth rates $y_{t-j+1} y_{t-j}$ for $j = 2, \ldots, L-1$, whenever those rates are finite. (A key observation is that when all past growth rates are, say, equal to $y \neq 0$, the estimate β_{2t} is equal to y^2, whereas the actual growth rate is $y_t = \Omega(y)$; see (30) or (31). The claim then follows by a rewording of the proof of Proposition 2.)

Remark 2. The contracting condition $|\Omega'(\lambda_1)| < 1$ that we use in part (2) of Proposition 2 and in Corollary 3 is more restrictive than in Marcet and Sargent (1988, 1989), and it may be worthwhile to reflect briefly on the reasons for this discrepancy. In their multidimensional stochastic setup, the "models" of the world that traders have in their minds when forming their expectations are indexed by a vector β of unknown parameters, whereas the corresponding actual temporary equilibrium dynamics are *characterized by the vector* $\Omega(\beta)$. Self-fulfilling expectations are defined

[10] The divergence they found may, in view of the findings of this chapter, be interpreted as convergence, for some set of initial conditions, to the root $\lambda_1 = 0$.

as a fixed point β^* of the map Ω, as in the text here. At each date, traders form an estimate β_t through recursive weighted least squares on all past observations (as in (24), but with a variable, increasing memory). Marcet and Sargent then get the analogue of Corollary 3 (with β^* in place of λ_1) under the condition that all eigenvalues of the Jacobian matrix $D\Omega(\beta^*)$ have a *real part* less than 1. This would correspond in our framework to $\Omega'(\lambda_1)<1$ (for an extensive use of that criterion as a selection device in linear stochastic expectations models, see Evans, 1983, 1985, 1989; Evans and Honkapohja, 1989). Marcet and Sargent derive their results, however, for weighted least squares with weights as in (24) satisfying $\alpha_{tj}=\alpha_{t-j}>0$, where the sequence α_t is increasing and tends to 1, whereas $t(\alpha_t-\alpha_{t-1})$ is bounded above as t goes to $+\infty$ (see Marcet and Sargent, 1989, Assumption A.4, p. 343). Although our framework is more limited and involves a bounded memory, our analysis suggests strongly that their condition is model-specific and would no longer be sufficient for a more general class of weighted estimators as in (23) or (24). In our model, the only robust condition is $|\Omega'(\lambda_1)|<1$, as shown by Corollary 2. In a multidimensional setup, the corresponding condition would be that all eigenvalues of $D\Omega(\beta^*)$ have a *modulus* less than 1.

3 Conclusion

We showed, within the framework of a simple deterministic example, that if the agents of an economic system try to learn the dynamic laws of their environment, and in so doing are ready to extrapolate from past data a large enough range of past growth rates of the state variable, then the resulting actual temporary equilibrium dynamics with learning will diverge for an open set of initial conditions. Our findings suggest that convergence to self-fulfilling expectations can be obtained in a decentralized setup only by restricting arbitrarily the kind of regularities that the traders are prepared to extract from past observations. It remains to be seen how these findings can be extended to more general multidimensional frameworks.

REFERENCES

Benassy, J. P. and M. Blad. 1989. "On Learning and Rational Expectations in an Overlapping Generations Model." *Journal of Economic Dynamics and Control* 13: 379–400.

Bray, M. 1982. "Learning, Estimation, and the Stability of Rational Expectations." *Journal of Economic Theory* 26: 318–39.

1983. "Convergence to Rational Expectations Equilibrium." In *Individual Forecasting and Aggregate Outcomes,* R. Frydman and E. Phelps, Eds. Cambridge: Cambridge University Press, pp. 123–32.

Bray, M., and N. Savin. 1986. "Rational Expectations Equilibria, Learning and Model Specification." *Econometrica* 54: 1129-60.

Calvo, G. 1988. "Passive Money and Idiosyncratic Expectations." Mimeo, University of Pennsylvania, Philadelphia.

Canning, D. 1989. "Convergence to Equilibrium in a Sequence of Games with Learning." STICERD D.P. No. 190, London School of Economics.

Champsaur, P. 1983. "On the Stability of Rational Expectations Equilibria." CORE D.P. No. 8324, Université Catholique de Louvain, Belgium. French version in *Cahiers du Séminaire d'Econométrie* 26 (1984): 47-65.

Crawford, V. 1974. "Learning the Optimal Strategy in Zero-Sum Games." *Econometrica* 42: 885-91.

1983. *Essays in Economic Theory.* New York: Garland.

1985. "Learning Behavior and Mixed Strategy Nash Equilibria." *Journal of Economic Behavior and Organization* 6: 69-78.

1988. "Learning and Mixed Strategy Equilibria in Evolutionary Games." D.P. No. 88-53, University of California, San Diego.

de Canio, S. 1979. "Rational Expectations and Learning from Experience." *Quarterly Journal of Economics* 93: 47-57.

Evans, G. 1983. "The Stability of Rational Expectations in Macroeconomic Models." In *Individual Forecasting and Aggregate Outcomes,* R. Frydman and E. Phelps, Eds. Cambridge: Cambridge University Press, pp. 69-94.

1985. "Expectational Stability and the Multiple Equilibria Problem in Linear Rational Expectations Models." *Quarterly Journal of Economics* 100: 1217-34.

1989. "The Fragility of Sunspots and Bubbles." *Journal of Monetary Economics* 18: 147-57.

Evans, G., and S. Honkapohja. 1989. "On the Robustness of Bubbles in Linear RE Models." STICERD D.P. No. 189, London School of Economics.

Fourgeaud, C., C. Gouriéroux, and J. Pradel. 1986. "Learning Procedures and Convergence to Rationality." *Econometrica* 54: 854-68.

Frydman, R. 1982. "Toward an Understanding of Market Processes." *American Economic Review* 72: 652-68.

Fuchs, G. 1976. "Asymptotic Stability of Stationary Temporary Equilibria and Changes in Expectations." *Journal of Economic Theory* 13: 201-16.

1977a. "Formation of Expectations: A Model in Temporary General Equilibrium Theory." *Journal of Mathematical Economics* 4: 167-88.

1977b. "Dynamic Role and Evolution of Expectations." In *Systèmes Dynamiques et Modèles Economiques,* Paris: Editions du CNRS.

1979a. "Dynamics of Expectations in Temporary General Equilibrium Theory." *Journal of Mathematical Economics* 6: 229-52.

1979b. "Is Error Learning Behaviour Stabilizing?" *Journal of Economic Theory* 20: 300-17. Reprinted in *Temporary Equilibrium. Selected Readings,* J. M. Grandmont, Ed. New York: Academic Press, (1988) pp. 286-303.

Fuchs, G., and G. Laroque. 1976. "Dynamics of Temporary Equilibria and Expectations." *Econometrica* 44: 1157-78. Reprinted in *Temporary Equilibrium. Selected Readings,* J. M. Grandmont, Ed. New York: Academic Press, (1988) pp. 249-70.

Fudenberg, D., and D. Kreps. 1988. "A Theory of Learning, Experimentation, and Equilibrium in Games." Mimeo, Massachusetts Institute of Technology, Cambridge, MA, and Stanford University.

Gouriéroux, C., J. J. Laffont, and A. Monfort. 1983. "Révision adaptative des anticipations et convergence vers les anticipations rationnelles." *Economie Appliquée* 36: 9–26.

Grandmont, J. M. 1977. "Temporary General Equilibrium Theory." *Econometrica* 45: 535–72. Reprinted in *Temporary Equilibrium. Selected Readings,* J. M. Grandmont, Ed. New York: Academic Press, (1988) pp. 3–40.

1985. "On Endogenous Competitive Business Cycles." *Econometrica* 53: 995–1045.

Grandmont, J. M., and G. Laroque. 1986. "Stability of Cycles and Expectations." *Journal of Economic Theory* 40: 138–51.

1990. "Stability, Expectations and Predetermined Variables." In *Essays in Honour of E. Malinvaud,* Vol. 1, P. Champsaur et al., Eds. Cambridge, MA: The MIT Press.

Guesnerie, R., and M. Woodford. 1989. "Stability of Cycles with Adaptive Learning Rules." Mimeo, DELTA, EHESS, Paris.

Jordan, J. 1986. "Convergence to Rational Expectations in a Stationary Linear Game." Mimeo, University of Minnesota, Minneapolis.

Kurz, M. 1989. "Bounded Ability of Agents to Learn the Equilibrium Price Process of a Complex Economy." IMSS TR No. 540, Stanford University.

Ljung, L., and T. Söderström. 1983. *Theory and Practice of Recursive Identification.* Cambridge, MA: The MIT Press.

Lucas, R. E., Jr. 1986. "Adaptive Behavior and Economic Theory." *Journal of Business* 59: 401–26.

Marcet, A., and T. Sargent. 1988. "The Fate of Systems with 'Adaptive' Expectations." *American Economic Review* 78: 168–72.

1989. "Convergence of Least Squares Learning Mechanisms in Self-Referential Linear Stochastic Models." *Journal of Economic Theory* 48: 337–68.

Shapley, L. 1964. "Some Topics in Two-Person Games." In *Advances in Game Theory,* M. Dresher, L. Shapley, and A. Tucker, Eds. Princeton: Princeton University Press.

Tillman, G. 1983. "Stability in a Simple Pure Consumption Loan Model." *Journal of Economic Theory* 30: 315–29. Reprinted in *Temporary Equilibrium. Selected Readings,* J. M. Grandmont, Ed. New York: Academic Press, (1988) pp. 271–85.

1985. "Existence and Stability of Rational Expectations Equilibria in a Simple Overlapping Generations Model." *Journal of Economic Theory* 36: 333–51.

Wickens, M. 1982. "Are Time Series Forecasts Self-Falsifying? A Study of Expectations Formation." Mimeo, University of Southampton.

Woodford, M. 1990. "Learning to Believe in Sunspots." *Econometrica* 58: 277–307.

CHAPTER 12

On the uniqueness of equilibrium once again

Andreu Mas-Colell

1 Introduction

This chapter has two objectives. First, we present a survey of the state of the art in the theory of uniqueness of Walrasian equilibrium. Second, we try to push forward its frontier, especially for the case of general production economies. Roughly speaking, we take up the topic where it was left by Kehoe (1985b).

The plan of the chapter is as follows. In Sections 2 and 3, we gather a number of basic concepts and facts about the aggregate excess demand of an economy. The exposition is taken from Mas-Colell (1985, Section 5.7), and we refer there for further analysis and basic references.

In Sections 4 and 5, we study the situation where the distribution of wealth is price-independent (collinear endowments). We emphasize uniqueness conditions that involve only the demand side of the economy or, what comes to the same thing, conditions for the fulfillment of the Weak Axiom of Revealed Preference in the aggregate. It turns out to be more convenient to focus on the stronger property of monotone excess demand (precise definitions are given in Section 2) because the latter aggregates better across consumers.

In these sections, we give main billing to the Mitiushin–Polterovich theorem, a beautiful result that deserves to be much better known. The

Sections 1 to 6 constitute a revision and extension of "Large Substitution Effects and the Uniqueness of Equilibrium," presented and distributed at the March 9, 1986 NSF-NBER General Equilibrium Conference held at Berkeley, California. In particular, both Examples 1 and 2 are taken from there. In turn, the Berkeley presentation was based, in part, on material contained in a Fisher–Schultz lecture delivered at the 1985 Boston meeting of the Econometric Society. Sections 7 to 10 are new.

I want to thank T. Kehoe, H. Leland, J. Nachbar, A. Schleifer, and V. W. Polterovich for different varieties of help and comments.

The financial support of the NSF is gratefully acknowledged.

theorem gives sufficient conditions on concave, C^2 utility functions for individual demand (income fixed to equal 1) to be monotone (with collinear endowments this then carries over to aggregate excess demand). It can be looked at as a concrete expression of the idea that the substitution effects dominate the income effects. What is remarkable is the simplicity of the (simplest) condition: $-[x \cdot \partial^2 u(x)x / x \cdot \partial u(x)] \leq 4$ for all x. Interestingly, an example will show that 4 is indeed the magic number for the purposes of uniqueness theory.

Our conclusion from Sections 4 and 5 is that as long as the distribution of income is price-independent, there are reasonable classes of conditions involving only the demand side of the economy and guaranteeing the uniqueness of equilibrium.

In Section 6, we look at the general case of noncollinear endowment (especially relevant in a production context). Unfortunately, the previous conclusion is then overturned. We present an extremely simple and nonpathological example with two consumers and linear utilities (in a four-commodity world) where the Weak Axiom fails to be satisfied in the aggregate. The discussion of the example tells us that there is little room for any attempt to get fruitful uniqueness conditions involving only the excess demand function: A minimally satisfactory theory will have to involve both consumption and production conditions.

In Sections 7 to 9, we pursue an approach in this direction. It consists in reducing the production economy (assumed to be of the constant return, no joint-production type) to an exchange economy for factors of production and exploit then either the general theory of the previous sections specialized to the exchange case (this leads to conditions involving factor intensities) or theories, such as gross substitution, specific to exchange economies. This last line is perhaps the most promising and leads to the main contribution of this chapter, which is Theorem 3 in Section 9. By using index theory, the theorem shows that uniqueness obtains if every utility and production function is *super Cobb–Douglas*. The concept of a super Cobb–Douglas function $h(x)$ is introduced in this chapter, and is defined by the property that at every x there is a Cobb–Douglas function h_x such that $h_x(x) = h(x)$ and $h_x(x') \leq h(x')$ for x' close to x. Of course, this includes the Cobb–Douglas case (which is dealt with in Theorem 2 of Section 8 as a step toward Theorem 3), but the extension to the super Cobb–Douglas situation adds considerable flexibility. See Section 9 for details.

Finally, in Section 10 we spell out some of the convergence implications of the uniqueness theory for dynamic economies. These constitute an important part of the initial motivation for this chapter.

2 Aggregate excess demand: Basic properties

This section describes a number of standard concepts on aggregate excess-demand functions. See Mas-Colell (1985, Section 5.7) for further details and references.

For l the number of commodities, a function $f: R^l_{++} \to R^l$ is an *excess-demand function* if it is continuous, homogeneous of degree 0, and satisfies Walras's law (i.e., $p \cdot f(p) = 0$ for all p).

Definition 1. *The excess-demand function f satisfies the* Weak Axiom (WA) *if* $q \cdot f(p) \leq 0$ *and* $p \cdot f(q) \leq 0$ *implies* $f(p) = f(q)$.

Definition 2. *The excess-demand function f is* monotone *with respect to the normalizing vector* $z \geq 0$, $z \neq 0$, *if* $(f(p) - f(q)) \cdot (p - q) \leq 0$ *whenever* $p \cdot z = q \cdot z = 1$ (*it is* strictly monotone *if the inequality is strict for* $p \neq q$).

An excess-demand function f that is monotone with respect to some z also satisfies the Weak Axiom (to verify this is a simple and useful exercise). The economic interpretation of the two properties is clear: the WA is the law of demand (prices and quantities move in opposite directions) for compensated price changes, whereas monotonicity is the law of demand for any kind of (normalized) price change.

If the excess-demand function was generated by a single preference-maximizing consumer, then it would satisfy the WA but not necessarily monotonicity (thus, it is immediate from the definition that strict Giffen goods cannot arise for $l = 2$). For aggregation purposes, however, monotonicity is a better behaved property. As is well known, by adding up excess-demand functions generated from utility maximization (and satisfying, therefore, the WA), one can lose any significant restriction (see Shafer and Sonnenschein, 1982). On the other hand, the sum of two excess-demand functions monotone with respect to a common normalizing factor z is monotone with respect to the same factor. It would be nice if one could get rid of the normalizing factor in the definition of monotonicity. But this cannot be done. In fact, if $f(p) \neq 0$, there is always a q such that $(f(p) - f(q)) \cdot (p - q) > 0$ (this is easy to verify graphically for $l = 2$).

Consider the two commodities case. Then (strict) monotonicity has a simple geometric interpretation. It says that the offer curve, that is, the set $f(R^l_{++})$, projects in a one-to-one manner into some one-dimensional subspace with positive normal (the projection is taken in the direction of the normal). Thus, the offer curves in Figure 1(a) and 1(b) (resp. Figure 1(c)) are (resp. is not) compatible with monotonicity with respect to some z.

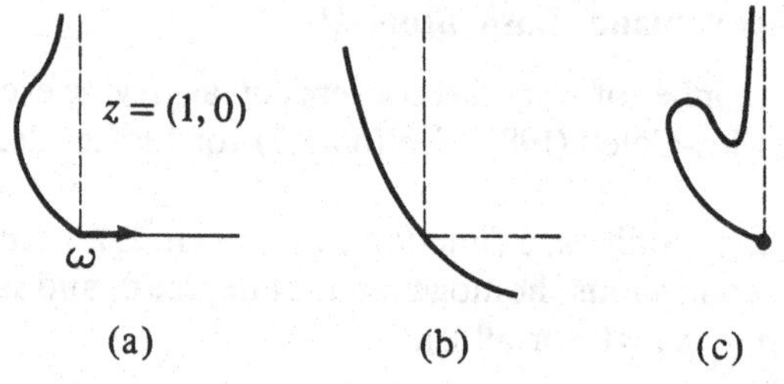

Figure 1.

Suppose now that the excess-demand function f is C^1. Then one can give natural sufficient conditions in terms of derivatives for the properties of interest. Precisely, a sufficient condition for the WA is that $v \cdot \partial f(p) v < 0$ whenever $p \cdot v = 0$, $v \neq 0$, *and* $v \cdot f(p) = 0$. A sufficient condition for monotonicity with respect to z is that $v \cdot \partial f(p) v < 0$ whenever $v \neq 0$, $z \cdot v = 0$. Abusing language somewhat, we will refer to such conditions as negative (or positive) definiteness. Although this is not an aspect to be emphasized in this chapter, we want to mention that these conditions remain valid if f is merely Lipschitzian (as would be the case if boundary consumption at the individual level were allowed) and the conditions are required whenever $\partial f(p)$ exists.

The relevance of the Weak Axiom (and, therefore, of monotonicity) to the uniqueness question is the following. If f satisfies the WA, then for any closed and convex cone $Y \subset R^l$, the set of price vectors p such that $p \cdot Y \leq 0$ and $f(p) \in Y$ is convex. This means that for the typical case of a regular economy, where the set of (normalized) equilibrium price vectors is discrete, the WA implies the uniqueness of equilibrium. Conversely, if f does not satisfy the WA (for, say, the price vectors p, q), then there is a production cone Y $(= \{x : q \cdot x \leq 0 \text{ and } p \cdot x \leq 0\})$ yielding an economy (f, Y) for which the equilibrium is not unique (this observation is due to H. Scarf).

Therefore, the WA is the minimal property on excess-demand functions that has uniqueness implications irrespective of the (constant returns) technology it is coupled with. Thus, any uniqueness condition involving only the consumption side of the economy can be presented as a sufficiency condition for the WA. Those are the conditions we will focus on in the next four sections. Because of the better aggregation properties of monotonicity, these often translate into the search of sufficiency conditions for the latter.

3 Decomposition of aggregate demand effects

We will now assume that the excess-demand function f is generated from a population of N consumers. Each consumer i is characterized by a vector of initial endowments ω_i and a demand function $h_i(p, w_i)$ defined on $R^l_{++} \times R_{++}$. Thus, $f(p) = \sum_i (h_i(p, p \cdot \omega_i) - \omega_i)$.

For every i and p, we can define

$$\theta_i(p) = \frac{1}{\sum_j p \cdot \omega_j} p \cdot \omega_i \quad \text{(the income share)},$$

$$c_i(p) = (\partial_w h_i(p, p \cdot \omega_i))^T \quad \text{(column vector of income effects)},$$

and

$$S_i(p) = \partial_p h_i(p, p \cdot \omega_i) + c_i(p)(h_i(p, p \cdot \omega_i))^T \quad \text{(matrix of substitution effects)}.$$

Correspondingly, we define the aggregate substitution effect matrix $S(p) = \sum_i S_i(p)$, and the weighted average income effect vector $c(p) = \sum_i \theta_i c_i(p)$.

Finally, we define two covariancelike matrices measuring the association across consumers of the deviation of individual income effect from its mean, that is, $c_i(p) - c(p)$, with, respectively, the deviations of (weighted) individual demand from its mean and the deviations of (weighted) initial endowments from its mean. Precisely, the matrices are defined as

$$C_h(p) = \sum_i p \cdot \omega_i [c_i(p) - c(p)] \left[\frac{1}{p \cdot \omega_i} h_i(p, p \cdot \omega_i) - \frac{1}{p(\sum_j \omega_j)} \sum_j h_j(p, p \cdot \omega_j) \right]^T,$$

$$C_\omega(p) = \sum_i p \cdot \omega_i [c_i(p) - c(p)] \left[\frac{1}{p \cdot \omega_i} \omega_i - \frac{1}{p(\sum_j \omega_j)} \sum_j \omega_j \right]^T,$$

and they will be called, respectively, the *expenditure distribution effect matrix* and the *endowment distribution effect matrix*. Note that if there is no dispersion of income effects, that is, if $c_i(p) = c(p)$ for all i, then $C_h(p) = C_\omega(p) = 0$. Similarly, if initial endowments are collinear, that is, if $\omega_i = \theta_i(p)(\sum_j \omega_j)$, then $C_\omega(p) = 0$.

The relevance of all this is that the expression

$$\partial f(p) = \sum_i [\partial_p h_i(p, p \cdot \omega_i) + c_i(p) \omega_i^T]$$

can readily be transformed into

$$\partial f(p) = S(p) - c(p) f^T(p) + C_h(p) - C_\omega(p).$$

This decomposition into four effects will allow a systematic study of the factors affecting the fulfillment of the WA by f. Of course, decompositions of this sort are not new. I follow Mas-Colell (1985, Section 5.7), but see there for earlier references (e.g., Jerison, 1982).

We saw in the previous section that the WA will hold if, for all p, $\partial f(p)$ is negative definite on $\{v: p\cdot v = f(p)\cdot v = 0\}$. So let $p\cdot v = f(p)\cdot v = 0$. Then $v\cdot\partial f(p)v<0$ will obtain if $v\cdot S(p)v + v\cdot C_h(p)v + v\cdot C_\omega(p)v < 0$. But $v\cdot S(p)v = \sum_i v\cdot S_i(p)v$ and $v\cdot S_i(p)v<0$ follows from preference maximization (negative definiteness of the individual substitution matrix). Therefore, assuming the preference maximizations hypothesis, $v\cdot S(p)v<0$ will always hold. The key effects are, therefore, the distribution effects matrices.

In the next two sections, we will assume that the distribution of income is price-independent or, equivalently, that initial endowments are collinear (those have been called *"distribution economies"* by Malinvaud, 1969). Then $C_\omega(p)=0$ and so we only have to worry about the expenditure matrix.

In Section 4, we discuss conditions under which $v\cdot C_h(p)v>0$. In Section 5, we discuss conditions under which $v\cdot S(p)v - v\cdot C_h(p)v<0$.

In Section 6, we bring C_ω into the picture and consider the case where the distribution of income is not price-independent.

4 Expenditure distribution effects: Engel curves conditions

In this section, we investigate the possibility that $C_h(p)$ is positive definite.

The positive definiteness of $C_h(p)$ has a clear interpretation. The vectors $c_i(p) = \partial_{w_i} h_i(p, p\cdot\omega_i)$ and $(1/p\cdot\omega_i)h_i(p, p\cdot\omega_i)$ can be viewed, respectively, as income marginal and income average propensities to consume. Thus, $C_h(p)$ positive definite means that on average (with the weight of every consumer being its expenditure), consumers have a higher than average marginal consumption for the commodities for which they have a higher than average consumption. Marginal and average tend to go together.

One can find arguments making positive association plausible (e.g., if the average is high, then the marginal must have been high somewhere) or implausible (e.g., if the average is high, then we are relatively satiated and the marginal should be low). The truth of the matter is that introspection will not settle this question. The author of this chapter is fairly sure he consumes more books and newspapers than the mean of the population. But although for books his marginal consumption is also probably higher than the mean (hence, positive association), for newspapers it is, on account of satiation, definitely lower (hence, negative association).

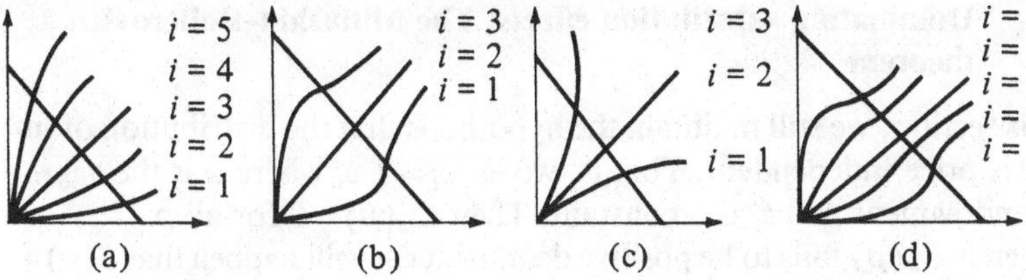

Figure 2.

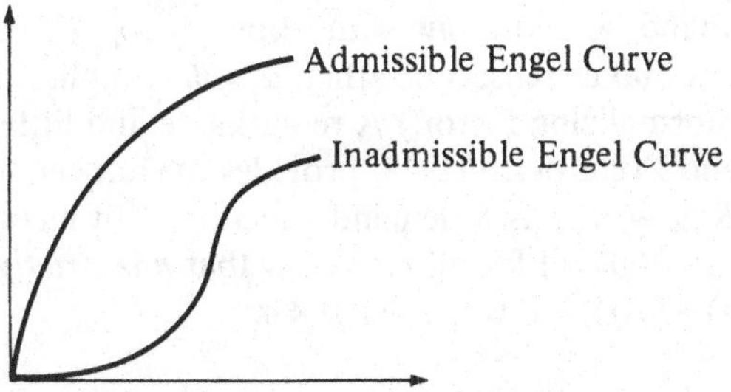

Figure 3.

Summarizing: The positive association issue is very much an empirical matter. For a recent econometric treatment, see Hildenbrand and Hildenbrand (1986).

For a fixed price vector, and assuming for simplicity that all consumers have the same income, Figure 2 represents families of population's Engel curves (for $l = 2$). Figure 2(a) and 2(c) (resp. 2(b) and 2(d)) display positive (resp. negative) association at the given price vector and income.

Suppose, to look at another limiting example, that all consumers have identical preferences. Then it follows from Hildenbrand (1983) that $C_h(p)$ will be positive definite if the distribution of income is nonincreasing on an interval $[0, b]$. (Strictly speaking, this requires a continuum of consumers. Also, the result is stronger: $\partial f(p)$ itself is negative definite.) In Freixas and Mas-Colell (1987), it is shown that if one wants the positive definiteness of $C_h(p)$ for any distribution of income on an interval $[a, b]$, then the sufficient and (in a certain sense) necessary conditions on the Engel curve associated with p is that (i) it be contained on a plane through the origin, and (ii) it display a uniform curvature condition (see Figure 3). These conditions do not guarantee the positive definiteness of $\partial f(p)$; hence, they only yield the WA.

5 Dominating substitution effects: The Mitiushin–Polterovich theorem

In this section, we still maintain the hypothesis that the distribution of income is price-independent. That is, we let $\omega_i = \theta_i \omega$, where ω is the aggregate endowment and θ_i is a constant. Then $C_\omega(p) = 0$ for all p.

Even if $C_h(p)$ fails to be positive definite, it can still happen that $S(p) + C_h(p)$, or even $\partial f(p) = S_p(p) - c(p) f^T(p) + C_h(p)$, be negative definite. This will occur if, informally, substitution effects dominate income effects.

The question is most naturally posed at the individual level: Are there conditions on the individual preferences of consumer i guaranteeing that individual excess demand be monotone with respect to ω_i? (This choice of normalizing factors makes sense since then $\omega_i = \theta_i \omega$ implies the existence of a common normalizing factor.) A remarkable and little known result of Mitiushin and Polterovich (1978) provides the answer.

Suppose that $h: R^l_{++} \to R^l_{++}$ is a demand function with income normalized to 1, that is, $p \cdot h(p) = 1$ for all p. We say that h is *strictly monotone* if $(p-q)\cdot(h(p)-h(q)) < 0$ whenever $p \neq q$.

Theorem 1. *If the C^1 demand function $h: R^l_{++} \to R^l_{++}$ (income is fixed to equal 1) is generated by the C^2, monotone, concave utility function u: $R^l_{++} \to R^l_{++}$, then a sufficient condition for the strict monotonicity of h is that*

$$\sigma(x) = -\frac{x \cdot \partial^2 u(x) x}{x \cdot \partial u(x)} < 4 \quad \textit{for all } x.$$

Proof: Mitiushin and Polterovich's proof is so simple that I would like to give it. Define $g: R^l_{++} \to R^l_{++}$ by $g(x) = [1/x \cdot \partial u(x)] \partial u(x)$, that is, $g(x)$ is collinear to $\partial u(x)$ and $x \cdot g(x) = 1$. Because $h(\cdot)$ and $g(\cdot)$ are inverses to each other, h will be strictly monotone if and only if $g(\cdot)$ is also (i.e., $(x-y)\cdot(g(x)-g(y)) < 0$ whenever $x \neq y$). A sufficient condition for the latter is that $w \cdot \partial g(x) w < 0$ for all x and $w \neq 0$.

Let $w \neq 0$ and denote $q = \partial u(x)$, $A = \partial^2 u(x)$. We can assume $q \cdot w = q \cdot x$. Differentiating, we get

$$(q \cdot x)^2 w \cdot \partial g(x) w = (q \cdot x) w \cdot Aw - (q \cdot w)(x \cdot Aw) - (w \cdot q)^2.$$

Since $q \cdot w > 0$, we have sign $w \cdot \partial g(x) w = \text{sign}\{w \cdot Aw - x \cdot Aw - w \cdot q\}$. But $w \cdot Aw - x \cdot Aw = (w - \frac{1}{2}x) \cdot A(w - \frac{1}{2}x) - \frac{1}{4} x \cdot Ax < -\frac{1}{4} x \cdot Ax < q \cdot x = q \cdot w$ and so $w \cdot \partial g(x) w < 0$. □

If $f_i: R \to R^l$ is an excess-demand function generated by a utility function as in the theorem and the endowments ω_i, then f_i is strictly monotone with respect to the vector ω_i because $f_i(p)=h(p)$ whenever $p \cdot \omega_i = 1$. Therefore, if all utility functions satisfy the conditions of the theorem and endowments are collinear, it follows that there exists a common normalizing factor ω and so the aggregate f will be strictly monotone with respect to ω.

Note that if the utility function u is homogeneous of degree 1, then $\sigma(x)=0$ for all x. Hence, the theorem covers the homothetic case (the case where, so to speak, the income effects are globally so well-behaved that no help is needed from substitution effects). The sufficiency condition "$\sigma(x)<4$ for all x" is not ordinal, that is, it depends on the utility representations. The least concave representation of Debreu (1976) provides, if it is C^2, the best candidate for the sufficiency test. In fact, the following is true: If for the least concave representation we have $\sigma(x)>4$ at all x, then h is not monotone. For an ordinal version of the condition, see Kannai (1987).

To gain some further understanding of the theorem, suppose that u is additively separable, that is, $u(x)=\sum_j u_j(x^j)$. Then the condition $\sigma(x)<4$ for all x is equivalent to $-[x_j u_j''(x_j)/u_j'(x)]<4$ for all x and j (see Section 7 for a discussion of the case when we have <1 instead of <4). If we were dealing with a von Neumann–Morgenstern utility theory over state-contingent income (so that $u_j(x_j)=\pi_j v(x_j)$, where π_j is the probability of state j and $v(\cdot)$ is the Bernouilli utility), then $-[x_j u_j''(x_j)/u_j'(x_j)]$ is the coefficient of relative risk aversion at x_j. Hence, the sufficiency condition for monotonicity is that this coefficient be less than (or equal to) 4. Apparently, this is not an implausible figure in applications (see, e.g., Friend and Blume, 1975; Grossman and Shiller, 1981; Leland, 1986; Kimball, 1988). As an incidental matter, it is worth mentioning that, as one would expect, this monotonicity result extends to the continuum-of-states case and it is thus likely that it can be used to establish uniqueness results for some general equilibrium models with financial securities.

Why the number 4? The proof makes clear where it comes from. Still one could imagine that all we are getting is a sufficiency condition and that behind it lurks a more sensible number. Surprisingly, the next example (which is the only original contribution of this section) shows that 4 is very much the magic number as far as uniqueness is concerned.

Example 1. There are two commodities and two consumers, A and B. Initial endowments are $\omega_A=\omega_B=(2,2)$. Utility functions are

$$u_A(x_1,x_2)=x_1+\frac{(4-\epsilon)^{\sigma_A}}{1-\sigma_A}x_2^{1-\sigma_A},$$

$$u_B(x_1,x_2)=\frac{(4-\epsilon)^{\sigma_B}}{1-\sigma_B}x_1^{1-\sigma_B}+x_2,$$

where

$$\sigma_A = \frac{\ln(1-\epsilon)}{\ln(4-\epsilon)-\ln 4}, \qquad \sigma_B = \frac{-\ln(1-\epsilon)}{\ln(4-\epsilon)-\ln(4-2\epsilon)},$$

and $\epsilon > 0$ is small.

Note that the upper bound for the "relative risk aversion" coefficients is $\max\{\sigma_A, \sigma_B\}$ and that $\sigma_A \to 4$, $\sigma_B \to 4$ as $\epsilon \to 0$ (use l'Hospital's rule to verify this). Both utility functions are linear with respect to some commodity and so they are minimally concave.

This economy has three equilibria. To make the lack of uniqueness point it is enough to exhibit two of them:

(I) $p_1 = 1$, $p_2 = 1$, $x_A = (\epsilon, 4-\epsilon)$, $x_B = (4-\epsilon, \epsilon)$,

(II) $p_1 = 1$, $p_2 = 1-\epsilon$, $x_A = (2\epsilon, 4)$, $x_B = (4-2\epsilon, 0)$.

It is easy to check that both (I) and (II) satisfy the feasibility, budget constraint, and first-order conditions.

As observed by Mitiushin and Polterovich (1978), Theorem 1 remains valid if the consumption set is not R^l_{++} but an arbitrary closed, convex cone $\Gamma \subset R^l_{++}$. To see this, note that for any p, $x = h(p)$ and $g(x)$ defined as in the proof of the theorem, the vector $g(x) - p$ supports Γ at x, that is, $(g(x)-p)\cdot(y-x) \le 0$ for any $y \in Y$. Similarly, for $y = h(q)$, we have $(g(y)-q)\cdot(x-y) \le 0$. Therefore,

$$(p-q)\cdot(h(p)-h(q)) = (p-q)\cdot(x-y) \le (g(x)-g(y))\cdot(x-y) < 0,$$

the last inequality following from the proof of the theorem. (I am grateful to V. Polterovich for clarifying this implication for me.)

Remark 1. For simplicity, we have avoided the study of correspondences. This is the only reason to require the strict concavity of utility functions. But it should be clear that with the proper definition of monotonicity ($(p-q)\cdot(x-y) \le 0$ for $x \in h(p)$, $y \in h(q)$), the previous results remain valid without strict concavity.

6 Noncollinear endowments

From the previous two sections, we could conclude that as long as the distribution of income is price-independent, we have a broad class of reasonable conditions guaranteeing the uniqueness of equilibrium.

As we will see, the situation changes drastically when initial endowments are not collinear. It is thus perhaps not surprising that the possibility of multiplicity has been taken most seriously in fields such as international trade, where differences of endowments are of the essence (see, e.g., Meade, 1952).

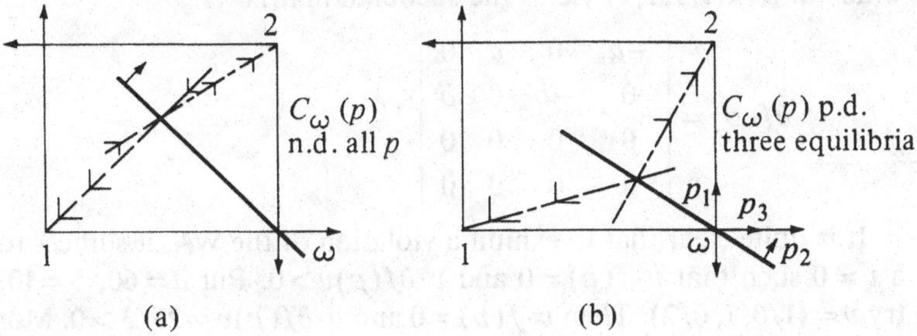

Figure 4.

Of course, there is no added complication if the covariance matrix $C_\omega(p)$ is negative definite, namely, if the marginal propensities to consume are negatively correlated with endowments. This means that people would rather consume what they don't have, which would tend to make for a lot of trade. Thus, informally, we could say that uniqueness is more likely in models that generate a large volume of trade. This is also an intuition present in international trade theory (e.g., Jones, 1970). See Figure 4 for an illustration. We will comment more on this in Section 7 when discussing production economies.

So far, so good. Lower-dimensional cases can, however, be misleading. The following two-consumers four-commodities example (taken from Mas-Colell, 1986) illustrates the difficulty we face. The utility functions in the example are as nice as they can be: linear (thus, globally, substitution effects are infinite and demand is gross substitute). Nonetheless, the weak axiom will be violated.

Example 2.

$$l=4,\ N=2;$$

$$u_1(x_1)=x_1^1, \qquad \omega_1=(0,0,a,0);$$

$$u_2(x_2)=x_2^2, \qquad \omega_2=(0,0,0,b).$$

Things could not be simpler. Endowments are only held in commodities not desired for consumption and the two agents specialize in the consumption of different commodities (in fact, there is a complete disjointness with consumer 1 living over commodities 1 and 3 and consumer 2 over 2 and 4).

Aggregate excess demand is

$$f(p)=\left(\frac{p_3}{p_1}a, \frac{p_4}{p_1}b, -a, -b\right),$$

which at $p=(1,1,1,1)$ yields the Jacobian matrix

$$\partial f(p)=\begin{bmatrix} -a & 0 & a & 0 \\ 0 & -b & 0 & b \\ 0 & 0 & 0 & 0 \\ 0 & 0 & 0 & 0 \end{bmatrix}.$$

It is quite clear that to exhibit a violation of the WA, it suffices to find a $v\neq 0$ such that $v\cdot f(p)=0$ and $v\cdot\partial f(p)v>0$. Put $a=60$, $b=10$, and try $v=(1/6,1,0,2)$. Then $v\cdot f(p)=0$ and $v\cdot\partial f(p)v=25/3>0$. More directly, try the price vector $p'=(25,30,24,36)$, $p''=(23,18,24,12)$. Then $f(p')=(1440/25,12,-60,-10)$ and $f(p'')=(1440/23,20/3,-60,-10)$. Hence, $p'f(p'')<0$, $p''\cdot f(p')<0$, a violation of the WA. Incidentally, it is a trivial matter to perturb the economy so as to replace the zero entries of $\partial f(p)$ by nonzero ones. To make this into a nonuniqueness example, we should specify appropriate production technologies. Because the WA is violated, we know that these exist. We point out that they can also be chosen to verify a no-joint production condition (see the technique used in Section 8).

The culprit of $v\cdot\partial f(p)v>0$ is twofold. First, $S(p)=0$, that is, there are no working substitution effects at p (this is an unavoidable consequence of assuming large substitution effects globally: consumption is pushed toward the boundary where the substitution effects are in fact nil). The matrix $C_h(p)$ is well-behaved, but $C_\omega(p)$ is quite bad. Economically, what goes on could be explained thus. If we raise p_4 by two units and p_2 by only one, then the second consumer will increase his demand of the second good (the income effect is positive). Demand and price move, therefore, in the same direction. The price change, however, is not compensated. To make it compensated in the aggregate (and this is what matters), we could try to raise the price of commodity 1 up to the point where the loss of real income by consumer 1 equals the gain by consumer 2 determined by the change of the second and fourth prices. Now, if the demand of consumer 1 is relatively large, it will only take a tiny change of the first price to accomplish this and so one may hope that when estimated quantitatively, the conclusion that prices and quantities move in the same direction is preserved. This is indeed what happens.

How particular is this example? Obviously, there is nothing pathological about it. What is essential is that when projected on the commodities never demanded, the vectors ω_1 and ω_2 be linearly independent. Suppose that these commodities are the last m. Let us assume that $c_1(p)\neq c(p_2)$. Then we can find a v_1 such that $v_1\cdot c_1(p)\neq v_1\cdot c_2(p)$ and $v_1^{l-m+1}=\cdots=v_1^l=0$. This means that, when projected on the last m coordinates,

$$(v_1\cdot c_1(p))\omega_1+(v_2\cdot c_2(p))\omega_2 \quad\text{and}\quad \omega_1+\omega_2$$

are linearly independent. Therefore, we can find a v_2 with $v_2^1 = \cdots = v_2^{l-m} = 0$ such that $v_2 \cdot (\omega_1 + \omega_2) = v_1 \cdot f(p)$ and

$$v_2 \cdot ((v_1 \cdot c_1(p))\omega_1 + (v_2 \cdot c_2(p))\omega_2) = -v_1 \cdot \partial f(p) v_1 + 1.$$

But then letting $v = v_1 + v_2$, we have $v \cdot f(p) = v_1 \cdot f(p) - v_2 \cdot (\omega_1 + \omega_2) = 0$ and $v \cdot \partial f(p) v = v_1 \cdot \partial f(p) v_1 + v_1 \cdot (c_1(p)\omega_1^T + c_2(p)\omega_2^T) v_2 = 1 > 0$. Summarizing: The WA can only hold if $c_1(p) = c_2(p)$ for all p. It is worthwhile to mention, however, that if we impose some natural restriction on technologies (such as, perhaps, no joint production), it is not at all clear that nonuniqueness examples can then be automatically generated from the violation of the WA.

For further extensions in the line of the last paragraph, see Grodal and Hildenbrand (1988) and Hildenbrand (1989).

There is some sense in which a randomly chosen economy will not have nondemanded commodities (see Kehoe, 1985a). Economies, however, do not come at random and in a production context the existence of nondemanded commodities seems a most natural phenomenon. Moreover, those are likely to be factors of production asymmetrically distributed across the population.

There is another sense in which the economy of Example 2 is special: It is the union of two disjoint economies. Again, the violation of the WA is a general feature of these economies (see Kehoe, 1986). Suppose that $f(\cdot)$ and $g(\cdot)$ are the excess demands for the two economies. Then we can choose q, q' and p, p' such that $q \cdot f(q') < 0$ and $p \cdot f(p') < 0$. Hence, if $\alpha > 0$ is large enough, $p \cdot f(\alpha p') + \alpha q \cdot f(q') < 0$ and $\alpha p' \cdot f(p) + q' \cdot f(q) < 0$. In other words, the disjoint union of f and g violates the WA at $(p, \alpha q)$ and $(\alpha p', q')$. Of course, the fact that the economies are disjoint in consumption and endowments does not mean that they cannot be linked via the (unspecified) technology.

The conclusions we draw from the example (we emphasize again its simplicity: two consumers and linear utilities!) is that with noncollinear endowments, an attack on the uniqueness question for general production economies based entirely on demand conditions (or, in other words, via the WA) is most unpromising. Production conditions must enter the picture. The next three sections will take them into account.

7 Exchange economies and gross substitution

We now consider a very special production restriction, namely, there is no production at all. We then know that the price vector p is an equilibrium if and only if $f(p) = 0$. Can we use this information on the nature of equilibrium to sharpen the previous results?

There is a clear sense in which this can be done. The negative definiteness conditions: "$v \cdot \partial f(p)v < 0$ for $v \neq 0$, $p \cdot v = 0$" need only be required at equilibrium, that is, whenever $f(p) = 0$. This is a well-known consequence of mathematical index theory (see Dierker, 1972; Varian, 1975; Mas-Colell, 1985). In fact, the weaker property: "whenever $f(p) = 0$ a $(l-1) \times (l-1)$ principal minor of $\partial f(p)$ has sign $(-1)^{l-1}$" will do. The more interesting question, however, is: Is there some significant condition on individual agents' characteristics that would yield negative definiteness at equilibrium without necessarily giving it outside of equilibrium?

As it turns out (all this is well known), there is such a condition, namely, gross substitution, that is, the diagonal (resp. off-diagonal) entries of $\partial f(p)$ are negative (resp. positive). For the negative definiteness implication at equilibrium, see, for example, McKenzie (1960). Any example of a gross substitute excess demand violating the Weak Axiom (such as Example 2 in Section 6) is also an example of a gross substitute excess demand violating negative definiteness at some price (Example 2 of Section 6 improves on the classical example of Kehoe, 1985b, in two respects: the elasticity of substitution is infinite rather than 1 and the number of consumers is 2 rather than 4).

Undoubtedly, for highly disaggregated models, gross substitution is most implausible. But for aggregate models, while restrictive, it is not strained. For two commodities, it precisely means that substitution effects dominate income effects. More generally, gross substitution should be thought of as a stronger property than monotonicity. On the precise relationship between the two properties, we can make the following comments:

1. Both properties are preserved under aggregation with the advantage on the side of gross substitution that there is no need to keep track of normalizing factors.
2. In the two-commodity world, an excess demand function f satisfies gross substitution if and only if it is monotone for any normalizing factor $z \geq 0$, $z \neq 0$. In Figure 1(a), there is an example of an excess demand for $l = 2$, which is monotone only with respect to some z (and is not gross substitute). In Figure 1(b), there is a gross substitute example.
3. In a two-commodity world with homothetic preferences, gross substitution obtains if the elasticity of substitution is everywhere larger than 1 (see Fisher, 1972).
4. If there are more than three commodities, gross substitution does not imply monotonicity (see Example 2 in Section 6). For $l = 3$, I do not know (see Kehoe and Mas-Colell, 1984, for the Weak Axiom).

5. Suppose that f is the excess-demand function generated by some ω and the C^1 demand function $h(p,w)$. If demand is normal, that is, if $\partial_w h(p,w) \geq 0$ for all (p,w), and f is gross substitute, then f is also monotone with respect to ω (see Polterovich and Spivak, 1986).
6. Suppose that f is the excess-demand function generated by some ω and the C^2 separable utility function $u(x) = \sum_i u_i(x_i)$. If $-[x_i u_i''(x_i)/u_i'(x_i)] < 1$ for all x_i and i, then f is gross substitute (see Varian, 1985, for a proof and a history of this result; see also Slutzky, 1915, Section 10). Monotonicity with respect to ω will also obtain. This follows from the observation in number 5 or from the fact that $-[x_i u_i''(x_i)/u_i'(x_i)] < 4$ for all x_i and i suffices (see Section 5).

Is gross substitution a helpful property for the study of more general production economies? We will see in the next section that it is, but only after the production economy has been reduced to an exchange one. Any attempt at a direct application faces the difficulty that the firms' demand functions for inputs cannot be expected to be gross substitutes. Indeed, with a technology close to constant returns, an increase in the price of an input has a negative effect on the supply of output and, therefore, on the demand of all other inputs (see Rader, 1972).

8 Reducing production economies to exchange economies

In this section, we will consider production economies of a particularly simple type, namely, those characterized by constant returns no-joint production technologies.

Without loss of generality, we will assume that the l commodities are of two types: (a) factors of production (r in number) owned by consumers and not entering their utility functions, and (b) consumption, or possibly intermediate, goods (m in number). By expanding the set of commodities and technologies, it is always possible to adopt this format. Of course, $l = m + r$.

These are N consumers with utility functions $u_i : R_+^m \to R$ and endowment vectors $\omega_i \in R_+^r$. Also, for every $j \leq m$, there is a convex production cone $Y_j \subset R^l$ with the property that at most the jth component of any $y \in Y_j$ can be positive. (Thus, we can as well identify Y_j with the production function for good j.) For every $z \in R_+^r$, let $A(z) = \{x \in R_+^m : (x, -z) \in \sum_{j=1}^m Y_j\}$. We assume that this convex set is closed and bounded. Finally, we restrict ourselves to economies where at equilibrium every consumption good is produced.

There is a simple, and familiar (it is usually attributed to T. Rader), way to associate with the production economy defined by u_i, ω_i, Y_j a *reduced-factor exchange economy* on the space of factors of production. We simply let agent i have endowments ω_i and utility function $u_i^*(z_i) = \max\{u_i(x_i) : x_i \in A(z_i)\}$. From now on, we will use an asterisk (*) to denote reference to the reduced economy. Under standard conditions on the original utility functions and technologies, the reduced-factor exchange economy generates an aggregate excess-demand function $f^*(p)$. The key fact is that the zeros of this excess demand correspond exactly to the equilibrium factor prices of the original production economy (by the nonsubstitution theorem, consumption good prices are uniquely determined from factor prices). The idea of studying the production economy by means of the reduced exchange economy goes back to at least Taylor (1938) and it has since been used many times. See, for example, Chapter 9 by J. Drèze in this volume.

Once reduced to the exchange case, we have two approaches to uniqueness: (i) the weak-axiom-based theory, and (ii) the gross-substitution-based theory. We comment on them in turn.

The weak-axiom theory still awaits careful development. What is needed is that $C_h^*(p)$ and $C_\omega^*(p)$ be, respectively, positive (and negative) semidefinite. The positive semidefiniteness of $C_h^*(p)$ will follow from considerations similar to the ones in Sections 4 and 5 once one takes into account that many properties are preserved in going from u_i to u_i^* (e.g., if u_i is homogenous of degree 1, so is u_i^*; the relationship between $\sigma^*(\cdot)$ and $\sigma(\cdot)$ – see Theorem 1 – needs to be investigated). The negative semidefiniteness of $C_\omega^*(p)$ will depend now on factor-intensity considerations (built into the definition of u_i^*). Informally, $C_\omega^*(p)$ will be negative semidefinite if, on average, consumers have a higher marginal propensity to consume commodities whose production is relatively more intensive on factors they are less endowed with than the mean of the population. In a world with two factors (say, capital and labor), two goods (say, necessities and luxuries), and two classes (say, poor and rich; the poor consumer needs relatively more necessities than the rich), this would say that the production of necessities must be more capital-intensive than the production of luxuries (for a similar insight, see Jones, 1972). Clearly, requirements of this sort may create problems in applications (thanks to T. Kehoe for this observation).

As for the gross-substitution theory, perhaps it can be said that if the number of factors is not large, then it may be the condition most often satisfied in practice. The difficulty raised in the previous section does not arise and it is, in fact, not a ridiculously implausible condition. In terms of primitives, we have, for example, the following theorem.

Theorem 2. *If every utility function u_i and every technology Y_j is of the Cobb–Douglas variety, then the utility functions u_i^* of the reduced-factor exchange economies are also Cobb–Douglas.*

Proof: Let $\beta \in R_+^m$ be the vector of Cobb–Douglas coefficients of u_i. Denote by E and F, respectively, the $m \times m$ and $r \times m$ matrices of coefficients corresponding to the technologies. If there are no intermediate goods, then $E=0$. We can assume that $(I-E)^{-1}$ exists.

For any vector of factor prices $q \in R^r$, let $b_q \in R_+^r$ be the vector of expenditure shares solving the problem: "Max $u_i^*(z)$ s.t. $q \cdot z \leq 1$." Because of the definition of u_i^*, the solution of this problem can be attained by means of a price vector $p \in R_+^m$, a consumption that solves "Max $u_i(x_i)$ s.t. $p \cdot x_i \leq 1$" and production vectors (one for every technology) that are profit-maximizing with respect to (p, q). But then a standard computation from input–output analysis gives $b_q = F(I-E)^{-1}\beta$. Therefore, the factor demand budget shares are independent of the factor prices. Since this independence is a characterizing property of Cobb–Douglas, we have reached our conclusion. □

The implication of Theorem 2 is that $f^*(\cdot)$ will satisfy the (weak) gross-substitute property and, thus, the equilibrium will be unique (strictly speaking, this is correct only if the economy is regular). Cobb–Douglas exchange economies have been extensively studied (see Afriat, 1987; and Eaves, 1985). For the production case, it is hard to believe that the previous uniqueness result is not in the literature, but I have been unable to find a reference. The result has also been obtained (simultaneously and independently) by Jerison (1988).

In the next section, we will provide a generalization of the uniqueness implication of Theorem 2 to a more general class of preferences and technologies.

We conclude this section with a remark. Theorem 2 excludes the possibility that agents have endowments of consumption goods. This is with loss of generality because the expansion trick referred to at the beginning of the section will not preserve the Cobb–Douglas character of the technologies. However, in the terminology of the next section, it preserves the super Cobb–Douglas character and thus the uniqueness implication is covered by Theorem 3 in the next section (see example (b) in Section 9).

9 Super Cobb–Douglas economies

In this section, we generalize the uniqueness implication of Theorem 2 to the equilibria of (regular) no-joint production economies, where, in a precise sense, preferences and technologies exhibit as much substitution as in a Cobb–Douglas world.

Definition 3. *The function $h: R^s_+ \to R$ is* super Cobb–Douglas *if at every $x \geq 0$, there is a Cobb–Douglas function $h_x: R^s_+ \to R$ such that $h_x(x) = h(x)$ and $h_x(x') \leq h(x')$ for all x' in a neighborhood of x.*

A concave, super Cobb–Douglas function is necessarily homogeneous of degree 1 and C^1 on R^s_{++}. Also, the Cobb–Douglas function h_x is entirely determined by $h(x)$ and $\partial h(x)$.

If h is continuous and C^2 on R^s_{++}, the super Cobb–Douglas property can be equivalently formulated as: "For every $x \gg 0$, let h_x be the (unique) Cobb–Douglas function with $h_x(x) = h(x)$, $\partial h_x(x) = \partial h(x)$. Then $\partial^2 h(x) - \partial^2 h_x(x)$ is positive semidefinite."

It is of interest to point out that the excess-demand function generated by a super Cobb–Douglas utility function does not need to satisfy the gross-substitute property.

Examples of super Cobb–Douglas functions include the following.

(a) All the C.E.S. functions with elasticity of substitution coefficient larger or equal to one (compare with John, 1989).

(b) Any function obtained as a nesting of super Cobb–Douglas functions. Specifically, suppose that $h^j: R^q \to R_+$, $j \leq s$, and $g: R^s \to R_+$ are super Cobb–Douglas. Then $G(x) = g(h^1(x), \ldots, h^s(x))$: $R^q \to R$ is also super Cobb–Douglas. Indeed, at any x' close to x, we have

$$G(x') = g(h^1(x'), \ldots, h^s(x')) \geq g_v(h^1(x'), \ldots, h^s(x'))$$
$$\geq g_v(h^1_x(x'), \ldots, h^s_x(x')),$$

where $v = (h^1(x), \ldots, h^s(x))$ and, of course, $g_v(h^1_x(x'), \ldots, h^s_x(x'))$ is a Cobb–Douglas function. As a particular case, note that a sum of super Cobb–Douglas functions is super Cobb–Douglas.

(c) Suppose that $h^1, h^2: R^s_+ \to R$ are concave, super Cobb–Douglas functions. Then the function $h: R^s_+ \to R$ defined by

$$h(x) = \max\{h_1(x_1) + h_2(x_2): x_1 + x_2 \leq x\}$$

is also (by way of proof, note that the graph of h is the convex hull of the graphs of h^1 and h^2). Because of this, the theory of this section allows implicitly for technological substitution (among super Cobb–Douglas technologies) in the production of any good.

The proof of the following result will rely again on the concept of a reduced factor exchange economy.

Theorem 3. *Suppose that every utility function u_i and every technology Y_j is super Cobb–Douglas. Then every (regular) economy has a unique equilibrium.*

Proof: We understand that the concept of regularity includes the differentiability of the relevant functions.

The proof will be by means of index theory (see Mas-Colell, 1985, Chap. 5, for an account). Namely, we will show that if f^* is the excess demand of the reduced exchange economy and $f^*(\bar{q})=0$, then the determinant of $(-1)^{(r-1)}\partial f^*(\bar{q})$, when viewed as a map from $T_q=\{v\in R^r: q\cdot v=0\}$ to itself, is necessarily nonnegative. For this it suffices that $\partial f^*(\bar{q})$ be negative semidefinite (n.s.d.).

For every q, let $c_j(q)$ be the minimum cost at which one unit of consumption good j can be produced. By the nonsubstitution theorem, this is a well-defined concept. Put $c(q)=(c_1(q),\dots,c_m(q))$. Denote by $B(q)$ the $r\times m$ matrix of cost-minimizing total (i.e., direct and indirect) factor requirements. Of course, $\partial c(q)=B^T(q)$ (Roy's identity). Let $b_j(q)$ be the jth column of $B(q)$ and put $E(q)=[B(q),I]$, an $r\times(m+r)$ matrix.

The excess demand of the nonreduced economy is denoted $f(p,q)$.

Direct computation yields

$$\partial f^*(q)=\sum_{j=1}^{m} f_j(c(q),q)\partial_q b_j(q)+E(q)\partial f(c(q),q)E^T(q).$$

Suppose that we now consider the Cobb–Douglas economy associated with the consumptions and productions of the equilibrium $\bar{q}$ (i.e., we take locally minorizing Cobb–Douglas functions with the same values at the given consumption and production). From now on a hat (ˆ) denotes reference to the Cobb–Douglas economy.

Because of the minorizing property, we have: (a) $c_j(q)\le\hat{c}_j(q)$ for q near $\bar{q}$ and $c_j(\bar{q})=\hat{c}_j(\bar{q})$. Therefore, $\partial_q b_j(\bar{q})-\partial_q\hat{b}_j(\bar{q})$ is n.s.d. for every j. Similarly, if we denote by $S_i(p,q)$ the substitution matrix of i, we have (b) $S_i(c(\bar{q}),\bar{q})-\hat{S}_i(c(\bar{q}),\bar{q})$ is n.s.d. for every i. Denote $\gamma_j=f_j(c(\bar{q}),\bar{q})\ge 0$. Observe that because of the homogeneity of the utility functions, the income effects of the original and the Cobb–Douglas economies are the same. Of course, the same is true for the values γ_j and the matrix $E(\bar{q})$.

Substituting, we have

$$\partial f^*(\bar{q})=\partial\hat{f}^*(\bar{q})+\sum_j\gamma_j(\partial_q b_j(\bar{q})-\partial_q\hat{b}_j(\bar{q}))$$
$$+\sum_i E(\bar{q})(S_i(c(\bar{q}),\bar{q})-\hat{S}_i(c(\bar{q}),\bar{q}))E^T(\bar{q}).$$

By the observation of the last paragraph, the second and third terms of this sum are n.s.d. matrices. As for the first, note that $\hat{f}^*(\bar{q})=0$ and, by Theorem 2, $\hat{f}^*$ is generated by a Cobb–Douglas exchange economy. Therefore, $\partial\hat{f}^*(\bar{q})$ is also n.s.d. (see Section 7). We conclude that, as we wanted, $\partial f^*(\bar{q})$ is n.s.d. □

As a final remark, we point out that, as the proof makes clear, the super Cobb–Douglas character of the economy is a sufficient, but far from necessary, condition. The crucial condition is that, so to speak, the economy be Cobb–Douglas in the average (the precise average, however, depends on endogenously generated variables).

10 Some remarks on equilibrium dynamics

So far, we have concerned ourselves with static economies. However, part of the motivation for this work is the observation that there seems to be a correspondence between uniqueness conditions for static economies and conditions for the asymptotic convergence of equilibrium trajectories in stationary dynamic economies (i.e., the turnpike property). For example, in Kehoe et al. (1986), it is shown that gross substitution yields the turnpike property in exchange, stationary, overlapping generations economies. While it can be presumed that this correspondence is very general (e.g., Drandakis, 1963), the fact of the matter is that very little is known about it. It appears to be an area well deserving of further research.

In this section, we add a further piece of evidence. Consider an overlapping generations economy (with production). Generation t has an excess-demand function $f_t(p_t, p_{t+1})$ and a production set Y_t. We assume stationarity, that is, f_{t+1} and Y_{t+1} are generated from f_t, Y_t by a shift operator. Suppose that the economy admitted an equilibrium cycle in prices, that is, suppose there are $(p_1, \ldots, p_n) \in R^{ln}$ such that the price sequence $p_t = p_{\text{mod}_n t}$ supports an equilibrium allocation. We could then define a pseudo-static economy over R^{ln} by replacing the mod n shift of f_{n-1}, Y_{n-1} for f_n, Y_n (observe, incidentally, that the resulting economy cannot have a price-independent distribution of income). Because any mod n shift of $(p_1, \ldots, p_n)$ is an equilibrium of this economy, we can conclude that the pseudo-static economy can have a unique equilibrium only if the cycle is trivial, that is, $p_1 = \cdots = p_n$. Also, there can be only one stationary equilibrium price sequence. Therefore Theorem 3 (Section 9) has the following consequence.

Corollary 1. *If the generation's characteristics of the (stationary) economy are generated from super Cobb–Douglas utility and production functions, then there is at most one stationary equilibrium price sequence and there can be no nontrivial cyclical equilibrium price sequences.*

Corollary 1 is only a very partial result. It begs to be extended in several directions:

1. The corollary yields the uniqueness of the so-called monetary steady states (i.e., stationary price sequences). What about the uniqueness of the nonmonetary ones (i.e., constantly inflationary or deflationary price sequences)?
2. Does the turnpike property - that is, the asymptotic convergence to a steady state - also follow?
3. Can the result be extended to the case of infinitely lived agents and production sets?
4. In a more speculative vein: Does the super Cobb-Douglas property rule out the possibility of stationary stochastic ("sunspot") equilibria?

REFERENCES

Afriat, S. 1987. *Logic of Choice and Economic Theory.* Oxford: Clarendon Press.

Debreu, G. 1976. "Least Concave Utility Functions." *Journal of Mathematical Economics* 3: 121-9.

Dierker, E. 1972. "Two Remarks on the Number of Equilibria of an Economy." *Econometrica* 40: 951-3.

Drandakis, E. 1963. "Factor Substitution in a Two Sector Model of Growth." *Review of Economic Studies* 30: 217-28.

Eaves, C. 1985. "Finite Solutions of Price Markets with Cobb-Douglas Utilities." *Mathematical Programming Study* 23: 1-14.

Fisher, F. 1972. "Gross Substitutes and the Utility Function." *Journal of Economic Theory* 4: 82-7.

Freixas, X., and A. Mas-Colell. 1987. "Engel Curves Leading to the Weak Axiom in the Aggregate." *Econometrica* 55: 515-32.

Friend, I., and M. E. Blume. 1975. "The Demand for Risky Assets." *American Economic Review* 65: 900-22.

Grodal, B., and W. Hildenbrand. 1989. "The Weak Axiom of Revealed Preferences in a Productive Economy." *Review of Economic Studies* 56: 635-9.

Grossman, S., and R. Shiller. 1981. "The Determinants of the Variability of Stock Prices." *American Economic Review* 71: 222-7.

Hildenbrand, W. 1983. "On the 'Law of Demand.'" *Econometrica* 51: 997-1020.

1989. "The Weak Axiom of Revealed Preferences for Market Demand Is Strong." *Econometrica* 57: 979-87.

Hildenbrand, K., and W. Hildenbrand. 1986. "On the Mean Effect: A Data Analysis of the U.K. Family Expenditure Survey." In *Contributions to Mathematical Economics,* W. Hildenbrand and A. Mas-Colell, Eds. Amsterdam: North-Holland, Chap. 14.

Jerison, M. 1982. "The Representative Consumer and the Weak Axiom When the Distribution of Income is Fixed." Working Paper No. 150, State University of New York at Albany.

1988. Private communication.

John, R. 1989. *Two-Sector-CES Model.* Manuscript, Bonn.

Jones, R. 1970. "The Transfer Problem Revisited." *Econometrica* 38: 178–85.
1972. "Activity Analysis and Real Incomes: Analogies With Production Models." *Journal of International Economics* 2: 277–302.
Kannai, Y. 1987. "A Characterization of Monotone Individual Demand Function." *Journal of Mathematical Economics* 18: 87–94.
Kehoe, T. 1985a. "A Numerical Investigation of Multiplicity of Equilibria." *Mathematical Programming Study* 23: 240–58.
1985b. "Multiplicity of Equilibrium and Comparative Statics." *Quarterly Journal of Economics* 100: 119–48.
1986. "Gross Substitutability and the Weak Axiom of Revealed Preference." Forthcoming in *Journal of Mathematical Economics*.
Kehoe, T., D. Levine, A. Mas-Colell, and M. Woodford. 1986. "Gross Substitutability in Large Square Economies." Forthcoming in *Journal of Economic Theory*.
Kehoe, T., and A. Mas-Colell. 1984. "An Observation on Gross Substitutability and the Weak Axiom of Revealed Preference." *Economics Letters* 15: 241–3.
Kimball, M. 1988. "Precautionary Saving and the Marginal Propensity to Consume." Mimeo, University of Michigan, Ann Arbor.
Leland, H. 1986. Personal communication.
Malinvaud, E. 1969. *Leçons de Théorie Microéconomique*. Paris: Dunod.
Mas-Colell, A. 1985. *The Theory of General Economic Equilibrium, A Differentiable Approach*. Cambridge: Cambridge University Press.
1986. "Large Substitution Effect and the Uniqueness of Equilibrium." Mimeo, University of California at Berkeley.
McKenzie, L. 1960. "Matrices with Dominant Diagonal and Economic Theory." In *Mathematical Methods in the Social Sciences, 1959*, K. Arrow, S. Karlin, and P. Suppes, Eds. Stanford: Stanford University Press, pp. 47–62.
Meade, J. 1952. *A Geometry of International Trade*. London: Allen and Unwin.
Mitiushin, L. G., and V. W. Polterovich. 1978. "Criteria for Monotonicity of Demand Functions" (in Russian). *Ekonomika i Matematicheskie Metody* 14: 122–8.
Polterovich, V. W., and V. A. Spivak. 1983. "Gross Substitutability of Point-to-Set Correspondences." *Journal of Mathematical Economics* 11: 117–40.
Rader, T. 1972. "General Equilibrium Theory with Complementary Factors." *Journal of Economic Theory* 4: 372–80.
Shafer, W., and H. Sonnenschein. 1982. "Market Demand and the Excess Demand Functions." In *Handbook of Mathematical Economics*, Vol. II, K. Arrow and M. Intriligator, Eds. Amsterdam: North-Holland, Chap. 14.
Slutzky, E. 1915. "Sulla Teoria del Bilancio del Consumatore." *Giornale degli Economisti* 51: 19–23.
Taylor, F. M. 1938. "The Guidance of Production in a Socialist State." In *On the Economic Theory of Socialism*, B. Lippincot, Ed. Minneapolis: University of Minnesota Press, pp. 39–54.
Varian, H. 1975. "A Third Remark on the Number of Equilibria of an Economy." *Econometrica* 43: 985–6.
1985. "Additive Utility and Gross Substitutes." Mimeo, University of Michigan, Ann Arbor.

PART IV

Employment, imperfect competition, and macroeconomics

CHAPTER 13

Risk sharing, the minimum wage, and the business cycle

Jean-Pierre Danthine and John B. Donaldson

1 Introduction

This chapter constructs a dynamic general equilibrium model in which labor incomes are influenced by risk-sharing considerations and borrowing restrictions. We show that the dynamic properties of such an economy, in which the sharing of income and risk is effected solely via the labor market, are consistent with the principal stylized facts of the business cycle. We consider a situation in which workers are unable to borrow against their future income. This capital-market imperfection is seen to alter the workings of the labor market whereby the latter substitutes as the vehicle for income and risk reallocation. The implications of this substitution for labor markets have been highlighted in the implicit contracts literature. Our objective here is to show how the introduction of such a consideration affects the time-series properties of a specific dynamic, multiagent general equilibrium model.

Our dynamic context is a variant of the one good stochastic growth model. This identifies us as following in the tradition of the real business cycle (RBC) literature (see, e.g., Kydland and Prescott, 1982; and Hansen, 1985a). We do this not only because the enormous flexibility of the RBC methodology allows us to incorporate simple contracting phenomenon in a natural way, but also because the RBC literature has a well-developed sense of model evaluation: comparing the covariance/variance matrix of the model's artificial time series with that of the U.S. economy.

We wish to acknowledge the helpful comments of Tom Cooley, Jacques Drèze, Nils Gottfries, G. Hansen, Finn Kydland, Rajnish Mehra, Lars Svensson, and Philippe Weil. Computing resources were generously provided by the Center for the Study of Futures Markets, Columbia University. Financial support from the Faculty Research Fund, Graduate School of Business, Columbia University, and the Fonds National de le Recherche Scientifique, Switzerland, is also gratefully acknowledged. Yu-Hua Chu provided superb programming assistance. This paper was prepared for the conference honoring Jacques Drèze, Louvain-la-Neuve, Belgium, June 9-10, 1989.

The second ingredient in what follows is a (static) model of labor contracting proposed by Drèze (1986, 1989). In Drèze's model, ex ante optimal income and risk-sharing arrangements may imply wage discrimination between old and young workers, and the institution of a (state-dependent) minimum wage resulting in unemployment. Socially desirable unemployment compensation is paid out of the proceeds of a tax on employer's profits.

The present chapter can thus be more precisely viewed as an attempt to integrate simple non-Walrasian contracting theory into the RBC paradigm. Although we believe such an exercise is of considerable interest on a purely theoretical and methodological level, that is not our only justification for undertaking such a study. Indeed, we believe non-Walrasian model features have considerable potential for explaining certain macroeconomic phenomena that have, to date, not yet been entirely successfully rationalized in the literature. The most important of these phenomena concerns the observed low variability of wages relative to employment found in U.S. and other countries' time-series data.[1] Time series generated by the simplest RBC model – the one good neoclassical stochastic growth model with a labor–leisure choice – have exactly the opposite property: wages vary much more than employment. This confounding of model prediction by the actual data is the so-called "wage–employment variability paradox."

Several resolutions have been proposed to this paradox. The first, and probably most controversial, was Kydland and Prescott's (1982) suggestion that the puzzle itself was evidence of a larger willingness on the part of economic agents to intertemporally substitute work and leisure across time than is implied by the standard time-additive utility function. Their proposal – to work with a modified utility function – was met with much skepticism on the part of labor economists, who declared themselves unable to find in the data traces of the required level of intertemporal substitutability. In another paper, the same authors – Kydland and Prescott (1988a) – show that taking due account of the variable work week of capital would also go a long way toward resolving the paradox. Following yet another trail, Hansen (1985) explores, quite successfully, the implications of the nonconvexity of the consumer-worker's choice set due to the impossibility of continuously adjusting the length of the work day, that is, he considers the implications of accepting as a fact the observation that most people have a limited menu of work schedules (full time or not at all).

[1] Kydland and Prescott (1988b) argue that this is due in large part to mismeasurement and that quality-adjusted hours – which they argue persuasively is the more appropriate measure of labor input – vary much less than aggregate hours.

In our first venture into non-Walrasian RBC modeling (Danthine and Donaldson, 1990a), we have argued that the wage–employment variability paradox suggests a need to integrate non-Walrasian elements into the RBC paradigm. We first tested the potential of efficiency wage considerations to account for the low variability of wages relative to employment. We showed that efficiency wage features, while leading naturally to unemployment, do not necessarily produce relative wage rigidities in the business-cycle sense and, for realistic levels of unemployment, do not appear necessarily to resolve the paradox. This chapter follows upon that first attempt. It is motivated by the observation that another major class of non-Walrasian labor market models - those with labor contracting - is "designed" to produce relative wage rigidities and, in that sense, is more likely to give rise to a satisfactory RBC model. (This class of models is known, however, to be less satisfactory in explaining unemployment.) This hypothesis must be examined not only in light of its actual impact on the variability of employment and wages, but also with respect to its compatibility with the other stylized facts of the business cycle. Our first question can thus be cast as follows: Assuming any observed wage rigidity is the result of risk-sharing considerations motivated by capital-market imperfections, can we account for the relative variability of employment and wages while also retaining the desirable features of simpler Walrasian RBC models?

Now the contract literature to date is very large (see Rosen, 1985, for a survey) and it is not possible to relate our work to all its many individual strands. Generally speaking, the economy's investment decision has not been modeled in this literature, whereas it is an emphasis of our formulation. Difficulties in obtaining clear-cut comparative statics results in the context of a capital-accumulation model with labor contracting (noted in Rosen, 1985) encourage the numerical approach we adopt. Those papers perhaps most directly related to our work are McDonald and Solow (1981), Osano (1988), and Wright (1988). Wright's (1988) setup (infinitely lived firms and finitely lived workers) is similar to our own, although he does not consider capital accumulation; as a result, the optimality of contract equilibrium that he obtains does not carry over to our setting. Osano (1988) also considers a closely related model but with infinitely lived firms and workers; he proves that an appropriately defined contract equilibrium supports the social optimum. No attempt is made to characterize this equilibrium, however, which is another emphasis of this chapter. Lastly, McDonald and Solow (1981) consider a model of a firm and union bargaining over a wage contract where the outcome is subject to certain equity conventions. Although they deal in a static partial equilibrium setting, their results support the possibility that short-term contracts could lead to fluctuations in employment with relatively stable wages.

An outline of the chapter is as follows: Section 2 proposes a dynamic model into which optimal risk sharing can be explicitly incorporated; as outlined before, this involves merging a model proposed by Drèze (1989) into a basic RBC paradigm. Section 3 describes the algorithm by which we compute this equilibrium, and Section 4 details a summary of our numerical results. Section 5 is reserved for concluding comments.

2 Model formulation

Optimal risk sharing requires that the ratio of agents' marginal utilities of consumption be constant across all states of nature. Such an optimal allocation of risks will generally be prevented if some subset of agents is restricted from participating in the financial markets. Under our formulation, workers are prohibited from borrowing and lending. This special form of market incompleteness is in the spirit of the observation that a worker's main wealth is nondiversifiable human capital and that firm-specific human capital (especially) does not collateralize consumption loans in modern economies. Such a constraint will have significant spillover effects on the workings of other markets as agents attempt to reallocate risks in other ways. We focus on the institution of the labor market as a vehicle for reallocating risks and we hypothesize the existence of a social contract whereby extremes of income inequality are to be avoided.

2.1 *Firms, workers, and equilibrium*

There are J identical firms, each producing the unique commodity with the same constant-returns-to-scale technology as described by a production function of the form $f(k_t, l_t^0, l_t)\Gamma_t$, where k_t denotes firm-specific capital, Γ_t the economywide shock to technology (common to all firms), and l_t^0 and l_t, respectively, denote firm levels of old and young labor employed (all period t levels). In general, a lowercase variable will denote firm- or individual-specific levels of that variable and uppercase variables denote economywide aggregates.

Firms are owned by infinitely lived dynasties of entrepreneurs (capitalists) who are entitled to the residual profits from production.[2] Capitalists' consumption and savings decisions solve the following standard problem:

[2] We intend that the infinitely lived dynasty be a proxy for a family for which each generation internalizes the utility of its heirs. Barro (1974) demonstrates that such an organization will behave collectively like the infinitely lived agent we postulate.

$$\max_{\{(c_t),(z_t)\}} E\left(\sum_{t=0}^{\infty} \beta^t V(c_t)\right)$$
$$\text{s.t.} \quad c_t + z_t \leq \pi(k_t, K_t, \Gamma_t) \tag{1}$$
$$k_{t+1} = (1-\Omega)k_t + z_t, \quad k_0 \text{ given,}$$

where $V(\cdot)$ denotes the period utility function of a representative capitalist, c_t and z_t, respectively, his period t consumption and investment, β his period discount factor, Ω the period depreciation rate, and E the expectations operator. The expression $\pi(k_t, K_t, \Gamma_t)$ is the period profit function of a representative capitalist with individual capital stock k_t when the state of the economy is summarized by the aggregate capital stock K_t and shock Γ_t. The specifics of this function will be described in a moment.

Problem (1) contains the core of our model's dynamics and is similar to previous RBC models in that respect. Note, however, that under our interpretation, unlike more standard models, the production and investment decisions are made by the same economic agent. These investment decisions, in turn, are significantly affected by the existence of non-Walrasian labor-market institutions described in what follows.

Workers do not own stocks and cannot borrow or lend. They thus consume their wages. Workers live T periods with $2L/T$ new workers being born and the same number of (old) workers, $2L/T$, dying at each date. There is, thus, a stationary population of $2L$ workers of which the fraction ξ is viewed as "young" unskilled apprentices and the fraction $(1-\xi)$ is viewed as "old" skilled workers. In what follows, we will choose $\xi = \frac{1}{2}$ while noting that the implied "midlife discontinuity" – graduating from unskilled to skilled status – can simply be viewed as marking the conclusion of an extensive training program. Alternatively, skill levels could be smoothed out by allowing several different skill designations and modifying the production technology accordingly. Every worker, young or old, is assumed to supply one unit of labor inelastically in each period of his life.

We assume that firms offer efficient labor contracts to old workers. Such contracts must clearly specify full employment since there is no disutility to work. Each of the J firms thus employs, in equilibrium, its share $(1/J)$ of the total supply of old workers. These contracts further imply optimal risk sharing between the risk-averse old workers and the less risk-averse capitalists; consequently, they must be of the form

$$l_t^0 = \frac{L_t^0}{J} = \frac{L^0}{J}, \tag{2}$$

with $W^0(K_t, \Gamma_t)$, the period t wage paid by all firms to old workers, satisfying, for all t,

$$u'(W^0(K_t,\Gamma_t))=\theta V'(c(k_t,K_t,\Gamma_t)), \tag{3}$$

where $c(k_t,K_t,\Gamma_t)$ solves problem (1). Here $u(\cdot)$ denotes the period utility function of a representative worker (old and young) and

$$k_t=\frac{K_t}{J}. \tag{4}$$

Equation (4) anticipates the fact that in equilibrium, each of the identical firms will hold the same amount of capital. As before, K_t and Γ_t are the economywide state variables.

The parameter θ governs the relative income shares of capitalists and old workers and may be viewed as reflecting, ex post, their relative bargaining strengths. In the spirit of the implicit contract literature, θ will be fixed at a level such that profit earners will voluntarily enter into such contracts. This means, specifically, that θ will be chosen so that the expected utility ($EV(\cdot)$) of the profit earners in the presence of contracting with old workers will be no less than what would be the case if the wages of the old were governed by Walrasian determination.

Following Drèze (1989), we next depart from the optimal-contracting literature by postulating the impossibility of contractual relationships between firms and young workers.[3] We thus assume, in effect, that for a portion of the labor force, efficient risk sharing cannot be achieved privately. Firms decide, on a purely profit-maximizing basis, how much young labor to hire for the current period given their current capital stock and ex post to the realization of the value of the technology shock. That is, the level of young employment, $L(K_t,\Gamma_t)$ in each state of the economy (K_t,Γ_t), is given by

$$L(K_t,\Gamma_t)=Jl_t, \tag{5}$$

where l_t solves

$$f_3\left(k_t,\frac{L^0}{J},l_t\right)\Gamma_t=W(K_t,\Gamma_t) \tag{6}$$

with $k_t=K_t/J$. Here $W(K_t,\Gamma_t)$ denotes the state-contingent wage of the young workers and it is to the origins of this wage that we now turn.

Given incomplete capital markets, Walrasian wage determination in the young "casual" labor market may entail considerable income variability and an inefficient allocation of income risk. Most real-world economies have developed institutions designed to prevent extremes of income

[3] Together with the incomplete-markets assumption, this is our crucial hypothesis. In its absence, the competitive equilibrium of our economy would again be a Pareto optimum and the dynamics of all our aggregates would be as in the pure Walrasian analogue.

inequality. Accordingly, we postulate the existence, in our artificial economy, of a system combining a minimum wage with unemployment compensation financed by a tax on firm profits. The state-contingent minimum wage $W(K_t, \Gamma_t)$ and unemployment compensation $TX(K_t, \Gamma_t)$ maximize the following social welfare function.

For every (K, Γ), $W(K, \Gamma)$, and $TX(K, \Gamma)$, solve

$$\max_{\{W(K,\Gamma),TX(K,\Gamma)\}} \lambda JV(C(K,\Gamma)) + L^0 u(W^0(K,\Gamma)) + L(K,\Gamma)u(W(K,\Gamma)) + [L - L(K,\Gamma)]u(TX(K,\Gamma)) \quad (7)$$

subject to

	multipliers
(a) $W(K,\Gamma) \geq TX(K,\Gamma)$	(μ)
(b) $L \geq L(K,\Gamma)$	(Φ)

with $L(K,\Gamma)$ determined by equations (5) and (6) given $W(K,\Gamma)$, and $W^0(K,\Gamma)$ satisfying equation (3).

Here $C(K,\Gamma)$ is the consumption of the representative capitalist at equilibrium. The solution to (7) can be viewed as the social contract arrived at through a bargaining process between firm owners and young workers, where the institutional arrangement is common knowledge, the constraints are agreed upon by all the participants, and the relative bargaining power is summarized by the parameter λ.

Notice that the solution to (7) is a schedule that defines the optimal wages to the young and old and unemployment benefits to the unemployed young in every state. We therefore write $W(K,\Gamma)$, $W^0(K,\Gamma)$, and $TX(K,\Gamma)$ to emphasize that these quantities need not be identical across states.

As our analysis to follow demonstrates, the solution to problem (7) will impose the condition that $W(K,\Gamma) = TX(K,\Gamma)$ whenever there is unemployment. If constraint (7a) had alternatively been written as $W(K,\Gamma) \geq \epsilon TX(K,\Gamma)$ for $\epsilon > 1$ a constant, then unemployment would be ex ante voluntary but ex post involuntary for the unemployed.

Before characterizing the solution to this problem, we now conclude the previous discussion by describing the profit and consumption functions of the representative profit-earners and by making precise the equilibrium concept appropriate to this model.

The profit function $\pi(k_t, K_t, \Gamma_t)$ can be written as

$$\pi(k_t, K_t, \Gamma_t) = \max_{l_t}[f(k_t, l_t^0, l_t)\Gamma_t - l_t^0 W^0(K_t, \Gamma_t) - l_t W(K_t, \Gamma_t) - tx(K_t, \Gamma_t)], \quad (8)$$

where $tx(K_t, \Gamma_t)$ is the individual firm's share of the total tax burden levied to finance unemployment compensation. In equilibrium, one must have

$$Jtx(K,\Gamma) = (L - L(K,\Gamma))TX(K,\Gamma) \tag{9}$$

for every state (K,Γ). It is important to note that for each individual firm, the tax tx is a lump-sum amount that is unrelated to the firm's employment policy and is thus not experience-related.

Problem (1) together with (8) is a standard dynamic programming formulation. By using Bellman's optimality principle, it can be shown to be equivalent to finding the value function $Q(k_t, K_t, \Gamma_t)$, where

$$\begin{aligned} Q(k_t, K_t, \Gamma_t) \\ = \max_{0 \le z_t \le \pi(k_t, K_t, \Gamma_t)} \Big\{ & V(\pi(k_t, K_t, \Gamma_t) - z_t) \\ & + \beta \int Q((1-\Omega)k_t + z_t, K_{t+1}, \Gamma_{t+1})\, dH(\Gamma_{t+1}; \Gamma_t) \Big\}, \end{aligned} \tag{10}$$

for appropriate laws of motion on the aggregate state variables, which we assume are known to the profit-earners (rational expectations):

$$K_{t+1} = (1-\Omega)K_t + Z(K_t, \Gamma_t) \tag{10a}$$

(law of motion on aggregate investment), and the conditional distribution of Γ_{t+1} given Γ_t, according to the known probability distribution $dH(\Gamma_{t+1}; \Gamma_t)$.

In terms of our previous discussion, note also the identity $c(k, K, \Gamma) = \pi(k, K, \Gamma) - z = \pi(k, K, \Gamma) - z(k, K, \Gamma)$.

This seemingly simple formulation belies the complex interactions between the profit-earners' and the workers' problems. Indeed, the optimal wage and employment schedules for workers of both generations depend upon the form of the aggregate investment function $Z(K_t, \Gamma_t)$, and in turn, the form of the aggregate investment function – being the sum of individual investment decisions – depends upon the choice of factor wages in the next time period. A continuous function $Q(\cdot)$, as defined in (10), will exist under the customary conditions, including the continuity and concavity of $u(\cdot)$, $V(\cdot)$, and $f(\cdot)$ as well as the continuity of the $W(\cdot)$, $W^0(\cdot)$, and $tx(\cdot)$ functions. For a precise description of the sufficient conditions and the associated existence proof, the reader is referred to Danthine and Donaldson (1990b).

Assuming differentiability of $Q(\cdot)$, the optimal $z(k_t, K_t, \Gamma_t)$ function that solves (10) is characterized via the standard first-order condition:

$$\begin{aligned} & V'(\pi(k_t, K_t, \Gamma_t) - z_t) \\ & = \beta \int Q_1((1-\Omega)k_t + z_t, K_{t+1}, \Gamma_{t+1})\, dH(\Gamma_{t+1}; \Gamma_t). \end{aligned} \tag{11}$$

By application of the envelope theorem,

$$Q_1(k_t, K_t, \Gamma_t) = V'(\pi(k_t, K_t, \Gamma_t) - z_t)[\pi_1(k_t, K_t, \Gamma_t) + (1-\Omega)]$$
$$= V'(\pi(k_t, K_t, \Gamma_t) - z_t)[f_1(k_t, l_t^0, l_t)\Gamma_t + (1-\Omega)]. \quad (12)$$

Note that this formulation differs from those in which we can express the consumer-investor's (the profit-earner's) income as the sum of his wage income and his capital rental income, the latter expressed as the marginal product of capital (the competitive return on capital) multiplied by his capital holdings. This is for two reasons. First, the profit-earners do not provide explicit labor services in this formulation. Second, and more significantly, optimal risk sharing between workers and profit-earners may force the residual profit to differ from the return on capital even in the presence of constant returns. Thus, we view profit-earners as entrepreneurs who contribute whatever capital they have to the production process every period and who receive in return the residual profit after wages and unemployment taxes have been paid. We also note that this reverses the roles normally assigned to firms and workers in more conventional RBC paradigms.

We may now use the homogeneity of the J profit earners, together with the constant-returns-to-scale assumption

$$Jf\left(\frac{K_t}{J}, \frac{L^0}{J}, \frac{L_t}{J}\right) = f(K_t, L^0, L_t), \quad (13)$$

to express aggregate profits as

$$\Pi(K_t, \Gamma_t) = f(K_t, L^0, L(K_t, \Gamma_t))\Gamma_t - W^0(K_t, \Gamma_t)L^0$$
$$- W(K_t, \Gamma_t)L(K_t, \Gamma_t) - TX(K_t, \Gamma_t)(L - L(K_t, \Gamma_t)). \quad (14)$$

Aggregate consumption of the profit-earners is then given by

$$C_t = \Pi(K_t, \Gamma_t) - Z(K_t, \Gamma_t). \quad (15)$$

The aggregate investment function $Z(K_t, \Gamma_t)$ is thus defined recursively by the equation:

$$V'(C_t) = V'(\Pi(K_t \Gamma_t) - Z(K_t, \Gamma_t))$$
$$= \beta \int V'(\Pi(K_{t+1}, \Gamma_{t+1}) - Z(K_{t+1}, \Gamma_{t+1}))$$
$$\times [f_1(K_{t+1}, L^0, L(K_{t+1}, \Gamma_{t+1}))\Gamma_{t+1} + (1-\Omega)]\, dH(\Gamma_{t+1}; \Gamma_t), \quad (16)$$

in conjunction with the law of motion on aggregate capital (equation (10a)), and equation (6) defining the aggregate demand for young labor.

Our notion of equilibrium can now be spelled out.

Definition. *Equilibrium in this model is a quadruple of continuous functions* $W(K_t, \Gamma_t)$, $W^0(K_t, \Gamma_t)$, $TX(K_t, \Gamma_t)$, *and* $Z(K_t, \Gamma_t)$ *that simultaneously solve problem* (7) *and equation* (16) *for all values of* (K_t, Γ_t) *in the feasible range.*

Now the existence of equilibrium can be guaranteed only if the technology and preferences satisfy substantially restrictive assumptions. A detailed consideration of existence issues is not the focus of this chapter, so the reader is once again referred to Danthine and Donaldson (1990b).

An issue still remaining is whether the equilibrium defined for this economy is optimal. The answer to this question turns out, of course, to be negative. It is clear that the minimum wage mechanism cannot restore a first best optimum. Implicitly, we have assumed costs in ascertaining the creditworthiness of workers as well as the reliability of young workers vis-à-vis contract fulfillment. These costs have to be borne. Specifically, the unemployment insurance scheme for young workers will force wages to the young above their Walrasian levels in certain states of nature, giving rise to unemployment and lost output (income) in those states. This reduction in total income and the fact that the unemployment insurance tax is financed solely by profit-earners together reduce the profit-earner's income relative to what it would be in the corresponding constrained optimum (that for which there is risk sharing for older workers and young workers are paid their Walrasian wage in every state of nature). Since in this class of models investment is typically a normal good, we would thus expect investment to be reduced (a fact confirmed by our simulation results).

2.2 *Equilibrium characterization*

Problem (7) together with (16) represent an adaptation of Drèze's contracting model (1989, Appendix 5) embedded in a dynamic context. Like Drèze (1989), the solution to (7) can take one of two forms. In "good" states of the world (those with favorable shocks and a high level of capital), the demand for labor will be sufficient to ensure full employment of the young at a Walrasian (equilibrium) wage that is above the minimum wage acceptable given the equity considerations captured by the social welfare function in (7). In that case, constraint (a) is not binding ($\mu = 0$), and constraint (b) is ($\Phi > 0$) with $L = L(K, \Gamma)$.

We will not explore this possibility, but rather concentrate on those sets of parameters for which, in all (stationary) states of the world, constraint

(a) is binding ($\mu > 0$) and $W(K,\Gamma) = TX(K,\Gamma)$ and, consequently, constraint (b) is not ($\Phi > 0$ and $L > L(K,\Gamma)$); that is, unemployment is positive. It can be shown that the wages of the young will then fall short of the wages of the old ($W(K,\Gamma) \leq W^0(K,\Gamma)$) in these states. For this second case, the precise first-order conditions for (7) are

$$-\lambda V'(\cdot)\left[(L(K,\Gamma)+TX(K,\Gamma))\frac{\partial L(K,\Gamma)}{\partial W(K,\Gamma)}\right]+u'(\cdot)L(K,\Gamma)+\mu=0, \quad (17a)$$

$$-\lambda V'(\cdot)[L-L(K,\Gamma)]+u'(\cdot)[L-L(K,\Gamma)]-\mu=0, \quad (17b)$$

where we have omitted the obvious arguments for economy of presentation.

Rearranging (17b) gives

$$[u'(\cdot)-\lambda V'(\cdot)][L-L(K,\Gamma)]=\mu, \quad (18)$$

which shows μ to be positive (i.e., $W(K,\Gamma) = TX(K,\Gamma)$) only if there cannot be full employment of workers at the efficient wage. Substituting (18) into (17a), one also obtains

$$[u'(\cdot)-\lambda V'(\cdot)]L(K,\Gamma)+\lambda V'(\cdot)\frac{\partial L(\cdot)}{\partial W(\cdot)}TX(K,\Gamma)=0, \quad \text{or} \quad (19)$$

$$u'(\cdot)=\lambda V'(\cdot)\left[1-\frac{W(K,\Gamma)}{L(K,\Gamma)}\frac{\partial L(K,\Gamma)}{\partial W(K,\Gamma)}\right], \quad (20)$$

$$=\lambda V'(\cdot)\left[1-\frac{L(K,\Gamma)}{L}\cdot n_{LW}\right], \quad (21)$$

where n_{LW} is the wage elasticity of (young) labor demand. Equation (21) is Drèze's (1989) equation A.50, which, as he shows, results from equating the marginal gain for workers of an increase in the minimum wage, $Lu'(\cdot)$, to the marginal loss of profit earners,

$$\lambda V'(\cdot)\left[L-\frac{W(K,\Gamma)\partial L(K,\Gamma)}{\partial W(K,\Gamma)}\right],$$

the latter being the loss of income due to the higher wage payment or the higher unemployment tax (L) plus the loss of output due to the reduced employment:

$$-f_3(K,L^0,L(K,\Gamma))\Gamma\frac{\partial L(K,\Gamma)}{\partial W(K,\Gamma)}=-W(K,\Gamma)\frac{\partial L(K,\Gamma)}{\partial W(K,\Gamma)}.$$

This concludes our formal discussion of the model and our notion of equilibrium. We next proceed to an overview of the numerical algorithm by which equilibrium is calculated.

3 Numerical procedure

The task before us is to solve problem (7) and equation (16) simultaneously for a given set of model parameters ($\alpha, \beta, \Omega, p, \bar{\Gamma}, \underline{\Gamma}, \gamma, \nu, \theta, \lambda$ – to be defined shortly). This was accomplished via a recursive iteration procedure that acts on the form of the investment function, thereby generating the equilibrium $Z(K,\Gamma)$ as the limit of a monotone increasing sequence of approximating functions. All calculations were performed on a (K,Γ) grid partition of a neighborhood surrounding the certainty capital stock steady state. The maximum distance between any two partition elements – the "norm" of the partition – was ranged between 0.005 and 0.02. The procedure is as follows: First, choose $Z_0(K,\Gamma)\equiv 0$. Using this $Z_0(K,\Gamma)$, solve problem (7) to determine the corresponding wage and employment functions, $W_0(K,\Gamma)$, $W_0^0(K,\Gamma)$, and $L_0(K,\Gamma)$. This is a matter of solving at most a system of two nonlinear equations. Standard subroutines are available for this purpose.

Using these latter functions, next solve equation (16) – which characterizes the equilibrium function – to obtain a $Z_1(K,\Gamma)$. The $Z_1(K,\Gamma)$ is obtained in a somewhat novel way. Since our solution process for problem (7) requires an explicit functional form for the $Z(K,\Gamma)$ function and since the standard procedures for solving equation (16) provide an equilibrium $\tilde{Z}_1(K,\Gamma)$ defined only on a discrete set of capital-stock-shock pairs (a partition of the state space), we chose to approximate the true $Z_1(K,\Gamma)$ in the following manner. Given the $\tilde{Z}_1(K,\Gamma)$, we regressed investment as a function of the capital stock and shock to technology, for all (K,Γ) pairs in the same neighborhood of the steady state, to obtain an expression of the form $Z_1(K,\Gamma)=\alpha+\hat{B}K+\hat{D}\Gamma$. Work by Christiano (1988) as well as ourselves (Danthine, Donaldson, and Mehra, 1989) is persuasive that $Z_1(K,\Gamma)$ so obtained is a good approximation to $\tilde{Z}_1(K,\Gamma)$. Our procedures for obtaining $\tilde{Z}_1(K,\Gamma)$ as the discrete solution to equation (16) follow along the lines of techniques described in Danthine and Donaldson (1990a) and Coleman (1989).

Using the $Z_1(K,\Gamma)$, we next solve problem (7) again to secure a new set of wage and employment functions $W_1(K,\Gamma)$, $W_1^0(K,\Gamma)$, and $L_2(K,\Gamma)$. From these latter functions, a new $Z_2(K,\Gamma)$ is obtained as a solution to equation (16) and the process repeats itself. We thereby construct a sequence of monotonic increasing functions that is bounded above and thus convergent. The corresponding sequences of wage functions $\{W_n^0(K,\Gamma)\}$ and $\{W_n(K,\Gamma)\}$ are each monotone decreasing and similarly converge; $\{L_n(K,\Gamma)\}$ is also monotone increasing (via equations (5) and (6)) and convergent.

By using the equilibrium investment function $Z(K,\Gamma)$ thus obtained, the time series of capital stock was generated as per (10a) for a specified (see what follows) sequence of random technology shocks. With all wage and quantity expressions defined as functions of K and Γ, the corresponding time series for the variables followed accordingly.

By using the same set of parameters, this entire procedure was then followed by a nearly identical one yet for which $W^0(K,\Gamma)$ was set equal to the marginal product of old workers in every state, with the wages of the young still governed by the same insurance agreement specified in problem (7). If the $E(V(\cdot))$ so obtained in this second simulation equals or falls slightly short of the $E(V(\cdot))$ obtained in the prior first simulation, the risk-sharing contracts for old workers were deemed incentive compatible: firms would voluntarily enter into such contracts as they are welfare noninferior for their owners. If the reverse were true (i.e., the introduction of the contract reduced the welfare of the profit-earners), θ was increased until the incentive compatibility relationship was restored.

As for functional forms, we choose $V(c)=\ln(c)$ and $u(c)=c^{\gamma}/\gamma$, and $f(K, L^0, L)\Gamma$ was assumed to be of the form $MK^{\alpha}(L_0^{1-\nu}L^{\nu})^{1-\alpha}\Gamma$. The shock to technology Γ was required to follow a two-state Markov process with transition probability matrix

$$\begin{array}{cc} & \Gamma_{t+1}=\bar{\Gamma} \qquad \underline{\Gamma} \\ \Gamma_t = \begin{array}{c}\bar{\Gamma}\\ \underline{\Gamma}\end{array} & \begin{bmatrix} p & 1-p \\ 1-p & p \end{bmatrix}\end{array}$$

with p, $\bar{\Gamma}$, and $\underline{\Gamma}$ parameters of choice. The discipline imposed on the choice of this subset of parameters was twofold: (i) that p be chosen high enough that the pattern of autocorrelations of output lagged with itself over several periods resembles the analogous pattern for output of the U.S. economy and (ii) that $\underline{\Gamma}, \bar{\Gamma}$ be chosen so that the standard deviation of (detrended) output for the model economy again approximated its counterpart for the U.S. economy. These considerations (especially (ii)) led us to choose $\bar{\Gamma}=1.009$ and $\underline{\Gamma}=0.992$, with $p=0.9$. By way of comparison, we note that in order for our shock process to match the first and second unconditional moments of Kydland and Prescott's (1982), we would have had to choose $\bar{\Gamma}=1.02$, $\underline{\Gamma}=0.98$, and $p=0.97$. In particular, the shocks would have had to be much higher. This observation suggests that the "transmission mechanism" in an economy with the types of restrictions to trades we have imposed is more powerful than its analogue for purely Walrasian models. We view this as especially significant because with proper accounting (in the Solow tradition) of the size of technology shocks, existing Walrasian paradigms are unable to account fully for the observed variability of output.

We next considered β, α, and Ω; by following Kydland and Prescott (1982), these were fixed at, respectively, 0.99, 0.36, and 0.10 (see Kydland and Prescott, 1982, for the complete rationale). The choice of the β value to be 0.99, in particular, gives an average period return to physical capital of 4%, which is approximately what is annually observed for the U.S. economy. This implies that our model period corresponds to one quarter.

The remaining parameters were more difficult to fix unambiguously. To our knowledge, there is no convincing study that attempts to measure the coefficient of relative risk aversion (CRRA) of shareholders vis-à-vis nonshareholders. In conformity with previous work, we use a logarithmic utility function for the profit-earners. We further adopt the intuitive assumption that those who choose not to be entrepreneurs are more risk-averse than those who do. The results reported in what follows correspond to a value of $\gamma = -6$, which we view as being in the admissible range $[-2, -10]$ in light of earlier microstudies, notably Drèze (1981). In the absence of hard empirical evidence on ν, the fraction of total labor income going to "casual" young workers as opposed to workers under contract, we simply fix ν at $\frac{1}{2}$. The parameter M is purely a scale parameter; it was chosen to fix the level of unemployment in the range of 4 to 10%, which is reasonable for what has been observed for the U.S. economy. As noted earlier, the parameter θ was determined entirely endogenously with and without risk-sharing labor contracts to the old as being the same. Lastly, the parameter λ determined the degree of income inequality between profit-earners and young workers. It was similarly endogenously determined in such a way as to given reasonable relative income allocations.

4 Numerical results

We first provide a statistical summary of the U.S. economy – our reference case – and then present a detailed comparative overview of the model's performance with special attention to the "wage–employment variability paradox."

Aggregate time series for the U.S. economy display certain statistical regularities, a replication of which constitutes the base test that a potentially valid model should pass. Table 1 summarizes these statistics for a representative post-war time period (3rd quarter 1955 through 1st quarter 1984).

As is evident from the first column of figures in Table 1, investment varies proportionately much more than output, and consumption and capital stock vary less so. Hours are substantially more variable than

Table 1. *Statistical properties: U.S. economy*

Series	Standard deviation (%)	Correlation with output
Output	1.76	1.00
Consumption	1.29	0.85
Investment	8.60	0.92
Capital stock	0.63	0.04
Hours (employment)	1.66	0.76
Productivity (average)	1.18	0.42

Source: Hansen (1985; Table 1); the results are derived from quarterly data that have been detrended using the Hodrick and Prescott (1980) filter methodology.

productivity (output/hours). The second column of figures shows that consumption and investment are especially highly correlated with output; the same is true of hours and, to a somewhat lesser extent, productivity. Note also that capital stock is essentially uncorrelated with output. Although not reported in the table, (detrended) output is highly intertemporally autocorrelated: its correlation with its one- and two-quarter lagged values is, respectively, 0.84 and 0.57 (cf. Kydland and Prescott, 1982).

Table 2 presents the analogous contract model statistics for a representative set of parameters.

There are a number of aspects of this case that deserve comment.

1. First and foremost, the wage–employment variability paradox appears essentially solved. The puzzle can be summarized by first noting that for U.S. data, (detrended) hours vary essentially as much as output, and the ratio of the standard deviation of hours to the standard deviation of (average) productivity is about 1.3 (1.6/1.18). For the basic Walrasian stochastic growth model, however, hours and productivity each vary approximately half as much as output, with the latter ratio being close to 1. In our risk-sharing model, hours vary slightly more than output and the hours–productivity relative variability ratio is 5.56 (1.78/0.32). Although this latter result is extreme and in a sense goes way overboard, we deem it acceptable given the strong assumptions we have adopted (no borrowing by workers, yet full insurance via the labor market), assumptions that would have to be relaxed in a more realistic version of the model. The small variation in average productivity is also due in part to the extremely small productivity shocks required to produce output variation identical to that for the U.S. economy.

Table 2. *Model statistics: Basic aggregates*[a]

Series	Undetrended (a)[c]	Undetrended (b)[d]	Detrended[b] (a)[c]	Detrended[b] (b)[d]
Output	4.39	1.00	1.76	1.00
Total consumption	2.72	0.61	0.80	−0.74
(i) Profit-earner consumption	18.72	0.92	2.76	0.88
(ii) Old worker consumption	3.71	0.78	1.35	0.37
(iii) Young worker consumption	2.67	−0.38	2.00	−0.95
(iv) Total worker consumption	2.18	0.44	0.90	−0.80
Investment	13.92	0.89	8.90	0.98
Capital stock	6.97	0.84	0.65	0.01
Total hours	3.01	0.91	1.78	0.98
(i) Young hours	6.02	0.91	3.72	0.98
Productivity (average)	2.14	0.83	0.32	0.05

Welfare measures and related statistics

Mean values		Welfare	
Output	1.16	Average utility[e]	
Total consumption	0.86	(i) Profit-earners	−3.33
(i) Profit-earner consumption	0.04	(ii) Old workers	−32.19
(ii) Old worker consumption	0.42	(iii) Young workers	−37.17
(iii) Young worker consumption	0.40		
Investment	0.304		
Capital stock	11.6		
Young hours	0.90		
Unemployment rate (young)	10%		

[a] $M=0.49$, $\lambda=7$, $\gamma=-6.00$, $\nu=0.50$, $\theta=16$, $p=0.9$, $\underline{\Gamma}=0.992$, $\bar{\Gamma}=1.009$.
[b] Detrended using Hodrick and Prescott (1980) methodology.
[c] (a) Standard deviation (%).
[d] (b) Correlation with output.
[e] Average utility per time period.

2. This resolution of the "business cycle puzzle" does not affect the ability of the model to replicate the other major stylized facts. The relative variability of the aggregate output, consumption, and investment series thus corresponds generally to the observations made before for the U.S. economy. This is especially encouraging as it shows that the integration of "real-worldlike" institutional arrangements designed to promote income and risk sharing into the standard paradigm can be accomplished without losing the latter's most attractive features.

3. The performance of the model in terms of the observed correlations is generally superior to what is obtained in pure Walrasian models, with one exception. On the positive side, investment is highly correlated with output and capital stock is essentially uncorrelated with output, as per the data. Hours are more highly correlated with output than what is observed for the U.S. economy, but in this regard our model performs no worse than the other Walrasian paradigms (e.g., Hansen's (1985) indivisible labor economy and Kydland and Prescott's (1982) time-to-build economy display similar correlations of 0.98 and 0.95, respectively). With regard to average productivity, its correlation with output is substantially lower than that of hours and, in this sense, the model is more respectful of the data than the Walrasian paradigms (Hansen's, 1985, and Kydland and Prescott's models give nearly identical correlations of, respectively, 0.86 and 0.87 along this dimension). We note the substantial effect that detrending has on many of these correlations.

4. On the negative side, young worker consumption (wages) is negatively correlated with output, a by-product of the minimum wage mechanism in conjunction with the no-borrowing constraint. This effect is substantially strengthened by the detrending process. With young worker consumption more variable than old worker consumption (detrended series) and highly countercyclical, the stochastic pattern of young worker consumption relative to output dominates that of old workers, resulting in countercyclical total worker consumption as well. (The fact that total worker consumption is significantly less variable than either of its constituent components further illustrates the disparate wage patterns of the different worker groups.) With capitalists' consumption (dividends) small relative to worker consumption, this same countercyclical effect carries over to the total consumption series as well. Note that this latter property is, to a significant extent, a phenomenon of detrending, and is not evident in the unfiltered data. That being said, it must nevertheless be acknowledged that even for unfiltered data, the total consumption–output correlation is too low relative to the data, a fact again attributable to the excessive power of our income-stabilization mechanisms. A weaker mechanism is apparently called for. Alternatively, this unattractive feature of the model could also be eliminated if the proportion of the worker population represented by young unskilled workers were lowered to a more realistic level.

5. Dunlop (1938) and Tarshis (1939) have criticized both classical and Keynesian labor-market theories for predicting, counterfactually, that average productivity and hours worked should be strongly negatively correlated with output. As documented by Christiano and Eichenbaum (1990), this same correlation is highly positive – normally above 0.9 – for typical

RBC models. For the U.S. economy, however, these series are essentially uncorrelated. A similar result is observed for our model as well as in the case presented in Table 2; the correlation of hours and productivity is −0.13, a dramatic improvement vis-à-vis earlier models. Excessive emphasis should not perhaps be placed on replicating this particular stylized fact, however, as it appears peculiar to the United States alone. Indeed, Danthine and Donaldson (1990c) report, for a large selection of countries, that the hours–average productivity correlation is typically strongly negative; for example, this correlation is −0.55 for Germany and −0.50 for the United Kingdom, and even ranging to a level of −0.70 for Australia. These latter observations appear to increase the attractiveness of our modeling perspective vis-à-vis standard RBC formulations.

With regard to the correlation of total wages and hours, our model predicts a value of −0.81, which again differs substantially from Walrasian RBC models where it is highly positive. The data are again somewhat ambiguous in this regard: Danthine and Donaldson report a range of −0.58 to +0.41 for this variable across their sample of countries. Generally speaking, however, they find this correlation to be mildly positive. Our result again reflects the extreme naiveté of our assumption. Note that for our formulation, the correlations of wages and hours or average productivity and hours can differ substantially (as reported) because wages under contracting need bear no direct relationship to marginal (and thus average) productivity.

6. Lastly, we emphasize the impact of agent heterogeneity by comparing the behavior of the different components of aggregate consumption. In particular, although the standard deviation of aggregate consumption generally conforms to U.S. observations, it is simultaneously compatible with one segment of the population, profit-earners, experiencing a much larger consumption variability. This property, in our view, has potentially interesting implications, especially for the magnitude of equity premium. In the same vein - and as noted earlier - the variation in total wages is much smaller than the variation in either of its components.

5 Concluding comments

In this chapter, we have proposed a dynamic macroeconomic model with non-Walrasian features that is able successfully to mimic the major stylized facts of the business cycle. The income and risk-sharing considerations we have introduced furthermore appear to provide a natural resolution to one of the outstanding puzzles: the wage–employment variability paradox. By constructing a non-Walrasian model with a *suboptimal* equilibrium path that is observationally equivalent to existing pure Walrasian RBC models, we have also substantially softened the assertion that business-cycle fluctuations of necessity result from the optimal responses of economic agents to uncertainty in the rate of technological change. We have also demonstrated the versatility of the RBC methodology and the possibility of extending it to accommodate a wide range of phenomena.

REFERENCES

Barro, R. 1974. "Are Government Bonds Net Wealth?" *Journal of Political Economy* 85: 1095–117.

Christiano, L. J. 1988. "Solving a Particular Growth Model by Linear Quadratic Approximation and Value Function Iteration." Working paper No. 415, Federal Reserve Bank of Minneapolis Research Department.

Christiano, L. J., and M. Eichenbaum. 1990. "Current Real Business Cycle Theories and Aggregate Labor Market Fluctuations." Mimeo, Northwestern University, Evanston, Illinois.

Coleman, W. J. 1989. "Equilibrium in an Economy with Capital and Taxes on Production." Working paper, Federal Reserve Board of Governors, Washington, D.C.

Danthine, J. P., J. B. Donaldson, and R. Mehra. 1989. "On Some Computational Aspects of Equilibrium Business Cycle Theory." *Journal of Economic Dynamics and Control.*

Danthine, J. P., and J. B. Donaldson. 1990a. "Efficiency Wages and the Business Cycle Puzzle." *European Economic Review* 34: 1275–1301.

1990b. "Risk Sharing, the Minimum Wage, and the Business Cycle." First Boston working paper, Columbia University, New York.

1990c. "Methodological and Empirical Issues in Real Business Cycle Theory." Mimeo, Columbia University, New York.

Drèze, J. H. 1981. "Inferring Risk Tolerance from Deductibles in Insurance Contracts." *The Geneva Papers on Risk and Insurance* 20: 48–52.

1986. "Work Sharing: Some Theory and Recent European Experience." *Economic Policy* 3: 562–619.

1989. *Labor Management, Contracts, and Capital Markets: A General Equilibrium Approach,* Yrjo Johnsson Lectures. Oxford: Blackwell.

Dunlop, John T. 1938. "The Movement of Real and Money Wage Rates." *Economic Journal* 48: 413–34.

Hansen, G. D. 1985. "Indivisible Labor and the Business Cycle." *Journal of Monetary Economics* 16: 309–27.

Hodrick, R. J., and E. C. Prescott. 1980. "Post-War U.S. Business Cycles." Working paper, Carnegie-Mellon University, Pittsburgh.

Kydland, F., and E. C. Prescott. 1982. "Time to Build and Aggregate Fluctuations." *Econometrica* 50: 1345–70.

1988a. "The Workweek of Capital and Its Cyclical Implications." *The Journal of Monetary Economics* 21: 343–60.

1988b. "Cyclical Movement of the Labor Input and Its Real Wages." Working paper No. 413, Federal Reserve Bank of Minneapolis Research Department.

McDonald, I. M., and R. M. Solow. 1981. "Wage Bargaining and Employment." *American Economic Review* 71: 896–908.

Osano, H. 1988. "Real Business Cycles in a Dynamic Labor Contract Equilibrium." Department of Economics Discussion Paper 809, Northwestern University, Evanston, Illinois.

Rosen, S. 1985. "Implicit Contracts: A Survey." *Journal of Economic Literature* 23: 1144–75.

Tarshis, L. 1939. "Changes in Real and Money Wage Rates." *Economic Journal* 49: 150–4.

Wright, R. D. 1988. "The Observational Implications of Labor Contracts in a Dynamic General Equilibrium Model." *Journal of Labor Economics* 6: 530–51.

CHAPTER 14

A medium-term employment equilibrium

Edmond Malinvaud

Extensive reflection on how the level of employment is determined occurred during the past decade and a half, particularly so in Western Europe. Although a good deal of agreement seems to exist on many aspects of this determination, we cannot say that the central models of macroeconomic theory now provide a fully appropriate framework for studying it. Speaking in honor of Jacques Drèze, who is so much motivated by the problem, provides an excellent occasion for trying to contribute to its solution or more modestly for explaining my own thoughts on how to analyze medium-term employment trends.

For short-term analysis, we may be satisfied with the recent reformulation, extension and econometric application of the Keynesian equilibrium. The fruitfulness of this work is well exemplified by the progress of the European Unemployment Programme as reported in J. Drèze and C. Bean (1990). But many questions and policy issues concerning employment have such a time horizon that the class generated by fixed-price equilibria no longer is directly suitable. The possibility then exists to work out the dynamics of such equilibria. I do not want to dismiss it, but will not discuss it here. Suffice it to say that it is hardly used in applications because of its difficulties. When considering medium-run issues, people argue essentially in static terms.

My purpose here is to exhibit the kind of equilibrium that I believe to be appropriate as a framework for such arguments and to derive from it some comparative statics results. The effects here involved concern a medium-term horizon, a notion that is somewhat flexible, probably between five and ten years, but sometimes also a little less or a little more. One of our concerns should be to detect how the relative strength of various effects evolves when the horizon is pushed farther ahead. I will venture some conjectures in this respect.

The specification of any equilibrium can go more or less deep into the modeling of behaviors and interactions, especially in macroeconomics, where large simplifications are unavoidable. For my presentation here, I think it wise to begin with the consideration of the most compact and simple expression of the model, then to concentrate attention on one of its two main ingredients, first in general terms (Section 2) before I give to it a simple mathematical expression (Section 3). The main comparative statics results will be discussed in Section 4. The last part of the chapter will deal a little more precisely with the formation of aggregate demand for goods.[1]

1 Real wages and employment

When discussing why unemployment differs between countries or historical periods, it is a rather common practice now among economists to focus on the simultaneous determination of the real wage rate and the volume of employment. Two relations between these variables are said to exist, representing, respectively, the outcome of the wage-bargaining process and the outcome of the working of the economic system for a given real wage rate. These relations can be plotted as curves on a graph like Figure 1, with the real wage W as abscissa and employment L as ordinate. The equilibrium is defined by the crossing point of the two curves.

I must first explain why I am accepting this simple expression of the process that determines employment in the medium run. For doing so,

[1] This chapter deals with the concern that has been motivating many of my thoughts during this decade, namely, understanding the interplay between real wages and employment. The reader may then wonder how this chapter relates to those of my earlier publications that touched on the same subject. The simple theoretical structure that is here given aims at making explicit the framework within which I have occasionally discussed some important aspects of actual unemployment problems. The closest to this structure was the model displayed in Malinvaud (1983) and used in Malinvaud (1982). There are, however, important differences in both the scope of the two models and their specification. In 1983, real factor prices were taken as exogenous and only one other exogenous variable was introduced, the autonomous demand for goods; here the real wage and interest rates are endogenous, while the role of various types of exogenous shocks is sketched. In 1983, the model was dynamic and intended to show why initial effects could go in the reverse direction of longer-term effects; here I am working with a static model suited for the study of medium-term effects and simply pointing to the changes to be brought into the specification and its results when the length of the horizon is changed. In 1983, the model assumed a Keynesian equilibrium with an admittedly extreme specification of the demand for goods; here the market for goods may be viewed as being cleared and a more flexible form of the demand function is assumed with a discussion of its effects. Finally, equations (1) and (2) somewhat differ from the equations used in 1983 for the representation of producers' decisions, as a result of my work in the meantime (Malinvaud, 1987, 1989). Perhaps I should also explain my insistence in studying the role of real wages on employment. It comes from my dissatisfaction when I witness that, on this important issue, no agreement seems to have been reached in our profession.

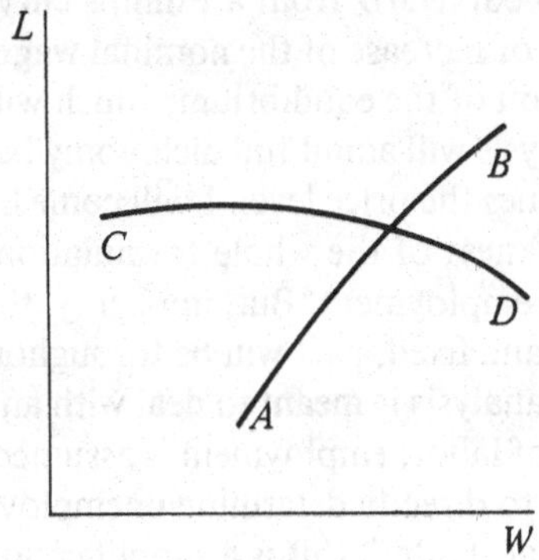

Figure 1.

it is convenient to give easy names to the two relations, even though any denomination would be misleading if its meaning in this context were not correctly understood. I will speak of "the bargaining equilibrium" for the first relation (curve *AB*) and of "the economic equilibrium" for the second (curve *CD*). The shape I am giving to this second curve will be one of the main points of my subsequent discussion.

Using such a compact representation is tantamount to assuming that the phenomenon described by each of the two curves has some autonomy and that the real wage and employment are the two most relevant economic variables that enter it. As for the economic equilibrium, I hope this will appear as a natural outcome of the next section. Let us then briefly consider the representation of the bargaining equilibrium.

Curve *AB* exhibits the notion that bargaining determines the real wage rate and that the level of employment then plays an important role. The objection was raised that employers, employees, and trade unions bargain on the nominal rate, whereas the real rate follows as a consequence of what the price level happens to be (I read Solow, 1986, as making this point). It seems to me that this objection has little force in most countries of the world, where bargaining takes great account of expected price increases and where unanticipated shocks to the cost of living are quickly shifted to wages, not to mention the case of explicit escalator clauses. Since we are concerned here with medium-term determination, the real wage certainly is a more direct outcome of bargaining than the nominal rate. Incidentally, I note that the wage equation of the second phase of the European Unemployment Programme turns out to describe an error-correction mechanism to a relationship that links the real wage to the level of unemployment, as well as to labor productivity (see Drèze and Bean, 1990).

We must, of course, distinguish curve *AB* from a Phillips curve that would determine the short-run rate of increase of the nominal wage. This curve will not appear in the definition of the equilibrium, which will concern only real magnitudes. The analysis will admit full dichotomy between the real economy and what determines the price level. I will come back at the end of the chapter on this weakness of the whole formulation.

Figure 1 relates W to the level of employment. But, implicitly, the supply of labor is assumed exogenous and fixed, as it will be throughout this chapter. More precisely, the whole analysis is meant to deal with an economy experiencing an excess supply of labor; employment is assumed to be equal to the demand for labor and to directly determine unemployment, which then need not explicitly appear. I admit this is a simplification, but one that seems to be warranted in the present instance.

The fact that the outcome of the bargaining process depends on unemployment is well accepted in the labor economics literature, as reported, for instance, in Farber (1986). I do not think I need to argue any longer for it; all the more so because I am ready to be eclectic about the exact rationale behind the bargaining process.

I must, however, recognize that Figure 1 may be somewhat misleading in conveying the notion of a fixed relationship. It is not so much that curve *AB* may shift as a consequence of exogenous changes in the bargaining institutions or in bargaining behavior, a possibility that is certainly well understood, but rather that it is probably not fully autonomous with respect to the economic equilibrium.

Curve *AB* may shift if, for instance, government succeeds in inducing social partners to accept lower real wages, or, alternatively, if a stronger centralization of trade unions or a better coordination between them leads them to give more weight to the employment objective, perhaps because they are less exclusively concerned with insiders' interests. Analyzing the outcome of such shifts is precisely what the formal apparatus presented here should permit.

But one must realize that the position of the *AB* curve ought to depend also on firms' ability to pay and on workers' aspirations, which are related to what they judge to be economically feasible. In some cases, this consideration may be accounted for again by shifts of the *AB* curve; this is the correct solution whenever a change in economic prospects may be taken as exogenous with respect to the problem that is analyzed. But changes in firms' resources and in workers' aspirations may also be a consequence of changes in the values taken by some of the variables determined by the economic equilibrium. These variables ought to be present beside L among the arguments of the function determining W, precisely the function graphed as *AB* (for instance, labor productivity has been recognized previously as a significant argument).

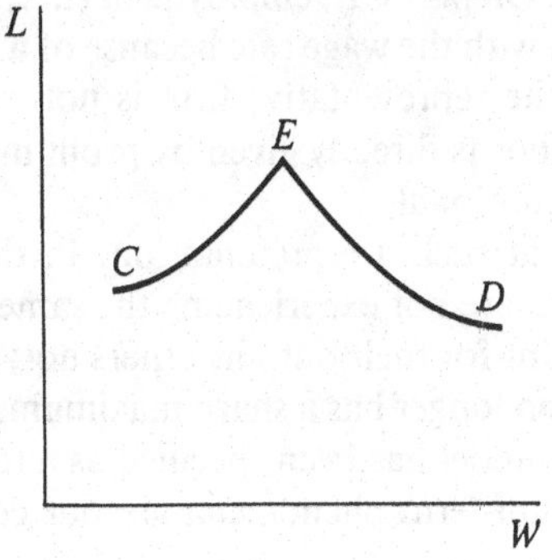

Figure 2.

Of course, this remark simply shows the inescapable limits of two-dimensional graphs. In algebraic formulas, the difficulty will easily be taken into account. But a warning was necessary. Actually, my interest here mainly concerns analysis of the relationship from W to L induced by the economic equilibrium. This is the reason why I will not pretend to be more precise at this stage on the exact form of the function that ought to represent how the bargaining process determines the real wage rate. I will introduce an hypothesis about it in Section 4.

I must, however, still point to the fact that Figure 1 differs from a graph that would confront a notional demand for labor to something akin to a supply of labor with W and L as coordinates, a kind of graph that has unfortunately reappeared in macroeconomics. I claim that my definitions of the two equilibria pictured by curves AB and CD give these curves as much autonomy as is feasible in two dimensions and more significance than exists in the alternative representations I just mentioned.

2 The economic equilibrium

Perhaps the best way to introduce what I mean by the economic equilibrium is to refer first to the fixed-price short-term Barro–Grossman equilibrium. Comparative statics analysis of this equilibrium under a fixed price level leads to Figure 2 if this level is high enough for an excess supply of labor to remain at all wage rates. Part CE corresponds to a Keynesian equilibrium with an excess supply of goods,[2] and part ED to a classical

[2] In my version of the Barro–Grossman model (Malinvaud, 1977), the labor supply increases with the wage rate and unemployment is not decreasing all along CE. But this last feature may be taken as a weakness of the model.

equilibrium with an excess demand. On part *CE*, employment (i.e., the effective demand for labor) increases with the wage rate because of a higher demand for goods; on part *ED*, the representative firm is not market-constrained, and its demand for labor is directly given by profit maximization and has been referred to as notional.

Of course, we should not stop at such a representation. In the first place, at a given wage rate, all firms are not experiencing the same situation, some facing a market constraint for their output, others not; aggregation smoothes curve *CD*, which no longer has a sharp maximum. More importantly, the Barro–Grossman model has been specified as a tool for short-term analysis, whereas medium-term phenomena are our concern here.

This change of emphasis requires that we explicitly consider the impact of the real wage on the capital stock that firms will decide to hold. I should like to show that, although the analysis has to be significantly different, curve *CD* can still be defined and is still likely to have a maximum, particularly so when "the medium run" is not too long. The assumption of an excess supply of labor will be maintained throughout.

Let us briefly consider the capital decisions of firms. For given demand and costs prospects, which of course are somewhat uncertain, firms must choose productive capacities and techniques of production. If expected real costs are low so that the profitability of production is high, firms will be induced to plan for a rather large productive capacity and to accept the risk that it remain partly idle if demand turns out to be not as good as the highest expectations now made for it; in the opposite case of a low profitability, firms will be more modest and will accept the risk of leaving a larger part of their market to foreign competitors. They will invest little, and even scrap part of their existing capacity. Similarly, if the expected real cost of labor is high relative to other costs, and particularly to the cost of capital, firms will choose labor-saving techniques, whereas they would be less eager to do so if the relative cost of labor were lower. For these two reasons, as long as the prospects concerning the demand for goods are assumed to be given, the demand for labor that will materialize later, when the capital equipment will be in operation, will be a decreasing function of the now expected real labor cost.

But a complete argument must take into account both the formation of the demand for goods and the interference of nonlabor costs. I will try to show in Section 5 that, even in a medium-run context, the demand for goods should be an increasing function of the real wage rate: I will discuss in the next section how this contributes in shaping curve *CD*. For the time being, I will just add a few words on the role of the cost of capital. This cost should be taken here as endogenous because, other things being

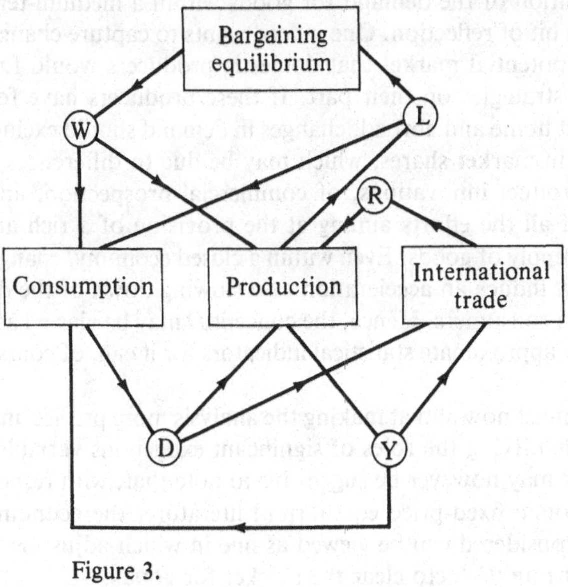

Figure 3.

equal, an increase in labor costs should lead to an increase also in the cost of capital.

A higher labor cost induces a lower productive capacity. Given the level of demand, this implies a lower surplus or a larger deficit of the foreign trade balance. This must be compensated by a larger net capital inflow from abroad. Given the interest rates on the international capital market, the domestic interest rate and the cost of capital must be higher. An increase in the capital cost reduces profitability, and hence has a depressing effect on capacity building; but it also leads to a decrease in the relative cost of labor, and hence to a lower capital–labor substitution than would otherwise have occurred. These two effects go in opposite directions as to their impact on the future demand for labor. The formulas presented in the following section, however, imply that the favorable substitution effect is unlikely to be strong enough to reverse the sign of the effect of the real wage on the demand for labor.

Figure 3 illustrates the main relations that consideration of the economic equilibrium must involve, as a consequence of the preceding remarks. Besides the real wage rate W and employment L, we find the aggregate demand for goods D determined mainly by the consumption sector, output Y determined by the production sector, and the real cost of capital R resulting mainly from the economic transactions with the rest of the world.

The exact definition of the demand for goods within a medium-term analysis requires a bit of reflection. One indeed wants to capture changes in the size of the potential market that domestic producers would face under unchanged strategies on their part. If these producers have foreign competitors at home and abroad, changes in demand should exclude progressive shifts in market shares, which may be due to differences in the intensity of product innovations, of commercial prospection, and, more generally, of all the efforts aiming at the provision of a rich and quickly available supply of goods. Even within a closed economy, changes in such efforts may induce an acceleration or a slowing down of the demand coming from consumers. Hence, the concept D may be viewed as a latent variable; but approximate statistical indicators for it can, of course, be computed.

Our discussion must now aim at making the analysis more precise and, in particular, at identifying the roles of significant exogenous variables. Before doing so, it may however be suggestive to note that, with respect to the macroeconomic fixed-price equilibrium literature, the economic equilibrium here considered can be viewed as one in which adjustments of the real interest rate de facto clear the market for goods.

3 Aggregate demand, real wage, and the demand for labor: A stylized model

Let us now consider a model exhibiting the interplay between the main relations but remaining as simple as possible for the sake of clarity. It will be written on the logarithms of the variables, denoted as lowercase letters: l, d, y, and w will, respectively, refer to the demand for labor, the demand for goods, output, and the real wage; r will be alternatively either the logarithm of the real cost of capital or the real interest rate.

This is a static equilibrium model intended for the study of a phenomenon that has important time, uncertainty, and irregularity dimensions. The variables then loosely refer to expected values as well as to medium-run averages. In the model of the production sector that I studied elsewhere (Malinvaud, 1987, 1989) and whose results I will use here, I have been more careful. I hope this will be taken as a sufficient excuse.[3]

[3] The two main approximations made in equations (1) and (2) for simplicity's sake are worth mentioning. First, the formulation pays no attention to whatever freedom firms have in fixing the prices of their goods; this is unavoidable with a model directly specified in real terms; alternatively, we may say that price-making behavior is thought of here as being part of the bargaining equilibrium. Second, equation (2) neglects indirect effects related to changes in the rate of utilization of capacity. Both these points are studied in the references quoted before, from which I drew the conclusion that the approximations were admissible for the purpose of the model discussed here.

The two following equations represent the behavior of firms concerning their capital equipment and their subsequent current operations:

$$y = d + f(w, r; z_1), \tag{1}$$

$$l = y + g(r - w; z_2). \tag{2}$$

The function f, which is decreasing in w and r, gives the effect of profitability: a high profitability induces a high average degree of satisfaction of demand and high market shares of domestic producers. The exogenous variable z_1 is meant to represent any outside influence on the relationship. I will consider it here as measuring the degree of uncertainty faced by firms as to future demand; f will then be a decreasing function of z_1.

$$f'_w < 0, \qquad f'_r < 0, \qquad f'_z < 0. \tag{3}$$

The function g characterizes the determination of the labor input-output coefficient, the inverse of labor productivity. It is written here as a function of $r - w$, the logarithm of the relative cost of capital with respect to labor, which is an admissible approximation; the function is increasing. It is also assumed to be a decreasing function of the exogenous variable z_2, which measures exogenous factors acting on labor productivity.[4] The constant-returns-to-scale assumption embodied in equation (2), as well as in equation (1), is taken as admissible for medium-term analysis.

$$g'_r > 0; \qquad g'_z < 0. \tag{4}$$

For the subsequent argument, it is useful to have some idea about the likely orders of magnitude of the derivatives of functions f and g with respect to w and r. This is easy for g'_r. In long-run analysis, this derivative would be taken as equal to the product of the elasticity of output with respect to capital and of the elasticity of substitution of capital for labor (so g'_r should be perhaps close to 0.2). But for medium-term analysis, a lower value must be preferred because of the putty-clay features of the technology. The shorter the time horizon, the lower will g'_r have to be.

The values of the negative partial derivatives f'_r and f'_w must depend very much on the point in the (w, r) plane at which they are evaluated. Very high unit costs would make production a losing activity; so, beyond a "factor-price frontier," output Y would be zero; the function f would not be defined. When (w, r) tends to this frontier from within, f must

[4] The exogenous shifts in labor productivity captured by z_2 should be understood as concerning foreign producers as well as domestic ones. An exogenous improvement in productivity at home but not abroad would be favorable to competitiveness, hence, it means both an increase in z_2 and a decrease in z_1, that is, an exogenous increase in output. The distinction should be kept in mind in the interpretation of the following comparative statics results.

tend to $-\infty$, hence, also its derivatives. On the other hand, when (w, r) is such that production is very profitable as long as it can be sold, output must be hardly sensitive to small changes of w and r; then f_r' and f_w' must be very close to zero (I have some figures about this nonlinearity of f in Malinvaud, 1987).

The formation of demand will be discussed in Section 5. But we may at this stage take it as being an increasing function of output, the real wage and autonomous demand z_3, but as a decreasing function of the real interest:

$$d = d(y, w, r; z_3), \tag{5}$$

$$1 > d_y' > 0, \qquad d_w' > 0, \qquad d_r' < 0, \qquad d_z' > 0. \tag{6}$$

The values of the derivatives of this function are also relevant; I will argue that d_w' is a decreasing function of profitability in the reference situation; $1-d_y'$ and d_w' must be considered as having lower values at longer time horizons.

Combining (1), (2), and (5) leads to a relation that explains the demand for labor as a function of factor costs and exogenous variables. Let us write this function as

$$l = m(w, r; z_1, z_2, z_3). \tag{7}$$

One easily computes the partial derivatives of this function:

$$\frac{\partial m}{\partial w} = \frac{f_w' + d_w'}{1 - d_y'} - g_r', \tag{8}$$

$$\frac{\partial m}{\partial r} = \frac{f_r' + d_r'}{1 - d_y'} + g_r', \tag{9}$$

$$\frac{\partial m}{\partial z_1} = \frac{f_z'}{1 - d_y'}, \qquad \frac{\partial m}{\partial z_2} = g_z', \qquad \frac{\partial m}{\partial z_3} = \frac{d_z'}{1 - d_y'}. \tag{10}$$

The derivatives with respect to the exogenous variables are quite natural: An exogenous increase in uncertainty (z_1) or in the factors that favorably act on labor productivity (z_2) depresses the demand for labor; but an increase in autonomous demand (z_3) stimulates it.

The roles of the real wage and interest rates are more ambiguous. When profitability is very low, that is, when factor costs are very high, the negative derivatives of function f must dominate, so that the demand for labor must be a decreasing function of both the real wage and the real interest. On the contrary, when profitability is satisfactory, the derivatives of function f are negligible: the demand effect and the substitution effect then go in opposite directions. But, at least for time horizons that are not too long, the demand effect of the real wage is likely to dominate its substitution effect; the demand for labor must then be an increasing function of the real wage rate.

We must also consider how the domestic real interest rate is determined, in relation with the international capital market. I will write this relation as

$$r = r^* + h(d-y), \qquad h' > 0, \tag{11}$$

in which r^* is the foreign real rate, an exogenous variable, and the function h is increasing. One should note that $d-y$ is not the trade deficit, but the logarithm of the ratio between demand D and output Y. This gives a little more flexibility in the definition of h, since, for instance, some imports of primary or intermediate inputs may have to be proportional to output. Considering the present international mobility of capital, one should think that the derivative h' is not very high, and we may assume that it is smaller than 1.

Combining (1) and (11) implies the existence of a relation between the capital cost and the labor cost:

$$r = s(w; z_1, r^*). \tag{12}$$

The relation makes sense only if r appears as an increasing function of r^* and w, which requires

$$1 + h'f_r' > 0. \tag{13}$$

Determination of the domestic rate r would be essentially unstable if this inequality failed to hold: An increase in the foreign rate r^*, after being transmitted to r, would entail such a fall of output and such a subsequent reaction on r that this reaction would be larger than the original increase in r^*, thus generating an explosive process. Ruling out this possibility should be seen as a restriction on the domain to which the model applies; point (w, r) should not be too close to the factor-price frontier.

The partial derivatives of the function s are

$$\frac{\partial s}{\partial w} = \frac{-h'f_w'}{1+h'f_r'}, \qquad \frac{\partial s}{\partial z_1} = \frac{-h'f_z'}{1+h'f_r'}, \qquad \frac{\partial s}{\partial r^*} = \frac{1}{1+h'f_r'}. \tag{14}$$

The domestic real interest rate is increasing with the real wage rate, with the degree of domestic business uncertainty, and with the foreign real interest rate.

Taking this relationship into account in equation (7) gives another function, this one determining the demand for labor from a single endogenous variable, the real wage rate, and from a number of exogenous variables:

$$l = n(w; z_1, z_2, z_3, r^*). \tag{15}$$

This is the function graphed as *CD* on Figure 1 and defining what I called the economic equilibrium.

The elasticity of the demand for labor with respect to the real wage rate is derived from (8), (9), and (14):

$$\frac{\partial n}{\partial w}=\frac{(1-h'd_r')f_w'}{(1+h'f_r')(1-d_y')}+\frac{d_w'}{1-d_y'}-\frac{1+h'f_w'}{1+h'f_r'}g_r'. \tag{16}$$

It is made of three terms that can be called, respectively, the profitability effect, the demand effect, and the substitution effect. The demand effect is unchanged when compared with (8). In case of a good profitability, the derivatives f_w' and f_r' are negligible and the substitution effect also is unchanged. Otherwise, it is somewhat reduced (f_w' has a larger absolute value than f_r', essentially because labor cost takes a larger share than capital cost in total cost). For the reason given earlier about equality (8), I conclude that the demand effect dominates and that the elasticity (16) is positive at low wage rates, at least when the time horizon is not too long. On the other hand, the negative profitability effect should be more important in (16) than in (8), since the numerator is multiplied by a number larger than 1 and the denominator by a number smaller than 1. This reflects the fact that a rise of the real wage induces a loss of competitiveness, and hence a rise in real interest, which further deteriorates profitability. At high wage rates, the profitability effect must dominate and the demand for labor be a decreasing function of the real wage rate. This discussion thus summarizes my arguments in support of the shape given to curve *CD* in Figure 1.

The impacts of changes in exogenous variables on the position of this curve may now be characterized by the following formulas:

$$\frac{\partial n}{\partial z_1}=\frac{f_z'[1-h'd_r'-h'g_r'(1-d_y')]}{(1-d_y')(1+h'f_r')}<0. \tag{17}$$

(In the square brackets of the numerator, the last term is much smaller than 1.)

$$\frac{\partial n}{\partial z_2}=g_z'<0, \qquad \frac{\partial n}{\partial z_3}=\frac{d_z'}{1-d_y'}>0, \tag{18}$$

$$\frac{\partial n}{\partial r^*}=\frac{\partial m}{\partial r}\cdot\frac{\partial s}{\partial r^*}. \tag{19}$$

An increase in business uncertainty or in productivity deteriorates the demand for labor (remember, however, footnote 4), but an increase in the autonomous demand for goods improves it. An increase in the foreign interest rate would be favorable to the demand for labor only if the substitution effect would dominate, which is unlikely.

4 Comparative statics properties of the full equilibrium

In order to complete the discussion, we must introduce into it the bargaining equilibrium. I suggest the following specification:

$$w = b(l, y-l, r; z_4). \tag{20}$$

The real wage resulting from bargaining is assumed to depend on the level of employment and on whatever exogenous factors act on the bargaining process (z_4). It also depends on employers' ability to pay, which is related to labor productivity and to the cost of capital. The direction of these effects is clear:

$$b_l' > 0, \quad b_y' > 0, \quad b_r' < 0, \quad b_z' > 0 \tag{21}$$

(b_l' being the derivative of function b with respect to its first argument).

Substituting (2) and (12) into (20), one derives a function that relates the real wage rate to employment and exogenous variables:

$$w = a(l; z_1, z_2, z_4, r^*). \tag{22}$$

The partial derivatives of this new function are defined by

$$\frac{\partial a}{\partial l} = b_l'[1 - b_y' g_r' - s_w'(b_r' - b_y' g_r')]^{-1} > 0. \tag{23}$$

(In the square brackets, the second term is too small to reverse the sign.)

$$\frac{\partial a}{\partial z_1} = \frac{\partial a}{\partial l} \cdot \frac{\partial s}{\partial z_1} \cdot \frac{b_r' - g_r' b_y'}{b_l'} < 0, \tag{24}$$

$$\frac{\partial a}{\partial z_2} = -\frac{\partial a}{\partial l} \cdot \frac{b_y' g_z'}{b_l'} > 0, \qquad \frac{\partial a}{\partial z_4} = \frac{\partial a}{\partial l} \cdot \frac{b_z'}{b_l'} > 0, \tag{25}$$

$$\frac{\partial a}{\partial r^*} = \frac{\partial a}{\partial l} \cdot \frac{\partial s}{\partial r^*} \cdot \frac{b_r' - g_r' b_y'}{b_l'} < 0. \tag{26}$$

This specification of the outcome of the bargaining process implies that the real wage is an increasing function of employment, but also a decreasing function of business uncertainty and the foreign real interest rate, whereas it is an increasing function of exogenous shocks to productivity or to the bargaining process in favor of labor.

At this stage, we may view the two curves *AB* and *CD* of Figure 1 as representing, respectively, the functions *a* given by (22) and *n* given by (15). We may then proceed to a qualitative discussion of the comparative statics properties that ought to follow from the equilibrium conditions embodied in these two functions. The conclusions can be supported by an algebraic discussion that will not be given here (it assumes that, if the equilibrium is in the ascending part of curve CD, the slope of this curve is there smaller than that of curve AB; this may be viewed as an innocuous stability condition).

An increase in the autonomous demand for goods (z_3) shifts upward curve CD and leaves curve AB unchanged. It is unambiguously favorable to both employment and the real wage.

An exogenous action on bargaining in favor of labor (z_4) leaves curve CD unchanged and shifts curve AB to the right. It induces an increase of the real wage. This may be favorable to employment; it will be so if the demand effect dominates in (16), which is likely to happen if profitability is good but not otherwise.

An increase in business uncertainty (z_1) shifts curve AB to the left and curve CD downward. It unambiguously decreases the real wage. Moreover the shift of the AB curve is likely to be smaller than that of the CD curve; hence, employment ought to fall also, particularly at low real wages.

An increase in productivity at home as well as abroad (z_2) shifts curve AB to the right and curve CD downward. Employment then decreases, except in the unlikely case when simultaneously the real wage would be low, the demand effect of wages would be high, and bargaining would pay great attention to labor productivity. The effect on the real wage is ambiguous; actually, its sign is the same as that of $b_y' - b_l'$: the wage rate increases when, in the bargaining process, its elasticity with respect to productivity is larger than its elasticity with respect to employment.

An increase in foreign interest rates (r^*), or, equivalently, an exogenous decrease in competitiveness, shifts curve AB to the left; the direction of the shift of curve CD is ambiguous unless the real wage is high, in which case curve CD shifts downward. This leads to a decrease of the real wage, except in the very unlikely case in which the following inequality would hold:

$$g_r'\left(1-\frac{b_y'}{b_l'}\right) > -\frac{b_r'}{b_l'} - \frac{f_r'+d_r'}{1-d_y'}. \tag{27}$$

The impact on employment is, however, quite ambiguous and depends on the exact values of many derivatives considered here. The simultaneous increase in interest rates and decrease in wage rates has a favorable substitution effect; but the latter may be dominated by the outcome of the demand effect and the profitability effect, both of which have ambiguous directions.

Can these comparative statics results bring some light for the explanation of the employment trends experienced in Europe during the last two decades? I think so. Without trying to be precise, I may argue along the following lines, which will perhaps suggest how the theoretical model of this chapter could be transposed to a more directly applicable econometric model.

The change from 1970 to 1977 can be characterized mainly by (i) the social unrest and malaise that weakened the position of employers in the wage-bargaining process (z_4 increased), (ii) the new uncertainties of the world economy (z_1 increased), and (iii) the deflationary impact of the first oil shock (z_3 decreased). Two of these changes, those of z_1 and z_3, clearly depressed the demand for labor, whereas the third one had an ambiguous effect on employment, but could not be strong enough to reverse the direction of the shift. The global effect on the real wage was weak, since it combined an upward push because of z_4 with a downward one because of z_1 and z_3. The exogenous decrease in the rate of growth of productivity, which was smaller in Europe than in the rest of the industrial world, somewhat reduced the unfavorable impact on the demand for labor, since it had a positive effect on z_2 and a negative one on z_1.

The change from 1977 to 1983 combined a strong deflation, due to the second oil shock and to the reversal of the direction of demand management policies, with a sharp rise in world real interest rates: z_3 decreased, and r^* increased. From the theoretical discussion, we may conclude that this naturally depressed both the demand for labor and the real wage rate.

The change from 1983 to 1989 can be characterized mainly by (i) an increase in world demand, the U.S. policy stance, and the decrease in the oil price dominating the depressive effect of international indebtedness; and (ii) a change of attitude of the European people, which gave more power to firms in the wage-bargaining process (z_3 increased and z_4 decreased). Starting from a situation of low business profitability, these two changes improved the demand for labor; the global effect on the real wage rate was small since z_3 and z_4 acted in opposite directions.

5 A closer look to the formation of demand

Aggregate demand was assumed to obey equation (5), the partial derivatives of function d being constrained by inequalities (6). My reasons for making this assumption come from what I believed I learned from economic theory and econometrics. Since many people have drawn about the same lessons as I did, the assumption probably appeared natural to most readers. But the facts do not seem to be yet so well established that any further examination of the issue would be worthless. I am therefore going to consider it now, paying particular attention to the medium-term perspective of this chapter and to the type of effects that has been stressed in the preceding sections. I approached the matter differently on another occasion (Malinvaud, 1986). I do not claim that either one of these two pieces makes a significant contribution to a body of literature that ought to be evaluated in full. But at least they present my own way of dealing with the problem.[5]

It is convenient here to view aggregate demand D as being the sum of four parts, an exogenous autonomous demand A that comes from government and abroad, an investment demand and two consumption demands coming, respectively, from two groups of consumers. The first group lives on accumulated wealth and receives in particular the part of profits that is distributed by firms; one may call the consumers of this group either old, or inactive, or capitalist, according to tastes. The second group lives on labor income, but takes into account its life-cycle needs; one may speak of these consumers as being young or active, or still as being the workers. Speaking of two groups of consumers obviously dramatizes the real situation; the main point is to distinguish between two types of income and two types of needs.[6] Transfer payments will be neglected here as elsewhere in this chapter.

Investment demand will be written as $YI(W,R)$, the rate of investment being a function of labor and capital costs. This is obviously a decreasing function of the cost of capital R. It will also be a decreasing function of the cost of labor W if the negative profitability effect dominates the positive substitution effect. Investment demand is assumed to be proportional to output, the accelerator phenomenon being neglected, an unavoidable consequence of the static nature of the model.

The real incomes of old consumers may be assumed to be positively related to the real interest rate R and to the cash flow of firms P:

$$P = (1 - WG - I)Y, \tag{28}$$

where G is simply the exponential of the function g of equation (2). Consumption C_1 of old consumers will then be written as[7]

[5] My treatment (Malinvaud, 1986) was limited to consumption demand. It was then rightly pointed out by A. Lindbeck in the discussion that the whole demand for goods must be considered when one wants to analyze the impact that changes in income distribution have on the macroeconomic equilibrium. The present section may thus appear as a useful complement to my previous article. Remember, however, how the demand for goods was defined at the end of Section 2: as a result of this definition, changes in market shares induced by changes in labor costs are not considered as implying changes in aggregate demand; they are taken care of by equation (1).

[6] In a previous unpublished work on the subject of this section, I worked out the overlapping generations structure corresponding to the distinction between the two groups of consumers. The mathematics looked to me as too difficult to be reproduced here, since it did not bring at the end more hindsight than the simple-minded discussion that follows.

[7] Capital gains resulting from retained earnings of the firms are neglected here. Their role was discussed in Malinvaud (1986).

$$C_1 = E(R, P), \tag{29}$$

with

$$E'_R > 0, \qquad 1 > E'_P > 0. \tag{30}$$

On the other hand, the incomes X of young consumers will be given by

$$X = WGY. \tag{31}$$

Their consumption C_2 will be given by the function

$$C_2 = H(R, X), \tag{32}$$

with

$$H'_R < 0, \qquad H'_X > 0. \tag{33}$$

(The first inequality may be disputed but plays little role in this chapter.)

An important hypothesis seems to me to follow from existing econometric knowledge and from the theoretical discussion of my previous article: even in the medium run, a shift of the income distribution from wages to profits has a negative impact on consumption, hence:

$$H'_X > E'_P. \tag{34}$$

However, the difference between these two derivatives is likely to decrease when one considers longer time horizons, because E'_P should increase, whereas, in any case, H'_X is close to 1.

Taking into account the hypotheses made previously, one can write C_1 and C_2 as functions of Y, W, and R.

$$C_1 = F(Y, W, R), \qquad C_2 = J(Y, W, R), \tag{35}$$

with

$$F'_Y = (1 - WG - I)E'_P, \qquad J'_Y = WGH'_X, \tag{36}$$

$$F'_W = -Y(G + WG'_W + I'_W)E'_P, \qquad J'_W = Y(G + WG'_W)H'_X, \tag{37}$$

$$F'_R = E'_R - Y(WG'_R + I'_R)E'_P, \qquad J'_R = H'_R + YWG'_R H'_X. \tag{38}$$

Considering aggregate demand, we may write

$$D = D(Y, W, R; A), \tag{39}$$

with

$$D'_Y = E'_P + WG(H'_X - E'_P) + I(1 - E'_P), \tag{40}$$

$$D'_W = Y(G + WG'_W)(H'_X - E'_P) + YI'_W(1 - E'_P), \tag{41}$$

$$D'_R = E'_R + H'_R + YWG'_R(H'_X - E'_P) + YI'_R(1 - E'_P). \tag{42}$$

Let us now consider, in the light of these expressions, the hypotheses made in Section 3 about the function d written on logarithms. The derivative D'_W should be positive because of (34), of the fact that the elasticity of G with respect to W has a small absolute value, and of the fact that, in I'_W, the profitability and the substitution effects go in opposite directions. However, this derivative D'_W should be all the more small as the medium run is longer and as the real wage is higher, hence, the profitability effect on investment is larger; it is even conceivable that the derivative becomes negative when profitability is low and the horizon is not short, a point made by A. Lindbeck in the discussion of my previous article.

The expression of D'_R is the sum of four terms, two of which may be taken as positive and two as negative. Assuming this derivative to be negative amounts to recognizing a dominant role to the negative effect on investment and/or to the depressing effect of a high interest rate on the consumption of young consumers. Such an assumption may look more conjectural than the one made for D'_W but one should notice that it played only a minor role in Section 3.

On the other hand, the weights respectively given to the substitution effect and the profitability effect in the demand for labor depended in Section 3 on $1-d'_y$. To know how high is the elasticity of D with respect to Y then is important. Expression (40) shows that D'_Y is increasing with E'_P (it would tend to 1 if both E'_P and H'_X would also tend to 1). We may, therefore, think that the elasticity d'_y increases with the length of the time horizon.

6 Concluding comments

This chapter has proposed a framework for the analysis of medium-run trends of employment. The main role in this framework is played by the relation showing how the demand for labor is likely to vary as a function of the real wage rate, when all the requirements of the economic equilibrium are taken into account. In particular, the reasons for the shape given to curve CD in Figure 1 had to be clarified. We have seen that at high wage rates, the demand for labor should be decreasing because of an acceleration of the substitution of capital for labor, because of a reduction in productive capacities and market shares, a reduction reinforced by the induced increase in interest rates, and, finally, because the counteracting demand effect would then be small. But at low wage rates, the relative strengths of the demand effect and the profitability effect are reversed, whereas the substitution effect remains small; the demand for labor should then be increasing with the wage rate.

The shape of the demand-for-labor schedule may appear paradoxical. Indeed, it implies that, under some exogenous conditions, the economic equilibrium is incompatible with full employment, no matter what wage bargaining is ready to accept. Most economists would not find such a statement paradoxical for short-term analysis, which has to reckon with all the rigidities of the economic system. But it is more surprising that it could still hold for medium-term analysis. In this respect, two comments may be added.

First, I have suggested that, as the time horizon extends farther into the future, the ascending part of the labor-demand schedule recedes: The substitution of capital for labor will have a larger impact because of a fuller replacement of existing capacities; the demand effect may become less significant because profits also are progressively spent. We may then say that the paradox disappears in long-run analysis.

Second, wage bargaining does not act only on the real wage rate. It also plays a role in the speed of inflation, a higher inflation rate normally resulting from more difficulties faced by labor and management when trying to reach some form of an agreement. This consideration makes the analysis of this chapter somewhat incomplete. My excuse for the lacuna is simple: I did not think I had anything significant to contribute on this occasion about the role of the price level on employment. Clearly, if the net impact of real wealth effects is viewed as favorable to aggregate demand, one ought to take this fact into account in analyzing the results of a shift to more reasonable wage bargains, which will reduce not only the real wage rate but also the inflation rate in the medium run. However, about the price level other considerations immediately come to mind; introducing them would take us too far away from the theme of this chapter.

REFERENCES

Drèze, J., and C. Bean. 1990. "European Unemployment: Lessons from a Multi-Country Econometric Study." In *Unemployment and Wage Determination in Europe,* B. Holmlund and K.-G. Löfgren, Eds. Oxford: Blackwell.

Farber, H. 1986. "The Analysis of Union Behavior." In *Handbook of Labor Economics,* O. Ashenfelter and R. Layard, Eds. Amsterdam: North-Holland.

Malinvaud, E. 1977. *The Theory of Unemployment Reconsidered.* Oxford: Blackwell.

1982. "Wages and Employment." *The Economic Journal* 92: 1–12.

1983. "Notes on Growth Theory with Imperfectly Flexible Prices." In *Modern Macroeconomic Theory,* J.-P. Fitoussi, Ed. Oxford: Blackwell, pp. 93–114.

1986. "Pure Profits as Forced Savings." *Scandinavian Journal of Economics* 88: 109–30. Also in *Growth and Distribution,* V. Bergström, S. Honkapohja, and J. Södersten, Eds. Oxford: Blackwell, pp. 137–58.

1987. "Capital productif, incertitudes et profitabilité." *Annales d'Economie et de Statistique* 5: 1–36.

1989. "Profitability and Factor Demands under Uncertainty." *De Economist* 137: 2–15.

Solow, R. 1986. "Unemployment: Getting the Questions Right." *Economica* 53 (Supplement).

CHAPTER 15

Optimal government policy in a macroeconomic model with imperfect competition and rational expectations

Jean-Pascal Benassy

1 Introduction

The purpose of this chapter is to show in a macroeconomic framework how the existence of imperfect competition on various markets changes the normative rules for government spending and taxation as compared to those that would prevail in a world of perfect competition.

There are by now already quite a number of macroeconomic models with imperfect competition in the literature.[1] It was shown notably that allocations in such imperfectly competitive equilibria had inefficiency properties quite akin to those encountered in Keynesian excess-supply models (Benassy, 1977, 1987, 1990; Negishi, 1977). It was also shown, however, that they nevertheless reacted in a Walrasian manner to monetary injections[2] (Benassy, 1987; Dixon, 1987), and that public spending policies had crowding-out effects similar to those prevailing in Walrasian models (Snower, 1983). Such similarities with the Walrasian model cease to hold, however, as soon as normative rules for budget policies are considered. In particular, as we will see in what follows, the traditional "first best" rule, which consists here in equating the marginal utilities of public and private consumption, must be amended to account for imperfect competition.

In a model such as the one we will consider, expectations specification is quite important; we will assume rational expectations – more specifically,

I wish to thank L. A. Gérard-Varet and H. Sneessens for their comments on a first version of this paper.

[1] See notably Benassy (1977, 1982, 1987, 1990), Negishi (1977, 1979), Hart (1982), Weitzman (1982, 1985), Snower (1983), D'Aspremont, Dos Santos, and Gerard-Varet (1985), Dehez (1985), Svensson (1986), Blanchard and Kiyotaki (1987), Sneessens (1987), and Silvestre (1988).

[2] Monetary injections considered here are of the traditional "helicopter" type and not open-market operations.

perfect foresight - since the model is deterministic. In a model with both price makers and price takers, this means that price takers will correctly anticipate the prices they will face in the future, whereas price makers will correctly anticipate the demand forthcoming at prices set by them. Let us turn now to a more detailed description of the model.

2 The model

We will consider here a very simple overlapping generations model with fiat money. The agents in presence are aggregate consumers and firm, and the government. The firm has a production function in period t, $y_t = F(l_t)$, the same in all periods. The representative consumers live two periods each. The consumer born in period t lives in periods t and $t+1$. He works an amount l_t in the first period, consumes amounts c_t and c'_{t+1} of the private good and benefits in the first period from the amount g_t of public spending. The utility function of this aggregate consumer is $U(c_t, c'_{t+1}, l_0 - l_t, g_t)$, where l_0 is the total amount of work available to the young consumer. As an example, we will consider in the appendix a Cobb-Douglas utility function:

$$U = \alpha_1 \log c_t + \alpha_2 \log c'_{t+1} + \alpha_3 \log(l_0 - l_t) + \alpha_4 \log g_t.$$

The consumer faces two budget constraints in periods t and $t+1$:

$$p_t c_t + m_{t+1} = w_t l_t + \pi_t - p_t \tau_t,$$

$$p_{t+1} c'_{t+1} = m_{t+1},$$

where p_t and p_{t+1} are the prices in t and $t+1$, respectively, and w_t is the wage. Profits π_t equal $p_t y_t - w_t l_t$, τ_t is the real level of taxes in t, and m_{t+1} is the quantity of money saved by the consumer when young and transferred to period $t+1$. The quantity of money at the beginning of period t is thus m_t. In what follows, we will actually collapse these constraints in an intertemporal budget constraint:

$$p_t c_t + p_{t+1} c'_{t+1} = w_t l_t + \pi_t - p_t \tau_t,$$

with, in addition, $p_{t+1} c'_{t+1} = m_{t+1}$.

The government chooses the two policy variables g_t and τ_t. Any budget deficit is financed by monetary creation, so that

$$m_{t+1} - m_t = p_t (g_t - \tau_t).$$

In what follows, we will essentially study stationary states with constant g_t and τ_t, and study optimal policies with respect to these variables.

2.1 *Walrasian equilibrium*

We will now characterize the long-run Walrasian equilibrium associated with constant policy parameters g and τ. Since the economy is stationary, we can suppress the time indexes. We will write p and p' for p_t and p_{t+1}. Accordingly, the consumer maximizes $U(c, c', l_0 - l, g)$ subject to the intertemporal budget constraint

$$pc + p'c' = wl + \pi - p\tau, \tag{1}$$

which yields the traditional Kuhn–Tucker conditions

$$\frac{\partial U}{\partial c} = \lambda p, \qquad \frac{\partial U}{\partial c'} = \lambda p', \qquad \frac{\partial U}{\partial (l_0 - l)} = \lambda w, \tag{2}$$

where λ is the consumer's marginal utility of income. Similarly, the firm maximizes profit $\pi = py - wl$ subject to the production function $y = F(l)$, which yields

$$F'(l) = \frac{w}{p}. \tag{3}$$

The goods market equilibrium equation is written

$$c + c' + g = y = F(l). \tag{4}$$

Finally, we have to write that the value of purchases by old consumers is equal to the quantity of money, that is,

$$pc' = m, \tag{5}$$

where m is the quantity of money at the beginning of the period considered. We will assume that equations (1)–(5) admit a unique solution, so that the endogenous variables p, p', w, l, y, c, c', and λ are functions of the exogenous variables m, g, and τ. It is immediately trivial to note that p, p', and w are homogeneous of degree 1 in m, whereas the other "real" variables are homogeneous of degree 0.

2.2 *First best*

An interesting "benchmark" allocation to which one may want to compare various equilibrium allocations is the "stationary first-best" one, which is obtained as a solution of the program:

$$\text{Maximize } U(c, c', l_0 - l, g) \quad \text{s.t. } c + c' + g \le F(l),$$

for which the first-order conditions yield:

$$\frac{\partial U}{\partial c}=\frac{\partial U}{\partial c'}=\frac{\partial U}{\partial g}=\frac{1}{F'(l)}\cdot\frac{\partial U}{\partial(l_0-l)}. \tag{6}$$

It is easy to see that this first-best allocation can be obtained as a competitive allocation (equations (1)–(5)), where government policy g and τ would be determined by the two supplementary equations

$$g=\tau \quad \text{and} \quad \frac{\partial U}{\partial g}=\frac{\partial U}{\partial c}, \tag{7}$$

where we see that the government would balance its budget and choose the same value of g that the consumer would have freely chosen; that is, the government would choose its level of spending so as to equate the marginal utilities of public and private consumption, which we call here the first-best rule. We will now see how this may be modified by the presence of imperfect competition, and turn first to the description of the imperfectly competitive equilibrium.

3 The imperfectly competitive equilibrium

We will now move to our imperfectly competitive framework and assume that the firm sets the price, whereas the young consumer sets the wage. We will assume to start with that they do so by taking into account isoelastic perceived demand curves. This will greatly simplify the exposition, and we will see in Section 6 that such demand curves can actually arise as objective demand curves with adequately modified (but more complex) utility and production functions.

Let us start with the firm and assume that it faces a family of perceived demand curves of the form $Ap^{-\eta}$, where $\eta>1$ is the absolute value of the elasticity of the demand curve and A is a "position" parameter. The program of the firm is thus

$$\text{Maximize } py-wl \quad \text{s.t.} \quad \begin{cases} y=F(l), \\ y\leq Ap^{-\eta}, \end{cases}$$

whose first-order conditions yield, after eliminating A:

$$F'(l)=\frac{\eta}{\eta-1}\frac{w}{p}, \tag{8}$$

which replaces equation (3). Note that when we use an objective demand curve (Section 6), the parameter η is the absolute value of the elasticity of this curve with respect to p.

Similarly, assume that the consumer faces a demand for his labor of the form $Bw^{-\epsilon}$, with $\epsilon>1$. The maximization program is

$$\text{Maximize } U(c,c',l_0-l,g) \text{ s.t. } \begin{cases} pc+p'c'=wl+\pi-p\tau, \\ l\leq Bw^{-\epsilon}, \end{cases}$$

whose first-order conditions yield, after elimination of B:

$$\frac{\partial U}{\partial c}=\lambda p, \qquad \frac{\partial U}{\partial c'}=\lambda p', \qquad \frac{\partial U}{\partial(l_0-l)}=\lambda w\left(\frac{\epsilon-1}{\epsilon}\right), \tag{9}$$

which replace equation (1). The other relations remain valid and we recall them without comment:

$$pc+p'c'=wl+\pi-p\tau, \tag{10}$$

$$c+c'+g=y=F(l), \tag{11}$$

$$pc'=m. \tag{12}$$

Equations (8)–(12) define the imperfectly competitive equilibrium, in which the variables p, p', w, l, y, c, c', and λ are functions of g, τ, m, and, of course, of the parameters ϵ and η. As an example, the appendix gives some detailed computations for the Cobb–Douglas example indicated previously.

A quick examination of these equations shows us that, whatever the values of g and τ, the stationary first-best allocation can never be attained as an imperfectly competitive equilibrium.[3] Indeed, combining equations (8) and (9), we obtain

$$F'(l)\frac{\partial U}{\partial c}=\frac{\eta}{\eta-1}\cdot\frac{\epsilon}{\epsilon-1}\frac{\partial U}{\partial(l_0-l)},$$

which clearly contradicts the conditions for first-best optimality given in equation (6). We will thus carry a "second-best" analysis, and see how imperfect competition affects the optimal government policy.

4 Welfare analysis: Balanced budget

Let us first consider the optimal government policy assuming a balanced budget, that is, $g\equiv\tau$. The government aims at maximizing the stationary utility $U(c,c',l_0-l,g)$, where all the arguments are themselves functions of g and τ. Differentiation with respect to g (remember, we assume $\tau=g$) yields:

[3] Of course, it is well known that the first-best could be obtained if, in addition to the policy tools we consider, the government were allowed to proportionately subsidize labor and goods, and to tax individually in a lump-sum manner the "excess revenues" so generated. But this would suppose an extremely high degree of interventionism that we implicitly exclude in this study.

$$\frac{\partial U}{\partial c}\cdot\frac{\partial c}{\partial g}+\frac{\partial U}{\partial c'}\cdot\frac{\partial c'}{\partial g}+\frac{\partial U}{\partial l}\cdot\frac{\partial l}{\partial g}+\frac{\partial U}{\partial g}=0. \tag{13}$$

With $g=\tau$, nominal money and thus nominal prices are stationary, so that $p'=p$, and (9) is rewritten:

$$\frac{\partial U}{\partial c}=\lambda p, \qquad \frac{\partial U}{\partial c'}=\lambda p, \qquad \frac{\partial U}{\partial(l_0-l)}=\lambda w\left(1-\frac{1}{\epsilon}\right). \tag{14}$$

Combining (13) and (14), we obtain immediately

$$\frac{\partial U}{\partial g}=\lambda p\left[\frac{w}{p}\left(1-\frac{1}{\epsilon}\right)\frac{\partial l}{\partial g}-\frac{\partial c}{\partial g}-\frac{\partial c'}{\partial g}\right]. \tag{15}$$

Now differentiate equation (11) with respect to g. We obtain

$$\frac{\partial c}{\partial g}+\frac{\partial c'}{\partial g}+1=F'(l)\frac{\partial l}{\partial g}. \tag{16}$$

Combining (8), (15), and (16), we finally obtain the formula

$$\frac{\partial U}{\partial g}=\lambda p\left[1-\left(\frac{\epsilon+\eta-1}{\epsilon\eta}\right)F'(l)\frac{\partial l}{\partial g}\right], \tag{17}$$

where again $\partial l/\partial g$ must be understood as a "balanced budget multiplier," that is, $\partial l/\partial g+\partial l/\partial\tau$. The Cobb-Douglas computations in the appendix show an example where this multiplier is strictly positive, in competitive and imperfectly competitive frameworks as well.

In order to discuss this formula, let us first note that if the consumer were to choose the level of g, he would choose a level such that $\partial U/\partial g=\lambda p$, that is, he would equate the marginal utilities of private and public consumption, since both have the same price p. What formula (17) thus tells us is that, if $\partial l/\partial g>0$, government spending (and taxes) will be pushed beyond the point that would be freely chosen by the consumer as soon as either ϵ or η is short of infinity, that is, as soon as there is some market power in goods or labor markets. We should note that in the perfectly competitive case (i.e., ϵ and η infinite), we find the traditional result that $\partial U/\partial g=\lambda p=\partial U/\partial c$.

The intuition for this striking result is quite straightforward. Market power leads to an inefficiently low level of activity. If $\partial l/\partial g$ is positive, an increase in g has two effects: (a) it directly increases utility as $\partial U/\partial g>0$, and (b) it reduces the inefficiencies associated with the too low level of activity. Therefore, the government, which takes into account effects (a) and (b), will choose a level of g different from that which would be chosen by the consumer, who only considers (a).

5 Welfare analysis: Unbalanced budget

We will now assume that g and τ are independent variables. We may thus have monetary creation or destruction, and, therefore, stationary inflation or deflation. Let us first differentiate utility $U(c, c', l_0 - l, g)$ with respect to τ:

$$\frac{\partial U}{\partial c}\cdot\frac{\partial c}{\partial \tau}+\frac{\partial U}{\partial c'}\cdot\frac{\partial c'}{\partial \tau}+\frac{\partial U}{\partial l}\cdot\frac{\partial l}{\partial \tau}=0. \tag{18}$$

Combining this with (8) and (9), and dividing by λp, we obtain

$$\frac{\partial c}{\partial \tau}+\frac{p'}{p}\frac{\partial c'}{\partial \tau}-\left(\frac{\epsilon-1}{\epsilon}\right)\left(\frac{\eta-1}{\eta}\right)F'(l)\frac{\partial l}{\partial \tau}=0. \tag{19}$$

Furthermore, differentiating (11) with respect to τ yields

$$\frac{\partial c}{\partial \tau}+\frac{\partial c'}{\partial \tau}=F'(l)\frac{\partial l}{\partial \tau}. \tag{20}$$

Subtracting (19) from (20), we obtain

$$\frac{\partial c'}{\partial \tau}\left(1-\frac{p'}{p}\right)=\left[1-\left(\frac{\epsilon-1}{\epsilon}\right)\left(\frac{\eta-1}{\eta}\right)\right]F'(l)\frac{\partial l}{\partial \tau}. \tag{21}$$

If $\partial c'/\partial \tau$ and $\partial l/\partial \tau$ are both positive (which is the case, for example, in the Cobb–Douglas case), this shows that as soon as there is market power, the government should engineer a permanent deflation, which will be obtained by running a permanent budget surplus, since

$$\left(1-\frac{p'}{p}\right)c'=\tau-g.$$

Let us now differentiate the utility function with respect to g. We obtain

$$\frac{\partial U}{\partial c}\cdot\frac{\partial c}{\partial g}+\frac{\partial U}{\partial c'}\cdot\frac{\partial c'}{\partial g}+\frac{\partial U}{\partial l}\cdot\frac{\partial l}{\partial \tau}+\frac{\partial U}{\partial g}=0. \tag{22}$$

Combining (22), (8), and (9) yields

$$\frac{\partial U}{\partial g}=\lambda p\left[\left(\frac{\epsilon-1}{\epsilon}\right)\left(\frac{\eta-1}{\eta}\right)F'(l)\frac{\partial l}{\partial g}+\frac{\partial c}{\partial g}-\frac{p'}{p}\frac{\partial c'}{\partial g}\right].$$

Differentiating (11) with respect to g yields

$$\frac{\partial c}{\partial g}+\frac{\partial c'}{\partial g}+1=F'(l)\frac{\partial l}{\partial g}.$$

Combining the last two equations, we obtain

$$\frac{\partial U}{\partial g}=\lambda p\left[1-\left(\frac{\epsilon+\eta-1}{\epsilon\eta}\right)F'(l)\frac{\partial l}{\partial g}+\left(1-\frac{p'}{p}\right)\frac{\partial c'}{\partial g}\right],$$

and using the expression for $(1-p'/p)$ found in (21),

$$\frac{\partial U}{\partial g}=\lambda p\left[1-\left(\frac{\epsilon+\eta-1}{\epsilon\eta}\right)F'(l)\left(\frac{\partial l}{\partial g}-\frac{\partial c'}{\partial g}\cdot\frac{\partial l}{\partial \tau}\bigg/\frac{\partial c'}{\partial \tau}\right)\right]. \tag{23}$$

We see that the results are not as clear-cut here as in the balanced budget case. In the particular case of the Cobb–Douglas utility function, we have

$$\frac{\partial l}{\partial g}=0, \qquad \frac{\partial c'}{\partial g}=-1, \qquad \frac{\partial l}{\partial \tau}>0, \qquad \frac{\partial c'}{\partial \tau}>0,$$

and therefore

$$\frac{\partial U}{\partial g}<\lambda p=\frac{\partial U}{\partial c}.$$

6 Objective demand curves

Up to now, the argument has been conducted in the framework of an imperfectly competitive equilibrium with isoelastic subjective demand curves and representative consumers and firm. We will now show that the very same results can be obtained in a model with objective demand curves and explicitly decentralized agents. In particular, isoelastic demand curves will be obtained through adequate use of C.E.S. subutility indexes.[4]

Let us now assume there are n households, indexed by $i=1,\dots,n$, and n firms, indexed by $j=1,\dots,n$, n being a large number. Firm j produces a specific output, also indexed by j, according to the production function

$$y_j=F(l_j)=F\left[n\left(\frac{1}{n}\sum_{i=1}^{n} l_{ij}^{(\epsilon-1)/\epsilon}\right)^{\epsilon/(\epsilon-1)}\right], \tag{24}$$

where F is the same production function as in the previous sections, l_{ij} is the amount of consumer i's labor employed by firm j, and l_j is a C.E.S. index of the l_{ij}'s. Firm j chooses the price p_j of output j so as to maximize its profit.

Household i sells a specific type of labor, also indexed by i, and has a utility function

$$U_i=U(c_i,c_i',l_0-l_i,g_i), \tag{25}$$

[4] This method is used, for example in Dixit and Stiglitz (1977), Weitzman (1985), and Blanchard and Kiyotaki (1987). Quite more general formulations are found in Benassy (1987, 1991).

where U is the same utility function as in the previous sections, l_i is the amount of labor sold by consumer i, c_i, c_i', and g_i are indexes of i's consumptions, respectively equal to

$$c_i = n\left(\frac{1}{n}\sum_{j=1}^{n} c_{ij}^{(\eta-1)/\eta}\right)^{\eta/(\eta-1)}, \tag{26a}$$

$$c_i' = n\left(\frac{1}{n}\sum_{j=1}^{n} c_{ij}'^{(\eta-1)/\eta}\right)^{\eta/(\eta-1)}, \tag{26b}$$

$$g_i = n\left(\frac{1}{n}\sum_{j=1}^{n} g_{ij}^{(\eta-1)/\eta}\right)^{\eta/(\eta-1)}, \tag{26c}$$

where c_{ij} is the amount of good j consumed by consumer i in the first period of his life, and so on. We will assume that the utility function U is separable in (c_i, c_i'), $l_0 - l_i$, and g_i, and that the indifference curves in (c_i, c_i') are homothetic. Household i chooses w_i in order to maximize his utility.

Following the methodology developed in Benassy (1987, 1988, 1990), we will compute the objective demand curves as the demand arising at a fixed-price equilibrium corresponding to any set of prices and wages (and, of course, government policies).

Let us start with the old household, which arrives with a quantity of money m_i. He wants to maximize his consumption index c_i', as given by equation (26b), subject to his budget constraint:

$$\sum_{j=1}^{n} p_j c_{ij}' = m_i.$$

The solution of this program is

$$c_{ij}' = \frac{m_i}{nP}\left(\frac{p_j}{P}\right)^{-\eta}, \tag{27}$$

where P is the price index corresponding to the C.E.S. function

$$P = \left(\frac{1}{n}\sum_{j=1}^{n} p_j^{1-\eta}\right)^{1/(1-\eta)}. \tag{28}$$

Assume the government has chosen for household i a level g_i of the index of government consumption. The corresponding specific demand for each good, g_{ij}, will be that which minimizes cost subject to this value of g_i, which yields immediately

$$g_{ij} = \frac{g_i}{n}\left(\frac{p_j}{P}\right)^{-\eta}. \tag{29}$$

Consider now the young household i. His optimization program is

$$\text{Maximize } U_i(c_i, c_i', l_0 - l_i, g_i) \quad \text{s.t.}$$

$$\sum_{j=1}^{n} p_j c_{ij} + \sum_{j=1}^{n} p_j' c_{ij}' = w_i l_i + \pi_i - T_i,$$

where the right-hand side is exogenous, T_i is the nominal level of taxes, and π_i the share of profits going to household i. Given the assumptions made on U (homotheticity, separability), the solution will be such that

$$\sum_{j=1}^{n} p_j c_{ij} = \theta(P'/P)(w_i l_i + \pi_i - T_i), \tag{30}$$

where θ, the propensity to consume, is between 0 and 1, P is the price index of this period, and P' that of the next one.

Maximization of c_i under budget constraint (30) yields the individual demands c_{ij}:

$$c_{ij} = \frac{1}{nP}\left(\frac{p_j}{P}\right)^{-\eta} \theta(w_i l_i + \pi_i - T_i). \tag{31}$$

Output y_j is the sum of demands:

$$y_j = \sum_{i=1}^{n} c_{ij} + \sum_{i=1}^{n} c_{ij}' + \sum_{i=1}^{n} g_{ij},$$

which using (27), (29), and (31) yields

$$y_j = \frac{1}{nP}\left(\frac{p_j}{P}\right)^{-\eta} \left[\sum_{i=1}^{n} m_i + P\sum_{i=1}^{n} g_i + \theta \sum_{i=1}^{n} (w_i l_i + \pi_i - T_i)\right].$$

Let us now use the identity

$$\sum_{i=1}^{n} (w_i l_i + \pi_i) = \sum_{j=1}^{n} p_j y_j.$$

We obtain the following expression for y_j:

$$y_j = \frac{1}{nP}\left(\frac{p_j}{P}\right)^{-\eta} \left[\sum_{i=1}^{n} (m_i + Pg_i - \theta T_i) + \theta \sum_{j=1}^{n} p_j y_j\right]. \tag{32}$$

Premultiplying (32) by p_j and summing over j, we obtain

$$\sum_{j=1}^{n} p_j y_j = \frac{1}{1-\theta}\left[\sum_{i=1}^{n} (m_i + Pg_i - \theta T_i)\right],$$

which, plugged back into (32), yields the objective demand for good j:

$$Y_j = \frac{1}{n}\left(\frac{p_j}{P}\right)^{-\eta} \frac{1}{1-\theta}\left[\sum_{i=1}^{n} \frac{m_i + Pg_i - \theta T_i}{P}\right]. \tag{33}$$

If n is large, P and P' (and thus θ) can be taken as given by firm j, and thus the objective demand for firm j's output is isoelastic with elasticity $-\eta$.

To find the objective demand for labor i, let us first consider the optimization program of some firm j at given wages and prices:

$$\text{Maximize } p_j y_j - \sum_{i=1}^{n} w_i l_{ij} \quad \text{s.t.} \quad y_j = F(l_j),$$

where l_j is the C.E.S. index of equation (24) and the firm takes p_j, y_j, and the wages as given. The solution in l_{ij} of this program is easily found as

$$l_{ij} = \frac{1}{n}\left(\frac{w_i}{W}\right)^{-\epsilon} F^{-1}(y_j), \tag{34}$$

where W is the wage index corresponding to the C.E.S. index:

$$W = \left(\frac{1}{n}\sum_{i=1}^{n} w_i^{1-\epsilon}\right)^{1/(1-\epsilon)}. \tag{35}$$

Summing the expressions in (34) over all j's, we obtain immediately the objective demand for labor i:

$$L_i = \frac{1}{n}\left(\frac{w_i}{W}\right)^{-\epsilon} \sum_{j=1}^{n} F^{-1}(Y_j), \tag{36}$$

where the expression for Y_j is that found in (33). Again, for large n, W can be considered as exogenous by household i, and the objective demand for labor i is isoelastic with elasticity $-\epsilon$.

To obtain the "representative-agent" representation of the previous sections, it is now enough to assume full symmetry among households, that is,

$$m_i = m, \qquad g_i = g, \qquad T_i = P\tau,$$

in which case the objective demand curve for good j further simplifies as

$$Y_j = \left(\frac{p_j}{P}\right)^{-\eta} \frac{1}{1-\theta}\left(\frac{m}{P} + g - \theta\tau\right), \tag{37}$$

the objective demand for labor i still being given by equation (36).

8 Conclusions

We have seen in this chapter that the presence of imperfect competition in various markets substantially modifies the normative rules for government spending and taxation. Whereas in a competitive setting the government equates the marginal utility for public and private consumption, that is, chooses the same level that would have been freely chosen by the consumer, in an imperfectly competitive framework the government will often choose a different level of public spending and taxation than that given by the "first-best" rule seen before.

We saw in particular that in case of a balanced budget, the government would generally choose a level of spending different from that which the private sector would have chosen, in order to alleviate the inefficiences due to a too low level of activity, itself due to imperfect competition. It is interesting to remark, however, that although the allocation has inefficiency properties very akin to those of a Keynesian underemployment equilibrium, the mechanism through which this "second-best" balanced budget rule operates is fairly un-Keynesian, as it essentially works through an increase in the supply of labor and of production, that is, a supply-side effect.[5] Still other un-Keynesian effects appear in that, when spending and taxation are allowed to differ, we found that the government could be led to run a budget surplus rather than a traditional "Keynesian" deficit.

We should point out at this stage that, in order not to introduce any other distortions than those due to imperfect competition, we worked throughout with lump-sum nondistortionary taxation. Clearly distortionary taxation, which is more realistic, could introduce further effects, which should be an interesting topic for further study.

Clearly, this investigation is only a first step, but it shows that we must expect quite different normative prescriptions for imperfectly competitive as compared to perfectly competitive economies. It also shows that even in situations which at first glance might appear as characterized by a generalized excess supply and underemployment of resources, one should investigate supply-side as well as demand-side policies.

Appendix

In this appendix, we will compute explicitly a number of relevant multipliers in the case where the consumer's utility function has the particular Cobb–Douglas form:

$$U=\alpha_1 \log c+\alpha_2 \log c'+\alpha_3 \log(l_0-l)+\alpha_4 \log g.$$

In such a case, equation (9) yield

$$\frac{\alpha_1}{c}=\lambda p, \qquad \frac{\alpha_2}{c'}=\lambda p', \qquad \frac{\alpha_3}{l_0-l}=\lambda w\left(\frac{\epsilon-1}{\epsilon}\right),$$

[5] Note that spending policies may also work through other channels, for example, a change in the elasticity of total demand. This well-known mechanism is, of course, nonoperative here as private and public demand have constant and identical elasticities.

which, combined with the budget equation (10), yield the following relations, calling $\beta_3 = \epsilon\alpha_3/(\epsilon-1)$:

$$pc = \frac{\alpha_1}{\alpha_1+\alpha_2+\beta_3}(wl_0+\pi-p\tau),$$

$$p'c' = \frac{\alpha_2}{\alpha_1+\alpha_2+\beta_3}(wl_0+\pi-p\tau),$$

$$w(l_0-l) = \frac{\beta_3}{\alpha_1+\alpha_2+\beta_3}(wl_0+\pi-p\tau),$$

which, using $\pi = py - wl$, can be rewritten

$$c = \frac{\alpha_1}{\alpha_1+\alpha_2}(y-\tau), \tag{A.1}$$

$$\frac{p'c'}{p} = \frac{\alpha_2}{\alpha_1+\alpha_2}(y-\tau), \tag{A.2}$$

$$\frac{w}{p}(l_0-l) = \frac{\beta_3}{\alpha_1+\alpha_2}(y-\tau). \tag{A.3}$$

Equation (A.3) together with $y = F(l)$ and equation (8) yield

$$\frac{\eta-1}{\eta}F'(l)(l_0-l) = \frac{\beta_3}{\alpha_1+\alpha_2}[F(l)-\tau]. \tag{A.4}$$

We thus find that l is a function of τ only, and by differentiation of (A.4) that $\partial l/\partial\tau > 0$ and $\partial l/\partial g = 0$. Note that the $\partial l/\partial g$ of Section 4 is a balanced-budget one, thus equal to $\partial l/\partial g + \partial l/\partial\tau$, which is positive.

Now from (A.1), we find that c is a function of τ only, and

$$\frac{\partial c}{\partial\tau} = \frac{\alpha_1}{\alpha_1+\alpha_2}\left(\frac{\partial y}{\partial\tau}-1\right).$$

Finally, the equation $c+c'+g=y$ yields c' as

$$c'(\tau,g) = y(\tau)-c(\tau)-g,$$

so that

$$\frac{\partial c'}{\partial g} = -1, \qquad \frac{\partial c'}{\partial\tau} = \frac{\partial y}{\partial\tau} - \frac{\partial c}{\partial\tau} = \frac{\alpha_2}{\alpha_1+\alpha_2}\frac{\partial y}{\partial\tau} + \frac{\alpha_1}{\alpha_1+\alpha_2} > 0.$$

REFERENCES

Benassy, J. P. 1977. "A neoKeynesian Model of Price and Quantity Determination in Disequilibrium." In *Equilibrium and Disequilibrium in Economic Theory,* G. Schwödiauer, Ed. Boston: Reidel, pp. 511–44.

1982. *The Economics of Market Disequilibrium.* New York: Academic Press.

1987. "Imperfect Competition, Unemployment and Policy." *European Economic Review* 31: 417–26.
1988. "The Objective Demand Curve in General Equilibrium with Price Makers." *The Economic Journal* 98 (Supplement): 37–49.
1990. "Non-Walrasian Equilibria, Money and Macroeconomics." In *Handbook of Monetary Economics,* B. Friedman and F. H. Hahn, Eds. Amsterdam: North-Holland, pp. 103–69.
1991. "Microeconomic Foundations and Properties of a Macroeconomic Model with Imperfect Competition." In *Issues in Contemporary Economics, Volume 1, Markets and Welfare,* K. J. Arrow, Ed. London: Macmillan, pp. 121–38.
Blanchard, O., and N. Kiyotaki. 1987. "Monopolistic Competition and the Effects of Aggregate Demand." *American Economic Review* 77: 647–66.
D'Aspremont, C., R. Dos Santos, and L. A. Gerard-Varet. 1985. "On Monopolistic Competition and Involuntary Unemployment," CORE Discussion paper, Louvain, Belgium.
Dehez, P. 1985. "Monopolistic Equilibrium and Involuntary Unemployment." *Journal of Economic Theory* 36: 160–6.
Dixit, A. K., and J. E. Stiglitz. 1977. "Monopolistic Competition and Optimum Product Diversity." *American Economic Review* 67: 297–308.
Dixon, H. 1987. "A Simple Model of Imperfect Competition with Walrasian Features." *Economic Journal* 39: 134–60.
Hart, O. D. 1982. "A Model of Imperfect Competition with Keynesian Features." *Quarterly Journal of Economics* 97: 109–38.
Negishi, T. 1977. "Existence of an Underemployment Equilibrium." In *Equilibrium and Disequilibrium in Economic Theory,* G. Schwödiauer, Ed. Boston: Reidel, pp. 497–510.
1979. *Microeconomic Foundations of Keynesian Macroeconomics.* Amsterdam: North-Holland.
Silvestre, J. 1988. "Undominated Prices in the Three Good Model." *European Economic Review* 32: 161–78.
Sneessens, H. 1987. "Investment and the Inflation-Unemployment Trade Off in a Macroeconomic Rationing Model with Monopolistic Competition." *European Economic Review* 31: 781–815.
Snower, D. 1983. "Imperfect Competition, Unemployment and Crowding Out." *Oxford Economic Papers* 35: 569–84.
Svensson, L. E. O. 1986. "Sticky Goods Prices, Flexible Asset Prices, Monopolistic Competition and Monetary Policy." *Review of Economic Studies* 53: 385–405.
Weitzman, M. 1982. "Increasing Returns and the Foundations of Unemployment Theory." *Economic Journal* 92: 787–804.
1985. "The Simple Macroeconomics of Profit Sharing." *American Economic Review* 75: 937–52.

CHAPTER 16

Imperfect competition, rational expectations, and unemployment

Claude d'Aspremont, Rodolphe Dos Santos Ferreira, and Louis-André Gérard-Varet

1 Introduction

Different results have recently pointed out the fact that in a standard, macrotype, general equilibrium model, unemployment may occur when the labor market is competitive but there is imperfect competition in the goods markets (d'Aspremont, Dos Santos Ferreira, and Gérard-Varet, 1984, 1989a, 1989b, 1990; Dehez, 1985; Silvestre, 1988). A common feature of these papers is to consider models either "static" or "temporary," making the result dependent upon specific assumptions imposed on the price expectations behind the scene. The question arises to investigate whether similar results still hold in a "dynamic" equilibrium framework under "rational expectations."

Schultz (1989) addresses the question in a simple overlapping generations model. The economy is endowed with a sector structure, where imperfect competitive markets in each sector are described as in Hart (1982), excluding intersectoral price effects and assuming that the firms correctly disregard any income feedback effect on the aggregate demand possibly generated by their strategic choices. Schultz's (1989) central result is that in a "rational expectation equilibrium," no matter how big the fixed labor supply is, there will always be a sufficiently small but positive wage rate such that if actual wages are below the critical rate, then there is full employment in equilibrium. Thus, with a competitive labor market, there exists a full-employment stationary equilibrium at a positive wage rate, despite the imperfect competition in the goods markets. As in Hart (1982), unemployment can only be due to downwards rigidity of wages. This is the conclusion we want to question here.

We thank Birgit Grodal and Yves Younès for most valuable comments on a preliminary version. We are, of course, fully responsible for any remaining errors and imperfections.

We start in Section 2 with an overlapping generations model, where, as in Schultz (1989), firms behave noncompetitively in an economy à la Hart. It singles out how much the impossibility of "involuntary unemployment" in rational expectation equilibrium depends upon the specific structure assumed for the economy. In Sections 3 and 4, we remove this structure by allowing correctly perceived income feedback effects ("Ford effects"). We show that even though the economy has a stationary Walrasian equilibrium, it may possibly exhibit instances for which there exists under imperfect competition only an inflationary equilibrium with increasing unemployment or a noninflationary equilibrium where unemployment prevails infinitely often. Section 5 extends the results to a case of monopolistic competition with consumers spending in more than one sector, so that intersectoral price effects come into the picture.

2 A simple overlapping generations model with imperfect competition

Let us consider a simple overlapping generations model. Time goes from 0 to infinity and in each period t there are three commodities: a produced good, labor, and money. We consider first a single representative sector containing n $(n \geq 2)$ infinitely living firms, each producing output y by means of labor l according to the same production function $y = f(l)$. We assume that $f: \mathbb{R}_+ \to \mathbb{R}_+$ is twice continuously differentiable, increasing, concave, and such that $f(0) = 0$. In Section 5, we will consider the multisectoral case.

Consumers live for two periods and all behave according to the same utility function U defined on $\mathbb{R}^2_+$, depending only upon current and future consumption, homothetic, increasing, strictly quasiconcave, and such that indifference curves do not cut the axes. In each period, consumers may be workers or capitalists or both. Each young worker has one unit of labor that can be used as input by the firms. Profits of the firms are distributed among young capitalists. Old workers are retired and old capitalists have given over their shares to the young capitalists. At date $t = 0$, there is a young generation and a generation already old that possesses the sector total endowment of money $M > 0$, which will remain constant over time.

Consider a young consumer, either worker or capitalist, having one unit of income (wages or profits). Given the current money price $p > 0$, if he expects the price for the next period to be $\hat{p} > 0$, his demand for present consumption is determined by a function $H(p, \hat{p})$, which is twice differentiable and such that

H is homogeneous of degree -1.

$$\text{For any } \hat{p}>0,\ \lim_{p\to 0} H(p,\hat{p})=\infty \text{ and } \lim_{p\to\infty} H(p,\hat{p})=0. \tag{1}$$

$$\text{For any } (p,\hat{p})\gg 0,\ 0<pH(p,\hat{p})<1 \text{ and } H_p'(p,\hat{p})<0.$$

Because young consumers have identical homothetic utilities, the income distribution does not matter. On the other hand, old consumers, either workers or capitalists, only spend their money holdings. Thus, given the stock M of money, the aggregate demand for the produced goods, for a conjecture I about the current money income, is given by

$$D(p,\hat{p},I)=H(p,\hat{p})I+\frac{M}{p}. \tag{2}$$

All firms hold the same expectations for future price $\hat{p}$ as the consumers.

By using (2), the (Marshallian) elasticity of the aggregate demand, for a conjecture I, is given by

$$-\frac{pD_p'(p,\hat{p},I)}{D(p,\hat{p},I)}=\frac{-pH_p'(p,\hat{p})I+M/p}{H(p,\hat{p})I+M/p}. \tag{3}$$

Let $\theta=p/\hat{p}$ be the expected real interest factor. We have

$$\alpha(\theta)\equiv\theta H(\theta,1)=pH(p,\hat{p}),\ \text{the propensity of the young to consume,}$$

$$\eta(\theta)\equiv-\frac{\theta H_p'(\theta,1)}{H(\theta,1)}=-\frac{pH_p'(p,\hat{p})}{H(p,\hat{p})},\ \text{the elasticity of the young's demand,} \tag{4a}$$

and

$$\sigma(\theta)\equiv\left(\frac{d}{d\theta}\frac{1-\theta H(\theta,1)}{H(\theta,1)}\right)\frac{\theta}{[1-\theta H(\theta,1)]/H(\theta,1)}$$

$$=-\left(1+\frac{H_p'(\theta,1)}{H(\theta,1)^2}\right)\frac{\theta H(\theta,1)}{(1-\theta H(\theta,1))}=\frac{\eta(\theta)-\alpha(\theta)}{1-\alpha(\theta)}, \tag{4b}$$

standing for the elasticity of intertemporal substitution.

When the conjecture about I is "correct," we must have

$$I=pH(p,\hat{p})I+M,$$

that is,

$$I=\frac{M}{1-pH(p,\hat{p})}=\frac{M}{1-\alpha(\theta)}. \tag{5}$$

Thus, under the assumption that I is correctly conjectured, using (4a), (5), and (3) gives

$$-\frac{pD_p'(p,\hat{p},M/(1-\alpha(\theta)))}{D(p,\hat{p},M/(1-\alpha(\theta)))}=\frac{\alpha(\theta)\eta(\theta)+(1-\alpha(\theta))}{\alpha(\theta)+(1-\alpha(\theta))}$$
$$=\alpha(\theta)\eta(\theta)+(1-\alpha(\theta))\equiv\Delta(\theta). \qquad (6)$$

When, under (5), the conjecture about the income is correct, the elasticity of the total demand is a weighted average of two demand elasticities, the young's $\eta(\theta)$ weighted by the propensity to consume $\alpha(\theta)$, and the old's, trivially 1, weighted by the propensity to save $1-\alpha(\theta)$.

Let us assume that, at any point in time, firms take as given the money wage $w\geq 0$, hold the same expectation for future price $\hat{p}>0$ as the consumers, know the amount $L>0$ of labor available in the sector as well as the aggregate demand function D, with all having the same (correct) conjectured income I. Firms act as Cournot oligopolists and, in this section, we assume that they do not consider that their choice of an output may affect the incomes of the consumer. Alternatively, one could see the economy as organized in the spirit of Hart (1982), that is, an economy that contains a large number of identical sectors, with each worker or capitalist in a sector consuming in some other sector and consumers being uniformly distributed. This motivates the following definition (where $D^{-1}(\cdot,\hat{p},I^*)(y)$ denotes the inverse total demand function, for given $\hat{p}$ and I^*, evaluated at the quantity y, and where l^* is the equilibrium amount of labor in each firm).

Definition 1. *A symmetric temporary equilibrium at given* $(w,\hat{p})$ *is a triple* $(l^*,p^*,I^*)\gg 0$ *such that*

(i) $l^*\in \underset{l\in[0,L-(n-1)l^*]}{\operatorname{argmax}} \; D^{-1}(\cdot,\hat{p},I^*)((n-1)f(l^*)+f(l))f(l)-wl;$

(ii) $p^*=D^{-1}(\cdot,\hat{p},I^*)(nf(l^*));$

(iii) $I^*=p^*nf(l^*).$

As in previous work, this definition leaves open the way in which the wage w is fixed. It could be in a noncompetitive way (as in Hart, 1982, where the wage is fixed by workers' unions) or in a competitive way. In the latter case, whenever unemployment prevails at all positive wages, the wage is fixed at zero. Our results will apply to both cases.

It is easy to see that the elasticity of total demand is at equilibrium (under correct conjecture) necessarily larger than $1/n$. Using (6) and (4b), we have

$$\Delta(\theta)=\begin{cases}1+\alpha(\theta)[1-\alpha(\theta)][\sigma(\theta)-1]\geq 1 & \text{if } \sigma(\theta)\geq 1,\\ \qquad\qquad\qquad\qquad \geq 1+\frac{\sigma(\theta)-1}{4}=\frac{3}{4}+\frac{\sigma(\theta)}{4} & \text{if } \sigma(\theta)<1,\end{cases} \qquad (7)$$

and since $\sigma(\theta)$ is positive, $\Delta(\theta)$ is lower bounded by $\frac{3}{4}$, which is larger than $1/n$ for $n \geq 2$. This observation will be used to show that in this economy, full employment is always attained when the money wage is low enough.

Theorem 1. *There exists a positive wage $\bar{w}$ such that for any sequence $(w^t, \hat{p}^t)$ with $0 \leq w^t \leq \bar{w}$ and $\hat{p}^t > 0$ at all t, every sequence of symmetric temporary equilibria (l^t, p^t, I^t) given $(w^t, \hat{p}^t)$ has full employment in each period, that is, $l^t = L/n$ for every t.*

Proof: By the first-order condition for profit maximization, any symmetric temporary equilibrium (l^t, p^t, I^t) given $(w^t, \hat{p}^t)$, which is such that $l^t < L/n$, must verify

$$p^t\left(1 - \frac{1/n}{\Delta(p^t/\hat{p}^t)}\right) = \frac{w^t}{f'(l^t)}. \tag{8}$$

By (ii) and (iii) in Definition 1, we must have (using (5))

$$p^t = \frac{1}{1-\alpha(p^t/\hat{p}^t)} \frac{M}{nf(l^t)} > \frac{M}{nf(L/n)}. \tag{9}$$

Using (7), (8), (9), and the concavity of f, we get $(n \geq 2)$

$$w^t = p^t\left(1 - \frac{1/n}{\Delta(p^t/\hat{p}^t)}\right) f'(l^t) > \frac{f'(L/n)}{f(L/n)} \frac{M}{n} \frac{3n-4}{3n} \equiv \bar{w} > 0. \tag{10}$$

Thus, taking $\bar{w}$ as given by (10), we cannot have both $w^t \leq \bar{w}$ for all t and $l^t < L/n$ at some t. This gives the result. □

This result strengthens Schultz's (1989) conclusion since it holds whether price expectations are fulfilled or not. The crucial point is that the marginal revenue $p[1 - 1/(n\Delta(p/\hat{p}))]$ remains positive whatever may be the value of p, once producers' conjectures on I are correct. Since $\Delta(p/\hat{p})$ is a weighted average of the young and old consumers' demand elasticities (see (6)) and as the former may be a priori arbitrarily small, the result is, in particular, obtained because the latter is always equal to 1. But this fact arises here because consumers buy in only one representative sector. The same conclusion can be reached with several sectors when the consumers have a rigid spending structure eliminating all price cross-effects, as in d'Aspremont et al. (1989a). However, as soon as individuals consume goods produced in more than one sector and have utility functions with elasticity of intersectoral substitution less than 1, the elasticity of the old consumers' demand will also be less than 1, suggesting that Theorem 1 no longer holds without further assumptions.

Looking for the consequences of intersectoral complementarity is a natural step in the present investigation. However, we start showing in the next section that once firms rightly take account of all income feedback effects, unemployment may arise, for any wage sequence, in a dynamic equilibrium under perfect foresight, even when consumers devote their income to the consumption of only one good.

3 Ford effects and the possibility of inflationary equilibria with increasing unemployment

Allowing for all income feedback effects (the so-called Ford effects) leads, in a one-sector economy, to a correctly conjectured demand function, which, using (2) and (5), is

$$\tilde{D}(p,\hat{p})=\frac{1}{1-pH(p,\hat{p})}\frac{M}{p}. \tag{11}$$

The corresponding Marshallian elasticity is (using (4))

$$\begin{aligned}-\frac{p\tilde{D}'_p(p,\hat{p})}{\tilde{D}(p,\hat{p})}&=-\frac{pH(p,\hat{p})+p^2H'_p(p,\hat{p})}{1-pH(p,\hat{p})}+1\\&=1-\frac{\alpha(\theta)(1-\eta(\theta))}{1-\alpha(\theta)}=1-\alpha(\theta)(1-\sigma(\theta))\\&=\alpha(\theta)\sigma(\theta)+(1-\alpha(\theta))\equiv\tilde{\Delta}(\theta).\end{aligned} \tag{12}$$

Comparing (12) and (6), we see that the elasticity of intertemporal substitution $\sigma(\theta)$ takes the place of the elasticity of the young consumers' demand $\eta(\theta)$ in the weighted average of elasticities. As $\eta(\theta)$ is itself a weighted average of 1 and $\sigma(\theta)$, with the same weights (see (4b)), changing weights cannot indefinitely decrease $\Delta(\theta)$. This is no longer the case with the weighted average in (12), where $1-\alpha(\theta)$ and $\sigma(\theta)$ can simultaneously be chosen small. Thus, contrary to $\Delta(\theta)$, $\tilde{\Delta}(\theta)$ may take arbitrarily low values, making clear why Theorem 1 cannot hold without further assumptions. Let us first introduce appropriate solution concepts.

Definition 2. *A temporary equilibrium with Ford effects at given* $(w,\hat{p})$ *is a vector* $(l_1^*,\dots,l_j^*,\dots,l_n^*,p^*)\gg 0$ *such that*

(i) $l_j^*\in \underset{l_j\in[0,L-\sum_{i\neq j}l_i^*]}{\operatorname{argmax}}\ \tilde{D}^{-1}(\cdot,\hat{p})\Big(\sum_{i\neq j}f(l_i^*)+f(l_j)\Big)f(l_j)-wl_j,$ $(j=1,\dots,n);$

(ii) $p^*=\tilde{D}^{-1}(\cdot,\hat{p})\Big(\sum_i f(l_i^*)\Big).$

Consider the first-order condition for profit maximization of firm j (according to (i)):

$$p^*\left(1-\frac{f(l_j^*)}{\sum_i f(l_i^*)}\frac{1}{\tilde{\Delta}(p^*/\hat{p})}\right)\geq\frac{w}{f'(l_j^*)}$$

$$\text{with an equality if } l_j^*<L-\sum_{i\neq j} l_i^*. \quad (13)$$

As the left-hand side is decreasing in l_j^* once we keep aggregate output $\sum_i f(l_i^*)$ constant, and as the right-hand side is nondecreasing, first-order conditions can be satisfied with equality only if the employment is the same for all firms. Thus, unemployment equilibria are always symmetric. Symmetry can only be broken in full-employment equilibria when labor is unequally allocated among firms. But then, either nothing is essentially lost by ignoring asymmetry (when the production function is linear) or unequal allocation of labor implies inefficiency (when the production function is strictly concave). This justifies our sticking henceforward to symmetric equilibria, denoted by an ordered pair $(l^*, p^*) \gg 0$.

Definition 3. *A symmetric perfect foresight equilibrium with Ford effects associated with a sequence* (w^t) *of nonnegative wages is a sequence* (l^t, p^t) *of symmetric temporary equilibria with Ford effects given* $(w^t, \hat{p}^t)$ *such that, for every* t, $p^{t+1}=\hat{p}^t$.

Let us also recall that if, in the economy, firms behave competitively, a stationary Walrasian equilibrium can be defined as a triple (l^*, p^*, w^*), where $l^*=L/n$, $p^*=[1/1-\alpha(1)][M/nf(l^*)]$, and $w^*=p^*f'(l^*)$. It is immediate to see the following theorem.

Theorem 2. *There exists a stationary Walrasian equilibrium with positive wage (and price).*

This is in sharp contrast with what may happen when the firms are imperfect competitors, as shown by the results in this section and in the next section.

We actually have the first observation that under imperfect competition with Ford effects, if the demand elasticity $\tilde{\Delta}(\theta)$ can only take values larger than or equal to $1/n$ (leading to nonnegative marginal revenue) when the real interest factor θ is less than 1, then any perfect foresight equilibrium is strongly inflationary, in the sense that the inflation rate is bounded away from zero. Also, excluding by assumption that the demand grow to infinity along an inflationary path, the supply must shrink to zero. More precisely, we have the following theorem.

Theorem 3. *If $\tilde{\Delta}(\theta) < 1/n$ for all $\theta \in [1, \infty[$, and if $\lim_{\theta \to 0} \alpha(\theta) < 1$, then any perfect foresight equilibrium with Ford effects, associated with any sequence of nonnegative wages, converges to zero employment and infinite price.*

Proof: For any sequence (w^t) of nonnegative wages, take any symmetric perfect foresight equilibrium with Ford effects (l^t, p^t). By the first-order condition for profit maximization, we have, for every t,

$$p^t\left(1 - \frac{1/n}{\tilde{\Delta}(p^t/\hat{p}^t)}\right) \geq \frac{w^t}{f'(l^t)} \quad \text{with an equality if } l^t < \frac{L}{n}. \tag{14}$$

This implies $\tilde{\Delta}(p^t/\hat{p}^t) \geq 1/n$, so that by assumption and by continuity of $\tilde{\Delta}$, $p^t/\hat{p}^t \equiv \theta^t \leq \underline{\theta}$ for some $\underline{\theta} < 1$ and every t. As $p^{t+1} = \hat{p}^t$, (p^t) is an increasing sequence. It is unbounded; otherwise it would be convergent, implying $\lim_{t \to \infty} \theta^t = 1 > \underline{\theta}$. As $\lim_{t \to \infty} p^t = \infty$, we get, using (5) and the equality $I^t = p^t n f(l^t)$, that $f(l^t)$, and hence l^t, tends to 0. Indeed by (1), since $\lim_{\theta \to 0} \alpha(\theta) < 1$, $\alpha(\theta)$ is bounded away from 1. To conclude, notice that if symmetry is broken for some t, it is still the case that the profit maximization condition imposes $\tilde{\Delta}(p^t/\hat{p}^t) \geq \max_j \{f(l_j^t)/\Sigma_i f(l_i^t)\} \geq 1/n$. Thus, the same argument leads to the conclusion that l_j^t tends to 0, for all j. □

In previous work, and for different contexts (d'Aspremont et al., 1984, 1989a, 1989b, 1990; Dehez, 1985; Silvestre, 1988), involuntary unemployment is obtained for small values of M/L. In the present framework, L and M are arbitrary, only constant over time. It remains that the first assumption of the theorem is increasingly difficult to satisfy as the number of firms increases. At the limit, for n arbitrarily large, it cannot be fulfilled.

It should be noticed that Theorem 3 would also apply to the case of elastic labor supply, at least if the utility function is separable in consumption and leisure. Of course, equilibria converging to zero employment might in that case avoid unemployment, labor supply decreasing along with the real wage. Yet such equilibria would still rightly be associated with a notion of involuntary underemployment (with respect to the Walrasian equilibrium employment level).

Also, the present result depends upon the assumption that firms are profit maximizers. This assumption, which is the natural one in an economy à la Hart, where all shareholders expend in other sectors, ceases to be warranted in a one-sector economy, where shareholders' purchasing power directly depends upon the price in the sector. As a matter of fact, it can be shown that if firms maximize shareholders' utility, the first-order necessary condition is always satisfied at full employment for a low enough money wage, whatever the expected real interest rate θ. This leads us back to the same type of result as Theorem 1.

However, in a multisectoral case, where all price cross-effects are included and the old consumers spend their money holdings on various produced goods, a result similar to Theorem 3 is compatible with shareholders' utility maximization. This is demonstrated in Section 5.

The quite strong result of Theorem 3 would not have any interest if its assumptions were ruling out existence of perfect foresight equilibria with Ford effects. Theorem 4 will give sufficient conditions for having such equilibria; we will then exhibit a class of examples satisfying these conditions together with the assumptions of Theorem 3. But first we need the following lemma.

Lemma 1. *Assume that* $\theta\tilde{\Delta}'(\theta)/\tilde{\Delta}(\theta) \geq -|1-\tilde{\Delta}(\theta)|$, $0<\theta<\infty$. *Given any sequence* (w^t) *of nonnegative wages, if a sequence* (l^t, p^t) *satisfies* (14) *with* $\hat{p}^t = p^{t+1}$, *for every t, together with* $l^t \leq L/n$ *and*

$$p^t = \frac{1}{1-\alpha(p^t/p^{t+1})}\frac{M}{nf(l^t)}, \tag{15}$$

then it is a symmetric perfect foresight equilibrium with Ford effects associated with (w^t).

Proof: Clearly (14) is the first-order necessary condition for profit maximization in the symmetric case (i.e., (i) in Definition 2) and, using (11), (15) corresponds to (ii) in Definition 2. Since marginal cost is nondecreasing in l, by concavity of f, (14) is sufficient for a maximum if the marginal revenue (namely, the left-hand side of (14)) is nonincreasing in l (nondecreasing in p) whenever nonnegative. Using $\tilde{D}(p^t, p^{t+1}) = nf(l^t)$, we get the following expression for the marginal revenue:

$$p^t\left[1-\frac{1}{\tilde{\Delta}(p^t/p^{t+1})}\left(1-\frac{(n-1)f(l^t)}{\tilde{D}(p^t,p^{t+1})}\right)\right].$$

Thus, by differentiating with respect to p^t, we obtain

$$\begin{aligned}
&1-\frac{1}{\tilde{\Delta}(\theta^t)}\left(1-\frac{(n-1)f(l^t)}{\tilde{D}(p^t,p^{t+1})}\right)\left(1-\frac{\tilde{\Delta}'(\theta^t)}{\tilde{\Delta}(\theta^t)}\theta^t\right)+\frac{(n-1)f(l^t)}{\tilde{D}(p^t,p^{t+1})}\\
&\geq 2\frac{(n-1)f(l^t)}{\tilde{D}(p^t,p^{t+1})}>0 \qquad \text{if } \tilde{\Delta}(\theta^t)\geq 1,\\
&\geq 2\left[1-\frac{1}{\tilde{\Delta}(\theta^t)}\left(1-\frac{(n-1)f(l^t)}{\tilde{D}(p^t,p^{t+1})}\right)\right]\geq 0 \quad \text{if } \tilde{\Delta}(\theta^t)<1. \qquad \square
\end{aligned}$$

We may now give conditions under which symmetric perfect foresight equilibria with Ford effects exist where unemployment tends *monotonically* to zero (so that full employment can be maintained at most in the first period), *whatever* may be the (nonincreasing) path of the money wages.

Theorem 4. *Assume that the production function is $f(l)=l^a$, with $0<a\le 1$. If $\tilde{\Delta}$ satisfies the assumption of Lemma 1, with $\tilde{\Delta}(1)<1/n$ and $\tilde{\Delta}(\theta)$ taking values larger than $1/n$ for some $\theta<1$, then, for any nonincreasing sequence of nonnegative wages, there exists a continuum of symmetric perfect foresight equilibria with Ford effects converging monotonically to zero employment and infinite price.*

Proof: Consider, first, the case of a nonincreasing sequence (w^t) of positive zero wages. Using (14) (as an equality) and (15), we have, with the specification of f:

$$l^t=\frac{aM}{nw^t}\left[1-\frac{1/n}{\tilde{\Delta}(\theta^t)}\right]\frac{1}{1-\alpha(\theta^t)}. \tag{16}$$

Applying (15) to t and $t-1$ gives

$$1-\alpha(\theta^{t+1})=\theta^t(1-\alpha(\theta^t))\frac{f(l^t)}{f(l^{t+1})}. \tag{17}$$

The elasticity of $\theta^t(1-\alpha(\theta^t))$ is (using (4) and (12)) given by

$$1-\frac{\alpha'(\theta^t)\theta^t}{1-\alpha(\theta^t)}=1-\frac{\alpha(\theta^t)[1-\eta(\theta^t)]}{1-\alpha(\theta^t)}=\tilde{\Delta}(\theta^t)>0, \tag{18}$$

and thus $\theta^t(1-\alpha(\theta^t))$ is increasing in θ^t. So, from (17), we get for $\theta^t<1$

$$1-\alpha(\theta^{t+1})<[1-\alpha(1)]\frac{f(l^t)}{f(l^{t+1})}. \tag{19}$$

The elasticity of the left-hand side of (17) being $\tilde{\Delta}(\theta^{t+1})-1$ (see (18)), it is decreasing in θ^{t+1} whenever $\tilde{\Delta}(\theta^{t+1})<1$. By continuity of $\tilde{\Delta}$, as $\tilde{\Delta}(1)<1/n$ and $\tilde{\Delta}(\theta)>1/n$ for some $\theta<1$, there exist $\underset{\sim}{\theta}$ and $\underline{\theta}$ satisfying $0\le\underset{\sim}{\theta}<\underline{\theta}<1$ and such that (see Figure 1)

$$\tilde{\Delta}(\underline{\theta})=\frac{1}{n} \quad\text{and}\quad \frac{1}{n}<\tilde{\Delta}(\theta)<1 \quad\text{if } \underset{\sim}{\theta}<\theta<\underline{\theta} \tag{20a}$$

and (by positivity of the wage w^0 in period 0)

$$\frac{aM}{nw^0}\left[1-\frac{1/n}{\tilde{\Delta}(\theta)}\right]\frac{1}{1-\alpha(\theta)}\le\frac{L}{n} \quad\text{if } \underset{\sim}{\theta}<\theta<\underline{\theta}. \tag{20b}$$

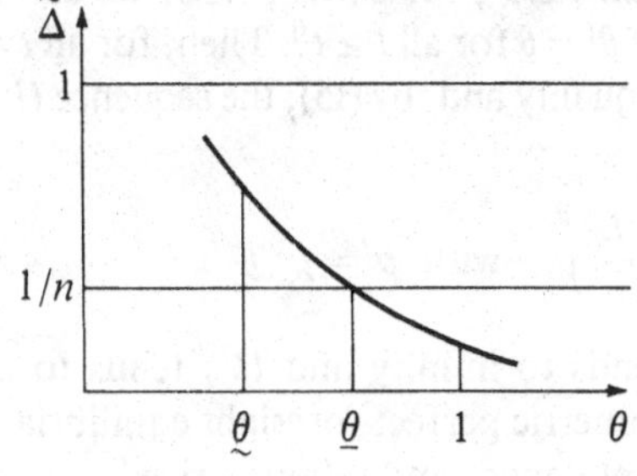

Figure 1.

Let $\omega^t \equiv w^t/w^{t+1}$; by (16) and (17) and using again the specification of f, we get

$$[1-\alpha(\theta^{t+1})]^{1-a}\left[1-\frac{1/n}{\tilde{\Delta}(\theta^{t+1})}\right]^a$$

$$=(\omega^t)^{-a}\theta^t[1-\alpha(\theta^t)]^{1-a}\left[1-\frac{1/n}{\tilde{\Delta}(\theta^t)}\right]^a. \quad (21)$$

Denote $G(\theta) \equiv [1-\alpha(\theta)]^{1-a}[1-1/n\tilde{\Delta}(\theta)]^a$. Clearly, as $\omega^t \geq 1$ for all t (the sequence of money wages is nonincreasing), the right-hand side of equation (21) belongs to the interval $]0, \sup_{\theta \in]\underset{\sim}{\theta}, \underline{\theta}[} G(\theta)[$ for any θ^t in $]\underset{\sim}{\theta}, \underline{\theta}[$ (notice that $(\omega^t)^{-a}\theta^t$ is less than 1 in this interval). Since the left-hand side of (21) takes all values in $]0, \sup_{\theta \in]\underset{\sim}{\theta}, \underline{\theta}[} G(\theta)[$ for θ^{t+1} varying from $\underset{\sim}{\theta}$ to $\underline{\theta}$ (by continuity of G and as $G(\underline{\theta})=0$, by (20a)), equation (21) always has a solution in θ^{t+1}, belonging to $]\underset{\sim}{\theta}, \underline{\theta}[$, for any θ^t in the same interval.

Thus, beginning with an arbitrary θ^0 in $]\underset{\sim}{\theta}, \underline{\theta}[$, we can always find a sequence (θ^t) of points belonging to this interval and such that equation (21) is verified for all t. Given w^0 and θ^0, l^0 is determined by (16), taking account of (20b). By (20a), $\tilde{\Delta}(\theta^t)<1$, so that $1-\alpha(\theta^t)$ is decreasing in θ^t, for all t as argued before. Hence, (19) leads to $f(l^t)>f(l^{t+1})$ and so to $l^t>l^{t+1}$. Thus, given any nonincreasing sequence (w^t), equation (21) determines (not necessarily uniquely) the sequence (θ^t) associated with any θ^0 in $]\underset{\sim}{\theta}, \underline{\theta}[$. Equation (16) then determines the sequence (l^t) of which we know that $l^0 \leq L/n$ and that it is decreasing (notice that (21) and (16) imply (17)). The sequence (p^t), which is increasing, is finally determined by (15). We know by Lemma 1 that the sequence (l^t, p^t) is an equilibrium. As (p^t) is increasing, it must be unbounded, otherwise it would converge, implying $\lim_{t\to\infty}\theta^t=1>\underset{\sim}{\theta}$, a contradiction. As α is increasing for θ in $]\underset{\sim}{\theta}, \underline{\theta}[$, $\alpha(\theta^t)$ is bounded away from 1, and equation (15) then implies that l^t tends to 0.

In the case where $w^t=0$, for all $t \geq t^0$, for some $t^0 \geq 0$, we can construct θ^t as before for $t<t^0$ and let $\theta^t=\underline{\theta}$ for all $t \geq t^0$. Then, for all $t \geq t^0$, $\tilde{\Delta}(\theta^t)=1/n$, (14) is satisfied as an equality and, by (15), the sequence (l^t, p^t) must simply satisfy, for all $t \geq t^0$,

$$n(l^t)^a = \frac{1}{1-\alpha(\underline{\theta})}\frac{M}{p^t} \leq n\left(\frac{L}{n}\right)^a, \quad \text{with } p^t = p^0\underline{\theta}^{-t}.$$

Since $\underline{\theta}<1$, the sequence (p^t) tends to infinity and (l^t) tends to zero. Again, we get a continuum of symmetric perfect foresight equilibria converging monotonically to zero employment and infinite price. □

It remains to show examples of demand functions satisfying the assumptions of Theorem 4. If the intertemporal utility function has constant elasticity σ belonging to the interval $]0, 1/n[$, straightforward calculations yield:

$$\begin{aligned} \alpha(\theta) &= \frac{1}{1+A\theta^{\sigma-1}} \quad \text{and} \\ \tilde{\Delta}(\theta) &= \frac{\sigma+A\theta^{\sigma-1}}{1+A\theta^{\sigma-1}}, \quad \text{with } 0<A<\frac{1-n\sigma}{n-1}, \end{aligned} \tag{22}$$

by assumption on the parameter A. It is immediate that $\tilde{\Delta}$ is a decreasing function, equal to $1/n$ for $\theta=\underline{\theta}\equiv[(1-n\sigma)/A(n-1)]^{1/(\sigma-1)}<1$, and always less than 1. Also

$$\begin{aligned} \frac{\tilde{\Delta}'(\theta)\theta}{\tilde{\Delta}(\theta)} &= -\frac{(1-\sigma)^2 A\theta^{\sigma-1}}{(1+A\theta^{\sigma-1})(\sigma+A\theta^{\sigma-1})} \\ &= [\tilde{\Delta}(\theta)-1]\frac{(1-\sigma)A\theta^{\sigma-1}}{\sigma+A\theta^{\sigma-1}} > \tilde{\Delta}(\theta)-1, \end{aligned}$$

so that the assumption of Lemma 1 is satisfied. Hence, the example fulfills all conditions required on $\tilde{\Delta}$ by Theorems 3 and 4.

Another example is given by the following expression for σ:

$$\sigma(\theta) = \frac{c}{c+\theta}, \quad \text{with } 0<c<\frac{1}{n-1}.$$

A straightforward computation, using (12) and (18), gives

$$\alpha(\theta) = \frac{c+\theta}{A+c+\theta} \quad \text{and} \quad \tilde{\Delta}(\theta) = \frac{A+c}{A+c+\theta}, \quad \text{with } 0<A<\frac{1}{n-1}-c, \tag{23}$$

by assumption on A. It is again seen that $\tilde{\Delta}$ is decreasing, equal to $1/n$ for $\theta=\underline{\theta}\equiv(n-1)(A+c)<1$, always less than 1, and such that

$$\frac{\tilde{\Delta}'(\theta)\theta}{\tilde{\Delta}(\theta)} = -\frac{\theta}{A+c+\theta} = \tilde{\Delta}(\theta) - 1,$$

satisfying, as for the first example, the assumption of Lemma 1.

These examples make clear the fact that unemployment in the economy arises because of unfavorable combinations of two factors: an insufficient number n of firms and a too strong intertemporal complementarity (given by weak values of σ). The more firms in the economy, the more complementarity is required to support the conclusion. It should be noticed that a third factor plays in the present context an unusual but significant role in the occurrence of unemployment: a *high* propensity to consume, giving weight to young consumers' demand.

4 On noninflationary unemployment equilibria

The conclusions resulting from Theorem 3 rely on the strong assumption that equilibrium values of the real interest factor θ are necessarily less than 1. If θ cannot be equal to 1 in equilibrium, but may take values larger than 1, then inflationary unemployment equilibria still exist (see Theorem 4) but noninflationary equilibria, possibly with full employment, are no longer excluded. Only deflationary equilibria (i.e., for every t, $\theta^t > 1$) are impossible, since the supply is upper bounded and the demand is unbounded (at a given stock of money $M > 0$), so that equilibrium prices cannot go to 0.

We will consider now equilibria such that θ takes values both larger and smaller than 1, excluding stationarity (since, by assumption, the marginal revenue will be negative for θ equal to 1). With nonstationary prices, full employment and, more generally, constant supply may still require sequences (θ^t) for which the marginal revenue is negative for some t. Theorem 5 gives conditions for which this is the case, showing that unemployment (or inefficient allocation of labor) necessarily arises infinitely often. However, allowing output (and hence demand) to fluctuate, we can get under the same conditions sequences (θ^t) such that the marginal revenue is always positive, so that efficient full employment may arise at some points in time, as illustrated by Theorem 6. We have first the following theorem.

Theorem 5. *If*

(i) $\tilde{\Delta}(1) < 1/n$ *and, for every* θ *in* $]1,\infty[$ *such that* $\tilde{\Delta}(\theta) \geq 1/n$ *and* $\tilde{\Delta}(1/\theta) \geq 1/n$, $\theta(1-\alpha(\theta)) > 1-\alpha(1/\theta)$; *and if*

(ii) $\tilde{\Delta}(\theta) \geq 1$ *implies*

$$\theta(1-\alpha(\theta)) > \sup_{\theta' \in]0,\infty[} (1-\alpha(\theta')) \quad \textit{or}$$

$$\theta(1-\alpha(\theta))<\inf_{\theta'\in]0,\infty[}(1-\alpha(\theta')),$$

then any symmetric perfect foresight equilibrium with Ford effects, for any sequence (w_t) *of nonnegative wages, has unemployment in an infinite number of periods.*

Proof: Take an equilibrium (l^t, p^t) having unemployment only in finitely many periods; then for some $\bar{t}$, full employment prevails at any $t \geq \bar{t}$, implying by the first-order condition for profit maximization that $\tilde{\Delta}(\theta^t) \geq 1/n$. With a stationary production, (15) gives for $t \geq \bar{t}$ (see (17))

$$\theta^t[1-\alpha(\theta^t)]=1-\alpha(\theta^{t+1}). \tag{24}$$

By (18), the left-hand side of this equation is increasing in θ^t. Let $\underset{\sim}{\theta}$ be the largest value of θ in $]0,1[$ such that $\tilde{\Delta}(\theta)=1$; $\underset{\sim}{\theta}=0$ if $\tilde{\Delta}(\theta)<1$ for all $\theta\in$ $]0,1[$. Also let $\tilde{\theta}$ be the smallest value of θ in $]1,\infty[$ such that $\tilde{\Delta}(\theta)=1$; $\tilde{\theta}=\infty$ if $\tilde{\Delta}(\theta)<1$ for all $\theta\in]1,\infty[$. By assumption (ii), equality (24) cannot be satisfied for $\theta^t\in]0,\underset{\sim}{\theta}]$ or $\theta^t\in]\tilde{\theta},\infty[$. As $\tilde{\Delta}(\theta)<1$ for $\theta\in]\underset{\sim}{\theta},\tilde{\theta}[$ by definition, the right-hand side of equation (24) is decreasing in θ^{t+1} whenever $\theta^{t+1}\in]\underset{\sim}{\theta},\tilde{\theta}[$ (its elasticity is equal to $\tilde{\Delta}(\theta^{t+1})-1<0$). Thus, we can define a decreasing function F such that $F(\theta^t)$ is the solution in θ^{t+1} of equation (24) that belongs to the inverval $[\underset{\sim}{\theta},\tilde{\theta}]$. The domain of F is included (possibly strictly) in $[\underset{\sim}{\theta},\tilde{\theta}]$. Clearly, the sequence (θ^t) must satisfy, for all $t\geq\bar{t}$, $\theta^{t+1}=F(\theta^t)$.

As F is decreasing, its iterated $F\circ F$ is increasing in its own domain (which may be strictly included in the domain of F). Hence,

$$\theta^{t+2}=F\circ F(\theta^t)\gtrless\theta^t$$

implies

$$\theta^{t+4}=F\circ F(\theta^{t+2})\gtrless F\circ F(\theta^t)=\theta^{t+2}.$$

By induction, we see that $\theta^{t+2}\neq\theta^t$ implies monotonicity of the subsequence $(\theta^{t+\tau})_\tau$, for τ even. Suppose that this subsequence is unbounded. Then it must be the case that $\lim_{\theta\to\infty}\theta[1-\alpha(\theta)]\leq 1$ (as $\theta[1-\alpha(\theta)]$ is increasing and equality (24) must be satisfied for all t). Thus we have that $\lim_{\theta\to\infty}[1-\alpha(\theta)]=0$ and, by l'Hospital's rule (and again by increasingness of $\theta[1-\alpha(\theta)]$):

$$\lim_{\theta\to\infty}\frac{1-\alpha(\theta)}{1/\theta}=\lim_{\theta\to\infty}\frac{\alpha'(\theta)\theta}{1/\theta}\in]0,1],$$

implying

$$\lim_{\theta\to\infty}\frac{\alpha'(\theta)\theta}{1-\alpha(\theta)}=\lim_{\theta\to\infty}[1-\tilde{\Delta}(\theta)]=1$$

(using (18)), so that $\lim_{\theta\to\infty}\tilde{\Delta}(\theta)=0$. This is inconsistent with positive production, which implies $\tilde{\Delta}(\theta)\geq 1/n$. Thus, the subsequence $(\theta^{t+\tau})_\tau$, for τ even, is bounded for any t (implying in particular that the sequence (θ^t) is bounded) and monotonic and hence converges. Suppose it converges to 0. Then, since by (9) the price $p^{t+\tau}$ is bounded away from 0, $(p^{t+\tau+1})_\tau$, for τ even, must go to infinity and either $(l^{t+\tau+1})_\tau$, for τ even, tends to 0, contradicting the assumption of full employment, or $(\alpha(\theta^{t+\tau+1}))_\tau$, for τ even, tends to 1, implying that $(\theta^{t+\tau+1})_\tau$, for τ even, tends to infinity (since $\alpha(\cdot)$ is increasing) in contradiction to the fact that (θ^t) is bounded. Therefore, the subsequence $(\theta^{t+\tau})_\tau$, for τ even, converges to some positive θ^*. It cannot be a stationary point since 1 is the only fixed point of F and by assumption (i) in the theorem, $\tilde{\Delta}(1)<1/n$ excludes positive production. Hence, θ^* is a periodic point of period 2. Equation (24) and the condition $\theta^*=F\circ F(\theta^*)$ give

$$F(\theta^*)\theta^*[1-\alpha(\theta^*)]=F(\theta^*)[1-\alpha(F(\theta^*))]=1-\alpha(\theta^*).$$

It implies (without loss of generality) $F(\theta^*)=1/\theta^*<1$. By assumption (i) in the theorem, $\tilde{\Delta}(\theta^*)<1/n$ or $\tilde{\Delta}(1/\theta^*)<1/n$, which contradicts the assumption that full employment prevails at any $t\geq\bar{t}$. □

In order to substantiate the preceding result, we will now strengthen the assumptions of Theorem 4 in two directions: first, to get only equilibria monotonically converging to zero employment and infinite price, and second, to get, in addition, at least one periodic equilibrium such that full employment prevails every two periods for a constant appropriate money wage.

Theorem 6. *Suppose that the assumptions of Theorem 4, ensuring the existence of symmetric perfect foresight equilibria with Ford effects converging monotonically to zero employment and infinite price, are satisfied. If, in addition,*

(i) $\tilde{\Delta}(\theta)<1$ *for any* $\theta>0$, *and* $\tilde{\Delta}(\theta)<1/n$ *for any* $\theta>1$,

then these are the only possible equilibria. However, if

(ii) $\lim_{\theta\to\infty}\tilde{\Delta}(\theta)>1/n$ *and, for* $0<\underline{\theta}<1$ *and* $\bar{\theta}>1/\underline{\theta}$, $\tilde{\Delta}(\theta)\leq 1/n$ *if and only if* $\theta\in[\underline{\theta},\bar{\theta}]$,

then there exist also, for some constant positive wage, some symmetric perfect foresight equilibria with Ford effects generating a cycle in prices of period 2: $\theta^t=\theta^*=1/\theta^{t+1}$ *for some* θ^* *in* $]0,\underline{\theta}[$. *Moreover, full employment prevails at most every two periods whenever*

$$\theta[1-\alpha(\theta)] \neq 1-\alpha\left(\frac{1}{\theta}\right) \quad \textit{for } \theta < \frac{1}{\bar{\theta}}. \tag{25}$$

Proof: It is clear that, under (i), we get only equilibria converging monotonically to zero employment and infinite price. Indeed, then we exclude $\theta^t > 1$ and, using (19) as in the proof of Theorem 4, we must have $l^t > l^{t+1}$, for all t, because α is increasing when $\tilde{\Delta}$ is upper bounded by 1. Also, (p^t) is unbounded and so (l^t) converges to zero.

Now, under (ii), using conditions (14) and (15) and following the argument in the proof of Theorem 4, we get from equation (21) applied to $\omega^t = 1$ (since w is constant) that, for $G(\theta) \equiv (1-\alpha(\theta))^{1-a}(1-1/n\tilde{\Delta}(\theta))^a$:

$$G(\theta^{t+1}) = \theta^t G(\theta^t). \tag{26}$$

Stationary solutions for this equation (such as 1, $\underline{\theta}$, and $\bar{\theta}$) are inadmissible since they imply, with $w^* > 0$, zero employment (by assumption, the marginal revenue is nonpositive for $\theta \in [\underline{\theta}, \bar{\theta}]$ and any positive production). However, take (θ^t) such that for all t, $\theta^{t+2} = \theta^t \neq \theta^{t+1}$, namely, a cycle of period 2. Then we have

$$\theta^{t+1}\theta^t G(\theta^t) = \theta^{t+1} G(\theta^{t+1}) = G(\theta^{t+2}) = G(\theta^t).$$

Because $G(\theta^t)$ must be positive with $w^* > 0$ (otherwise the marginal revenue would be nonpositive), we obtain $\theta^{t+1} = 1/\theta^t$. Such cycles are obtained looking at the solution θ^* in $]0, \underline{\theta}[$ of the equation

$$\Gamma(\theta) \equiv G\left(\frac{1}{\theta}\right) - \theta G(\theta) = 0. \tag{27}$$

When θ tends to zero, $\Gamma(\theta)$ tends to a positive limit or to zero by positive values. Indeed, as $\theta(1-\alpha(\theta))$ is increasing and since, by assumption, $\lim_{\theta\to\infty} \tilde{\Delta}(\theta) > 1/n$, we have

$$\begin{aligned}\lim_{\theta\to 0} \theta^{a-1}\Gamma(\theta) &= \lim_{\theta\to 0}\left\{\left(\frac{1}{\theta}\right)^{1-a} G\left(\frac{1}{\theta}\right) - \theta^a G(\theta)\right\} \\ &= \lim_{\theta\to\infty}\{\theta^{1-a}G(\theta)\} \\ &= \lim_{\theta\to\infty}\left\{[\theta(1-\alpha(\theta))]^{1-a}\left[1-\frac{1/n}{\tilde{\Delta}(\theta)}\right]^a\right\} > 0.\end{aligned}$$

As $1/\bar{\theta} < \underline{\theta}$, we also have, by assumption and by continuity of $\tilde{\Delta}$:

$$\Gamma\left(\frac{1}{\bar{\theta}}\right) = G(\bar{\theta}) - \left(\frac{1}{\bar{\theta}}\right)G\left(\frac{1}{\bar{\theta}}\right) = -\left(\frac{1}{\bar{\theta}}\right)G\left(\frac{1}{\bar{\theta}}\right) < 0.$$

By continuity of Γ, equation (27) has a solution θ^* in $]0, \underline{\theta}[$ such that $\bar{\theta} < 1/\theta^*$ (see Figure 2).

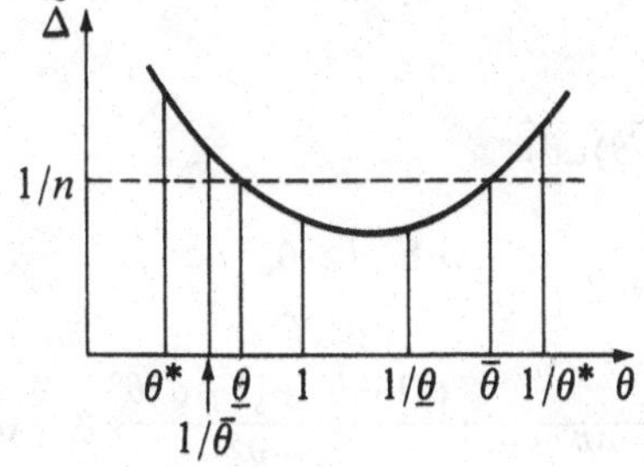

Figure 2.

We thus have, for any constant positive wage w^*, positive labor-demand levels determined by (16), say, l^* and l_*, respectively, associated with θ^* and $1/\theta^*$. Taking $w^*>0$ such that $\max\{l_*, l^*\} \leq L/n$, we get an equilibrium where full employment prevails at most every two periods. Indeed, $l^* = l_*$ is ruled out by (25) (see (17)). □

Let us finally give an example of a demand function such that unemployment prevails infinitely often in all equilibria, increases monotonically in some of them, but alternates with full employment in at least one two-period cycle. A sufficient condition for Lemma 1 is that $\sigma(\theta)$ be nondecreasing and upper bounded by 2. To see this, observe that with (12) and (18) the assumption of Lemma 1 is equivalent to

$$\alpha(\theta)\sigma'(\theta)\theta \geq -[|1-\tilde{\Delta}(\theta)|\tilde{\Delta}(\theta)+(1-\tilde{\Delta}(\theta))(\sigma(\theta)-\tilde{\Delta}(\theta))]. \quad (28)$$

Now, if $\sigma(\theta)>1$, implying $\tilde{\Delta}(\theta)>1$, then the right-hand side of (28) becomes (by (12)):

$$-(\tilde{\Delta}(\theta)-1)[2\tilde{\Delta}(\theta)-\sigma(\theta)] = -(\tilde{\Delta}(\theta)-1)[(1-\alpha(\theta))(2-\sigma(\theta))+\alpha(\theta)\sigma(\theta)] < 0,$$

since $\sigma(\theta)\leq 2$ by assumption. If $\sigma(\theta)<1$, implying $\sigma(\theta)<\tilde{\Delta}(\theta)<1$, then the right-hand side of (28) is again negative. Hence, the inequality holds in both cases when $\sigma'(\theta)\geq 0$.

The restrictions on σ are fulfilled and $\sigma(1)<1/n$ when the elasticity of substitution σ is

$$\sigma(\theta)=\frac{bc+d\theta^{\delta}}{c+\theta^{\delta}}, \quad 0<b<\frac{1}{n}<d\leq 2, \; c>\frac{d-1/n}{1/n-b}, \text{ and } \delta>0. \quad (29)$$

Notice that the examples of Section 3 can also be derived from the same function σ, with the parameter values $d=b<1/n$ (leading to (22)) and

$d=0$, $b=\delta=1$ (leading to (23)). An easy computation with (12) and (18) gives

$$\alpha(\theta)=\frac{1}{1+\theta^{-1}\exp(\int(\sigma(\theta)/\theta)\,d\theta)}$$

$$=\frac{1}{1+A(c+\theta^{\delta})^{(d-b)/\delta}\theta^{b-1}},\quad \text{with } A>0, \tag{30a}$$

and

$$\tilde{\Delta}(\theta)=1-\frac{1}{1+A(c+\theta^{\delta})^{(d-b)/\delta}\theta^{b-1}}\cdot\frac{c(1-b)+(1-d)\theta^{\delta}}{c+\theta^{\delta}}. \tag{30b}$$

Clearly, $H(\theta,1)\equiv\alpha(\theta)/\theta$ satisfies conditions (1). Also,

$$\tilde{\Delta}(1)<\frac{1}{n}\quad\text{if } A<\frac{n}{(n-1)}\frac{1}{(c+1)^{(d-b)/\delta}}\left[\frac{1}{n}-\frac{bc+d}{c+1}\right] \tag{30c}$$

and, for the given values of the parameters, $\tilde{\Delta}$ satisfies the assumptions of Theorem 4.

Take for simplicity numerical values for the parameters

$$A=0.11,\qquad b=0.02,\qquad c=4,\qquad d=1,\qquad \delta=5,\qquad n=3.$$

As σ is strictly increasing and tends to $d=1$ when θ goes to infinity, σ and hence $\tilde{\Delta}$ are always less than 1: assumption (ii) of Theorem 5 is thus trivially satisfied. It can also be checked that $\tilde{\Delta}(\theta)\geq\frac{1}{3}$ if and only if $\theta\leq\underline{\theta}=0.300$ or $\theta\geq\bar{\theta}=1.023$, with $\theta(1-\alpha(\theta))>1-\alpha(1/\theta)$ if and only if $0.335=\theta^*<\theta<1$ or $\theta>1/\theta^*=2.981$. Since $\theta^*>\underline{\theta}$, $\theta(1-\alpha(\theta))>1-\alpha(1/\theta)$ holds for $\theta>1/\underline{\theta}>1/\theta^*$, that is, for all $\theta\in]1,\infty[$ such that $\tilde{\Delta}(1/\theta)\geq 1/n$, so that assumption (i) of Theorem 5 is also satisfied. By Theorem 5, all equilibria have unemployment infinitely often. However, as $\underline{\theta}\bar{\theta}<1$, Theorem 6 does not hold.

Consider a second numerical example where A, b, and c have the same values as before and where $d=1.02$, $\delta=1$, $n=2$, and $a=1$ (linear technology). Again we have $\tilde{\Delta}(\theta)\geq\frac{1}{2}$ if and only if $\theta<\underline{\theta}'=0.927$ or $\theta>\bar{\theta}'=1.599$ with $\theta(1-\alpha(\theta))>1-\alpha(1/\theta)$ if and only if $0.719=\theta^{*\prime}<\theta<1$ or $\theta>1/\theta^{*\prime}=1.391$. Since $1/\theta^{*\prime}<\bar{\theta}'$, we get $\theta(1-\alpha(\theta))>1-\alpha(1/\theta)$ for $\theta>\bar{\theta}'>1/\theta^{*\prime}$, that is, for every $\theta\in]1,\infty[$ such that $\tilde{\Delta}(\theta)\geq 1/n$, verifying assumption (i) of Theorem 5. Because $\sigma(196)=1$ and σ is increasing, and because $196(1-\alpha(196))=21.738$, assumption (ii) is also fulfilled so that Theorem 5 applies. But in this case, since $\underline{\theta}'\bar{\theta}'>1$, we also have Theorem 6(ii). The equation $\theta[1-1/n\tilde{\Delta}(\theta)]=1-1/n\tilde{\Delta}(1/\theta)$ corresponding to (27) (with $a=1$) has two solutions $\theta^{**}=0.421$ and $1/\theta^{**}=2.373$ lying, respectively, in each one of the two admissible intervals where $\tilde{\Delta}(\theta)>1/n$. For some constant positive wage rate, full employment will alternate with unemployment.

These examples illustrate that as soon as intertemporal complementarity sufficiently decreases when the real interest factor becomes large, full employment may prevail at some periods. Still, for values of the real interest factor close to 1, complementarity may remain too large (and propensity to consume too high) for full employment to be permanently guaranteed.

5 The case of monopolistic competition

We want to consider now whether the results of the two preceding sections can be extended to the case of an economy where there are m ($m \geq 2$) sectors with one firm in each sector. Consumers who live for two periods now spend their wealth in all sectors. All consumers behave according to the same intertemporally separable utility function $U(u(c), u(\hat{c}))$ with $c \in \mathbb{R}_+^m$ and $\hat{c} \in \mathbb{R}_+^m$ standing, respectively, for the present and future consumption. As in the original model, U is homothetic, increasing, strictly quasiconcave, and such that the indifference curves do not cut the axes. All other technical assumptions are maintained. A supplementary condition is that u is a CES function, namely:

$$u(c) = \left(\sum_{i=1}^{m} c_i^{(\rho-1)/\rho} \right)^{\rho/(\rho-1)},$$

where $\rho > 0$, $\rho \neq 1$ is the intersectoral elasticity of substitution.

By two-stage maximization, consumption in each period is derived first. Present consumption is, for x units of expenditure, given by

$$c_i = \frac{1}{m}\left(\frac{p_i}{P}\right)^{-\rho} \frac{x}{P}, \tag{31}$$

with $P \equiv ((1/m)\sum_{k=1}^{m} p_k^{1-\rho})^{1/(1-\rho)}$ being the average current price. A similar expression holds for $\hat{c}_i$ given future expenditures $\hat{x}$ and the average future price $\hat{P}$. Let x/P and $\hat{x}/\hat{P}$ be the present and future real aggregate consumption. Second-stage maximization can be formulated in terms of some linear transformation of $U(x/P, \hat{x}/\hat{P})$. This gives, using (2) and (31), the aggregate demand for goods in the ith sector:

$$\begin{aligned} D^i(p_i, P, \hat{P}, I) &= \frac{1}{m}\left(\frac{p_i}{P}\right)^{-\rho}\left[H(P, \hat{P})I + \frac{M}{P}\right] \\ &= \frac{1}{m}\left(\frac{p_i}{P}\right)^{-\rho} D(P, \hat{P}, I). \end{aligned} \tag{32}$$

Since $I = \sum_{i=1}^{m} p_i D^i(p_i, P, \hat{P}, I) = PD(P, \hat{P}, I)$, incorporating the Ford effects leads to a modified aggregate demand function (using (11) and letting $\alpha(P/\hat{P}) = PH(P, \hat{P})$):

$$\tilde{D}^i(p_i, P, \hat{P}) = \frac{1}{m}\left(\frac{p_i}{P}\right)^{-\rho}\left[\frac{1}{1-\alpha(P/\hat{P})}\frac{M}{P}\right]$$
$$= \frac{1}{m}\left(\frac{p_i}{P}\right)^{-\rho}\tilde{D}(P, \hat{P}). \tag{33}$$

The corresponding price elasticity is (using (12)):

$$-\frac{p_i \tilde{D}^{i'}_{p_i}(p_i, P, \hat{P})}{\tilde{D}^i(p_i, P, \hat{P})} = \rho\left(1 - \frac{\partial P}{\partial p_i}\frac{p_i}{P}\right) + \tilde{\Delta}\left(\frac{P}{\hat{P}}\right)\frac{\partial P}{\partial p_i}\frac{p_i}{P}$$
$$= \rho\left(1 - \frac{1}{m}\left(\frac{p_i}{P}\right)^{1-\rho}\right) + \tilde{\Delta}\left(\frac{P}{\hat{P}}\right)\frac{1}{m}\left(\frac{p_i}{P}\right)^{1-\rho}$$
$$\equiv \tilde{\Delta}^i\left(\frac{p_i}{P}, \frac{P}{\hat{P}}\right). \tag{34}$$

The firms set the prices in the goods markets taking the money wage $w \geq 0$ as given. All firms use the same technology f and share with the consumers the same expectation $\hat{P} > 0$ about average future price.

Take the point of view of firm j. Given $\hat{P}$ and the vector $p_{-j} = (p_i)_{i \neq j}$ of prices set by others, the admissible strategies of j, as constrained by the amount $L > 0$ of labor available in the economy, are given by

$$\mathcal{P}(p_{-j}, \hat{P}) = \left\{p_j \in \mathbb{R}_+ : \sum_{i=1}^{m} f^{-1}(\tilde{D}^i(p_i, P, \hat{P})) \leq L\right\}. \tag{35}$$

We will use the same solution concept as the one used in d'Aspremont et al. (1990) to deal with the present version of monopolistic competition. This is as follows.

Definition 4. *A multisectoral temporary equilibrium at given* $(w, \hat{P})$ *is a vector* $(l_1^*, \ldots, l_j^*, \ldots, l_m^*, p_1^*, \ldots, p_j^*, \ldots, p_m^*) > 0$ *such that for any* $j = 1, \ldots, m$,

(i) $p_j^* \in \underset{p_j \in \mathcal{P}(p_{-j}^*, \hat{P})}{\operatorname{argmax}} \; p_j \tilde{D}^j(p_j, P^j, \hat{P}) - wf^{-1}(\tilde{D}^j(p_j, P^j, \hat{P}))$,

where $P^j \equiv \left[\frac{1}{m}\left(p_j^{1-\rho} + \sum_{k \neq j} p_k^{*1-\rho}\right)\right]^{1/(1-\rho)}$;

(ii) $l_j^* = f^{-1}(\tilde{D}^j(p_j^*, P^*, \hat{P}))$.

Consider a multisectoral temporary equilibrium with unemployment: equilibrium prices must be interior to the firms' admissible strategy sets. Take firm j. First-order conditions imply

$$\tilde{D}^j(p_j^*, P^*, \hat{P})\left(1 - \tilde{\Delta}^j\left(\frac{p_j^*}{P^*}, \frac{P^*}{\hat{P}}\right)\left[1 - \frac{w/p_j^*}{f'(f^{-1}(\tilde{D}^j(p_j^*, P^*, \hat{P})))}\right]\right) = 0. \tag{36}$$

P^* being taken as fixed and the term in square brackets being nondecreasing in p_j^*, if $\tilde{\Delta}^j$ is increasing in p_j^*, there is at most one value of p_j^*, the same for all j, which satisfies (36). This is indeed the case whenever $\rho < 1$ or $\tilde{\Delta}(P^*/\hat{P}) < \rho$ (see (34) and notice that (36) implies $\tilde{\Delta}^j \geq 1$). Thus, under that condition, unemployment equilibria are symmetric. There are clearly nonsymmetric equilibria with full employment, but then labor is inefficiently allocated at equilibrium. Thus, we again stick to symmetric temporary equilibria denoted $(l^*, p^*) \gg 0$; this motivates the following adaptation of Definition 3:

Definition 5. *A symmetric multisectoral equilibrium with perfect foresight associated with a sequence (w^t) of nonnegative wages is a sequence (l^t, p^t) of symmetric multisectoral temporary equilibria given $(w^t, \hat{P}^t)$ such that, for every t, $p^{t+1} = P^{t+1} = \hat{P}^t$.*

The existence of a stationary Walrasian equilibrium (Theorem 2) is easily obtained in the present context: m has only to be substituted to n in the argument. In order to extend the strongest result on unemployment of Theorem 3, the assumption on $\tilde{\Delta}$ must be modified. As shown in the proof of Lemma 2 that follows, first-order conditions for profit maximization require that, in any multisectoral temporary equilibrium, whether symmetric or not, the price elasticity in every sector be not less than 1, as soon as $\rho < 1$ or $\tilde{\Delta}(\theta) \geq \rho(m-1)/m$, for all θ. By (34), $\tilde{\Delta}^j(p_j/P, P/\hat{P}) \geq 1$ holds for every j (as required by first-order conditions in any multisectoral temporary equilibrium) only if $\tilde{\Delta}(P/\hat{P}) \geq m-(m-1)\rho$. Then to extend Theorem 3, one must replace the condition $\tilde{\Delta}(P/\hat{P}) < 1/n$ by the condition $\tilde{\Delta}(P/\hat{P}) < m-(m-1)\rho$. Observe first that the requirements on $\tilde{\Delta}$ cannot be fulfilled unless $\rho < m^2/(m^2-1)$. As the number of sectors increases, intersectoral substitutability must be progressively lower if we want to get unemployment in the sense of Theorem 3. On the other hand, if there is intersectoral complementarity (i.e., $\rho < 1$), increasing the number of sectors makes unemployment more plausible. A second observation is that the result does not rely on symmetry. Under the new condition on $\tilde{\Delta}$ (ruling out values of P^t/P^{t+1} larger than some $\underline{\theta} < 1$) it is the case that, in any multisectoral equilibrium with perfect foresight, the demand in any sector must go to zero with P^t going to infinity (as long as the marginal propensity to consume α is bounded away from 1). Indeed, by definition of P, if $\rho > 1$, all prices tend to infinity, implying by (33) the conclusion. If $\rho < 1$, then by (34) no price tends to zero, which by (33) again gives the conclusion.

We now turn to the extension to monopolistic competition of Theorems 4, 5, and 6. The following result, which provides a necessary and sufficient condition for the existence of a symmetric multisectoral equilibrium with perfect foresight, will take the place of Lemma 1.

Lemma 2. *Assume* $\theta\tilde{\Delta}'(\theta) \geq -(\tilde{\Delta}(\theta)-\rho)(\tilde{\Delta}(\theta)-1)$ *for all* $\theta \in]0,\infty[$, *and also that* $\tilde{\Delta}(\theta) \geq \rho(m-1)/m$ *unless* $\rho < 1$. *Then, given any sequence* (w^t) *of positive wages, any positive sequence* (l^t, p^t) *satisfies, for every* t, $l^t \leq L/m$ *and*

$$p^t\left(1-\frac{m}{(m-1)\rho+\tilde{\Delta}(p^t/p^{t+1})}\right) \geq \frac{w^t}{f'(l^t)} \tag{37}$$

(with an equality if $l^t < L/m$*), as well as*

$$p^t = \frac{1}{1-\alpha(p^t/p^{t+1})}\frac{M}{mf(l^t)}, \tag{38}$$

if and only if it is a symmetric multisectoral equilibrium with perfect foresight associated with (w^t).

Proof: By symmetry and using (33), condition (38) is equivalent to (ii) in Definition 4. For the case $l^t < L/m$ condition (37) is, under quasiconcavity of the profit function, equivalent to (i) in Definition 4 and is easily obtained with (36), (34), and symmetry. To show that the profit function is quasiconcave under convexity of the cost function, it is sufficient to prove that, whenever positive, the marginal revenue $p_j(1-1/\tilde{\Delta}^j)$ of producer j is decreasing in quantity, that is, increasing in p_j. By (34) and assumption on $\tilde{\Delta}$, we have:

$$\begin{aligned} p_j\frac{d\tilde{\Delta}^j}{dp_j} &= (\tilde{\Delta}-\rho)(1-\rho)\frac{1}{m}\left(\frac{p_j}{P}\right)^{1-\rho} \\ &\quad + \frac{\partial P}{\partial p_j}\frac{p_j}{P}\left[(\tilde{\Delta}-\rho)(\rho-1)\frac{1}{m}\left(\frac{p_j}{P}\right)^{1-\rho} + \frac{1}{m}\left(\frac{p_j}{P}\right)^{1-\rho}\tilde{\Delta}'\frac{P}{\hat{P}}\right] \\ &\geq \frac{1}{m}\left(\frac{p_j}{P}\right)^{1-\rho}(\tilde{\Delta}-\rho)\left[1-\rho+\frac{1}{m}\left(\frac{p_j}{P}\right)^{1-\rho}(\rho-\tilde{\Delta})\right] \\ &= (\tilde{\Delta}^j-\rho)(1-\tilde{\Delta}^j). \end{aligned}$$

Thus, for $\tilde{\Delta}^j > 1$,

$$\begin{aligned} p_j\frac{d[p_j(1-1/\tilde{\Delta}^j)]/dp_j}{p_j(1-1/\tilde{\Delta}^j)} &= 1+\frac{p_j(d\tilde{\Delta}^j/dp_j)}{\tilde{\Delta}^j(\tilde{\Delta}^j-1)} \\ &\geq 1+\frac{\rho-\tilde{\Delta}^j}{\tilde{\Delta}^j} = \frac{\rho}{\tilde{\Delta}^j} > 0, \end{aligned}$$

giving the quasiconcavity of the profit function.

Let us consider now the case $l' = L/m$. To prove necessity we show that in a temporary equilibrium (whether symmetric or not) it must be the case that for any producer j, profit should be nondecreasing in quantity or, equivalently, nonincreasing in price. Suppose on the contrary that, for some producer j, its profit is increasing in p_j, that is, using (34),

$$1-\frac{1}{(1/m)(p_j/P)^{1-\rho}(\tilde{\Delta}(P/\hat{P})-\rho)+\rho}<\frac{w}{p_j f'(l_j)}. \tag{39}$$

Hence, at equilibrium, p_j is constrained from above and so labor demand must be nondecreasing in p_j:

$$\begin{aligned}
&p_j\frac{\partial}{\partial p_j}\sum_{i=1}^{m} f^{-1}(\tilde{D}^i(p_i,P,\hat{P}))\\
&=\sum_{i=1}^{m}\frac{\tilde{D}^i(p_i,P,\hat{P})}{f'(f^{-1}(\tilde{D}^i(p_i,P,\hat{P})))}\left(\frac{\partial\tilde{D}^i(p_i,P,\hat{P})}{\partial P}\frac{P}{\tilde{D}^i(p_i,P,\hat{P})}\right)\left(\frac{\partial P}{\partial p_j}\frac{p_j}{P}\right)\\
&\quad+\frac{\tilde{D}^j(p_j,P,\hat{P})}{f'(f^{-1}(\tilde{D}^j(p_j,P,\hat{P})))}\left(\frac{\partial\tilde{D}^j(p_j,P,\hat{P})}{\partial p_j}\frac{p_j}{\tilde{D}^j(p_j,P,\hat{P})}\right)\\
&=\rho\left(\sum_{i=1}^{m}\frac{f(l_i)}{f'(l_i)}\right)\\
&\quad\times\left[\left(1-\frac{\tilde{\Delta}(P/\hat{P})}{\rho}\right)\frac{1}{m}\left(\frac{p_j}{P}\right)^{(1-\rho)}-\frac{f(l_j)/f'(l_j)}{\sum_{i=1}^{m}(f(l_i)/f'(l_i))}\right]\geq 0.
\end{aligned}\tag{40}$$

For this inequality to hold, we must have $\tilde{\Delta}(P/\hat{P})<\rho$.

If $\rho<1$, the left-hand side of (39) is negative for every j; thus, each p_j is constrained from above and (40) must hold for all j. By adding over all j, we get from (40)

$$\rho\left(\sum_{i=1}^{m}\frac{f(l_i)}{f'(l_i)}\right)\left(\frac{-\tilde{\Delta}(P/\hat{P})}{\rho}\right)\geq 0,$$

leading to a contradiction.

If $\rho>1$, the left-hand side of (39) is increasing in p_j, taking P as fixed; so that if the inequality (39) holds for some producer then it necessarily holds for the producer choosing the smallest price p_i (the largest l_i). But then the left-hand side of (40) is strictly upper bounded by

$$\rho\left(\sum_{i=1}^{m}\frac{f(l_i)}{f'(l_i)}\right)\left(1-\frac{\tilde{\Delta}(P/\hat{P})}{\rho}-\frac{1}{m}\right)\leq 0,$$

using the assumption $\tilde{\Delta}(\theta)\geq\rho(m-1)/m$. This gives again a contradiction to (40).

Let us now prove sufficiency. First observe that symmetry makes the left-hand side of (40) negative so that (37) with a strict inequality gives, for any j, a local constrained maximum. It remains to show that it also gives a global constrained maximum. By quasiconcavity of the profit function, such a maximum can only be reached for $p_j \leq p_i = p_k$ and any $i, k \neq j$. Recall that with f increasing and concave,

$$\frac{f(l_j)/f'(l_j)}{\sum_{i=1}^{m}(f(l_i)/f'(l_i))}$$

is increasing in l_j, hence decreasing in p_j, so that the left-hand side of (40) is, for $p_j \leq p_i = p_k$, upper bounded by

$$\rho\left(\sum_{i=1}^{m}\frac{f(l_i)}{f'(l_i)}\right)\frac{1}{m}\left[\left(1-\frac{\tilde{\Delta}(P/\hat{P})}{\rho}\right)\left(\frac{p_j}{P}\right)^{1-\rho}-1\right].$$

The term in square brackets is upper bounded by $(p_j/P)^{1-\rho}-1$, which is negative for $\rho<1$ and any $p_j<p_i=p_k$ $(i,k\neq j)$. Also, the same term is, for $\rho>1$ and $p_j>0$, strictly upper bounded by $[1-\tilde{\Delta}(P/\hat{P})/\rho]m-1$, which is nonpositive by assumption on $\tilde{\Delta}$.

Hence, in both cases, total labor demand is decreasing in p_j, so that no price below p^t (the price chosen by all other firms) belongs to the admissible strategy set $\mathcal{P}((p^t), P^{t+1})$, when (37) is satisfied for $l^t = L/m$. □

Using Lemma 2 instead of Lemma 1, and replacing $1/n$ by $m-(m-1)\rho$ as the relevant bound on $\tilde{\Delta}$, Theorems 4, 5, and 6 apply to monopolistic competition together with the restriction that ρ be less than 1 or $\tilde{\Delta}$ be lower bounded by $\rho(m-1)/m$. As a matter of fact, the transposition of the proofs is immediate when there is intersectoral substitutability - since $\rho>1$ implies $m-(m-1)\rho<1$. But the proof of Theorem 4 must be modified in the case $\rho<1$, as it relies upon the fact that $1/n<1$. Also, in this case of intersectoral complementarity, the present extension to monopolistic competition reinforces the unemployment result of Theorem 5 (see Theorem 7).

The proof of Theorem 4, which exhibits symmetric perfect foresight equilibria, where unemployment monotonically goes to zero (whatever the path of money wages), cannot be immediately transposed in the case $\rho<1$, since it relies on the property that $\tilde{\Delta}$ must take values less than 1. But from (37), taken as an equality, and from (38) we get, for $f(l)=l^a$,

$$\hat{G}(\theta^{t+1}) = (\omega^t)^{-a}\theta^t\hat{G}(\theta^t), \tag{41}$$

with

$$\hat{G}(\theta) \equiv [1-\alpha(\theta)]^{1-a}\left[1-\frac{m}{(m-1)\rho+\tilde{\Delta}(\theta)}\right]^a$$

and

$$\theta^t \equiv \frac{p^t}{p^{t+1}}, \qquad \omega^t \equiv \frac{w^t}{w^{t+1}}.$$

Now take $\underline{\theta}<1$, such that $\tilde{\Delta}(\underline{\theta})=m-(m-1)\rho$, and consider an interval $]\theta,\underline{\theta}[$, where $\tilde{\Delta}(\theta)>m-(m-1)\rho>1$. Clearly, $\hat{G}(\underline{\theta})=0$ and $\hat{G}(\theta)>0$ for $\theta\in]\theta,\underline{\theta}[$. If θ is chosen close enough to $\underline{\theta}$, then $\hat{G}$ is decreasing in the same interval. As $(\omega^t)^{-a}\theta^t<1$ by assumption on the sequence (ω^t) and because $\theta^t<\underline{\theta}<1$ in any equilibrium, $\hat{G}(\theta^{t+1})<\hat{G}(\theta^t)$, implying $\theta^{t+1}>\theta^t$. Since α is a decreasing function whenever $\tilde{\Delta}$ is larger than 1, we get, from (38) and using this inequality,

$$1-\alpha(\theta^t)<1-\alpha(\theta^{t+1})=\theta^t[1-\alpha(\theta^t)]\frac{f(l^t)}{f(l^{t+1})}<[1-\alpha(\theta^t)]\frac{f(l^t)}{f(l^{t+1})},$$

implying $l^{t+1}<l^t$ as required.

With intersectoral complementarity and assuming some intertemporal substitutability, we have the analogue of Theorem 5, for the case $\rho<1$.

Theorem 7. *If $\tilde{\Delta}(1)<m-(m-1)\rho$, and*

$$\lim_{\theta\to 0}\alpha(\theta)<1 \quad \textit{or} \quad \lim_{\theta\to 0}\tilde{\Delta}(\theta)<m-(m-1)\rho,$$

and, moreover, $\tilde{\Delta}(\theta)>1$ for any $\theta\in]0,\infty[$, then any symmetric multisectoral equilibrium with perfect foresight has unemployment in an infinite number of periods.

Proof: Any symmetric multisectoral equilibrium with perfect foresight having unemployment in only a finite number of periods must verify, for any large enough t, equation (24):

$$\theta^t[1-\alpha(\theta^t)]=1-\alpha(\theta^{t+1}).$$

The only positive stationary value of θ satisfying this equality is 1. By differentiating both sides of this equation, we get (according to (18)):

$$d\theta^t[1-\alpha(\theta^t)]\tilde{\Delta}(\theta^t)=d\theta^{t+1}[1-\alpha(\theta^{t+1})]\frac{\tilde{\Delta}(\theta^{t+1})-1}{\theta^{t+1}},$$

so that, as $\tilde{\Delta}(\theta)>1$ for any positive value of θ, the previous equation defines implicitly θ^{t+1} as an increasing function of θ^t, such that, for $\theta^{t+1}=\theta^t=1$, $d\theta^{t+1}/d\theta^t=\tilde{\Delta}(1)/[\tilde{\Delta}(1)-1]>1$. Hence, $\theta^t>1$ (respectively, $\theta^t<1$) implies $\theta^{t+1}>\theta^t$ (respectively, $\theta^{t+1}<\theta^t$). Since, by assumption on $\tilde{\Delta}(1)$ and referring to the proof of Lemma 2, no temporary equilibrium with positive employment is possible with θ in a small neighborhood of 1, any symmetric perfect foresight equilibrium with full employment must be either deflationary with prices tending to zero or inflationary with prices tending to infinity. By (33), such equilibria are obviously ruled out: Deflationary equilibria would mean unbounded production, and inflationary equilibria are incompatible with full employment, unless $\alpha(\theta^t)$ tends to 1, which is excluded by assumption. □

There are examples of intertemporal utility functions satisfying the assumptions of Theorems 3 and 4 for which all symmetric multisectoral equilibria with perfect foresight converge to zero employment and infinite price. Consider any utility function generating the following elasticity of intertemporal substitution:

$$\sigma(\theta)=1+\frac{d\theta^{\delta}}{\theta^{2\delta}-b\theta^{\delta}+c}, \tag{42}$$

with

$$0<c<\frac{b}{2}<\sqrt{c}<1, \quad d>0, \quad \text{and} \quad 0<\delta\leq(1-\rho)\sqrt{1-\frac{b^2}{4c}}.$$

This expression for σ leads (by (12) and (18)) to a marginal propensity to consume when young:

$$\alpha(\theta)=\frac{1}{1+Ae^{g(\theta)}}, \tag{43a}$$

with

$$g(\theta)\equiv\frac{2d}{\delta\sqrt{4c-b^2}}\tan^{-1}\left(\frac{2\theta^{\delta}-b}{\sqrt{4c-b^2}}\right) \quad \text{and} \quad 0<A\leq\exp(-\lim_{\theta\to\infty}g(\theta)),$$

and to an elasticity of aggregate demand:

$$\tilde{\Delta}(\theta)=1+\frac{1}{1+Ae^{g(\theta)}}\frac{d\theta^{\delta}}{\theta^{2\delta}-b\theta^{\delta}+c}. \tag{43b}$$

A standard computation gives

$$\tilde{\Delta}'(\theta)\theta=-\frac{d\theta^{\delta}[(1+Ae^{g(\theta)})\delta(\theta^{2\delta}-c)+Ae^{g(\theta)}d\theta^{\delta}]}{(1+Ae^{g(\theta)})^2(\theta^{2\delta}-b\theta^{\delta}+c)^2}, \tag{44}$$

not less than

$$-(\tilde{\Delta}(\theta)-1)(\tilde{\Delta}(\theta)-\rho)=-\frac{d\theta^{\delta}[(1+Ae^{g(\theta)})(1-\rho)(\theta^{2\delta}-b\theta^{\delta}+c)-d\theta^{\delta}]}{(1+Ae^{g(\theta)})^2(\theta^{2\delta}-b\theta^{\delta}+c)^2},$$

as $\delta(\theta^{2\delta}-c)\leq(1-\rho)(\theta^{2\delta}-b\theta^{\delta}+c)$ and $Ae^{g(\theta)}\leq1$, by assumption on the relevant parameter values, so that the condition of Lemma 2 is satisfied. Also, as g is bounded, α is bounded away from 0 and 1, and the revised Theorem 3 applies if we assume

$$d<(1+Ae^{g(1)})(1-b+c)(m-1)(1-\rho),$$

entailing that $\tilde{\Delta}(1)<m-(m-1)\rho$. Notice that $\tilde{\Delta}$ is decreasing for $\theta>1$ (by (44)), as $c<1$. In order to apply the revised Theorem 4, one must check that $\tilde{\Delta}$ takes values larger than $m-(m-1)\rho$ for some $\theta<1$, say, for $\theta=(b/2)^{1/\delta}$. By (43) this is indeed the case if

$$d>(1+A)\left[\frac{4c-b^2}{2b}\right](m-1)(1-\rho).$$

Observe that this inequality does not contradict the preceding restriction on d, as $g(1)>0$, and $1-b+c>(4c-b^2)/2b$ (because $b>2c$).

To conclude this discussion, let us go back to the question of firms' objectives already mentioned in Section 3. It was observed in that section that maximizing profits conforms to shareholders' interests only in an economy à la Hart, where shareholders buy the goods in any other sector. We could also have considered such an economy in the present context. We can apply the argument to an economy with $m+1$ sectors, where consumers are uniformly distributed among sectors as workers or capitalists and buy goods in the m sectors in which they are not income earners; one only has to substitute the elasticity Δ, as defined in (6), to the elasticity $\tilde{\Delta}$ of aggregate demands, which takes account of Ford effects. We know by (7) that Δ cannot be less than $\frac{3}{4}$. But this is no obstacle to apply Theorem 3 or Theorem 7, leading to involuntary unemployment, as soon as the elasticity of intersectoral substitution ρ is less than 1.

We may as well consider that the firms maximize the shareholders' utility. Assuming that the utility function U is homogeneous of degree 1, aggregation of shareholders' utilities becomes straightforward, leading to producer j's objective function:

$$\Phi(p_j, p_{-j}, \hat{P}) \equiv U\left(H(P,\hat{P}), \frac{1-PH(P,\hat{P})}{\hat{P}}\right)\Pi_j,$$

where Π_j is producer j's profits. Now the derivative of this function with respect to p_j is

$$\Phi'_{p_j} = U\frac{\partial \Pi_j}{\partial p_j} + \frac{\Pi_j}{p_j}\frac{\partial P}{\partial p_j}\frac{p_j}{P}\left[U'_1 H'_P P - U'_2 \frac{P}{\hat{P}}(H + H'_P P)\right].$$

By homogeneity of degree 1 of U and the first-order condition of maximization of U, we have $U = (U'_1/P)PH + (U'_2/\hat{P})(1-PH) = U'_1/P = U'_2/\hat{P}$, so that

$$\begin{aligned}\frac{1}{U}\Phi'_{p_j} &= \frac{\partial \Pi_j}{\partial p_j} - \frac{\Pi_j}{p_j}\frac{1}{m}\left(\frac{p_j}{P}\right)^{1-\rho}\alpha \\ &= \tilde{D}^j\left\{1 - \tilde{\Delta}^j\left[1 - \frac{w/p_j}{f' \circ f^{-1} \circ \tilde{D}^j}\right]\right. \\ &\quad \left. - \frac{1}{m}\left(\frac{p_j}{P}\right)^{1-\rho}\alpha\left[1 - \frac{w/p_j}{f' \circ f^{-1} \circ \tilde{D}^j}\frac{f' \circ f^{-1} \circ \tilde{D}^j}{\tilde{D}^j} f^{-1} \circ \tilde{D}^j\right]\right\},\end{aligned}$$

using the expression for $\partial \Pi_j/\partial p_j$ in the left-hand side of (36) and the definition of Π_j as given in condition (i) of Definition 4. Letting a be the elasticity of the production function, we finally get, using (34):

$$\frac{p_j}{U\tilde{D}^j}\Phi'_{p_j} = p_j\left[1-\tilde{\Delta}^j-\frac{1}{m}\left(\frac{p_j}{P}\right)^{1-\rho}\alpha\right] + \frac{w}{f'\circ f^{-1}\circ\tilde{D}^j}\left[\tilde{\Delta}^j+\frac{1}{m}\left(\frac{p_j}{P}\right)^{1-\rho}\alpha a\circ f^{-1}\circ\tilde{D}^j\right]$$

$$= p_j\left[1-\rho-\frac{1}{m}\left(\frac{p_j}{P}\right)^{1-\rho}(\alpha+\tilde{\Delta}-\rho)\right] + \frac{w}{f'\circ f^{-1}\circ\tilde{D}^j}\left[\rho+\frac{1}{m}\left(\frac{p_j}{P}\right)^{1-\rho}(\alpha a\circ f^{-1}\circ\tilde{D}^j+\tilde{\Delta}-\rho)\right]. \quad (45)$$

Now, the first term

$$p_j\left[1-\rho-\frac{1}{m}\left(\frac{p_j}{P}\right)^{1-\rho}(\alpha+\tilde{\Delta}-\rho)\right] = p_j\left[(1-\rho)\left(1-\frac{1}{m}\left(\frac{p_j}{P}\right)^{1-\rho}\right)-\alpha\sigma\frac{1}{m}\left(\frac{p_j}{P}\right)^{1-\rho}\right] \quad (46)$$

is always negative for $\rho > 1$, so that the objective function is decreasing in p_j (increasing in l_j) for a low enough money wage w. Hence, unemployment can only be ascribed in this case to excessively high wages, not to unfavorable expectations of future prices, leading to Schultz's (1989) conclusion. But this is no longer true when intersectoral complementarity ($\rho < 1$) is assumed. For values of the expected real interest factor $P/\hat{P}$ such that

$$\alpha\left(\frac{P}{\hat{P}}\right)\sigma\left(\frac{P}{\hat{P}}\right) < (m-1)(1-\rho),$$

the right-hand side of (46) is positive for some producer, say, j, choosing the smallest price p_j (the largest l_j), and hence his objective function is increasing in p_j. It is then clear by (40) that an increase in p_j will increase the payoff of producer j while decreasing employment, so that one cannot be in the presence of an equilibrium. Results such as Theorems 3 and 7 can be applied to the present context of shareholders' utility maximization with the inequality $\tilde{\Delta}(\theta) < m-(m-1)\rho$ replaced by $\tilde{\Delta}(\theta)+\alpha(\theta) < m-(m-1)\rho$ (or, equivalently, by $\alpha(\theta)\sigma(\theta) < (m-1)(1-\rho)$). The condition is stronger but not at all inconsistent with our other assumptions, once we have multiplicity of sectors ($m > 1$) and intersectoral complementarity ($\rho < 1$).

6 Conclusion

We have shown examples of overlapping generations models where unemployment arises in all perfect foresight equilibria because of imperfect competition features of the goods markets. Depending upon the values of the real interest factor, the economy goes monotonically to zero employment at a (strong) inflationary equilibrium or exhibits unemployment in an infinite number of periods at a noninflationary equilibrium. In any case, imperfect competition, the number of firms, and the degree of intertemporal (or intersectoral) complementarity form the crux of the matter.

REFERENCES

d'Aspremont, C., R. Dos Santos Ferreira, and L.-A. Gérard-Varet. 1984. "Oligopoly and Involuntary Unemployment," CORE Discussion Paper No. 8408.

1989a. "Unemployment in a Cournot Model with Ford Effects." *Recherches Economiques de Louvain* 55: 33–60.

1989b. "Unemployment in an Extended Oligopoly Model." *Oxford Economic Papers* 41: 490–505.

1990. "Monopolistic Competition and Involuntary Unemployment." *Quarterly Journal of Economics* 105: 895–919.

Dehez, P. 1985. "Monopolistic Equilibrium and Involuntary Unemployment." *Journal of Economic Theory* 36: 160–5.

Hart, O. D. 1982. "A Model of Imperfect Competition with Keynesian Features." *Quarterly Journal of Economics* 97: 109–38.

Schultz, C. 1989. "The Impossibility of 'Involuntary Unemployment' in an Overlapping Generations Model with Rational Expectations." Dicussion Paper No. 89-18, Institute of Economics, University of Copenhagen.

Silvestre, J. 1990. "There May Be Unemployment When the Labor Market Is Competitive and the Output Market Is Not." *Economic Journal* 100: 899–913.

CHAPTER 17

Competition for customers

Egbert Dierker

1 Introduction

Price competition à la Bertrand on a market for a homogeneous product implies that a firm can, by lowering its price, attract all potential customers simultaneously. We would like to emphasize that this is independent of preferences or demand functions consumers may have for the good offered on the market. The basic feature is the competition for customers by undercutting prices as long as profits stay positive. Thus, if competition takes the extremely strong form as in Bertrand's comment on Cournot, the usual worries about the arbitrariness of individual preferences and, therefore, of the profit function remain irrelevant.

Since it is implausible to assume that the presence of only two firms in a market suffices to enforce perfect competition, it is generally thought that price competition is better suited for a market in which differentiated products are traded. When we replace the homogeneous good by a set of differentiated products, consumers no longer simultaneously switch to the firm with the lowest price. In this situation, the size of a firm's clientele grows continuously if the firm lowers its price. This growth has a strong influence on the firm's profit function. Indeed, we will assume that the dependence of the size of a firm's clientele on the prices charged plays a dominant role for the firm's profit function. We feel that the competition for customers is, as in the pure Bertrand case, the driving force behind strategic price setting on an oligopolistic market. For instance, the price of gasoline at a filling station in a competitive environment is sometimes reduced not to encourage the average customer to use more gasoline, but

I would like to thank I. Bomze, H. Dierker, W. Hildenbrand, W. Neuefeind, K. Podczeck, M. Quinzii, K. Schürger, and W. Trockel for helpful remarks and discussions. I am particularly indebted to J. Thisse for many valuable suggestions. Support from the Deutsche Forschungsgemeinschaft, Gottfried-Wilhelm-Leibniz-Förderpreis, and the Sonderforschungsbereich 303 at the University of Bonn is gratefully acknowledged.

rather to increase the firm's market share. Therefore, the competition for customers has to be studied when one wants to explain how market prices evolve. This chapter may be seen as a step toward a better understanding of the functioning of a market with a given finite number of firms that interact by setting prices in a noncooperative way.

To avoid the drastic jump in demand occurring in Bertrand competition when a firm undercuts prices, we focus attention on the *distribution of consumers' characteristics*. It is crucial for a firm to know how many customers it can attract by a price reduction. The need to study distributions of agents' characteristics has long been emphasized by Debreu and, in particular, by W. Hildenbrand. We would like to mention Hildenbrand (1983), where the distribution of expenditures (income) plays a central role. The present work is also influenced by a paper on price-dispersed preferences (cf. Dierker, Dierker, and Trockel, 1984). The object studied in this chapter may be called a *price-dispersed Bertrand discontinuity*.

We ask how the individual discontinuities must be distributed so that the optimal strategy of a firm in response to the prices charged by its opponents is uniquely defined. If uniqueness obtains, then the optimal response is a continuous function and Brouwer's fixed-point theorem can be used to show the existence of an equilibrium in pure strategies. The fundamental problems pointed out by Roberts and Sonnenschein (1977) disappear in this case. We derive the uniqueness of the optimal response and establish the quasiconcavity of a firm's profit function with respect to its own price.[1]

The quasiconcavity of profit functions is essential when one wants to show the existence of Nash equilibria in pure strategies. Observations on real markets do not seem to support the view that the strategy of a firm can be any probability measure on the firm's price space. The choice of an optimal mixed strategy is such a complex task in the present context that its interpretation as a description of the actual behavior of a firm appears implausible. In our opinion, it is much more appropriate to think of an equilibrium as a situation in which prices are publicly posted and no firm regrets its decision to announce a certain price after it has observed the prices posted by its opponents.

Furthermore, the quasiconcavity of a firm's profit function is also important for the actual decision making of a firm since it allows a firm to

[1] H. Dierker (1986) has established the existence of Nash equilibria in pure strategies for an oligopoly model with differentiated products and price-setting firms. This is done by deriving the concavity (not just quasiconcavity as in this chapter) of profits from certain assumptions on the distribution of consumers' wealth and preferences. Moreover, her approach differs from the present one in that she does not focus on the discrete-choice aspect and her distributional assumptions are dissimilar in nature from the ones given here.

achieve a globally optimal response by local considerations. In order to find its optimal strategy, the firm only has to decrease (or increase) its price as long as this procedure increases its profits. By comparison, the task of finding a globally optimal strategy is much more demanding if it is not known in which direction to search and whether an optimum is a local or a global one.

Intuitively, one expects three effects to occur when a firm lowers its price:

1. the firm gains more clients,
2. the firm gets less money per unit sold,
3. the demand of the firm's customers varies.

We will make assumptions on the distribution of consumers' characteristics in order to control the first effect. The second effect is clear and will not cause problems. The third effect, however, is ambiguous since microeconomic theory hardly imposes any restriction at all. As we have argued before, we think that this effect is of secondary importance. In order to concentrate on the dependence of the market shares on prices, it is convenient to assume that the expenditures spent on this market are constant, whereas product prices vary in the relevant range. If a considerable proportion of consumers reacts to a small price variation by turning to another firm, then the total demand for a firm's product mainly depends on effects 1 and 2, and the neglect of effect 3 presents a legitimate simplification.[2]

By focusing on effect 1, the *basic questions* can be formulated as follows:

> Which properties of the distribution of consumers' characteristics, in particular those that describe the choice of a firm or a brand, lead to quasiconcave profit functions?
>
> Why are these properties meaningful?

In Section 2, we will present an example, which relates to a standard model of discrete choice, in order to get a particular solution to the first question. A more general solution to this question will be given in Section 3.

Moreover, we will argue in Section 3 that the second question can be viewed in the following way: The discontinuity of demand in a pure Bertrand setting is caused by the rates of substitution (RS) of consumers between the products of the individual firms all being equal to 1 and, hence, equal to each other. If one introduces product differentiation, then the RS are no longer identical and the discontinuity disappears. Product differentiation thus leads to perturbations of the individual RS. In view of the

[2] For a treatment of the problem including effect 3, see Proposition 6 in Section 3.

pure Bertrand case, in which the equality of all RS is most important, it seems natural to us to assume that the perturbed RS exhibit a certain tendency toward equality. More precisely, we will assume that *more equal perturbations are more likely*. To capture this idea we will use the concept of Schur concavity. We will see in Section 3 that Schur concavity gives rise to properties of the distribution of consumers' characteristics that entail quasiconcave profit functions provided that effect 3 is dominated by effect 1.

There are several models of product differentiation. Anderson, de Palma, and Thisse (1989) discuss some linkages between them. An extensive discussion of stochastic choice and stochastic utility models including foundations of the highly popular logit model is given in de Palma and Thisse (1989).

After the completion of the research presented in this chapter, I became aware of the fact that Caplin and Nalebuff (1991a) have independently and simultaneously treated the question of the existence of pure strategy equilibria in a closely related way. They devote a large part of their paper to the analysis of markets in which consumers buy one unit of an indivisible good and explicitly consider the characteristics of the brands that are produced. Their paper also presents a nice discussion in which various models of product differentiation are seen from a unifying perspective. They establish the existence of equilibria in pure strategies for a large class of markets and provide some uniqueness results.

The results in their paper (1991a), in their companion paper on social choice (1991b) as well as the ones in this chapter essentially rely on the same development in mathematics; see, for example, Prékopa (1973) or Uhrin (1984) and the references therein. A partial difference between the goals of their paper (1989a) and this chapter is the following. Their main concern is to unify and extend in an essential way the previously known results by making rather weak assumptions, whereas we are more interested in exploring why certain assumptions on the distribution of consumers' characteristics appear natural when one wants to describe market shares. To this end, they focus on generalizations of the concept of concavity, whereas, as mentioned before, we use the idea that the individual RS tend to be equal in order to describe suitable distributions of consumers' characteristics.

2 Basic model and example

The purpose of this section is to describe the basic structure of our model of an oligopolistic market and to illustrate its subsequent analysis by means of an example. In the example, the distribution of customers among firms is given by a logit specification. The logit approach is widely used in the area of applied discrete-choice analysis because of its computational simplicity. More recently, the logit method has also been applied to problems of oligopoly theory (see, e.g., de Palma et al., 1985, for an application to the problem of spatial competition).

We will consider a market for a differentiated product where different variants, called brands, are sold by different firms. We assume that each firm offers just one brand. Therefore, a brand and its producer will be labeled in the same way. It suffices to assume that there are three firms in the market under consideration, since it turns out that dealing with four or more firms does not require more than an obvious change in notation. The case of duopoly is a little bit simpler than that of three or more firms and can easily be derived along the same lines.

On the formal level, the three brands will be treated as three different goods. A good as well as its producer is indexed by $j \in \{1, 2, 3\}$. In addition, there is a composite commodity, denoted by 0, which serves as numéraire. Hence, price vectors take the form $(1, p_1, p_2, p_3) \in \mathbb{R}^4_{++}$.

Firms' costs are expressed with respect to the numéraire good, which is considered as the unique input in each firm's production process. Since we do not deal with entry considerations, which we imagine as having occurred in the past, we need not allow for fixed costs or other kinds of nonconvexities and can assume constant returns. The constant unit cost of firm j is denoted c_j, $j = 1, 2, 3$.

Although differences in quality between goods 1, 2, and 3 are not explicitly ruled out, they do not play a central role in our model. However, in order to avoid the extreme case considered by Bertrand, it is important that competition is mitigated by (horizontal) product differentiation. We think of a typical consumer as buying only one of the three goods. His decision to select a particular good will, of course, depend on prices. At some critical price constellation, he will switch from one good to another one. Due to product differentiation and diversity of taste, different consumers will in general switch between goods at different price systems. Each firm considers the prices of the other goods as given and wants to set its own price in such a way that it attracts as many customers as required by profit maximization.

Next we describe the consumers by an atomless probability space $(A, \mathcal{A}, \mu)$. For each consumer $a \in A$, there are two critical price ratios, $r^a_{1,2}$ and $r^a_{1,3}$, which describe a's preference for good 1 vis-à-vis good 2 and 3, respectively. At price ratio $p_1/p_2 > r^a_{1,2}$ (or $p_1/p_3 > r^a_{1,3}$) consumer a prefers good 2 (or good 3) to good 1. On the other hand, if $p_1/p_2 \leq r^a_{1,2}$ and $p_1/p_3 \leq r^a_{1,3}$, then a chooses good 1. Since the distribution of the rates $r^a_{i,j}$ of substitution is supposed to be absolutely continuous with respect to

Lebesgue measure, the specification of a's choice in case of equality in the previous relations can be arbitrary. The distribution of $r_{1,2}$ and $r_{1,3}$ is of central importance for firm 1, since it describes the reaction of potential customers to a variation of p_1 given p_2 and p_3.[3]

Similarly, from the viewpoint of firm 2 (or firm 3), there are critical price ratios $r^a_{2,1}$ and $r^a_{2,3}$ (or $r^a_{3,1}$ and $r^a_{3,2}$) that describe the switches in demand relevant for firm 2 (or firm 3). Consistency requires that $r^a_{i,j} = (r^a_{j,i})^{-1}$ for $i \neq j$ and $r^a_{i,j} \cdot r^a_{j,k} = r^a_{i,k}$ for any permutation (i, j, k) of $(1, 2, 3)$. The latter equality reflects the fact that $p_i/p_j \cdot p_j/p_k = p_i/p_k$.

Assume that firms 2 and 3 have set the prices for their products equal to $\bar{p}_2$ and $\bar{p}_3$, respectively, and consider firm 1's problem to respond optimally to $(\bar{p}_2, \bar{p}_3)$. If firm 1 charges p_1, then its set of customers is

$$C(p_1) = \left\{ a \in A \,\middle|\, r^a_{1,2} \geq \frac{p_1}{\bar{p}_2} \text{ and } r^a_{1,3} \geq \frac{p_1}{\bar{p}_3} \right\}.$$

Let $f(p_1, a)$ denote the demand of agent $a \in C(p_1)$ for good 1 at $(1, p_1, \bar{p}_2, \bar{p}_3)$. Then the aggregate demand for good 1 at p_1 is

$$F(p_1) = \int_{C(p_1)} f(p_1, a)\mu(da).$$

Observe that aggregation of demand takes place with respect to the set $C(p_1)$, which itself varies when the strategic variable p_1 of firm 1 does. The classical case of pure Bertrand competition, in which all consumers switch simultaneously, is completely governed by the discontinuous variation of $C(p_1)$. In the present model with product differentiation, the dependence of C on p_1 will also play the dominant role.

We assume that F is differentiable. Differentiation of profits $(p_1 - c_1) \times F(p_1)$ leads to a first-order condition, which can be written as

$$\frac{p_1}{p_1 - c_1} = -\frac{F'(p_1)}{F(p_1)} p_1 \quad \text{for } p_1 > c_1.$$

Note that the left-hand side of the formula is monotonically decreasing. Hence, the optimal response of firm 1 is uniquely determined if we can establish that the right-hand side is (weakly) monotonically increasing. Therefore, we will focus attention on the monotonicity of the right-hand side in the sequel. If the right-hand side is monotonically increasing, then the logarithm of the profit considered as a function of $\log p_1$ is concave. Consequently, the profit function itself is quasiconcave.

[3] W. Hildenbrand has called my attention to a paper by Novshek and Sonnenschein (1979) that develops the demand theory for consumption sectors in which switching at critical price ratios occurs. Novshek and Sonnenschein, however, do not study the role of particular assumptions on the distribution of critical price ratios for aggregate demand.

It is apparent from the definition of $F(p_1)$ that the right-hand side can be decomposed into two terms describing two separate effects:

- the first effect relies upon *the change of firm 1's clientele* $C(p_1)$ in dependence of the price p_1 charged;
- the second effect, obtained by differentiation under the integral sign, corresponds to the variation of demand by the consumers belonging to the *fixed* set $C(p_1)$ of customers.[4]

It seems to us that *the competition for customers,* which is captured by the first effect, *is crucial for the conflict among price setting firms* on an oligopolistic market. Compared to this type of competition, the goal of diverting money away from other goods, which are represented by the numéraire in our model, toward the firm's own market is of secondary importance. For instance, a car producer will price its standard compact car in such a way that it can compete with similar cars produced by other firms and not in order to induce people to spend less on other goods such as food or housing and more on compact cars. Thus, we will mostly disregard the second effect in favor of the first (see, however, Proposition 6 and the corresponding discussion).

A clear-cut way to eliminate the second effect is to assume

$$p_1 \int_{C(p_1)} \frac{\partial}{\partial p_1} f_1(p_1, a)\mu(da) \cdot \left[\int_{C(p_1)} f(p_1, a)\mu(da) \right]^{-1} = -1.$$

This assumption expresses, in a strict way, the idea that a firm can increase its revenue only by attracting more customers because the amount of money spent per customer is fixed for a given set $C(p_1)$. Since the customers gained by a firm are lost by one of its rivals, the assumption reflects our intention to focus on the conflict among oligopolists in the spirit of Bertrandlike undercutting of prices. A weaker assumption will be given in Proposition 6 in the next section.

It remains to discuss the effect caused by the influence of p_1 on firm 1's clientele $C(p_1)$. For that purpose, we first have to specify the distribution of the critical price ratios $r_{i,j}$. The following procedure relies upon the concept of price-dispersed preferences (cf. Dierker et al., 1984, or Trockel, 1984).

Intuitively speaking, the preference of agent a for good 1 vis-à-vis the other goods is influenced by various attributes of goods 1, 2, and 3. In particular, any attribute of good 1 will, in general, affect a's rates of substitution between good 1 and the remaining goods. The result is the same as if good 1 would have been measured in some other unit, the size of

[4] We implicitly assume that differentiation and integration can be interchanged.

which reflects the weight agent a attaches to the attribute. We will summarize all effects on consumer a caused by all attributes of good 1 by some positive factor q_1^a, which stretches or shrinks the 1-axis of the commodity space. It would be a tremendous task to describe all attributes and all their implications for the consumers in detail and then to derive the desired properties of the distribution of consumers' characteristics. Therefore, we will start out by considering directly the distribution of q_1, which is a determinant of the distribution of the critical price ratios $r_{1,2}$ and $r_{1,3}$.

Similarly, there are many attributes of goods 2 and 3 that different consumers will typically like or dislike in different ways. They give rise to positive random variables q_2 and q_3 acting multiplicatively on axis 2 and axis 3, respectively. In other words, consumer a can be viewed as having the utility function u^a given by

$$u^a(x_0, x_1, x_2, x_3) = v^a\left(x_0, \frac{x_1}{q_1^a} + \frac{x_2}{q_2^a} + \frac{x_3}{q_3^a}\right)$$

for some $v^a: \mathbb{R}_+^2 \to \mathbb{R}$.

Now assume that, without the preference diversification just described, we are in the case of pure Bertrand competition in which all rates of substitution between goods i and j coincide. It will be no restriction to assume that all rates of substitution are equal to 1 in the unperturbed Bertrand case (see the remark after Proposition 4 in Section 3). Then a's rate of substitution between goods i and j after preference diversification has taken place is given by $r_{i,j}^a = q_j^a / q_i^a$. Thus, we can describe firm 1's clientele in terms of (q_1^a, q_2^a, q_3^a) as follows:

$$C(p_1) = \left\{ a \in A \,\middle|\, \frac{q_2^a}{q_1^a} \geq \frac{p_1}{\bar{p}_2} \text{ and } \frac{q_3^a}{q_1^a} \geq \frac{p_1}{\bar{p}_3} \right\}.$$

The measure μ on A induces a distribution of the random vector (q_1^a, q_2^a, q_3^a). In the next section, we will impose qualitative assumptions on this distribution. For a better understanding and motivation of these assumptions, we will now describe a particular example in some detail.

It is convenient to first transform our basic variables by using logarithms. This is due to the fact that the stretching factors q_j act multiplicatively and, therefore, their logarithms act additively. We define

$$t_j^a = -\log q_j^a \quad \text{for } j = 1, 2, 3,$$

$$\beta_j = -\log \bar{p}_j \quad \text{for } j = 2, 3, \quad \text{and}$$

$$\tau_1 = -\log p_1.$$

We assume in our *logit example* that the t_j are independently distributed with densities

$$\rho_j(t_j) = e^{-(t_j-\alpha_j)} \cdot \exp(-e^{-(t_j-\alpha_j)}), \quad j=1,2,3.$$

Readers who are familiar with standard applications of the logit method will observe that we use it to model the distribution of random perturbations q_j that act multiplicatively rather than, as usual, additively because the densities ρ_j refer to logarithms. This specification has the advantage that *preferences are monotone* in the sense that the random variables q_j are always positive. Otherwise, if the previous ρ_j were the density of q_j itself rather than that of $\log q_j$, it would happen for a positive fraction of consumers that, say, q_1^a is positive and large, whereas q_2^a is negative and has a large absolute value. Such a consumer a would find brand 2 very undesirable and simultaneously feel a strong urge to consume brand 1. In the present context, the additive procedure would yield a somewhat extreme picture of an oligopolistic market if brands are similar enough.

The density ρ_j is unimodal with mode α_j. The corresponding distribution function is given by $\exp(-e^{-(t_j-\alpha_j)})$. The "double exponential" form makes it rather easy to handle this expression. We will make use of the following two salient features of this class of distributions, which are sometimes called Gumbel distributions:

1. The maximum of two independent random variables with Gumbel distribution is Gumbel distributed;
2. the difference of two independent random variables with Gumbel distribution has a logistic distribution.

More precisely, we will use these two properties in the following form:

(i) Let t_2 and t_3 be independent random variables with distributions as specified before. Define

$$m_1 = \max(t_2+\beta_2, t_3+\beta_3).$$

Then the distribution function of m_1 is given by

$$\begin{aligned}\text{Prob}(m_1 \leq \eta) &= \exp(-e^{-(\eta-\alpha_2-\beta_2)}) \cdot \exp(-e^{-(\eta-\alpha_3-\beta_3)}) \\ &= \exp[-e^{-\eta}(e^{\alpha_2+\beta_2}+e^{\alpha_3+\beta_3})] \\ &= \exp[-e^{-(\eta-\gamma)}],\end{aligned}$$

where $e^{\gamma} = e^{\alpha_2+\beta_2}+e^{\alpha_3+\beta_3}$.

(ii) If t_1 and m_1 are independent random variables distributed as stated before, then the distribution function of $m_1 - t_1$ is given by

$$\text{Prob}\{m_1 - t_1 \leq \tau_1\} = \frac{e^{\tau_1+\alpha_1}}{e^{\tau_1+\alpha_1}+e^{\gamma}}.$$

The last formula is obtained by an elementary calculation. Standard references for the logit method are McFadden (1974, 1981).

Observe that

$$\mu(C(p_1)) = \mu\left\{a \in A \,\middle|\, \frac{q_j^a}{q_1^a} \geq \frac{p_1}{\bar{p}_j} \text{ for } j=2 \text{ and } j=3\right\}$$

$$= \mu\{a \in A \mid t_j^a + \beta_j - t_1^a \leq \tau_1 \text{ for } j=2 \text{ and } j=3\}$$

$$= \mu\{a \in A \mid m_1^a - t_1^a \leq \tau_1\},$$

where m_1 is defined as in (i).

The *market share of firm 1* in terms of customers at price $p_1 = e^{-\tau_1}$ is

$$S(\tau_1) = \mu(C(e^{-\tau_1})).$$

Thus, we get in our logit example

$$S(\tau_1) = \frac{e^{\tau_1+\alpha_1}}{e^{\tau_1+\alpha_1}+e^{\gamma}}.$$

Remember that it is our goal to show that the elasticity $|F'(p_1)/F(p_1)|p_1$ increases when p_1 does, as this monotonicity property implies the uniqueness of the optimal price for firm 1. The substitution $p_1 = e^{-\tau_1}$ yields

$$-\frac{dF(p_1)}{dp_1} \cdot \frac{p_1}{F(p_1)} = \frac{dF(e^{-\tau_1})}{d\tau_1} \cdot \frac{1}{F(e^{-\tau_1})}.$$

To relate this expression to the market share $S(\tau_1)$ we make the following assumption. Define the set of *marginal clients* as

$$\partial C(p_1) = \left\{a \in C(p_1) \,\middle|\, r_{1,2}^a = \frac{p_1}{\bar{p}_2} \text{ or } r_{1,3}^a = \frac{p_1}{\bar{p}_3}\right\}.$$

Since it is our aim in this section to present the essence of the argument yielding continuous reaction functions, we assume that the average demand function $\bar{f}_{C(p_1)}(p_1)$ of all clients $a \in C(p_1)$ is equal to the average demand $\bar{f}_{\partial C(p_1)}(p_1)$ of the marginal clients $a \in \partial C(p_1)$.[5]

The assumption $\bar{f}_C = \bar{f}_{\partial C}$ is satisfied in the case in which every consumer spends a fixed (but individual) amount of money on the oligopolistic market, provided that the distribution of (q_1, q_2, q_3) and hence that of the critical price ratios is independent of the amount spent. We will address the question of how one can incorporate more general demand patterns in the next section (see Proposition 6 and the discussion thereafter). It should be clear, though, that one does need assumptions on consumers' demand in an essential way in order to rule out the non-existence phenomenon, which has been forcefully pointed out by Roberts and Sonnenschein (1977).

[5] Conditional expectations are defined up to null sets only. If $\bar{f}_{\partial C(p_1)}(p_1) = \bar{f}_{C(p_1)}(p_1)$ a.e., we might as well specify $\bar{f}_{\partial C}$ in such a way that it always coincides with $\bar{f}_C$.

Since

$$C(p_1) = C(e^{-\tau_1}) = \bigcup_{t_1 \le \tau_1} \partial C(e^{-t_1}),$$

we have

$$F(e^{-\tau_1}) = \int_{-\infty}^{\tau_1} \bar{f}_{\partial C(e^{-t_1})}(e^{-\tau_1}) \cdot S'(t_1)\, dt_1.$$

Therefore, under the usual assumptions (see Dieudonné, 1969, p. 177ff.),

$$\frac{dF(e^{-\tau_1})}{d\tau_1} = \int_{-\infty}^{\tau_1} \frac{\partial}{\partial \tau_1} \bar{f}_{\partial C(e^{-t_1})}(e^{-\tau_1}) \cdot S'(t_1)\, dt_1 + \bar{f}_{\partial C(e^{\tau_1})}(e^{-\tau_1}) \cdot S'(\tau_1)$$

$$= \int_{C(e^{-\tau_1})} \frac{\partial}{\partial \tau_1} f(e^{-\tau_1}, a) \mu(da) + \bar{f}_{\partial C(e^{-\tau_1})}(e^{-\tau_1}) \cdot S'(\tau_1).$$

Using our assumptions imposed upon consumers' demand, that is to say $\bar{f}_C = \bar{f}_{\partial C}$, and the assumption that the elasticity of mean demand aggregated over the fixed set $C(p_1)$ of customers equals -1, we get

$$\frac{1}{F(e^{-\tau_1})} \cdot \frac{dF(e^{-\tau_1})}{d\tau_1} = 1 + \frac{S'(\tau_1)}{S(\tau_1)}$$

$$= 1 + \frac{d}{d\tau_1} \log S(\tau_1).$$

Thus, we obtain the following result, which is independent of the logit specification:

> *The elasticity* $|F'(p_1)/F(p_1)|p_1$ *is monotonically increasing in* p_1 *if* $\log S(\tau_1)$ *is concave. This property holds in the logit example.*[6]

One checks easily that $\log S(\tau_1)$ actually is (strictly) concave in the case of the logit example carried out before, where

$$S(\tau_1) = e^{\tau_1 + \alpha_1} \cdot (e^{\tau_1 + \alpha_1} + e^{\gamma})^{-1},$$

since e^{γ} and $e^{\tau_1 + \alpha_1}$ must be positive. However, despite the great popularity of logit models in discrete choice analysis, I am not aware of any compelling reason that explains why logit models are the "correct" ones. One could, for instance, argue that the probit model, which is based on the normal distribution instead of the Gumbel, is not less appropriate than the logit model. Actually, it turns out that the desired concavity of $\log S(\tau_1)$ also holds true for the probit model. In the next section, we will address

[6] The concavity of $\log S(\tau_1)$ is closely related to the notion of an increasing hazard rate, which is sometimes used in oligopoly theory for similar purposes. The goal of this chapter is to present assumptions on the distribution of preferences that yield an increasing hazard rate.

the question of how one can qualitatively describe classes of distributions that work as well as the logit example.

3 Results: What can we learn from the logit example?

We are now going to investigate which properties of the logit model are important for the concavity of $\log S(\tau_1)$ and, therefore, for the uniqueness of optimal prices to be charged by a firm. Observe that the logit model exhibits the following features:

(a) the random variables t_1, t_2, and t_3 are independently distributed;
(b) they obey the same probability law (Gumbel distribution);
(c) the logarithms of the densities ρ_j (as well as of the associated distribution functions) are concave.

These properties are also satisfied by the (independent) probit model. However, we will see that less is required in order to obtain that $\log S(\tau_1)$ is concave.

First, we will show that *one need not worry at all about the particular functional form* of the densities ρ_j, when one focuses on (a) and (b). More precisely, in the independently and identically distributed (i.i.d.) case, it suffices to assume that the joint density $\rho = \rho_1 \cdot \rho_2 \cdot \rho_3$ (with $\rho_1 = \rho_2 = \rho_3$) is unimodal. Since unimodality is, by itself, a rather weak assumption, the fundamental requirements here are stochastic independence and symmetry in terms of identical distributions.

Then we will argue that one need not require (b). To do so, we will use the concept of Schur concavity, which is closely related to that of unimodality in the case of independent random variables. Again we conclude that (c) holds. If (c) holds, then $\log S(\tau_1)$ will be concave, where $S(\tau_1)$ denotes firm 1's market share. This is due to the fact that the concavity of logarithms is maintained when one goes through the procedure of describing $S(\tau_1)$ starting from the distribution of (t_1, t_2, t_3). This is illustrated by properties (i) and (ii) in the logit example of Section 2, where explicit formulas have been given.

Finally, we will see that one does not in fact need the independence property (a) to derive from a condition similar to (c) that $\log S(\tau_1)$ is concave. However, one is then confronted with the question of why (c) should hold when neither (a) nor (b) do. To our regret, we have no satisfactory answer to offer here.

A function $g: \mathbb{R}^n \to \mathbb{R}_+$ is *log concave* iff $\log g$ is concave, that is to say iff for all $x, y \in \mathbb{R}^n$ and for every $0 < \lambda < 1$, we have $g(\lambda x + (1-\lambda)y) \geq g(x)^\lambda \cdot (g(y))^{1-\lambda}$. A density $\rho: \mathbb{R}^n \in \mathbb{R}_+$ is *unimodal* iff all upper contour sets $\{t \in \mathbb{R}^n \mid \rho(t) \geq c\}$ are convex.[7] Whenever convenient, we assume the functions under consideration to be continuously differentiable.

Observe that by a suitable choice of the units in which the commodities are measured, all modes α_j in the logit example can be normalized to zero so that the distributions of t_1, t_2, and t_3 become identical. We put $t = (t_1, t_2, t_3)$.

Proposition 1. *Assume that t_1, t_2, and t_3 are independently and identically distributed (i.i.d.). Let the joint density $\rho = \rho_1 \cdot \rho_2 \cdot \rho_3$ be unimodal, continuously differentiable and positive. Then the densities $\rho_1 = \rho_2 = \rho_3$ are log concave.*

Though the proof is contained in Marshall and Olkin (1974, p. 1190ff.), we want to outline the argument here, since it relies on an interesting observation that is useful for later purposes. Recall that a function g: $\mathbb{R}^n \to \mathbb{R}$ is *Schur concave* iff $g(x) \geq g(y)$ whenever x is majorized by y. The vector x is majorized by y iff $\sum_{j=1}^n x_j = \sum_{j=1}^n y_j$ and, for any $1 \leq k \leq n$, the sum of the k smallest components of x is at least as large as the sum of the k smallest components of y. In other words, thinking of x and y as distributions of a given total income among n individuals, x is majorized by y if the distribution of x is at least as equal as that of y in the sense of Lorenz dominance. Since the comparison of vectors by majorization involves rearrangements of their components according to size, Schur concave functions are necessarily permutation-symmetric. Moreover, the set of all points x majorized by a given point y is equal to the convex hull of all points obtained by permuting the components of y.

By assumption, ρ is unimodal and permutation-symmetric. Consider an upper contour set U defined by $\rho(t) \geq c$. The permutation-symmetric convex set U, which is centered around a point with all components equal, enjoys a certain degree of equality of vector components. More precisely, if x is majorized by y and $y \in U$, then $x \in U$. Thus, unimodality implies Schur concavity in this framework.

The classical inequality of I. Schur, which characterizes Schur concavity for differentiable functions, states that

$$(\partial_i \rho(t) - \partial_j \rho(t))(t_i - t_j) \leq 0$$

for all vectors t and for all $i \neq j$. In particular, for $i = 1$, $j = 2$, and $\rho(t) = \rho_1(t_1)\rho_2(t_2)\rho_3(t_3)$, we get, provided $t_2 > t_1$,

$$\rho_3(t_3)[\rho_1'(t_1)\rho_2(t_2) - \rho_1(t_1)\rho_2'(t_2)] \geq 0.$$

[7] The support of g or ρ can be a convex subset of $\mathbb{R}^n$. Also note that unimodality corresponds to quasiconcavity.

It follows that $\rho_1'(t_1)/\rho_1(t_1) \geq \rho_2'(t_2)/\rho_2(t_2)$ for $t_2 > t_1$. Since $\rho_1 = \rho_2 = \rho_3$, this inequality expresses the log concavity of densities, which was to be shown.

Remark 1. The assumption that ρ is C^1 and positive has only been made to express log concavity in terms of a derivative. It suffices to assume $\rho_1 = \rho_2 = \rho_3$ to be continuous densities. For convenience, we will disregard differentiability questions in the sequel.

Apart from its being a useful tool in the proof of Proposition 1, we find the concept of Schur concavity very appealing in the context of Bertrandlike competition. The reason is that *Schur concavity captures the idea of equality in a suitable way and it is precisely the equality of the rates of substitution that lies at the heart of pure Bertrand competition.* If there are preference perturbations t_j^a due to product differentiation, one wants to express the idea that these perturbations exhibit a certain tendency toward equality. This idea can be extended beyond the case of i.i.d. perturbations t_j^a by using the concept of Schur concavity in the following way.

We now drop the assumption that t_1, t_2, and t_3 are identically distributed. Since we still assume stochastic independence of t_1, t_2, and t_3, and since the product of log concave functions is log concave, it suffices to consider each t_j separately. Suppose two consumers, a and a', are independently drawn at random from the population A. For every j, this random draw gives rise to a distribution of a pair of perturbations $(t_j^a, t_j^{a'})$ with density $\rho_j(t_j^a) \cdot \rho_j(t_j^{a'})$. The Schur concavity of this density $\rho_j \cdot \rho_j$ has the following interpretation. Consider two realizations $(\bar{t}_j^a, \bar{t}_j^{a'})$ and $(\tilde{t}_j^a, \tilde{t}_j^{a'})$ such that $\bar{t}_j^a + \bar{t}_j^{a'} = \tilde{t}_j^a + \tilde{t}_j^{a'}$. Assume that the first realization exhibits more equality than the second in the sense that $\tilde{t}_j^a \leq \bar{t}_j^a \leq \bar{t}_j^{a'} \leq \tilde{t}_j^{a'}$. Then

$$\rho_j(\tilde{t}_j^a) \cdot \rho_j(\tilde{t}_j^{a'}) \leq \rho_j(\bar{t}_j^a) \cdot \rho_j(\bar{t}_j^{a'}).$$

In this way Schur concavity of $\rho_j(t_j^a) \cdot \rho_j(t_j^{a'})$ expresses the idea that *more equal perturbations are more likely.* The density $\rho_j(t_j^a) \cdot \rho_j(t_j^{a'})$ increases along any line on which the total perturbation $t_j^a + t_j^{a'}$ is kept fixed, when one approaches the diagonal where $t_j^a = t_j^{a'}$. This interpretation also shows the close relation between Schur concavity and unimodality. With regard to the interpretation just given, we think that Schur concavity is a reasonable assumption in the context of Bertrandlike competition and state the following proposition.

Proposition 2. *Let the density $(t_j, t_j') \mapsto \rho_j(t_j) \cdot \rho_j(t_j')$ be Schur-concave. Then ρ_j is log concave.*

Again, this proposition is implied by Marshall and Olkin (1974); see, in particular, their Remark 2.2. The mathematical argument is the same as that underlying Proposition 1.

Remark 2. If ρ_j is log concave, then $(t_j^1, \dots, t_j^n) \mapsto \prod_{k=1}^n \rho_j(t_j^k)$ is Schur concave and vice versa. Therefore, we could as well consider independent random draws of n rather than two consumers for any natural number n.

Corollary 1. *If the assumptions of Proposition 2 hold for all j, then the product density $\rho = \rho_1 \cdot \rho_2 \cdot \rho_3$ is log concave.*

Observe that stochastic independence has been used in two different ways. In Proposition 2, independence refers to a random draw of two persons and not to the independence of t_1, t_2, and t_3, which was required in Proposition 1. If the t_j's are dependent, one can still use the idea behind Proposition 2 as follows. Consider the two agents a and a' independently drawn from the population A. Remember that $m_1 = \max(t_2 + \beta_2, t_3 + \beta_3)$ and that the critical clients of firm 1 at $p_1 = e^{-\tau_1}$ are characterized by $m_1 - t_1 = \tau_1$. Let $m_1^a - t_1^a$ and $m_1^{a'} - t_1^{a'}$ indicate the prices at which agent a and a' switch firms, respectively. Denote the density of $m_1 - t_1$ by ζ and assume that $m_1^a - t_1^a$ and $m_1^{a'} - t_1^{a'}$ tend to be equal (in the sense of Schur concavity).

Proposition 3. *If the density $\zeta(m_1 - t_1) \cdot \zeta(m_1' - t_1')$ is Schur concave, then $S(\tau_1)$ is log concave.*

Proof: The log concavity of the density ζ follows by the argument used before. Note that S is the distribution function associated with the density ζ. The following elementary lemma completes the proof.

Lemma 1. *Let ζ be a log concave density on $\mathbb{R}$. Then the distribution function associated with ζ is log concave.*

Proof: Put

$$c(x) = \log \zeta(x)$$

and define

$$f(x) = \log \int_{-\infty}^{x} e^{c(\xi)} \, d\xi.$$

We have to show that f is concave due to the fact that c is so. Differentiation yields that $f'' \leq 0$ if

$$c'(x)\cdot\int_{-\infty}^{x} e^{c(\xi)}\,d\xi \le e^{c(x)}.$$

Since c is concave, we have

$$c'(x)\cdot\int_{-\infty}^{x} e^{c(\xi)}\,d\xi \le \int_{-\infty}^{x} c'(\xi)\cdot e^{c(\xi)}\,d\xi = e^{c(x)}. \qquad \square$$

Proposition 4. *If t_1, t_2, and t_3 are independent random variables with log concave densities, then $S(\tau_1)$ is log concave.*

Observe that Proposition 4 applies in the situation of Proposition 1 and that of Corollary 1 to Proposition 2.

Remark 3. The definition of firm 1's clientele and, hence, that of $S(\tau_1)$ has been formulated for a given specification of the units in which the goods are measured. Furthermore, we have assumed that in the unperturbed pure Bertrand case, the rates of substitution between goods 1, 2, and 3 all equal 1. Since the result that $S(\tau_1)$ is log concave is derived from the log concavity of certain densities and since the transformation $g(x) = f(x+\text{const.})$ preserves log concavity, the normalizations made do not affect the argument. This fact is not surprising since there is a close relation to the concept of an elasticity, which has suitable invariance properties.

Proof of Proposition 4: Since $t_2+\beta_2$ and $t_3+\beta_3$ have log concave densities, the corresponding distribution functions are log concave according to Lemma 1. It follows from stochastic independence that the distribution function M_1 of $m_1 = \max(t_2+\beta_2, t_3+\beta_3)$ is the product of two log concave functions and hence log concave. According to Theorem 7 of Prékopa (1973), the convolution of two log concave functions is log concave. Since $C(e^{-\tau_1}) = \{a \in A \mid m_1^a - t_1^a \le \tau_1\}$, the proposition is proven. $\square$

Until now we have assumed Schur concavity together with stochastic independence to obtain the log concavity of $S(\tau_1)$. The next proposition states that, without any independence assumption, $S(\tau_1)$ is log concave provided ρ is so.

Proposition 5. *Let ρ denote the joint density of (t_1, t_2, t_3). Assume ρ is log concave. Then $S(\tau_1)$ is log concave.*

Proof: Define the convex set

$$K = \{(t_1, t_2, t_3) \in \mathbb{R}^3 \mid t_j + \beta_j - t_1 \le 0 \text{ for } j=2 \text{ and } j=3\}.$$

Furthermore, define $f: \mathbb{R}^3 \times \mathbb{R} \to \mathbb{R}_+$ by

$$f(t_1, t_2, t_3, \tau_1) = \rho(t_1 + \tau_1, t_2, t_3).$$

Since $\log \rho$ is concave, $\log f$ is, too. We have

$$\begin{aligned} S(\tau_1) &= \mu\{a \in A \mid t_j^a + \beta_j - t_1 \leq \tau_1 \text{ for } j = 2, 3\} \\ &= \mu\{a \in A \mid t_j^a + \beta_j - (t_1^a + \tau_1) \leq 0 \text{ for } j = 2, 3\} \\ &= \int_K \rho(t_1 + \tau_1, t_2, t_3)\, dt_1 dt_2 dt_3 \\ &= \int_K f(t_1, t_2, t_3, \tau_1)\, dt_1 dt_2 dt_3. \end{aligned}$$

By Theorem 6 of Prékopa (1973) this integral is a log-concave function of τ_1. □

It is not difficult to give examples of classes of log concave densities. For instance, it is shown in Barndorff-Nielsen (1978, Chapter 9.5) that exponential families, which play a role in mathematical statistics, have log concave densities under some conditions.[8]

It would be desirable to have a class of plausible stochastic processes that describe random perturbations of preferences and that give rise to a log concave joint density ρ of (t_1, t_2, t_3). In this context, we would like to mention that the behavior of the degree of concavity under convolutions is well understood (cf. Uhrin, 1984, in particular Theorem 2.1).[9] The developments in mathematics, however, have not led to a satisfactory foundation of discrete theory until now.

Eventually, we turn to a different subject. Remember that we have made simplifying assumptions in Section 2 that have allowed us to reduce the consideration of $[F'(p_1)/F(p_1)]p_1$ to that of $\log S(\tau_1)$. We are going to ask ourselves how Proposition 5 can be extended so as to take demand itself into account. For that purpose we have to spell out explicitly how the stretching factors q_j, which affect individual preferences, are related to demand. The following discussion proceeds along the lines of Dierker et al. (1984). The book by Trockel (1984, in particular the drawing on p. 110 and its context) will be a useful reference. Note, however, that the following formulation will be on a more aggregate level.

We can split the total decision of a consumer into two independent parts. As usual, we give the description from the viewpoint of firm 1. The first part concerns the amounts of good 1 and of the numéraire good that are bought by the consumer, provided he becomes a customer of firm 1.

[8] I am grateful to I. Bomze for this reference.

[9] I owe this reference to K. Schürger.

This decision is affected by the stretching factor q_1, but not by q_2 and q_3. The second part is the decision of whether to buy from firm 1 or not. Here q_2 and q_3 become effective in addition to q_1.

Consider the reduced commodity space consisting of goods 0 and 1 only and let $f(p_1 | q_1)$ denote the mean demand for good 1 at prices $(1, p_1)$, the mean being taken over all consumers a with $q_1^a = q_1$. Stretching the 1-axis by the factor q_1 induces a change of preferences and hence of demand. For instance, if the 1-axis is stretched by the factor $q_1 = 2$, then the demand for good 1 doubles if the price p_1 is accordingly adjusted – that is to say, if p_1 is set equal to half of its original value, provided that perturbations occur independently of preferences. This consideration can be summarized in the formula

$$f\left(\frac{p_1}{q_1}\middle| q_1\right) = q_1 \cdot f(p_1 | 1),$$

or, equivalently,

$$f(p_1 | q_1) = q_1 \cdot f(p_1 \cdot q_1 | 1).$$

This formula is now used to compute $-[F'(p_1)/F(p_1)] \cdot p_1$. We substitute $\tau_1 = -\log p_1$ and $\Phi(\tau_1) = F(e^{-\tau_1})$ and must compute $(\log \Phi(\tau_1))'$. To compute $\Phi(\tau_1)$ for given $\bar{p}_2 = e^{-\beta_2}$ and $\bar{p}_3 = e^{-\beta_3}$, we put

$$\phi(\tau_1 | t_1) = f(e^{-\tau_1} | e^{-t_1}).$$

The formula at the end of the last paragraph then becomes

$$\phi(\tau_1 | t_1) = e^{-t_1} \phi(e^{-(\tau_1 + t_1)} | 0).$$

Now we have to take into account how many consumers decide to buy the product of firm 1. Since the customers of firm 1 are characterized by $m_1 \le \tau_1 + t_1$, their weight for given t_1 equals $M_1(\tau_1 + t_1)$. Since t_1 occurs with density $\rho_1(t_1)$, we get

$$\Phi(\tau_1) = \int_{\mathbb{R}} \phi(e^{-(\tau_1 + t_1)} | 0) \cdot M_1(\tau_1 + t_1) \cdot e^{-t_1} \rho_1(t_1)\, dt_1.$$

This integral represents a convolution. Hence, we obtain the following proposition by Theorem 7 of Prékopa (1973).

Proposition 6. *If $\phi(e^{-(\tau_1 + t_1)} | 0) \cdot M_1(\tau_1 + t_1)$ and $\rho_1(t_1)$ are log concave, then $\Phi(\tau_1)$ is log concave.*

Proposition 6 states a condition under which the optimal response of firm 1 to $(\bar{p}_2, \bar{p}_3)$ is unique. Let us compare Proposition 6 with Proposition 4, where demand does not appear explicitly. Since e^{-t_1} is log linear, the essential difference between $\Phi(\tau_1)$ and $S(\tau_1)$ consists of the factor $\phi(e^{-(\tau_1+t_1)}|0)$, which describes how consumers' demand depends on $p_1 = e^{-\tau_1}$. We know that $\log M_1$ is concave under the conditions of Proposition 4. It is required in Proposition 6 that even $\log\phi + \log M_1$ is concave. Of course, this is the case if $(\log\phi)'$ is nonincreasing in τ_1 or, in other terms, if the elasticity $|f'(p_1|1)/f(p_1|1)|p_1$ is monotonically nondecreasing in p_1. Examples are provided by the C.E.S. utility function. Note, however, that Proposition 6 allows for changes of this elasticity "in the wrong direction" as long as the concavity of $\log M_1$ is strong enough to counterbalance these changes.

The concavity of $\log M_1$ in terms of the second derivative depends on the distribution of the perturbations t_j. Suppose that the distribution becomes more concentrated because, for instance, every t_j is replaced by αt_j, $0<\alpha<1$. Then $\log M_1$ becomes "more concave." One would expect that, roughly speaking, a strong concentration of the t_j's will help to overcome a possibly adverse effect of the demand ϕ. In other words, a fiercer competition among the firms due to a lesser degree of product differentiation is helpful when one wants to establish the log concavity of the demand for a brand and, thereby, the existence of an equilibrium in pure strategies.

Moreover, the uniqueness of the optimal response of firm 1 does not only depend on the log concavity of $\Phi(\tau_1)$, but also on the derivative of $p_1/(p_1-c_1)$ (see Section 2). If competition becomes fiercer, then the relevant range of p_1 shrinks closer to c_1. The closer p_1 and c_1, the larger $|[d/dp_1][p_1/(p_1-c_1)]| = |c_1/(c_1-p_1)|$. This argument provides additional support for the intuition that fierce competition helps to obtain continuous reaction functions.

In the present chapter, we have shown how the uniqueness of the optimal response of a firm to the prices charged by its rivals can be deduced from assumptions on the distribution of consumers' characteristics, provided the size of a firm's clientele is the essential determinant of its profits. This condition has been given a precise meaning in Proposition 6. Using the concept of Schur concavity to express a certain tendency of preference perturbations toward equality, we have argued that the distributional assumptions we made appear reasonable in view of the pure Bertrand case, which is characterized by the complete equality of the individual rates of substitution between brands. However, in order to do so we had to assume stochastic independence.

Although the mathematical results such as those of Prékopa (1973) lend themselves naturally to applications in models of oligopolistic competition with price-setting firms, we do not have a satisfactory theory of Bertrand–Nash equilibria at present. In particular, one would like to know better why the distribution of consumers' characteristics can be assumed to have the properties used to establish the existence of an equilibrium in pure strategies. We hope that this chapter will stimulate research in this area.

REFERENCES

Anderson, S., A. de Palma, and J. Thisse. 1989. "Demand for Differentiated Products, Discrete Choice Models, and the Characteristics Approach." *Review of Economic Studies* 56: 21–35.

Barndorff-Nielsen, O. 1978. *Information and Exponential Families in Statistical Theory.* New York: Wiley.

Caplin, A., and B. Nalebuff. 1991a. "Aggregation and Imperfect Competition: On the Existence of Equilibrium." Mimeo, Princeton University. *Econometrica,* forthcoming.

1991b. "Aggregation and Social Choice: A Mean-Voter Theorem." Mimeo, Princeton University. *Econometrica,* forthcoming.

de Palma, A., V. Ginsburgh, Y. Papageorgiu, and J. Thisse. 1985. "The Principle of Minimum Differentiation Holds under Sufficient Heterogeneity." *Econometrica* 53: 767–81.

de Palma, A., and J. Thisse. 1989. "Les modèles de choix discrets." *Annales d'Economie et de Statistique* 14: 151–90.

Dierker, H. 1986. "Existence of Nash Equilibrium in Pure Strategies in an Oligopoly with Price Setting Firms." Discussion paper, University of Bonn.

Dierker, E., H. Dierker, and W. Trockel. 1984. "Price-Dispersed Preferences and C^1 Mean Demand." *Journal of Mathematical Economics* 13: 11–42.

Dieudonné, J. 1969. *Foundations of Modern Analysis.* New York: Academic Press.

Hildenbrand, W. 1983. "On the 'Law of Demand.'" *Econometrica* 51: 997–1019.

Marshall, A., and I. Olkin. 1974. "Majorization in Multivariate Distributions." *The Annals of Statistics* 2: 1189–1200.

McFadden, D. 1974. "Conditional Logit Analysis of Qualitative Choice Behavior." In *Frontiers in Econometrics,* P. Zaremka, Ed. New York: Academic Press, pp. 105–42.

1981. "Econometric Models of Probabilistic Choice." In *Structural Analysis of Discrete Data with Econometric Applications,* C. Manski and D. McFadden, Eds. Cambridge, MA: The MIT Press, pp. 198–272.

Novshek, W., and H. Sonnenschein. 1979. "Marginal Consumers and Neoclassical Demand Theory." *Journal of Political Economy* 87: 1368–76.

Prékopa, A. 1973. "On Logarithmic Concave Measures and Functions." *Acta Scientiarum Mathematicarum* 34: 335–43.

Roberts, J., and H. Sonnenschein. 1977. "On the Foundations of the Theory of Monopolistic Competition." *Econometrica* 45: 101–13.

Trockel, W. 1984. *Market Demand.* Springer Lecture Notes in Economics and Mathematical Systems, 223. Berlin: Springer-Verlag.

Uhrin, B. 1984. "Some Remarks About the Convolution of Unimodal Functions." *The Annals of Probability* 12: 640–5.

PART V

Applied general equilibrium models

CHAPTER 18

Trade policy modeling with imperfectly competitive market structures

Alasdair Smith and Anthony J. Venables

1 Introduction

Trade policy has been one of the major areas of application of computable equilibrium models. In the work of Whalley (1985), Deardorff and Stern (1986), and others, we have seen the development of large-scale and highly sophisticated world models. These have been used to address a wide range of trade policy questions and to simulate the effects of trade liberalizations.

These models are based on the assumption that markets are perfectly competitive, yet in the last decade, theoretical research in international trade and trade policy has focused on imperfectly competitive market structures. This literature has generated important insights both with respect to the positive theory of trade and the theory of trade policy (for surveys of each of these, see Helpman and Krugman, 1985, 1989). The new approach to trade theory that is developed in this literature is now undergoing empirical application. Econometric work based on imperfectly competitive trade models is being undertaken, and there is now a rapidly growing literature on computable equilibrium models of trade and trade policy under imperfect competition (e.g., Cox and Harris, 1985; Baldwin and Krugman, 1988; Dixit, 1988; Smith and Venables, 1988).

There are, of course, many different theories of imperfect competition, and we know from the theoretical literature that both positive and normative results may be sensitive to model specification. The volume of intraindustry trade predicted by the theory depends on the extent to which markets are segmented. In some circumstances, the welfare effect of an export subsidy is positive or negative according as firms compete in quantities or in prices. This poses some problems for computable equilibrium modeling. Any model that has been constructed on the basis of a particular

This research was supported by U.K. ESRC Grant No. R000231763.

form of competitive interaction between firms must face the possibility that changing the form of the interaction might have dramatic effects on its results – even changing the sign of welfare effects. In the current state of knowledge, we are in no position to say with any confidence that one industry is best described by quantity competition and another by price competition. The best we can do is conduct sensitivity analysis with respect to the type of competitive interaction assumed to be taking place between firms.

In this chapter, we first discuss some of the alternative approaches to the numerical modeling of trade policy under imperfect competition that have been employed in the literature. We then undertake sensitivity analysis with respect to model structure and the form of competitive interaction between firms. By working with a single industry and a range of policy experiments, the sensitivity of results with respect to different modeling approaches is investigated. We conclude – albeit on the basis of the example of a single industry – that results are not as sensitive to the way in which imperfect competition is modeled as might have been feared.

2 Modeling imperfect competition

The methodology of computable equilibrium modeling is to construct a theoretical model, assemble a data set, and then choose parameters of the model such that the equilibrium of the model coincides with observed values of variables in the data set. The data set includes information of two types: parameters of the demand system and of technology, drawn from econometric or other forms of empirical research; and values of endogenous variables, including production, consumption, and trade. Calibration then involves selecting values of other parameters such that these endogenous variables are supported as an equilibrium of the model. If perfect competition is assumed, then prices are set equal to marginal costs, and other parameters are chosen such that at these prices, the levels of production and consumption supported by the model coincide with observed values.

Central to imperfect competition is the fact that price may exceed marginal cost in some industries. To incorporate this in the model, we need data on price–cost margins, and we need theory to inform us as to what behavior supports the observed price–cost margins. There are two possible sources of information on the relationship between price and marginal cost. First, it may be possible in some industries to obtain direct observations on each of these (e.g., Dixit, 1988). Second, even if this is not possible, estimates of the extent of returns to scale in the technology (giving a relationship between average and marginal cost) together with an assumption that the industry is in long-run equilibrium, so price is equal to average cost, gives the required information on the relationship between price and marginal cost (see, e.g., Baldwin and Krugman, 1988; Smith and Venables, 1988).

Given some observed price–marginal cost margin, how is this to be supported as an equilibrium of the model? There are three related issues here. First, how differentiated are products in the industry? Clearly, the more differentiated are the products of one firm from those of another, then the greater would theory predict the price–marginal cost margin to be. Second, how concentrated is the industry? An important aspect of this question is what is the appropriate level at which an industry is to be defined? General equilibrium modeling may require that industries are defined at a relatively aggregate level, while competitive interaction between firms may be taking place at the level of very much more narrowly defined products. In this case, we have to think of the industry as being composed of a number of subindustries, and concentration must be measured at the subindustry level. The third theoretical determinant of the price–marginal cost margin is the nature of the competitive interaction between these firms. Do firms collude, or do they compete in quantity, or in price?

An observation on the price–marginal cost margin can shed light on one of these issues only if there is other information, or maintained assumptions, on the other two. The literature has followed several different approaches here. For example, the work of Dixit on the U.S. automobile industry (Dixit, 1988) uses price–cost margins to infer the nature of competition conditional upon product differentiation and numbers of firms. To do this, Dixit assumes that all U.S.-produced cars are perfect substitutes in the U.S. market, as are all Japanese cars; cars from the two sources are imperfect substitutes for each other, with an estimated elasticity of substitution drawn from econometric work and set at 2. Data on the number of firms in the industry is readily available, although firms are of different sizes. This is handled by using the Herfindahl index to provide the number of equal-sized firms equivalent to the actual distribution of firms. Given product differentiation and numbers of firms, observed price–marginal cost margins then turn out to imply a degree of competition intermediate between Cournot behavior and Bertrand. This is summarized by a value of a conjectural variations parameter, and this conjectural variation is then held constant in the policy simulations that follow. A similar methodology is followed in Baldwin and Krugman's (1988) study of the market for 16K random-access memory chips. They argue that the product is inherently homogeneous, and obtain data on the number of firms. They they use observed price–cost margins (through the life cycle of the product) to infer the nature of competitive interaction. The conjectural variation so calibrated turns out to imply behavior significantly more collusive than Cournot.

An alternative approach is followed by Smith and Venables (1988). In this work, an assumption is imposed on the form of competition between firms, and, by using data on the Herfindahl equivalent number of firms in each industry, calibration solves for the degree of product differentiation in the industry that is consistent with observed price–cost margins. The advantages of this approach, as compared to calibrating competitive behavior, are twofold. First, conjectural variations are dispensed with: the equilibria under study are Nash equilibria. Second, the approach provides estimates of the measure of product differentiation in the industry – a measure that we do not otherwise have for the range of industries studied. The disadvantage of the approach is, of course, that it is only as good as the maintained assumption about the degree of concentration and the nature of competition. This means that sensitivity analysis is essential.

In order to investigate the sensitivity of results with respect to these assumptions, this chapter considers an application of the model of Smith and Venables (1988) to a particular industry. Details of the model are set out in the appendix, and we only sketch its structure here. It is a model of partial equilibrium, focusing on a single industry (or group of industries). Any particular firm is located in one country, but can export to all markets, so that it competes with other firms in its industry from all countries. Firms have increasing returns to scale, with the possibility of decreasing marginal cost as well as decreasing average cost. Products are differentiated, and demands are assumed to be isoelastic, with an elasticity of demand for total industry sales with respect to an industry price index denoted η, and an elasticity of demand for an individual product variety (given the industry price index) denoted ϵ. Products are more differentiated the lower is ϵ. The form of firms' perceived marginal revenue, and, hence, the relationship between price and marginal cost, then depends on the nature of the competitive interaction between firms. We will assume for the moment that firms compete in each national market separately, and consider the two cases of quantity and price competition. If firms are Cournot competitors, the equality of marginal revenue to marginal cost (for each firm in each market) takes the form

$$p\left[1-\frac{1}{\epsilon}+s\left\{\frac{1}{\epsilon}-\frac{1}{\eta}\right\}\right]=mc.$$

If they are Bertrand competitors, the analogous equation is

$$p\left[1-\frac{1}{\epsilon-s(\epsilon-\eta)}\right]=mc,$$

where p is price, s is the firm's share of the market, and mc is marginal cost.

Suppose now that given data on the price–marginal cost margin, firms' market shares s, and the overall demand elasticity η, these equations are used to calibrate the measure of product differentiation ϵ. What difference does the form of behavior make to the calibrated value of ϵ, the elasticity of demand for an individual variety? Consider as an example the case of the domestic electrical appliance industry (NACE 346), with the model disaggregated into a six-country structure – France, Germany, Italy, the United Kingdom, the rest of the EC, and the rest of the world. (Data on this industry and details of calibration are described in Smith and Venables, 1988.) We initially suppose that this industry is comprised of five separate and symmetric subindustries, this number being chosen such that each subindustry is of similar scale to the two largest narrowly defined product groups in the industry – washing machines and refrigerators. Each firm competes with other firms (from all countries) in its subindustry. Given estimates of returns to scale, the demand elasticity η, numbers of firms, and production, consumption and trade, we then calibrate the degree of product differentiation consistent with price–marginal cost margins. For Cournot behavior, we obtain $\epsilon = 10.77$, and for Bertrand behavior, $\epsilon = 7.78$. These relative magnitudes reflect the fact that Bertrand behavior is inherently more competitive than Cournot. A given price–marginal cost margin, therefore, must be supported by more market power being derived from product differentiation, that is, a lower value of ϵ.

These values of ϵ were obtained given the assumption that competitive interaction between firms was occurring not at the aggregate industry level, but rather within five separate subindustries. Now consider changing this assumption, and suppose that all firms in the industry compete in the same product range, that is, the industry consists of a single subindustry. Changing the number of subindustries in this way makes the industry very much more competitive. Since all firms in the industry now compete together, instead of one-fifth of the firms competing in each of five subindustries, the effect of this changed assumption is to decrease the market shares s by a factor of 5. With one subindustry and Cournot behavior, calibration produces $\epsilon = 7.65$; with Bertrand behavior this becomes $\epsilon = 7.28$.

We see from this that the measure of product differentiation varies substantially according to the maintained assumptions about the form of competition, and about the level of disaggregation necessary to capture competitive interaction between firms. When the industry is quite competitive (as is the case if we assume a single subindustry), then the difference between Cournot and Bertrand competition is small. If the industry is assumed to be more concentrated, so each firm has a substantial share of the market, then Cournot behavior provides a significant degree of market power, so that the data are consistent with a substantially lower degree of product differentiation.

These four cases give us different interpretations of the industry under study, ranging from Cournot behavior with a relatively high degree of concentration, to Bertrand behavior and a lower level of concentration. How sensitive are policy conclusions with respect to this variety of assumptions? To investigate this, we conducted four different policy experiments for this industry, the experiments being an import tariff, an export subsidy, a production subsidy, and a multilateral trade liberalization. Each experiment was conducted under each set of assumptions, that is, for each of the cases of quantity and price competition, with five subindustries and with a single one. Results are summarized in Tables 1 to 4.

The first experiment considered was imposition of a 5% U.K. ad valorem import tariff against imports from all the other countries in the model, that is, France, Germany, Italy, the rest of the EC, and the rest of the world. Of course, a tariff change of this type is not a legal policy option, but the experiment serves to illustrate some of the effects discussed in the theoretical literature. The results given are the changes in U.K. consumer surplus (ΔCS), U.K. government revenue (ΔGR), U.K. firms' profits ($\Delta\Pi$), and U.K. welfare (ΔW), defined as the sum of these three elements. Each of these changes is reported in million ECU at 1982 prices and, for comparison, total U.K. consumption of the industry's output in the base year amounted to 2174mECU. The percentage change in U.K. output from the industry is also given ($\Delta X\%$).

We learn several things from Table 1. The tariff brings welfare gains in all cases, both when the number of firms is held constant (oligopoly) and when entry and exit is permitted in each country until profits are restored to their base level (monopolistic competition). Gains are always larger under monopolistic competition than under oligopoly. Results vary across the four cases studied, but are of a similar order of magnitude in all cases. Three things about the differences between cases are worth noting. First, quantity changes are largest for the case of Cournot behavior and five subindustries; as was noted before, market shares in this case give firms significant market power, so the calibrated demand elasticity ϵ is relatively high. Second, the profit increase due to the tariff is relatively small if competition is relatively intense, so the increased market shares of domestic firms caused by the tariff translates into relatively small price increases; this small profit gain pulls down the overall welfare gain. Third, differences between the cases are smaller when entry and exit are allowed than under oligopoly.

Table 1. *5% U.K. import tariff*

	ΔCS^a	ΔGR^b	$\Delta \Pi^c$	ΔW^d	$\Delta X\%^e$
Oligopoly					
Cournot, 5 subindustries	−36.3	28.6	32.8	25.1	17.9
Bertrand, 5 subindustries	−31.1	31.5	18.4	18.8	14.3
Cournot, 1 subindustry	−30.7	31.6	27.7	28.6	14.2
Bertrand, 1 subindustry	−30.0	32.0	15.7	17.7	13.7
Monopolistic competition					
Cournot, 5 subindustries	0.9	24.6	0	25.5	26.4
Bertrand, 5 subindustries	1.2	28.5	0	29.7	20.8
Cournot, 1 subindustry	1.2	28.7	0	29.9	20.5
Bertrand, 1 subindustry	1.3	29.2	0	30.5	19.8

[a] ΔCS: change in consumer surplus, 1982mECU.
[b] ΔGR: change in government revenue, 1982mECU.
[c] $\Delta \Pi$: change in profits, 1982mECU.
[d] ΔW: change in consumer surplus + government revenue + profits.
[e] % change in production.

Table 2. *5% U.K. export subsidy*[a]

	ΔCS	ΔGR	$\Delta \Pi$	ΔW	$\Delta X\%$
Oligopoly					
Cournot, 5 subindustries	16.9	−27.1	14.8	4.6	21.7
Bertrand, 5 subindustries	11.3	−21.8	12.5	2.0	12.5
Cournot, 1 subindustry	11.1	−21.6	12.4	1.9	12.2
Bertrand, 1 subindustry	10.5	−21.1	12.3	1.7	11.3
Monopolistic competition					
Cournot, 5 subindustries	37.7	−30.0	0	7.7	29.7
Bertrand, 5 subindustries	37.0	−24.6	0	12.4	19.7
Cournot, 1 subindustry	37.3	−24.4	0	12.9	19.4
Bertrand, 1 subindustry	38.7	−24.0	0	14.7	18.7

[a] See Table 1 for definitions of terms.

The second experiment is a 5% U.K. export subsidy, and its effects are reported in Table 2. This is an interesting case because we know that, with a fixed number of firms, a small export subsidy will increase welfare if behavior is Cournot and the number of firms is relatively small. But a

Table 3. *1% U.K. production subsidy*[a]

	ΔCS	ΔGR	ΔΠ	ΔW	ΔX%
Oligopoly					
Cournot, 5 subindustries	20.3	−18.3	11.0	13.0	9.3
Bertrand, 5 subindustries	20.6	−17.9	8.0	10.7	7.1
Cournot, 1 subindustry	20.6	−17.9	7.9	10.6	7.0
Bertrand, 1 subindustry	20.7	−17.8	7.5	10.4	6.7
Monopolistic competition					
Cournot, 5 subindustries	34.0	−19.0	0	15.0	13.4
Bertrand, 5 subindustries	35.6	−18.6	0	17.0	10.7
Cournot, 1 subindustry	35.8	−18.6	0	17.2	10.6
Bertrand, 1 subindustry	36.5	−18.5	0	18.0	10.3

[a] See Table 1 for definitions of terms.

subsidy will reduce welfare if the number of firms is large enough, or if behavior is Bertrand, products are homogeneous and marginal cost is increasing (Eaton and Grossman, 1986). For the industry under study here, there is product differentiation and marginal costs are decreasing. It turns out that a 5% U.K. export subsidy raises U.K. welfare in *all* cases. As would be expected from theory, the gains are greatest with Cournot behavior and few firms, but they are small in all cases - under oligopoly the welfare gains never exceed 0.25% of the value of consumption. Under monopolistic competition, the export subsidy causes entry to occur making the industry more competitive and bringing gains to consumers. The total welfare gain is positive in all cases, but is now smallest for the case of Cournot behavior and a relatively high degree of concentration (five subindustries). This is because the high value of ϵ in this case implies a larger increase in export volume, so the revenue cost of the export subsidy is relatively large.

Table 3 reports the effect of a 1% U.K. production subsidy. As expected, this increases U.K. output, and raises both profits and consumer surplus. There is a net welfare gain from this experiment as the consumer price is brought closer to marginal cost, and the size of the gain is quite similar across the four oligopoly cases. Under monopolistic competition, entry occurs, making the industry more competitive and giving larger welfare gains; but, again, the size of the welfare change is similar across all four types of competition.

Table 4 studies the effects of reducing the real cost of intra-EC trade by an amount equal to 2.5% of the value of trade; this may be thought of

Table 4. *Reduction in the cost of intra-EC trade, equal to 2.5% of the value of trade*[a]

	ΔCS	ΔGR	$\Delta\Pi$	ΔW	$\Delta X\%$
Oligopoly					
Cournot, 5 subindustries	126	0	−42	84	2.1
Bertrand, 5 subindustries	95	0	−0.2	95	1.3
Cournot, 1 subindustry	92	0	2	94	1.2
Bertrand, 1 subindustry	88	0	9	97	1.2
Monopolistic competition					
Cournot, 5 subindustries	94	0	0	94	1.8
Bertrand, 5 subindustries	98	0	0	98	1.3
Cournot, 1 subindustry	99	0	0	99	1.3
Bertrand, 1 subindustry	104	0	0	104	1.3

[a] See Table 1 for definitions of terms.

as a possible representation of the effects of trade liberalization associated with the EC's internal market program. For this case, the results reported are for the EC as a whole (for which the base consumption of the product amounted to 11.4 bill ECU). Once again, we see that overall welfare results are not very sensitive to the nature of competition. However, the procompetitive effect of the policy has larger effect on firms' profits when behavior is Cournot, and when the industry is relatively concentrated.

These examples seem to suggest that policy conclusions are a good deal less sensitive to the way in which imperfect competition is modeled than a reading of the theoretical literature might suggest. Calibration and simulation under different assumptions about competition and about the degree of concentration never change either the sign or the order or magnitude of the welfare effects of policy experiments.

3 Modeling intraindustry trade

One of the major contributions coming from the literature on trade under imperfect competition is a satisfactory explanation of intraindustry trade. In order to support intraindustry trade, traditional computable equilibrium models based on perfect competition have to resort to the "Armington assumption," that products produced in one country are perceived as being different from those produced in another. One of the original motivations for research on international trade under imperfect competition was precisely to get away from this rather ad hoc explanation of intraindustry

Table 5. *Cournot behavior, segmented markets:* $\epsilon = 10.77$; *tariff equivalents, %*

	Consumed in				
Produced in	France	Germany	Italy	U.K.	Rest of EC
France	0	30.7	33.9	34.2	33.7
Germany	27.4	0	32.8	32.6	24.4
Italy	25.3	22.7	0	25.1	27.2
U.K.	36.4	33.1	40.4	0	27.7
Rest of EC	32.0	25.3	43.9	31.0	0

trade, and instead provide an explanation based on the underlying behavior of firms. However, there exist different ways of modeling international competition and the international organization of markets, and these different models give rise to different volumes of trade. Once again, we need to investigate the range of possibilities, and explore the sensitivity of our results with respect to this dimension of market organization.

The simplest form of international competition is that in which markets are internationally segmented. This was implicitly assumed before, and has become the benchmark case in much of the literature. The assumption means that each firm chooses its strategic variable on a country-by-country basis; for example, if firms are Cournot competitors, then each firm chooses its sales in a particular country taking as constant its rivals' sales in that (and all other) countries. Behavior of this type gives strong incentives for intraindustry trade, supporting trade even if all firms produce a homogeneous output (Brander and Krugman, 1983). However, inspection of data on actual trade volumes indicates that firms almost always have relatively larger shares in their home market than they do in export markets. For the observed trade volumes to be consistent with the theory, there must therefore be substantial barriers to trade. These barriers could be trade taxes, transport costs, or (if firms product differentiated products) national demand differences. Their magnitude can be illustrated by producing a single summary measure of the ad valorem equivalent of the barrier. For our example industry, NACE 346, these tariff equivalents are given in Table 5 for the five EC countries in the model. For example, the observed performance of French firms in the German market is consistent with segmented-market Cournot behavior if there is an implicit ad valorem barrier of 30.7% on French imports to Germany.

Table 6. *Capacity precommitment, price competition:* $\epsilon = 9.50$; *tariff equivalents, %*

	Consumed in				
Produced in	France	Germany	Italy	U.K.	Rest of EC
France	0	28.2	32.8	30.9	31.2
Germany	26.5	0	33.5	30.9	22.9
Italy	21.1	18.1	0	19.5	22.9
U.K.	38.9	35.3	44.0	0	28.8
Rest of EC	31.0	23.5	45.3	28.5	0

Alternative theories of international market organization predict lower volumes of trade for given parameter values. For example, consider the perfect equilibrium of the following two-stage game between firms. At the first stage, firms choose a total volume of output (or capacity) for supply to some set of markets in aggregate. At the second stage, firms choose price in each market separately, so segmented-market Bertrand equilibria are established, conditional upon total sales over the sum of the markets in question. It turns out that this game gives a lower volume of trade than does a segmented-market Cournot equilibrium (see the appendix, and for further details, Venables, 1990). Calibration of a given data set under this alternative hypothesis will, therefore, give different tariff equivalents, and these are described for NACE 346 in Table 6. In comparing Table 6 with Table 5, two things need to be noted. First, because the equilibrium supports a lower volume of trade, lower tariff equivalents are required to make the observed trade volumes consistent with this two-stage equilibrium. Second, the equilibrium of the two-stage game is also more competitive, in the sense of supporting lower-price cost margins, than is the equilibrium of the single-stage Cournot segmented-market game. This means that the calibrated measure of product differentiation ϵ is also lower now than in the previous case, dropping from 10.77 to 9.5. With a lower value of ϵ, larger price differences are required to reduce trade to observed levels. This tends to raise the calibrated tariff equivalents, and the difference between the numbers reported in Tables 5 and 6 is the outcome of these two forces.

Table 7 gives the matrix of tariff equivalents for a third possible form of international market game. This is the case of market integration, in which firms play a quantity game, choosing total supply to a set of markets.

Table 7. *Cournot behavior, segmented markets:* $\epsilon = 8.73$; *tariff equivalents, %*

	Consumed in				
Produced in	France	Germany	Italy	U.K.	Rest of EC
France	0	28.8	33.7	31.0	31.7
Germany	27.8	0	35.0	31.7	23.4
Italy	21.8	18.4	0	19.0	23.1
U.K.	42.0	38.2	47.1	0	30.8
Rest of EC	32.8	24.6	47.7	29.2	0

Deliveries of the output to each country is then undertaken by arbitrageurs, so the producer price (price net of transport costs) is equated in all countries (see the appendix). For given parameter values, this equilibrium supports a lower volume of trade than the previous two. However, it is also more competitive, in the sense of giving lower price–cost margins. The calibration procedure, therefore, gives a lower value of ϵ (=8.73), which means that high tariff equivalents are required to hold trade volumes down to their observed levels. These two forces give tariff equivalents that are in some cases higher and in other cases lower than those of Tables 5 and 6.

We have little evidence as to whether international markets are segmented, integrated, or in between - as with the international quantity game followed by segmented-market price game. Once again, therefore, it is important to try and assess the sensitivity of policy simulations with respect to these types of international competition. Tables 8 to 11 report the results of the previous four policy experiments under the hypotheses of Cournot segmented-market behavior (*C*, segmented, as in Table 5); a two-stage game with each firm choosing sales to the EC as a whole, followed by a segmented-market price competition (*C*, Bertrand, as in Table 6); the integrated-market case, where each firm chooses sales to the EC as a whole, and deliveries take place to equalize producer prices on sales in each national market (*C*, integrated, as in Table 7). In each of these cases, it is assumed that there are five subindustries, so the first case in Tables 8–11 is the same as the first case in Tables 1–4.

Consider, first, the U.K. import tariff (Table 8). It raises U.K. welfare in all cases, but, under oligopoly, the gain from the tariff is much reduced the more integrated are markets. The reason for this is that U.K. firms are less able to exploit their improved position in their domestic market

Table 8. *5% U.K. import tariff*[a]

	ΔCS	ΔGR	$\Delta\Pi$	ΔW	$\Delta X\%$
Oligopoly					
C, segmented	−36.3	28.6	32.8	25.1	17.9
C, Bertrand	−38.5	30.7	24.8	17.0	16.2
C, integrated	−37.3	31.8	18.4	12.9	15.4
Monopolistic competition					
C, segmented	0.9	24.6	0	25.5	26.4
C, Bertrand	−0.9	26.5	0	25.6	25.2
C, integrated	−0.3	27.8	0	27.5	24.0

[a] See Table 1 for definitions of terms.

Table 9. *5% U.K. export subsidy*[a]

	ΔCS	ΔGR	$\Delta\Pi$	ΔW	$\Delta X\%$
Oligopoly					
C, segmented	16.9	−27.1	14.8	4.6	21.7
C, Bertrand	16.8	−25.4	14.8	6.2	18.5
C, integrated	15.2	−24.2	14.3	5.3	16.1
Monopolistic competition					
C, segmented	37.7	−30.0	0	7.7	29.7
C, Bertrand	41.0	−29.1	0	11.9	27.8
C, integrated	41.4	−28.0	0	13.4	25.4

[a] See Table 1 for definitions of terms.

when they are only choosing a single strategic variable over all markets – as is the case when markets are integrated (see also Markusen and Venables, 1988). If free entry and exit are permitted, we see that the gains from the tariff are larger than is the case under oligopoly, and of a similar order of magnitude in all cases.

A U.K. export subsidy raises U.K. welfare in all cases (Table 9). The size of the welfare gain is small, and is similar in all cases. Under both oligopoly and monopolistic competition, the gain is smallest in the Cournot segmented-market case; this is because of the high value of the demand elasticity ϵ and, consequently, the large increase in export volume and high revenue cost of the policy. The production subsidy raises welfare in all cases (Table 10), and by amounts that differ rather little between cases.

Table 10. *1% U.K. production subsidy*[a]

	ΔCS	ΔGR	$\Delta\Pi$	ΔW	$\Delta X\%$
Oligopoly					
C, segmented	20.3	−18.3	11.0	13.0	9.3
C, Bertrand	20.3	−18.1	10.0	12.2	8.4
C, integrated	20.4	−18.1	9.3	11.6	7.9
Monopolistic competition					
C, segmented	34.0	−19.0	0	15.0	13.4
C, Bertrand	34.7	−19.0	0	15.7	12.9
C, integrated	35.5	−18.9	0	16.6	12.3

[a] See Table 1 for definitions of terms.

Table 11. *Reduction in the cost of intra-EC trade, equal to 2.5% of the value of trade*[a]

	ΔCS	ΔGR	$\Delta\Pi$	ΔW	$\Delta X\%$
Oligopoly					
C, segmented	126	0	−42	84	2.1
C, Bertrand	135	0	−22	113	1.9
C, integrated	126	0	−11	120	1.7
Monopolistic competition					
C, segmented	94	0	0	94	1.8
C, Bertrand	120	0	0	120	1.9
C, integrated	121	0	0	121	1.7

[a] See Table 1 for definitions of terms.

Finally, Table 11 reports the EC-wide experiment of reducing the real cost of trade within the community. Here we see that the gains from reducing the cost of trade become steadily larger the more integrated is the market structure. The reason for this is that this experiment brings an all-around increase in intra-EC trade volumes. It has already been noted that, given tariff equivalents, the segmented-market equilibrium has a higher volume of trade than does the integrated-market equilibrium; corresponding to this, the social value of an increase in trade volume is greater in the integrated-market case than the segmented-market case. We therefore see that the gains from reduced trade costs are up to 50% larger if markets are integrated than if they are segmented.

4 General equilibrium considerations

The preceding two sections have studied the sensitivity of policy conclusions with respect to some of the modeling choices faced by researchers in trade policy under imperfect competition. There are, of course, many other dimensions in which sensitivity analysis needs to be undertaken - for example, with respect to parameter values, and, importantly, with respect to choice of functional form for demand and cost functions.

The results presented in this chapter have all been derived from a model of partial equilibrium - that is, ignoring income effects and, more importantly, assuming that the industry under study can draw resources from other sectors of the economy at prices that are constant and equal to social marginal valuations. These assumptions are likely to introduce two significant sources of bias into the results presented. First, the assumption that the sector faces infinitely elastic input supply curves means that the quantity changes predicted by the model are exaggerated. General equilibrium considerations would introduce a positive slope into input supply functions and dampen these quantity effects. Second, welfare results depend on the assumption that resources drawn from other sectors are priced at their social marginal cost. Market prices of these inputs could be either above or below their social marginal cost. For example, if the resources are being drawn from other sectors that are themselves imperfectly competitive, and hence "too small" relative to a first-best optimum, then shadow prices of these resources will exceed their market prices. Conversely, if contraction of other sectors leads to terms of trade gains (or, more precisely, if tariffs in these sectors are set at less than their optimum value), then the shadow prices of inputs will be less than market prices. To incorporate these features fully would require the embedding of industry models of the type outlined before in a full multicountry general equilibrium framework.

5 Conclusions

Trade models based on perfectly competitive markets have but a single theory of competition on which to build. Trade models that incorporate imperfect competition have a wide range of possible theories from which elements can be drawn. One distinction between theories is the selection of the set of strategic variables open to firms. This chapter has explored the implications of having firms play four different sorts of game: (1) a segmented-market quantity game, where firms' strategic variables are quantities in each market; (2) a segmented-market price game; (3) an integrated-market quantity game, in which each firm's strategic variable is a single quantity for a set of markets, and delivery to national markets occurs by arbitrage; and (4) a two-stage game, with an integrated-market quantity choice followed by segmented-market price games.

A second distinction between theories is according to whether the number of players in the game is held constant or entry and exit of firms are permitted. For each of the previous models, this chapter presents results both for the case in which the number of firms is fixed (oligopoly) and when it is variable (monopolistic competition). These should not be viewed as competing theories, but rather as capturing a distinction between the short-run and long-run effects of policy.

A third issue that we have tried to capture in this chapter is one of aggregation. Imperfect competition raises aggregation issues that are not present in a perfectly competitive model, as we have to ask what level of industrial aggregation is appropriate to capture competition between firms in an "industry." The chapter addressed this issue by comparing results for two different levels of industrial aggregation.

The richness of the set of possibilities open is a potential source of problems for applied work on trade policy, since we are far away from having the sort of empirical work that will enable us to say with any confidence that one industry is adequately characterized by one sort of game and another industry is characterized by a different sort. This means that the applied trade policy researcher must use sensitivity analysis to assess the breadth of the range of possible outcomes. Working with the example of a single industry calibrated to a European data set, this chapter suggests that the welfare effects of a range of policy experiments are a good deal less sensitive to the way in which competition is modeled than might have been feared.

Appendix

The model underlying the simulations contained in this chapter has the following structure. There are J producing and consuming countries, and each industry has demands in country j generated from a subutility function

$$y_j = \left[\sum_{i=1}^{J} n_i m_i a_{ij}^{1/\epsilon} x_{ij}^{(\epsilon-1)/\epsilon} \right]^{\epsilon/(\epsilon-1)}, \quad \epsilon > 1, \ j = 1, \ldots, J, \qquad \text{(A.1)}$$

where n_i and x_{ij} are as defined in the text, m_i is the number of varieties produced per country i firm (held constant in simulations reported here), and the a_{ij} are demand parameters. y_j can be regarded as a quantity index of aggregate consumption of the industry output. Dual to the quantity index is a price index q_j taking the form

$$q_j = \left[\sum_{i=1}^{I} n_i m_i a_{ij} p_{ij}^{1-\epsilon} \right]^{1/(1-\epsilon)}, \quad j=1,\ldots,J, \tag{A.2}$$

and representing the price of the aggregate product, where the p_{ij} are the prices of the individual varieties. Income effects are ignored, so that demand for the aggregate product is a function only of the price index q_j. This demand function is isoelastic,

$$y_j = b_j q_j^{-\eta}, \quad j=1,\ldots,J, \tag{A.3}$$

where the b_j reflect the size of the respective country markets. Utility maximization implies that demand for individual product varieties depends both on the price of the individual variety and on the aggregate price index:

$$x_{ij} = a_{ij} \left(\frac{p_{ij}}{q_j} \right)^{-\epsilon} y_j = a_{ij} b_j p_{ij}^{-\epsilon} q_j^{\epsilon-\eta}, \quad i,j=1,\ldots,J. \tag{A.4}$$

The profits of a single representative country i firm are

$$\pi_i = m_i \sum_{j=1}^{J} x_{ij} p_{ij} (1-T_{ij}) - C_i(x_i, m_i), \quad i=1,\ldots,J, \tag{A.5}$$

where the T_{ij} are the ad valorem costs of selling in market j (transport costs or trade taxes, for example). The function C_i is the firm's cost function, assumed to depend on the output per variety $x_i = \sum_j x_{ij}$ and on the number of varieties m_i. The form of this function is a weighted average of functions linear and log linear in m_i and x_i.

If firms play a single-stage segmented-market game, then choice of sales in each market x_{ij} to maximize profits given the demand system, equations (A.1)–(A.4), gives first-order conditions:

$$p_{ij}(1-T_{ij}) \left(1 - \frac{1}{e_{ij}} \right) = \frac{1}{m_i} \frac{\partial C_i}{\partial x_i}, \quad i,j=1,\ldots,J, \tag{A.6}$$

where e_{ij} is the perceived elasticity of demand.

If firms are Cournot competitors, then this takes the form:

$$\frac{1}{e_{ij}} = \frac{1}{\epsilon} + \left(\frac{1}{\eta} - \frac{1}{\epsilon} \right) s_{ij}, \quad i,j=1,\ldots,J,$$

where s_{ij} is the share of a single firm from country i in the subindustry market j.

If firms are Bertrand competitors then

$$e_{ij} = \epsilon - (\epsilon - \eta) s_{ij}.$$

Section 3 considers the case when, instead of playing a single-stage game, firms play a two-stage game, choosing total output at the first stage and the distribution of output between markets at the second stage. If the second stage is a segmented-market price game (Table 6 and cases *C*, Bertrand), then at the second stage of the game each firm chooses its sales x_{ij} to maximize (A.5), taking as constant its total sales $x_i = \sum_{j=1}^{J} x_{ij}$ and the prices of other firms. This gives the first-order conditions:

$$p_{ij}(1-T_{ij})\left(1-\frac{1}{e_{ij}}\right)=p_{ik}(1-T_{ik})\left(1-\frac{1}{e_{ik}}\right), \quad i,j,k=1,\ldots,J, \qquad \text{(A.7)}$$

where $e_{ij} = \epsilon - (\epsilon - \eta)s_{ij}$.

At the first stage, each firm chooses total output x_i given other firms' total output and fully incorporating the reallocation of sales between markets implied by the second-stage equilibrium, equation (A.7).

If the second-stage game has fully integrated markets (Table 7 and cases *C*, integrated), then at the second stage sales x_{ij} are determined by arbitrage, given total x_i, so as to equate the producer price of a particular product in each market, that is, satisfying

$$p_{ij}(1-T_{ij}) = p_{ik}(1-T_{ik}), \quad i,j,k=1,\ldots,J. \qquad \text{(A.8)}$$

At the first stage, each firm chooses total output x_i given other firms' total output, and fully incorporating the reallocations of sales between markets implied by the second-stage equilibrium, equation (A.8).

REFERENCES

Baldwin, R., and P. R. Krugman. 1988. "Market Access and International Competition; a Simulation Study of 16K Random Access Memories." In *Empirical Methods for International Trade,* R. Feenstra, Ed. Cambridge, MA: The MIT Press.

Brander, J. A., and P. R. Krugman. 1983. "A Reciprocal Dumping Model of International Trade." *Journal of International Economics* 11: 1-14.

Cox, D., and R. Harris. 1985. "Trade Liberalisation and Industrial Organisation; Some Estimates for Canada." *Journal of Political Economy* 93: 115–45.

Deardorff, A. V., and R. Stern. 1986. *The Michigan Model of World Production and Trade.* Cambridge, MA: The MIT Press.

Dixit, A. K. 1984. "International Trade Policy for Oligopolistic Industries." *Economic Journal* (Supplement): 1-16.

1988. "Optimal Trade and Industrial Policies for the U.S. Automobile Industry." In *Empirical Methods for International Trade,* R. Feenstra, Ed. Cambridge, MA: The MIT Press.

Eaton, J., and G. Grossman. 1986. "Optimal Trade and Industrial Policy under Oligopoly." *Quarterly Journal of Economics* 101: 383–406.

Helpman, E., and P. R. Krugman. 1985. *Market Structure and Foreign Trade.* Cambridge, MA: The MIT Press.

1989. *Trade Policy and Market Structure.* Cambridge, MA: The MIT Press.

Markusen, J., and A. J. Venables. 1988. "Trade Policy with Increasing Returns and Imperfect Competition." *Journal of International Economics* 24: 299-316.

Smith, A., and A. J. Venables. 1988. "Completing the Internal Market in the European Community; Some Industry Simulations." *European Economic Review* 32: 1501-25.

Venables, A. J. 1990. "International Capacity Choice and National Market Games." *Journal of International Economics* 29: 23-42.

Whalley, J. 1985. *Trade Liberalisation among Major World Trading Areas.* Cambridge, MA: The MIT Press.

CHAPTER 19

Seminonparametric Bayesian estimation of consumer and factor demand models

William A. Barnett, John Geweke, and Michael Wolfe

1 Introduction

Recently, there has been growing interest in the possibility of using flexible functional forms to produce applied general equilibrium models that can incorporate economic theory under plausibly weak assumptions,[1] as opposed to the calibration approach, which uses very restrictive specifications for tastes and technology.[2] However, there are many unresolved problems in this area. Consider, for example, the concluding paragraph from Diewert and Wales (1988):

> We believe that semiflexible functional forms have a promising future in the context of constructing econometric applied general equilibrium models. Lau (1978), for example, criticized traditional calibration-type applied general equilibrium models that use Cobb–Douglas, Leontief or C.E.S. type functional forms due to their *a priori* imposition of unwarranted substitution elasticities. Lau preferred the econometric approach, utilizing flexible functional forms on both the producer and consumer side. However, calibration-type general equilibrium model builders have maintained that the econometric approach based on flexible forms cannot be implemented using time series data if the model has a large number of goods.

While Diewert and Wales then proposed a single possible parametric specification, we believe that a general modeling approach to this problem is needed. Such an approach (1) must be able to incorporate as much theoretical flexibility as can be supported by the available sample size, so that the depth of the parameterization must be dependent upon the sample size. The approach (2) must be able to impose the maintained economic

This research was partially supported by National Science Foundation grant SES 8305162 (Barnett) and SES 8908365 (Geweke) and by a grant from the Pew Foundation to Duke University. We are grateful to Milton D. Terrell for his valuable computational assistance in the estimation of the supply-side models.

[1] Examples include those cited in Jorgenson (1984).

[2] For a review of the calibration approach literature, see Shoven and Whalley (1984).

theory globally – especially if the model is to be used for forecasting into regions not necessarily known at the time that the model is estimated. And, finally, (3) iterative estimation algorithms capable of producing inferences having known properties must exist. An approach that goes far toward meeting all three of those requirements is the Bayesian estimation of the new AIM (asymptotically ideal model) specification produced from the Müntz–Szatz series expansion estimated seminonparametrically in infinite dimensional parameter space.

Condition (2) is critical to the resolution of the overfitting problem that is at the center of the calibration model builders' critique of the econometric approach to applied general equilibrium modeling. As observed before by Diewert and Wales, the issue is whether the econometric approach is applicable when there is a large number of goods relative to the sample size. In the language of econometrics, the issue is the potential overfitting that can be produced by undersized samples. However, if a modeling approach satisfies conditions (1) and (2) before, all of the information contained in the data can be extracted econometrically without the risk of overfitting, since a sequence of functions constrained everywhere to lie within the neoclassical functions space cannot produce a perfect fit regardless of the order of approximation or the depth of the parameterization, since globally increasing, concave functions cannot produce the irregular, oscillatory behavior needed to fit the noise in data. However, in practice, a blockwise weakly separable tree structure would have to be imposed upon the structure of a general equilibrium model to permit recursive blockwise inference at reasonable computational cost.[3]

Integrating consumer demand systems, output supply systems, and factor demand systems into a closed general equilibrium economy is a long-run objective of this research. However, at the present stage of development, our results are available only for a consumer demand system and for a factor demand system under constant returns to scale. In this chapter, we provide a unified presentation of those currently existing consumption and production modeling results. The specification for consumer demand and production modeling, along with an operational procedure for applying Bayesian estimation and inference methods, provides an important stepping stone toward full structural implementation within a theoretically and statistically coherent model of an economy.

As a result of the scope of this chapter, we have included two major self-contained sections, Sections 2 and 3. Section 2, which follows immediately, provides our completed results on consumer demand modeling

[3] Presently available methods of testing for blockwise weak separability have been investigated in Monte Carlo studies by Barnett and Choi (1989).

with Bayesian estimation of AIM, and Section 3 reports on our progress on Bayesian and maximum likelihood estimation of the AIM production model. Section 4 concludes the chapter.

2 AIM consumption modeling

2.1 *Introduction*

2.1.1 *The objectives*

In this section, we review our results on applying new operational methods in Bayesian inference to estimate the AIM consumer demand system seminonparametrically at its first two orders of approximation, AIM(1) and AIM(2).[4] The AIM model is produced from the Müntz–Szatz series expansion and has the advantage of yielding a demand system that can be restricted to be globally regular at all orders of approximation as well as in the limit. However, inference with the model is complicated because regularity can be imposed through the imposition of inequality constraints on parameters and by the fact that the likelihood function can be badly behaved without imposition of those regularity conditions.

As a result of these characteristics of the AIM model's structure, sampling theoretic methods are greatly compromised in principle. Although Barnett and Yue (1988b) have successfully computed maximum likelihood estimates for the AIM consumer demand model at its first three orders of approximation, AIM(1), AIM(2), and AIM(3), any inferences from that research beyond point estimation alone must be interpreted with great care, since sampling distributions are truncated and since the likelihood function under the maintained hypothesis need not be concave.

On the other hand, Bayesian methods are not at all compromised in principle by the existence of inequality constraints or of complex likelihood function properties. But, in practice, these complications render available algorithms for numerical integration impractical. In this chapter, we develop and apply the required three extensions of Geweke's generic operational methods for Bayesian inference (Geweke, 1986, 1988; Geweke and Terrell, 1990).[5] These three methodological innovations not only permit Bayesian estimation of the AIM sequence of demand systems, but, in addition, greatly expand the scope of applicability of Bayesian methods to include important common classes of problems that previously were completely intractable by either Bayesian or sampling theoretic methods.

[4] Earlier reports on our results with the AIM consumption model can be found in Barnett and Yue (1988b) and Barnett, Geweke, and Yue (1989).

[5] On this subject, also see Barnett, Geweke, and Yue (1989).

2.1.2 *The model*

The literature on using neoclassical economic theory in econometrics has followed a rocky road. For many years, the literature concentrated on the derivation and estimation of consumer demand systems, factor demand systems, and output supply systems from globally regular generating functions, such as the Cobb–Douglas and CES utility, indirect utility, production, and cost functions. Such globally regular functions are defined to satisfy everywhere the monotonicity and curvature conditions for rational neoclassical economic behavior. This approach reached its peak at the time that extensions to the CES model were being proposed.[6] However, that approach ran into a dead end when Uzawa (1962) proved that it is not possible to produce a model that simultaneously can attain arbitrary elasticities of substitution and also can be CES as the arguments of the function vary.

As a means of circumventing that dead end, attention initially turned to the use of nonintegrable models, which provide local approximations to demand and supply functions (i.e., to the decisions' solution functions, rather than to the generating functions). For many years, the double log model was popular in that regard. That literature reached its peak with Barnett's (1979a) version of the aggregated Rotterdam model, which can be derived under very weak assumptions on individual preferences. That model is particularly attractive, since its assumptions are not sufficiently strong to assure the existence of a representative consumer; and theorists, such as Debreu (1974) and Sonnenschein (1973), typically have argued that the assumptions for aggregate integrability are too strong to be useful. Barnett's version of the aggregate Rotterdam model solves that problem by recovering some but not all microeconomic theory at the aggregate level under assumptions just strong enough to recover some but not all of the microeconomic theory after aggregation. In agreement with the Debreu and Sonnenschein critique, Barnett's model is not integrable at the aggregate level, since, as demonstrated by Debreu and Sonnenschein, integrability cannot be recovered at the aggregate level under reasonable assumptions.

Nevertheless, despite the theoretical implausibility of all available assumption structures producing aggregate integrability, many important issues are most readily investigated under the assumption of aggregate integrability, since only then is all microeconomic theory available at the aggregate level. Barnett's version of the Rotterdam, not providing access to aggregate integrability, can only recover some microeconomic theory

[6] In particular, see Barnett's (1979b) blockwise weakly separable nested nonhomothetic CES utility tree.

at the aggregate level. Hence, the literature turned toward the use of local approximations to the generating functions themselves, so that duality theory would provide access to all of the implications of aggregate integrability. In this approach, the theoretical discomfort about the provable implausibility of aggregate integrability was at least nominally circumvented by appealing to the usefulness of aggregate integrability as a means of imposing plausible functional "regularity" upon aggregate demand systems.[7]

The result was the class of "flexible functional forms" such as the popular translog model, which can attain arbitrary elasticities at a point. To a high degree, these models have revolutionized microeconometrics by providing access to all neoclassical microeconomic theory in econometric applications – at least for those microeconometricians who are willing to accept Gorman's assumptions for the existence of a representative consumer at the aggregate level. These models completely escape from the dead end of the Uzawa Impossibility Theorem by providing the capability to attain arbitrary elasticities of substitution – although at only one point. But this escape is achieved at the cost of giving up global integrability completely. In fact, in a number of recent papers, it has been shown that the most popular flexible functional forms have very small regions of theoretical regularity and often perform poorly in Monte Carlo experiments.[8] We were left with the choice between models such as the CES, which are globally regular, but not locally flexible, and models such as the translog, which are locally flexible, but not theoretically regular.

A partial solution to this problem recently has been provided in the work of Barnett (1983a), Barnett and Lee (1985, 1987), and Barnett, Lee, and Wolfe (1985, 1987), who originated and analyzed the minflex Laurent model, and the work of Diewert and Wales (1987) and Blackorby, Schworm, and Fisher (1986), who originated and analyzed the Generalized Barnett model. The minflex Laurent model is both fully locally flexible and also regular over large regions, but not globally. The generalized

[7] It should be acknowledged that this justification for the use of integrable aggregate demand systems is poorly linked with theory. The effect of loss of aggregate integrability in theory is the introduction of distribution effects into aggregate demand systems. Since aggregate integrability is impossible in a demand system possessing distribution effects, aggregate integrability cannot be a useful functional "regularity" condition under those circumstances. Nevertheless, distribution effects rarely have been introduced into the specifications of aggregate demand systems, despite the theoretical internal contradiction created by not doing so.

[8] See, e.g., Barnett (1981, 1982, 1983a, 1983b, 1985); Barnett and Lee (1985, 1987); Barnett, Lee, and Wolfe (1985, 1987); White (1980); Wales (1977); Gallant (1981); Caves and Christensen (1980); Guilkey and Lovell (1980); and Guilkey, Lovell, and Sickles (1980).

Barnett model is fully globally regular and locally quasiflexible, in a sense that Diewert and Wales (1987) define, but not fully locally flexible. A further interesting contribution to these recent advances is Lewbel (1987). However, we still are left with a trade-off in deciding between minflex Laurent and generalized Barnett. But perhaps even more importantly, none of the models described before possesses any claim to global flexibility, and hence the flexible inference capabilities appear to be at a point, despite the fact that there do not exist any known statistical inference techniques that can impute an inference to a single point.

A path-breaking innovation in that regard has been provided by Gallant (1981, 1982) in his introduction of seminonparametric inference methods into econometrics.[9] His Fourier model possesses a global flexibility property in the sense that his model asymptotically can reach any continuous function, and his inferences do not maintain a specification containing a finite number of parameters, so that his asymptotic inferences are free from any specification error. However, the basis functions with which Gallant's model seeks to span the neoclassical function space are sines and cosines, despite the fact that such trigonometric functions are periodic and hence are far from neoclassical. Attaining theoretical regularity globally with that model, without reducing the span in an unacceptable manner, seems to be very difficult. Attaining regularity locally is possible, but far from easy, as has been observed by McFadden (1985). In addition, at fixed sample size, no uniquely best rule exists for selecting the number of terms. The reason is that use of an excessive number of terms in the unconstrained Fourier model produces overfitting, but the word "excessive" in this context is not defined.[10] Considerable educated judgment is needed to assure that the model's potentially very large number of terms is not "fitting" the noise about the true function. In short, the use of Gallant's model is best left to professional econometricians.[11] This

[9] See also Chalfant (1987).

[10] The most systematic approaches currently available to the choice of K for the Fourier model are those of Eastwood and Gallant (1987), who provide selection rules that differ depending upon whether large-sample or small-sample properties are sought. Each of the sequential truncation rules proposed in that paper, whether deterministic or adaptive, works well under some circumstances and poorly under others. The relevant circumstances are supplied by Eastwood and Gallant (1987). See also Gallant (1982) on the same subject.

[11] Computer code for imposing sufficient (but not necessary) curvature conditions on the Fourier model globally (but not also the monotonicity restrictions required for regularity) were provided by Gallant (1981). But that procedure reduces the model's span to a degree that is rejected by the data. A more promising approach to imposing curvature (but not also monotonicity) conditions on the Fourier model is provided by Gallant and Golub (1984). Although their procedure does not damage estimator consistency, their

limitation is unfortunate, since the original intent of this literature was to provide widespread availability of the constraints of microeconomic theory in applied research.

A possible solution was proposed by Barnett and Jonas (1983), who originated a multivariate version of the Müntz-Szatz series expansion, which not only is globally flexible in the same sense as Gallant's Fourier model, but also in principle permits *easy* imposition of theoretical regularity - *globally.* With imposed regularity, the series expansion always remains within the neoclassical space being spanned by the series' basis.[12] Overfitting of data is impossible with a series expansion that is globally regular at all orders of approximation, since globally regular functions are consistent with rational economic behavior and therefore not with the anomalous behavior exhibited by stochastic disturbances. A perfect fit to data (containing any amount of noise at all) is impossible, no matter how many terms are entered into the expansion. Hence, at fixed sample size, the number of terms can be increased iteratively until convergence of elasticity estimates. This combination of global regularity at all orders of approximation and of asymptotic global flexibility appears to be ideal. In fact, the expansion possesses all of the properties defined by McFadden (1985) to be desirable in demand modeling. Hence, the demand system derived from the Müntz–Szatz series expansion, when estimated seminonparametrically, has been named by Barnett and Yue (1988a, 1988b) as the *asymptotically ideal model* (AIM).

restrictions are not exclusively on the parameters, but rather are jointly on the parameters and on the data. Gallant and Golub's procedure could be imposed at a fine lattice of points, or in a more complex fashion within an arbitrary closed rectangular region. In the latter case, which to our knowledge has never been attempted, a nested double optimization is involved. Under their curvature restrictions, Gallant and Golub (1984) advocate a parametric bootstrap for inference.

It should be observed that overlooking the imposition of monotonicity is not a trivial matter. For example, the translog model under the imposition of the global curvature restrictions retains some amount of inference capability, However, if monotonicity as well as curvature are imposed globally, the translog's inference capabilities are totally lost, since the translog then collapses to the Cobb-Douglas, which has all fixed (nonestimable) elasticities.

Challenging procedures of the sort advocated by Gallant and Golub (1984) seem unavoidably necessary with the Fourier model, since the Fourier's basis functions (sines and cosines) used to span the neoclassical function space are not themselvces elements of that space. In contrast, the basis functions of the Müntz–Szatz series expansion that we use in what follows all lie within the space being spanned. Our regularity restrictions on the partial sums are imposed only on the parameters and do not depend upon the data. In fact, those restrictions are simply nonnegativity of the coefficients.

12 For a presentation of Müntz and Szatz's original theory regarding the univariate Müntz-Szatz series expansion, see Rudin (1966).

2.1.3 *The new Bayesian methods*

In this section, we report on the systematic estimation of the AIM consumer demand model by Bayesian estimation.[13] The Bayesian estimation, which is of central importance in this research, was accomplished through the use of fundamental new advances in constrained numerical integration. The new developments in Monte Carlo integration applied in this chapter permit Bayesian methods to be used in many common statistical applications that previously were beyond the capabilities of existing Bayesian and sampling theoretic methods, including inference with badly behaved nonconcave likelihood functions subject to binding inequality restrictions.

2.2 *The expansion*

Let $\lambda(k)=2^{-k}$ for $k=1,\ldots,\infty$, and let $\mathbb{N}=\{1,2,\ldots\}$ be the natural numbers. Define $\mathbf{x}$ to be the vector of consumption quantities, and $\mathbf{p}$ to be the vector of corresponding prices. Let $\mathbf{v}=\mathbf{p}/\mathbf{p}'\mathbf{x}$ be expenditure normalized prices, and let $f(\mathbf{v})$ be the reciprocal indirect utility function. Then the multivariate version of the Müntz–Szatz series model proposed by Barnett and Jonas (1983) is

$$f(\mathbf{v})=a_0+\sum_{k\in\mathbb{N}}\sum_{i=1}^{n}a_{ik}v_i^{\lambda(k)}+\sum_{k\in\mathbb{N}}\sum_{m\in\mathbb{N}}\left(\sum_{i=1}^{n}\sum_{j=1}^{n}a_{ijkm}v_i^{\lambda(k)}v_j^{\lambda(m)}\right)+\cdots,$$

where n is the number of goods, and $a_0, a_{ik}, a_{ijkm}, \ldots$ are parameters to be estimated for $i,j=1,\ldots,n$ and $k,m=1,\ldots,\infty$. In the current application of that expansion, we select $\Lambda=\{\lambda(k):\lambda(k)=2^{-k}, k\in\mathbb{N}\}$ to be the exponent set.[14] Sample size is designated by T.

In our application of the model that follows, the number of goods is $n=3$. The model then becomes

$$f(\mathbf{v})=a_0+\sum_{k\in\mathbb{N}}\sum_{i=1}^{3}a_{ik}v_i^{\lambda(k)}+\sum_{k\in\mathbb{N}}\sum_{m\in\mathbb{N}}\left(\sum_{i=1}^{3}\sum_{j=1}^{3}a_{ijkm}v_i^{\lambda(k)}v_j^{\lambda(m)}\right)$$
$$+\sum_{k\in\mathbb{N}}\sum_{m\in\mathbb{N}}\sum_{l\in\mathbb{N}}\left(\sum_{i=1}^{3}\sum_{j=1}^{3}\sum_{h=1}^{3}a_{ijhkml}v_i^{\lambda(k)}v_j^{\lambda(m)}v_h^{\lambda(l)}\right).$$

Since there are only three goods, interactions between four or more goods are impossible.

The partial sums (i.e., finite-order approximations) from this expansion for $K\in\mathbb{N}$ are defined by

[13] See also Barnett, Geweke, and Yue (1989).

[14] For a presentation of Müntz and Szatz's original theory regarding the univariate Müntz–Szatz, see Rudin (1966) and Barnett and Jonas (1983).

$$f_K(\mathbf{v}) = a_0 + \sum_{k=1}^{K}\sum_{i=1}^{3} a_{ik} v_i^{\lambda(k)} + \sum_{k=1}^{K}\sum_{m=1}^{K}\left(\sum_{i=1}^{3}\sum_{j=1}^{3} a_{ijkm} v_i^{\lambda(k)} v_j^{\lambda(m)}\right)$$
$$+ \sum_{k=1}^{K}\sum_{m=1}^{K}\sum_{l=1}^{K}\left(\sum_{i=1}^{3}\sum_{j=1}^{3}\sum_{h=1}^{3} a_{ijhkml} v_i^{\lambda(k)} v_j^{\lambda(m)} v_h^{\lambda(l)}\right).$$

The corresponding exponent set is $\Lambda = \{\lambda(k) : \lambda(k) = 2^{-k}, k = 1, \ldots, K\}$. Barnett and Yue (1988a) have proved that if a continuous function $g(\mathbf{v})$ and all of its first and second derivatives are in $\mathcal{L}_p$ space, then there exists a sequence of coefficients of the expansion such that f_K converges to g both pointwise and in Sobolev norm. Barnett and Yue also have shown that if g is bounded and continuous within its domain, then there exists a coefficient sequence such that f_K converges almost uniformly to g in $\mathcal{L}_\infty$ space, and the first- and second-order derivatives of f_K all converge almost uniformly to the corresponding derivatives of g in $\mathcal{L}_\infty$ space.[15] Under certain identifying assumptions, all elasticities are everywhere estimated consistently as $T \to \infty$, if $K = K(T)$ is selected to be a slowly increasing function of sample size and if the parameters are estimated by maximum likelihood estimation at each K.

Barnett and Yue's (1988a, 1988b) results are inspired by and closely resemble those proved by Gallant (1981, 1982, 1984) for the Fourier model, except that unlike the Fourier model, the Müntz–Szatz series partial sums *easily* can be forced to be *globally* regular at all orders of approximation as well as in the limit. Hence, in practice when global regularity is imposed, K can be increased at any preselected fixed sample size T until the elasticity estimates converge. The reason is that within the class of *globally regular* Müntz–Szatz partial sums, there is a limit to the goodness of fit that can be attained as K increases at fixed T, and an oscillatory fit is impossible from within the class of increasing, strictly concave functions. Hence, convergence of elasticity estimates as K increases at fixed T can be expected without the model having been permitted to "fit" the noise about the underlying true function.[16] If we repeat this process at each T, we should expect that the converged value of K at each T will be a slowly increasing function of T, so that our assumption about $K(T)$ will be satisfied.

By contrast, the number of terms in the unconstrained Fourier model cannot be increased to convergence in that manner, since without imposition of global regularity of the partial sums, an undersized sample

[15] This latter result can be acquired either as an independent proof or as a direct corollary to the result in Sobolev space.

[16] In addition, strong empirical evidence of the AIM model's inability to overfit has been acquired in our recent research with the AIM factor demand system, fitted to the Berndt and Wood data and to Monte Carlo data.

problem will arise.[17] Eventually, a perfect fit will be attained with a very irregular Fourier expansion, which treats the noise as if it were a reflection of erratic irrational behavior. Hence, with the Fourier model, the selection of the function $K(T)$ requires careful consideration of the risk of overfitting.

In fact, in recent years, even simple flexible functional forms such as the translog have been the source of controversy regarding their need often to violate maintained theoretical restrictions - that is, to overfit - in order to retain their local flexibility property. The importance of being able to impose or attain regularity globally, or at least over the convex closure of the data, has been demonstrated in recent research by Barnett (1981, 1982, 1983a, 1983b, 1985); Barnett and Lee (1985, 1987); Barnett, Lee, and Wolfe (1985, 1987); White (1980); Wales (1977); Gallant (1981); Caves and Christensen (1980); Guilkey and Lovell (1980); and Guilkey, Lovell, and Sickles (1980). Otherwise, the theoretical maintained hypothesis from which neoclassical demand system models are derived is violated and the properties of parametric inferences thereby are severely damaged. In addition to the severe inference problems now known to be produced by violation of the maintained theoretical hypothesis, models violating maintained theory are virtually useless in policy applications, as in producing policy simulations or in computation of cost-benefit or other welfare economic comparisons. For example, if the theoretical curvature conditions are violated, the behavioral implication is that consumers are locally minimizing utility subject to the budget constraint.

A particularly important positive contribution in that direction was recently produced by Diewert and Wales (1987) in creating their generalized Barnett model, which is both locally flexible and globally regular. In addition, as shown by Blackorby, Schworm, and Fisher (1986), that model is the only currently known parametric model that remains flexible under the null hypothesis of weak separability. Using the same basis functions, Barnett (1985) originated the minflex Laurent model, which is regular over large regions (most likely including the convex closure of the data).[18] The minflex Laurent model, although sacrificing some regularity relative to

[17] In principle, the Gallant and Golub (1984) procedure could be used to impose regularity on the Fourier model at a fine lattice of points, and then our procedure for selecting K could be applied. In fact, we believe that procedure would indeed be the best one to use with the Fourier, although that procedure is not the one advocated for the Fourier by Eastwood and Gallant (1987). However, we appreciate the difficulty of applying our data-based procedure for selecting K with the Fourier.

[18] Those regional regularity properties are displayed in Barnett and Lee (1985) and Barnett, Lee, and Wolfe (1985, 1987) for various typical cases. Barnett (1985) has proved theorems regarding the regular regions in general. The basis functions shared in common by the generalized Barnett model and by both versions of the minflex Laurent model (the minflex Laurent generalized Leontief model and the minflex Laurent translog model) are

the globally regular generalized Barnett model, possesses a stronger flexibility property than the generalized Barnett model. However, the flexibility properties of both of those models are inherently local, unlike the global spanning capabilities of models produced seminonparametrically in infinite dimensional parameter space, such as the Fourier and Müntz–Szatz series models. As a result, the capabilities of the generalized Barnett model and the minflex Laurent model are best judged relative to the capabilities of the earlier fully parametric models, such as the translog, rather than relative to the more ambitious capabilities of the class of seminonparametric models introduced into economics more recently by Gallant.

Barnett and Yue (1988a) have proved that the span of the Müntz–Szatz series is not reduced by deleting elements from the parameter arrays. As a result, we restrict consideration to the index sets $A=\{(i,j): i\neq j;\ i,j=1,2,3\}$ and $B=\{(i,j,h): i\neq j, j\neq h, i\neq h:\ i,j,h=1,2,3\}$, when producing the interaction terms in the expansion. The model then becomes

$$f_K(\mathbf{v})=a_0+\sum_{k=1}^{K}\sum_{i=1}^{3}a_{ik}v_i^{\lambda(k)}+\sum_{k=1}^{K}\sum_{m=1}^{K}\left(\sum\sum_{(i,j)\in A}a_{ijkm}v_i^{\lambda(k)}v_j^{\lambda(m)}\right)$$
$$+\sum_{k=1}^{K}\sum_{m=1}^{K}\sum_{l=1}^{K}\left(\sum\sum\sum_{(i,j,h)\in B}a_{ijhkml}v_i^{\lambda(k)}v_j^{\lambda(m)}v_h^{\lambda(l)}\right). \tag{1}$$

Deleting the diagonal elements in this manner is important. In addition to decreasing the number of parameters in any partial sum, deletion of the diagonal subsequence of parameters results in a model that is globally regular at all orders of approximation, if the parameters are nonnegative. Nonnegativity of the coefficients is not sufficient for regularity, when the diagonal terms are left in the expansion. Hence, when the model is in the form defined by (1), the model can be used easily to impose theoretical regularity. Whether imposed within the maintained hypothesis or only within a tested null hypothesis, neoclassical regularity imposed in this simple manner is imposed globally at every finite K as well as in the limit as $K\to\infty$. Convergence within the neoclassical function space is achieved without ever leaving that space with any function in the function sequence.[19] As a result, we believe that the Müntz–Szatz series model is very practical.

the basis functions of the Laurent series expansion, which can be viewed as the Taylor series basis augmented to include the corresponding terms with negative exponents.

19 When the sequence is estimated subject to the coefficient nonnegativity constraints, the consistency result in Barnett and Yue (1988a) necessarily becomes conditional upon the neoclassical function subspace spanned. That subspace excludes the nondifferentiable (although nevertheless increasing and concave) functions. See Barnett and Jonas (1983) regarding the need to exclude the nondifferentiable functions from the spanned space. However, the significance of this compromise in span should not be overemphasized, since the Sobolev norm and neoclassical elasticities are not defined without differentiability.

We have estimated the first two partial sums, $f_K(\mathbf{v})$, $K=1,2$. We call those partial sums Partial Sum 1 and Partial Sum 2, respectively.

2.3 *Partial Sum 1*

To acquire Partial Sum 1, substitute $K=1$ into equation (1). We find that Partial Sum 1 takes the following form:

$$\begin{aligned} f_{K=1}(\mathbf{v}) &= a_0 + \sum_{i=1}^{3} a_i v_i^{1/2} + \sum\sum_{(i,j)\in A} a_{ij} v_i^{1/2} v_j^{1/2} \\ &\quad + \sum\sum\sum_{(i,j,h)\in B} a_{ijh} v_i^{1/2} v_j^{1/2} v_h^{1/2} \\ &= a_0 + a_1 v_1^{1/2} + a_2 v_2^{1/2} + a_3 v_3^{1/2} + a_4 v_1^{1/2} v_2^{1/2} \\ &\quad + a_5 v_1^{1/2} v_3^{1/2} + a_6 v_2^{1/2} v_3^{1/2} + a_7 v_1^{1/2} v_2^{1/2} v_3^{1/2}, \end{aligned}$$

where $a_4 = a_{12} + a_{21}$; $a_5 = a_{13} + a_{31}$; $a_6 = a_{23} + a_{32}$; and $a_7 = a_{123} + a_{132} + a_{213} + a_{231} + a_{312} + a_{321}$. The exponent set is the singleton $\Lambda = \{\frac{1}{2}\}$.

To acquire the demand functions, we can use the modified Roy's identity:

$$\mathbf{x} = \frac{\nabla f_{K=1}(\mathbf{v})}{\mathbf{v}'\nabla f_{K=1}(\mathbf{v})},$$

where ∇ is the gradient operator. Define $\mathbf{s} = (s_1, s_2, s_3)'$ to be the expenditure shares, so that $s_i = p_i x_i / \mathbf{p}'\mathbf{x} = v_i x_i$. Then we have that

$$s_i = \frac{v_i\, \partial f_{K=1}/\partial v_i}{\mathbf{v}'\nabla f_{K=1}(\mathbf{v})} \tag{2}$$

for $i=1,2,3$. Differentiating $f_{K=1}$, we find that

$$2v_1 \frac{\partial f_{K=1}}{\partial v_1} = a_1 v_1^{1/2} + a_4 v_1^{1/2} v_2^{1/2} + a_5 v_1^{1/2} v_3^{1/2} + a_7 v_1^{1/2} v_2^{1/2} v_3^{1/2} \tag{3}$$

$$2v_2 \frac{\partial f_{K=1}}{\partial v_2} = a_2 v_2^{1/2} + a_4 v_1^{1/2} v_2^{1/2} + a_6 v_2^{1/2} v_3^{1/2} + a_7 v_1^{1/2} v_2^{1/2} v_3^{1/2} \tag{4}$$

$$2v_3 \frac{\partial f_{K=1}}{\partial v_3} = a_3 v_3^{1/2} + a_5 v_1^{1/2} v_3^{1/2} + a_6 v_2^{1/2} v_3^{1/2} + a_7 v_1^{1/2} v_2^{1/2} v_3^{1/2} \tag{5}$$

and, hence,

$$\begin{aligned} 2\sum_{i=1}^{3} v_i \frac{\partial f_{K=1}}{\partial v_i} &= a_1 v_1^{1/2} + a_2 v_2^{1/2} + a_3 v_3^{1/2} + 2a_4 v_1^{1/2} v_2^{1/2} + 2a_5 v_1^{1/2} v_3^{1/2} \\ &\quad + 2a_6 v_2^{1/2} v_3^{1/2} + 3a_7 v_1^{1/2} v_2^{1/2} v_3^{1/2} \end{aligned} \tag{6}$$

If we now let

$$S_i = v_i \frac{\partial f_{K=1}}{\partial v_i}$$

for $i=1,2,3$, and $S = S_1 + S_2 + S_3$, it follows from (2) that

$$s_i = \frac{S_i}{S} \tag{7}$$

for $i=1,2,3$. We can compute (7) by dividing (3) and (4) successively by (6). We need not estimate the s_3 share equation, since from s_1 and s_2, we can compute $s_3 = 1 - s_1 - s_2$.

When estimating equation (7), we use additive Gaussian errors and impose the parameter normalization $a_1 + a_2 + a_3 = 1$ to eliminate the parameter a_3.[20] A normalization is necessary, since each of the equations in (2) is homogeneous of degree zero in the parameters. With a_3 eliminated by normalization, the parameters that remain to be estimated are a_1, a_2, a_4, a_5, a_6, and a_7. So Partial Sum 1 has six free parameters.

2.4 *Partial Sum 2*

To acquire Partial Sum 2, set $K=2$ in equation (1), so that the exponent set becomes the double $\Lambda = \{\frac{1}{2}, \frac{1}{4}\}$. The result is

$$f_{K=2}(\mathbf{v}) = a_0 + \sum_{k=1}^{2} \sum_{i=1}^{3} a_{ik} v_i^{2^{-k}} + \sum_{k=1}^{2} \sum_{m=1}^{2} \left(\sum\sum_{(i,j)\in A} a_{ijkm} v_i^{2^{-k}} v_j^{2^{-m}} \right)$$

$$+ \sum_{k=1}^{2} \sum_{m=1}^{2} \sum_{l=1}^{2} \left(\sum\sum\sum_{(i,j,h)\in B} a_{ijhkml} v_i^{2^{-k}} v_j^{2^{-m}} v_h^{2^{-l}} \right).$$

In order to avoid the extensive multiple subscripting in the coefficients a_{ijhkml}, we reparameterize by stacking the coefficients as they appear in the expansion into a single vector of parameters, $\mathbf{b} = (b_0, \ldots, b_{26})$, containing the 27 coefficients in $f_{K=2}(\mathbf{v})$. The result is

$$\begin{aligned} f_{K=2}(\mathbf{v}) = {} & b_0 + b_1 v_1^{1/2} + b_2 v_2^{1/2} + b_3 v_3^{1/2} + b_4 v_1^{1/4} + b_5 v_2^{1/4} + b_6 v_3^{1/4} \\ & + b_7 v_1^{1/2} v_2^{1/2} + b_8 v_1^{1/2} v_2^{1/4} + b_9 v_1^{1/4} v_2^{1/2} + b_{10} v_1^{1/4} v_2^{1/4} \\ & + b_{11} v_1^{1/2} v_3^{1/2} + b_{12} v_1^{1/2} v_3^{1/4} + b_{13} v_1^{1/4} v_3^{1/2} + b_{14} v_1^{1/4} v_3^{1/4} \\ & + b_{15} v_2^{1/2} v_3^{1/2} + b_{16} v_2^{1/2} v_3^{1/4} + b_{17} v_2^{1/4} v_3^{1/2} + b_{18} v_2^{1/4} v_3^{1/4} \end{aligned}$$

20 Strictly speaking, the specification of Gaussian errors is incorrect, since shares must be in the unit interval. Following the convention in this literature, we retain the Gaussinity assumption for its analytical simplicity and to make our results comparable to the work of others. The interred variances for these errors are so small as to make the violation of the share restrictions academic (see Table 1). These problems could be avoided by using the logistic normal as the disturbance distribution (see Rossi, 1983).

$$+b_{19}v_1^{1/2}v_2^{1/2}v_3^{1/2}+b_{20}v_1^{1/4}v_2^{1/2}v_3^{1/2}+b_{21}v_1^{1/2}v_2^{1/4}v_3^{1/2}$$
$$+b_{22}v_1^{1/2}v_2^{1/2}v_3^{1/4}+b_{23}v_1^{1/2}v_2^{1/4}v_3^{1/4}+b_{24}v_1^{1/4}v_2^{1/2}v_3^{1/4}$$
$$+b_{25}v_1^{1/4}v_2^{1/4}v_3^{1/2}+b_{26}v_1^{1/4}v_2^{1/4}v_3^{1/4}.$$

If we now let

$$S_i=v_i\frac{\partial f_{K=2}}{\partial v_i}$$

for $i=1,2,3$, and $S=S_1+S_2+S_3$, we can substitute into (7) to derive the share equations, s_1 and s_2, where the numerators and denominator (multiplied by 4) are as follows:

$$4S_1=2b_1v_1^{1/2}+b_4v_1^{1/4}+2b_7v_1^{1/2}v_2^{1/2}+2b_8v_1^{1/2}v_2^{1/4}+b_9v_1^{1/4}v_2^{1/2}$$
$$+b_{10}v_1^{1/4}v_2^{1/4}+2b_{11}v_1^{1/2}v_3^{1/2}+2b_{12}v_1^{1/2}v_3^{1/4}+b_{13}v_1^{1/4}v_3^{1/2}$$
$$+b_{14}v_1^{1/4}v_3^{1/4}+2b_{19}v_1^{1/2}v_2^{1/2}v_3^{1/2}+b_{20}v_1^{1/4}v_2^{1/2}v_3^{1/2}$$
$$+2b_{21}v_1^{1/2}v_2^{1/4}v_3^{1/2}+2b_{22}v_1^{1/2}v_2^{1/2}v_3^{1/4}+2b_{23}v_1^{1/2}v_2^{1/4}v_3^{1/4}$$
$$+b_{24}v_1^{1/4}v_2^{1/2}v_3^{1/4}+b_{25}v_1^{1/4}v_2^{1/4}v_3^{1/2}+b_{26}v_1^{1/4}v_2^{1/4}v_3^{1/4}$$

and

$$4S_2=2b_2v_2^{1/2}+b_5v_2^{1/4}+2b_7v_1^{1/2}v_2^{1/2}+b_8v_1^{1/2}v_2^{1/4}+2b_9v_1^{1/4}v_2^{1/2}$$
$$+b_{10}v_1^{1/4}v_2^{1/4}+2b_{15}v_2^{1/2}v_3^{1/2}+2b_{16}v_2^{1/2}v_3^{1/4}+b_{17}v_2^{1/4}v_3^{1/2}$$
$$+b_{18}v_2^{1/4}v_3^{1/4}+2b_{19}v_1^{1/2}v_2^{1/2}v_3^{1/2}+2b_{20}v_1^{1/4}v_2^{1/2}v_3^{1/2}$$
$$+b_{21}v_1^{1/2}v_2^{1/4}v_3^{1/2}+2b_{22}v_1^{1/2}v_2^{1/2}v_3^{1/4}+b_{23}v_1^{1/2}v_2^{1/4}v_3^{1/4}$$
$$+2b_{24}v_1^{1/4}v_2^{1/2}v_3^{1/4}+b_{25}v_1^{1/4}v_2^{1/4}v_3^{1/2}+b_{26}v_1^{1/4}v_2^{1/4}v_3^{1/4}$$

and

$$4S=2b_1v_1^{1/2}+2b_2v_2^{1/2}+2b_3v_3^{1/2}+b_4v_1^{1/4}+b_5v_2^{1/4}+b_6v_3^{1/4}$$
$$+4b_7v_1^{1/2}v_2^{1/2}+3b_8v_1^{1/2}v_2^{1/4}+3b_9v_1^{1/4}v_2^{1/2}+2b_{10}v_1^{1/4}v_2^{1/4}$$
$$+4b_{11}v_1^{1/2}v_3^{1/2}+3b_{12}v_1^{1/2}v_3^{1/4}+3b_{13}v_1^{1/4}v_3^{1/2}+2b_{14}v_1^{1/4}v_3^{1/4}$$
$$+4b_{15}v_2^{1/2}v_3^{1/2}+3b_{16}v_2^{1/2}v_3^{1/4}+3b_{17}v_2^{1/4}v_3^{1/2}+2b_{18}v_2^{1/4}v_3^{1/4}$$
$$+6b_{19}v_1^{1/2}v_2^{1/2}v_3^{1/2}+5b_{20}v_1^{1/4}v_2^{1/2}v_3^{1/2}+5b_{21}v_1^{1/2}v_2^{1/4}v_3^{1/2}$$
$$+5b_{22}v_1^{1/2}v_2^{1/2}v_3^{1/4}+4b_{23}v_1^{1/2}v_2^{1/4}v_3^{1/4}+4b_{24}v_1^{1/4}v_2^{1/2}v_3^{1/4}$$
$$+4b_{25}v_1^{1/4}v_2^{1/4}v_3^{1/2}+3b_{26}v_1^{1/4}v_2^{1/4}v_3^{1/4}.$$

Using $s_3=1-s_1-s_2$, we can compute s_3 from the estimated equations for s_1 and s_2. We use additive errors in the share equations, and we use the parameter normalization $b_1+b_2+b_3=1$ to eliminate parameter b_3 by substitution. In addition, observe that parameter b_0 does not appear in the share equations. Hence, 25 free parameters remain to be estimated.

2.5 *Partial sum K and the asymptotically ideal model (AIM)*

In general, application of (2) to the Müntz–Szatz partial sums (1) at each K produces a sequence of systems of share equations. In the previous two sections, we have derived the first two such systems of share equations in that sequence. Barnett and Yue (1988a, 1988b) have named the full sequence of share equation systems, for all K, the AIM model (asymptotically ideal model). In the next section, we describe the estimation procedure and data that we use in this chapter in our first actual estimation of the AIM model for $K=1$ and $K=2$. For the Partial Sum 1 reciprocal indirect utility function, we call the corresponding AIM share equation system AIM(1), and for Partial Sum 2, we call the corresponding AIM share equations AIM(2). We acquire AIM(1) and AIM(2) from equation (7), with S_i and S in that equation acquired from Section 3 for AIM(1) and from Section 4 for AIM(2).

2.6 *Estimation procedure and data*

We assume an additive error structure in the share equations, with the vector of additive disturbances, ϵ_t, being distributed independently and identically as a multivariate normal with zero mean and covariance matrix Σ. We use the price and quantity data from Appendix D, Table D, of Barnett (1981, pp. 348–9). That table contains 62 observations on five goods from 1890 to 1955, with the war years 1942–5 deleted. We use the data on three of those five goods: perishables, semidurables, and durables. The two goods that we do not use from that data are services and leisure.

The consumption quantity data were divided by population, also from that table, to acquire the per-capita data used in this research. In addition, the data on the normalized prices, v_i, were rescaled to equal 1.0 in 1929 for each good i in a manner that left the factor shares unaffected by the rescaling of the normalized prices.[21]

Since the disturbances added to the share equations are designated by ϵ_t for observations $t=1, \ldots, T$, the sample disturbance covariance matrix is

$$\hat{\Sigma}=\frac{1}{T}\sum_{t=1}^{T}\epsilon_t\epsilon_t,$$

where $T=62$. The generalized variance of the fit is the determinant $|\hat{\Sigma}|$. Maximum likelihood estimates of the parameters of AIM(1) and AIM(2)

[21] In particular, the values of $p_i(t)$ were replaced by $p_i(t)/v_i(1929)$ and the values of $x_i(t)$ were replaced by $x_i(t)v_i(1929)$ for each good i and each observation t. As a result, $v_i(t)$ was rescaled to $v_i(t)/v_i(1929)$ and the values of $s_i(t)$ were unaffected by the rescaling.

can be acquired by minimizing the generalized variance of the fit, since maximizing the likelihood function with additive multivariate normal disturbances is equivalent to minimizing the generalized variance of the fit.[22]

2.7 *Computation of elasticities*

Elasticities of substitution can be computed from the formula

$$\sigma_{ij}=\left(\frac{\partial x_i}{\partial p_j}+x_j\frac{\partial x_i}{\partial m}\right)\frac{m}{x_i x_j}, \tag{8}$$

where $m=\mathbf{p}'\mathbf{x}$ is total expenditure. But since $s_i=v_i x_i$, we have for $i=1,2,3$ that

$$x_i=\frac{s_i m}{p_i}. \tag{9}$$

If we compute the first partial derivatives of (9) with respect to m and p_i $(i=1,2,3)$ and substitute back into (8), we get that

$$\sigma_{ij}=\left[\frac{1}{v_i}\frac{\partial s_i}{\partial p_j}+\frac{s_j}{v_j}\left(\frac{1}{v_i}\frac{\partial s_i}{\partial m}+\frac{s_i}{p_i}\right)\right]\frac{mv_iv_j}{s_is_j} \tag{10}$$

for $i\neq j$, and

$$\sigma_{ii}=\left[\frac{1}{v_i}\frac{\partial s_i}{\partial p_i}-\frac{s_i}{p_iv_i}+\frac{s_i}{v_i}\left(\frac{1}{v_i}\frac{\partial s_i}{\partial m}+\frac{s_i}{p_i}\right)\right]\frac{mv_i^2}{s_i^2} \tag{11}$$

for $i=1,2,3$.

Direct derivation of the income elasticities η_{i0} produces

$$\eta_{i0}=\frac{\partial x_i}{\partial m}\frac{m}{x_i}=\frac{m}{x_i}\left(\frac{1}{v_i}\frac{\partial s_i}{\partial m}+\frac{s_i}{p_i}\right).$$

So

$$\eta_{i0}=\frac{\partial s_i}{\partial m}\frac{m}{s_i}+1. \tag{12}$$

We could use numerical differentiation to produce the values of $\partial s_i/\partial m$ and $\partial s_i/\partial p_j$ for $i,j=1,2,3$ and substitute into (10), (11), and (12) to acquire the income and substitution elasticities, as was done by Barnett and Yue (1988b). However, with Bayesian estimation, we use the analytical formulas for the elasticities provided in Appendix C. The computation of elasticities is at the median observation of the exogenous variables,

[22] For a proof of the equivalency of maximizing the likelihood function and minimizing the generalized variance of the fit, see Barnett (1976), which also contains the proofs of the consistency, asymptotic normality, and asymptotic efficiency of the maximum likelihood estimators with the class of seemingly unrelated nonlinear equation systems.

which is for the year 1920. By computing the substitution and income elasticities, the compensated (Hicks–Allen) price elasticities ξ_{ij} are immediately available from $\xi_{ij} = s_j \sigma_{ij}$ for $i, j = 1, 2, 3$; and then the uncompensated (Cournot) price elasticities can be computed from the Slutsky equation:

$$\eta_{ij} = \xi_{ij} - s_j \eta_{i0}$$

for $i, j = 1, 2, 3$.

2.8 *The maximum likelihood estimates*

Barnett and Yue (1988b) have computed maximum likelihood estimates for AIM(1), AIM(2), and AIM(3). They used the same data that we use here for Bayesian estimation. Barnett and Yue's (1988b) findings were the following.

Within the class of globally regular Müntz–Szatz partial sums, Barnett and Yue (1988b) conclude that the constrained elasticity estimates converged versus K at $K=2$. That conclusion was indicated from inspection of the constrained elasticity estimates for AIM(1) and AIM(2). As a further check on that conjecture, Barnett and Yue (1988b) computed the maximum likelihood estimates for constrained AIM(3). The constrained AIM(3) model produced a maximized value for the likelihood function that was virtually identical to that acquired with constrained AIM(2) to within reasonable computer algorithmic precision. Similarly, the change in the elasticity estimates from constrained AIM(2) to constrained AIM(3) appeared to represent little more than computer noise. Although there was no gain from passing from AIM(2) to AIM(3), nothing is lost other than possibly some precision, since overfitting is impossible with constrained AIM.[23]

[23] To see the impossibility of overfitting, consider the following imaginary experiment. Suppose we search over the entire class of neoclassical (monotonically increasing, strictly quasiconcave, twice continuously differentiable) functions, and compute the generalized variance of the fit to our data for each function within that set of functions. We then have produced a corresponding set of values of the generalized variance of the fits. Now compute the infimum of that set. The infimum will be positive, since a perfect fit is impossible from within the class of neoclassical functions. As a result, the generalized variance of the fit of the AIM demand system must be bounded below by that infimum. We should expect that at any data point, the elasticities of the AIM system will tend to approach those of a neoclassical demand system having a generalized variance of its fit that is close to this infimum.

It is also interesting to observe that our implicit nested iteration automatically satisfies the conditions for seminonparametric inference. In producing our asymptotic inferences, we iterate on K until convergence of elasticities at each fixed sample size, while iteratively increasing sample size toward infinity. That procedure automatically increases K monotonically, but at a rate lower than the rate of increase in sample size. Those are precisely the conditions necessary to produce seminonparametric inferences asymptotically.

An interesting test is that of the unconstrained AIM(1) nested within the unconstrained AIM(2) as the maintained hypothesis. AIM(1) was rejected by Barnett and Yue (1988b) in this test.[24] This rejection provides further evidence of the lack of convergence of the elasticity estimates at $K=1$. Furthermore, AIM(2) was accepted when tested as a null nested within AIM(3). Hence, AIM(2) is accepted very decisively as the element of the AIM class most appropriate with this data. However, some caution is needed in interpreting this result, since in our current exploration of the likelihood function, reported in what follows, we find regions of poor behavior outside of the nonnegative orthant. As a result, we cannot be certain that the conditions for the usual sampling theoretic asymptotics are satisfied.

The Bayesian methods developed and applied in what follows have the ability to produce valid inferences with the AIM system and are not compromised by the behavior of the model or by the existence of binding constraints when the theoretical inequality constraints are imposed.

2.9 *Monte Carlo integration in Bayesian inference: Background*

In this study, we conduct Bayesian inference *conditional* on particular choices of K in the AIM(K) expansion. Hence, inference is parametric, and is a specific instance of the familiar statistical model in which the distribution of a vector of random variables $\mathbf{y}_T = (y_1, \dots, y_T)'$ is assumed to be known up to a vector of parameters $\boldsymbol{\theta} = (\theta_1, \dots, \theta_k)'$. The model may be expressed by the probability density function whose kernel is the likelihood function $L(\mathbf{y}_T \mid \boldsymbol{\theta})$, with the functional form of L known and $\boldsymbol{\theta}$ unknown. In Bayesian inference, the unknown vector of parameters $\boldsymbol{\theta}$ is regarded as random, and its distribution conditional on the observed vector $\mathbf{y}_T$ is derived. If $\pi(\boldsymbol{\theta})$ is the prior probability density of the parameters, the conditional distribution of $\boldsymbol{\theta}$ is $p(\boldsymbol{\theta} \mid \mathbf{y}_T) \propto L(\mathbf{y}_T \mid \boldsymbol{\theta}) \pi(\boldsymbol{\theta})$. Then $p(\boldsymbol{\theta} \mid \mathbf{y}_T)$ is the posterior density of $\boldsymbol{\theta}$. Virtually all Bayesian inference problems can be cast conveniently in the form of determining the expected value of a function of interest, $g(\boldsymbol{\theta})$, under the posterior: $E[g(\boldsymbol{\theta}) \mid \mathbf{y}_T] = \int_\Theta g(\boldsymbol{\theta}) p(\boldsymbol{\theta} \mid \mathbf{y}_T)\, d\boldsymbol{\theta}$, where Θ is the parameter space.

Among the attractions of Bayesian inference are its provision of a logically consistent approach in complex situations and its incorporation in decision theory.[25] However, there have been very substantial problems in the implementation of methods for Bayesian inference. These problems have been approached on a case-by-case basis, with limited development

[24] This conclusion perhaps should be qualified by observing that the asymptotic likelihood ratio test has been shown in Monte Carlo studies generally to be biased toward rejection.

[25] See, e.g., Berger and Wolpert (1984).

of generic methods. Analytical results have been obtained only in a limited set of cases, and computations have been slow relative to frequentist methods. The development of analytical generic methods is precluded by the intractability of the integrals in $E[g(\theta)\mid \mathbf{y}_T]$ that emerge in all but the very simplest problems.

The generic problem requires determination of

$$E[g(\theta)\mid \mathbf{y}_T]=\frac{\int_\Theta g(\theta)\pi(\theta)L(\mathbf{y}_T\mid\theta)\,d\theta}{\int_\Theta \pi(\theta)L(\mathbf{y}_T\mid\theta)\,d\theta}.$$

in Monte Carlo integration with importance sampling, a sequence of independent and identically distributed random vectors $\{\theta_j\}_{j=1}^n$ is drawn from an importance sampling density $I(\theta)$. Typically, n is on the order of 10^4. Heuristically, the importance sampling density should mimic the posterior density, and to this end we define the weight function $w(\theta)=p(\theta\mid\mathbf{y}_T)/I(\theta)$. The value of $\bar{g}_T=E[g(\theta)\mid\mathbf{y}_T]$ can be approximated numerically by

$$g_{n,T}=\frac{\sum_{i=1}^n g(\theta_i)w(\theta_i)}{\sum_{i=1}^n w(\theta_i)}, \tag{13}$$

as was first observed over 20 years ago by Hammersley and Handscomb (1964).[26]

Kloek and van Dijk (1978) conjectured that $n^{1/2}(g_{n,T}-\bar{g}_T)\Rightarrow N(0,\sigma_T^2)$ as $n\to\infty$, where n is the number of Monte Carlo replications and where $\Rightarrow$ is used to designate convergence in distribution. Kloek and van Dijk (1978) also provided a method of approximating σ_T^2 numerically. This is an important conjecture, for it allows routine evaluation of the numerical accuracy of $g_{n,T}$. More formally, Geweke (1989b) has proven that if $I(\theta)>0\ \forall\theta\in\Theta$, then $g_{n,T}\to\bar{g}_T$ almost surely as $n\to\infty$. If in addition, $E[w(\theta)]<\infty$, Geweke (1989b) has proven that it indeed is true that

$$n^{1/2}(g_{n,T}-\bar{g}_T)\Rightarrow N(0,\sigma_T^2) \tag{14}$$

as $n\to\infty$, where

$$\sigma_T^2=E\{[g(\theta)-\bar{g}_T]^2w(\theta)\}; \tag{15}$$

and if

$$\hat{\sigma}_{nT}^2=\frac{\sum_{i=1}^n[g(\theta_i)-g_{n,T}]^2w(\theta_i)^2}{[\sum_{i=1}^n w(\theta_i)]^2} \tag{16}$$

then

[26] Observe that if the Monte Carlo sampling were directly from the posterior, so that $w(\theta_i)=1$ for all i, then $g_{n,T}$ would reduce directly to $(1/n)\sum_{i=1}^n g(\theta_i)$, as would be the natural choice in that case.

$$n\hat{\sigma}_{nT}^2 \rightarrow \sigma_T^2 \tag{17}$$

almost surely as $n \rightarrow \infty$.[27] From (15), we see that the asymptotic variance of $g_{n,T}$ is $(1/n)\sigma_T^2$. Hence, from (17), it follows that the numerical accuracy of $g_{n,T}$ as an approximation to $\bar{g}_T$ can be evaluated from the square root of $\hat{\sigma}_{nT}^2$, which is called the "numerical standard error" of the Monte Carlo approximation.

The conditions for convergence guide the choice of $I(\theta)$ as an experimental design problem. Recently, readily applicable methods for analytical identification of families of importance sampling densities that satisfy the moment condition $E[w(\theta)] < \infty$ have been developed. See Geweke (1989b). In many econometric models, the multivariate t density has proved to be a useful foundation for the algorithmic construction of the logarithm of the importance sampling density. The degrees-of-freedom parameter is chosen so that the tails of the importance sampling density decline at the same, or a slower, rate than the tails of the posterior density. The mean is chosen to be the mode of the posterior density. The covariance matrix can be approximated by minus the inverse of the Hessian evaluated at the mode, but this approximation is often unsatisfactory. Substantial improvements can be achieved by first tailoring each axis of the Choleski decomposition of the negative inverse Hessian to match the shape of the posterior density, as documented in Geweke (1988).

It is important to evaluate the adequacy of any chosen importance sampling density. Since the asymptotic variance of $g_{n,T}$ is $(1/n)\sigma_T^2$, we know that the number of Monte Carlo replications with importance sampling to attain a given asymptotic variance for the approximation, $g_{n,T}$, is proportional to σ_T^2. A convenient benchmark importance sampling density is the posterior density itself. In all except very simple cases, it is impossible to sample directly from the posterior, but if it were possible, then the number of replications required to achieve a prescribed asymptotic variance for the unweighted approximation, $(1/n)\sum_{i=1}^n g(\theta_i)$, would be proportional to $\text{var}[g(\theta)]$, where the variance is taken using the posterior.[28] Therefore, define the *relative numerical efficiency* of the importance sampling density $I(\theta)$ for the function of interest $g(\theta)$ to be RNE $= \text{var}[g(\theta)]/\sigma_T^2$. Since $\text{var}[g(\theta)]$ may be computed routinely and σ_T^2 can be computed approximately from $n\hat{\sigma}_{nT}^2$ in accordance with (17), RNE can be estimated as a byproduct of Monte Carlo numerical integration with importance sampling.

[27] These results are specific to the use of the approximation $g_{n,T}$. In particular, the results would not hold if the unweighted mean, $(1/n)\sum_{i=1}^n g(\theta_i)$, were used as the approximation to $\bar{g}_T$. This, in fact, is the reason for the use of the approximation $g_{n,t}$ in the literature on Monte Carlo integration.

[28] To see this, simply substitute $w(\theta) = 1$ into equations (14) and (15).

The RNE indicates the relative cost of an importance sampling density and the scope for improvement: for example, if RNE = 0.4, then 25,000 replications will be required to achieve the same numerical accuracy that would have been achieved with 10,000 replications sampling directly from the posterior density. By using RNE as a criterion for evaluation, algorithmic construction of the importance sampling density has proven successful in a variety of problems with up to a score of parameters.[29] In these problems, the log posterior is frequently asymmetric and not well approximated by the multivariate t, but is concave near the mode. In some cases, inequality constraints are not satisfied by the mode, and in that event, a simple rejection method has been used to impose the constraints: replications are taken ignoring the constraints, and are then discarded if the constraints are not satisfied.

2.10 *Extensions of Monte Carlo integration methodology for the AIM consumer demand application*

2.10.1 *The issues*

The likelihood function for the AIM consumer demand application is constructed by assuming an additive, normally distributed disturbance for each share equation. Since the shares must sum to one, the disturbances must sum to zero. Hence, one share equation is redundant, and the likelihood function is invariant to the equation that is dropped. Consequently, any inference procedure based on the likelihood principle – including Bayesian inference – is invariant with respect to the equation eliminated. We, therefore, have a two-equation model. In AIM(1), there are 9 parameters, of which 6 are nonnegative; and in AIM(2), there are 28 parameters, of which 25 are nonnegative. In each case, normalization is achieved by taking the sum of coefficients on $v_1^{1/2}$, $v_2^{1/2}$, and $v_3^{1/2}$ to be unity. Our objective is to undertake Bayesian inference conditional on each of these models.[30]

The 2×2 disturbance covariance matrix is parameterized by the lower triangular Choleski decomposition of its inverse,

[29] See Geweke (1988, 1989a).

[30] We do not claim any inferences independent of the AIM(1) and AIM(2) parameterizations that we use. To do so rigorously would raise the difficulties inherent in placing a prior on an explicitly infinite dimensional parameter space. However, we conjecture that for the AIM parameterizations, convergence to the space of all regular functions occurs rapidly, so that conditions on a parameterization poses no practical specification problems. This conjecture is strongly supported by our most recent results with the production-side factor demand AIM model.

$$\Sigma^{-1} = LL'; \qquad L = \begin{bmatrix} l_1 & 0 \\ l_2 & l_3 \end{bmatrix}.$$

This imposes positive definiteness, and the posterior density of these parameters (l_1, l_2, l_3) is considerably more nearly normal than is the posterior density of the variances and covariances themselves. For an analytical motivation by analogy to the multivariate regression model, see Anderson (1984, pp. 254–7). We incorporate a diffuse prior, proportional to $|\Sigma^{-1}|$, for the seemingly unrelated regression model.

The nonnegativity constraints on the coefficients $\{a_i\}$ in AIM(1) or $\{b_i\}$ in AIM(2) are critical. Without these constraints, right-hand-side values of the share equations become unbounded for certain configurations of the parameters and certain observations. As a consequence, the log-likelihood function has many isolated singularities outside the nonnegative orthant for the coefficients. The poor behavior of the likelihood function outside of the nonnegative orthant is not surprising, since only within the nonnegative orthant is the model globally consistent with rational (transitive, consistent) decision making by the consumer.

In practice, the global posterior mode is very difficult to determine, and local behavior at the global mode provides no information about the behavior of the posterior density in the nonnegative orthant of the coefficients. Analytic first and second derivatives of the posterior density have been derived, and a modified Newton–Raphson method is employed to determine the posterior mode subject to the appropriate nonnegativity constraints. Details are provided in Appendix B.

The nonnegativity constraints, in conjunction with the nonconcavity of the posterior density, render this problem unsuited to tools for Bayesian inference developed heretofore. Coping with these novelties has required three innovations in existing methodology. These innovations, in turn, greatly expand the universe of practical applications for Bayesian inference. In particular, they permit Bayesian inference in classes of problems that often arise in applied econometrics but are completely intractable from a frequentist approach.

2.10.2 *Linear inequality constraints in high dimensions*

In high dimensions, the imposition of linear inequality constraints through rejection methods in Monte Carlo integration – as detailed in Geweke (1986) – can well be impractical, even for inequality constraints that are by any standard consistent with the data. A leading, instructive example is a posterior density centered at the origin and symmetric about the axes in k dimensions. Imposition of nonnegativity constraints on all parameters through rejection requires 2^k drawings, on average, for each retained value. For $k > 15$, it is necessary to develop a more efficient procedure. This necessity clearly is relevant to AIM(2), which has 25 nonnegative parameters. A result of this research is an algorithm for sampling from the multivariate normal or "t," with arbitrary globally satisfied linear inequality restrictions. The algorithm has been thoroughly tested, and execution time is nearly as fast as that of standard algorithms for drawing from an unconstrained multivariate normal or "t" of the same dimension. The method is documented and delineated in a separate technical report (Geweke and Terrell, 1990).

2.10.3 *Locally nonconcave posterior densities*

If the mode of the posterior density is on the boundary of the nonnegative orthant of the coefficients, the posterior need not be concave at that mode. If the constrained mode and the global (i.e., unconstrained) mode are within a concave region over which the posterior is well behaved, then it may be possible to center the importance sampling density at the global mode and sample while imposing the nonnegativity constraints as just described. That does not happen here: the likelihood is ill-behaved outside the nonnegative orthant; and the Hessian at the appropriately constrained mode has 2 positive eigenvalues (out of 9) in AIM(1) and 3 positive eigenvalues (out of 28) in AIM(2). The negative inverse of the Hessian, therefore, fails to provide a candidate covariance matrix for a multivariate "t" importance sampling density.

A covariance matrix appropriate for importance sampling in this situation may be constructed through the method of *iterative expansion of the importance sampling density.* This new, generic procedure should prove useful in many applications in which the likelihood function or posterior is locally ill-behaved. The method begins with a candidate negative inverse covariance matrix $\mathbf{H}$. In principle, $\mathbf{H}$ could be aribtrary. In practice, it is important that $\mathbf{H}$ not be too large, because iterative expansion weakly increases $\mathbf{H}$, in the sense that a quadratic form $\mathbf{z}'\mathbf{H}\mathbf{z}$ is nondecreasing at each iteration for arbitrary fixed $\mathbf{z}$. The iterative expansion algorithm proceeds as follows.

(i) Let $\hat{\boldsymbol{\theta}}$ be the constrained mode. Make one drawing $\mathbf{x}$ from a $N(\mathbf{0}, -\mathbf{H}^{-1})$ density, with the truncation restrictions appropriate to the nonnegativity constraints on $\boldsymbol{\theta} = \hat{\boldsymbol{\theta}} + \mathbf{x}$.

(ii) Let v denote the difference between the value of the log-posterior evaluated at the constrained mode and at $\boldsymbol{\theta}$. If a normal importance sampling density $N(\hat{\boldsymbol{\theta}}, \mathbf{H})$ matches the posterior at $\boldsymbol{\theta}$, then $-\mathbf{x}'\mathbf{H}\mathbf{x} = 2v$. The critical aspect of importance sampling density construction is that the tails of the importance sampling density be at least as thick as the tails of the posterior.[31] Hence, if $-\mathbf{x}'\mathbf{H}\mathbf{x} \geq 2v$ (or, in the applications here, if $-\mathbf{x}'\mathbf{H}\mathbf{x} \geq 2v+\epsilon$, with $\epsilon = 10^{-4}$), return to step (i). Otherwise proceed with step (iii).

(iii) Let $\mathbf{\Sigma} = -\mathbf{H}^{-1}$, where $\mathbf{H}$ is the negative inverse covariance matrix in step (i). Take the new negative inverse covariance matrix to be of the form $\mathbf{H}^* = -(\mathbf{\Sigma} + q\mathbf{x}\mathbf{x}')^{-1}$; that is, the covariance matrix will be "stretched" in the direction of the point at which the importance sampling density is too thin relative to the posterior. The standard decomposition

$$\mathbf{H}^* = -(\mathbf{\Sigma} + q\mathbf{x}\mathbf{x}')^{-1} = \mathbf{H} - \mathbf{H}\mathbf{x}\mathbf{x}'\mathbf{H}/(\mathbf{x}'\mathbf{H}\mathbf{x} + q^{-1})$$

is convenient, since it obviates the need to invert any matrices. The parameter q is chosen so that $-\mathbf{x}'\mathbf{H}^*\mathbf{x} = 2v$, that is, $q = (\mathbf{x}'\mathbf{H}\mathbf{x} + 2v)/2v\mathbf{x}'\mathbf{H}\mathbf{x}$. Hence,

$$\mathbf{H}^* = \mathbf{H} - \mathbf{H}\mathbf{x}\mathbf{x}'\mathbf{H}(\mathbf{x}'\mathbf{H}\mathbf{x} + 2v)/(\mathbf{x}'\mathbf{H}\mathbf{x})^2.$$

(iv) Set $\mathbf{H} = \mathbf{H}^*$ and return to step (i).

At the conclusion of the iterations, the logarithm of the importance sampling density is taken to be the multivariate "t" with mean $\hat{\boldsymbol{\theta}}$, covariance matrix $-H^{-1}$, and degrees of freedom appropriate to the tail behavior of the log-posterior with the appropriate nonnegativity constraints.

Iterative expansion of the importance sampling density is successful if it leads to an importance sampling density in which the weights $w(\boldsymbol{\theta}_i)$ have no extraordinarily large values in the subsequent n iterations that construct the numerical approximation to $E[g(\boldsymbol{\theta})]$. Since $w(\boldsymbol{\theta}_i) \propto \exp[-2v/\mathbf{x}'\mathbf{H}\mathbf{x}]$ in the notation of step (ii), this means that success will depend on the initial approximation to the negative inverse covariance matrix and the number of iterations executed in the iterative expansion. The next section reports choices suitable for the problem at hand. As more experience is acquired with iterative expansion, it seems reasonable that it will become possible to make these choices algorithmically, that is, without ad hoc interventions for each application.

2.10.4 *Mixed rejection, weighted sampling, and oversampling in Monte Carlo integration*

Two practical difficulties remain. The first is that, with the importance sampling density constructed as described and with a locally nonconcave posterior, the weights $w(\boldsymbol{\theta}_i)$ will be exceedingly small for many sampled points. This characteristic would appear to arise for any well-behaved importance sampling density constructed to avoid undersampling (i.e.,

[31] See Geweke (1989b).

constructed to avoid "thin tails" relative to the posterior), given a non-concave posterior. In principle, this is not a problem. However, in many applications – including the ones taken up in this chapter – a very substantial portion of computing time is devoted to evaluation of functions of interest and accumulation of terms in (13) and (16); if most weights are very small, then most computing time is devoted to terms that are of negligible consequence for the results. A second concern arises from the desirability of retaining sampled values $g(\theta_i)$ and corresponding weights $w(\theta_i)$, so as to construct fractiles or plot posterior densities. If most weights are very small, then large amounts of disk space are devoted to terms that are, again, of negligible consequence for the final reporting.

The "small-weight" problem is easily obviated. To simplify the description, suppose that the importance sampling density and posterior are each scaled to have the value unity at their modes. Because the importance sampling density is constructed by iterative expansion, few values of $w(\theta)$ will exceed unity and many will be quite small – values of 10^{-5} or 10^{-6} may be typical. Choose a value $b<1$ (in the applications here, $b=0.1$). If $w(\theta_i)\geq b$, the drawing is retained and used in the expressions (13) and (16). If $w(\theta_i)<b$, the drawing is retained with probability $w(\theta_i)/b$, and discarded otherwise. If retained, then the weight b is assigned to the draw-in (13) and (16).

Despite the iterative expansion of the importance sampling density, the second difficulty that may remain is that large weights $w(\theta_i)$ may turn up, corresponding to "nuggets" of mass in the posterior density. Rather than use such drawings directly, it is better to explore the posterior density in the region of the nugget. This is accomplished by constructing a k-dimensional rectangle in the parameter space of the form of the Cartesian product $(\theta_1-\zeta_1,\theta_1+\zeta_1)\times(\theta_2-\zeta_2,\theta_2+\zeta_2)\times\cdots\times(\theta_k-\zeta_k,\theta_k+\zeta_k)$. If $w(\theta_i)\geq 2$, the original drawing is discarded, and m uniformly distributed drawings θ_{ij} from this k-dimensional rectangle are made, where m is the greatest integer contained in $w(\theta_i)$; and each drawing is assigned the weight $p(\theta_{ij})=[w(\theta_i)/m]\cdot[p(\theta_{ij})/p(\theta_i)]$. The vector $\zeta=(\zeta_1,\zeta_2,\ldots,\zeta_k)'$ is inversely proportional to the gradient evaluated at θ_i. In the applications taken up here, the constant of proportionality is 0.2. Experimentation with this choice in these, and a variety of other applications, clearly is desirable.

2.11 *Procedures and results for Bayesian inference with AIM*(1) *and AIM*(2)

2.11.1 *Procedures*

Diffuse, improper priores were used. For AIM(1), the prior is flat over the entire relevant range for all parameters: the unit simplex for a_1, a_2, and

a_3; the positive orthant for $a_4, \ldots, a_7$; the positive orthant for l_1 and l_3; and the real line for l_2. For AIM(2), the prior is flat on the unit simplex for a_1, a_2, and a_3; on the positive orthant for l_1 and l_3; and on the real line for l_2. For AIM(2), the prior on $b_4, \ldots, b_{26}$ is $\text{IIDN}(0,1)$, truncated to the positive orthant.

A systematic search for local and global posterior modes was conducted by generating random initial values of the parameters and then using the modified Newton–Raphson method described in Appendix B to determine the mode.[32] Random initial values of the parameters were generated as follows. The values $\{a_1, a_2, a_3\}$ or $\{b_1, b_2, b_3\}$ were sampled from the unit simplex (in accordance with the parameter normalization) by setting a_i or b_i to $z_i^2/\sum_{j=1}^{3} z_j^2$ with $z_i \sim \text{IIDN}(0,1)$ for $i = 1,2,3$; while for $i > 3$, we sampled $a_i \sim z_i^2$, $b_i \sim z_i^2$ with $z_i \sim \text{IIDN}(0,1)$. The initial values of the l_i were set to their maximum posterior values conditional on the model's coefficients.

In AIM(1), two modes were detected, for the first time at the first and third of 2,000 trials, respectively. The posterior p.d.f. at one mode is 7.25×10^{15} times as high as at the other, so the lower one can be ignored in constructing the importance sampling density. The additional prior $a_i \sim \text{IIDN}(0,1)$ for $i > 3$ was then removed, and the mode of the original posterior density was determined. There was little change.

In AIM(2), two modes were also detected, at the first and second of 573 trials, respectively. The posterior density at one mode is 1.91 times the density at the other. For reasons best portrayed in Figure 1, page 467, however, exceptional treatment of multimodality is not required. Each mode is on the boundary of the parameter space, and a line passing through the two points intersects the parameter space only between the points. Since the minimum along this line is close to and scarcely lower than the lower mode, the lower mode can be ignored.

The Hessians of the log-posteriors at their modes are not negative definite, since there are two positive eigenvalues in AIM(1) and three positive eigenvalues in AIM(2). To construct an initial candidate Hessian for iterative expansion of the posterior density in AIM(1), the cross-partial derivatives between parameters on the boundary of the parameter space and those in the interior were set to zero. The resulting matrix was negative definite. In AIM(2), the same procedure was used, and, in addition, the cross partial derivatives between all parameters on the boundary of the

32 With occasional random initial values of the parameters, the Newton–Raphson method led to exponent overflow and terminated the search process. For reasons not yet understood, these problems were not encountered in Barnett and Yue's (1988b) work with the same data, but with a different optimization program used on a Cyber mainframe computer.

parameter space were set to zero to attain a negative definite initial candidate Hessian.

Iterative expansion of the importance sampling density in AIM(1) was applied for 10,000 iterations organized into ten successive groups of 1,000 each. The Hessian $\mathbf{H}^*$ was continuously updated within each group as detailed in the previous section, and the density $N(0, -\mathbf{H}^{-1})$ for drawing $\mathbf{x}$ was modified at the end of each group by setting $\mathbf{H} = \mathbf{H}^*$. The Hessian was revised 27 times following this procedure, with no revisions in the last 4,000 iterations.

The candidate Hessian for AIM(2) produced a covariance matrix that was too large: no revisions occurred, and subsequent Monte Carlo integration using the importance sampling density constructed from the candidate Hessian led to small RNE values. The original, candidate Hessian was then scaled by values greater than unity (thus *shrinking* the original candidate covariance matrix) until revisions occurred. The value 2.56 produced 304 revisions in 40,000 iterations (organized into groups of 1,000 as with AIM(1)) with little updating in the last 10,000 iterations. With these importance sampling densities, $n = 12{,}000$ iterations was employed for AIM(1) and 16,000 for AIM(2).

2.11.2 *AIM*(1) *results*

Table 1 provides findings for parameters and functions of interest in AIM(1). With isolated exceptions, posterior means are determined to three places of computational precision past the decimal and reported in the table to four decimal places. Clearly, the Monte Carlo computational error is entirely negligible, since the data themselves in economics are rarely accurate to three decimal places, and estimates of elasticities rarely are even reported to more than one or two decimal places. RNE is typically about 50% – that is, numerical accuracy is about what it would have been with 6,000 drawings directly from the posterior (had that been possible), as is reflected in numerical standard errors between 1 and 2% of posterior standard deviations.

The parameters $\{a_i\}$ and $\{l_i\}$ are technical constructs of no direct use, but the findings for them illustrate several aspects of Bayesian inference subject to inequality constraints. The parameters a_1, a_2, and a_3 are well within the unit simplex to which they are constrained. Their distributions are nearly symmetric, and the usual rules of thumb for imputing confidence intervals from mean and standard deviation are adequate. Parameters a_4 and a_5 are regular and internal at the mode, but are close enough (within two standard deviations, or less) to the boundary of the parameter space such that rules of thumb for inference are not reliable. Observe that because of the nonnegativity constraints, the mode is less than the

Table 1. *Bayesian inference in AIM(1) consumer demand*[a]

Parameter or function	Posterior			Numerical accuracy		Posterior quantiles				
	Mode	Mean	St. dev.	Num. S.E.	RNE (%)	1%	10%	50%	90%	99%
a_1	0.3552	0.3391	0.0268	0.0003	50.7	0.2684	0.3038	0.3410	0.3714	0.3946
a_2	0.4051	0.4254	0.0270	0.0004	39.6	0.3790	0.3944	0.4218	0.4610	0.5070
a_3	0.2396	0.2355	0.0259	0.0003	56.7	0.1698	0.2023	0.2360	0.2681	0.2927
a_4	0.0608	0.0827	0.0330	0.0005	43.8	0.0255	0.0437	0.0789	0.1280	0.1801
a_5	0.1450	0.2040	0.0726	0.0010	41.5	0.0814	0.1208	0.1930	0.2986	0.4326
$a_6 \times 10^2$	0.0000	0.2146	0.2499	0.0028	66.2	0.0015	0.0191	0.1339	0.5007	1.1843
$a_7 \times 10^2$	0.0000	0.0110	0.0104	0.0001	52.7	0.0001	0.0011	0.0078	0.0256	0.0449
$l_1 \times 10^{-2}$	0.1505	0.1461	0.0311	0.0004	53.4	0.0943	0.1094	0.1407	0.1914	0.2272
$l_2 \times 10^{-2}$	−0.3576	−0.3163	0.0126	0.0016	50.7	−0.5517	−0.4678	−0.3306	−0.1421	0.0043
$l_3 \times 10^{-2}$	0.4248	0.4271	0.0855	0.0011	54.1	0.2490	0.3143	0.4287	0.5406	0.6087
$\|\Sigma\| \times 10^5$	0.2448	0.2891	0.0766	0.0009	62.3	0.1586	0.2021	0.2779	0.3906	0.5228
σ_{11}	−1.014	−1.0934	0.1196	0.0016	48.8	−1.435	−1.251	−1.081	−0.9545	−0.8727
σ_{12}	0.5094	0.5098	0.0045	0.0001	52.0	0.4998	0.5042	0.5096	0.5158	0.5201
σ_{13}	0.5754	0.6092	0.0429	0.0006	40.0	0.5407	0.5614	0.6016	0.6660	0.7414
σ_{22}	−0.6635	−0.6300	0.0470	0.0007	40.7	−0.7213	−0.6875	−0.6333	−0.5671	−0.5083
σ_{23}	0.4725	0.4632	0.0140	0.0002	43.9	0.4230	0.4443	0.4655	0.4789	0.4861
σ_{33}	−1.748	−1.8024	0.2340	0.0028	56.8	−2.489	−2.101	−1.779	−1.528	−1.368
η_{10}	0.9853	0.9778	0.0104	0.0001	40.8	0.9423	0.9643	0.9797	0.9889	0.9932
η_{20}	1.0198	1.0274	0.0092	0.0001	41.7	1.0113	1.0165	1.0261	1.0396	1.0551
η_{30}	0.9851	0.9777	0.0110	0.0002	44.9	0.9424	0.9628	0.9801	0.9896	0.9942

ξ_{11}	−0.3491	−0.3622	0.0178	0.0002	46.2	−0.4124	−0.3859	−0.3607	−0.3406	−0.3275
ξ_{12}	0.2176	0.2237	0.0091	0.0001	42.1	0.2059	0.2124	0.2231	0.2361	0.2461
ξ_{13}	0.1316	0.1385	0.0131	0.0002	55.5	0.1096	0.1226	0.1377	0.1556	0.1708
ξ_{21}	0.1753	0.1700	0.0103	0.0001	54.7	0.1446	0.1563	0.1705	0.1826	0.1930
ξ_{22}	−0.2834	−0.2757	0.0106	0.0002	39.4	−0.2943	−0.2881	−0.2769	−0.2614	−0.2459
ξ_{23}	0.1080	0.1057	0.0119	0.0001	55.4	0.0757	0.0905	0.1060	0.1208	0.1315
ξ_{31}	0.1981	0.2027	0.0142	0.0002	53.9	0.1744	0.1858	0.2016	0.2212	0.2434
ξ_{32}	0.2018	0.2031	0.0029	–	43.5	0.1968	0.1995	0.2029	0.2067	0.2105
ξ_{33}	−0.3999	−0.4058	0.0143	0.0002	50.6	−0.4424	−0.4246	−0.4051	−0.3879	−0.3764
η_{11}	−0.6883	−0.6883	0.0087	0.0001	62.5	−0.7097	−0.6995	−0.6882	−0.6772	−0.6687
η_{12}	−0.2033	−0.2052	0.0050	0.0001	46.1	−0.2182	−0.2120	−0.2048	−0.1991	−0.1951
η_{13}	−0.0937	−0.0843	0.0157	0.0002	43.4	−0.1156	−0.1036	−0.0855	−0.0634	−0.0444
η_{21}	−0.1757	−0.1725	0.0092	0.0001	59.5	−0.1940	−0.1840	−0.1727	−0.1605	−0.1507
η_{22}	−0.7189	−0.7266	0.0105	0.0002	40.8	−0.7553	−0.7408	−0.7256	−0.7139	−0.7070
η_{23}	−0.1251	−0.1283	0.0105	0.0001	61.9	−0.1529	−0.1416	−0.1282	−0.1151	−0.1037
η_{31}	−0.1410	−0.1232	0.0209	0.0003	41.7	−0.1611	−0.1479	−0.1256	−0.0956	−0.0623
η_{32}	−0.2189	−0.2258	0.0102	0.0001	40.5	−0.2533	−0.2395	−0.2249	−0.2134	−0.2066
η_{33}	−0.6251	−0.6287	0.0105	0.0001	61.7	−0.6531	−0.6421	−0.6285	−0.6155	−0.6041

[a] Table is based on 12,000 Monte Carlo iterations with importance sampling, as described in the text. Values less than 5×10^{-5} are denoted by "–". The column "Mode" indicates the value of the parameter or function of interest at the mode of the posterior density. "Num. S.E." is the numerical standard error, which is the square root of $\hat{\sigma}^2_{nT}$ computed from equation (16).

median is less than the mean for these parameters. The rightward skewness of their posterior distributions is also evident in the fractiles. For parameters a_6 and a_7, whose modes are on the boundary of the parameter space, these effects are much more pronounced. The effects derived in Geweke (1986, Result 2) for severely constrained parameters are dominant here: the posterior standard deviation is about the same as the mean, and the entire posterior distribution is well approximated by the exponential.

The functions of interest are the various elasticities, computed at 1920 prices and income. For each nine-dimensional parameter vector $\boldsymbol{\theta}_i$ generated in the Monte Carlo replications, these elasticities were computed using the analytical results obtained and set forth in Appendix C. Since these relationships are exact, the posterior moments and fractiles reported here are also exact, up to the numerical accuracy indicated. Thus, in spite of the highly nonlinear parameterization of AIM(1), and the highly nonlinear nature of the mapping from these parameters to the elasticities (see Appendix C), the posterior means for the elasticities reported here are (with a couple of exceptions) exact to three places of computational accuracy.

The posterior is least informative about the elasticities of substitutions, σ_{ij}. A centered, 98% confidence interval for the σ_{ij} has a range (width) exceeding 0.20 in a majority of cases. Moreover, the posteriors tend to be asymmetric. By contrast, the income elasticities η_{i0} are well determined. They are all near unity, but clearly η_{20} exceeds unity, whereas η_{10} and η_{30} are less than unity. The range of a centered 98% confidence interval for the η_{i0} is about 0.05. The compensated (Hicks–Allen) price elasticities ξ_{ij} are not quite as well determined, since 98% of their mass typically is spread over a range of 0.04 to 0.10. The uncompensated (Cournot) elasticities η_{ij} are about as well determined as the income elasticities.

2.11.3 *AIM*(2) *results*

Table 2 provides findings for parameters and functions of interest in AIM(2). With occasional exceptions, posterior means have been computed to three decimal places of accuracy. RNE is again about 50%, so that the numerical accuracy from 16,000 iterations with an importance sampling density is about that accuracy that would have been achieved from 8,000 iterations with sampling directly from the posterior (had that been possible).

There is abundant evidence that the posterior density in AIM(2) is highly irregular. Of the parameters (b_1, b_2, b_5, b_6, b_{12}, and b_{22}) that are within the interior of the parameter space at the posterior mode, only for b_{12} is the mode of the posterior density within two standard deviations of the posterior mean. With the other parameters, the mode is up to five standard deviations from the mean. This phenomenon carries over to the elasticities: evaluated at the posterior mode, the elasticities are rarely within the 98% confidence interval for those functions. This behavior results from binding nonnegativity constraints in many dimensions, since then the posterior mode is in an isolated corner of the parameter space.

Inferences from AIM(2) on the whole are quite different from inferences from AIM(1). Of the 27 functions of interest, 98% confidence intervals from the two models overlap in only seven cases. Indeed, confidence intervals for the functions of interest in AIM(2) are generally on the order of half the length of those in AIM(1), and the confidence interval lengths in AIM(1) already were short. The decrease in the lengths of those confidence intervals is evident from the usually decreased posterior standard deviations of the elasticity estimates. These results are particularly noteworthy, since the number of parameters in AIM(2) is much larger than the number in AIM(1). The substantial change in inferences produced by moving from AIM(1) to AIM(2), along with the usually increased precision of the elasticity estimates, suggests that the expansion from AIM(1) to AIM(2) does much to provide more specification flexibility for this data set. These results are consistent with those of Barnett and Yue (1988b), whose maximum likelihood estimation results produced converged inferences with AIM(N) for $N \geq 2$, but not for $N = 1$.

2.12 *Conclusion*

In this section, we report on successful estimation of AIM(1) and AIM(2) with consumption data on three goods. Our approach is a Bayesian estimation with Monte Carlo integration using importance sampling. We produce and apply new advances in that generic numerical inference methodology to permit use of inequality constraints. In addition, our new algorithms are applicable even when the likelihood function is poorly behaved, as can be the case when consumer decisions are made in the irrational manner that can be implied by the AIM model outside of its globally theoretically valid subset of the parameter space (the nonnegative orthant). These new numerical Bayesian methods build upon those of Geweke (1986, 1988, 1989b).

Since Barnett and Yue (1988b) verified that passing to AIM(3) with our data produces no gains, the results in this chapter include no results for AIM(3). Having successfully estimated AIM with our Bayesian methods, we next plan to apply those methods to produce exact odds ratios for hypothesis testing with AIM. We thereby will be able to produce a direct test of the theoretical regularity conditions. We also plan to estimate a version of AIM that is between AIM(1) and AIM(2); the approach is to

Table 2. *Bayesian inference in AIM(2) consumer demand*[a]

Parameter or function	Posterior			Numerical accuracy		Posterior quantiles				
	Mode	Mean	St. dev.	Num. S.E.	RNE (%)	1%	10%	50%	90%	99%
b_1	0.8033	0.9106	0.0530	0.0006	45.5					
b_2	0.1967	0.0511	0.0488	0.0006	45.1					
b_3	0.0000	0.0382	0.0258	0.0003	47.9					
b_4	0.0000	0.0456	0.0300	0.0003	50.3					
b_5	0.9822	1.5549	0.1510	0.0017	48.6					
b_6	0.9371	1.1762	0.1094	0.0013	47.3					
b_7	0.0000	0.0116	0.0007	–	46.6					
b_8	0.0000	0.1036	0.0491	0.0006	48.8					
b_9	0.0000	0.0037	0.0024	–	49.3					
b_{10}	0.0000	0.1558	0.0872	0.0010	46.7					
b_{11}	0.0000	0.0009	0.0006	–	51.7					
b_{12}	0.0724	0.1171	0.0536	0.0006	48.0					
b_{13}	0.0000	0.0044	0.0034	–	52.4					
b_{14}	0.0000	0.0717	0.0498	0.0006	48.0					
b_{15}	0.0000	0.0002	0.0002	–	50.7					
b_{16}	0.0000	0.0017	0.0012	–	49.9					
b_{17}	0.0000	0.0026	0.0021	–	51.4					
b_{18}	0.0000	0.0251	0.0185	0.0002	49.1					
b_{19}	0.0000	–	–	–	50.2					
b_{20}	0.0000	–	–	–	49.7					
b_{21}	0.0000	–	–	–	50.6					
b_{22}	0.0005	0.0001	0.0001	–	53.8					
b_{23}	0.0000	0.0013	0.0010	–	51.5					
b_{24}	0.0000	0.0003	0.0002	–	50.1					
b_{25}	0.0000	0.0004	0.0003	–	48.9					
b_{26}	0.0000	0.0040	0.0033	–	47.9					
$l_1 \times 10^{-2}$	0.5131	0.4795	0.0569	0.0006	53.3					

$l_2 \times 10^{-2}$	0.5778	0.5237	0.1064	0.0011	53.5					
$l_3 \times 10^{-2}$	0.5679	0.5340	0.0552	0.0006	53.7					
$\|\Sigma\| \times 10^6$	0.1178	0.1640	0.0540	0.0006	57.0					
σ_{11}	−2.240	−1.9475	0.0567	0.0006	51.4	−2.089	−2.014	−1.951	−1.873	−1.8098
σ_{12}	0.5288	0.6082	0.0202	0.0002	49.9	0.5599	0.5817	0.6076	0.6369	0.6486
σ_{13}	0.5731	0.6059	0.0185	0.0002	44.0	0.5701	0.5850	0.6042	0.6298	0.6434
σ_{22}	−0.8766	−0.8682	0.0322	0.0004	49.1	−0.9425	−0.9130	−0.8664	−0.8275	−0.8006
σ_{23}	0.7820	0.7881	0.0086	0.0001	41.9	0.7688	0.7793	0.7886	0.7971	0.8041
σ_{33}	−1.266	−1.6005	0.0677	0.0007	52.0	−1.779	−1.690	−1.599	−1.516	−1.4572
η_{10}	0.8078	0.8205	0.0078	0.0001	49.2	0.8039	0.8110	0.8201	0.8307	0.8410
η_{20}	1.0357	1.0557	0.0048	0.0001	44.4	1.0450	1.0504	1.0558	1.0611	1.0675
η_{30}	1.0609	1.0562	0.0065	0.0001	46.5	1.0419	1.0481	1.0566	1.0640	1.0712
ξ_{11}	−0.4408	−0.4628	0.0114	0.0001	49.1	−0.4883	−0.4785	−0.4631	−0.4480	−0.4379
ξ_{12}	0.2335	0.2738	0.0093	0.0001	50.7	0.2506	0.2619	0.2738	0.2855	0.2924
ξ_{13}	0.2073	0.1890	0.0071	0.0001	46.3	0.1748	0.1803	0.1885	0.1979	0.2065
ξ_{21}	0.1041	0.1447	0.0068	0.0001	51.3	0.1295	0.1357	0.1446	0.1535	0.1591
ξ_{22}	−0.3869	−0.3906	0.0082	0.0001	47.7	−0.4070	−0.4017	−0.3904	−0.3802	−0.3725
ξ_{23}	0.2829	0.2460	0.0074	0.0001	49.4	0.2262	0.2325	0.2465	0.2548	0.2613
ξ_{31}	0.1128	0.1441	0.0068	0.0001	44.5	0.1308	0.1360	0.1439	0.1514	0.1597
ξ_{32}	0.3452	0.3548	0.0078	0.0001	47.2	0.3358	0.3451	0.3549	0.3640	0.3704
ξ_{33}	−0.4580	−0.4989	0.0074	0.0001	52.8	−0.5153	−0.5086	−0.4992	−0.4891	−0.4822
η_{11}	−0.5998	−0.6579	0.0142	0.0002	49.0	−0.6869	−0.6774	−0.6576	−0.6396	−0.6259
η_{12}	−0.1231	−0.0955	0.0090	0.0001	48.6	−0.1157	−0.1075	−0.0958	−0.0827	−0.0788
η_{13}	−0.0849	−0.0670	0.0056	0.0001	46.5	−0.0790	−0.0741	−0.0672	−0.0598	−0.0559
η_{21}	−0.0997	−0.1063	0.0046	0.0001	49.2	−0.1163	−0.1124	−0.1066	−0.1000	−0.0973
η_{22}	−0.8442	−0.8659	0.0062	0.0001	43.5	−0.8744	−0.8719	−0.8664	−0.8593	−0.8449
η_{23}	−0.0918	−0.0083	0.0028	–	49.4	−0.0902	−0.0868	−0.0835	−0.0800	−0.0767
η_{31}	−0.0960	−0.1070	0.0043	–	47.8	−0.1160	−0.1123	−0.1071	−0.1015	−0.0965
η_{32}	−0.1231	−0.1206	0.0044	0.0001	42.0	−0.1313	−0.1247	−0.1207	−0.1160	−0.1115
η_{33}	−0.8418	−0.8285	0.0043	–	47.1	−0.8365	−0.8338	−0.8288	−0.8231	−0.8167

[a] Table is based on 16,000 Monte Carlo iterations with importance sampling, as described in the text. Values less than 5×10^{-5} are denoted by "–". The omitted entries were not computed to keep disk storage requirements within reasonable bounds. "Num. S.E." is the numerical standard error, which is the square root of $\hat{\sigma}^2_{nT}$ computed from equation (16).

estimate AIM(2) with a lower prior variance on the coefficients of the "higher-order" terms than on the coefficients of the terms that also appear in AIM(1). Such an approach can permit smooth transition from AIM(1) to AIM(2), and then analogously to AIM(3) with larger sample sizes, as the prior variance on the coefficients of the "higher-order" terms is increased.

3 Production

3.1 *The expansion*

Let $\lambda(k)=2^{-k}$ for $k=1,\ldots,\infty$, and let $\mathbb{N}=\{1,2,\ldots\}$ be the natural numbers. Define $\mathbf{x}$ to be the vector of factor demand quantities and $\mathbf{p}$ to be the vector of corresponding factor prices. Let y be the firm's output; and let $C(y,\mathbf{p})$ be the firm's cost function. We begin with the constant returns-to-scale case. In that case, there exists a factor-price aggregator function $P(\mathbf{p})$ such that $C(y,\mathbf{p})=yP(\mathbf{p})$. The function P often is called the "unit-cost function," since $P(\mathbf{p})$ is the minimum cost of production per unit of y produced, as is immediately evident from $C(y,\mathbf{p})=yP(\mathbf{p})$.

The Müntz–Szatz series expansion, as defined in the mathematics literature, and as originally provided by Müntz and Szatz, is a univariate expansion. The multivariate version of the Müntz–Szatz series expansion applied before to consumption modeling would produce the following specification for a firm's unit cost function $P(\mathbf{p})$ in the two-factor case:

$$P(\mathbf{p})=a_0+\sum_{k\in\mathbb{N}}\sum_{i=1}^{N}a_{ik}p_i^{\lambda(k)}+\sum_{k\in\mathbb{N}}\sum_{m\in\mathbb{N}}\left(\sum_{i=1}^{N}\sum_{j=1}^{N}a_{ijkm}p_i^{\lambda(k)}p_j^{\lambda(m)}\right),$$

where $N=2$ is the number of factors of production, and $a_0, a_{ik}, a_{ijkm},\ldots$ are parameters to be estimated for $i,j=1,\ldots,N$ and $k,m=1,\ldots,\infty$, and $\Lambda=\{\lambda(k):k\in\mathbb{N}\}$ is the exponent set. For the Müntz–Szatz theorem to apply, the exponents must satisfy the condition $\sum_{k=1}^{n}(1/\lambda(k))=\infty$. In Section 2, the exponent set was selected to be $\Lambda=\{\lambda(k):\lambda(k)=2^{-k},\ k\in\mathbb{N}\}$. We use the same exponent set here. Sample size is designated by T.

At present, we are considering only the two-factor case. We proceed to the three-factor case at a later date.

The partial sums (i.e., finite-order approximations) from this expansion for $n\in\mathbb{N}$ are defined by

$$P_n(\mathbf{p})=a_0+\sum_{k=1}^{n}\sum_{i=1}^{N}a_{ik}p_i^{\lambda(k)}+\sum_{k=1}^{n}\sum_{m=1}^{n}\left(\sum_{i=1}^{N}\sum_{j=1}^{N}a_{ijkm}p_i^{\lambda(k)}p_j^{\lambda(m)}\right).$$

The corresponding exponent set again is $\Lambda=\{\lambda(k):\lambda(k)=2^{-k},\ k=1,\ldots,n\}$. We will be interested in the first four partial sums.

The span of that multivariate expansion is the entire space of continuous functions. Furthermore, Barnett and Yue (1988a) have shown that the span is not reduced by deleting the diagonal elements of the parameter matrices and imposing symmetry on those matrices. Although this expansion proved appropriate for indirect utility functions in consumer demand modeling before, a denser multivariate generalization of the Müntz–Szatz series expansion is needed for modeling cost functions. The reason is that cost functions must be linearly homogeneous in factor prices. The expansion defined before does not satisfy that restriction. In addition, if linear homogeneity is imposed on the previous expansion, the span of the expansion is reduced to a strict subset of the set of linearly homogeneous functions. We want an expansion that will span the entire space of linearly homogeneous functions.

In particular, we must put the diagonal terms back into the expansion, and we also must add in all of the remaining interaction terms up to order 2^n for each partial sum n. In producing the Müntz–Szatz indirect utility function for consumer demand modeling, we had included interactions only up to order N, regardless of n. Once we have produced our new denser multivariate version of the Müntz–Szatz series expansion, we can impose linear homogeneity without contracting the span to a strict subset of the space of linearly homogeneous functions. Prior to imposing linear homogeneity, the only other restrictions we can impose upon the parameter matrices is symmetry. We then are assured that the subsequent imposition of linear homogeneity will reduce the span only to exactly the space of linearly homogeneous functions. Proceeding in that manner, we acquire the following series as our linearly homogeneous expansion.

3.2 *The linearly homogeneous multivariate Müntz–Szatz series expansion*

Let N be the number of factors of production. For use with partial sum n of our expansion, define the following set of 2^n-dimensional points:

$$A_n = \{(i_1, i_2, \ldots, i_{2^n}) : i_1, i_2, \ldots, i_{2^n} \in \{1, 2, \ldots, N\};\ i_1 \leq i_2 \leq i_3 \leq \cdots \leq i_{2^n}\}. \tag{18}$$

The nth partial sum of our expansion of the unit cost function $P(\mathbf{p})$ is defined by

$$P_n(\mathbf{p}) = \sum_{\mathbf{z} \in A_n} a_{\mathbf{z}} \prod_{i=1}^{2^n} p_{i_j}^{2^{-n}}. \tag{19}$$

Hence, the full expansion of the unit-cost function is

$$P(\mathbf{p}) = \lim_{n\to\infty} P_n(\mathbf{p}) = \lim_{n\to\infty} \sum_{\mathbf{z} \in A_n} a_{\mathbf{z}} \prod_{j=1}^{2^n} p_{i_j}^{2^{-n}}. \tag{20}$$

Although these formulas are appropriate methods of generating the expansion and its partial sums, the use of the subscript $\mathbf{z}$ is awkward when the expansion is written out. For example, when writing out Partial Sum 3, we have that $2^n = 8$. Hence, in that case, each subscript $\mathbf{z} = (i_1, i_2, \ldots, i_{2^n})$ has eight digits. The use of eight-digit subscripts with each coefficient in a model takes up too much space on the page. Hence, after producing the partial sums, we simply stack the coefficients into a single vector and resubscript them sequentially from 1.

Formally speaking, this amounts to the following change in notation. Let $\#A_n$ be the cardinal number of the set A_n. Then

$$P_n(\mathbf{p}) = \sum_{\mathbf{z} \in A_n} a_{k(\mathbf{z})} \prod_{j=1}^{2^n} p_{i_j}^{2^{-n}}, \tag{21}$$

where $k(\mathbf{z}) = 1, 2, \ldots, \#A_n$, with $k(\mathbf{z}_1) \neq k(\mathbf{z}_2)$ if $\mathbf{z}_1 \neq \mathbf{z}_2$. Observe that the sum of the exponents is $(2^n)(2^{-n}) = 1$. As a result, the expansion is globally linearly homogeneous in $\mathbf{p}$ at each n as well as in the limit as $n \to \infty$. This property is required by economic theory for every cost function and every unit-cost function.

A unit-cost function must have the following properties: it must be strictly concave and increasing, as well as linearly homogeneous in $\mathbf{p}$. Expansion (20) is globally linearly homogeneous and spans the space of linearly homogeneous functions, since its basis functions are dense in that space. We can impose concavity and monotonicity on the coefficients by requiring all of the coefficients to be nonnegative. As we will see, the conditional factor demand estimating equations will be fully linear.

The reason that nonnegativity of the coefficients assures neoclassical properties globally is the following. Consider the basis functions, $\prod_{j=1}^{2^n} p_{i_j}^{2^{-n}}$. Clearly, $p_{i_j}^{2^{-n}}$ is increasing and concave in its one variable for any fixed n. Hence, by Theorem 1 of Berge (1963, p. 207), it follows that $\prod_{j=1}^{2^n} p_{i_j}^{2^{-n}}$ is increasing and quasiconcave jointly in all of its variables at any fixed n. But $\prod_{j=1}^{2^n} p_{i_j}^{2^{-n}}$ also is linearly homogeneous, since the sum of its exponents is 1.0. Hence, it follows from Theorem 3 of Berge (1963, p. 208) that $\prod_{j=1}^{2^n} p_{i_j}^{2^{-n}}$ is increasing and concave.[33]

3.3 *Derivation of the conditional factor demand equations*

To acquire the conditional factor demand functions $\mathbf{x}(y, \mathbf{p})$, we can use Shepherd's lemma:

$$\mathbf{x} = \frac{\partial C_n(y, \mathbf{p})}{\partial \mathbf{p}},$$

[33] See also the "Application" of Berge (1963, p. 209).

where $C_n(y, \mathbf{p}) = y \partial P_n(\mathbf{p})$ holds in our current assumption of constant returns to scale. Hence, we have that

$$\mathbf{x} = y \frac{\partial P_n(\mathbf{p})}{\partial \mathbf{p}}.$$

Dividing both sides by y and adding the disturbances ϵ, we get the input-output equations

$$\frac{\mathbf{x}}{y} = \frac{\partial P_n(\mathbf{p})}{\partial \mathbf{p} + \epsilon}. \tag{22}$$

We estimate those N input–output equations with additive disturbances and with nonnegativity imposed on all coefficients. Since those equations, unlike consumer demand equations, are not linearly dependent, we do not delete an arbitrary equation; we estimate all N equations jointly. We assume that the vector of additive disturbances, ϵ_t, is distributed independently and identically as a multivariate normal with zero mean and covariance matrix Σ. The endogenous variables are the input–output ratios $\mathbf{x}/y$. The exogenous variables are the factor prices $\mathbf{p}$. We have a closed-form system of seemingly unrelated regression equations.

The system of factor demand functions produced by applying Shepherd's lemma to the nth partial sum of the cost function $C_n(y, \mathbf{p})$ will be called the AIM(n) factor demand system, and the resulting input–output system, (22), will be called the AIM(n) input–output system.

3.4 *The partial sums*

By using equation (21), we now explicitly produce the first four partial sums of our expansion of the cost function in the two-factor case, and by using Shepherd's lemma, we derive the AIM(n), $n = 1, 2, 3, 4$, conditional factor demand functions.[34] To estimate AIM(n), all that remains is to divide each factor demand function through by output y to produce the input–output equations, (22), and then estimate the coefficients subject to the nonnegativity constraints.

AIM(1): exponent set $\Lambda = \{\frac{1}{2}\}$, 3 parameters.

$$C_{n=1}(y, \mathbf{p}) = yP_{n=1}(\mathbf{p}) = y(\alpha_1 p_1 + \alpha_2 p_2 + \alpha_3 p_1^{1/2} p_2^{1/2}); \tag{23}$$

[34] To minimize the risk of algebraic error in producing these expansions from the general form (21) and in the differentiation required to apply Shepherd's lemma, Michael Wolfe has developed a computer program using an AI tool called Reduce, which does all of the symbolic logic and differentiation analytically from the general form (21) and Shepherd's lemma.

$$\frac{\partial C_{n=1}(y,\mathbf{p})}{\partial p_1}=y(\alpha_1+\tfrac{1}{2}\alpha_3 p_1^{-1/2}p_2^{1/2}),$$

$$\frac{\partial C_{n=1}(y,\mathbf{p})}{\partial p_2}=y(\alpha_2+\tfrac{1}{2}\alpha_3 p_1^{1/2}p_2^{-1/2}).$$

Notice that $C_{n=1}(y,\mathbf{p})$ is *exactly* Diewert's generalized Leontief model. Hence, AIM(1) is the generalized Leontief factor demand system. Furthermore, for $n>1$, the generalized Leontief model is a completely nested special case, since AIM(1) is nested in AIM(n) for all $n>1$.

AIM(2): exponent set $\Lambda=\{\frac{1}{2},\frac{1}{4}\}$, 5 parameters.

$$C_{n=2}(y,\mathbf{p})=yP_{n=2}(\mathbf{p})=y(\alpha_1 p_1+\alpha_2 p_2+\alpha_3 p_1^{3/4}p_2^{1/4}+\alpha_4 p_1^{1/2}p_2^{1/2}+\alpha_5 p_1^{1/4}p_2^{3/4}); \tag{24}$$

$$\frac{\partial C_{n=2}(y,\mathbf{p})}{\partial p_1}=y(\alpha_1+\tfrac{3}{4}\alpha_3 p_1^{-1/4}p_2^{1/4}+\tfrac{1}{2}\alpha_4 p_1^{-1/2}p_2^{1/2}+\tfrac{1}{4}\alpha_5 p_1^{-3/4}p_2^{3/4}),$$

$$\frac{\partial C_{n=2}(y,\mathbf{p})}{\partial p_2}=y(\alpha_2+\tfrac{1}{4}\alpha_3 p_1^{3/4}p_2^{-3/4}+\tfrac{1}{2}\alpha_4 p_1^{1/2}p_2^{-1/2}+\tfrac{3}{4}\alpha_5 p_1^{1/4}p_2^{-1/4}).$$

AIM(3): exponent set $\Lambda=\{\frac{1}{2},\frac{1}{4},\frac{1}{8}\}$, 9 parameters.

$$\begin{aligned}C_{n=3}&(y,\mathbf{p})\\ &=yP_{n=3}(\mathbf{p})=y(\alpha_1 p_1+\alpha_2 p_2+\alpha_3 p_1^{7/8}p_2^{1/8}\\ &\qquad+\alpha_4 p_1^{3/4}p_2^{1/4}+\alpha_5 p_1^{5/8}p_2^{3/8}+\alpha_6 p_1^{1/2}p_2^{1/2}\\ &\qquad+\alpha_7 p_1^{3/8}p_2^{5/8}+\alpha_8 p_1^{1/4}p_2^{3/4}+\alpha_9 p_1^{1/8}p_2^{7/8});\end{aligned} \tag{25}$$

$$\begin{aligned}\frac{\partial C_{n=3}(y,\mathbf{p})}{\partial p_1}&=y(\alpha_1+\tfrac{7}{8}\alpha_3 p_1^{-1/8}p_2^{1/8}+\tfrac{3}{4}\alpha_4 p_1^{-1/4}p_2^{1/4}+\tfrac{5}{8}\alpha_5 p_1^{-3/8}p_2^{3/8}\\ &\quad+\tfrac{1}{2}\alpha_6 p_1^{-1/2}p_2^{1/2}+\tfrac{3}{8}\alpha_7 p_1^{-5/8}p_2^{5/8}+\tfrac{1}{4}\alpha_8 p_1^{-3/4}p_2^{3/4}\\ &\quad+\tfrac{1}{8}\alpha_9 p_1^{-7/8}p_2^{7/8}),\end{aligned}$$

$$\begin{aligned}\frac{\partial C_{n=3}(y,\mathbf{p})}{\partial p_2}&=y(\alpha_2+\tfrac{1}{8}\alpha_3 p_1^{7/8}p_2^{-7/8}+\tfrac{1}{4}\alpha_4 p_1^{3/4}p_2^{-3/4}+\tfrac{3}{8}\alpha_5 p_1^{5/8}p_2^{-5/8}\\ &\quad+\tfrac{1}{2}\alpha_6 p_1^{1/2}p_2^{-1/2}+\tfrac{5}{8}\alpha_7 p_1^{3/8}p_2^{-3/8}+\tfrac{3}{4}\alpha_8 p_1^{1/4}p_2^{-1/4}\\ &\quad+\tfrac{7}{8}\alpha_9 p_1^{1/8}p_2^{-1/8}).\end{aligned}$$

To illustrate how these partial sums were produced, consider the correspondence between (21) and (25) for the first few terms of $P_{n=3}(\mathbf{p})$. Since $n=3$, we have that $\mathbf{z}=(i_1,i_2,\ldots,i_{2n})=(i_1,i_2,\ldots,i_8)$, and $\prod_{j=1}^{2^n}p_{i_j}^{2^{-n}}=\prod_{j=1}^{8}p_{i_j}^{1/8}$. For one such octuple $\mathbf{z}$, consider $\mathbf{z}=(1,1,1,1,1,1,1,1)$. Then $i_j=1$ for all j, so that $\prod_{j=1}^{8}p_{i_j}^{1/8}=\prod_{j=1}^{8}p_1^{1/8}=p_1$, which produces the first term in the expansion of $P_{n=3}(\mathbf{p})$ in equation (25). In the same way, setting $\mathbf{z}=(2,2,2,2,2,2,2,2)$ produces the second term in equation (25).

Table 3. *Bayesian inference in AIM*(1), *Berndt–Wood production data*[a]

Parameter or function	Classical inference MLE	S.E.	Bayesian inference Posterior mean	Posterior st. dev.	Numerical S.E.
α_1	0.0133	0.853	0.2068	0.1542	0.0058
α_2	0.1383	0.972	0.3526	0.1735	0.0068
α_3	1.406	0.578	1.0029	0.3217	0.0116
l_{11}	22.54	3.17	22.9167	2.9964	0.0617
l_{22}	5.459	0.765	5.2051	0.7079	0.0157
l_{21}	−13.15	2.21	−11.9206	2.0876	0.0601
ξ_K	−0.4904		−0.3501	0.1113	0.0040
ξ_L	−0.4204		−0.2989	0.0962	0.0035
ξ_{KL}	0.4904		0.3501	0.1113	0.0040
ξ_{LK}	0.4204		0.2989	0.0962	0.0035
σ_K	−1.0624		−0.7602	0.2405	0.0088
σ_L	−0.7806		−0.5541	0.1794	0.0064
σ_{KL}	0.9107		0.6489	0.2074	0.0075

[a] In maximum likelihood estimation, the coefficients α_j have been constrained to be positive through the use of a penalized likelihood function, and hence the point estimates are not exact maximum likelihood. Standard errors (S.E.) are produced in the usual way from the second derivatives of the penalized likelihood function. In the Bayesian estimation columns, see the footnotes to Tables 1 and 2 for the explanations of notation. The abbreviation "st. dev." stands for standard deviation.

The third term is produced by setting $\mathbf{z} = (1,1,1,1,1,1,1,2)$, so that $\prod_{j=1}^{8} p_{i_j}^{1/8}$ becomes $p_1^{1/8}p_1^{1/8}p_1^{1/8}p_1^{1/8}p_1^{1/8}p_1^{1/8}p_1^{1/8}p_2^{1/8} = p_1^{7/8}p_2^{1/8}$. Similarly, the fourth term was produced by setting $\mathbf{z} = (1,1,1,1,1,1,2,2)$, etc.

3.5 *Empirical findings*

We estimate the AIM factor demand system for two factors of production and constant returns to scale with the widely studied Berndt and Wood data set for U.S. manufacturing, 1947–77. The Berndt and Wood data have been extended by Morrison and subsequently by Epstein and Yatchew. Our data source is Epstein and Yatchew (1985), which contains data on output (value added) and on two factors of production: labor and capital. We subscript labor to be the first factor and capital to be the second factor. These results will be supplemented in later research with findings from an extended AIM model permitting nonconstant returns to scale and technical progress.

Constrained maximum likelihood estimates using AIM(1), AIM(2), AIM(3), and AIM(4) are presented in Tables 3, 4, 5, and 6, respectively.

Table 4. *Classical inference in AIM(2), Berndt–Wood production data*[a]

Parameter or function	MLE	S.E.
α_1	0.0284	0.554
α_2	0.0194	0.646
α_3	0.0498	1.46
α_4	1.143	2.398
α_5	0.3170	1.949
l_{11}	22.53	3.34
l_{22}	5.462	0.812
l_{21}	−13.17	2.238
ξ_K	−0.4933	
ξ_L	−0.4229	
ξ_{KL}	0.4933	
ξ_{LK}	0.4229	
σ_K	−1.0687	
σ_L	−0.7854	
σ_{KL}	0.9161	

[a] The coefficients α_j have been constrained to be positive through the use of a penalized likelihood function, and hence the point estimates are not exact maximum likelihood. Standard errors (S.E.) are produced in the usual way from the second derivatives of the penalized likelihood function.

The standard errors corresponding to these estimates are produced in the usual way from the inverse of the Hessian of the log-likelihood function evaluated at the maximum. In the case of constrained estimates, this means that a conventional interpretation of reported standard errors would carry with it the implicit assumption that binding constraints are known to be binding a priori in the population. Since this is not the case, we do not report such standard errors. Even the standard errors for AIM(1), in which no constraints are binding, must be interpreted with some care, since the point estimate of α_1 is within one standard error of the constraint boundaries.

In addition to maximum likelihood estimates of parameters and (where appropriate) asymptotic standard errors, these tables also indicate the values of elasticities evaluated at the mean of the sample. Of course, it is the elasticity estimates rather than the parameter estimates that bear comparison across the orders of expansion. The elasticity estimates corresponding to the constrained maximum likelihood estimates are virtually

Table 5. *Classical inference in AIM(3), Berndt–Wood production data*[a]

Parameter or function	MLE	S.E.
α_1	0.0219	0.604
α_2	0.0126	0.408
α_3	0.0298	0.902
α_4	0.0499	1.50
α_5	0.1207	2.80
α_6	0.6086	1.30
α_7	0.6091	4.49
α_8	0.0788	2.44
α_9	0.0265	0.836
l_{11}	22.55	3.28
l_{22}	5.459	0.791
l_{21}	−13.15	2.32
ξ_K	−0.4914	
ξ_L	−0.4210	
ξ_{KL}	0.4914	
ξ_{LK}	0.4210	
σ_K	−1.0647	
σ_L	−0.7819	
σ_{KL}	0.9127	

[a] The coefficients α_j have been constrained to be positive through the use of a penalized likelihood function, and hence the point estimates are not exact maximum likelihood. Standard errors (S.E.) are produced in the usual way from the second derivatives of the penalized likelihood function.

identical across the three orders of expansion. This similarity of the three models for relative prices in the range of the data is also reflected in the maximum likelihood estimate of the variance matrix of the disturbances, and in the value of the log-likelihood function at the maximum. It is clear that AIM has converged at the first order of expansion.

For AIM(2) and AIM(3), the inequality constraints on the α_i are binding. However, the fit of the model to the data does not improve when the inequality constraints are removed: there is little change in the value of the variance matrix of the disturbances, and the value of the log-likelihood function increases by less than one. Interestingly, at the unconstrained maximum likelihood estimate, the regularity conditions are satisfied for each point in the sample space; and, therefore, following a procedure like the one proposed in Gallant and Golub (1984) to impose regularity

Table 6. *Classical inference in AIM(4), Berndt–Wood production data*[a]

Parameter or function	MLE	S.E.
α_1	0.0107	0.335
α_2	0.0125	0.527
α_3	0.0160	0.527
α_4	0.0241	0.805
α_5	0.0398	1.30
α_6	0.0753	2.31
α_7	0.0176	0.598
α_8	0.0105	0.358
α_9	0.8382	8.65
α_{10}	0.2622	8.29
α_{11}	0.1090	3.66
α_{12}	0.0591	1.90
α_{13}	0.0142	1.31
α_{14}	0.0263	0.839
α_{15}	0.0197	0.611
α_{16}	0.0155	0.471
α_{17}	0.0127	0.401
l_{11}	22.57	3.30
l_{22}	5.454	0.808
l_{21}	−13.14	2.37
ξ_K	−0.4964	
ξ_L	−0.4204	
ξ_{KL}	0.4964	
ξ_{LK}	0.4204	
σ_K	−1.0827	
σ_L	−0.7763	
σ_{KL}	0.9168	

[a] The coefficients α_i have been constrained to be positive through the use of a penalized likelihood function, and hence the point estimates are not exact maximum likelihood. Standard errors (S.E.) are produced in the usual way from the second derivatives of the penalized likelihood function.

over the sample would leave the unconstrained estimates unchanged. In addition, the stronger global regularity sufficient conditions embodied in the constraints $\alpha_i \geq 0$ are consistent with the information in the sample, as is evident from the small change in the log-likelihood function when the inequality conditions are imposed. Although imposition of those

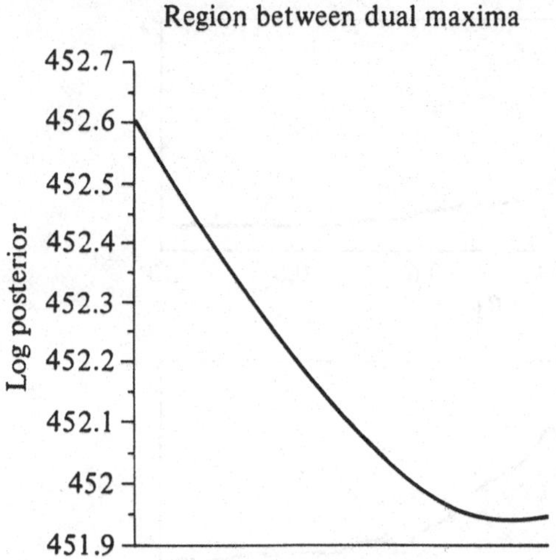

Figure 1. Profile of the logarithm of the posterior density, as it appears along a line between the two local modes for AIM(2).

sufficient conditions is not necessary to attain regional regularity in any of the cases that we considered, the inequality constraints proved to be computationally convenient in producing Bayesian estimates, since it is preferable for the numerical integration to be conducted entirely within a regular subset of the parameter space. With fixed data, the model surely is not globally regular everywhere in the data space, although the model is necessarily regular within the nonnegative orthant of the parameter space.

Because of the convergence of AIM at the first order of expansion, we confine Bayesian inference to AIM(1). The results, presented in Table 6, were obtained from 100,000 Monte Carlo iterations. Posterior means for both parameter values and for elasticities evaluated at the sample mean differ substantively from the maximum likelihood estimates. This difference can be traced to the fact that the nonnegativity constraint on α_1 was nearly binding, inducing a discrepancy between the mode and mean of the posterior density. For the computational reasons mentioned before, we produced the Bayesian estimates only under the parametric nonnegativity constraints.

Further insight is provided by Figure 1, which presents approximations to the posterior density constructed from the application of a standard cubic smoothing spline to a subsample of parameter values from the Monte Carlo iterations. The modes of these functions correspond closely

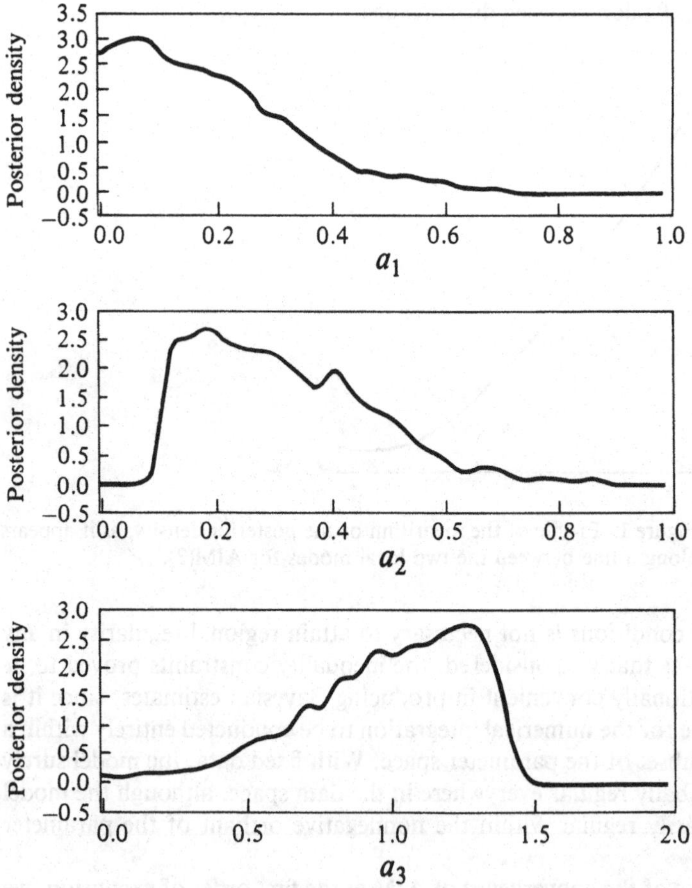

Figure 2. Posterior densities of parameters, AIM(1).

to the maximum likelihood estimates. However, this result is not a logical necessity, since the graphs in Figure 1 are of marginal posteriors, acquired by integrations over the posterior, and not profiles (i.e., "slices") through the posterior density. Figure 1 indicates the extreme difficulty in interpreting maximum likelihood estimates or posterior modes as point estimates of parameters in this data set. The posterior density of each function of interest should be examined directly.

Inference was undertaken at the sample mean for conditional factor demand elasticities (the ξ_j's) and for Allen elasticities of substitution (the σ_j's). Formulas for those elasticities are supplied in Barnett, Geweke,

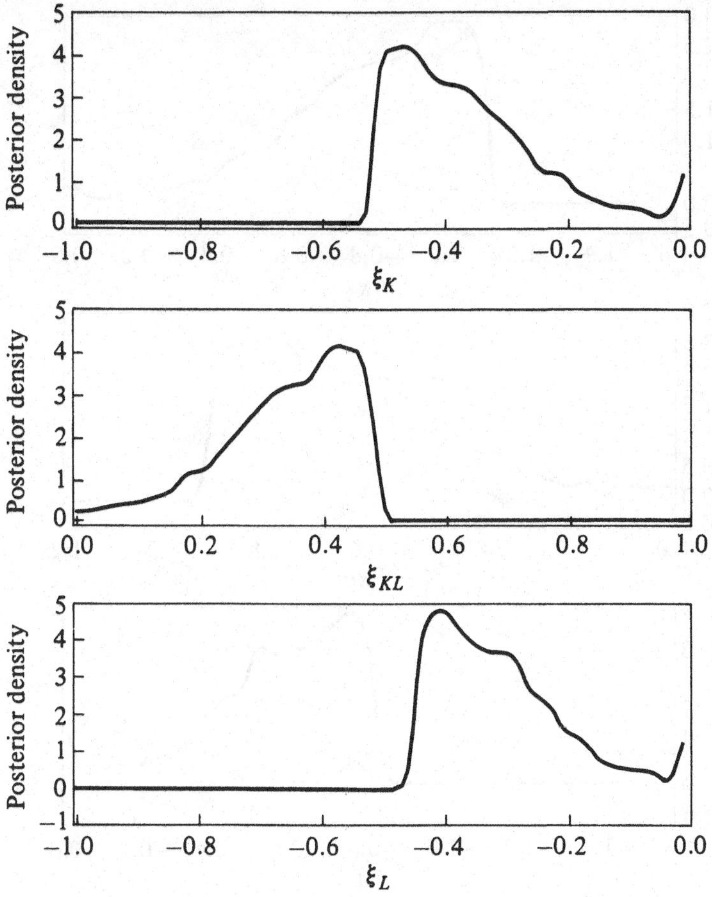

Figure 3. Posterior densities of factor price elasticities ξ_{ij} of AIM(1) conditional factor demand.

and Wolfe (1990, Appendix A). Posterior densities for these elasticities and the parameters are presented in Figures 2, 3, and 4. These graphs again underscore the extreme nonnormality of functions of interest in this model. Indeed, if these results characterize other data sets as well, careful reinterpretation of the results in the extensive neoclassical econometric literature may be appropriate.

In future work, we plan to compute odds ratios for the nonnegativity restrictions on the parameters, and to verify the validity of the model's inferences by replacing the extended Berndt–Wood data by Monte Carlo

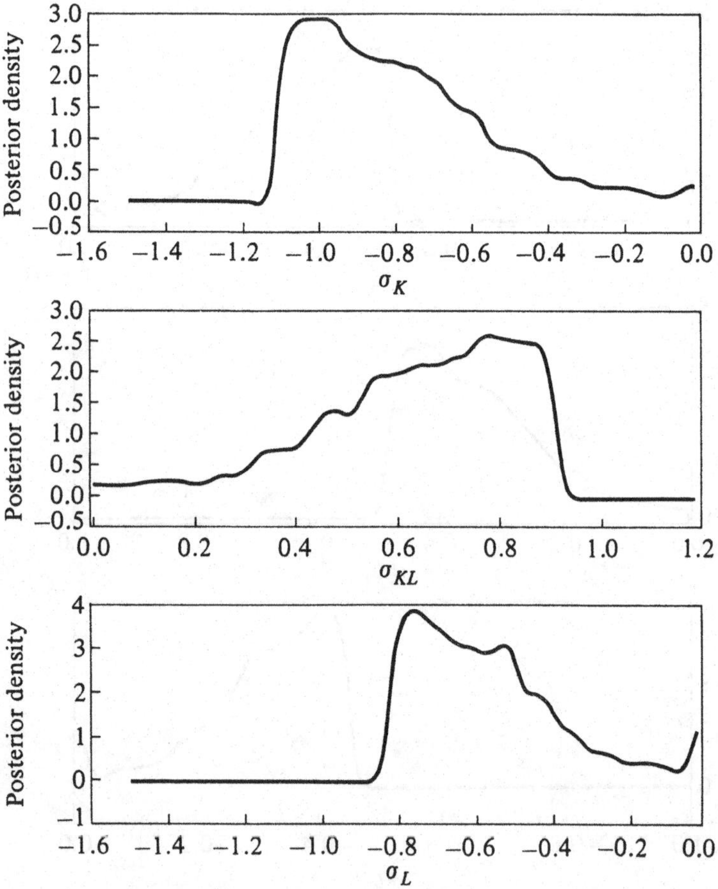

Figure 4. Posterior densities of Allen elasticities of substitution σ_{ij} for AIM(1).

data generated from a Cobb–Douglas technology. We also contemplate using the AIM conditional factor demand system in consumer demand modeling. To do so, one need only replace output by real income (i.e., real expenditure on consumer goods) and factor prices by consumer goods prices. Our conditional factor demand system then becomes Hicksian compensated consumer demands. Comparison of our findings in this chapter with those in Barnett and Yue (1988b) and in Barnett, Geweke, and Yue (1989) suggest that the likelihood function produced from Hicksian demand is better behaved than the likelihood functions produced from Marshallian demand.

5 Conclusions

It is our belief that the AIM sequence of consumption and factor demand equations provides a fruitful specification for future research on seminonparametric modeling of demand systems and eventually for modeling of general equilibrium systems. The AIM model, being produced from a power series, contains no nonneoclassical trigonometric functions. The ability to impose global regularity at all orders of approximation, as well as at convergence, is a particular merit of AIM. Furthermore, when global regularity is imposed at all orders of approximation, overfitting is impossible. Hence, the number of terms can be increased at fixed sample size until elasticity estimates converge. This procedure is in contrast with the usual seminonparametric procedure of selecting an arbitrary rule in advance for fixing the number of terms as a function of sample size.

In short, the AIM model, with our approach to numerical Bayesian estimation, makes the capabilities of seminonparametric inference available and practical in demand systems modeling, when testing for or imposing global theoretical regularity is needed. Furthermore, the new algorithmic developments in numerical Bayesian methodology introduced in this chapter greatly expand upon the capabilities of Bayesian statistics and should permit Bayesian methods to be used in large classes of important inference problems to which neither Bayesian nor sampling theoretic methods previously were applicable.

Our results on factor demand were substantially easier to acquire than on the demand side. The primary reason is that the imposition of linear homogeneity on tastes is a severe assumption, which we have not imposed, whereas the imposition of constant returns to scale on technology has some merits, at least as a starting point in investigating technology. The resulting difference in estimation complexity should be no surprise, since the popular translog model similarly produces a better behaved linear factor demand specification than its nonlinear consumer demand specification, when linear homogeneity is not imposed upon tastes. One implication of our results may be that reliable inference with consumer demand systems in general may be even more difficult than previously believed.

On the other hand, our results in estimation of technology converge rapidly and convincingly as the order of the approximation K increases. In addition, the theoretical restrictions, although not yet tested, seem strongly to be accepted. The reason is that in the AIM(1) case, none of the restrictions was binding. Although some constraints were binding for the higher-order partial sums, the elasticity estimates already had converged against order of approximation of AIM(1). In short, our existing results strongly suggest that the constant returns-to-scale version of AIM provides a highly useful method for accurate inference regarding constant returns-to-scale technologies.

Once this line of research is complete, we believe that it will provide a unified approach to producing applied general equilibrium models of substantial global flexibility as well as global theoretical regularity and will fully solve the overfitting problem that has hampered the use of flexible functional forms in applied general equilibrium modeling.

Appendix A: Approximate inequality constrained asymptotic likelihood ratio test

In this appendix, we show that the tail area of the test of global regularity produced from an approximate procedure is always less than would be produced, if the sampling distribution of the test statistic under the null were derived subject to the actual theoretical inequality constraints on the model's parameters. As a result, that test of theory is biased toward rejection of the neoclassical theory and, hence, provides a conservative test when it accepts the theory. These results are relevant to interpretation of the sampling theoretic results in Barnett and Yue (1988b).

Let the observations on the normalized prices be $\mathbf{v}_t$, $t=1,\dots,T$, and define $\mathbf{z}=(\mathbf{v}_1',\dots,\mathbf{v}_T')'$. Let the observations on the expenditure shares be $\mathbf{s}=(\mathbf{s}_1',\dots,\mathbf{s}_T')'$, where $\mathbf{s}_t=(s_{1t},s_{2t})'$. Then the likelihood function can be denoted by $L(\boldsymbol{\alpha}\,|\,\mathbf{s},\mathbf{z})$, where $\boldsymbol{\alpha}\in\mathbb{R}^N$ is the parameter vector. Define the likelihood ratio by

$$Y_T=\frac{\sup_{\boldsymbol{\alpha}\geq\mathbf{0}} L(\boldsymbol{\alpha}\,|\,\mathbf{s},\mathbf{z})}{\sup_{\boldsymbol{\alpha}\in\mathbb{R}^N} L(\boldsymbol{\alpha}\,|\,\mathbf{s},\mathbf{z})}. \tag{A.1}$$

Then the asymptotic likelihood ratio test statistic is $-2\log Y_T$. For the form taken by that test statistic as a function of the values of the generalized variance of the fit, rather than as a function of the values of the likelihood function, see Barnett (1981, p. 95).

Let Y be a random variable such that $-2\log Y_T$ converges in distribution to Y as $T\to\infty$, if the null hypothesis that $\boldsymbol{\alpha}\geq\mathbf{0}$ is true. Suppose that we knew the distribution of Y, so that we could use Y_T to produce an asymptotic test of the null hypothesis that $\boldsymbol{\alpha}\geq\mathbf{0}$. The asymptotic tail area of the test would be $\tau=P[Y>-2\log Y_T]$, where Y_T is computed from equation (A.1) using the observations on $(\mathbf{s},\mathbf{z})$. See Barnett (1981, p. 95). We would reject the null, if τ were small, perhaps less than 0.05.

Although that test would be straightforward, we nevertheless cannot use it directly, since we do not know the limiting distribution of $-2\log Y_T$, so we do not know the distribution of Y. However, consider the alternative test statistic

$$\tilde{Y}_T = \frac{\sup_{\alpha \in G} L(\alpha \mid \mathbf{s}, \mathbf{z})}{\sup_{\alpha \in \mathbb{R}^N} L(\alpha \mid \mathbf{s}, \mathbf{z})}, \tag{A.2}$$

where the parameter vector $\boldsymbol{\alpha}$ has been arbitrarily partitioned such that $\boldsymbol{\alpha} = (\alpha_1, \alpha_2)'$ with $\alpha_2 \in \mathbb{R}^\rho$, and where $G = \{\alpha \in \mathbb{R}^N: \boldsymbol{\alpha}_1 \geq \mathbf{0},\ \boldsymbol{\alpha}_2 = \mathbf{0}\}$. Then, clearly, $\tilde{Y}_T \leq Y_T$ for any possible data on $(\mathbf{s}, \mathbf{z})$.

Let $\tilde{Y}$ be a random variable such that $-2\log \tilde{Y}_T$ converges in distribution to $\tilde{Y}$ as $T \to \infty$, if $\alpha_2 = 0$ is true. Consider the tail area $\tilde{\tau} = P[\tilde{Y} > -2\log \tilde{Y}_T]$, where $\tilde{Y}_T$ is computed from (A.2) using the data $(\mathbf{s}, \mathbf{z})$. Since $\tilde{Y}_T \leq Y_T$, we know that $-2\log \tilde{Y}_T \geq -2\log Y_T$, and hence that

$$[\tilde{Y} > -2\log \tilde{Y}_T] \subset [\tilde{Y} > -2\log Y_T].$$

It follows immediately that

$$P[\tilde{Y} > -2\log \tilde{Y}_T] \leq P[\tilde{Y} > -2\log Y_T],$$

so that

$$\tau = P[\tilde{Y} > -2\log \tilde{Y}_T], \tag{A.3}$$

But since $\tilde{Y}_T \leq Y_T$, we know that $\tilde{Y} \leq Y$ [a.s.]. Hence, $[\tilde{Y} > -2\log Y_T] \subset [Y > -2\log Y_T]$, and, therefore, $P[\tilde{Y} > -2\log Y_T] \leq \tau$. From (A.3), we see immediately that

$$\tau \leq \tilde{\tau}. \tag{A.4}$$

In the applied literature on maximum likelihood estimation, it is common to ignore the truncation of test statistic sampling distributions caused by nonbinding inequality constraints on parameters, as opposed to binding corner solutions on parameters. In accordance with that convention, we assume that

$$\tilde{\tau} \approx P[Z > -2\log \tilde{Y}_T], \tag{A.5}$$

where Z is the limiting distribution of $-2\log Z_T$, which is defined by

$$Z_T = \frac{\sup_{\alpha_2 \geq 0} L(\alpha \mid \mathbf{s}, \mathbf{z})}{\sup_{\alpha \in \mathbb{R}^N} L(\alpha \mid \mathbf{s}, \mathbf{z})},$$

with $\boldsymbol{\alpha}_1$ unconstrained in the numerator.

Under assumption (A.5), the approximate test uses $\tilde{Y}_T$ as the test statistic, since by using the $\chi^2(\rho)$ distribution for the distribution of $\tilde{Y}$, we implicitly are assuming that the equality $\boldsymbol{\alpha}_2 = 0$ would have remained binding for all possible realizations of the random vector $\mathbf{s}$. Hence, from (A.4), we see that acceptance of the null hypothesis that $\boldsymbol{\alpha} \geq \mathbf{0}$ based upon the approximate test statistic $-2\log \tilde{Y}_T$ is conservative, since a large tail area $\tilde{\tau}$ implies that the tail area τ is even larger.

Appendix B: The likelihood function, gradient, and Hessian

B. *Objective*

This appendix provides the necessary information for formation of the log-posterior density, gradient, and Hessian for the AIM consumer demand models of any order. This is done in two steps. The first step develops this information for any system of seemingly unrelated regressions that is nonlinear in the parameters. Therefore, it is applicable to a very wide variety of models. The second step develops the specifics for the functional form in the AIM demand systems.

B.1 *Seemingly unrelated regression models nonlinear in the parameters*

To develop notation, let the ith observation for the jth equation be

$$y_{ij}=f_j(\mathbf{x}_i,\boldsymbol{\beta})+\epsilon_{ij},\quad j=1,\ldots,m;\ i=1,\ldots,T,$$

where y_{ij} is the ith observation on the jth dependent variable, $\mathbf{x}_i$ is the ith observation on the vector of exogenous variables for the system, ϵ_{ij} is the disturbance corresponding to the ith observation on the jth equation, and $\boldsymbol{\beta}$ is a vector of unknown coefficients for the system. Vector notation will be used whenever possible to simplify the derivations, and to this end, let

$$\mathbf{y}_j=(y_{1j},\ldots,y_{nj})'=[f_j(\mathbf{x}_1,\boldsymbol{\beta})+\epsilon_1,\ldots,f_j(\mathbf{x}_n,\boldsymbol{\beta})+\epsilon_T]'=\mathbf{F}_j(\mathbf{x},\boldsymbol{\beta})+\epsilon_j.$$

For further compactness, let

$$\mathbf{F}(\mathbf{x},\boldsymbol{\beta})=[\mathbf{F}_1(\mathbf{x},\boldsymbol{\beta})',\ldots,\mathbf{F}_m(\mathbf{X},\boldsymbol{\beta})']',$$

$$\epsilon=(\epsilon_1',\ldots,\epsilon_m')',\quad \text{and}\quad \mathbf{y}=(\mathbf{y}_1',\ldots,\mathbf{y}_m')'.$$

The statistical assumption is

$$(\epsilon_{i1},\ldots,\epsilon_{im})'\sim \text{IIDN}(\mathbf{0},\boldsymbol{\Sigma}),\quad i=1,\ldots,n.$$

Let the inverse of the positive definite variance matrix $\boldsymbol{\Sigma}$ have lower triangular Choleski factorization $\boldsymbol{\Sigma}^{-1}=\mathbf{LL}'$, with the diagonal elements of $\mathbf{L}$ being positive.

With a diffuse prior, the kernel of the log-posterior density takes the form

$$\log\{|\boldsymbol{\Sigma}^{-1}|^{r/2}\}-\tfrac{1}{2}[\mathbf{y}-\mathbf{F}(\mathbf{x},\boldsymbol{\beta})]'(\boldsymbol{\Sigma}^{-1}\otimes\mathbf{I}_T)[\mathbf{y}-\mathbf{F}(\mathbf{x},\boldsymbol{\beta})]$$

$$=r\sum_{j=1}^{m}\log(l_{jj})-\tfrac{1}{2}\{(\mathbf{L}'\otimes\mathbf{I}_T)[\mathbf{y}-\mathbf{F}(\mathbf{x},\boldsymbol{\beta})]\}'\{(\mathbf{L}'\otimes\mathbf{I}_T)[\mathbf{y}-\mathbf{F}(\mathbf{x},\boldsymbol{\beta})]\}.$$

This expression involves the inner product of the vector

$$
\begin{aligned}
(\mathbf{L}'\otimes\mathbf{I}_n)[\mathbf{y}-\mathbf{F}(\mathbf{x},\boldsymbol{\beta})]
&= \begin{bmatrix} l_{11}\mathbf{I}_T & l_{21}\mathbf{I}_T & \cdots & l_{m2}\mathbf{I}_T \\ \mathbf{0} & l_{22}\mathbf{I}_T & \cdots & l_{m2}\mathbf{I}_T \\ \vdots & \vdots & \ddots & \vdots \\ \mathbf{0} & \mathbf{0} & \cdots & l_{mm}\mathbf{I}_T \end{bmatrix}
\begin{pmatrix} \mathbf{y}_1-\mathbf{F}_1(\mathbf{x},\boldsymbol{\beta}) \\ \mathbf{y}_2-\mathbf{F}_2(\mathbf{x},\boldsymbol{\beta}) \\ \vdots \\ \mathbf{y}_m-\mathbf{F}_m(\mathbf{x},\boldsymbol{\beta}) \end{pmatrix} \\
&= \begin{pmatrix} \Sigma_{u=1}^{m} l_{u1}[\mathbf{y}_u-\mathbf{F}_u(\mathbf{x},\boldsymbol{\beta})] \\ \Sigma_{u=2}^{m} l_{u2}[\mathbf{y}_u-\mathbf{F}_u(\mathbf{x},\boldsymbol{\beta})] \\ \vdots \\ l_{mm}[\mathbf{y}_m-\mathbf{F}_m(\mathbf{x},\boldsymbol{\beta})] \end{pmatrix},
\end{aligned}
$$

and, consequently, the log posterior density may be written

$$
\begin{aligned}
&g(\boldsymbol{\beta}, l_{11}, l_{21}, \ldots, l_{mm}) \\
&\quad = r\sum_{j=1}^{m}\log(l_{jj}) - \frac{1}{2}\sum_{i=1}^{n}\sum_{j=1}^{m}\sum_{u=j}^{m}\sum_{v=j}^{m} l_{uj}[u_{iu}-f_u(\mathbf{x}_i,\boldsymbol{\beta})]\,l_{uj}[u_{iu}-f_u(\mathbf{x}_i,\boldsymbol{\beta})].
\end{aligned}
$$

By denoting the vector of first derivatives of $f_u(\mathbf{x}_i, \boldsymbol{\beta})$ with respect to $\boldsymbol{\beta}$ by $\mathbf{f}_u^{(1)}(\mathbf{x}_i, \boldsymbol{\beta})$, the matrix of second derivatives of $f_u(\mathbf{x}_i, \boldsymbol{\beta})$ with respect to $\boldsymbol{\beta}$ by $\mathbf{f}_u^{(2)}(\mathbf{x}_i, \boldsymbol{\beta})$, and the residual term for the ith observation in the uth equation by $e_{iu}(\mathbf{x}_i, \boldsymbol{\beta}) = y_{iu} - f_u(\mathbf{x}_i, \boldsymbol{\beta})$, the first and second partial derivatives of $g(\boldsymbol{\beta}, l_{11}, l_{21}, \ldots, l_{mm})$ may be written as follows:

$$
\begin{aligned}
\frac{\partial g}{\partial \boldsymbol{\beta}} &= \frac{1}{2}\sum_{i=1}^{T}\sum_{j=1}^{m}\sum_{u=j}^{m}\sum_{v=j}^{m}[f_u^{(1)}(\mathbf{x}_i,\boldsymbol{\beta})\,l_{uj}l_{vj}e_{iv}(\mathbf{x}_i,\boldsymbol{\beta}) \\
&\qquad + f_v^{(1)}(\mathbf{x}_i,\boldsymbol{\beta})\,l_{vj}l_{uj}e_{iu}(\mathbf{x}_i,\boldsymbol{\beta})], \\
\frac{\partial g}{\partial l_{pq}} &= r\delta_{p,q}l_{pq}^{-1} - \frac{1}{2}\sum_{i=1}^{T}\sum_{v=q}^{m} e_{ip}(\mathbf{x}_i,\boldsymbol{\beta})\,l_{vq}e_{iv}(\mathbf{x}_i,\boldsymbol{\beta}), \\
\frac{\partial^2 g}{\partial\boldsymbol{\beta}\,\partial\boldsymbol{\beta}'} &= \frac{1}{2}\sum_{i=1}^{T}\sum_{j=1}^{m}\sum_{u=j}^{m}\sum_{v=j}^{m}\{\mathbf{f}_u^{(2)}(\mathbf{x}_i,\boldsymbol{\beta})\,l_{uj}l_{vj}e_{iv}(\mathbf{x}_i,\boldsymbol{\beta}) \\
&\qquad - f_u^{(1)}(\mathbf{x}_i,\boldsymbol{\beta})\,l_{uj}l_{vj}f_v^{(1)}(\mathbf{x}_i,\boldsymbol{\beta})' \\
&\qquad + f_v^{(2)}(\mathbf{x}_i,\boldsymbol{\beta})\,l_{vj}l_{uj}e_{iu}(\mathbf{x}_i,\boldsymbol{\beta}) \\
&\qquad - f_v^{(1)}(\mathbf{x}_i,\boldsymbol{\beta})\,l_{vj}l_{uj}f_u^{(1)}(\mathbf{x}_i,\boldsymbol{\beta})'\}, \\
\frac{\partial^2 g}{\partial\boldsymbol{\beta}\,\partial l_{pq}} &= \frac{1}{2}\sum_{i=1}^{T}\Big\{\sum_{u=q}^{m}[f_u^{(1)}(\mathbf{x}_i,\boldsymbol{\beta})\,l_{uq}e_{ip}(\mathbf{x}_i;\boldsymbol{\beta}) + f_p^{(1)}(\mathbf{x}_i,\boldsymbol{\beta})\,l_{uq}e_{iu}(\mathbf{x}_i,\boldsymbol{\beta})] \\
&\qquad + \sum_{v=q}^{m}[f_p^{(1)}(\mathbf{x}_i,\boldsymbol{\beta})\,l_{vq}e_{iv}(\mathbf{x}_i,\boldsymbol{\beta}) + f_v^{(1)}(\mathbf{x}_i,\boldsymbol{\beta})\,l_{vq}e_{ip}(\mathbf{x}_i,\boldsymbol{\beta})]\Big\}, \\
\frac{\partial^2 g}{\partial l_{pq}\,\partial l_{st}} &= rl_{pq}^{-2}\delta_{p,s}\delta_{q,t}\delta_{p,q} - \delta_{q,t}\sum_{i=1}^{T} e_{ip}(\mathbf{x}_i,\boldsymbol{\beta})\,e_{is}(\mathbf{x}_i,\boldsymbol{\beta})
\end{aligned}
$$

B.2 *Specialization to the functional form in the AIM demand systems*

The functional form of each share equation in the AIM demand systems is

$$s_{ij} = \frac{\sum_{l=0}^{k} \beta_l c_{jl} x_{il}}{\sum_{l=0}^{k} \beta_l z_{il}} + \epsilon_{ij},$$

where all values except ϵ_{ij} and the β_l are known, and $\beta_0 = 1$. Thus,

$$f_{ju}^{(1)}(\mathbf{x}_i, \boldsymbol{\beta}) = \frac{(\sum_{l=0}^{k} \beta_l z_{il}) c_{ju} x_{iu} - (\sum_{l=0}^{k} \beta_l c_{jl} x_{il}) z_{iu}}{(\sum_{l=0}^{k} \beta_l z_{il})^2},$$

$$f_{juv}^{(2)}(\mathbf{x}_i, \boldsymbol{\beta}) = \frac{-(\sum_{l=0}^{k} \beta_l z_{il})(z_{iv} c_{ju} x_{iu} + z_{iu} c_{jv} x_{iv}) + 2 z_{iv} z_{iu} \sum_{l=0}^{k} \beta_l c_{jl} x_{il}}{(\sum_{l=0}^{k} \beta_l z_{il})^3}.$$

These derivations and the coding of the routines that implement them have been thoroughly cross-checked by comparing analytical and numerical results. The routine that evaluates the posterior density was coded in 128-bit as well as 64-bit arithmetic. The high-precision variant was used to form numerical first and second derivatives of the log posterior density (as well as some intermediate products in the process of debugging). These were compared with the results of the routines that directly implement the analytical first and second derivatives.

B.3 *Determining the mode of the posterior for density*

The posterior density is maximized using the Newton–Raphson method, modified to account for the nonnegativity constraints on certain of the parameters. This method has proven to be computationally efficient, so that maximization requires only a few minutes on a 32-bit minicomputer programmed in double precision, even for AIM(2).

At each step in the Newton–Raphson iterative procedure, some parameters are included (i.e., free to be changed) and some are excluded (set to their boundary value, $\beta_l = 0$). Let $\boldsymbol{\theta}_i$ be the vector of included variables at the ith step, $\mathbf{g}(\boldsymbol{\theta}_i)$ the first derivative of the log-posterior density with respect to this vector, and $\mathbf{H}(\boldsymbol{\theta}_i)$ the matrix of second derivatives with respect to this vector. Let $\mathbf{H}^*(\boldsymbol{\theta}_i)$ be a matrix constructed from $\mathbf{H}(\boldsymbol{\theta}_i)$ by subtracting the term 2ϵ from each of its eigenvalues and recomputing the matrix, where ϵ is the largest eigenvalue of $\mathbf{H}(\boldsymbol{\theta}_i)$ if $\mathbf{H}(\boldsymbol{\theta}_i)$ is not negative definite, and zero otherwise. Then the direction of search in the ith step is $\mathbf{d}_i = -\mathbf{H}^*(\boldsymbol{\theta}_i)^{-1}\mathbf{g}(\boldsymbol{\theta}_i)$. The updated vector is $\boldsymbol{\theta}_{i+1} = \boldsymbol{\theta}_i + s_i \mathbf{d}_i$, where the step size s_i is 1, if $\boldsymbol{\theta}_{i+1}$ satisfies all inequality constraints and the value of the log-posterior density at $\boldsymbol{\theta}_{i+1}$ is greater than at $\boldsymbol{\theta}_i$. If constraints are violated at this point, then s_i is chosen to be the largest value consistent with inequality constraints. Step size is repeatedly halved, if necessary, until the log-posterior density at $\boldsymbol{\theta}_{i+1}=\boldsymbol{\theta}_i+s_i\mathbf{d}_i$ exceeds the value at $\boldsymbol{\theta}_i$. If an inequality constraint is binding on a parameter in θ_{i+1}, then that parameter is excluded and iterations continue.

Iterations proceed in this fashion until $-\mathbf{g}(\boldsymbol{\theta}_i)\mathbf{H}^*(\boldsymbol{\theta}_i)^{-1}\mathbf{g}(\boldsymbol{\theta}_i)$ is quite small. When the convergence criterion is satisfied, the gradient vector for each excluded parameter is examined. As soon as one excluded parameter for which the gradient is positive is found, that one parameter is added to the vector of included variables, and iteration continues.

Appendix C: Computation of elasticities

C.1 *Consumer demand case*

The systematic part of a share equation can be written

$$s_j=\frac{\sum_{i=0}^k \beta_i c_{ji} x_i}{\sum_{i=0}^k \beta_i d_i x_i}=\frac{\tau_j}{\gamma},$$

where β_i is a_i in AIM(1) or b_i in AIM(2); x_i is a product of powers of the v_j, as indicated in Sections 2.3 and 2.4; and the c_{ji} and d_i are known constants, as indicated in Sections 2.3 and 2.4. Let $r_j=p_j$, $j=1,2,3$; and let $r_4=m$. Then

$$\frac{\partial s_j}{\partial r_n}=\gamma^{-2}\sum_{i=0}^k \beta_i(\gamma c_{ji}-\tau_j d_i)\frac{\partial x_i}{\partial r_n},$$

and, in turn,

$$\frac{\partial x_i}{\partial r_n}=\sum_{l=1}^3\left[\frac{\partial x_i}{\partial v_l}\right]\left[\frac{\partial v_l}{\partial r_n}\right].$$

In matrix notation,

$$\mathbf{U}=\mathbf{EGH}$$

with

$$u_{jn}=\frac{\partial s_j}{\partial r_n},$$

$$e_{ji}=\gamma^{-2}\beta_i(\gamma c_{ji}-\tau_j d_i),$$

$$g_{il}=\frac{\partial x_i}{\partial v_l},$$

$$h_{ln}=\frac{\partial v_l}{\partial r_n}.$$

The g_{il} may be computed from the expressions given in Sections 4 and 5; $h_{ln}=\delta_{l,n}m^{-1}$ $(n=1,2,3)$; and $h_{l4}=-p_l m^{-2}$.

Given **U**, elasticities may be computed as indicated in Section 2.8. The advantage of this approach is that only **E** depends on the unknown parameters. The matrices **G** and **H** may be computed in advance and need not be recomputed at each iteration of Monte Carlo integration.

C.2 *Production case*

See Barnett, Geweke, and Wolfe (1990, Appendix A).

REFERENCES

Anderson, T. W. 1984. *An Introduction to Multivariate Statistical Analysis,* 2d Ed. New York: Wiley.

Barnett, W. A. 1976. "Maximum Likelihood and Iterated Aitken Estimation of Nonlinear Systems of Equations." *Journal of the American Statistical Association* 71: 354–60.

1979a. "Theoretical Foundations for the Rotterdam Model." *Review of Economic Studies* 46: 109–30.

1979b. "Recursive Subaggregation and a Generalized Hypocycloidal Demand Model." *Econometrica* 45: 1117–36.

1981. *Consumer Demand and Labor Supply.* Amsterdam: North-Holland.

1982. "The Flexible Laurent Demand System." In *Proceedings of the 1982 American Statistical Association Meetings.* Washington, D.C.: American Statistical Association, pp. 82–9.

1983a. "New Indices of Money Supply and the Flexible Laurent Demand System." *Journal of Business and Economic Statistics* 1: 7–23.

1983b. "Definitions of 'Second Order Approximation' and of 'Flexible Functional Form.'" *Economics Letters* 12: 31–5.

1985. "The Minflex Laurent Translog Flexible Functional Form." *Journal of Econometrics* 30: 33–44.

Barnett, W. A., and Seungmook Choi. 1989. "A Monte Carlo Study of Tests of Blockwise Weak Separability." *Journal of Business and Economic Statistics* 7: 363–77.

Barnett, W. A., John Geweke, and Michael Wolfe. In press. "Seminonparametric Bayesian Estimation of the Asymptotically Ideal Production Model." *Journal of Econometrics.*

Barnett, W. A., John Geweke, and Piyu Yue. 1991. "Seminonparametric Bayesian Estimation of the Asymptotically Ideal Model: The AIM Consumer Demand System." In *Nonparametric and Semiparametric Methods in Econometrics and Statistics,* Proceedings of the Fifth International Symposium in Economic Theory and Econometrics, William Barnett, James Powell, and George Tauchen, Eds. Cambridge: Cambridge University Press.

Barnett, W. A., and Andrew Jonas. 1983. "The Müntz-Szatz Demand System: An Application of A Globally Well Behaved Series Expansion." *Economics Letters* 11: 337–42.

Barnett, W. A., and Y. W. Lee. 1985. "The Global Properties of the Minflex Laurent, Generalized Leontief, and Translog Flexible Functional Forms." *Econometrica* 53: 1421–37.

1987. "The Laurent Series Approach to Structural Modeling." *European Journal of Operations Research* 30: 270-9.

Barnett, W. A., Y. W. Lee, and M. D. Wolfe. 1985. "The Three-Dimensional Global Properties of the Minflex Laurent, Generalized Leontief, and Translog Flexible Functional Forms." *Journal of Econometrics* 30: 3-31.

1987. "The Global Properties of the Two Minflex Laurent Flexible Functional Forms." *Journal of Econometrics* 36: 281-98.

Barnett, W. A., and Piyu Yue. 1988a. "The Asymptotically Ideal Model (AIM)." Working paper.

1988b. "Seminonparametric Estimation of the Asymptotically Ideal Model: The AIM Demand System." In *Nonparametric and Robust Inference,* Advances in Econometrics, Vol. 7, George Rhodes and Thomas Fomby, Ed. Greenwich, CN: JAI Press, pp. 229-52.

Berge, Claude. 1963. *Topological Spaces.* New York: Macmillan.

Berger, J. O., and R. L. Wolpert. 1984. *The Likelihood Principle.* Hayward, CA: The Institute of Mathematical Statistics.

Blackorby, C., Daniel Primont, and R. R. Russell. 1978. *Duality, Separability, and Functional Structure.* New York: Elsevier North-Holland.

Blackorby, C., W. Schworm, and T. Fisher. 1986. "Testing for the Existence of Input Aggregates in an Economy Production Function." University of British Columbia, Vancouver, processed.

Caves, D., and L. Christensen. 1980. "Global Properties of Flexible Functional Forms." *American Economic Review* 70: 422-32.

Chalfant, James A. 1987. "A Globally Flexible, Almost Ideal Demand System." *Journal of Business and Economic Statistics* 5: 233-42.

Debreu, G. 1974. "Excess Demand Functions." *Journal of Mathematical Economics* 1: 15-21.

Diewert, W. E., and T. J. Wales. 1987. "Flexible Functional Forms and Global Curvature Conditions." *Econometrica* 55: 43-68.

1988. "A Normalized Quadratic Semiflexible Functional Form." *Journal of Econometrics* 37: 327-42.

Eastwood, Brian J., and A. Ronald Gallant. 1987. "Adaptive Truncation Rules for Seminonparametric Estimators that Achieve Asymptotic Normality." Working Paper, Graduate School of Business, University of Chicago.

Epstein, Larry, and Adonis Yatchew. 1985. "The Empirical Determination of Technology and Expectations." *Journal of Econometrics* 27: 235-58.

Gallant, A. Ronald. 1981. "On the Bias in Flexible Functional Forms and An Essentially Unbiased Form: The Fourier Flexible Form." *Journal of Econometrics* 15: 211-45.

1982. "Unbiased Determination of Production Technologies." *Journal of Econometrics* 20: 285-323.

1984. "The Fourier Flexible Form." *American Journal of Agricultural Economics* 66: 204-8.

Gallant, A. Ronald, and Gene H. Golub. 1984. "Imposing Curvature Restrictions on Flexible Functional Forms." *Journal of Econometrics* 267: 295-321.

Gallant, A. Ronald, and Douglas W. Nychka. 1987. "Semi-Nonparametric Maximum Likelihood Estimation." *Econometrica* 55: 363-90.

Geweke, J. 1986. "Exact Inference in the Inequality Constrained Normal Linear Regression Model." *Journal of Applied Econometrics* 1: 127-42.

1988. "Exact Inference in Models with Autoregressive Conditional Heteroskedasticity." In *Dynamic Econometric Modeling,* Proceedings of the Third

International Symposium in Economic Theory and Econometrics, W. Barnett, E. Berndt, and H. White, Eds. Cambridge: Cambridge University Press, pp. 73–104.

1989a. "Modelling with Normal Polynomial Expansions." In *Economic Complexity: Chaos, Sunspots, Bubbles, and Nonlinearity,* Proceedings of the Fourth International Symposium in Economic Theory and Econometrics, Cambridge: Cambridge University Press, pp. 337–60.

1989b. "Exact Inference in Econometric Models Using Monte Carlo Integration." *Econometrica* 57: 1317–40.

Geweke, J., and M. D. Terrell. 1990. "Efficient Methods for Sampling from Truncated Multivariate Normal Distributions." Working paper, Duke University, Durham, NC.

Guilkey, D., and C. Lovell. 1980. "On the Flexibility of the Translog Approximation." *International Economic Review* 21: 137–47.

Guilkey, D., C. Lovell, and C. Sickles. 1980. "A Comparison of the Performance of Three Flexible Functional Forms." *International Economic Review* 24: 591–616.

Hammersley, J. M., and D. C. Handscomb. 1964. *Monte Carlo Methods.* London: Methuen.

Jorgenson, Dale. 1984. "Econometric Methods for Applied General Equilibrium Analysis." In *Applied General Equilibrium Analysis,* Herbert E. Scarf and John B. Shoven, Eds. Cambridge: Cambridge University Press, 139–203.

Kloek, T., and H. K. van Dijk. 1978. "Bayesian Estimates of Equation System Parameters: An Application of Integration by Monte Carlo." *Econometrica* 46: 1–19.

Lau, Lawrence J. 1978. "Testing and Imposing Monotonicity, Convexity, and Quasiconvexity Constraints." In *Production Economics: A Dual Approach to Theory and Applications,* Vol. 1, Melvin Fuss and Daniel McFadden, Eds. Amsterdam: North-Holland, pp. 16–28.

Lewbel, Arthur. 1987. "Fractional Demand Systems." *Journal of Econometrics* 36: 311–38.

McFadden, Daniel. 1985. "Specification of Econometrica Models." Presidential Address, Fifth World Congress of the Econometric Society, Cambridge, Massachusetts.

Rossi, Peter E. 1983. "Specification and Analysis of Econometric Production Models." Ph.D. dissertation, University of Chicago.

Rudin, Walter. 1966. *Real and Complex Analysis.* New York: McGraw-Hill.

Shoven, John B., and John Whalley. 1984. "Applied General Equilibrium Models of Taxation and International Trade: An Introduction and Survey." *Journal of Economic Literature* 22: 1007–51.

Sonnenschein, H. 1973. "The Utility Hypothesis and Market Demand Theory." Western Economic Journal 1: 404–10.

Uzawa, H. 1962. "Production Functions with Constant Elasticities of Substitution." *Review of Economic Studies* 29: 291–9.

Wales, T. J. 1977. "On the Flexibility of Flexible Functional Forms: An Empirical Approach." *Journal of Econometrics* 5: 183–93.

White, Halbert. 1980. "Using Least Squares to Approximate Unknown Regression Functions." *International Economic Review* 21: 149–70.